NEW YORK LEGISLATURE

NEW YORK
CONSOLIDATED LAWS

PENAL LAW

2022 EDITION

D1607163

WEST HARTFORD
LEGAL PUBLISHING

Part 1 - GENERAL PROVISIONS 7

    Title A - GENERAL PURPOSES, RULES OF CONSTRUCTION, AND DEFINITIONS 7

    Article 1 - GENERAL PURPOSES 7

    Article 5 - GENERAL RULES OF CONSTRUCTION AND APPLICATION 7

    Article 10 - DEFINITIONS 7

    Title B - PRINCIPLES OF CRIMINAL LIABILITY 9

    Article 15 - CULPABILITY 9

    Article 20 - PARTIES TO OFFENSES AND LIABILITY THROUGH ACCESSORIAL CONDUCT 10

    Title C - DEFENSES 11

    Article 25 - DEFENSES IN GENERAL 11

    Article 30 - DEFENSE OF INFANCY 11

    Article 35 - DEFENSE OF JUSTIFICATION 12

    Article 40 - OTHER DEFENSES INVOLVING LACK OF CULPABILITY 14

Part 2 - SENTENCES 15

    Title E - SENTENCES 15

    Article 55 - CLASSIFICATION AND DESIGNATION OF OFFENSES 15

    Article 60 - AUTHORIZED DISPOSITIONS OF OFFENDERS 16

    Article 65 - SENTENCES OF PROBATION, CONDITIONAL DISCHARGE AND UNCONDITIONAL DISCHARGE 27

    Article 70 - SENTENCES OF IMPRISONMENT 32

    Article 80 - FINES 56

    Article 85 - SENTENCE OF INTERMITTENT IMPRISONMENT 58

Part 3 - SPECIFIC OFFENSES 59

    Title G - ANTICIPATORY OFFENSES 59

    Article 100 - CRIMINAL SOLICITATION 59

    Article 105 - CONSPIRACY 60

    Article 110 - ATTEMPT 61

    Article 115 - CRIMINAL FACILITATION 62

Title H - OFFENSES AGAINST THE PERSON INVOLVING PHYSICAL INJURY, SEXUAL CONDUCT, RESTRAINT AND INTIMIDATION 62

Article 120 - ASSAULT AND RELATED OFFENSES 62

Article 121 - STRANGULATION AND RELATED OFFENSES 69

Article 125 - HOMICIDE AND RELATED OFFENSES 70

Article 130 - SEX OFFENSES 76

Article 135 - KIDNAPPING, COERCION AND RELATED OFFENSES 82

Title I - OFFENSES INVOLVING DAMAGE TO AND INTRUSION UPON PROPERTY 85

Article 140 - BURGLARY AND RELATED OFFENSES 85

Article 145 - CRIMINAL MISCHIEF AND RELATED OFFENSES 86

Article 150 - ARSON 89

Title J - OFFENSES INVOLVING THEFT 90

Article 155 - LARCENY 90

Article 156 - OFFENSES INVOLVING COMPUTERS; DEFINITION OF TERMS 93

Article 158 - WELFARE FRAUD 96

Article 160 - ROBBERY 97

Article 165 - OTHER OFFENSES RELATING TO THEFT 98

Title K - OFFENSES INVOLVING FRAUD 104

Article 170 - FORGERY AND RELATED OFFENSES 104

Article 175 - OFFENSES INVOLVING FALSE WRITTEN STATEMENTS 106

Article 176 - INSURANCE FRAUD 108

Article 177 - HEALTH CARE FRAUD 110

Article 178 - CRIMINAL DIVERSION OF PRESCRIPTION MEDICATIONS AND PRESCRIPTIONS 111

Article 179 - CRIMINAL DIVERSION OF MEDICAL MARIHUANA 112

Article 180 - BRIBERY NOT INVOLVING PUBLIC SERVANTS, AND RELATED OFFENSES 113

Article 185 - FRAUDS ON CREDITORS 115

Article 187 - RESIDENTIAL MORTGAGE FRAUD 116

Article 190 - OTHER FRAUDS 116

4

Title L - OFFENSES AGAINST PUBLIC ADMINISTRATION 123

Article 195 - OFFICIAL MISCONDUCT AND OBSTRUCTION OF PUBLIC SERVANTS GENERALLY 123

Article 200 - BRIBERY INVOLVING PUBLIC SERVANTS AND RELATED OFFENSES 124

Article 205 - ESCAPE AND OTHER OFFENSES RELATING TO CUSTODY 126

Article 210 - PERJURY AND RELATED OFFENSES 128

Article 215 - OTHER OFFENSES RELATING TO JUDICIAL AND OTHER PROCEEDINGS 130

Title M - OFFENSES AGAINST PUBLIC HEALTH AND MORALS 135

Article 220 - CONTROLLED SUBSTANCES OFFENSES 135

Article 221 - OFFENSES INVOLVING MARIHUANA 142

Article 222 - CANNABIS 143

Article 225 - GAMBLING OFFENSES 146

Article 230 - PROSTITUTION OFFENSES 151

Article 235 - OBSCENITY AND RELATED OFFENSES 155

Title N - OFFENSES AGAINST PUBLIC ORDER, PUBLIC SENSIBILITIES AND THE RIGHT TO PRIVACY 157

Article 240 - OFFENSES AGAINST PUBLIC ORDER 157

Article 241 - HARASSMENT OF RENT REGULATED TENANTS 164

Article 242 - OFFENSES AGAINST SERVICE ANIMALS AND HANDLERS 165

Article 245 - OFFENSES AGAINST PUBLIC SENSIBILITIES 166

Article 250 - OFFENSES AGAINST THE RIGHT TO PRIVACY 167

Title O - OFFENSES AGAINST MARRIAGE, THE FAMILY, AND THE WELFARE OF CHILDREN AND INCOMPETENTS 170

Article 255 - OFFENSES AFFECTING THE MARITAL RELATIONSHIP 170

Article 260 - OFFENSES RELATING TO CHILDREN, DISABLED PERSONS AND VULNERABLE ELDERLY PERSONS 171

Article 263 - SEXUAL PERFORMANCE BY A CHILD 175

Title P - OFFENSES AGAINST PUBLIC SAFETY 176

Article 265 - FIREARMS AND OTHER DANGEROUS WEAPONS 176

Article 270 - OTHER OFFENSES RELATING TO PUBLIC SAFETY 191

Article 275 - OFFENSES RELATING TO UNAUTHORIZED RECORDING.................194

Part 4 - ADMINISTRATIVE PROVISIONS...196

Title W - PROVISIONS RELATING TO FIREARMS, FIREWORKS, PORNOGRAPHY EQUIPMENT AND VEHICLES USED IN THE TRANSPORTATION OF GAMBLING RECORDS 196

Article 400 - LICENSING AND OTHER PROVISIONS RELATING TO FIREARMS ...196

Article 405 - LICENSING AND OTHER PROVISIONS RELATING TO FIREWORKS207

Article 410 - SEIZURE AND FORFEITURE OF EQUIPMENT USED IN PROMOTING PORNOGRAPHY 212

Article 415 - SEIZURE AND FORFEITURE OF VEHICLES, VESSELS AND AIRCRAFT USED TO TRANSPORT OR CONCEAL GAMBLING RECORDS 213

Article 420 - SEIZURE AND DESTRUCTION OF UNAUTHORIZED RECORDINGS OF SOUND AND FORFEITURE OF EQUIPMENT USED IN THE PRODUCTION THEREOF 214

Article 450 - DISPOSAL OF STOLEN PROPERTY..214

Title X - ORGANIZED CRIME CONTROL ACT 216

Article 460 - ENTERPRISE CORRUPTION 216

Article 470 - MONEY LAUNDERING 220

Article 480 - CRIMINAL FORFEITURE - FELONY CONTROLLED SUBSTANCE OFFENSES 228

Title Y - HATE CRIMES ACT OF 2000..231

Article 485 - HATE CRIMES 231

Title Y-1 - Enacted without title heading 233

Article 490 - TERRORISM 233

Title Y-2 - CORRUPTING THE GOVERNMENT 237

Article 496 - CORRUPTING THE GOVERNMENT 237

Title Z - LAWS REPEALED; TIME OF TAKING EFFECT..238

Article 500 - LAWS REPEALED; TIME OF TAKING EFFECT 238

6

Part 1 - GENERAL PROVISIONS
Title A - GENERAL PURPOSES, RULES OF CONSTRUCTION, AND DEFINITIONS
Article 1 - GENERAL PURPOSES
Section 1.00 - Short title
This chapter shall be known as the "Penal Law."
N.Y. Penal Law § 1.00

Section 1.05 - General purposes
The general purposes of the provisions of this chapter are:
1. To proscribe conduct which unjustifiably and inexcusably causes or threatens substantial harm to individual or public interests;
2. To give fair warning of the nature of the conduct proscribed and of the sentences authorized upon conviction;
3. To define the act or omission and the accompanying mental state which constitute each offense;
4. To differentiate on reasonable grounds between serious and minor offenses and to prescribe proportionate penalties therefor;
5. To provide for an appropriate public response to particular offenses, including consideration of the consequences of the offense for the victim, including the victim's family, and the community; and
6. To insure the public safety by preventing the commission of offenses through the deterrent influence of the sentences authorized, the rehabilitation of those convicted, the promotion of their successful and productive reentry and reintegration into society, and their confinement when required in the interests of public protection.
N.Y. Penal Law § 1.05

Article 5 - GENERAL RULES OF CONSTRUCTION AND APPLICATION
Section 5.00 - Penal law not strictly construed
The general rule that a penal statute is to be strictly construed does not apply to this chapter, but the provisions herein must be construed according to the fair import of their terms to promote justice and effect the objects of the law.
N.Y. Penal Law § 5.00
Section 5.05 - Application of chapter to offenses committed before and after enactment
1. The provisions of this chapter shall govern the construction of and punishment for any offense defined in this chapter and committed after the effective date hereof, as well as the construction and application of any defense to a prosecution for such an offense.
2. Unless otherwise expressly provided, or unless the context otherwise requires, the provisions of this chapter shall govern the construction of and punishment for any offense defined outside of this chapter and committed after the effective date thereof, as well as the construction and application of any defense to a prosecution for such an offense.
3. The provisions of this chapter do not apply to or govern the construction of and punishment for any offense committed prior to the effective date of this chapter, or the construction and application of any defense to a prosecution for such an offense. Such an offense must be construed and punished according to the provisions of law existing at the time of the commission thereof in the same manner as if this chapter had not been enacted.
N.Y. Penal Law § 5.05
Section 5.10 - Other limitations on applicability of this chapter
1. Except as otherwise provided, the procedure governing the accusation, prosecution, conviction and punishment of offenders and offenses is not regulated by this chapter but by the criminal procedure law.
2. This chapter does not affect any power conferred by law upon any court-martial or other military authority or officer to prosecute and punish conduct and offenders violating military codes or laws.
3. This chapter does not bar, suspend, or otherwise affect any right or liability to damages, penalty, forfeiture or other remedy authorized by law to be recovered or enforced in a civil action, regardless of whether the conduct involved in such civil action constitutes an offense defined in this chapter.
4. Sections 120.45, 120.50, 120.55, 120.60 and 240.25, subdivisions two and three of section 240.26, and sections 240.70 and 240.71 of this chapter (a) do not apply to conduct which is otherwise lawful under the provisions of the National Labor Relations Act as amended, the National Railway Labor Act as amended, or the Federal Employment Labor Management Act as amended, and (b) do not bar any conduct, including, but not limited to, peaceful picketing or other peaceful demonstration, protected from legal prohibition by the federal and state constitutions.
N.Y. Penal Law § 5.10

Article 10 - DEFINITIONS
Section 10.00 - Definitions of terms of general use in this chapter
Except where different meanings are expressly specified in subsequent provisions of this chapter, the following terms have the following meanings:
1. "Offense" means conduct for which a sentence to a term of imprisonment or to a fine is provided by any law of this state or by any law, local law or ordinance of a political subdivision of this state, or by any order, rule or regulation of any governmental instrumentality authorized by law to adopt the same.
2. "Traffic infraction" means any offense defined as "traffic infraction" by section one hundred fifty-five of the vehicle and traffic law.

3. "Violation" means an offense, other than a "traffic infraction, " for which a sentence to a term of imprisonment in excess of fifteen days cannot be imposed.

4. "Misdemeanor" means an offense, other than a "traffic infraction, " for which a sentence to a term of imprisonment in excess of fifteen days may be imposed, but for which a sentence to a term of imprisonment in excess of one year cannot be imposed.

5. "Felony" means an offense for which a sentence to a term of imprisonment in excess of one year may be imposed.

6. "Crime" means a misdemeanor or a felony.

7. "Person" means a human being, and where appropriate, a public or private corporation, an unincorporated association, a partnership, a government or a governmental instrumentality.

8. "Possess" means to have physical possession or otherwise to exercise dominion or control over tangible property.

9. "Physical injury" means impairment of physical condition or substantial pain.

10. "Serious physical injury" means physical injury which creates a substantial risk of death, or which causes death or serious and protracted disfigurement, protracted impairment of health or protracted loss or impairment of the function of any bodily organ.

11. "Deadly physical force" means physical force which, under the circumstances in which it is used, is readily capable of causing death or other serious physical injury.

12. "Deadly weapon" means any loaded weapon from which a shot, readily capable of producing death or other serious physical injury, may be discharged, or a switchblade knife, pilum ballistic knife, metal knuckle knife, dagger, billy, blackjack, plastic knuckles, or metal knuckles.

13. "Dangerous instrument" means any instrument, article or substance, including a "vehicle" as that term is defined in this section, which, under the circumstances in which it is used, attempted to be used or threatened to be used, is readily capable of causing death or other serious physical injury.

14. "Vehicle" means a "motor vehicle", "trailer" or "semi-trailer," as defined in the vehicle and traffic law, any snowmobile as defined in the parks and recreation law, any aircraft, or any vessel equipped for propulsion by mechanical means or by sail.

15. "Public servant" means (a) any public officer or employee of the state or of any political subdivision thereof or of any governmental instrumentality within the state, or (b) any person exercising the functions of any such public officer or employee. The term public servant includes a person who has been elected or designated to become a public servant.

16. "Juror" means any person who is a member of any jury, including a grand jury, impaneled by any court in this state or by any public servant authorized by law to impanel a jury. The term juror also includes a person who has been drawn or summoned to attend as a prospective juror.

17. "Benefit" means any gain or advantage to the beneficiary and includes any gain or advantage to a third person pursuant to the desire or consent of the beneficiary.

18. "Juvenile offender" means

(1) a person thirteen years old who is criminally responsible for acts constituting murder in the second degree as defined in subdivisions one and two of section 125.25 of this chapter or such conduct as a sexually motivated felony, where authorized pursuant to section 130.91 of the penal law; and

(2) a person fourteen or fifteen years old who is criminally responsible for acts constituting the crimes defined in subdivisions one and two of section 125.25 (murder in the second degree) and in subdivision three of such section provided that the underlying crime for the murder charge is one for which such person is criminally responsible; section 135.25 (kidnapping in the first degree); 150.20 (arson in the first degree); subdivisions one and two of section 120.10 (assault in the first degree); 125.20 (manslaughter in the first degree); subdivisions one and two of section 130.35 (rape in the first degree); subdivisions one and two of section 130.50 (criminal sexual act in the first degree); 130.70 (aggravated sexual abuse in the first degree); 140.30 (burglary in the first degree); subdivision one of section 140.25 (burglary in the second degree); 150.15 (arson in the second degree); 160.15 (robbery in the first degree); subdivision two of section 160.10 (robbery in the second degree) of this chapter; or section 265.03 of this chapter, where such machine gun or such firearm is possessed on school grounds, as that phrase is defined in subdivision fourteen of section 220.00 of this chapter; or defined in this chapter as an attempt to commit murder in the second degree or kidnapping in the first degree, or such conduct as a sexually motivated felony, where authorized pursuant to section 130.91 of the penal law.

19. For the purposes of section 260.30 and 120.01 of this chapter the term "child day care provider" shall be defined as provided for in section three hundred ninety of the social services law.

20. For purposes of sections 120.13, 120.18, 125.11, 125.21 and 125.22 of this chapter, the term "peace officer" means a peace officer as defined in subdivision one, two, three, four, six, twelve, thirteen, fifteen, sixteen, seventeen, eighteen, nineteen, twenty, twenty-one, twenty-three, twenty-three-a, twenty-four, twenty-five, twenty-six, twenty-eight, twenty-nine, thirty, thirty-one, thirty-two, thirty-four, thirty-five, thirty-six, forty-three, forty-five, forty-seven, forty-eight, forty-nine, fifty-one, fifty-two, fifty-eight, sixty-one, as added by chapter two hundred fifty-seven of the laws of nineteen hundred ninety-two, sixty-one, as added by chapter three hundred twenty-one of the laws of nineteen hundred ninety-two, sixty-two, as added by chapter two hundred four of the laws of nineteen hundred ninety-three, sixty-two, as added by chapter six hundred eighty-seven of the laws of nineteen hundred ninety-three, sixty-three, as amended by chapter six hundred thirty-eight of the laws of two thousand three, sixty-four, sixty-five, sixty-eight, as added by chapter one hundred sixty-eight of the laws of two thousand, sixty-eight, as added by chapter three hundred eighty-one of the laws of two thousand, seventy, seventy-one, seventy-four, as added by chapter five hundred forty-eight of the laws of two thousand one, seventy-five, as added by chapter three hundred twenty-one of the laws of two thousand two, seventy-five, as added

by chapter six hundred twenty-three of the laws of two thousand two, seventy-seven, as added by chapter three hundred sixty-seven of the laws of two thousand four, seventy-eight or seventy-nine, as added by chapter two hundred forty-one of the laws of two thousand four, of section 2.10 of the criminal procedure law, as well as any federal law enforcement officer defined in section 2.15 of the criminal procedure law.

21. "Drug trafficking felony" means any of the following offenses defined in article two hundred twenty of this chapter: violation of use of a child to commit a controlled substance offense as defined in section 220.28; criminal sale of a controlled substance in the fourth degree as defined in section 220.34; criminal sale of a controlled substance in the third degree as defined in section 220.39; criminal sale of a controlled substance in the second degree as defined in section 220.41; criminal sale of a controlled substance in the first degree as defined in section 220.43; criminal sale of a controlled substance in or near school grounds as defined in section 220.44; unlawful manufacture of methamphetamine in the second degree as defined in section 220.74; unlawful manufacture of methamphetamine in the first degree as defined in section 220.75; or operating as a major trafficker as defined in section 220.77.

N.Y. Penal Law § 10.00

Amended by New York Laws 2019, ch. 34,Sec. 2, eff. 5/30/2019.

Amended by New York Laws 2013, ch. 1,Sec. 26, eff. 3/16/2013.

Title B - PRINCIPLES OF CRIMINAL LIABILITY

Article 15 - CULPABILITY

Section 15.00 - Culpability; definitions of terms

The following definitions are applicable to this chapter:

1. "Act" means a bodily movement.

2. "Voluntary act" means a bodily movement performed consciously as a result of effort or determination, and includes the possession of property if the actor was aware of his physical possession or control thereof for a sufficient period to have been able to terminate it.

3. "Omission" means a failure to perform an act as to which a duty of performance is imposed by law.

4. "Conduct" means an act or omission and its accompanying mental state.

5. "To act" means either to perform an act or to omit to perform an act.

6. "Culpable mental state" means "intentionally" or "knowingly" or "recklessly" or with "criminal negligence," as these terms are defined in section 15.05.

N.Y. Penal Law § 15.00

Section 15.05 - Culpability; definitions of culpable mental states

The following definitions are applicable to this chapter:

1. "Intentionally." A person acts intentionally with respect to a result or to conduct described by a statute defining an offense when his conscious objective is to cause such result or to engage in such conduct.

2. "Knowingly." A person acts knowingly with respect to conduct or to a circumstance described by a statute defining an offense when he is aware that his conduct is of such nature or that such circumstance exists.

3. "Recklessly." A person acts recklessly with respect to a result or to a circumstance described by a statute defining an offense when he is aware of and consciously disregards a substantial and unjustifiable risk that such result will occur or that such circumstance exists. The risk must be of such nature and degree that disregard thereof constitutes a gross deviation from the standard of conduct that a reasonable person would observe in the situation. A person who creates such a risk but is unaware thereof solely by reason of voluntary intoxication also acts recklessly with respect thereto.

4. "Criminal negligence." A person acts with criminal negligence with respect to a result or to a circumstance described by a statute defining an offense when he fails to perceive a substantial and unjustifiable risk that such result will occur or that such circumstance exists. The risk must be of such nature and degree that the failure to perceive it constitutes a gross deviation from the standard of care that a reasonable person would observe in the situation.

N.Y. Penal Law § 15.05

Section 15.10 - Requirements for criminal liability in general and for offenses of strict liability and mental culpability

The minimal requirement for criminal liability is the performance by a person of conduct which includes a voluntary act or the omission to perform an act which he is physically capable of performing. If such conduct is all that is required for commission of a particular offense, or if an offense or some material element thereof does not require a culpable mental state on the part of the actor, such offense is one of "strict liability." If a culpable mental state on the part of the actor is required with respect to every material element of an offense, such offense is one of "mental culpability."

N.Y. Penal Law § 15.10

Section 15.15 - Construction of statutes with respect to culpability requirements

1. When the commission of an offense defined in this chapter, or some element of an offense, requires a particular culpable mental state, such mental state is ordinarily designated in the statute defining the offense by use of the terms "intentionally," "knowingly," "recklessly" or "criminal negligence," or by use of terms, such as "with intent to defraud" and "knowing it to be false," describing a specific kind of intent or knowledge. When one and only one of such terms appears in a statute defining an offense, it is presumed to apply to every element of the offense unless an intent to limit its application clearly appears.

2. Although no culpable mental state is expressly designated in a statute defining an offense, a culpable mental state may nevertheless be required for the commission of such offense, or with respect to some or all of the material elements thereof,

if the proscribed conduct necessarily involves such culpable mental state. A statute defining a crime, unless clearly indicating a legislative intent to impose strict liability, should be construed as defining a crime of mental culpability. This subdivision applies to offenses defined both in and outside this chapter.

N.Y. Penal Law § 15.15

Section 15.20 - Effect of ignorance or mistake upon liability

1. A person is not relieved of criminal liability for conduct because he engages in such conduct under a mistaken belief of fact, unless:

(a) Such factual mistake negatives the culpable mental state required for the commission of an offense; or

(b) The statute defining the offense or a statute related thereto expressly provides that such factual mistake constitutes a defense or exemption; or

(c) Such factual mistake is of a kind that supports a defense of justification as defined in article thirty-five of this chapter.

2. A person is not relieved of criminal liability for conduct because he engages in such conduct under a mistaken belief that it does not, as a matter of law, constitute an offense, unless such mistaken belief is founded upon an official statement of the law contained in (a) a statute or other enactment, or (b) an administrative order or grant of permission, or (c) a judicial decision of a state or federal court, or (d) an interpretation of the statute or law relating to the offense, officially made or issued by a public servant, agency or body legally charged or empowered with the responsibility or privilege of administering, enforcing or interpreting such statute or law.

3. Notwithstanding the use of the term "knowingly" in any provision of this chapter defining an offense in which the age of a child is an element thereof, knowledge by the defendant of the age of such child is not an element of any such offense and it is not, unless expressly so provided, a defense to a prosecution therefor that the defendant did not know the age of the child or believed such age to be the same as or greater than that specified in the statute.

4. Notwithstanding the use of the term "knowingly" in any provision of this chapter defining an offense in which the aggregate weight of a controlled substance or marihuana is an element, knowledge by the defendant of the aggregate weight of such controlled substance or marihuana is not an element of any such offense and it is not, unless expressly so provided, a defense to a prosecution therefor that the defendant did not know the aggregate weight of the controlled substance or marihuana.

N.Y. Penal Law § 15.20

Section 15.25 - Effect of intoxication upon liability

Intoxication is not, as such, a defense to a criminal charge; but in any prosecution for an offense, evidence of intoxication of the defendant may be offered by the defendant whenever it is relevant to negative an element of the crime charged.

N.Y. Penal Law § 15.25

Article 20 - PARTIES TO OFFENSES AND LIABILITY THROUGH ACCESSORIAL CONDUCT

Section 20.00 - Criminal liability for conduct of another

When one person engages in conduct which constitutes an offense, another person is criminally liable for such conduct when, acting with the mental culpability required for the commission thereof, he solicits, requests, commands, importunes, or intentionally aids such person to engage in such conduct.

N.Y. Penal Law § 20.00

Section 20.05 - Criminal liability for conduct of another; no defense

In any prosecution for an offense in which the criminal liability of the defendant is based upon the conduct of another person pursuant to section 20.00, it is no defense that:

1. Such other person is not guilty of the offense in question owing to criminal irresponsibility or other legal incapacity or exemption, or to unawareness of the criminal nature of the conduct in question or of the defendant's criminal purpose or to other factors precluding the mental state required for the commission of the offense in question; or

2. Such other person has not been prosecuted for or convicted of any offense based upon the conduct in question, or has previously been acquitted thereof, or has legal immunity from prosecution therefor; or

3. The offense in question, as defined, can be committed only by a particular class or classes of persons, and the defendant, not belonging to such class or classes, is for that reason legally incapable of committing the offense in an individual capacity.

N.Y. Penal Law § 20.05

Section 20.10 - Criminal liability for conduct of another; exemption

Notwithstanding the provisions of sections 20.00 and 20.05, a person is not criminally liable for conduct of another person constituting an offense when his own conduct, though causing or aiding the commission of such offense, is of a kind that is necessarily incidental thereto. If such conduct constitutes a related but separate offense upon the part of the actor, he is liable for that offense only and not for the conduct or offense committed by the other person.

N.Y. Penal Law § 20.10

Section 20.15 - Convictions for different degrees of offense

Except as otherwise expressly provided in this chapter, when, pursuant to section 20.00, two or more persons are criminally liable for an offense which is divided into degrees, each person is guilty of such degree as is compatible with his own culpable mental state and with his own accountability for an aggravating fact or circumstance.

N.Y. Penal Law § 20.15

Section 20.20 - Criminal liability of corporations

1. As used in this section:

(a) "Agent" means any director, officer or employee of a corporation, or any other person who is authorized to act in behalf of the corporation.

(b) "High managerial agent" means an officer of a corporation or any other agent in a position of comparable authority with respect to the formulation of corporate policy or the supervision in a managerial capacity of subordinate employees.

2. A corporation is guilty of an offense when:

(a) The conduct constituting the offense consists of an omission to discharge a specific duty of affirmative performance imposed on corporations by law; or

(b) The conduct constituting the offense is engaged in, authorized, solicited, requested, commanded, or recklessly tolerated by the board of directors or by a high managerial agent acting within the scope of his employment and in behalf of the corporation; or

(c) The conduct constituting the offense is engaged in by an agent of the corporation while acting within the scope of his employment and in behalf of the corporation, and the offense is (i) a misdemeanor or a violation, (ii) one defined by a statute which clearly indicates a legislative intent to impose such criminal liability on a corporation, or (iii) any offense set forth in title twenty-seven of article seventy-one of the environmental conservation law.

N.Y. Penal Law § 20.20

Section 20.25 - Criminal liability of an individual for corporate conduct

A person is criminally liable for conduct constituting an offense which he performs or causes to be performed in the name of or in behalf of a corporation to the same extent as if such conduct were performed in his own name or behalf.

N.Y. Penal Law § 20.25

Title C - DEFENSES

Article 25 - DEFENSES IN GENERAL

Section 25.00 - Defenses; burden of proof

1. When a "defense," other than an "affirmative defense," defined by statute is raised at a trial, the people have the burden of disproving such defense beyond a reasonable doubt.

2. When a defense declared by statute to be an "affirmative defense" is raised at a trial, the defendant has the burden of establishing such defense by a preponderance of the evidence.

N.Y. Penal Law § 25.00

Article 30 - DEFENSE OF INFANCY

Section 30.00 - [SeeNew York Laws2017, ch.59,Sec.WWW-106subsection b for further contingencies for 10/1/2019]Infancy

1. Except as provided in subdivisions two and three of this section, a person less than seventeen, or commencing October first, two thousand nineteen, a person less than eighteen years old is not criminally responsible for conduct.

2. A person thirteen, fourteen or, fifteen years of age is criminally responsible for acts constituting murder in the second degree as defined in subdivisions one and two of section 125.25 and in subdivision three of such section provided that the underlying crime for the murder charge is one for which such person is criminally responsible or for such conduct as a sexually motivated felony, where authorized pursuant to section 130.91 of this chapter; and a person fourteen or, fifteen years of age is criminally responsible for acts constituting the crimes defined in section 135.25 (kidnapping in the first degree); 150.20 (arson in the first degree); subdivisions one and two of section 120.10 (assault in the first degree); 125.20 (manslaughter in the first degree); subdivisions one and two of section 130.35 (rape in the first degree); subdivisions one and two of section 130.50 (criminal sexual act in the first degree); 130.70 (aggravated sexual abuse in the first degree); 140.30 (burglary in the first degree); subdivision one of section 140.25 (burglary in the second degree); 150.15 (arson in the second degree); 160.15 (robbery in the first degree); subdivision two of section 160.10 (robbery in the second degree) of this chapter; or section 265.03 of this chapter, where such machine gun or such firearm is possessed on school grounds, as that phrase is defined in subdivision fourteen of section 220.00 of this chapter; or defined in this chapter as an attempt to commit murder in the second degree or kidnapping in the first degree, or for such conduct as a sexually motivated felony, where authorized pursuant to section 130.91 of this chapter.

3. A person sixteen or commencing October first, two thousand nineteen, seventeen years of age is criminally responsible for acts constituting:

(a) a felony, as defined in subdivision five of section 10.00 of this chapter;

(b) a traffic infraction, as defined in subdivision two of section 10.00 of this chapter;

(c) a violation, as defined in subdivision three of section 10.00 of this chapter;

(d) a misdemeanor as defined in subdivision four of section 10.00 of this chapter, but only when the charge for such misdemeanor is:

(i) accompanied by a felony charge that is shown to have been committed as a part of the same criminal transaction, as defined in subdivision two of section 40.10 of the criminal procedure law;

(ii) results from reduction or dismissal in satisfaction of a charge for a felony offense, in accordance with a plea of guilty pursuant to subdivision four of section 220.10 of the criminal procedure law; or

(iii) a misdemeanor defined in the vehicle and traffic law.

4. In any prosecution for an offense, lack of criminal responsibility by reason of infancy, as defined in this section, is a defense.

N.Y. Penal Law § 30.00
Amended by New York Laws 2017, ch. 59,Sec. WWW-38, eff. 10/1/2018.

Article 35 - DEFENSE OF JUSTIFICATION

Section 35.00 - Justification; a defense

In any prosecution for an offense, justification, as defined in sections 35.05 through 35.30, is a defense.
N.Y. Penal Law § 35.00

Section 35.05 - Justification; generally

Unless otherwise limited by the ensuing provisions of this article defining justifiable use of physical force, conduct which would otherwise constitute an offense is justifiable and not criminal when:

1. Such conduct is required or authorized by law or by a judicial decree, or is performed by a public servant in the reasonable exercise of his official powers, duties or functions; or

2. Such conduct is necessary as an emergency measure to avoid an imminent public or private injury which is about to occur by reason of a situation occasioned or developed through no fault of the actor, and which is of such gravity that, according to ordinary standards of intelligence and morality, the desirability and urgency of avoiding such injury clearly outweigh the desirability of avoiding the injury sought to be prevented by the statute defining the offense in issue. The necessity and justifiability of such conduct may not rest upon considerations pertaining only to the morality and advisability of the statute, either in its general application or with respect to its application to a particular class of cases arising thereunder. Whenever evidence relating to the defense of justification under this subdivision is offered by the defendant, the court shall rule as a matter of law whether the claimed facts and circumstances would, if established, constitute a defense.
N.Y. Penal Law § 35.05

Section 35.10 - Justification; use of physical force generally

The use of physical force upon another person which would otherwise constitute an offense is justifiable and not criminal under any of the following circumstances:

1. A parent, guardian or other person entrusted with the care and supervision of a person under the age of twenty-one or an incompetent person, and a teacher or other person entrusted with the care and supervision of a person under the age of twenty-one for a special purpose, may use physical force, but not deadly physical force, upon such person when and to the extent that he reasonably believes it necessary to maintain discipline or to promote the welfare of such person.

2. A warden or other authorized official of a jail, prison or correctional institution may, in order to maintain order and discipline, use such physical force as is authorized by the correction law.

3. A person responsible for the maintenance of order in a common carrier of passengers, or a person acting under his direction, may use physical force when and to the extent that he reasonably believes it necessary to maintain order, but he may use deadly physical force only when he reasonably believes it necessary to prevent death or serious physical injury.

4. A person acting under a reasonable belief that another person is about to commit suicide or to inflict serious physical injury upon himself may use physical force upon such person to the extent that he reasonably believes it necessary to thwart such result.

5. A duly licensed physician, or a person acting under a physician's direction, may use physical force for the purpose of administering a recognized form of treatment which he or she reasonably believes to be adapted to promoting the physical or mental health of the patient if (a) the treatment is administered with the consent of the patient or, if the patient is under the age of eighteen years or an incompetent person, with the consent of the parent, guardian or other person entrusted with the patient's care and supervision, or (b) the treatment is administered in an emergency when the physician reasonably believes that no one competent to consent can be consulted and that a reasonable person, wishing to safeguard the welfare of the patient, would consent.

6. A person may, pursuant to the ensuing provisions of this article, use physical force upon another person in self-defense or defense of a third person, or in defense of premises, or in order to prevent larceny of or criminal mischief to property, or in order to effect an arrest or prevent an escape from custody. Whenever a person is authorized by any such provision to use deadly physical force in any given circumstance, nothing contained in any other such provision may be deemed to negate or qualify such authorization.
N.Y. Penal Law § 35.10

Section 35.15 - Justification; use of physical force in defense of a person

1. A person may, subject to the provisions of subdivision two, use physical force upon another person when and to the extent he or she reasonably believes such to be necessary to defend himself, herself or a third person from what he or she reasonably believes to be the use or imminent use of unlawful physical force by such other person, unless:

(a) The latter's conduct was provoked by the actor with intent to cause physical injury to another person; or

(b) The actor was the initial aggressor; except that in such case the use of physical force is nevertheless justifiable if the actor has withdrawn from the encounter and effectively communicated such withdrawal to such other person but the latter persists in continuing the incident by the use or threatened imminent use of unlawful physical force; or

(c) The physical force involved is the product of a combat by agreement not specifically authorized by law.

2. A person may not use deadly physical force upon another person under circumstances specified in subdivision one unless:

(a) The actor reasonably believes that such other person is using or about to use deadly physical force. Even in such case, however, the actor may not use deadly physical force if he or she knows that with complete personal safety, to oneself and others he or she may avoid the necessity of so doing by retreating; except that the actor is under no duty to retreat if he or she is:

(i) in his or her dwelling and not the initial aggressor; or

(ii) a police officer or peace officer or a person assisting a police officer or a peace officer at the latter's direction, acting pursuant to section 35.30; or

(b) He or she reasonably believes that such other person is committing or attempting to commit a kidnapping, forcible rape, forcible criminal sexual act or robbery; or

(c) He or she reasonably believes that such other person is committing or attempting to commit a burglary, and the circumstances are such that the use of deadly physical force is authorized by subdivision three of section 35.20.

N.Y. Penal Law § 35.15

Section 35.20 - Justification; use of physical force in defense of premises and in defense of a person in the course of burglary

1. Any person may use physical force upon another person when he or she reasonably believes such to be necessary to prevent or terminate what he or she reasonably believes to be the commission or attempted commission by such other person of a crime involving damage to premises. Such person may use any degree of physical force, other than deadly physical force, which he or she reasonably believes to be necessary for such purpose, and may use deadly physical force if he or she reasonably believes such to be necessary to prevent or terminate the commission or attempted commission of arson.

2. A person in possession or control of any premises, or a person licensed or privileged to be thereon or therein, may use physical force upon another person when he or she reasonably believes such to be necessary to prevent or terminate what he or she reasonably believes to be the commission or attempted commission by such other person of a criminal trespass upon such premises. Such person may use any degree of physical force, other than deadly physical force, which he or she reasonably believes to be necessary for such purpose, and may use deadly physical force in order to prevent or terminate the commission or attempted commission of arson, as prescribed in subdivision one, or in the course of a burglary or attempted burglary, as prescribed in subdivision three.

3. A person in possession or control of, or licensed or privileged to be in, a dwelling or an occupied building, who reasonably believes that another person is committing or attempting to commit a burglary of such dwelling or building, may use deadly physical force upon such other person when he or she reasonably believes such to be necessary to prevent or terminate the commission or attempted commission of such burglary.

4. As used in this section, the following terms have the following meanings:

(a) The terms "premises," "building" and "dwelling" have the meanings prescribed in section 140.00;

(b) Persons "licensed or privileged" to be in buildings or upon other premises include, but are not limited to:

(i) police officers or peace officers acting in the performance of their duties; and

(ii) security personnel or employees of nuclear powered electric generating facilities located within the state who are employed as part of any security plan approved by the federal operating license agencies acting in the performance of their duties at such generating facilities. For purposes of this subparagraph, the term "nuclear powered electric generating facility" shall mean a facility that generates electricity using nuclear power for sale, directly or indirectly, to the public, including the land upon which the facility is located and the safety and security zones as defined under federal regulations.

N.Y. Penal Law § 35.20

Section 35.25 - Justification; use of physical force to prevent or terminate larceny or criminal mischief

A person may use physical force, other than deadly physical force, upon another person when and to the extent that he or she reasonably believes such to be necessary to prevent or terminate what he or she reasonably believes to be the commission or attempted commission by such other person of larceny or of criminal mischief with respect to property other than premises.

N.Y. Penal Law § 35.25

Section 35.27 - Justification; use of physical force in resisting arrest prohibited

A person may not use physical force to resist an arrest, whether authorized or unauthorized, which is being effected or attempted by a police officer or peace officer when it would reasonably appear that the latter is a police officer or peace officer.

N.Y. Penal Law § 35.27

Section 35.30 - Justification; use of physical force in making an arrest or in preventing an escape

1. A police officer or a peace officer, in the course of effecting or attempting to effect an arrest, or of preventing or attempting to prevent the escape from custody, of a person whom he or she reasonably believes to have committed an offense, may use physical force when and to the extent he or she reasonably believes such to be necessary to effect the arrest, or to prevent the escape from custody, or in self-defense or to defend a third person from what he or she reasonably believes to be the use or imminent use of physical force; except that deadly physical force may be used for such purposes only when he or she reasonably believes that:

(a) The offense committed by such person was:

(i) a felony or an attempt to commit a felony involving the use or attempted use or threatened imminent use of physical force against a person; or

(ii) kidnapping, arson, escape in the first degree, burglary in the first degree or any attempt to commit such a crime; or

(b) The offense committed or attempted by such person was a felony and that, in the course of resisting arrest therefor or attempting to escape from custody, such person is armed with a firearm or deadly weapon; or

(c) Regardless of the particular offense which is the subject of the arrest or attempted escape, the use of deadly physical force is necessary to defend the police officer or peace officer or another person from what the officer reasonably believes to be the use or imminent use of deadly physical force.

2. The fact that a police officer or a peace officer is justified in using deadly physical force under circumstances prescribed in paragraphs (a) and (b) of subdivision one does not constitute justification for reckless conduct by such police officer or peace officer amounting to an offense against or with respect to innocent persons whom he or she is not seeking to arrest or retain in custody.

3. A person who has been directed by a police officer or a peace officer to assist such police officer or peace officer to effect an arrest or to prevent an escape from custody may use physical force, other than deadly physical force, when and to the extent that he or she reasonably believes such to be necessary to carry out such police officer's or peace officer's direction, unless he or she knows that the arrest or prospective arrest is not or was not authorized and may use deadly physical force under such circumstances when:

(a) He or she reasonably believes such to be necessary for self-defense or to defend a third person from what he or she reasonably believes to be the use or imminent use of deadly physical force; or

(b) He or she is directed or authorized by such police officer or peace officer to use deadly physical force unless he or she knows that the police officer or peace officer is not authorized to use deadly physical force under the circumstances.

4. A private person acting on his or her own account may use physical force, other than deadly physical force, upon another person when and to the extent that he or she reasonably believes such to be necessary to effect an arrest or to prevent the escape from custody of a person whom he or she reasonably believes to have committed an offense and who in fact has committed such offense; and may use deadly physical force for such purpose when he or she reasonably believes such to be necessary to:

(a) Defend himself, herself or a third person from what he or she reasonably believes to be the use or imminent use of deadly physical force; or

(b) Effect the arrest of a person who has committed murder, manslaughter in the first degree, robbery, forcible rape or forcible criminal sexual act and who is in immediate flight therefrom.

5. A guard, police officer or peace officer who is charged with the duty of guarding prisoners in a detention facility, as that term is defined in section 205.00, or while in transit to or from a detention facility, may use physical force when and to the extent that he or she reasonably believes such to be necessary to prevent the escape of a prisoner from a detention facility or from custody while in transit thereto or therefrom.

N.Y. Penal Law § 35.30

Article 40 - OTHER DEFENSES INVOLVING LACK OF CULPABILITY

Section 40.00 - Duress

1. In any prosecution for an offense, it is an affirmative defense that the defendant engaged in the proscribed conduct because he was coerced to do so by the use or threatened imminent use of unlawful physical force upon him or a third person, which force or threatened force a person of reasonable firmness in his situation would have been unable to resist.

2. The defense of duress as defined in subdivision one of this section is not available when a person intentionally or recklessly places himself in a situation in which it is probable that he will be subjected to duress.

N.Y. Penal Law § 40.00

Section 40.05 - Entrapment

In any prosecution for an offense, it is an affirmative defense that the defendant engaged in the proscribed conduct because he was induced or encouraged to do so by a public servant, or by a person acting in cooperation with a public servant, seeking to obtain evidence against him for purpose of criminal prosecution, and when the methods used to obtain such evidence were such as to create a substantial risk that the offense would be committed by a person not otherwise disposed to commit it. Inducement or encouragement to commit an offense means active inducement or encouragement. Conduct merely affording a person an opportunity to commit an offense does not constitute entrapment.

N.Y. Penal Law § 40.05

Section 40.10 - Renunciation

1. In any prosecution for an offense, other than an attempt to commit a crime, in which the defendant's guilt depends upon his criminal liability for the conduct of another person pursuant to section 20.00, it is an affirmative defense that, under circumstances manifesting a voluntary and complete renunciation of his criminal purpose, the defendant withdrew from participation in such offense prior to the commission thereof and made a substantial effort to prevent the commission thereof.

2. In any prosecution for criminal facilitation pursuant to article one hundred fifteen, it is an affirmative defense that, prior to the commission of the felony which he facilitated, the defendant made a substantial effort to prevent the commission of such felony.

3. In any prosecution pursuant to section 110.00 for an attempt to commit a crime, it is an affirmative defense that, under circumstances manifesting a voluntary and complete renunciation of his criminal purpose, the defendant avoided the commission of the crime attempted by abandoning his criminal effort and, if mere abandonment was insufficient to accomplish such avoidance, by taking further and affirmative steps which prevented the commission thereof.

4. In any prosecution for criminal solicitation pursuant to article one hundred or for conspiracy pursuant to article one hundred five in which the crime solicited or the crime contemplated by the conspiracy was not in fact committed, it is an affirmative defense that, under circumstances manifesting a voluntary and complete renunciation of his criminal purpose, the defendant prevented the commission of such crime.

5. A renunciation is not "voluntary and complete" within the meaning of this section if it is motivated in whole or in part by (a) a belief that circumstances exist which increase the probability of detection or apprehension of the defendant or another participant in the criminal enterprise, or which render more difficult the accomplishment of the criminal purpose, or (b) a decision to postpone the criminal conduct until another time or to transfer the criminal effort to another victim or another but similar objective.

N.Y. Penal Law § 40.10

Section 40.15 - Mental disease or defect

In any prosecution for an offense, it is an affirmative defense that when the defendant engaged in the proscribed conduct, he lacked criminal responsibility by reason of mental disease or defect. Such lack of criminal responsibility means that at the time of such conduct, as a result of mental disease or defect, he lacked substantial capacity to know or appreciate either:

1. The nature and consequences of such conduct; or

2. That such conduct was wrong.

N.Y. Penal Law § 40.15

Part 2 - SENTENCES

Title E - SENTENCES

Article 55 - CLASSIFICATION AND DESIGNATION OF OFFENSES

Section 55.00 - Applicability of article

The provisions of this article govern the classification and designation of every offense, whether defined within or outside of this chapter.

N.Y. Penal Law § 55.00

Section 55.05 - Classifications of felonies and misdemeanors

1. Felonies. Felonies are classified, for the purpose of sentence, into five categories as follows:

(a) Class A felonies;

(b) Class B felonies;

(c) Class C felonies;

(d) Class D felonies; and

(e) Class E felonies.

Class A felonies are subclassified, for the purpose of sentence, into two categories as follows: subclass I and subclass II, to be known as class A-I and class A-II felonies, respectively.

2. Misdemeanors. Misdemeanors are classified, for the purpose of sentence, into three categories as follows:

(a) Class A misdemeanors;

(b) Class B misdemeanors; and

(c) Unclassified misdemeanors.

N.Y. Penal Law § 55.05

Section 55.10 - Designation of offenses

1. Felonies.

(a) The particular classification or subclassification of each felony defined in this chapter is expressly designated in the section or article defining it.

(b) Any offense defined outside this chapter which is declared by law to be a felony without specification of the classification thereof, or for which a law outside this chapter provides a sentence to a term of imprisonment in excess of one year, shall be deemed a class E felony.

2. Misdemeanors.

(a) Each misdemeanor defined in this chapter is either a class A misdemeanor or a class B misdemeanor, as expressly designated in the section or article defining it.

(b) Any offense defined outside this chapter which is declared by law to be a misdemeanor without specification of the classification thereof or of the sentence therefor shall be deemed a class A misdemeanor.

(c) Except as provided in paragraph (b) of subdivision three, where an offense is defined outside this chapter and a sentence to a term of imprisonment in excess of fifteen days but not in excess of one year is provided in the law or ordinance defining it, such offense shall be deemed an unclassified misdemeanor.

3. Violations. Every violation defined in this chapter is expressly designated as such. Any offense defined outside this chapter which is not expressly designated a violation shall be deemed a violation if:

(a) Notwithstanding any other designation specified in the law or ordinance defining it, a sentence to a term of imprisonment which is not in excess of fifteen days is provided therein, or the only sentence provided therein is a fine; or

(b) A sentence to a term of imprisonment in excess of fifteen days is provided for such offense in a law or ordinance enacted prior to the effective date of this chapter but the offense was not a crime prior to that date.

4. Traffic infraction. Notwithstanding any other provision of this section, an offense which is defined as a "traffic infraction" shall not be deemed a violation or a misdemeanor by virtue of the sentence prescribed therefor.

N.Y. Penal Law § 55.10

Article 60 - AUTHORIZED DISPOSITIONS OF OFFENDERS

Section 60.00 - Applicability of provisions

1. The sentences prescribed by this article shall apply in the case of every offense, whether defined within or outside of this chapter.

2. The sole provision of this article that shall apply in the case of an offense committed by a juvenile offender is section 60.10 of this article and no other provisions of this article shall be deemed or construed to apply in any such case.

N.Y. Penal Law § 60.00

Section 60.01 - Authorized dispositions; generally

1. Applicability. Except as otherwise specified in this article, when the court imposes sentence upon a person convicted of an offense, the court must impose a sentence prescribed by this section.

2. Revocable dispositions.

(a) The court may impose a revocable sentence as herein specified:

(i) the court, where authorized by article sixty-five, may sentence a person to a period of probation or to a period of conditional discharge as provided in that article; or

(ii) the court, where authorized by article eighty-five, may sentence a person to a term of intermittent imprisonment as provided in that article.

(b) A revocable sentence shall be deemed a tentative one to the extent that it may be altered or revoked in accordance with the provisions of the article under which it was imposed, but for all other purposes shall be deemed to be a final judgment of conviction.

(c) In any case where the court imposes a sentence of probation, conditional discharge, or a sentence of intermittent imprisonment, it may also impose a fine authorized by article eighty.

(d) In any case where the court imposes a sentence of imprisonment not in excess of sixty days, for a misdemeanor or not in excess of six months for a felony or in the case of a sentence of intermittent imprisonment not in excess of four months, it may also impose a sentence of probation or conditional discharge provided that the term of probation or conditional discharge together with the term of imprisonment shall not exceed the term of probation or conditional discharge authorized by article sixty-five of this chapter. The sentence of imprisonment shall be a condition of and run concurrently with the sentence of probation or conditional discharge.

3. Other dispositions. When a person is not sentenced as specified in subdivision two, or when a sentence specified in subdivision two is revoked, the sentence of the court must be as follows:

(a) A term of imprisonment; or

(b) A fine authorized by article eighty, provided, however, that when the conviction is of a class B felony or of any felony defined in article two hundred twenty, the sentence shall not consist solely of a fine; or

(c) Both imprisonment and a fine; or

(d) Where authorized by section 65.20, unconditional discharge as provided in that section; or

(e) Following revocation of a sentence of conditional discharge imposed pursuant to section 65.05 of this chapter or paragraph (d) of subdivision two of this section, probation as provided in section 65.00 of this chapter or to the sentence of imprisonment and probation as provided for in paragraph (d) of subdivision two of this section.

4. In any case where a person has been sentenced to a period of probation imposed pursuant to section 65.00 of this chapter, if the part of the sentence that provides for probation is revoked, the court must sentence such person to imprisonment or to the sentence of imprisonment and probation as provided for in paragraph (d) of subdivision two of this section.

N.Y. Penal Law § 60.01

Section 60.02 - Authorized disposition; youthful offender

When a person is to be sentenced upon a youthful offender finding, the court must impose a sentence as follows:

(1) If the sentence is to be imposed upon a youthful offender finding which has been substituted for a conviction of an offense other than a felony, the court must impose a sentence authorized for the offense for which the youthful offender finding was substituted, except that if the youthful offender finding was entered pursuant to paragraph (b) of subdivision one of section 720.20 of the criminal procedure law, the court must not impose a definite or intermittent sentence of imprisonment with a term of more than six months; or

(2) If the sentence is to be imposed upon a youthful offender finding which has been substituted for a conviction for any felony, the court must impose a sentence authorized to be imposed upon a person convicted of a class E felony provided, however, that the court must not impose a sentence of conditional discharge or unconditional discharge if the youthful offender finding was substituted for a conviction of a felony defined in article two hundred twenty of this chapter.

(3) [Repealed]

(4) Notwithstanding any other provision of law in this section, if the sentence is to be imposed upon a youthful offender finding which has been substituted for a conviction of prostitution or loitering for the purposes of prostitution provided that the person does not stand charged with loitering for the purpose of patronizing a prostitute, and such offense occurred when the person was sixteen or seventeen years of age, the court must impose a sentence authorized to be imposed upon a person convicted of a violation as defined in subdivision three of section 10.00 of the penal law and where the court imposes a revocable sentence authorized for a violation may order any of the specialized services enumerated in title eight-A of article six of the social services law or other appropriate services made available to persons in need of supervision in accordance with article seven of the family court act.

N.Y. Penal Law § 60.02

16

Amended by New York Laws 2020, ch. 144,Sec. 4, eff. 8/24/2020.
Amended by New York Laws 2014, ch. 402,Sec. 6, eff. 10/16/2014.

Section 60.04 - Authorized disposition; controlled substances and marihuana felony offenses

1. Applicability. Notwithstanding the provisions of any law, this section shall govern the dispositions authorized when a person is to be sentenced upon a conviction of a felony offense defined in article two hundred twenty or two hundred twenty-one of this chapter or when a person is to be sentenced upon a conviction of such a felony as a multiple felony offender as defined in subdivision five of this section.

2. Class A felony. Every person convicted of a class A felony must be sentenced to imprisonment in accordance with section 70.71 of this title, unless such person is convicted of a class A-II felony and is sentenced to probation for life in accordance with section 65.00 of this title.

3. Class B felonies. Every person convicted of a class B felony must be sentenced to imprisonment in accordance with the applicable provisions of section 70.70 of this chapter, a definite sentence of imprisonment with a term of one year or less or probation in accordance with section 65.00 of this chapter provided, however, a person convicted of criminal sale of a controlled substance to a child as defined in section 220.48 of this chapter must be sentenced to a determinate sentence of imprisonment in accordance with the applicable provisions of section 70.70 of this chapter or to a sentence of probation in accordance with the opening paragraph of paragraph (b) of subdivision one of section 65.00 of this chapter.

4. Alternative sentence. Where a sentence of imprisonment or a sentence of probation as an alternative to imprisonment is not required to be imposed pursuant to subdivision two, three or five of this section, the court may impose any other sentence authorized by section 60.01 of this article, provided that when the court imposes a sentence of imprisonment, such sentence must be in accordance with section 70.70 of this title. Where the court imposes a sentence of imprisonment in accordance with this section, the court may also impose a fine authorized by article eighty of this title and in such case the sentence shall be both imprisonment and a fine.

5. Multiple felony offender. Where the court imposes a sentence pursuant to subdivision three of section 70.70 of this chapter upon a second felony drug offender, as defined in paragraph (b) of subdivision one of section 70.70 of this chapter, it must sentence such offender to imprisonment in accordance with the applicable provisions of section 70.70 of this chapter, a definite sentence of imprisonment with a term of one year or less, or probation in accordance with section 65.00 of this chapter, provided, however, that where the court imposes a sentence upon a class B second felony drug offender, it must sentence such offender to a determinate sentence of imprisonment in accordance with the applicable provisions of section 70.70 of this chapter or to a sentence of probation in accordance with the opening paragraph of paragraph (b) of subdivision one of section 65.00 of this chapter. When the court imposes sentence on a second felony drug offender pursuant to subdivision four of section 70.70 of this chapter, it must impose a determinate sentence of imprisonment in accordance with such subdivision.

6. Substance abuse treatment. When the court imposes a sentence of imprisonment which requires a commitment to the state department of corrections and community supervision upon a person who stands convicted of a controlled substance or marihuana offense, the court may, upon motion of the defendant in its discretion, issue an order directing that the department of corrections and community supervision enroll the defendant in the comprehensive alcohol and substance abuse treatment program in an alcohol and substance abuse correctional annex as defined in subdivision eighteen of section two of the correction law, provided that the defendant will satisfy the statutory eligibility criteria for participation in such program. Notwithstanding the foregoing provisions of this subdivision, any defendant to be enrolled in such program pursuant to this subdivision shall be governed by the same rules and regulations promulgated by the department of corrections and community supervision, including without limitation those rules and regulations establishing requirements for completion and those rules and regulations governing discipline and removal from the program. No such period of court ordered corrections based drug abuse treatment pursuant to this subdivision shall be required to extend beyond the defendant's conditional release date.

7.

a. Shock incarceration participation. When the court imposes a sentence of imprisonment which requires a commitment to the department of corrections and community supervision upon a person who stands convicted of a controlled substance or marihuana offense, upon motion of the defendant, the court may issue an order directing that the department of corrections and community supervision enroll the defendant in the shock incarceration program as defined in article twenty-six-A of the correction law, provided that the defendant is an eligible incarcerated individual, as described in subdivision one of section eight hundred sixty-five of the correction law. Notwithstanding the foregoing provisions of this subdivision, any defendant to be enrolled in such program pursuant to this subdivision shall be governed by the same rules and regulations promulgated by the department of corrections and community supervision, including without limitation those rules and regulations establishing requirements for completion and such rules and regulations governing discipline and removal from the program.

b.

(i) In the event that an incarcerated individual designated by court order for enrollment in the shock incarceration program requires a degree of medical care or mental health care that cannot be provided at a shock incarceration facility, the department, in writing, shall notify the incarcerated individual, provide a proposal describing a proposed alternative-to-shock-incarceration program, and notify him or her that he or she may object in writing to placement in such alternative-to-shock-incarceration program. If the incarcerated individual objects in writing to placement in such alternative-to-shock-incarceration program, the department of corrections and community supervision shall notify the sentencing court, provide such proposal to the court, and arrange for the incarcerated individual's prompt appearance before the court. The court shall provide the proposal and notice of a court appearance to the people, the incarcerated individual and the appropriate defense attorney. After considering the proposal and any submissions by the parties, and after a reasonable opportunity for the people, the incarcerated individual and counsel to be heard, the court may modify its sentencing order accordingly, notwithstanding the provisions of section 430.10 of the criminal procedure law.

(ii) An incarcerated individual who successfully completes an alternative-to-shock-incarceration program within the department of corrections and community supervision shall be treated in the same manner as a person who has successfully completed the shock incarceration program, as set forth in subdivision four of section eight hundred sixty-seven of the correction law.

N.Y. Penal Law § 60.04

Amended by New York Laws 2021, ch. 322,Sec. 102, eff. 8/2/2021.

Section 60.05 - Authorized dispositions; other class A, B, certain C and D felonies and multiple felony offenders

1. Applicability. Except as provided in section 60.04 of this article governing the authorized dispositions applicable to felony offenses defined in article two hundred twenty or two hundred twenty-one of this chapter or in section 60.13 of this article governing the authorized dispositions applicable to felony sex offenses defined in paragraph (a) of subdivision one of section 70.80 of this title, this section shall govern the dispositions authorized when a person is to be sentenced upon a conviction of a class A felony, a class B felony or a class C, class D or class E felony specified herein, or when a person is to be sentenced upon a conviction of a felony as a multiple felony offender.

2. Class A felony. Except as provided in subdivisions three and four of section 70.06 of this chapter, every person convicted of a class A felony must be sentenced to imprisonment in accordance with section 70.00 of this title, unless such person is convicted of murder in the first degree and is sentenced in accordance with section 60.06 of this article.

3. Class B felony. Except as provided in subdivision six of this section, every person convicted of a class B violent felony offense as defined in subdivision one of section 70.02 of this title, must be sentenced to imprisonment in accordance with such section 70.02; and, except as provided in subdivision six of this section, every person convicted of any other class B felony must be sentenced to imprisonment in accordance with section 70.00 of this title.

4. Certain class C felonies. Except as provided in subdivision six, every person convicted of a class C violent felony offense as defined in subdivision one of section 70.02 of this title, must be sentenced to imprisonment in accordance with section 70.02 of this title; and, except as provided in subdivision six of this section, every person convicted of the class C felonies of: attempt to commit any of the class B felonies of bribery in the first degree as defined in section 200.04, bribe receiving in the first degree as defined in section 200.12, conspiracy in the second degree as defined in section 105.15 and criminal mischief in the first degree as defined in section 145.12; criminal usury in the first degree as defined in section 190.42, rewarding official misconduct in the first degree as defined in section 200.22, receiving reward for official misconduct in the first degree as defined in section 200.27, attempt to promote prostitution in the first degree as defined in section 230.32, promoting prostitution in the second degree as defined in section 230.30, arson in the third degree as defined in section 150.10 of this chapter, must be sentenced to imprisonment in accordance with section 70.00 of this title.

5. Certain class D felonies. Except as provided in subdivision six of this section, every person convicted of the class D felonies of assault in the second degree as defined in section 120.05, strangulation in the second degree as defined in section 121.12 or attempt to commit a class C felony as defined in section 230.30 of this chapter, must be sentenced in accordance with section 70.00 or 85.00 of this title.

6. Multiple felony offender. When the court imposes sentence upon a second violent felony offender, as defined in section 70.04, or a second felony offender, as defined in section 70.06, the court must impose a sentence of imprisonment in accordance with section 70.04 or 70.06, as the case may be, unless it imposes a sentence of imprisonment in accordance with section 70.08 or 70.10.

7. Fines. Where the court imposes a sentence of imprisonment in accordance with this section, the court also may impose a fine authorized by article eighty and in such case the sentence shall be both imprisonment and a fine.

8. Shock incarceration participation.

(a) When the court imposes a determinate sentence of imprisonment pursuant to subdivision three of section 70.02 of this chapter or subdivision six of section 70.06 of this chapter upon a person who stands convicted either of burglary in the second degree as defined in subdivision two of section 140.25 of this chapter or robbery in the second degree as defined in subdivision one of section 160.10 of this chapter, or an attempt thereof, upon motion of the defendant, the court may issue an order directing that the department of corrections and community supervision enroll the defendant in the shock incarceration program as defined in article twenty-six-A of the correction law, provided that the defendant is an eligible inmate, as described in subdivision one of section eight hundred sixty-five of the correction law. Notwithstanding the foregoing provisions of this subdivision, any defendant to be enrolled in such program pursuant to this subdivision shall be governed by the same rules and regulations promulgated by the department of corrections and community supervision, including without limitation those rules and regulations establishing requirements for completion and such rules and regulations governing discipline and removal from the program.

(b) Paragraph (b) of subdivision seven of section 60.04 of this article shall apply in the event an inmate designated by court order for enrollment in the shock incarceration program requires a degree of medical care or mental health care that cannot be provided at a shock incarceration facility.

N.Y. Penal Law § 60.05

Amended by New York Laws 2019, ch. 55,Sec. KK-1, eff. 5/12/2019.

18

§ 60.06 Authorized disposition; murder in the first degree offenders;

N.Y. Penal Law § 60.06

Section 60.07 - Authorized disposition; criminal attack on operators of for-hire vehicles

1. Notwithstanding any other provision of law to the contrary, when a court has found, pursuant to the provisions of section 200.61 of the criminal procedure law, both that a person has been convicted of a specified offense as defined in subdivision two of this section and the victim of such offense was operating a for-hire vehicle in the course of providing for-hire vehicle services at the time of the commission of such offense, the sentence of imprisonment imposed upon conviction for such offense shall be the sentence authorized by the applicable provisions of article seventy of this chapter, provided, however, that the minimum term of an indeterminate sentence or minimum determinate sentence shall be not less than three years nor more than five years greater than the minimum term or sentence otherwise required to be imposed pursuant to such provisions. The provisions of this subdivision shall not apply where the court, having regard to the nature and circumstances of the crime and the history and character of the defendant, finds on the record that such additional term or sentence would be unduly harsh and that not imposing such additional term or sentence would be consistent with the public safety and would not deprecate the seriousness of the crime.

2. For purposes of this section:

(a) the term "specified offense" shall mean an attempt to commit murder in the second degree as defined in section 125.25 of this chapter, gang assault in the first degree as defined in section 120.07 of this chapter, gang assault in the second degree as defined in section 120.06 of this chapter, assault in the first degree as defined in section 120.10 of this chapter, manslaughter in the first degree as defined in section 125.20 of this chapter, manslaughter in the second degree as defined in section 125.15 of this chapter, robbery in the first degree as defined in section 160.15 of this chapter, robbery in the second degree as defined in section 160.10 of this chapter, or the attempted commission of any of the following offenses: gang assault in the first degree as defined in section 120.07, assault in the first degree as defined in section 120.10, manslaughter in the first degree as defined in section 125.20 or robbery in the first degree as defined in section 160.15;

(b) the term "for-hire vehicle" shall mean a vehicle designed to carry not more than five passengers for compensation and such vehicle is a taxicab, as defined in section one hundred forty-eight-a of the vehicle and traffic law, a livery, as such term is defined in section one hundred twenty-one-e of the vehicle and traffic law, or a "black car", as such term is defined in paragraph (g) of this subdivision;

(c) the term "livery car base" shall mean a central facility, wherever located, that dispatches a livery operator to both pick-up and discharge passengers in the state;

(d) "for-hire vehicle services" shall mean:

(i) with respect to a taxicab, the transport of passengers pursuant to a license or permit issued by a local authority by a person duly authorized to operate such taxicab;

(ii) with respect to a livery, the transport of passengers by a livery operator while affiliated with a livery car base; or

(iii) with respect to a "black car", the transport of passengers by a "black car operator" pursuant to dispatches from or by a central dispatch facility regardless of where the pick-up and discharge occurs, and, with respect to dispatches from or by a central dispatch facility located outside the state, all dispatches involving a pick-up in the state, regardless of where the discharge occurs.

(e) "livery operator" shall mean the registered owner of a livery, as such term is defined in section one hundred twenty-one-e of the vehicle and traffic law, or a driver designated by such registered owner to operate the registered owner's livery as the registered owner's authorized designee, where such registered owner or driver provides services while affiliated with a livery car base;

(f) "black car operator" shall mean the registered owner of a "black car" or a driver designated by such registered owner to operate the registered owner's black car as the registered owner's authorized designee; and

(g) "black car" shall mean a for-hire vehicle dispatched from a central facility, which has certified to the satisfaction of the department of state pursuant to article six-F of the executive law that more than ninety percent of the central facility's for-hire business is on a payment basis other than direct cash payment by a passenger.

N.Y. Penal Law § 60.07

Section 60.08 - Authorized dispositions; resentencing of certain controlled substance offenders

Any person convicted of an offense and sentenced to prison for an indeterminate sentence, the minimum of which was at least one year and the maximum of which was life imprisonment, which sentence was imposed pursuant to chapter two hundred seventy-six, two hundred seventy-seven, two hundred seventy-eight, or ten hundred fifty-one of the laws of nineteen hundred seventy-three, and for which such sentence was imposed upon conviction of the crime of criminal possession of a controlled substance in the first degree, criminal possession of a controlled substance in the second degree, criminal possession of a controlled substance in the third degree, criminal sale of a controlled substance in the first degree, criminal sale of a controlled substance in the second degree, or criminal sale of a controlled substance in the third degree, and the sole controlled substance involved was methadone, may apply, upon notice to the appropriate district attorney, for resentencing in the court which originally imposed sentence.

N.Y. Penal Law § 60.08

Section 60.09 - Authorized dispositions; resentencing of certain persons convicted of specified controlled substance offenses

a. Any person convicted of an offense as defined in section 115.05, 220.16, 220.18, 220.39 or 220.41 of this chapter or of an attempt thereof, for an act committed on or after September first, nineteen hundred seventy-three but prior to the date on which the provisions of this section become effective, may, upon notice to the appropriate district attorney, apply for resentencing in the court which originally imposed sentence. Such resentencing shall be in accordance with the provisions of subdivision (b) of this section and shall include credit for any jail time incurred upon the subject conviction as well as credit for any period of incarceration incurred pursuant to the sentence originally imposed.

b. A court, upon an application specified in subdivision (a) of this section may resentence a person as follows:

(i) if the conviction was for a class A-III offense the court may impose a new maximum term which shall be no less than three times the amount of the minimum term imposed in the original sentence and no more than twenty-five years;

(ii) if the conviction was for a class A-II offense the court may impose a new minimum term which shall be no less than three years imprisonment and no more than eight and one-third years;

(iii) upon resentence of a person as specified in paragraph (i) of this subdivision the court shall resentence the person to the same minimum term previously imposed;

(iv) upon resentence of a person as specified in paragraph (ii) of this subdivision the court shall impose a maximum term of life imprisonment;

(v) if the conviction was for an offense as specified in section 115.05 of this chapter and the offense which was the object of the criminal facilitation was a class A-III felony then the court shall set aside the conviction and substitute it with a conviction for violation of section 115.01 or 115.00 of this chapter, whichever is appropriate under the facts of the case, and impose a sentence in accordance with those provisions.

c. Upon resentence as provided in this section the court may not impose a sentence greater than the sentence previously imposed.

N.Y. Penal Law § 60.09

Section 60.10 - Authorized disposition; juvenile offender

1. When a juvenile offender is convicted of a crime, the court shall sentence the defendant to imprisonment in accordance with section 70.05 or sentence him upon a youthful offender finding in accordance with section 60.02 of this chapter.

2. Subdivision one of this section shall apply when sentencing a juvenile offender notwithstanding the provisions of any other law that deals with the authorized sentence for persons who are not juvenile offenders. Provided, however, that the limitation prescribed by this section shall not be deemed or construed to bar use of a conviction of a juvenile offender, other than a juvenile offender who has been adjudicated a youthful offender pursuant to section 720.20 of the criminal procedure law, as a previous or predicate felony offender under section 70.04, 70.06, 70.08 or 70.10, when sentencing a person who commits a felony after he has reached the age of sixteen.

N.Y. Penal Law § 60.10

Section 60.10-A - [SeeNew York Laws2017, ch.59,Sec.WWW-106subsection b for further contingencies for 10/1/2019]Authorized disposition; adolescent offender

When an adolescent offender is convicted of an offense, the court shall sentence the defendant to any sentence authorized to be imposed on a person who committed such offense at age eighteen or older. When a sentence is imposed, the court shall consider the age of the defendant in exercising its discretion at sentencing.

N.Y. Penal Law § 60.10-A

Added by New York Laws 2017, ch. 59,Sec. WWW-41, eff. 10/1/2018.

Section 60.11 - Authorized dispositions; criminal possession of a weapon in the fourth degree

When a person is to be sentenced upon a conviction of the crime of criminal possession of a weapon in the fourth degree as defined in subdivision one of section 265.01 as a result of a plea of guilty entered in satisfaction of an indictment or count thereof charging the defendant with the class D violent felony offense of criminal possession of a weapon in the third degree as defined in subdivision four of section 265.02, the court must sentence the defendant in accordance with the provisions of section 70.15.

N.Y. Penal Law § 60.11

Section 60.11A - Authorized dispositions; certain criminal possession of a weapon in the third degree offenders

When a person is to be sentenced upon conviction of the crime of criminal possession of a weapon in the third degree as defined in subdivision ten of section 26502 of this chapter, the court must sentence such defendant to a determinate sentence as provided in subparagraph (ii) of paragraph (c) of subdivision three of section 7002 of this chapter, unless a greater minimum sentence is otherwise required by another provision of this chapter

N.Y. Penal Law § 60.11A

Added by New York Laws 2013, ch. 1,Sec. 26-a, eff. 3/16/2013.

Section 60.12 - Authorized disposition; alternative sentence domestic violence cases

1. Notwithstanding any other provision of law, where a court is imposing sentence upon a person pursuant to section 70.00, 70.02 , 70.06 or subdivision two or three of section 70.71 of this title, other than for an offense defined in section 125.26, 125.27, subdivision five of section 125.25, or article 490 of this chapter, or for an offense which would require such person to register as a sex offender pursuant to article six-C of the correction law, an attempt or conspiracy to commit any such offense, and is authorized or required pursuant to sections 70.00, 70.02, 70.06 or subdivision two or three of section 70.71 of this title to impose a sentence of imprisonment , the court, upon a determination following a hearing that (a) at the time of the instant offense, the defendant was a victim of domestic violence subjected to substantial physical, sexual or

psychological abuse inflicted by a member of the same family or household as the defendant as such term is defined in subdivision one of section 530.11 of the criminal procedure law; (b) such abuse was a significant contributing factor to the defendant's criminal behavior; (c) having regard for the nature and circumstances of the crime and the history, character and condition of the defendant, that a sentence of imprisonment pursuant to section 70.00, 70.02 or 70.06 of this title would be unduly harsh may instead impose a sentence in accordance with this section. A court may determine that such abuse constitutes a significant contributing factor pursuant to paragraph (b) of this subdivision regardless of whether the defendant raised a defense pursuant to article thirty-five, article forty, or subdivision one of section 125.25 of this chapter. At the hearing to determine whether the defendant should be sentenced pursuant to this section, the court shall consider oral and written arguments, take testimony from witnesses offered by either party, and consider relevant evidence to assist in making its determination. Reliable hearsay shall be admissible at such hearings.

2. Where a court would otherwise be required to impose a sentence pursuant to section 70.02 of this title, the court may impose a definite sentence of imprisonment of one year or less, or probation in accordance with the provisions of section 65.00 of this title, or may fix a determinate term of imprisonment as follows:

(a) For a class B felony, the term must be at least one year and must not exceed five years;

(b) For a class C felony, the term must be at least one year and must not exceed three and one-half years;

(c) For a class D felony, the term must be at least one year and must not exceed two years; and

(d) For a class E felony, the term must be one year and must not exceed one and one-half years.

3. Where a court would otherwise be required to impose a sentence for a class A felony offense pursuant to section 70.00 of this title, the court may fix a determinate term of imprisonment of at least five years and not to exceed fifteen years.

4. Where a court would otherwise be required to impose a sentence for a class A felony offense pursuant to subparagraph (i) of paragraph (b) of subdivision two of section 70.71 of this title, the court may fix a determinate term of imprisonment of at least five years and not to exceed eight years.

5. Where a court would otherwise be required to impose a sentence for a class A felony offense pursuant to subparagraph (i) of paragraph (b) of subdivision three of section 70.71 of this title, the court may fix a determinate term of imprisonment of at least five years and not to exceed twelve years.

6. Where a court would otherwise be required to impose a sentence for a class A felony offense pursuant to subparagraph (ii) of paragraph (b) of subdivision two of section 70.71 of this title, the court may fix a determinate term of imprisonment of at least one year and not to exceed three years.

7. Where a court would otherwise be required to impose a sentence for a class A felony offense pursuant to subparagraph (ii) of paragraph (b) of subdivision three of section 70.71 of this title, the court may fix a determinate term of imprisonment of at least three years and not to exceed six years.

8. Where a court would otherwise be required to impose a sentence pursuant to subdivision six of section 70.06 of this title, the court may fix a term of imprisonment as follows:

(a) For a class B felony, the term must be at least three years and must not exceed eight years;

(b) For a class C felony, the term must be at least two and one-half years and must not exceed five years;

(c) For a class D felony, the term must be at least two years and must not exceed three years;

(d) For a class E felony, the term must be at least one and one-half years and must not exceed two years.

9. Where a court would otherwise be required to impose a sentence for a class B, C, D or E felony offense pursuant to section 70.00 of this title, the court may impose a sentence in accordance with the provisions of subdivision two of section 70.70 of this title.

10. Except as provided in subdivision seven of this section, where a court would otherwise be required to impose a sentence pursuant to subdivision three of section 70.06 of this title, the court may impose a sentence in accordance with the provisions of subdivision three of section 70.70 of this title.

11. Where a court would otherwise be required to impose a sentence pursuant to subdivision three of section 70.06 of this title, where the prior felony conviction was for a felony offense defined in section 70.02 of this title, the court may impose a sentence in accordance with the provisions of subdivision four of section 70.70 of this title.

N.Y. Penal Law § 60.12

Amended by New York Laws 2019, ch. 55,Sec. WW-1, eff. 5/14/2019.

Amended by New York Laws 2019, ch. 31,Sec. 1, eff. 5/14/2019.

Section 60.13 - Authorized dispositions; felony sex offenses

When a person is to be sentenced upon a conviction for any felony defined in article one hundred thirty of this chapter, including a sexually motivated felony, or patronizing a person for prostitution in the first degree as defined in section 230.06 of this chapter, aggravated patronizing a minor for prostitution in the third degree as defined in section 230.11 of this chapter, aggravated patronizing a minor for prostitution in the second degree as defined in section 230.12 of this chapter, aggravated patronizing a minor for prostitution in the first degree as defined in section 230.13 of this chapter, incest in the second degree as defined in section 255.26 of this chapter, or incest in the first degree as defined in section 255.27 of this chapter, or a felony attempt or conspiracy to commit any of these crimes, the court must sentence the defendant in accordance with the provisions of section 70.80 of this title.

N.Y. Penal Law § 60.13

Amended by New York Laws 2015, ch. 368,Sec. 2, eff. 1/19/2016.

Section 60.20 - Authorized dispositions; traffic infraction

1. When a person is convicted of a traffic infraction, the sentence of the court shall be as follows:

(a) A period of conditional discharge, as provided in article sixty-five; or

(b) Unconditional discharge as provided in section 65.20; or

(c) A fine or a sentence to a term of imprisonment, or both, as prescribed in and authorized by the provision that defines the infraction; or

(d) A sentence of intermittent imprisonment, as provided in article eighty-five.

2. Where a sentence of conditional discharge is imposed for a traffic infraction, all incidents of the sentence shall be the same as would be applicable if the sentence were for a violation.

N.Y. Penal Law § 60.20

Section 60.21 - Authorized dispositions; driving while intoxicated or aggravated driving while intoxicated

Notwithstanding paragraph (d) of subdivision two of section 60.01 of this article, when a person is to be sentenced upon a conviction for a violation of subdivision two, two-a or three of section eleven hundred ninety-two of the vehicle and traffic law, the court may sentence such person to a period of imprisonment authorized by article seventy of this title and shall sentence such person to a period of probation or conditional discharge in accordance with the provisions of section 65.00 of this title and shall order the installation and maintenance of a functioning ignition interlock device. Such period of probation or conditional discharge shall run consecutively to any period of imprisonment and shall commence immediately upon such person's release from imprisonment.

N.Y. Penal Law § 60.21

Section 60.25 - Authorized dispositions; corporation

When a corporation is convicted of an offense, the sentence of the court shall be as follows:

(a) A fine authorized by section 80.10; or

(b) Where authorized by section 65.05, a period of conditional discharge as provided in that section; or

(c) Where authorized by section 65.20, unconditional discharge as provided in that section.

In any case where a corporation has been sentenced to a period of conditional discharge and such sentence is revoked, the court shall sentence the corporation to pay a fine.

N.Y. Penal Law § 60.25

Section 60.27 - Restitution and reparation

1. In addition to any of the dispositions authorized by this article, the court shall consider restitution or reparation to the victim of the crime and may require restitution or reparation as part of the sentence imposed upon a person convicted of an offense, and after providing the district attorney with an opportunity to be heard in accordance with the provisions of this subdivision, require the defendant to make restitution of the fruits of his or her offense or reparation for the actual out-of-pocket loss caused thereby and, in the case of a violation of section 190.78, 190.79, 190.80, 190.82 or 190.83 of this chapter, any costs or losses incurred due to any adverse action taken against the victim. The district attorney shall where appropriate, advise the court at or before the time of sentencing that the victim seeks restitution or reparation, the extent of injury or economic loss or damage of the victim, and the amount of restitution or reparation sought by the victim in accordance with his or her responsibilities under subdivision two of section 390.50 of the criminal procedure law and article twenty-three of the executive law. The court shall hear and consider the information presented by the district attorney in this regard. In that event, or when the victim impact statement reports that the victim seeks restitution or reparation, the court shall require, unless the interests of justice dictate otherwise, in addition to any of the dispositions authorized by this article that the defendant make restitution of the fruits of the offense and reparation for the actual out-of-pocket loss and, in the case of a violation of section 190.78, 190.79, 190.80, 190.82 or 190.83 of this chapter, any costs or losses incurred due to any adverse action, caused thereby to the victim. In the event that restitution or reparation are not ordered, the court shall clearly state its reasons on the record. Adverse action as used in this subdivision shall mean and include actual loss incurred by the victim, including an amount equal to the value of the time reasonably spent by the victim attempting to remediate the harm incurred by the victim from the offense, and the consequential financial losses from such action.

2. Whenever the court requires restitution or reparation to be made, the court must make a finding as to the dollar amount of the fruits of the offense and the actual out-of-pocket loss to the victim caused by the offense. In making this finding, the court must consider any victim impact statement provided to the court. If the record does not contain sufficient evidence to support such finding or upon request by the defendant, the court must conduct a hearing upon the issue in accordance with the procedure set forth in section 400.30 of the criminal procedure law.

3. The provisions of sections 420.10, 420.20 and 420.30 of the criminal procedure law shall apply in the collection and remission of restitution and reparation.

4. For purposes of the imposition, determination and collection of restitution or reparation, the following definitions shall apply:

(a) the term "offense" shall include the offense for which a defendant was convicted, as well as any other offense that is part of the same criminal transaction or that is contained in any other accusatory instrument disposed of by any plea of guilty by the defendant to an offense.

(b) the term "victim" shall include the victim of the offense, the representative of a crime victim as defined in subdivision six of section six hundred twenty-one of the executive law, an individual whose identity was assumed or whose personal identifying information was used in violation of section 190.78, 190.79 or 190.80 of this chapter, or any person who has suffered a financial loss as a direct result of the acts of a defendant in violation of section 190.78, 190.79, 190.80, 190.82 or 190.83 of this chapter, a good samaritan as defined in section six hundred twenty-one of the executive law and the office of victim services or other governmental agency that has received an application for or has provided financial assistance or compensation to the victim. A victim shall also mean any owner or lawful producer of a master recording, or a trade association that represents such owner or lawful producer, that has suffered injury as a result of an offense as defined in article two hundred seventy-five of this chapter.

5.

(a) Except upon consent of the defendant or as provided in paragraph (b) of this subdivision, or as a condition of probation or conditional discharge as provided in paragraph (g) of subdivision two of section 65.10 of this chapter, the amount of restitution or reparation required by the court shall not exceed fifteen thousand dollars in the case of a conviction for a felony, or ten thousand dollars in the case of a conviction for any offense other than a felony. Notwithstanding the provisions of this subdivision, if an officer of a school district is convicted of violating any section of article one hundred fifty-five of this chapter where the victim of such crime is such officer's school district, the court may require an amount of restitution up to the full amount of the fruits of the offense or reparation up to the full amount of the actual out-of-pocket loss suffered by the victim, provided further that in such case the provisions of paragraph (b) of this subdivision shall not apply.

(b) The court in its discretion may impose restitution or reparation in excess of the amounts specified in paragraph (a) of this subdivision, provided however that the amount in excess must be limited to the return of the victim's property, including money, or the equivalent value thereof; and reimbursement for medical expenses actually incurred by the victim prior to sentencing as a result of the offense committed by the defendant.

6. Any payment made as restitution or reparation pursuant to this section shall not limit, preclude or impair any liability for damages in any civil action or proceeding for an amount in excess of such payment.

7. In the event that the court requires restitution or reparation to be made to a person and that person dies prior to the completion of said restitution or reparation, the remaining payments shall be made to the estate of the deceased.

8. The court shall in all cases where restitution or reparation is imposed direct as part of the disposition that the defendant pay a designated surcharge of five percent of the entire amount of a restitution or reparation payment to the official or organization designated pursuant to subdivision eight of section 420.10 of the criminal procedure law. The designated surcharge shall not exceed five percent of the amount actually collected. Upon the filing of an affidavit of the official or organization designated pursuant to subdivision eight of section 420.10 of the criminal procedure law demonstrating that the actual cost of the collection and administration of restitution or reparation in a particular case exceeds five percent of the entire amount of the payment or the amount actually collected, as the case may be, the court shall direct that the defendant pay an additional surcharge of not more than five percent of the entire amount of a restitution or reparation payment to such official or organization, or the actual cost of collection or administration, whichever is less unless, upon application of the defendant, the court determines that imposition of such additional surcharge would cause undue hardship to the defendant, or any other person who is financially supported by the defendant, or would otherwise not be in the interest of justice. Such additional surcharge, when added to the initial five percent surcharge, shall not exceed ten percent of the amount actually collected.

9. If the offense of which a person is convicted is a class A, class B, class C, or class D felony involving the sale of a controlled substance, as defined in article two hundred twenty of this chapter, and no other victim who is a person is seeking restitution in the case, the term "victim" as used in this section, in addition to its ordinary meaning, shall mean any law enforcement agency of the state of New York or of any subdivision thereof which has expended funds in the purchase of any controlled substance from such person or his agent as part of the investigation leading to such conviction. Any restitution which may be required to be made to a law enforcement agency pursuant to this section shall be limited to the amount of funds expended in the actual purchase of such controlled substance by such law enforcement agency, less the amount of any funds which have been or will be recovered from any other source, and shall not include a designated surcharge pursuant to subdivision eight of this section. Any law enforcement agency seeking restitution pursuant to this section shall file with the court and the district attorney an affidavit stating that funds expended in the actual purchase of a controlled substance for which restitution is being sought have not been and will not be recovered from any other source or in any other civil or criminal proceeding. Any law enforcement agency receiving restitution pursuant to this section shall promptly transmit to the commissioner of the division of criminal justice services a report stating the dollar amount of the restitution received.

10. If the offense of which a person is convicted is defined in section 150.10, 150.15 or 150.20 of this chapter, and no other victim who is a person is seeking restitution in the case, the term "victim" as used in this section, in addition to its ordinary meaning, shall mean any municipality or volunteer fire company which has expended funds or will expend funds for the purpose of restoration, rehabilitation or clean-up of the site of the arson. Any restitution which may be required to be made to a municipality or volunteer fire company pursuant to this section shall be limited to the amount of funds reasonably expended or to be expended for the purpose of restoration, rehabilitation or cleanup of the site of the arson, less the amount of any funds which have been or will be recovered from any other source, and shall not include a designated surcharge pursuant to subdivision eight of this section. Any municipality or volunteer fire company seeking restitution pursuant to this section shall file with the court, district attorney and defense counsel an affidavit stating that the funds reasonably expended or to be expended for which restitution is being sought have not been and will not be recovered from any other source or in any other civil or criminal proceeding. For the purposes of this subdivision, "volunteer fire company" means a fire company as defined in paragraph a of subdivision two of section one hundred of the general municipal law.

11. Notwithstanding any other provision of this section to the contrary, when a person is convicted of harming an animal trained to aid a person with a disability in the second degree as defined in section 195.11 of this chapter, or harming an animal trained to aid a person with a disability in the first degree as defined in section 195.12 of this chapter, the court, in

addition to any other sentence, shall order the payment of restitution to the person with a disability who was aided by such animal.

12. If the offense of which a person is convicted is defined in section 155.25, 155.30, 155.35, 155.40 or 155.42 of this chapter, and the property taken is timber, the court may upon conviction, in addition to any other sentence, direct the defendant to pay the rightful owner of such timber an amount equal to treble the stumpage value of the timber stolen as defined in section 71-0703 of the environmental conservation law and for any permanent and substantial damage caused to the land or the improvements thereon as a result of such violation. Such reparations shall be of such kind, nature and extent as will reasonably restore the lands affected by the violation to their condition immediately before the violation and may be made by physical restoration of such lands and/or by the assessment of monetary payment to make such restoration.

13. If the offense of which a person is convicted is defined in section 240.50, subdivision one or two of section 240.55, section 240.60, section 240.61, section 240.62 or section 240.63 of this chapter, and no other victim who is a person is seeking restitution in the case, the term "victim" as used in this subdivision, in addition to the ordinary meaning, shall mean any school, municipality, fire district, fire company, fire corporation, ambulance association, ambulance corporation, or other legal or public entity engaged in providing emergency services which has expended funds for the purpose of responding to a false report of an incident or false bomb as defined in section 240.50, subdivision one or two of section 240.55, section 240.60, section 240.61, section 240.62, or section 240.63 of this chapter. Any restitution which may be required to be made to a victim pursuant to this subdivision shall be limited to the amount of funds reasonably expended for the purpose of responding to such false report of incident or false bomb, less the amount of any funds which have been or will be recovered from any other source and shall not include a designated surcharge pursuant to subdivision eight of this section. Any victim seeking restitution pursuant to this subdivision shall file with the court, district attorney and defense counsel an affidavit stating that the funds reasonably expended for which restitution is being sought have not been and will not be recovered from any other source or in any other civil or criminal proceeding, except as provided for by section 3-112 of the general obligations law.

14. Where a transfer of probation has occurred pursuant to section 410.80 of the criminal procedure law and the probationer is subject to a restitution condition, the department of probation in the county in which the order of restitution was imposed shall notify the appropriate district attorney. Upon notification by the department of probation, such district attorney shall file a certified copy of the judgment with the clerk of the county in the receiving jurisdiction for purposes of establishing a first lien and to permit institution of civil proceedings pursuant to the provisions of subdivision six of section 420.10 of the criminal procedure law.

N.Y. Penal Law § 60.27

Amended by New York Laws 2013, ch. 356,Sec. 1, eff. 9/27/2013.

Section 60.28 - Authorized disposition; making graffiti and possession of graffiti instruments

When a person is convicted of an offense defined in section 145.60 or 145.65 of this chapter, or of an attempt to commit such offense, and the sentence imposed by the court for such conviction includes a sentence of probation or conditional discharge, the court shall, where appropriate, include as a condition of such sentence the defendant's successful participation in a graffiti removal program pursuant to paragraph (h) of subdivision two of section 65.10 of this chapter.

N.Y. Penal Law § 60.28

Section 60.29 - Authorized disposition; cemetery desecration

When a person is convicted of an offense defined in section 145.22 or 145.23 of this chapter or of an attempt to commit such an offense, and the sentence imposed by the court for such conviction includes a sentence of probation or conditional discharge, such sentence shall, where appropriate, be in accordance with paragraph (h) of subdivision two of section 65.10 of this article as such section relates to cemetery crime.

N.Y. Penal Law § 60.29

Section 60.30 - Civil penalties

This article does not deprive the court of any authority conferred by law to decree a forfeiture of property, suspend or cancel a license, remove a person from office, or impose any other civil penalty and any appropriate order exercising such authority may be included as part of the judgment of conviction.

N.Y. Penal Law § 60.30

Section 60.35 - Mandatory surcharge, sex offender registration fee, DNA databank fee, supplemental sex offender victim fee and crime victim assistance fee required in

certain cases.

1.

(a) Except as provided in section eighteen hundred nine of the vehicle and traffic law and section 27.12 of the parks, recreation and historic preservation law, whenever proceedings in an administrative tribunal or a court of this state result in a conviction for a felony, a misdemeanor, or a violation, as these terms are defined in section 10.00 of this chapter, there shall be levied at sentencing a mandatory surcharge, sex offender registration fee, DNA databank fee and a crime victim assistance fee in addition to any sentence required or permitted by law, in accordance with the following schedule:

(i) a person convicted of a felony shall pay a mandatory surcharge of three hundred dollars and a crime victim assistance fee of twenty-five dollars;

(ii) a person convicted of a misdemeanor shall pay a mandatory surcharge of one hundred seventy-five dollars and a crime victim assistance fee of twenty-five dollars;

(iii) a person convicted of a violation shall pay a mandatory surcharge of ninety-five dollars and a crime victim assistance fee of twenty-five dollars;

(iv) a person convicted of a sex offense as defined by subdivision two of section one hundred sixty-eight-a of the correction law or a sexually violent offense as defined by subdivision three of section one hundred sixty-eight-a of the correction law shall, in addition to a mandatory surcharge and crime victim assistance fee, pay a sex offender registration fee of fifty dollars.

(v) a person convicted of a designated offense as defined by subdivision seven of section nine hundred ninety-five of the executive law shall, in addition to a mandatory surcharge and crime victim assistance fee, pay a DNA databank fee of fifty dollars.

(b) When the felony or misdemeanor conviction in subparagraphs (i), (ii) or (iv) of paragraph (a) of this subdivision results from an offense contained in article one hundred thirty of this chapter, incest in the third, second or first degree as defined in sections 255.25, 255.26 and 255.27 of this chapter or an offense contained in article two hundred sixty-three of this chapter, the person convicted shall pay a supplemental sex offender victim fee of one thousand dollars in addition to the mandatory surcharge and any other fee.

2. Where a person is convicted of two or more crimes or violations committed through a single act or omission, or through an act or omission which in itself constituted one of the crimes or violations and also was a material element of the other, the court shall impose a mandatory surcharge and a crime victim assistance fee, and where appropriate a supplemental sex offender victim fee, in accordance with the provisions of this section for the crime or violation which carries the highest classification, and no other sentence to pay a mandatory surcharge, crime victim assistance fee or supplemental sex offender victim fee required by this section shall be imposed. Where a person is convicted of two or more sex offenses or sexually violent offenses, as defined by subdivisions two and three of section one hundred sixty-eight-a of the correction law, committed through a single act or omission, or through an act or omission which in itself constituted one of the offenses and also was a material element of the other, the court shall impose only one sex offender registration fee. Where a person is convicted of two or more designated offenses, as defined by subdivision seven of section nine hundred ninety-five of the executive law, committed through a single act or omission, or through an act or omission which in itself constituted one of the offenses and also was a material element of the other, the court shall impose only one DNA databank fee.

3. The mandatory surcharge, sex offender registration fee, DNA databank fee, crime victim assistance fee, and supplemental sex offender victim fee provided for in subdivision one of this section shall be paid to the clerk of the court or administrative tribunal that rendered the conviction. Within the first ten days of the month following collection of the mandatory surcharge, crime victim assistance fee, and supplemental sex offender victim fee, the collecting authority shall determine the amount of mandatory surcharge, crime victim assistance fee, and supplemental sex offender victim fee collected and, if it is an administrative tribunal, or a town or village justice court, it shall then pay such money to the state comptroller who shall deposit such money in the state treasury pursuant to section one hundred twenty-one of the state finance law to the credit of the criminal justice improvement account established by section ninety-seven-bb of the state finance law. Within the first ten days of the month following collection of the sex offender registration fee and DNA databank fee, the collecting authority shall determine the amount of the sex offender registration fee and DNA databank fee collected and, if it is an administrative tribunal, or a town or village justice court, it shall then pay such money to the state comptroller who shall deposit such money in the state treasury pursuant to section one hundred twenty-one of the state finance law to the credit of the general fund. If such collecting authority is any other court of the unified court system, it shall, within such period, pay such money attributable to the mandatory surcharge or crime victim assistance fee to the state commissioner of taxation and finance to the credit of the criminal justice improvement account established by section ninety-seven-bb of the state finance law. If such collecting authority is any other court of the unified court system, it shall, within such period, pay such money attributable to the sex offender registration fee and the DNA databank fee to the state commissioner of taxation and finance to the credit of the general fund.

4. Any person who has paid a mandatory surcharge, sex offender registration fee, DNA databank fee, a crime victim assistance fee or a supplemental sex offender victim fee under the authority of this section based upon a conviction that is subsequently reversed or who paid a mandatory surcharge, sex offender registration fee, DNA databank fee, a crime victim assistance fee or supplemental sex offender victim fee under the authority of this section which is ultimately determined not to be required by this section shall be entitled to a refund of such mandatory surcharge, sex offender registration fee, DNA databank fee, crime victim assistance fee or supplemental sex offender victim fee uponn application, in the case of a town or village court, to the state comp troller. The state comptroller shall require such proof as is necessary in order to determine whether a refund is required by law. In all otherr cases, such application shall be made to the department, agency or court that collected such surcharge or fee. Such department, agency or court shall initiate the refund process and the state comptroller shall pay the refund pursuant to subdivision fifteen of section eight of the state finance law.

5.[Effective until September 1, 2023]

(a) When a person who is convicted of a crime or violation and sentenced to a term of imprisonment has failed to pay the mandatory surcharge, sex offender registration fee, DNA databank fee, crime victim assistance fee or supplemental sex offender victim fee required by this section, the clerk of the court that rendered the conviction shall notify the superintendent or the municipal official of the facility where the person is confined. The superintendent or the municipal official shall cause any amount owing to be collected from such person during his or her term of imprisonment from moneys to the credit of an incarcerated individuals' fund or such moneys as may be earned by a person in a work release program pursuant to section eight hundred sixty of the correction law. Such moneys attributable to the mandatory surcharge or crime victim assistance fee shall be paid over to the state comptroller to the credit of the criminal justice improvement account established by section ninety-seven- bb of the state finance law and such moneys attributable to the sex offender registration fee or DNA databank fee shall be paid over to the state comptroller to the credit of the general fund, except that any such moneys collected which are surcharges, sex offender registration fees, DNA databank fees, crime victim assistance fees or supplemental sex offender victim fees levied in relation to convictions obtained in a town or village justice court shall be paid within thirty days after the receipt thereof by the superintendent or municipal official of the facility to the justice of the court in which the conviction was obtained. For the purposes of collecting such mandatory surcharge, sex offender registration fee, DNA databank fee, crime victim assistance fee, and supplemental sex offender victim fee, the state shall be legally entitled to the money to the credit of an incarcerated individuals' fund or money which is earned by an incarcerated individual in a work release program. For purposes of this subdivision, the term " incarcerated individuals' fund" shall mean moneys in the possession of an incarcerated individual at the time of his or her admission into such facility, funds earned by him or her as provided for in section one hundred eighty-seven of the correction law and any other funds received by him or her or on his or her behalf and deposited with such superintendent or municipal official.

(b) The incarceration fee provided for in subdivision two of section one hundred eighty-nine of the correction law shall not be assessed or collected if any order of restitution or reparation, fine, mandatory surcharge, sex offender registration fee, DNA databank fee, crime victim assistance fee or supplemental sex offender victim fee remains unpaid. In such circumstances, any monies which may lawfully be withheld from the compensation paid to a prisoner for work performed while housed in a general confinement facility in satisfaction of such an obligation shall first be applied toward satisfaction of such obligation.

5.[Effective September 1, 2023] When a person who is convicted of a crime or violation and sentenced to a term of imprisonment has failed to pay the mandatory surcharge, sex offender registration fee, DNA databank fee, crime victim assistance fee or supplemental sex offender victim fee required by this section, the clerk of the court that rendered the conviction shall notify the superintendent or the municipal official of the facility where the person is confined. The superintendent or the municipal official shall cause any amount owing to be collected from such person during his or her term of imprisonment from moneys to the credit of an incarcerated individuals' fund or such moneys as may be earned by a person in a work release program pursuant to section eight hundred sixty of the correction law. Such moneys attributable to the mandatory surcharge or crime victim assistance fee shall be paid over to the state comptroller to the credit of the criminal justice improvement account established by section ninety-seven- bb of the state finance law and such moneys attributable to the sex offender registration fee or DNA databank fee shall be paid over to the state comptroller to the credit of the general fund, except that any such moneys collected which are surcharges, sex offender registration fees, DNA databank fees, crime victim assistance fees or supplemental sex offender victim fees levied in relation to convictions obtained in a town or village justice court shall be paid within thirty days after the receipt thereof by the superintendent or municipal official of the facility to the justice of the court in which the conviction was obtained. For the purposes of collecting such mandatory surcharge, sex offender registration fee, DNA databank fee, crime victim assistance fee and supplemental sex offender victim fee, the state shall be legally entitled to the money to the credit of an incarcerated individuals' fund or money which is earned by an incarcerated individual in a work release program. For purposes of this subdivision, the term " incarcerated individuals' fund" shall mean moneys in the possession of an incarcerated individual at the time of his or her admission into such facility, funds earned by him or her as provided for in section one hundred eighty-seven of the correction law and any other funds received by him or her or on his or her behalf and deposited with such superintendent or municipal official.

6. Notwithstanding any other provision of this section, where a person has made restitution or reparation pursuant to section 60.27 of this article, such person shall not be required to pay a mandatory surcharge or a crime victim assistance fee.

7. Notwithstanding the provisions of subdivision one of section 60.00 of this article, the provisions of subdivision one of this section shall not apply to a violation under any law other than this chapter.

8. Subdivision one of section 130.10 of the criminal procedure law notwithstanding, at the time that the mandatory surcharge, sex offender registration fee or DNA databank fee, crime victim assistance fee or supplemental sex offender victim fee is imposed a town or village court may, and all other courts shall, issue and cause to be served upon the person required to pay the mandatory surcharge, sex offender registration fee or DNA databank fee, crime victim assistance fee or supplemental sex offender victim fee, a summons directing that such person appear before the court regarding the payment of the mandatory surcharge, sex offender registration fee or DNA databank fee, crime victim assistance fee or supplemental sex offender victim fee, if after sixty days from the date it was imposed it remains unpaid. The designated date of appearance on the summons shall be set for the first day court is in session falling after the sixtieth day from the imposition of the mandatory surcharge, sex offender registration fee or DNA databank fee, crime victim assistance fee or supplemental sex offender victim fee. The summons shall contain the information required by subdivision two of section 130.10 of the criminal procedure law except that in substitution for the requirement of paragraph (c) of such subdivision the summons shall state that the person served must appear at a date, time and specific location specified in the summons if after sixty days from the date of issuance the mandatory surcharge, sex offender registration fee or DNA databank fee, crime victim assistance fee or supplemental sex offender victim fee remains unpaid. The court shall not issue a summons under this subdivision to a person who is being sentenced to a term of confinement in excess of sixty days in jail or in the department of corrections and community supervision. The mandatory surcharges, sex offender registration fee and DNA databank fees, crime victim assistance fees and supplemental sex offender victim fees for those persons shall be governed by the provisions of section 60.30 of this article.

9. Notwithstanding the provisions of subdivision one of this section, in the event a proceeding is in a town or village court, such court shall add an additional five dollars to the surcharges imposed by such subdivision one.

10. [Repealed]

N.Y. Penal Law § 60.35

Amended by New York Laws 2021, ch. 322,Sec. 103-a, eff. 8/2/2021.
Amended by New York Laws 2021, ch. 322,Sec. 103, eff. 8/2/2021.
Amended by New York Laws 2021, ch. 55,Sec. A-8, eff. 4/19/2021.
Amended by New York Laws 2020, ch. 144,Sec. 3, eff. 8/24/2020.
Amended by New York Laws 2020, ch. 55,Sec. A-8, eff. 4/3/2020.
Amended by New York Laws 2019, ch. 55,Sec. O-8, eff. 4/12/2019.
Amended by New York Laws 2017, ch. 55,Sec. A-8, eff. 4/20/2017.
Amended by New York Laws 2015, ch. 55,Sec. B-8, eff. 4/13/2015.
Amended by New York Laws 2013, ch. 525,Sec. 1, eff. 12/18/2013.

Section 60.36 - Authorized dispositions; driving while intoxicated offenses

Where a court is imposing a sentence for a violation of subdivision two, two-a, or three of section eleven hundred ninety-two of the vehicle and traffic law pursuant to sections 65.00 or 65.05 of this title and, as a condition of such sentence, orders the installation and maintenance of an ignition interlock device, the court may impose any other penalty authorized pursuant to section eleven hundred ninety-three of the vehicle and traffic law.

N.Y. Penal Law § 60.36

Section 60.37 - Authorized disposition; certain offenses

When a person has been charged with an offense and the elements of such offense meet the criteria of an "eligible offense" and such person qualifies as an "eligible person" as such terms are defined in section four hundred fifty-eight-l of the social services law, the court may, as a condition of adjournment in contemplation of dismissal in accordance with section 170.55 of the criminal procedure law, or a condition of probation or a conditional discharge, direct that the defendant participate in an education reform program pursuant to subdivision two of section four hundred fifty-eight-l of the social services law.

N.Y. Penal Law § 60.37

Article 65 - SENTENCES OF PROBATION, CONDITIONAL DISCHARGE AND UNCONDITIONAL DISCHARGE

Section 65.00 - Sentence of probation

1. Criteria.

(a) Except as otherwise required by section 60.04 or 60.05 of this title, and except as provided by paragraph (b) hereof, the court may sentence a person to a period of probation upon conviction of any crime if the court, having regard to the nature and circumstances of the crime and to the history, character and condition of the defendant, is of the opinion that:

(i) Institutional confinement for the term authorized by law of the defendant is or may not be necessary for the protection of the public;

(ii) the defendant is in need of guidance, training or other assistance which, in his case, can be effectively administered through probation supervision; and

(iii) such disposition is not inconsistent with the ends of justice.

(b) The court, with the concurrence of either the administrative judge of the court or of the judicial district within which the court is situated or such administrative judge as the presiding justice of the appropriate appellate division shall designate, may sentence a person to a period of probation upon conviction of a class A-II felony defined in article two hundred twenty, the class B felony defined in section 220.48 of this chapter or any other class B felony defined in article two hundred twenty of this chapter where the person is a second felony drug offender as defined in paragraph (b) of subdivision one of section 70.70 of this chapter, if the prosecutor either orally on the record or in a writing filed with the indictment recommends that the court sentence such person to a period of probation upon the ground that such person has or is providing material assistance in the investigation, apprehension or prosecution of any person for a felony defined in article two hundred twenty or the attempt or the conspiracy to commit any such felony, and if the court, having regard to the nature and circumstances of the crime and to the history, character and condition of the defendant is of the opinion that:

(i) Institutional confinement of the defendant is not necessary for the protection of the public;

(ii) The defendant is in need of guidance, training or other assistance which, in his case, can be effectively administered through probation supervision;

(iii) The defendant has or is providing material assistance in the investigation, apprehension or prosecution of a person for a felony defined in article two hundred twenty or the attempt or conspiracy to commit any such felony; and

(iv) Such disposition is not inconsistent with the ends of justice.

[Effective until September 1, 2023] Provided, however, that the court shall not, except to the extent authorized by paragraph (d) of subdivision two of section 60.01 of this chapter, impose a sentence of probation in any case where it sentences a defendant for more than one crime and imposes a sentence of imprisonment for any one of the crimes, or where the defendant is subject to an undischarged indeterminate or determinate sentence of imprisonment which was imposed at a previous time by a court of this state and has more than one year to run.

[Effective September 1, 2023] Provided, however, that the court shall not, except to the extent authorized by paragraph (d) of subdivision two of section 60.01 of this chapter, impose a sentence of probation in any case where it sentences a defendant for more than one crime and imposes a sentence of imprisonment for any one of the crimes, or where the defendant is subject to an undischarged indeterminate or reformatory sentence of imprisonment which was imposed at a previous time by a court of this state and has more than one year to run.

2. Sentence. When a person is sentenced to a period of probation the court shall, except to the extent authorized by paragraph (d) of subdivision two of section 60.01 of this chapter, impose the period authorized by subdivision three of this section and shall specify, in accordance with section 65.10, the conditions to be complied with. The court may modify or enlarge the conditions or, if the defendant commits an additional offense or violates a condition, revoke the sentence at any time prior to the expiration or termination of the period of probation.

3. Periods of probation. Unless terminated sooner in accordance with the criminal procedure law, the period of probation shall be as follows:

(a)

(i) For a felony, other than a class A-II felony defined in article two hundred twenty of this chapter or the class B felony defined in section 220.48 of this chapter, or any other class B felony defined in article two hundred twenty of this chapter committed by a second felony drug offender, or a sexual assault, the period of probation shall be a term of three, four or five years;

(ii) For a class A-II felony drug offender as defined in paragraph (a) of subdivision one of section 70.71 of this chapter as described in paragraph (b) of subdivision one of this section, or a class B felony committed by a second felony drug offender described in paragraph (b) of subdivision one of this section, the period of probation shall be life and for a class B felony defined in section 220.48 of this chapter, the period of probation shall be twenty-five years;

(iii) For a felony sexual assault, the period of probation shall be ten years.

(b)

(i) For a class A misdemeanor, other than a sexual assault, the period of probation shall be a term of two or three years;

(ii) For a class A misdemeanor sexual assault, the period of probation shall be six years.

(c) For a class B misdemeanor, the period of probation shall be one year, except the period of probation shall be no less than one year and no more than three years for the class B misdemeanor of public lewdness as defined in section 245.00 of this chapter;

(d) For an unclassified misdemeanor, the period of probation shall be a term of two or three years if the authorized sentence of imprisonment is in excess of three months, otherwise the period of probation shall be one year.

For the purposes of this section, the term "sexual assault" means an offense defined in article one hundred thirty or two hundred sixty-three, or in section 255.25, 255.26 or 255.27 of this chapter, or an attempt to commit any of the foregoing offenses.

4. If during the periods of probation referenced in subparagraph (i) of paragraph (a), subparagraph (i) of paragraph (b) and paragraph (d) of subdivision three of this section an alleged violation is sustained following a hearing pursuant to section 410.70 of the criminal procedure law and the court continues or modifies the sentence, the court may extend the remaining period of probation up to the maximum term authorized by this section. Provided, however, a defendant shall receive credit for the time during which he or she was supervised under the original probation sentence prior to any declaration of delinquency and for any time spent in custody pursuant to this article for an alleged violation of probation.

5. In any case where a court pursuant to its authority under subdivision four of section 60.01 of this chapter revokes probation and sentences such person to imprisonment and probation, as provided in paragraph (d) of subdivision two of section 60.01 of this chapter, the period of probation shall be the remaining period of the original probation sentence or one year whichever is greater.

N.Y. Penal Law § 65.00

Amended by New York Laws 2021, ch. 55,Sec. A-19, eff. 4/19/2021.
Amended by New York Laws 2020, ch. 55,Sec. A-19, eff. 4/3/2020.
Amended by New York Laws 2019, ch. 55,Sec. O-19, eff. 4/12/2019.
Amended by New York Laws 2017, ch. 55,Sec. A-19, eff. 4/20/2017.
Amended by New York Laws 2015, ch. 55,Sec. B-19, eff. 4/13/2015.
Amended by New York Laws 2014, ch. 17,Sec. 1, eff. 2/9/2014.
Amended by New York Laws 2013, ch. 556,Sec. 1 to Sec. 4, eff. 2/9/2014.
See New York Laws 2014, ch. 17, Sec. 4.

Section 65.05 - Sentence of conditional discharge

1. Criteria.

(a) Except as otherwise required by section 60.05, the court may impose a sentence of conditional discharge for an offense if the court, having regard to the nature and circumstances of the offense and to the history, character and condition of the defendant, is of the opinion that neither the public interest nor the ends of justice would be served by a sentence of imprisonment and that probation supervision is not appropriate.

(b) When a sentence of conditional discharge is imposed for a felony, the court shall set forth in the record the reasons for its action.

2. Sentence. Except to the extent authorized by paragraph (d) of subdivision two of section 60.01 of this chapter, when the court imposes a sentence of conditional discharge the defendant shall be released with respect to the conviction for which the sentence is imposed without imprisonment or probation supervision but subject, during the period of conditional discharge, to such conditions as the court may determine. The court shall impose the period of conditional discharge authorized by subdivision three of this section and shall specify, in accordance with section 65.10, the conditions to be complied with. If a defendant is sentenced pursuant to paragraph (e) of subdivision two of section 65.10 of this chapter, the court shall require the administrator of the program to provide written notice to the court of any violation of program participation by the defendant. The court may modify or enlarge the conditions or, if the defendant commits an additional

offense or violates a condition, revoke the sentence at any time prior to the expiration or termination of the period of conditional discharge.

3. Periods of conditional discharge. Unless terminated sooner in accordance with the criminal procedure law, the period of conditional discharge shall be as follows:

(a) Three years in the case of a felony; and

(b) One year in the case of a misdemeanor or a violation.

Where the court has required, as a condition of the sentence, that the defendant make restitution of the fruits of his or her offense or make reparation for the loss caused thereby and such condition has not been satisfied, the court, at any time prior to the expiration or termination of the period of conditional discharge, may impose an additional period. The length of the additional period shall be fixed by the court at the time it is imposed and shall not be more than two years. All of the incidents of the original sentence, including the authority of the court to modify or enlarge the conditions, shall continue to apply during such additional period.

N.Y. Penal Law § 65.05

Section 65.10 - Conditions of probation and of conditional discharge

1. In general. The conditions of probation and of conditional discharge shall be such as the court, in its discretion, deems reasonably necessary to insure that the defendant will lead a law-abiding life or to assist him to do so.

2. Conditions relating to conduct and rehabilitation. When imposing a sentence of probation or of conditional discharge, the court shall, as a condition of the sentence, consider restitution or reparation and may, as a condition of the sentence, require that the defendant:

(a) Avoid injurious or vicious habits;

(b) Refrain from frequenting unlawful or disreputable places or consorting with disreputable persons;

(c) Work faithfully at a suitable employment or faithfully pursue a course of study or of vocational training that will equip him for suitable employment;

(d) Undergo available medical or psychiatric treatment and remain in a specified institution, when required for that purpose;

(e) Participate in an alcohol or substance abuse program or an intervention program approved by the court after consultation with the local probation department having jurisdiction, or such other public or private agency as the court determines to be appropriate;

(e-1) Participate in a motor vehicle accident prevention course. The court may require such condition where a person has been convicted of a traffic infraction for a violation of article twenty-six of the vehicle and traffic law where the commission of such violation caused the serious physical injury or death of another person. For purposes of this paragraph, the term "motor vehicle accident prevention course" shall mean a motor vehicle accident prevention course approved by the department of motor vehicles pursuant to article twelve-B of the vehicle and traffic law;

(f) Support his dependents and meet other family responsibilities;

(g) Make restitution of the fruits of his or her offense or make reparation, in an amount he can afford to pay, for the actual out-of-pocket loss caused thereby. When restitution or reparation is a condition of the sentence, the court shall fix the amount thereof, the manner of performance, specifically state the date when restitution is to be paid in full prior to the expiration of the sentence of probation and may establish provisions for the early termination of a sentence of probation or conditional discharge pursuant to the provisions of subdivision three of section 410.90 of the criminal procedure law after the restitution and reparation part of a sentence of probation or conditional discharge has been satisfied. The court shall provide that in the event the person to whom restitution or reparation is to be made dies prior to the completion of said restitution or reparation, the remaining payments shall be made to the estate of the deceased.

(g-1) [Repealed]

(h) Perform services for a public or not-for-profit corporation, association, institution or agency, including but not limited to services for the division of substance abuse services, services in an appropriate community program for removal of graffiti from public or private property, including any property damaged in the underlying offense, or services for the maintenance and repair of real or personal property maintained as a cemetery plot, grave, burial place or other place of interment of human remains. Provided however, that the performance of any such services shall not result in the displacement of employed workers or in the impairment of existing contracts for services, nor shall the performance of any such services be required or permitted in any establishment involved in any labor strike or lockout. The court may establish provisions for the early termination of a sentence of probation or conditional discharge pursuant to the provisions of subdivision three of section 410.90 of the criminal procedure law after such services have been completed. Such sentence may only be imposed upon conviction of a misdemeanor, violation, or class D or class E felony, or a youthful offender finding replacing any such conviction, where the defendant has consented to the amount and conditions of such service;

(i) If a person under the age of twenty-one years, (i) resides with his parents or in a suitable foster home or hostel as referred to in section two hundred forty-four of the executive law, (ii) attends school, (iii) spends such part of the period of the sentence as the court may direct, but not exceeding two years, in a facility made available by the division for youth pursuant to article nineteen-G of the executive law, provided that admission to such facility may be made only with the prior consent of the division for youth, (iv) attend a non-residential program for such hours and pursuant to a schedule prescribed by the court as suitable for a program of rehabilitation of youth, (v) contribute to his own support in any home, foster home or hostel;

(j) Post a bond or other security for the performance of any or all conditions imposed;

(k) Observe certain specified conditions of conduct as set forth in an order of protection issued pursuant to section 530.12 or 530.13 of the criminal procedure law.

(k-1) Install and maintain a functioning ignition interlock device, as that term is defined in section one hundred nineteen-a of the vehicle and traffic law, in any vehicle owned or operated by the defendant if the court in its discretion determines that such a condition is necessary to ensure the public safety. The court may require such condition only where a person has been convicted of a violation of subdivision two, two-a or three of section eleven hundred ninety-two of the vehicle and traffic law, or any crime defined by the vehicle and traffic law or this chapter of which an alcohol-related violation of any provision of section eleven hundred ninety-two of the vehicle and traffic law is an essential element. The offender shall be required to install and operate the ignition interlock device only in accordance with section eleven hundred ninety-eight of the vehicle and traffic law.

(k-2)

(i) Refrain, upon sentencing for a crime involving unlawful sexual conduct committed against a metropolitan transportation authority passenger, customer, or employee or a crime involving assault against a metropolitan transportation authority employee, committed in or on any facility or conveyance of the metropolitan transportation authority or a subsidiary thereof or the New York city transit authority or a subsidiary thereof, from using or entering any of such authority's subways, trains, buses or other conveyances or facilities specified by the court for a period of up to three years, or a specified period of such probation or conditional discharge, whichever is less. For purposes of this section, a crime involving assault shall mean an offense described in article one hundred twenty of this chapter which has as an element the causing of physical injury or serious physical injury to another as well as the attempt thereof.

(ii) The court may, in its discretion, suspend, modify or cancel a condition imposed under this paragraph in the interest of justice at any time. If the person depends on the authority's subways, trains, buses, or other conveyances or facilities for trips of necessity, including, but not limited to, travel to or from medical or legal appointments, school or training classes or places of employment, obtaining food, clothing or necessary household items, or rendering care to family members, the court may modify such condition to allow for a trip or trips as in its discretion are necessary.

(iii) A person at liberty and subject to a condition under this paragraph who applies, within thirty days after the date such condition becomes effective, for a refund of any prepaid fare amounts rendered unusable in whole or in part by such condition including, but not limited to, a monthly pass, shall be issued a refund of the amounts so prepaid.

(l) Satisfy any other conditions reasonably related to his rehabilitation.

3. Conditions relating to supervision. When imposing a sentence of probation the court, in addition to any conditions imposed pursuant to subdivision two of this section, shall require as conditions of the sentence, that the defendant:

(a) Report to a probation officer as directed by the court or the probation officer and permit the probation officer to visit him at his place of abode or elsewhere;

(b) Remain within the jurisdiction of the court unless granted permission to leave by the court or the probation officer. Where a defendant is granted permission to move or travel outside the jurisdiction of the court, the defendant shall sign a written waiver of extradition agreeing to waive extradition proceedings where such proceedings are the result of the issuance of a warrant by the court pursuant to subdivision two of section 410.40 of the criminal procedure law based on an alleged violation of probation. Where any county or the city of New York incurs costs associated with the return of any probationer based on the issuance of a warrant by the court pursuant to subdivision two of section 410.40 of the criminal procedure law, the jurisdiction may collect the reasonable and necessary expenses involved in connection with his or her transport, from the probationer; provided that where the sentence of probation is not revoked pursuant to section 410.70 of the criminal procedure law no such expenses may be collected.

(c) Answer all reasonable inquiries by the probation officer and notify the probation officer prior to any change in address or employment.

4. Electronic monitoring. When imposing a sentence of probation the court may, in addition to any conditions imposed pursuant to subdivisions two and three of this section, require the defendant to submit to the use of an electronic monitoring device and/or to follow a schedule that governs the defendant's daily movement. Such condition may be imposed only where the court, in its discretion, determines that requiring the defendant to comply with such condition will advance public safety, probationer control or probationer surveillance. Electronic monitoring shall be used in accordance with uniform procedures developed by the office of probation and correctional alternatives.

4-a. Mandatory conditions for sex offenders.

(a) When imposing a sentence of probation or conditional discharge upon a person convicted of an offense defined in article one hundred thirty, two hundred thirty-five or two hundred sixty-three of this chapter, or section 255.25, 255.26 or 255.27 of this chapter, and the victim of such offense was under the age of eighteen at the time of such offense or such person has been designated a level three sex offender pursuant to subdivision six of section 168-l of the correction law, the court shall require, as a mandatory condition of such sentence, that such sentenced offender shall refrain from knowingly entering into or upon any school grounds, as that term is defined in subdivision fourteen of section 220.00 of this chapter, or any other facility or institution primarily used for the care or treatment of persons under the age of eighteen while one or more of such persons under the age of eighteen are present, provided however, that when such sentenced offender is a registered student or participant or an employee of such facility or institution or entity contracting therewith or has a family member enrolled in such facility or institution, such sentenced offender may, with the written authorization of his or her probation officer or the court and the superintendent or chief administrator of such facility, institution or grounds, enter such facility, institution or upon such grounds for the limited purposes authorized by the probation officer or the court and superintendent or chief officer. Nothing in this subdivision shall be construed as restricting any lawful condition of supervision that may be imposed on such sentenced offender.

(b) When imposing a sentence of probation or conditional discharge upon a person convicted of an offense for which registration as a sex offender is required pursuant to subdivision two or three of section one hundred sixty-eight-a of the correction law, and the victim of such offense was under the age of eighteen at the time of such offense or such person has been designated a level three sex offender pursuant to subdivision six of section one hundred sixty-eight-l of the correction law or the internet was used to facilitate the commission of the crime, the court shall require, as mandatory conditions of such sentence, that such sentenced offender be prohibited from using the internet to access pornographic material, access a commercial social networking website, communicate with other individuals or groups for the purpose of promoting sexual relations with persons under the age of eighteen, and communicate with a person under the age of eighteen when such offender is over the age of eighteen, provided that the court may permit an offender to use the internet to communicate with a person under the age of eighteen when such offender is the parent of a minor child and is not otherwise prohibited from communicating with such child. Nothing in this subdivision shall be construed as restricting any other lawful condition of supervision that may be imposed on such sentenced offender. As used in this subdivision, a "commercial social networking website" shall mean any business, organization or other entity operating a website that permits persons under eighteen years of age to be registered users for the purpose of establishing personal relationships with other users, where such persons under eighteen years of age may:

(i) create web pages or profiles that provide information about themselves where such web pages or profiles are available to the public or to other users; (ii) engage in direct or real time communication with other users, such as a chat room or instant messenger; and (iii) communicate with persons over eighteen years of age; provided, however, that, for purposes of this subdivision, a commercial social networking website shall not include a website that permits users to engage in such other activities as are not enumerated herein.

5. Other conditions. When imposing a sentence of probation the court may, in addition to any conditions imposed pursuant to subdivisions two, three and four of this section, require that the defendant comply with any other reasonable condition as the court shall determine to be necessary or appropriate to ameliorate the conduct which gave rise to the offense or to prevent the incarceration of the defendant.

5-a. Other conditions for sex offenders. When imposing a sentence of probation upon a person convicted of an offense for which registration as a sex offender is required pursuant to subdivision two or three of section one hundred sixty-eight-a of the correction law, in addition to any conditions required under subdivisions two, three, four, four-a and five of this section, the court may require that the defendant comply with a reasonable limitation on his or her use of the internet that the court determines to be necessary or appropriate to ameliorate the conduct which gave rise to the offense or to protect public safety, provided that the court shall not prohibit such sentenced offender from using the internet in connection with education, lawful employment or search for lawful employment.

N.Y. Penal Law § 65.10

Amended by New York Laws 2020, ch. 56,Sec. VV-1, eff. 7/2/2020.

Amended by New York Laws 2018, ch. 480,Sec. 2, eff. 6/26/2019.

Section 65.15 - Calculation of periods of probation and of conditional discharge

1. A period of probation or a period or additional period of conditional discharge commences on the day it is imposed. Multiple periods, whether imposed at the same or at different times, shall run concurrently.

2. When a person has violated the conditions of his or her probation or conditional discharge and is declared delinquent by the court, the declaration of delinquency shall interrupt the period of the sentence as of the date of the delinquency and such interruption shall continue until a final determination as to the delinquency has been made by the court pursuant to a hearing held in accordance with the provisions of the criminal procedure law. Any order for the installation and maintenance of a functioning ignition interlock device imposed pursuant to section 60.21 of this title shall remain in effect throughout the delinquency and the court may extend the period of such installation and maintenance by the period of the delinquency; provided, however, that the defendant shall get credit for any period where the device was installed and maintained during the delinquency.

3.[Effective until September 1, 2023] In any case where a person who is under a sentence of probation or of conditional discharge is also under an indeterminate or determinate sentence of imprisonment, imposed for some other offense by a court of this state the service of the sentence of imprisonment shall satisfy the sentence of probation or of conditional discharge unless the sentence of probation or of conditional discharge is revoked prior to the next to occur of parole or conditional release under, or satisfaction of, the sentence of imprisonment. Provided, however, that the service of an indeterminate or determinate sentence of imprisonment shall not satisfy a sentence of probation if the sentence of probation was imposed at a time when the sentence of imprisonment had one year or less to run.

3.[Effective September 1, 2023] In any case where a person who is under a sentence of probation or of conditional discharge is also under an indeterminate sentence of imprisonment, or a reformatory sentence of imprisonment authorized by section 75.00, imposed for some other offense by a court of this state the service of the sentence of imprisonment shall satisfy the sentence of probation or of conditional discharge unless the sentence of probation or of conditional discharge is revoked prior to the next to occur of parole or conditional release under, or satisfaction of, the sentence of imprisonment. Provided, however, that the service of an indeterminate or a reformatory sentence of imprisonment shall not satisfy a sentence of probation if the sentence of probation was imposed at a time when the sentence of imprisonment had one year or less to run.

N.Y. Penal Law § 65.15

Amended by New York Laws 2021, ch. 55,Sec. A-19, eff. 4/19/2021.
Amended by New York Laws 2020, ch. 55,Sec. A-19, eff. 4/3/2020.
Amended by New York Laws 2019, ch. 55,Sec. O-19, eff. 4/12/2019.
Amended by New York Laws 2017, ch. 55,Sec. A-19, eff. 4/20/2017.
Amended by New York Laws 2015, ch. 440,Sec. 1, eff. 11/21/2015.
Amended by New York Laws 2015, ch. 55,Sec. B-19, eff. 4/13/2015.

Section 65.20 - Sentence of unconditional discharge

1. Criteria. The court may impose a sentence of unconditional discharge in any case where it is authorized to impose a sentence of conditional discharge under section 65.05 if the court is of the opinion that no proper purpose would be served by imposing any condition upon the defendant's release.

When a sentence of unconditional discharge is imposed for a felony, the court shall set forth in the record the reasons for its action.

2. Sentence. When the court imposes a sentence of unconditional discharge, the defendant shall be released with respect to the conviction for which the sentence is imposed without imprisonment, fine or probation supervision. A sentence of unconditional discharge is for all purposes a final judgment of conviction.

N.Y. Penal Law § 65.20

Article 70 - SENTENCES OF IMPRISONMENT

Section 70.00 - Sentence of imprisonment for felony

1.[Effective until September 1, 2023] Indeterminate sentence. Except as provided in subdivisions four, five and six of this section or section 70.80 of this article, a sentence of imprisonment for a felony, other than a felony defined in article two hundred twenty or two hundred twenty-one of this chapter, shall be an indeterminate sentence. When such a sentence is imposed, the court shall impose a maximum term in accordance with the provisions of subdivision two of this section and the minimum period of imprisonment shall be as provided in subdivision three of this section.

1.[Effective September 1, 2023] Indeterminate sentence. Except as provided in subdivisions four and five of this section or section 70.80 of this article, a sentence of imprisonment for a felony, other than a felony defined in article two hundred twenty or two hundred twenty-one of this chapter, shall be an indeterminate sentence. When such a sentence is imposed, the court shall impose a maximum term in accordance with the provisions of subdivision two of this section and the minimum period of imprisonment shall be as provided in subdivision three of this section.

2. Maximum term of sentence. The maximum term of an indeterminate sentence shall be at least three years and the term shall be fixed as follows:

(a) For a class A felony, the term shall be life imprisonment;

(b) For a class B felony, the term shall be fixed by the court, and shall not exceed twenty-five years;

(c) For a class C felony, the term shall be fixed by the court, and shall not exceed fifteen years;

(d) For a class D felony, the term shall be fixed by the court, and shall not exceed seven years; and

(e) For a class E felony, the term shall be fixed by the court, and shall not exceed four years.

3. Minimum period of imprisonment. The minimum period of imprisonment under an indeterminate sentence shall be at least one year and shall be fixed as follows:

(a) In the case of a class A felony, the minimum period shall be fixed by the court and specified in the sentence.

(i) For a class A-I felony, such minimum period shall not be less than fifteen years nor more than twenty-five years; provided, however, that (A) where a sentence, other than a sentence of death or life imprisonment without parole, is imposed upon a defendant convicted of murder in the first degree as defined in section 125.27 of this chapter such minimum period shall be not less than twenty years nor more than twenty-five years, and, (B) where a sentence is imposed upon a defendant convicted of murder in the second degree as defined in subdivision five of section 125.25 of this chapter or convicted of aggravated murder as defined in section 125.26 of this chapter, the sentence shall be life imprisonment without parole, and, (C) where a sentence is imposed upon a defendant convicted of attempted murder in the first degree as defined in article one hundred ten of this chapter and subparagraph (i), (ii) or (iii) of paragraph (a) of subdivision one and paragraph (b) of subdivision one of section 125.27 of this chapter or attempted aggravated murder as defined in article one hundred ten of this chapter and section 125.26 of this chapter such minimum period shall be not less than twenty years nor more than forty years.

(ii) For a class A-II felony, such minimum period shall not be less than three years nor more than eight years four months, except that for the class A-II felony of predatory sexual assault as defined in section 130.95 of this chapter or the class A-II felony of predatory sexual assault against a child as defined in section 130.96 of this chapter, such minimum period shall be not less than ten years nor more than twenty-five years.

(b) For any other felony, the minimum period shall be fixed by the court and specified in the sentence and shall be not less than one year nor more than one-third of the maximum term imposed.

4. Alternative definite sentence for class D and E felonies. When a person, other than a second or persistent felony offender, is sentenced for a class D or class E felony, and the court, having regard to the nature and circumstances of the crime and to the history and character of the defendant, is of the opinion that a sentence of imprisonment is necessary but that it would be unduly harsh to impose an indeterminate or determinate sentence, the court may impose a definite sentence of imprisonment and fix a term of one year or less.

5. Life imprisonment without parole. Notwithstanding any other provision of law, a defendant sentenced to life imprisonment without parole shall not be or become eligible for parole or conditional release. For purposes of commitment and custody, other than parole and conditional release, such sentence shall be deemed to be an indeterminate sentence. A

defendant may be sentenced to life imprisonment without parole upon conviction for the crime of murder in the first degree as defined in section 125.27 of this chapter and in accordance with the procedures provided by law for imposing a sentence for such crime. A defendant who was eighteen years of age or older at the time of the commission of the crime must be sentenced to life imprisonment without parole upon conviction for the crime of terrorism as defined in section 490.25 of this chapter, where the specified offense the defendant committed is a class A-I felony; the crime of criminal possession of a chemical weapon or biological weapon in the first degree as defined in section 490.45 of this chapter; or the crime of criminal use of a chemical weapon or biological weapon in the first degree as defined in section 490.55 of this chapter; provided, however, that nothing in this subdivision shall preclude or prevent a sentence of death when the defendant is also convicted of the crime of murder in the first degree as defined in section 125.27 of this chapter. A defendant who was seventeen years of age or younger at the time of the commission of the crime may be sentenced, in accordance with law, to the applicable indeterminate sentence with a maximum term of life imprisonment. A defendant must be sentenced to life imprisonment without parole upon conviction for the crime of murder in the second degree as defined in subdivision five of section 125.25 of this chapter or for the crime of aggravated murder as defined in subdivision one of section 125.26 of this chapter. A defendant may be sentenced to life imprisonment without parole upon conviction for the crime of aggravated murder as defined in subdivision two of section 125.26 of this chapter.

6.[Repealed September 1, 2023] Determinate sentence. Except as provided in subdivision four of this section and subdivisions two and four of section 70.02, when a person is sentenced as a violent felony offender pursuant to section 70.02 or as a second violent felony offender pursuant to section 70.04 or as a second felony offender on a conviction for a violent felony offense pursuant to section 70.06, the court must impose a determinate sentence of imprisonment in accordance with the provisions of such sections and such sentence shall include, as a part thereof, a period of post-release supervision in accordance with section 70.45.

N.Y. Penal Law § 70.00

Amended by New York Laws 2021, ch. 55,Sec. A-19, eff. 4/19/2021.
Amended by New York Laws 2020, ch. 55,Sec. A-19, eff. 4/3/2020.
Amended by New York Laws 2019, ch. 55,Sec. O-19, eff. 4/12/2019.
Amended by New York Laws 2017, ch. 55,Sec. A-19, eff. 4/20/2017.
Amended by New York Laws 2017, ch. 59,Sec. WWW-40-a, eff. 10/1/2018.
Amended by New York Laws 2015, ch. 55,Sec. B-19, eff. 4/13/2015.

Section 70.02 - Sentence of imprisonment for a violent felony offense

1. Definition of a violent felony offense. A violent felony offense is a class B violent felony offense, a class C violent felony offense, a class D violent felony offense, or a class E violent felony offense, defined as follows:

(a) Class B violent felony offenses: an attempt to commit the class A-I felonies of murder in the second degree as defined in section 125.25, kidnapping in the first degree as defined in section 135.25, and arson in the first degree as defined in section 150.20; manslaughter in the first degree as defined in section 125.20, aggravated manslaughter in the first degree as defined in section 125.22, rape in the first degree as defined in section 130.35, criminal sexual act in the first degree as defined in section 130.50, aggravated sexual abuse in the first degree as defined in section 130.70, course of sexual conduct against a child in the first degree as defined in section 130.75; assault in the first degree as defined in section 120.10, kidnapping in the second degree as defined in section 135.20, burglary in the first degree as defined in section 140.30, arson in the second degree as defined in section 150.15, robbery in the first degree as defined in section 160.15, sex trafficking as defined in paragraphs (a) and (b) of subdivision five of section 230.34, sex trafficking of a child as defined in section 230.34 -a, incest in the first degree as defined in section 255.27, criminal possession of a weapon in the first degree as defined in section 265.04, criminal use of a firearm in the first degree as defined in section 265.09, criminal sale of a firearm in the first degree as defined in section 265.13, aggravated assault upon a police officer or a peace officer as defined in section 120.11, gang assault in the first degree as defined in section 120.07, intimidating a victim or witness in the first degree as defined in section 215.17, hindering prosecution of terrorism in the first degree as defined in section 490.35, criminal possession of a chemical weapon or biological weapon in the second degree as defined in section 490.40, and criminal use of a chemical weapon or biological weapon in the third degree as defined in section 490.47.

(b) Class C violent felony offenses: an attempt to commit any of the class B felonies set forth in paragraph (a) of this subdivision; aggravated criminally negligent homicide as defined in section 125.11, aggravated manslaughter in the second degree as defined in section 125.21, aggravated sexual abuse in the second degree as defined in section 130.67, assault on a peace officer, police officer, firefighter or emergency medical services professional as defined in section 120.08, assault on a judge as defined in section 120.09, gang assault in the second degree as defined in section 120.06, strangulation in the first degree as defined in section 121.13, aggravated strangulation as defined in section 121.13 -a, burglary in the second degree as defined in section 140.25, robbery in the second degree as defined in section 160.10, criminal possession of a weapon in the second degree as defined in section 265.03, criminal use of a firearm in the second degree as defined in section 265.08, criminal sale of a firearm in the second degree as defined in section 265.12, criminal sale of a firearm with the aid of a minor as defined in section 265.14, aggravated criminal possession of a weapon as defined in section 265.19, soliciting or providing support for an act of terrorism in the first degree as defined in section 490.15, hindering prosecution of terrorism in the second degree as defined in section 490.30, and criminal possession of a chemical weapon or biological weapon in the third degree as defined in section 490.37.

(c) Class D violent felony offenses: an attempt to commit any of the class C felonies set forth in paragraph (b); reckless assault of a child as defined in section 120.02, assault in the second degree as defined in section 120.05, menacing a police officer or peace officer as defined in section 120.18, stalking in the first degree, as defined in subdivision one of section

33

120.60, strangulation in the second degree as defined in section 121.12, rape in the second degree as defined in section 130.30, criminal sexual act in the second degree as defined in section 130.45, sexual abuse in the first degree as defined in section 130.65, course of sexual conduct against a child in the second degree as defined in section 130.80, aggravated sexual abuse in the third degree as defined in section 130.66, facilitating a sex offense with a controlled substance as defined in section 130.90, labor trafficking as defined in paragraphs (a) and (b) of subdivision three of section 135.35, criminal possession of a weapon in the third degree as defined in subdivision five, six, seven, eight, nine or ten of section 265.02, criminal sale of a firearm in the third degree as defined in section 265.11, intimidating a victim or witness in the second degree as defined in section 215.16, soliciting or providing support for an act of terrorism in the second degree as defined in section 490.10, and making a terroristic threat as defined in section 490.20, falsely reporting an incident in the first degree as defined in section 240.60, placing a false bomb or hazardous substance in the first degree as defined in section 240.62, placing a false bomb or hazardous substance in a sports stadium or arena, mass transportation facility or enclosed shopping mall as defined in section 240.63, aggravated unpermitted use of indoor pyrotechnics in the first degree as defined in section 405.18 , and criminal manufacture, sale, or transport of an undetectable firearm, rifle or shotgun as defined in section 265.50.

(d) Class E violent felony offenses: an attempt to commit any of the felonies of criminal possession of a weapon in the third degree as defined in subdivision five, six, seven or eight of section 265.02 as a lesser included offense of that section as defined in section 220.20 of the criminal procedure law, persistent sexual abuse as defined in section 130.53, aggravated sexual abuse in the fourth degree as defined in section 130.65-a, falsely reporting an incident in the second degree as defined in section 240.55 and placing a false bomb or hazardous substance in the second degree as defined in section 240.61.

2. Authorized sentence.

(a)[Effective until September 1, 2023] Except as provided in subdivision six of section 60.05, the sentence imposed upon a person who stands convicted of a class B or class C violent felony offense must be a determinate sentence of imprisonment which shall be in whole or half years. The term of such sentence must be in accordance with the provisions of subdivision three of this section.

(a)[Effective September 1, 2023] The sentence imposed upon a person who stands convicted of a class B or class C violent felony offense must be an indeterminate sentence of imprisonment. Except as provided in subdivision five of section 60.05, the maximum term of such sentence must be in accordance with the provisions of subdivision three of this section and the minimum period of imprisonment under such sentence must be in accordance with subdivision four of this section.

(b) Except as provided in paragraph (b-1) of this subdivision, subdivision six of section 60.05 and subdivision four of this section, the sentence imposed upon a person who stands convicted of a class D violent felony offense, other than the offense of criminal possession of a weapon in the third degree as defined in subdivision five, seven or eight of section 265.02 or criminal sale of a firearm in the third degree as defined in section 265.11, must be in accordance with the applicable provisions of this chapter relating to sentencing for class D felonies provided, however, that where a sentence of imprisonment is imposed which requires a commitment to the state department of corrections and community supervision, such sentence shall be a determinate sentence in accordance with paragraph (c) of subdivision three of this section.

(b-1) Except as provided in subdivision six of section 60.05, the sentence imposed upon a person who stands convicted of the class D violent felony offense of menacing a police officer or peace officer as defined in section 120.18 of this chapter must be a determinate sentence of imprisonment.

(c) Except as provided in subdivision six of section 60.05, the sentence imposed upon a person who stands convicted of the class D violent felony offenses of criminal possession of a weapon in the third degree as defined in subdivision five, seven , eight or nine of section 265.02, criminal sale of a firearm in the third degree as defined in section 265.11 or the class E violent felonies of attempted criminal possession of a weapon in the third degree as defined in subdivision five, seven , eight or nine of section 265.02 must be a sentence to a determinate period of imprisonment, or, in the alternative, a definite sentence of imprisonment for a period of no less than one year, except that:

(i) the court may impose any other sentence authorized by law upon a person who has not been previously convicted in the five years immediately preceding the commission of the offense for a class A misdemeanor defined in this chapter, if the court having regard to the nature and circumstances of the crime and to the history and character of the defendant, finds on the record that such sentence would be unduly harsh and that the alternative sentence would be consistent with public safety and does not deprecate the seriousness of the crime; and

(ii) the court may apply the provisions of paragraphs (b) and (c) of subdivision four of this section when imposing a sentence upon a person who has previously been convicted of a class A misdemeanor defined in this chapter in the five years immediately preceding the commission of the offense.

3. Term of sentence. The term of a determinate sentence for a violent felony offense must be fixed by the court as follows:

(a) For a class B felony, the term must be at least five years and must not exceed twenty-five years, provided, however, that the term must be: (i) at least ten years and must not exceed thirty years where the sentence is for the crime of aggravated assault upon a police officer or peace officer as defined in section 120.11 of this chapter; and (ii) at least ten years and must not exceed thirty years where the sentence is for the crime of aggravated manslaughter in the first degree as defined in section 125.22 of this chapter;

(b)For a class C felony, the term must be at least three and one-half years and must not exceed fifteen years, provided, however, that the term must be:

(i) at least seven years and must not exceed twenty years where the sentence is for the crime of aggravated manslaughter in the second degree as defined in section 125.21 of this chapter;

(ii) at least seven years and must not exceed twenty years where the sentence is for the crime of attempted aggravated assault upon a police officer or peace officer as defined in section 120.11 of this chapter;

(iii) at least three and one-half years and must not exceed twenty years where the sentence is for the crime of aggravated criminally negligent homicide as defined in section 125.11 of this chapter; and

(iv) at least five years and must not exceed fifteen years where the sentence is imposed for the crime of aggravated criminal possession of a weapon as defined in section 265.19 of this chapter;

(c) For a class D felony, the term must be at least two years and must not exceed seven years, provided, however, that the term must be:

(i) at least two years and must not exceed eight years where the sentence is for the crime of menacing a police officer or peace officer as defined in section 120.18 of this chapter; and

(ii) at least three and one-half years and must not exceed seven years where the sentence is imposed for the crime of criminal possession of a weapon in the third degree as defined in subdivision ten of section 265.02 of this chapter;

(d) For a class E felony, the term must be at least one and one-half years and must not exceed four years.

4.

(a) Except as provided in paragraph (b) of this subdivision, where a plea of guilty to a class D violent felony offense is entered pursuant to section 220.10 or 220.30 of the criminal procedure law in satisfaction of an indictment charging the defendant with an armed felony, as defined in subdivision forty-one of section 1.20 of the criminal procedure law, the court must impose a determinate sentence of imprisonment.

(b) In any case in which the provisions of paragraph (a) of this subdivision or the provisions of subparagraph (ii) of paragraph (c) of subdivision two of this section apply, the court may impose a sentence other than a determinate sentence of imprisonment, or a definite sentence of imprisonment for a period of no less than one year, if it finds that the alternate sentence is consistent with public safety and does not deprecate the seriousness of the crime and that one or more of the following factors exist:

(i) mitigating circumstances that bear directly upon the manner in which the crime was committed; or

(ii) where the defendant was not the sole participant in the crime, the defendant's participation was relatively minor although not so minor as to constitute a defense to the prosecution; or

(iii) possible deficiencies in proof of the defendant's commission of an armed felony.

(c) The defendant and the district attorney shall have an opportunity to present relevant information to assist the court in making a determination pursuant to paragraph (b) of this subdivision, and the court may, in its discretion, conduct a hearing with respect to any issue bearing upon such determination. If the court determines that a determinate sentence of imprisonment should not be imposed pursuant to the provisions of such paragraph (b), it shall make a statement on the record of the facts and circumstances upon which such determination is based. A transcript of the court's statement, which shall set forth the recommendation of the district attorney, shall be forwarded to the state division of criminal justice services along with a copy of the accusatory instrument.

N.Y. Penal Law § 70.02

Amended by New York Laws 2021, ch. 55,Sec. A-19, eff. 4/19/2021.
Amended by New York Laws 2020, ch. 94,Sec. 4, eff. 6/12/2020.
Amended by New York Laws 2020, ch. 55,Sec. A-19, eff. 4/3/2020.
Amended by New York Laws 2019, ch. 134,Sec. 5, eff. 1/26/2020.
Amended by New York Laws 2019, ch. 134,Sec. 4, eff. 1/26/2020.
Amended by New York Laws 2019, ch. 55,Sec. O-19, eff. 4/12/2019.
Amended by New York Laws 2018, ch. 476,Sec. 239, eff. 12/28/2018.
Amended by New York Laws 2018, ch. 189,Sec. 3, eff. 11/13/2018.
Amended by New York Laws 2017, ch. 55,Sec. A-19, eff. 4/20/2017.
Amended by New York Laws 2015, ch. 368,Sec. 3, eff. 1/19/2016.
Amended by New York Laws 2015, ch. 55,Sec. B-19, eff. 4/13/2015.
Amended by New York Laws 2013, ch. 1,Sec. 30, eff. 3/16/2013.
Amended by New York Laws 2013, ch. 1,Sec. 29, eff. 3/16/2013.
Amended by New York Laws 2013, ch. 1,Sec. 28, eff. 3/16/2013.
Amended by New York Laws 2013, ch. 1,Sec. 27, eff. 3/16/2013.

Section 70.04 - Sentence of imprisonment for second violent felony offender

1. Definition of second violent felony offender.

(a) A second violent felony offender is a person who stands convicted of a violent felony offense as defined in subdivision one of section 70.02 after having previously been subjected to a predicate violent felony conviction as defined in paragraph (b) of this subdivision.

(b) For the purpose of determining whether a prior conviction is a predicate violent felony conviction the following criteria shall apply:

(i) The conviction must have been in this state of a class A felony (other than one defined in article two hundred twenty) or of a violent felony offense as defined in subdivision one of section 70.02, or of an offense defined by the penal law in effect prior to September first, nineteen hundred sixty-seven, which includes all of the essential elements of any such felony, or in any other jurisdiction of an offense which includes all of the essential elements of any such felony for which a sentence to a term of imprisonment in excess of one year or a sentence of death was authorized and is authorized in this state irrespective of whether such sentence was imposed;

(ii) Sentence upon such prior conviction must have been imposed before commission of the present felony;

(iii) Suspended sentence, suspended execution of sentence, a sentence of probation, a sentence of conditional discharge or of unconditional discharge, and a sentence of certification to the care and custody of the division of substance abuse services, shall be deemed to be a sentence;

(iv) Except as provided in subparagraph (v) of this paragraph, sentence must have been imposed not more than ten years before commission of the felony of which the defendant presently stands convicted;

(v) In calculating the ten year period under subparagraph (iv), any period of time during which the person was incarcerated for any reason between the time of commission of the previous felony and the time of commission of the present felony shall be excluded and such ten year period shall be extended by a period or periods equal to the time served under such incarceration;

(vi) An offense for which the defendant has been pardoned on the ground of innocence shall not be deemed a predicate violent felony conviction.

2.[Effective until September 1, 2023] Authorized sentence. When the court has found, pursuant to the provisions of the criminal procedure law, that a person is a second violent felony offender the court must impose a determinate sentence of imprisonment which shall be in whole or half years. Except where sentence is imposed in accordance with the provisions of section 70.10, the term of such sentence must be in accordance with the provisions of subdivision three of this section.

2.[Effective September 1, 2023] Authorized sentence. When the court has found, pursuant to the provisions of the criminal procedure law, that a person is a second violent felony offender the court must impose an indeterminate sentence of imprisonment. Except where sentence is imposed in accordance with the provisions of section 70.10, the maximum term of such sentence must be in accordance with the provisions of subdivision three of this section and the minimum period of imprisonment under such sentence must be in accordance with subdivision four of this section.

3.[Effective until September 1, 2023] Term of sentence. The term of a determinate sentence for a second violent felony offender must be fixed by the court as follows:

(a) For a class B felony, the term must be at least ten years and must not exceed twenty-five years;

(b) For a class C felony, the term must be at least seven years and must not exceed fifteen years; and

(c) For a class D felony, the term must be at least five years and must not exceed seven years.

(d) For a class E felony, the term must be at least three years and must not exceed four years.

3.[Effective September 1, 2023] Maximum term of sentence. The maximum term of an indeterminate sentence for a second violent felony offender must be fixed by the court as follows:

(a) For a class B felony, the term must be at least twelve years and must not exceed twenty-five years;

(b) For a class C felony, the term must be at least eight years and must not exceed fifteen years; and

(c) For a class D felony, the term must be at least five years and must not exceed seven years.

(d) For a class E felony, the term must be at least four years.

4.[Effective September 1, 2023] Minimum period of imprisonment. The minimum period of imprisonment under an indeterminate sentence for a second violent felony offender must be fixed by the court at one-half of the maximum term imposed and must be specified in the sentence.

N.Y. Penal Law § 70.04

Amended by New York Laws 2021, ch. 55,Sec. A-19, eff. 4/19/2021.

Amended by New York Laws 2020, ch. 55,Sec. A-19, eff. 4/3/2020.

Amended by New York Laws 2019, ch. 55,Sec. O-19, eff. 4/12/2019.

Amended by New York Laws 2017, ch. 55,Sec. A-19, eff. 4/20/2017.

Amended by New York Laws 2015, ch. 55,Sec. B-19, eff. 4/13/2015.

Section 70.05 - Sentence of imprisonment for juvenile offender

1. Indeterminate sentence. A sentence of imprisonment for a felony committed by a juvenile offender shall be an indeterminate sentence. When such a sentence is imposed, the court shall impose a maximum term in accordance with the provisions of subdivision two of this section and the minimum period of imprisonment shall be as provided in subdivision three of this section. The court shall further provide that where a juvenile offender is under placement pursuant to article three of the family court act, any sentence imposed pursuant to this section which is to be served consecutively with such placement shall be served in a facility designated pursuant to subdivision four of section 70.20 of this article prior to service of the placement in any previously designated facility.

2. Maximum term of sentence. The maximum term of an indeterminate sentence for a juvenile offender shall be at least three years and the term shall be fixed as follows:

(a) For the class A felony of murder in the second degree, the term shall be life imprisonment;

(b) For the class A felony of arson in the first degree, or for the class A felony of kidnapping in the first degree the term shall be fixed by the court, and shall be at least twelve years but shall not exceed fifteen years;

(c) For a class B felony, the term shall be fixed by the court, and shall not exceed ten years;

(d) For a class C felony, the term shall be fixed by the court, and shall not exceed seven years; and

(e) For a class D felony, the term shall be fixed by the court and shall not exceed four years.

3. Minimum period of imprisonment. The minimum period of imprisonment under an indeterminate sentence for a juvenile offender shall be specified in the sentence as follows:

(a) For the class A felony of murder in the second degree, the minimum period of imprisonment shall be fixed by the court and shall be not less than five years but shall not exceed nine years provided, however, that where the sentence is for an offense specified in subdivision one or two of section 125.25 of this chapter and the defendant was fourteen or fifteen years old at the time of such offense, the minimum period of imprisonment shall be not less than seven and one-half years but shall not exceed fifteen years;

(b) For the class A felony of arson in the first degree, or for the class A felony of kidnapping in the first degree, the minimum period of imprisonment shall be fixed by the court and shall be not less than four years but shall not exceed six years; and

(c) For a class B, C or D felony, the minimum period of imprisonment shall be fixed by the court at one-third of the maximum term imposed.

N.Y. Penal Law § 70.05

Section 70.06 - Sentence of imprisonment for second felony offender

1. Definition of second felony offender.

(a) A second felony offender is a person, other than a second violent felony offender as defined in section 70.04, who stands convicted of a felony defined in this chapter, other than a class A-I felony, after having previously been subjected to one or more predicate felony convictions as defined in paragraph (b) of this subdivision.

(b) For the purpose of determining whether a prior conviction is a predicate felony conviction the following criteria shall apply:

(i) The conviction must have been in this state of a felony, or in any other jurisdiction of an offense for which a sentence to a term of imprisonment in excess of one year or a sentence of death was authorized and is authorized in this state irrespective of whether such sentence was imposed;

(ii) Sentence upon such prior conviction must have been imposed before commission of the present felony;

(iii) Suspended sentence, suspended execution of sentence, a sentence of probation, a sentence of conditional discharge or of unconditional discharge, and a sentence of certification to the care and custody of the division of substance abuse services, shall be deemed to be a sentence;

(iv) Except as provided in subparagraph (v) of this paragraph, sentence must have been imposed not more than ten years before commission of the felony of which the defendant presently stands convicted;

(v) In calculating the ten year period under subparagraph (iv), any period of time during which the person was incarcerated for any reason between the time of commission of the previous felony and the time of commission of the present felony shall be excluded and such ten year period shall be extended by a period or periods equal to the time served under such incarceration;

(vi) An offense for which the defendant has been pardoned on the ground of innocence shall not be deemed a predicate felony conviction.

2.[Effective until September 1, 2023] Authorized sentence. Except as provided in subdivision five or six of this section, or as provided in subdivision five of section 70.80 of this article, when the court has found, pursuant to the provisions of the criminal procedure law, that a person is a second felony offender the court must impose an indeterminate sentence of imprisonment. The maximum term of such sentence must be in accordance with the provisions of subdivision three of this section and the minimum period of imprisonment under such sentence must be in accordance with subdivision four of this section.

2.[Effective September 1, 2023] Authorized sentence. Except as provided in subdivision five of this section, or as provided in subdivision five of section 70.80 of this article, when the court has found, pursuant to the provisions of the criminal procedure law, that a person is a second felony offender the court must impose an indeterminate sentence of imprisonment. The maximum term of such sentence must be in accordance with the provisions of subdivision three of this section and the minimum period of imprisonment under such sentence must be in accordance with subdivision four of this section.

3.[Effective until September 1, 2023] Maximum term of sentence. Except as provided in subdivision five or six of this section, or as provided in subdivision five of section 70.80 of this article, the maximum term of an indeterminate sentence for a second felony offender must be fixed by the court as follows:

(a) For a class A-II felony, the term must be life imprisonment;

(b) For a class B felony, the term must be at least nine years and must not exceed twenty-five years;

(c) For a class C felony, the term must be at least six years and must not exceed fifteen years;

(d) For a class D felony, the term must be at least four years and must not exceed seven years; and

(e) For a class E felony, the term must be at least three years and must not exceed four years; provided, however, that where the sentence is for the class E felony offense specified in section 240.32 of this chapter, the maximum term must be at least three years and must not exceed five years.

3.[Effective September 1, 2023] Maximum term of sentence. Except as provided in subdivision five of this section, or as provided in subdivision five of section 70.80 of this article, the maximum term of an indeterminate sentence for a second felony offender must be fixed by the court as follows:

(a) For a class A-II felony, the term must be life imprisonment;

(b) For a class B felony, the term must be at least nine years and must not exceed twenty-five years;

(c) For a class C felony, the term must be at least six years and must not exceed fifteen years;

(d) For a class D felony, the term must be at least four years and must not exceed seven years; and

(e) For a class E felony, the term must be at least three years and must not exceed four years.

4. Minimum period of imprisonment.

(a) The minimum period of imprisonment for a second felony offender convicted of a class A-II felony must be fixed by the court at no less than six years and not to exceed twelve and one-half years and must be specified in the sentence, except that for the class A-II felony of predatory sexual assault as defined in section 130.95 of this chapter or the class A-II felony of predatory sexual assault against a child as defined in section 130.96 of this chapter, such minimum period shall be not less than ten years nor more than twenty-five years.

(b) Except as provided in paragraph (a), the minimum period of imprisonment under an indeterminate sentence for a second felony offender must be fixed by the court at one-half of the maximum term imposed and must be specified in the sentence.

6.[Repealed September 1, 2023] Determinate sentence. When the court has found, pursuant to the provisions of the criminal procedure law, that a person is a second felony offender and the sentence to be imposed on such person is for a violent felony offense, as defined in subdivision one of section 70.02, the court must impose a determinate sentence of imprisonment the term of which must be fixed by the court as follows:

(a) For a class B violent felony offense, the term must be at least eight years and must not exceed twenty-five years;

(b) For a class C violent felony offense, the term must be at least five years and must not exceed fifteen years;

(c) For a class D violent felony offense, the term must be at least three years and must not exceed seven years; and

(d) For a class E violent felony offense, the term must be at least two years and must not exceed four years.

7.[Repealed September 1, 2023] Notwithstanding any other provision of law, in the case of a person sentenced for a specified offense or offenses as defined in subdivision five of section 410.91 of the criminal procedure law, who stands convicted of no other felony offense, who has not previously been convicted of either a violent felony offense as defined in section 70.02 of this article, a class A felony offense or a class B felony offense, and is not under the jurisdiction of or awaiting delivery to the department of corrections and community supervision, the court may direct that such sentence be executed as a parole supervision sentence as defined in and pursuant to the procedures prescribed in section 410.91 of the criminal procedure law.

N.Y. Penal Law § 70.06

Amended by New York Laws 2021, ch. 55,Sec. A-19, eff. 4/19/2021.
Amended by New York Laws 2020, ch. 55,Sec. A-19, eff. 4/3/2020.
Amended by New York Laws 2019, ch. 55,Sec. O-19, eff. 4/12/2019.
Amended by New York Laws 2017, ch. 55,Sec. A-19, eff. 4/20/2017.
Amended by New York Laws 2015, ch. 55,Sec. B-19, eff. 4/13/2015.

Section 70.07 - Sentence of imprisonment for second child sexual assault felony offender

1. A person who stands convicted of a felony offense for a sexual assault against a child, having been subjected to a predicate felony conviction for a sexual assault against a child, must be sentenced in accordance with the provisions of subdivision four or five of this section.

2. A "sexual assault against a child" means a felony offense, other than persistent sexual abuse as defined in section 130.53 of this chapter, (a) the essential elements of which include the commission or attempted commission of sexual conduct, as defined in subdivision ten of section 130.00 of this chapter, (b) committed or attempted to be committed against a child less than fifteen years old.

3. For purposes of determining whether a person has been subjected to a predicate felony conviction under this section, the criteria set forth in paragraph (b) of subdivision one of section 70.06 shall apply provided however that for purposes of this subdivision, the terms "ten year" or "ten years", as provided in subparagraphs (iv) and (v) of paragraph (b) of subdivision one of such section 70.06, shall be "fifteen year" or "fifteen years". The provisions of section 400.19 of the criminal procedure law shall govern the procedures that must be followed to determine whether a person who stands convicted of a sexual assault against a child has been previously subjected to a predicate felony conviction for such a sexual assault and whether such offender was eighteen years of age or older at the time of the commission of the predicate felony.

4. Where the court has found pursuant to subdivision three of this section that a person who stands convicted of a felony offense defined in article one hundred thirty of this chapter for the commission or attempted commission of a sexual assault against a child has been subjected to a predicate felony conviction for a sexual assault against a child, the court shall sentence the defendant as follows:

(a) where the defendant stands convicted of such sexual assault against a child and such conviction is for a class A-II or class B felony offense, and the predicate conviction for such sexual assault against a child is for a class A-II, class B or class C felony offense, the court shall impose an indeterminate sentence of imprisonment, the maximum term of which shall be life and the minimum period of which shall be at least fifteen years and no more than twenty-five years;

(b) where the defendant stands convicted of such sexual assault against a child and the conviction is for a class C felony offense, and the predicate conviction for such sexual assault against a child is for a class A-II, class B or class C felony offense, the court shall impose a determinate sentence of imprisonment, the term of which must be at least twelve years and must not exceed thirty years; provided however, that if the court determines that a longer sentence is warranted, the court shall set forth on the record the reasons for such determination and, in lieu of imposing such sentence of imprisonment, may impose an indeterminate sentence of imprisonment, the maximum term of which shall be life and the minimum period of which shall be at least fifteen years and no more than twenty-five years;

(c) where the defendant stands convicted of such sexual assault against a child and the conviction is for a class B felony offense, and the predicate conviction for such sexual assault against a child is for a class D or class E felony offense, the court shall impose a determinate sentence of imprisonment, the term of which must be at least twelve years and must not exceed thirty years;

(d) where the defendant stands convicted of such sexual assault against a child and the conviction is for a class C felony offense, and the predicate conviction for such sexual assault against a child is for a class D or class E felony offense, the court shall impose a determinate sentence of imprisonment, the term of which must be at least ten years and must not exceed twenty-five years;

(e) where the defendant stands convicted of such sexual assault against a child and the conviction is for a class D felony offense, and the predicate conviction for such sexual assault against a child is for a felony offense, the court shall impose a determinate sentence of imprisonment, the term of which must be at least five years and must not exceed fifteen years; and

(f) where the defendant stands convicted of such sexual assault against a child and the conviction is for a class E felony offense, and the predicate conviction for such sexual assault against a child is for a felony offense, the court shall impose a determinate sentence of imprisonment, the term of which must be at least four years and must not exceed twelve years.

5. Notwithstanding subdivision four of this section, where the court has found pursuant to subdivision three of this section that a person: (a) stands convicted of a felony offense defined in article one hundred thirty of this chapter for the commission or attempted commission of a sexual assault against a child; and (b) has been subjected to a predicate felony conviction for sexual assault against a child as defined in subdivision two of this section; and (c) who was under the age of eighteen years at the time of the commission of such predicate felony offense, then the court may, in lieu of the sentence authorized by subdivision four of this section, sentence the defendant to a term of imprisonment in accordance with the sentence authorized for the instant felony offense pursuant to subdivision three of section 70.04 of this article. The court shall set forth on the record the reasons for such determination.

N.Y. Penal Law § 70.07

Section 70.08 - Sentence of imprisonment for persistent violent felony offender; criteria

1. Definition of persistent violent felony offender.

(a) A persistent violent felony offender is a person who stands convicted of a violent felony offense as defined in subdivision one of section 70.02 or the offense of predatory sexual assault as defined in section 130.95 of this chapter or the offense of predatory sexual assault against a child as defined in section 130.96 of this chapter, after having previously been subjected to two or more predicate violent felony convictions as defined in paragraph (b) of subdivision one of section 70.04 of this article.

(b) For the purpose of determining whether a person has two or more predicate violent felony convictions, the criteria set forth in paragraph (b) of subdivision one of section 70.04 shall apply.

2. Authorized sentence. When the court has found, pursuant to the provisions of the criminal procedure law, that a person is a persistent violent felony offender the court must impose an indeterminate sentence of imprisonment, the maximum term of which shall be life imprisonment. The minimum period of imprisonment under such sentence must be in accordance with subdivision three of this section.

3.[Effective until September 1, 2023] Minimum period of imprisonment. The minimum period of imprisonment under an indeterminate life sentence for a persistent violent felony offender must be fixed by the court as follows:

(a) For the class A-II felony of predatory sexual assault as defined in section 130.95 of this chapter or the class A-II felony of predatory sexual assault against a child as defined in section 130.96 of this chapter, the minimum period must be twenty-five years;

(a-1) For a class B felony, the minimum period must be at least twenty years and must not exceed twenty-five years;

(b) For a class C felony, the minimum period must be at least sixteen years and must not exceed twenty-five years;

(c) For a class D felony, the minimum period must be at least twelve years and must not exceed twenty-five years.

3.[Effective September 1, 2023] Minimum period of imprisonment. The minimum period of imprisonment under an indeterminate life sentence for a persistent violent felony offender must be fixed by the court as follows:

(a) For the class A-II felony of predatory sexual assault as defined in section 130.95 of this chapter or the class A-II felony of predatory sexual assault against a child as defined in section 130.96 of this chapter, the minimum period must be twenty-five years;

(a-1) For a class B felony, the minimum period must be at least ten years and must not exceed twenty-five years;

(b) For a class C felony, the minimum period must be at least eight years and must not exceed twenty-five years;

(c) For a class D felony, the minimum period must be at least six years and must not exceed twenty-five years.

N.Y. Penal Law § 70.08

Amended by New York Laws 2021, ch. 55,Sec. A-19, eff. 4/19/2021.
Amended by New York Laws 2020, ch. 55,Sec. A-19, eff. 4/3/2020.
Amended by New York Laws 2019, ch. 55,Sec. O-19, eff. 4/12/2019.
Amended by New York Laws 2017, ch. 55,Sec. A-19, eff. 4/20/2017.
Amended by New York Laws 2015, ch. 55,Sec. B-19, eff. 4/13/2015.

Section 70.10 - Sentence of imprisonment for persistent felony offender

1. Definition of persistent felony offender.

(a) A persistent felony offender is a person, other than a persistent violent felony offender as defined in section 70.08, who stands convicted of a felony after having previously been convicted of two or more felonies, as provided in paragraphs (b) and (c) of this subdivision.

(b) A previous felony conviction within the meaning of paragraph (a) of this subdivision is a conviction of a felony in this state, or of a crime in any other jurisdiction, provided:

(i) that a sentence to a term of imprisonment in excess of one year, or a sentence to death, was imposed therefor; and

(ii) that the defendant was imprisoned under sentence for such conviction prior to the commission of the present felony; and

(iii) that the defendant was not pardoned on the ground of innocence; and

(iv) that such conviction was for a felony offense other than persistent sexual abuse, as defined in section 130.53 of this chapter.

(c) For the purpose of determining whether a person has two or more previous felony convictions, two or more convictions of crimes that were committed prior to the time the defendant was imprisoned under sentence for any of such convictions shall be deemed to be only one conviction.

2. Authorized sentence. When the court has found, pursuant to the provisions of the criminal procedure law, that a person is a persistent felony offender, and when it is of the opinion that the history and character of the defendant and the nature and circumstances of his criminal conduct indicate that extended incarceration and life-time supervision will best serve the public interest, the court, in lieu of imposing the sentence of imprisonment authorized by section 70.00, 70.02, 70.04, 70.06 or subdivision five of section 70.80 for the crime of which such person presently stands convicted, may impose the sentence of imprisonment authorized by that section for a class A-I felony. In such event the reasons for the court's opinion shall be set forth in the record.

N.Y. Penal Law § 70.10

Section 70.15 - Sentences of imprisonment for misdemeanors and violation

1. Class A misdemeanor. A sentence of imprisonment for a class A misdemeanor shall be a definite sentence. When such a sentence is imposed the term shall be fixed by the court, and shall not exceed three hundred sixty-four days.

1-a.

(a) Notwithstanding the provisions of any other law, whenever the phrase "one year" or "three hundred sixty-five days" or "365 days" or any similar phrase appears in any provision of this chapter or any other law in reference to the definite sentence or maximum definite sentence of imprisonment that is imposed, or has been imposed, or may be imposed after enactment of this subdivision, for a misdemeanor conviction in this state, such phrase shall mean, be interpreted and be applied as three hundred sixty-four days.

(b) The amendatory provisions of this subdivision are ameliorative and shall apply to all persons who are sentenced before, on or after the effective date of this subdivision, for a crime committed before, on or after the effective date of this subdivision.

(c) Any sentence for a misdemeanor conviction imposed prior to the effective date of this subdivision that is a definite sentence of imprisonment of one year, or three hundred sixty-five days, shall, by operation of law, be changed to, mean and be interpreted and applied as a sentence of three hundred sixty-four days. In addition to any other right of a person to obtain a record of a proceeding against him or her, a person so sentenced prior to the effective date of this subdivision shall be entitled to obtain, from the criminal court or the clerk thereof, a certificate of conviction, as described in subdivision one of section 60.60 of the criminal procedure law, setting forth such sentence as the sentence specified in this paragraph.

(d) Any sentence for a misdemeanor conviction imposed prior to the effective date of this subdivision that is other than a definite sentence of imprisonment of one year may be set aside, upon motion of the defendant under section 440.20 of the criminal procedure law based on a showing that the judgment and sentence under the law in effect at the time of conviction imposed prior to the effective date of this subdivision is likely to result in collateral consequences, in order to permit the court to resentence the defendant in accordance with the amendatory provisions of this subdivision.

(e) Resentence by operation of law is without prejudice to an individual seeking further relief pursuant to paragraph (j) of subdivision one of section 440.10 of the criminal procedure law. Nothing in this section is intended to diminish or abrogate any rights or remedies otherwise available to the individual.

2. Class B misdemeanor. A sentence of imprisonment for a class B misdemeanor shall be a definite sentence. When such a sentence is imposed the term shall be fixed by the court, and shall not exceed three months.

3. Unclassified misdemeanor. A sentence of imprisonment for an unclassified misdemeanor shall be a definite sentence. When such a sentence is imposed the term shall be fixed by the court, and shall be in accordance with the sentence specified in the law or ordinance that defines the crime but, in any event, it shall not exceed three hundred sixty-four days.

4. Violation. A sentence of imprisonment for a violation shall be a definite sentence. When such a sentence is imposed the term shall be fixed by the court, and shall not exceed fifteen days.

In the case of a violation defined outside this chapter, if the sentence is expressly specified in the law or ordinance that defines the offense and consists solely of a fine, no term of imprisonment shall be imposed.

N.Y. Penal Law § 70.15

Amended by New York Laws 2019, ch. 59,Sec. MMM-1, eff. 4/12/2019.

Amended by New York Laws 2019, ch. 55,Sec. OO-2, eff. 4/12/2019.

Amended by New York Laws 2019, ch. 55,Sec. OO-1, eff. 4/12/2019.

Section 70.20 - Place of imprisonment

1.[Effective until September 1, 2023]

(a) Indeterminate or determinate sentence. Except as provided in subdivision four of this section, when an indeterminate or determinate sentence of imprisonment is imposed, the court shall commit the defendant to the custody of the state department of corrections and community supervision for the term of his or her sentence and until released in accordance with the law; provided, however, that a defendant sentenced pursuant to subdivision seven of section 70.06 shall be committed to the custody of the state department of corrections and community supervision for immediate delivery to a reception center operated by the department.

(b) The court in committing a defendant who is not yet eighteen years of age to the department of corrections and community supervision shall inquire as to whether the parents or legal guardian of the defendant, if present, will grant to the minor the capacity to consent to routine medical, dental and mental health services and treatment.

(c) Notwithstanding paragraph (b) of this subdivision, where the court commits a defendant who is not yet eighteen years of age to the custody of the department of corrections and community supervision in accordance with this section and no medical consent has been obtained prior to said commitment, the commitment order shall be deemed to grant the capacity to consent to routine medical, dental and mental health services and treatment to the person so committed.

(d) Nothing in this subdivision shall preclude a parent or legal guardian of an incarcerated individual who is not yet eighteen years of age from making a motion on notice to the department of corrections and community supervision pursuant to article twenty-two of the civil practice law and rules and section one hundred forty of the correction law, objecting to routine medical, dental or mental health services and treatment being provided to such incarcerated individual under the provisions of paragraph (b) of this subdivision.

(e) Nothing in this section shall require that consent be obtained from the parent or legal guardian, where no consent is necessary or where the defendant is authorized by law to consent on his or her own behalf to any medical, dental, and mental health service or treatment.

1.[Effective September 1, 2023]

(a) Indeterminate sentence. Except as provided in subdivision four of this section, when an indeterminate sentence of imprisonment is imposed, the court shall commit the defendant to the custody of the state department of corrections and community supervision for the term of his or her sentence and until released in accordance with the law.

(b) The court in committing a defendant who is not yet eighteen years of age to the department of corrections and community supervision shall inquire as to whether the parents or legal guardian of the defendant, if present, will grant to the minor the capacity to consent to routine medical, dental and mental health services and treatment.

(c) Notwithstanding paragraph (b) of this subdivision, where the court commits a defendant who is not yet eighteen years of age to the custody of the department of corrections and community supervision in accordance with this section and no medical consent has been obtained prior to said commitment, the commitment order shall be deemed to grant the capacity to consent to routine medical, dental and mental health services and treatment to the person so committed.

(d) Nothing in this subdivision shall preclude a parent or legal guardian of an incarcerated individual who is not yet eighteen years of age from making a motion on notice to the department of corrections and community supervision pursuant to article twenty-two of the civil practice law and rules and section one hundred forty of the correction law, objecting to routine medical, dental or mental health services and treatment being provided to such incarcerated individual under the provisions of paragraph (b) of this subdivision.

(e) Nothing in this section shall require that consent be obtained from the parent or legal guardian, where no consent is necessary or where the defendant is authorized by law to consent on his or her own behalf to any medical, dental, and mental health service or treatment.

2. Definite sentence. Except as provided in subdivision four of this section, when a definite sentence of imprisonment is imposed, the court shall commit the defendant to the county or regional correctional institution for the term of his sentence and until released in accordance with the law.

2-a. Sentence of life imprisonment without parole. When a sentence of life imprisonment without parole is imposed, the court shall commit the defendant to the custody of the state department of corrections and community supervision for the remainder of the life of the defendant.

3.[Effective until September 1, 2023] Undischarged imprisonment in other jurisdiction. When a defendant who is subject to an undischarged term of imprisonment, imposed at a previous time by a court of another jurisdiction, is sentenced to an additional term or terms of imprisonment by a court of this state to run concurrently with such undischarged term, as provided in subdivision four of section 70.25, the return of the defendant to the custody of the appropriate official of the other jurisdiction shall be deemed a commitment for such portion of the term or terms of the sentence imposed by the court of this state as shall not exceed the said undischarged term. The defendant shall be committed to the custody of the state department of corrections and community supervision if the additional term or terms are indeterminate or determinate or to the appropriate county or regional correctional institution if the said term or terms are definite for such portion of the term or terms of the sentence imposed as shall exceed such undischarged term or until released in accordance with law. If such additional term or terms imposed shall run consecutively to the said undischarged term, the defendant shall be committed as provided in subdivisions one and two of this section.

3.[Effective September 1, 2023] Undischarged imprisonment in other jurisdiction. When a defendant who is subject to an undischarged term of imprisonment, imposed at a previous time by a court of another jurisdiction, is sentenced to an additional term or terms of imprisonment by a court of this state to run concurrently with such undischarged term, as provided in subdivision four of section 70.25, the return of the defendant to the custody of the appropriate official of the other jurisdiction shall be deemed a commitment for such portion of the term or terms of the sentence imposed by the court of this state as shall not exceed the said undischarged term. The defendant shall be committed to the custody of the state department of corrections and community supervision if the additional term or terms are indeterminate or to the appropriate county or regional correctional institution if the said term or terms are definite for such portion of the term or terms of the sentence imposed as shall exceed such undischarged term or until released in accordance with law. If such additional term or terms imposed shall run consecutively to the said undischarged term, the defendant shall be committed as provided in subdivisions one and two of this section.

4.

(a) Notwithstanding any other provision of law to the contrary, a juvenile offender, adolescent offender, or a juvenile offender or adolescent offender who is adjudicated a youthful offender , who is given an indeterminate, determinate or a definite sentence, and who is under the age of twenty-one at the time of sentencing, shall be committed to the custody of

41

the commissioner of the office of children and family services who shall arrange for the confinement of such offender in secure facilities of the office; provided, however if an adolescent offender who committed a crime on or after the youth's sixteenth birthday receives a definite sentence not exceeding one year, the judge may order that the adolescent offender serve such sentence in a specialized secure juvenile detention facility for older youth certified by the office of children and family services in conjunction with the state commission of correction and operated pursuant to section two hundred eighteen-a of the county law. The release or transfer of such juvenile offenders or adolescent offenders from the office of children and family services shall be governed by section five hundred eight of the executive law.

(a-1) [Repealed]

(a-2) Notwithstanding any other provision of law to the contrary, a person sixteen years of age who commits a vehicle and traffic law offense that does not constitute an adolescent offender offense on or after October first, two thousand eighteen and a person seventeen years of age who commits such an offense on or after October first, two thousand nineteen who is sentenced to a term of imprisonment who is under the age of twenty-one at the time he or she is sentenced shall be committed to a specialized secure detention facility for older youth certified by the office of children and family services in conjunction with the state commission of correction.

(b) The court in committing a juvenile offender and youthful offender to the custody of the office of children and family services shall inquire as to whether the parents or legal guardian of the youth, if present, will consent for the office of children and family services to provide routine medical, dental and mental health services and treatment.

(c) Notwithstanding paragraph (b) of this subdivision, where the court commits an offender to the custody of the office of children and family services in accordance with this section and no medical consent has been obtained prior to said commitment, the commitment order shall be deemed to grant consent for the office of children and family services to provide for routine medical, dental and mental health services and treatment to the offender so committed.

(d) Nothing in this subdivision shall preclude a parent or legal guardian of an offender who is not yet eighteen years of age from making a motion on notice to the office of children and family services pursuant to article twenty-two of the civil practice law and rules objecting to routine medical, dental or mental health services and treatment being provided to such offender under the provisions of paragraph (b) of this subdivision.

(e) Nothing in this section shall require that consent be obtained from the parent or legal guardian, where no consent is necessary or where the offender is authorized by law to consent on his or her own behalf to any medical, dental and mental health service or treatment.

5. Subject to regulations of the department of health, routine medical, dental and mental health services and treatment is defined for the purposes of this section to mean any routine diagnosis or treatment, including without limitation the administration of medications or nutrition, the extraction of bodily fluids for analysis, and dental care performed with a local anesthetic. Routine mental health treatment shall not include psychiatric administration of medication unless it is part of an ongoing mental health plan or unless it is otherwise authorized by law.

N.Y. Penal Law § 70.20

Amended by New York Laws 2021, ch. 322,Sec. 104-a, eff. 8/2/2021.
Amended by New York Laws 2021, ch. 322,Sec. 104, eff. 8/2/2021.
Amended by New York Laws 2021, ch. 55,Sec. A-19, eff. 4/19/2021.
Amended by New York Laws 2020, ch. 55,Sec. G-1, eff. 6/2/2020.
Amended by New York Laws 2020, ch. 55,Sec. A-19, eff. 4/3/2020.
Amended by New York Laws 2019, ch. 55,Sec. O-19, eff. 4/12/2019.
Amended by New York Laws 2017, ch. 55,Sec. A-19, eff. 4/20/2017.
Amended by New York Laws 2017, ch. 59,Sec. WWW-43 and Sec. WWW-44, eff. 10/1/2018.
Amended by New York Laws 2015, ch. 55,Sec. B-19, eff. 4/13/2015.
Amended by New York Laws 2013, ch. 437,Sec. 1, eff. 10/23/2013.
See New York Laws 2020, ch. 55, Sec. G-6.

Section 70.25 - Concurrent and consecutive terms of imprisonment

1. Except as provided in subdivisions two, two-a and five of this section, when multiple sentences of imprisonment are imposed on a person at the same time, or when a person who is subject to any undischarged term of imprisonment imposed at a previous time by a court of this state is sentenced to an additional term of imprisonment, the sentence or sentences imposed by the court shall run either concurrently or consecutively with respect to each other and the undischarged term or terms in such manner as the court directs at the time of sentence. If the court does not specify the manner in which a sentence imposed by it is to run, the sentence shall run as follows:

(a)[Effective until September 1, 2023] An indeterminate or determinate sentence shall run concurrently with all other terms; and

(a)[Effective September 1, 2023] An indeterminate sentence shall run concurrently with all other terms; and

(b) A definite sentence shall run concurrently with any sentence imposed at the same time and shall be consecutive to any other term.

2. When more than one sentence of imprisonment is imposed on a person for two or more offenses committed through a single act or omission, or through an act or omission which in itself constituted one of the offenses and also was a material element of the other, the sentences, except if one or more of such sentences is for a violation of section 270.20 of this chapter, must run concurrently.

2-a.[Effective until September 1, 2023] When an indeterminate or determinate sentence of imprisonment is imposed pursuant to section 70.04, 70.06, 70.07, 70.08, 70.10, subdivision three or four of section 70.70, subdivision three or four of section 70.71 or subdivision five of section 70.80 of this article, or is imposed for a class A-I felony pursuant to section 70.00 of this article, and such person is subject to an undischarged indeterminate or determinate sentence of imprisonment imposed prior to the date on which the present crime was committed, the court must impose a sentence to run consecutively with respect to such undischarged sentence.

2-a.[Effective September 1, 2023] When an indeterminate or determinate sentence of imprisonment is imposed pursuant to section 70.04, 70.06, 70.07, 70.08, 70.10, subdivision three or four of section 70.70, subdivision three or four of section 70.71 or subdivision five of section 70.80 of this article, or is imposed for a class A-I felony pursuant to section 70.00 of this article, and such person is subject to an undischarged indeterminate sentence of imprisonment imposed prior to the date on which the present crime was committed, the court must impose a sentence to run consecutively with respect to such undischarged sentence.

2-b.[Effective until September 1, 2023] When a person is convicted of a violent felony offense committed after arraignment and while released on recognizance or bail, but committed prior to the imposition of sentence on a pending felony charge, and if an indeterminate or determinate sentence of imprisonment is imposed in each case, such sentences shall run consecutively. Provided, however, that the court may, in the interest of justice, order a sentence to run concurrently in a situation where consecutive sentences are required by this subdivision if it finds either mitigating circumstances that bear directly upon the manner in which the crime was committed or, where the defendant was not the sole participant in the crime, the defendant's participation was relatively minor although not so minor as to constitute a defense to the prosecution. The defendant and the district attorney shall have an opportunity to present relevant information to assist the court in making this determination and the court may, in its discretion, conduct a hearing with respect to any issue bearing upon such determination. If the court determines that consecutive sentences should not be ordered, it shall make a statement on the record of the facts and circumstances upon which such determination is based.

2-b.[Effective September 1, 2023] When a person is convicted of a violent felony offense committed after arraignment and while released on recognizance or bail, but committed prior to the imposition of sentence on a pending felony charge, and if an indeterminate sentence of imprisonment is imposed in each case, such sentences shall run consecutively. Provided, however, that the court may, in the interest of justice, order a sentence to run concurrently in a situation where consecutive sentences are required by this subdivision if it finds either mitigating circumstances that bear directly upon the manner in which the crime was committed or, where the defendant was not the sole participant in the crime, the defendant's participation was relatively minor although not so minor as to constitute a defense to the prosecution. The defendant and the district attorney shall have an opportunity to present relevant information to assist the court in making this determination and the court may, in its discretion, conduct a hearing with respect to any issue bearing upon such determination. If the court determines that consecutive sentences should not be ordered, it shall make a statement on the record of the facts and circumstances upon which such determination is based.

2-c. When a person is convicted of bail jumping in the second degree as defined in section 215.56 or bail jumping in the first degree as defined in section 215.57 committed after arraignment and while released on recognizance or bail in connection with a pending indictment or information charging one or more felonies, at least one of which he is subsequently convicted, and if an indeterminate sentence of imprisonment is imposed in each case, such sentences shall run consecutively. Provided, however, that the court may, in the interest of justice, order a sentence to run concurrently in a situation where consecutive sentences are required by this subdivision if it finds mitigating circumstances that bear directly upon the manner in which the crime was committed. The defendant and the district attorney shall have an opportunity to present relevant information to assist the court in making this determination and the court may, in its discretion, conduct a hearing with respect to any issue bearing upon such determination. If the court determines that consecutive sentences should not be ordered, it shall make a statement on the record of the facts and circumstances upon which such determination is based.

2-d. When a person is convicted of escape in the second degree as defined in section 205.10 or escape in the first degree as defined in section 205.15 committed after issuance of a securing order, as defined in subdivision five of section 500.10 of the criminal procedure law, in connection with a pending indictment or information charging one or more felonies, at least one of which he is subsequently convicted, and if an indeterminate sentence of imprisonment is imposed in each case, such sentences shall run consecutively. Provided, however, that the court may, in the interest of justice, order a sentence to run concurrently in a situation where consecutive sentences are required by this subdivision if it finds mitigating circumstances that bear directly upon the manner in which the crime was committed. The defendant and the district attorney shall have an opportunity to present relevant information to assist the court in making this determination and the court may, in its discretion, conduct a hearing with respect to any issue bearing upon such determination. If the court determines that consecutive sentences should not be ordered, it shall make a statement on the record of the facts and circumstances upon which such determination is based.

2-e. Whenever a person is convicted of course of sexual conduct against a child in the first degree as defined in section 130.75 or course of sexual conduct against a child in the second degree as defined in section 130.80 and any other crime under article one hundred thirty committed against the same child and within the period charged under section 130.75 or 130.80, the sentences must run concurrently.

2-f. Whenever a person is convicted of facilitating a sex offense with a controlled substance as defined in section 130.90 of this chapter, the sentence imposed by the court for such offense may be ordered to run consecutively to any sentence imposed upon conviction of an offense defined in article one hundred thirty of this chapter arising from the same criminal transaction.

2-g. Whenever a person is convicted of unlawful manufacture of methamphetamine in the third degree as defined in section 220.73 of this chapter, unlawful manufacture of methamphetamine in the second degree as defined in section 220.74 of this chapter, or unlawful manufacture of methamphetamine in the first degree as defined in section 220.75 of this chapter, or any attempt to commit any of such offenses, and such person is also convicted, with respect to such unlawful methamphetamine laboratory, of unlawful disposal of methamphetamine laboratory material as defined in section 220.76 of this chapter, the sentences must run concurrently.

3. Where consecutive definite sentences of imprisonment are not prohibited by subdivision two of this section and are imposed on a person for offenses which were committed as parts of a single incident or transaction, the aggregate of the terms of such sentences shall not exceed one year.

4. When a person, who is subject to any undischarged term of imprisonment imposed at a previous time by a court of another jurisdiction, is sentenced to an additional term or terms of imprisonment by a court of this state, the sentence or sentences imposed by the court of this state, subject to the provisions of subdivisions one, two and three of this section, shall run either concurrently or consecutively with respect to such undischarged term in such manner as the court directs at the time of sentence. If the court of this state does not specify the manner in which a sentence imposed by it is to run, the sentence or sentences shall run consecutively.

5.

(a)[Effective until September 1, 2023] Except as provided in paragraph (c) of this subdivision, when a person is convicted of assault in the second degree, as defined in subdivision seven of section 120.05 of this chapter, any definite, indeterminate or determinate term of imprisonment which may be imposed as a sentence upon such conviction shall run consecutively to any undischarged term of imprisonment to which the defendant was subject and for which he was confined at the time of the assault.

(a)[Effective September 1, 2023] Except as provided in paragraph (c) of this subdivision, when a person is convicted of assault in the second degree, as defined in subdivision seven of section 120.05 of this chapter, any definite or indeterminate term of imprisonment which may be imposed as a sentence upon such conviction shall run consecutively to any undischarged term of imprisonment to which the defendant was subject and for which he was confined at the time of the assault.

(b)[Effective until September 1, 2023] Except as provided in paragraph (c) of this subdivision, when a person is convicted of assault in the second degree, as defined in subdivision seven of section 120.05 of this chapter, any definite, indeterminate or determinate term of imprisonment which may be imposed as a sentence upon such conviction shall run consecutively to any term of imprisonment which was previously imposed or which may be prospectively imposed where the person was confined within a detention facility at the time of the assault upon a charge which culminated in such sentence of imprisonment.

(b)[Effective September 1, 2023] Except as provided in paragraph (c) of this subdivision, when a person is convicted of assault in the second degree, as defined in subdivision seven of section 120.05 of this chapter, any definite or indeterminate term of imprisonment which may be imposed as a sentence upon such conviction shall run consecutively to any term of imprisonment which was previously imposed or which may be prospectively imposed where the person was confined within a detention facility at the time of the assault upon a charge which culminated in such sentence of imprisonment.

(c) Notwithstanding the provisions of paragraphs (a) and (b) of this subdivision, a term of imprisonment imposed upon a conviction to assault in the second degree as defined in subdivision seven of section 120.05 of this chapter may run concurrently to any other term of imprisonment, in the interest of justice, provided the court sets forth in the record its reasons for imposing a concurrent sentence. Nothing in this section shall require the imposition of a sentence of imprisonment where it is not otherwise required by law.

N.Y. Penal Law § 70.25

Amended by New York Laws 2021, ch. 55,Sec. A-19, eff. 4/19/2021.
Amended by New York Laws 2020, ch. 55,Sec. A-19, eff. 4/3/2020.
Amended by New York Laws 2019, ch. 55,Sec. O-19, eff. 4/12/2019.
Amended by New York Laws 2017, ch. 55,Sec. A-19, eff. 4/20/2017.
Amended by New York Laws 2015, ch. 55,Sec. B-19, eff. 4/13/2015.

Section 70.30 - Calculation of terms of imprisonment

1.[Effective until September 1, 2023] An indeterminate or determinate sentence of imprisonment commences when the prisoner is received in an institution under the jurisdiction of the state department of corrections and community supervision. Where a person is under more than one indeterminate or determinate sentence, the sentences shall be calculated as follows:

[Effective September 1, 2023] An indeterminate sentence of imprisonment commences when the prisoner is received in an institution under the jurisdiction of the state department of corrections and community supervision. Where a person is under more than one indeterminate sentence, the sentences shall be calculated as follows:

(a)[Effective until September 1, 2023] If the sentences run concurrently, the time served under imprisonment on any of the sentences shall be credited against the minimum periods of all the concurrent indeterminate sentences and against the terms of all the concurrent determinate sentences. The maximum term or terms of the indeterminate sentences and the term or terms of the determinate sentences shall merge in and be satisfied by discharge of the term which has the longest unexpired time to run;

(a)[Effective September 1, 2023] If the sentences run concurrently, the time served under imprisonment on any of the sentences shall be credited against the minimum periods of all the concurrent sentences, and the maximum terms merge in and are satisfied by discharge of the term which has the longest unexpired time to run;

(b)[Effective until September 1, 2023] If the defendant is serving two or more indeterminate sentences which run consecutively, the minimum periods of imprisonment are added to arrive at an aggregate minimum period of imprisonment equal to the sum of all the minimum periods, and the maximum terms are added to arrive at an aggregate maximum term equal to the sum of all the maximum terms, provided, however, that both the aggregate maximum term and the aggregate minimum period of imprisonment shall be subject to the limitations set forth in paragraphs (e) and (f) of this subdivision, where applicable;

(b)[Effective September 1, 2023] If the sentences run consecutively, the minimum periods of imprisonment are added to arrive at an aggregate minimum period of imprisonment equal to the sum of all the minimum periods, and the maximum terms are added to arrive at an aggregate maximum term equal to the sum of all the maximum terms, provided, however, that both the aggregate maximum term and the aggregate minimum period of imprisonment shall be subject to the limitations set forth in paragraphs (c) and (d) of this subdivision, where applicable;

(c)[Effective until September 1, 2023] If the defendant is serving two or more determinate sentences of imprisonment which run consecutively, the terms of the determinate sentences are added to arrive at an aggregate maximum term of imprisonment, provided, however, that the aggregate maximum term of imprisonment shall be subject to the limitations set forth in paragraphs (e) and (f) of this subdivision, where applicable.

(c)[Effective September 1, 2023]

(i) Except as provided in subparagraph (ii) or (iii) of this paragraph, the aggregate maximum term of consecutive sentences imposed for two or more crimes, other than two or more crimes that include a class A felony, committed prior to the time the person was imprisoned under any of such sentences shall, if it exceeds twenty years, be deemed to be twenty years, unless one of the sentences was imposed for a class B felony, in which case the aggregate maximum term shall, if it exceeds thirty years, be deemed to be thirty years. Where the aggregate maximum term of two or more consecutive sentences is reduced by calculation made pursuant to this paragraph, the aggregate minimum period of imprisonment, if it exceeds one-half of the aggregate maximum term as so reduced, shall be deemed to be one-half of the aggregate maximum term as so reduced;

(ii) Notwithstanding subparagraph (i) of this paragraph, the aggregate maximum term of consecutive sentences imposed for the conviction of two violent felony offenses committed prior to the time the person was imprisoned under any of such sentences and one of which is a class B violent felony offense, shall, if it exceeds forty years, be deemed to be forty years;

(iii) Notwithstanding subparagraphs (i) and (ii) of this paragraph, the aggregate maximum term of consecutive sentences imposed for the conviction of three or more violent felony offenses committed prior to the time the person was imprisoned under any of such sentences and one of which is a class B violent felony offense, shall, if it exceeds fifty years, be deemed to be fifty years;

(d)[Effective until September 1, 2023] If the defendant is serving one or more indeterminate sentences of imprisonment and one or more determinate sentence of imprisonment which run consecutively, the minimum term or terms of the indeterminate sentence or sentences and the term or terms of the determinate sentence or sentences are added to arrive at an aggregate maximum term of imprisonment, provided, however, (i) that in no event shall the aggregate maximum so calculated be less than the term or maximum term of imprisonment of the sentence which has the longest unexpired time to run; and (ii) that the aggregate maximum term of imprisonment shall be subject to the limitations set forth in paragraphs (e) and (f) of this subdivision, where applicable.

(d)[Effective September 1, 2023] The aggregate maximum term of consecutive sentences imposed upon a juvenile offender for two or more crimes, not including a class A felony, committed before he has reached the age of sixteen, shall, if it exceeds ten years, be deemed to be ten years. If consecutive indeterminate sentences imposed upon a juvenile offender include a sentence for the class A felony of arson in the first degree or for the class A felony of kidnapping in the first degree, then the aggregate maximum term of such sentences shall, if it exceeds fifteen years, be deemed to be fifteen years. Where the aggregate maximum term of two or more consecutive sentences is reduced by a calculation made pursuant to this paragraph, the aggregate minimum period of imprisonment, if it exceeds one-half of the aggregate maximum term as so reduced, shall be deemed to be one-half of the aggregate maximum term as so reduced.

(e)[Effective until September 1, 2023]

(i) Except as provided in subparagraph (ii), (iii), (iv), (v), (vi) or (vii) of this paragraph, the aggregate maximum term of consecutive sentences, all of which are indeterminate sentences or all of which are determinate sentences, imposed for two or more crimes, other than two or more crimes that include a class A felony, committed prior to the time the person was imprisoned under any of such sentences shall, if it exceeds twenty years, be deemed to be twenty years, unless one of the sentences was imposed for a class B felony, in which case the aggregate maximum term shall, if it exceeds thirty years, be deemed to be thirty years. Where the aggregate maximum term of two or more indeterminate consecutive sentences is reduced by calculation made pursuant to this paragraph, the aggregate minimum period of imprisonment, if it exceeds one-half of the aggregate maximum term as so reduced, shall be deemed to be one-half of the aggregate maximum term as so reduced;

(ii) Where the aggregate maximum term of two or more consecutive sentences, one or more of which is a determinate sentence and one or more of which is an indeterminate sentence, imposed for two or more crimes, other than two or more crimes that include a class A felony, committed prior to the time the person was imprisoned under any of such sentences, exceeds twenty years, and none of the sentences was imposed for a class B felony, the following rules shall apply:

(A) if the aggregate maximum term of the determinate sentence or sentences exceeds twenty years, the defendant shall be deemed to be serving to a determinate sentence of twenty years.

(B) if the aggregate maximum term of the determinate sentence or sentences is less than twenty years, the defendant shall be deemed to be serving an indeterminate sentence the maximum term of which shall be deemed to be twenty years. In such instances, the minimum sentence shall be deemed to be ten years or six-sevenths of the term or aggregate maximum term of the determinate sentence or sentences, whichever is greater.

(iii) Where the aggregate maximum term of two or more consecutive sentences, one or more of which is a determinate sentence and one or more of which is an indeterminate sentence, imposed for two or more crimes, other than two or more crimes that include a class A felony, commmitted prior to the time the person was imprisoned under any of such sentences, exceeds thirty years, and one of the sentences was imposed for a class B felony, the following rules shall apply:

(A) if the aggregate maximum term of the determinate sentence or sentences exceeds thirty years, the defendant shall be deemed to be serving a determinate sentence of thirty years;

(B) if the aggregate maximum term of the determinate sentence or sentences is less than thirty years, the defendant shall be deemed to be serving an indeterminate sentence the maximum term of which shall be deemed to be thirty years. In such instances, the minimum sentence shall be deemed to be fifteen years or six-sevenths of the term or aggregate maximum term of the determinate sentence or sentences, whichever is greater.

(iv) Notwithstanding subparagraph (i) of this paragraph, the aggregate maximum term of consecutive sentences, all of which are indeterminate sentences or all of which are determinate sentences, imposed for the conviction of two violent felony offenses committed prior to the time the person was imprisoned under any of such sentences and one of which is a class B violent felony offense, shall, if it exceeds forty years, be deemed to be forty years

(v) Notwithstanding subparagraphs (ii) and (iii) of this paragraph, where the aggregate maximum term of two or more consecutive sentences, one or more of which is a determinate sentence and one or more of which is an indeterminate sentence, and where such sentences are imposed for the conviction of two violent felony offenses committed prior to the time the person was imprisoned under any such sentences and where one of which is a class B violent felony offense, the following rules shall apply:

(A) if the aggregate maximum term of the determinate sentence or sentences exceeds forty years, the defendant shall be deemed to be serving a determinate sentence of forty years;

(B) if the aggregate maximum term of the determinate sentence or sentences is less than forty years, the defendant shall be deemed to be serving an indeterminate sentence the maximum term of which shall be deemed to be forty years. In such instances, the minimum sentence shall be deemed to be twenty years or six-sevenths of the term or aggregate maximum term of the determinate sentence or sentences, whichever is greater.

(vi) Notwithstanding subparagraphs (i) and (iv) of this paragraph, the aggregate maximum term of consecutive sentences, all of which are indeterminate or all of which are determinate sentences, imposed for the conviction of three or more violent felony offenses committed prior to the time the person was imprisoned under any of such sentences and one of which is a class B violent felony offense, shall, if it exceeds fifty years, be deemed to be fifty years;

(vii) Notwithstanding subparagraphs (ii), (iii) and (v) of this paragraph, where the aggregate maximum term of two or more consecutive sentences, one or more of which is a determinate sentence and one or more of which is an indeterminate sentence, and where such sentences are imposed for the conviction of three or more violent felony offenses committed prior to the time the person was imprisoned under any such sentences and one of which is a class B violent felony offense, the following rules shall apply:

(A) if the aggregate maximum term of the determinate sentence or sentences exceeds fifty years, the defendant shall be deemed to be serving a determinate sentence of fifty years.

(B) if the aggregate maximum term of the determinate sentence or sentences is less than fifty years, the defendant shall be deemed to be serving an indeterminate sentence the maximum term of which shall be deemed to be fifty years. In such instances, the minimum sentence shall be deemed to be twenty-five years or six-sevenths of the term or aggregate maximum term of the determinate sentence or sentences, whichever is greater.

(viii) Notwithstanding any provision of this subdivision to the contrary where a person is serving two or more consecutive sentences, one or more of which is an indeterminate sentence and one or more of which is a determinate sentence, and if he would be eligible for a reduction provision pursuant to this subdivision if the maximum term or aggregate maximum term of the indeterminate sentence or sentences were added to the term or aggregate maximum term of the determinate sentence or sentences, the person shall be deemed to be eligible for the applicable reduction provision and the rules set forth in this subdivision shall apply.

(f)[Effective until September 1, 2023] The aggregate maximum term of consecutive sentences imposed upon a juvenile offender for two or more crimes, not including a class A felony, committed before he has reached the age of sixteen, shall, if it exceeds ten years, be deemed to be ten years. If consecutive indeterminate sentences imposed upon a juvenile offender include a sentence for the class A felony of arson in the first degree or for the class A felony of kidnapping in the first degree, then the aggregate maximum term of such sentences shall, if it exceeds fifteen years, be deemed to be fifteen years. Where the aggregate maximum term of two or more consecutive sentences is reduced by a calculation made pursuant to this paragraph, the aggregate minimum period of imprisonment, if it exceeds one-half of the aggregate maximum term as so reduced, shall be deemed to be one-half of the aggregate maximum term as so reduced.

2. Definite sentences. A definite sentence of imprisonment commences when the prisoner is received in the institution named in the commitment. Where a person is under more than one definite sentence, the sentences shall be calculated as follows:

(a) If the sentences run concurrently and are to be served in a single institution, the terms merge in and are satisfied by discharge of the term which has the longest unexpired time to run;

(b) If the sentences run consecutively and are to be served in a single institution, the terms are added to arrive at an aggregate term and are satisfied by discharge of such aggregate term, or by service of two years imprisonment plus any term imposed for an offense committed while the person is under the sentences, whichever is less;

(c) If the sentences run concurrently and are to be served in more than one institution, the term of each such sentence shall be credited with the portion of any concurrent term served after that sentence was imposed;

(d) If the sentences run consecutively and are to be served in more than one institution, the aggregate of the time served in all of the institutions shall not exceed two years plus any term imposed for an offense committed while the person is under the sentences.

2-a. Undischarged imprisonment in other jurisdiction. Where a person who is subject to an undischarged term of imprisonment imposed at a previous time by a court of another jurisdiction is sentenced to an additional term or terms of imprisonment by a court of this state, to run concurrently with such undischarged term, such additional term or terms shall be deemed to commence when the said person is returned to the custody of the appropriate official of such other jurisdiction where the undischarged term of imprisonment is being served. If the additional term or terms imposed shall run consecutively to the said undischarged term, such additional term or terms shall commence when the prisoner is received in the appropriate institution as provided in subdivisions one and two of this section. The term or terms of such imprisonment shall be calculated and such other pertinent provisions of this section applied in the same manner as where a person is under more than one sentence in this state as provided in this section.

3.[Effective until September 1, 2023] Jail time. The term of a definite sentence, a determinate sentence, or the maximum term of an indeterminate sentence imposed on a person shall be credited with and diminished by the amount of time the person spent in custody prior to the commencement of such sentence as a result of the charge that culminated in the sentence. In the case of an indeterminate sentence, if the minimum period of imprisonment has been fixed by the court or by the board of parole, the credit shall also be applied against the minimum period. The credit herein provided shall be calculated from the date custody under the charge commenced to the date the sentence commences and shall not include any time that is credited against the term or maximum term of any previously imposed sentence or period of post-release supervision to which the person is subject. Where the charge or charges culminate in more than one sentence, the credit shall be applied as follows:

(a) If the sentences run concurrently, the credit shall be applied against each such sentence;

(b) If the sentences run consecutively, the credit shall be applied against the aggregate term or aggregate maximum term of the sentences and against the aggregate minimum period of imprisonment.

In any case where a person has been in custody due to a charge that culminated in a dismissal or an acquittal, the amount of time that would have been credited against a sentence for such charge, had one been imposed, shall be credited against any sentence that is based on a charge for which a warrant or commitment was lodged during the pendency of such custody.

3.[Effective September 1, 2023] Jail time. The term of a definite sentence or the maximum term of an indeterminate sentence imposed on a person shall be credited with and diminished by the amount of time the person spent in custody prior to the commencement of such sentence as a result of the charge that culminated in the sentence. In the case of an indeterminate sentence, if the minimum period of imprisonment has been fixed by the court or by the board of parole, the credit shall also be applied against the minimum period. The credit herein provided shall be calculated from the date custody under the charge commenced to the date the sentence commences and shall not include any time that is credited against the term or maximum term of any previously imposed sentence or period of post-release supervision to which the person is subject. Where the charge or charges culminate in more than one sentence, the credit shall be applied as follows:

(a) If the sentences run concurrently, the credit shall be applied against each such sentence;

(b) If the sentences run consecutively, the credit shall be applied against the aggregate term or aggregate maximum term of the sentences and against the aggregate minimum period of imprisonment.

In any case where a person has been in custody due to a charge that culminated in a dismissal or an acquittal, the amount of time that would have been credited against a sentence for such charge, had one been imposed, shall be credited against any sentence that is based on a charge for which a warrant or commitment was lodged during the pendency of such custody.

4.[Effective until September 1, 2023] Good behavior time. Time allowances earned for good behavior, pursuant to the provisions of the correction law, shall be computed and applied as follows:

(a) In the case of a person serving an indeterminate or determinate sentence, the total of such allowances shall be calculated as provided in section eight hundred three of the correction law and the allowances shall be applied as provided in paragraph (b) of subdivision one of section 70.40;

(b) In the case of a person serving a definite sentence, the total of such allowances shall not exceed one-third of his term or aggregate term and the allowances shall be applied as a credit against such term.

4.[Effective September 1, 2023] Good behavior time. Time allowances earned for good behavior, pursuant to the provisions of the correction law, shall be computed and applied as follows:

(a) In the case of a person serving an indeterminate sentence, the total of such allowances shall not exceed one-third of his maximum or aggregate maximum term and the allowances shall be applied as provided in subdivision one (b) of section 70.40;

(b) In the case of a person serving a definite sentence, the total of such allowances shall not exceed one-third of his term or aggregate term and the allowances shall be applied as a credit against such term.

5. Time served under vacated sentence. When a sentence of imprisonment that has been imposed on a person is vacated and a new sentence is imposed on such person for the same offense, or for an offense based upon the same act, the new sentence shall be calculated as if it had commenced at the time the vacated sentence commenced, and all time credited against the vacated sentence shall be credited against the new sentence. In any case where a vacated sentence also includes a period of post-release supervision, all time credited against the period of post-release supervision shall be credited against the period of post-release supervision included with the new sentence. In the event a period of post-release supervision is not included with the new sentence, such period shall be credited against the new sentence.

6. Escape. When a person who is serving a sentence of imprisonment escapes from custody, the escape shall interrupt the sentence and such interruption shall continue until the return of the person to the institution in which the sentence was being served or, if the sentence was being served in an institution under the jurisdiction of the state department of corrections and community supervision, to an institution under the jurisdiction of that department. Any time spent by such person in custody from the date of escape to the date the sentence resumes shall be credited against the term or maximum term of the interrupted sentence, provided:

(a) That such custody was due to an arrest or surrender based upon the escape; or

(b) That such custody arose from an arrest on another charge which culminated in a dismissal or an acquittal; or

(c) That such custody arose from an arrest on another charge which culminated in a conviction, but in such case, if a sentence of imprisonment was imposed, the credit allowed shall be limited to the portion of the time spent in custody that exceeds the period, term or maximum term of imprisonment imposed for such conviction.

7.[Expires September 1, 2023] Absconding from temporary release or furlough program. When a person who is serving a sentence of imprisonment is permitted to leave an institution to participate in a program of work release or furlough program as such term is defined in section six hundred thirty-one of the correction law, or in the case of an institution under the jurisdiction of the state department of corrections and community supervision or a facility under the jurisdiction of the state office of children and family services to participate in a program of temporary release, fails to return to the institution or facility at or before the time prescribed for his or her return, such failure shall interrupt the sentence and such interruption shall continue until the return of the person to the institution in which the sentence was being served or, if the sentence was being served in an institution under the jurisdiction of the state department of corrections and community supervision or a facility under the jurisdiction of the state office of children and family services to an institution under the jurisdiction of that department or a facility under the jurisdiction of that office. Any time spent by such person in an institution from the date of his or her failure to return to the date his or her sentence resumes shall be credited against the term or maximum term of the interrupted sentence, provided:

(a) That such incarceration was due to an arrest or surrender based upon the failure to return; or

(b) That such incarceration arose from an arrest on another charge which culminated in a dismissal or an acquittal; or

(c) That such custody arose from an arrest on another charge which culminated in a conviction, but in such case, if a sentence of imprisonment was imposed, the credit allowed shall be limited to the portion of the time spent in custody that exceeds the period, term or maximum term of imprisonment imposed for such conviction.

N.Y. Penal Law § 70.30

Amended by New York Laws 2021, ch. 55,Sec. A-19, eff. 4/19/2021.
Amended by New York Laws 2020, ch. 55,Sec. A-19, eff. 4/3/2020.
Amended by New York Laws 2019, ch. 55,Sec. O-19, eff. 4/12/2019.
Amended by New York Laws 2017, ch. 55,Sec. A-19, eff. 4/20/2017.
Amended by New York Laws 2015, ch. 55,Sec. B-19, eff. 4/13/2015.

Section 70.35 - [Effective until September 1, 2023] Merger of certain definite and indeterminate or determinate sentences

The service of an indeterminate or determinate sentence of imprisonment shall satisfy any definite sentence of imprisonment imposed on a person for an offense committed prior to the time the indeterminate or determinate sentence was imposed, except as provided in paragraph (b) of subdivision five of section 70.25 of this article. A person who is serving a definite sentence at the time an indeterminate or determinate sentence is imposed shall be delivered to the custody of the state department of corrections and community supervision to commence service of the indeterminate or determinate sentence immediately unless the person is serving a definite sentence pursuant to paragraph (b) of subdivision five of section 70.25 of this article. In any case where the indeterminate or determinate sentence is revoked or vacated, the person shall receive credit against the definite sentence for each day spent in the custody of the state department of corrections and community supervision.

N.Y. Penal Law § 70.35

Amended by New York Laws 2021, ch. 55,Sec. A-19, eff. 4/19/2021.
Amended by New York Laws 2020, ch. 55,Sec. A-19, eff. 4/3/2020.
Amended by New York Laws 2019, ch. 55,Sec. O-19, eff. 4/12/2019.
Amended by New York Laws 2017, ch. 55,Sec. A-19, eff. 4/20/2017.
Amended by New York Laws 2015, ch. 55,Sec. B-19, eff. 4/13/2015.

Section 70.35 - [Effective September 1, 2023] Merger of certain definite and indeterminate sentences

The service of an indeterminate sentence of imprisonment shall satisfy any definite sentence of imprisonment imposed on a person for an offense committed prior to the time the indeterminate sentence was imposed, except as provided in paragraph (b) of subdivision five of section 70.25 of this article. A person who is serving a definite sentence at the time an indeterminate sentence is imposed shall be delivered to the custody of the state department of corrections and community supervision to commence service of the indeterminate sentence immediately unless the person is serving a definite sentence pursuant to paragraph (b) of subdivision five of section 70.25 of this article. In any case where the indeterminate sentence is revoked or vacated, the person shall receive credit against the definite sentence for each day spent in the custody of the state department of corrections and community supervision.

N.Y. Penal Law § 70.35

Amended by New York Laws 2021, ch. 55,Sec. A-19, eff. 4/19/2021.
Amended by New York Laws 2020, ch. 55,Sec. A-19, eff. 4/3/2020.
Amended by New York Laws 2019, ch. 55,Sec. O-19, eff. 4/12/2019.
Amended by New York Laws 2017, ch. 55,Sec. A-19, eff. 4/20/2017.
Amended by New York Laws 2015, ch. 55,Sec. B-19, eff. 4/13/2015.

Section 70.40 - Release on parole; conditional release; presumptive release

1. Indeterminate sentence.

(a)[Effective until September 1, 2023] Release on parole shall be in the discretion of the state board of parole, and such person shall continue service of his or her sentence or sentences while on parole, in accordance with and subject to the provisions of the executive law and the correction law.

(i) A person who is serving one or more than one indeterminate sentence of imprisonment may be paroled from the institution in which he or she is confined at any time after the expiration of the minimum or the aggregate minimum period of the sentence or sentences or, where applicable, the minimum or aggregate minimum period reduced by the merit time allowance granted pursuant to paragraph (d) of subdivision one of section eight hundred three of the correction law.

(ii) A person who is serving one or more than one determinate sentence of imprisonment shall be ineligible for discretionary release on parole.

(iii) A person who is serving one or more than one indeterminate sentence of imprisonment and one or more than one determinate sentence of imprisonment, which run concurrently may be paroled at any time after the expiration of the minimum period of imprisonment of the indeterminate sentence or sentences, or upon the expiration of six-sevenths of the term of imprisonment of the determinate sentence or sentences, whichever is later.

(iv) A person who is serving one or more than one indeterminate sentence of imprisonment and one or more than one determinate sentence of imprisonment which run consecutively may be paroled at any time after the expiration of the sum of the minimum or aggregate minimum period of the indeterminate sentence or sentences and six-sevenths of the term or aggregate term of imprisonment of the determinate sentence or sentences.

(v) Notwithstanding any other subparagraph of this paragraph, a person may be paroled from the institution in which he or she is confined at any time on medical parole pursuant to section two hundred fifty-nine-r or section two hundred fifty-nine-s of the executive law or for deportation pursuant to paragraph (d) of subdivision two of section two hundred fifty-nine-i of the executive law or after the successful completion of a shock incarceration program pursuant to article twenty-six-A of the correction law.

(a)[Effective September 1, 2023]

(i) A person who is serving one or more than one indeterminate sentence of imprisonment may be paroled from the institution in which he or she is confined at any time after the expiration of the minimum or the aggregate minimum period of imprisonment of the sentence or sentences or after the successful completion of a shock incarceration program, as defined in article twenty-six-A of the correction law, whichever is sooner. Release on parole shall be in the discretion of the state board of parole, and such person shall continue service of his or her sentence or sentences while on parole, in accordance with and subject to the provisions of the executive law and the correction law.

(ii) A person who is serving one or more than one indeterminate sentence of imprisonment may be paroled from the institution in which he or she is confined at any time after the expiration of the minimum or the aggregate minimum period of the sentence or sentences.

(b)[Effective until September 1, 2023] A person who is serving one or more than one indeterminate or determinate sentence of imprisonment shall, if he or she so requests, be conditionally released from the institution in which he or she is confined when the total good behavior time allowed to him or her, pursuant to the provisions of the correction law, is equal to the unserved portion of his or her term, maximum term or aggregate maximum term; provided, however, that (i) in no event shall a person serving one or more indeterminate sentence of imprisonment and one or more determinate sentence of imprisonment which run concurrently be conditionally released until serving at least six-sevenths of the determinate term of imprisonment which has the longest unexpired time to run and (ii) in no event shall a person be conditionally released prior to the date on which such person is first eligible for discretionary parole release. The conditions of release, including those governing post-release supervision, shall be such as may be imposed by the state board of parole in accordance with the provisions of the executive law.

Every person so released shall be under the supervision of the state department of corrections and community supervision for a period equal to the unserved portion of the term, maximum term, aggregate maximum term, or period of post-release supervision.

(b)[Effective September 1, 2023] A person who is serving one or more than one indeterminate sentence of imprisonment shall, if he or she so requests, be conditionally released from the institution in which he or she is confined when the total good behavior time allowed to him or her, pursuant to the provisions of the correction law, is equal to the unserved portion of his or her maximum or aggregate maximum term. The conditions of release, including those governing post-release supervision, shall be such as may be imposed by the state board of parole in accordance with the provisions of the executive law.

Every person so released shall be under the supervision of the department of corrections and community supervision for a period equal to the unserved portion of the maximum, aggregate maximum term, or period of post-release supervision.

(c)[Repealed September 1, 2023] A person who is serving one or more than one indeterminate sentence of imprisonment shall, if he or she so requests, be released from the institution in which he or she is confined if granted presumptive release pursuant to section eight hundred six of the correction law. The conditions of release shall be such as may be imposed by the state board of parole in accordance with the provisions of the executive law. Every person so released shall be under the supervision of the department of corrections and community supervision for a period equal to the unserved portion of his or her maximum or aggregate maximum term unless discharged in accordance with law.

2. Definite sentence. A person who is serving one or more than one definite sentence of imprisonment with a term or aggregate term in excess of ninety days, and is eligible for release according to the criteria set forth in paragraphs (a), (b) and (c) of subdivision one of section two hundred seventy-three of the correction law, may, if he or she so requests, be conditionally released from the institution in which he or she is confined at any time after service of sixty days of that term, exclusive of credits allowed under subdivisions four and six of section 70.30. In computing service of sixty days, the credit allowed for jail time under subdivision three of section 70.30 shall be calculated as time served. Conditional release from such institution shall be in the discretion of the parole board, or a local conditional release commission established pursuant to article twelve of the correction law, provided, however that where such release is by a local conditional release commission, the person must be serving a definite sentence with a term in excess of one hundred twenty days and may only be released after service of ninety days of such term. In computing service of ninety days, the credit allowed for jail time under subdivision three of section 70.30 of this article shall be calculated as time served. A conditional release granted under this subdivision shall be upon such conditions as may be imposed by the parole board, in accordance with the provisions of the executive law, or a local conditional release commission in accordance with the provisions of the correction law.

Conditional release shall interrupt service of the sentence or sentences and the remaining portion of the term or aggregate term shall be held in abeyance. Every person so released shall be under the supervision of the department of corrections and community supervision or a local probation department and in the custody of the local conditional release commission in accordance with article twelve of the correction law, for a period of one year. The local probation department shall cause complete records to be kept of every person released to its supervision pursuant to this subdivision. The department of corrections and community supervision may supply to a local probation department and the local conditional release commission custody information and records maintained on persons under the supervision of such local probation department to aid in the performance of its supervision responsibilities. Compliance with the conditions of release during the period of supervision shall satisfy the portion of the term or aggregate term that has been held in abeyance.

3. Delinquency.

(a) When a person is alleged to have violated the terms of presumptive release or parole and the state board of parole has declared such person to be delinquent, the declaration of delinquency shall interrupt the person's sentence as of the date of the delinquency and such interruption shall continue until the return of the person to an institution under the jurisdiction of the state department of corrections and community supervision.

(b) When a person is alleged to have violated the terms of his or her conditional release or post-release supervision and has been declared delinquent by the parole board or the local conditional release commission having supervision over such person, the declaration of delinquency shall interrupt the period of supervision or post-release supervision as of the date of the delinquency. For a conditional release, such interruption shall continue until the return of the person to the institution from which he or she was released or, if he or she was released from an institution under the jurisdiction of the state department of corrections and community supervision, to an institution under the jurisdiction of that department. Upon such return, the person shall resume service of his or her sentence. For a person released to post-release supervision, the provisions of section 70.45 shall apply.

(c) Any time spent by a person in custody from the time of delinquency to the time service of the sentence resumes shall be credited against the term or maximum term of the interrupted sentence, provided:

(i) that such custody was due to an arrest or surrender based upon the delinquency; or

(ii) that such custody arose from an arrest on another charge which culminated in a dismissal or an acquittal; or

(iii) that such custody arose from an arrest on another charge which culminated in a conviction, but in such case, if a sentence of imprisonment was imposed, the credit allowed shall be limited to the portion of the time spent in custody that exceeds the period, term or maximum term of imprisonment imposed for such conviction.

N.Y. Penal Law § 70.40

Amended by New York Laws 2021, ch. 55,Sec. A-19, eff. 4/19/2021.
Amended by New York Laws 2021, ch. 55,Sec. A-15, eff. 4/19/2021.
Amended by New York Laws 2020, ch. 55,Sec. A-19, eff. 4/3/2020.
Amended by New York Laws 2019, ch. 55,Sec. O-19, eff. 4/12/2019.
Amended by New York Laws 2019, ch. 55,Sec. O-15, eff. 4/12/2019.
Amended by New York Laws 2017, ch. 55,Sec. A-19, eff. 4/20/2017.
Amended by New York Laws 2017, ch. 55,Sec. A-15, eff. 4/20/2017.
Amended by New York Laws 2015, ch. 55,Sec. B-19, eff. 4/13/2015.
Amended by New York Laws 2015, ch. 55,Sec. B-15, eff. 4/13/2015.

Section 70.45 - Determinate sentence; post-release supervision

1. In general. When a court imposes a determinate sentence it shall in each case state not only the term of imprisonment, but also an additional period of post-release supervision as determined pursuant to this article. Such period shall commence as provided in subdivision five of this section and a violation of any condition of supervision occurring at any time during such period of post-release supervision shall subject the defendant to a further period of imprisonment up to the balance of the remaining period of post-release supervision, not to exceed five years; provided, however, that a defendant serving a term of post-release supervision for a conviction of a felony sex offense, as defined in section 70.80 of this article, may be subject to a further period of imprisonment up to the balance of the remaining period of post-release supervision. Such maximum limits shall not preclude a longer period of further imprisonment for a violation where the defendant is subject to indeterminate and determinate sentences.

1-a. When, following a final hearing, a time assessment has been imposed upon a person convicted of a felony sex offense who owes three years or more on a period of post-release supervision, imposed pursuant to subdivision two-a of this section, such defendant, after serving three years of the time assessment, shall be reviewed by the board of parole and may be re-released to post-release supervision only upon a determination by the board of parole made in accordance with subdivision two of section two hundred fifty-nine-i of the executive law. If re-release is not granted, the board shall specify a date not more than twenty-four months from such determination for reconsideration, and the procedures to be followed upon reconsideration shall be the same. If a time assessment of less than three years is imposed upon such a defendant, the defendant shall be released upon the expiration of such time assessment, unless he or she is subject to further imprisonment or confinement under any provision of law.

2. Period of post-release supervision for other than felony sex offenses. The period of post-release supervision for a determinate sentence, other than a determinate sentence imposed for a felony sex offense as defined in paragraph (a) of subdivision one of section 70.80 of this article, shall be five years except that:

(a) such period shall be one year whenever a determinate sentence of imprisonment is imposed pursuant to subdivision two of section 70.70 of this article or subdivision nine of section 60.12 of this title upon a conviction of a class D or class E felony offense;

(b) such period shall be not less than one year nor more than two years whenever a determinate sentence of imprisonment is imposed pursuant to subdivision two of section 70.70 of this article or subdivision nine of section 60.12 of this title upon a conviction of a class B or class C felony offense;

(c) such period shall be not less than one year nor more than two years whenever a determinate sentence of imprisonment is imposed pursuant to subdivision three or four of section 70.70 of this article upon conviction of a class D or class E felony offense or subdivision ten of section 60.12 of this title;

(d) such period shall be not less than one and one-half years nor more than three years whenever a determinate sentence of imprisonment is imposed pursuant to subdivision three or four of section 70.70 of this article upon conviction of a class B felony or class C felony offense or subdivision eleven of section 60.12 of this title;

(e) such period shall be not less than one and one-half years nor more than three years whenever a determinate sentence of imprisonment is imposed pursuant to subdivision three of section 70.02 of this article or subdivision two or eight of section 60.12 of this title upon a conviction of a class D or class E violent felony offense or subdivision four, five, six, or seven of section 60.12 of this title;

(f) such period shall be not less than two and one-half years nor more than five years whenever a determinate sentence of imprisonment is imposed pursuant to subdivision three of section 70.02 of this article or subdivision two or eight of section 60.12 of this title upon a conviction of a class B or class C violent felony offense.

2-a. Periods of post-release supervision for felony sex offenses. The period of post-release supervision for a determinate sentence imposed for a felony sex offense as defined in paragraph (a) of subdivision one of section 70.80 of this article shall be as follows:

(a) not less than three years nor more than ten years whenever a determinate sentence of imprisonment is imposed pursuant to subdivision four of section 70.80 of this article upon a conviction of a class D or class E felony sex offense;

(b) not less than five years nor more than fifteen years whenever a determinate sentence of imprisonment is imposed pursuant to subdivision four of section 70.80 of this article upon a conviction of a class C felony sex offense;

(c) not less than five years nor more than twenty years whenever a determinate sentence of imprisonment is imposed pursuant to subdivision four of section 70.80 of this article upon a conviction of a class B felony sex offense;

(d) not less than three years nor more than ten years whenever a determinate sentence is imposed pursuant to subdivision three of section 70.02 of this article upon a conviction of a class D or class E violent felony sex offense as defined in paragraph (b) of subdivision one of section 70.80 of this article;

(e) not less than five years nor more than fifteen years whenever a determinate sentence is imposed pursuant to subdivision three of section 70.02 of this article upon a conviction of a class C violent felony sex offense as defined in section 70.80 of this article;

(f) not less than five years nor more than twenty years whenever a determinate sentence is imposed pursuant to subdivision three of section 70.02 of this article upon a conviction of a class B violent felony sex offense as defined in section 70.80 of this article;

(g) not less than five years nor more than fifteen years whenever a determinate sentence of imprisonment is imposed pursuant to either section 70.04, section 70.06, or subdivision five of section 70.80 of this article upon a conviction of a class D or class E violent or non-violent felony sex offense as defined in section 70.80 of this article;

(h) not less than seven years nor more than twenty years whenever a determinate sentence of imprisonment is imposed pursuant to either section 70.04, section 70.06, or subdivision five of section 70.80 of this article upon a conviction of a class C violent or non-violent felony sex offense as defined in section 70.80 of this article;

(i) such period shall be not less than ten years nor more than twenty-five years whenever a determinate sentence of imprisonment is imposed pursuant to either section 70.04, section 70.06, or subdivision five of section 70.80 of this article upon a conviction of a class B violent or non-violent felony sex offense as defined in section 70.80 of this article; and

(j) such period shall be not less than ten years nor more than twenty years whenever any determinate sentence of imprisonment is imposed pursuant to subdivision four of section 70.07 of this article.

3. Conditions of post-release supervision. The board of parole shall establish and impose conditions of post-release supervision in the same manner and to the same extent as it may establish and impose conditions in accordance with the executive law upon persons who are granted parole or conditional release; provided that, notwithstanding any other provision of law, the board of parole may impose as a condition of post-release supervision that for a period not exceeding six months immediately following release from the underlying term of imprisonment the person be transferred to and participate in the programs of a residential treatment facility as that term is defined in subdivision six of section two of the correction law. Upon release from the underlying term of imprisonment, the person shall be furnished with a written statement setting forth the conditions of post-release supervision in sufficient detail to provide for the person's conduct and supervision.

4. Revocation of post-release supervision. An alleged violation of any condition of post-release supervision shall be initiated, heard and determined in accordance with the provisions of subdivisions three and four of section two hundred fifty-nine-i of the executive law.

5. Calculation of service of period of post-release supervision. A period or periods of post-release supervision shall be calculated and served as follows:

(a) A period of post-release supervision shall commence upon the person's release from imprisonment to supervision by the department of corrections and community supervision and shall interrupt the running of the determinate sentence or sentences of imprisonment and the indeterminate sentence or sentences of imprisonment, if any. The remaining portion of any maximum or aggregate maximum term shall then be held in abeyance until the successful completion of the period of post-release supervision or the person's return to the custody of the department of corrections and community supervision, whichever occurs first.

(b) Upon the completion of the period of post-release supervision, the running of such sentence or sentences of imprisonment shall resume and only then shall the remaining portion of any maximum or aggregate maximum term previously held in abeyance be credited with and diminished by such period of post-release supervision. The person shall then be under the jurisdiction of the department of corrections and community supervision for the remaining portion of such maximum or aggregate maximum term.

(c) When a person is subject to two or more periods of post-release supervision, such periods shall merge with and be satisfied by discharge of the period of post-release supervision having the longest unexpired time to run; provided, however, any time served upon one period of post-release supervision shall not be credited to any other period of post-release supervision except as provided in subdivision five of section 70.30 of this article.

(d) When a person is alleged to have violated a condition of post-release supervision and the department of corrections and community supervision has declared such person to be delinquent:

(i) the declaration of delinquency shall interrupt the period of post-release supervision; (ii) such interruption shall continue until the person is restored to post-release supervision; (iii) if the person is restored to post-release supervision without being returned to the department of corrections and community supervision, any time spent in custody from the date of delinquency until restoration to post-release supervision shall first be credited to the maximum or aggregate maximum term of the sentence or sentences of imprisonment, but only to the extent authorized by subdivision three of section 70.40 of this article. Any time spent in custody solely pursuant to such delinquency after completion of the maximum or aggregate maximum term of the sentence or sentences of imprisonment shall be credited to the period of post-release supervision, if any; and (iv) if the person is ordered returned to the department of corrections and community supervision, the person shall be required to serve the time assessment before being re-released to post-release supervision. In the event the balance of the remaining period of post-release supervision is six months or less, such time assessment may be up to six months unless a longer period is authorized pursuant to subdivision one of this section. The time assessment shall commence upon the issuance of a determination after a final hearing that the person has violated one or more conditions of supervision. While serving such assessment, the person shall not receive any good behavior allowance pursuant to section eight hundred three of the correction law. Any time spent in custody from the date of delinquency until return to the department of corrections and community supervision shall first be credited to the maximum or aggregate maximum term of the sentence or sentences of imprisonment, but only to the extent authorized by subdivision three of section 70.40 of this article. The maximum or aggregate maximum term of the sentence or sentences of imprisonment shall run while the person is serving such time assessment in the custody of the department of corrections and community supervision. Any time spent in custody solely pursuant to such delinquency after completion of the maximum or aggregate maximum term of the sentence or sentences of imprisonment shall be credited to the period of post-release supervision, if any.

(e) Notwithstanding paragraph (d) of this subdivision, in the event a person is sentenced to one or more additional indeterminate or determinate term or terms of imprisonment prior to the completion of the period of post-release supervision, such period of post-release supervision shall be held in abeyance and the person shall be committed to the custody of the department of corrections and community supervision in accordance with the requirements of the prior and additional terms of imprisonment.

(f) When a person serving a period of post-release supervision is returned to the department of corrections and community supervision pursuant to an additional consecutive sentence of imprisonment and without a declaration of delinquency, such period of post-release supervision shall be held in abeyance while the person is in the custody of the department of corrections and community supervision. Such period of post-release supervision shall resume running upon the person's re-release.

N.Y. Penal Law § 70.45

Amended by New York Laws 2019, ch. 31,Sec. 2, eff. 5/14/2019.

Section 70.70 - Sentence of imprisonment for felony drug offender other than a class A felony

1. For the purposes of this section, the following terms shall mean:

(a) "Felony drug offender" means a defendant who stands convicted of any felony, defined in article two hundred twenty or two hundred twenty-two of this chapter other than a class A felony.

(b) "Second felony drug offender" means a second felony offender as that term is defined in subdivision one of section 70.06 of this article, who stands convicted of any felony, defined in article two hundred twenty or two hundred twenty-two of this chapter other than a class A felony.

(c) "Violent felony" shall have the same meaning as that term is defined in subdivision one of section 70.02 of this article.

2. Except as provided in subdivision three or four of this section, a sentence of imprisonment for a felony drug offender shall be a determinate sentence as provided in paragraph (a) of this subdivision.

(a) Term of determinate sentence. Except as provided in paragraph (b) or (c) of this subdivision, the court shall impose a determinate term of imprisonment upon a felony drug offender which shall be imposed by the court in whole or half years, which shall include as a part thereof a period of post-release supervision in accordance with section 70.45 of this article. The terms of imprisonment authorized for such determinate sentences are as follows:

(i) for a class B felony, the term shall be at least one year and shall not exceed nine years, except that for the class B felony of criminal sale of a controlled substance in or near school grounds as defined in subdivision two of section 220.44 of this chapter or on a school bus as defined in subdivision seventeen of section 220.00 of this chapter or criminal sale of a controlled substance to a child as defined in section 220.48 of this chapter, the term shall be at least two years and shall not exceed nine years;

(ii) for a class C felony, the term shall be at least one year and shall not exceed five and one-half years;

(iii) for a class D felony, the term shall be at least one year and shall not exceed two and one-half years; and

(iv) for a class E felony, the term shall be at least one year and shall not exceed one and one-half years.

(b) Probation. Notwithstanding any other provision of law, the court may sentence a defendant convicted of a class B, class C, class D or class E felony offense defined in article two hundred twenty or two hundred twenty-two of this chapter to probation in accordance with the provisions of sections 60.04 and 65.00 of this chapter.

(c) Alternative definite sentence for class B, class C, class D, and class E felonies. If the court, having regard to the nature and circumstances of the crime and to the history and character of the defendant, is of the opinion that a sentence of imprisonment is necessary but that it would be unduly harsh to impose a determinate sentence upon a person convicted of a class C, class D or class E felony offense defined in article two hundred twenty or two hundred twenty-two of this chapter, or a class B felony defined in article two hundred twenty of this chapter, other than the class B felony defined in section 220.48 of this chapter, as added by a chapter of the laws of two thousand nine the court may impose a definite sentence of imprisonment and fix a term of one year or less.

(d) The court may direct that a determinate sentence imposed on a defendant convicted of a class B felony, other than the class B felony defined in section 220.48 of this chapter, pursuant to this subdivision be executed as a sentence of parole supervision in accordance with section 410.91 of the criminal procedure law.

3. Sentence of imprisonment for second felony drug offender.

(a) Applicability. This subdivision shall apply to a second felony drug offender whose prior felony conviction was not a violent felony.

(b) Authorized sentence. Except as provided in paragraphs (c), (d) and (e) of this subdivision, when the court has found pursuant to the provisions of section 400.21 of the criminal procedure law that a defendant is a second felony drug offender who stands convicted of a class B, class C, class D or class E felony offense defined in article two hundred twenty or two hundred twenty-two of this chapter the court shall impose a determinate sentence of imprisonment. Such determinate sentence shall include as a part thereof a period of post-release supervision in accordance with section 70.45 of this article. The terms of such determinate sentence shall be imposed by the court in whole or half years as follows:

(i) for a class B felony, the term shall be at least two years and shall not exceed twelve years;

(ii) for a class C felony, the term shall be at least one and one-half years and shall not exceed eight years;

(iii) for a class D felony, the term shall be at least one and one-half years and shall not exceed four years; and

(iv) for a class E felony, the term shall be at least one and one-half years and shall not exceed two years.

(c) Probation. Notwithstanding any other provision of law, the court may sentence a second felony drug offender convicted of a class B felony to lifetime probation in accordance with the provisions of section 65.00 of this chapter and may sentence a second felony drug offender convicted of a class C, class D or class E felony to probation in accordance with the provisions of section 65.00 of this chapter.

(d) Sentence of parole supervision. In the case of a person sentenced for a specified offense or offenses as defined in subdivision five of section 410.91 of the criminal procedure law, who stands convicted of no other felony offense, who has not previously been convicted of either a violent felony offense as defined in section 70.02 of this article, a class A felony offense or a class B felony offense, and is not under the jurisdiction of or awaiting delivery to the department of corrections and community supervision, the court may direct that a determinate sentence imposed pursuant to this subdivision shall be executed as a parole supervision sentence as defined in and pursuant to the procedures prescribed in section 410.91 of the criminal procedure law.

(e) Alternate definite sentence for class C, class D and class E felonies. If the court, having regard to the nature and circumstances of the crime and to the history and character of the defendant, is of the opinion that a sentence of imprisonment is necessary but that it would be unduly harsh to impose a determinate sentence upon a person convicted of a class C, class D or class E felony offense defined in article two hundred twenty or two hundred twenty-two of this chapter, the court may impose a definite sentence of imprisonment and fix a term of one year or less.

4. Sentence of imprisonment for second felony drug offender previously convicted of a violent felony.

(a) Applicability. This subdivision shall apply to a second felony drug offender whose prior felony conviction was a violent felony.

(b) Authorized sentence. When the court has found pursuant to the provisions of section 400.21 of the criminal procedure law that a defendant is a second felony drug offender whose prior felony conviction was a violent felony, who stands convicted of a class B, class C, class D or class E felony offense defined in article two hundred twenty or two hundred twenty-two of this chapter, the court shall impose a determinate sentence of imprisonment. Such determinate sentence shall include as a part thereof a period of post-release supervision in accordance with section 70.45 of this article. The terms of such determinate sentence shall be imposed by the court in whole or half years as follows:

(i) for a class B felony, the term shall be at least six years and shall not exceed fifteen years;

(ii) for a class C felony, the term shall be at least three and one-half years and shall not exceed nine years;

(iii) for a class D felony, the term shall be at least two and one-half years and shall not exceed four and one-half years; and

(iv) for a class E felony, the term shall be at least two years and shall not exceed two and one-half years.

N.Y. Penal Law § 70.70

Amended by New York Laws 2021, ch. 92,Sec. 19-d, eff. 3/31/2021.
Amended by New York Laws 2021, ch. 92,Sec. 19-c, eff. 3/31/2021.
Amended by New York Laws 2021, ch. 92,Sec. 19-b, eff. 3/31/2021.
Amended by New York Laws 2021, ch. 92,Sec. 19-a, eff. 3/31/2021.

Section 70.71 - Sentence of imprisonment for a class A felony drug offender

1. For the purposes of this section, the following terms shall mean:

(a) "Felony drug offender" means a defendant who stands convicted of any class A felony as defined in article two hundred twenty of this chapter.

(b) "Second felony drug offender" means a second felony offender as that term is defined in subdivision one of section 70.06 of this article, who stands convicted of and is to be sentenced for any class A felony as defined in article two hundred twenty of this chapter.

(c) "Violent felony offense" shall have the same meaning as that term is defined in subdivision one of section 70.02 of this article.

2. Sentence of imprisonment for a first felony drug offender.

(a) Applicability. Except as provided in subdivision three, four or five of this section, this subdivision shall apply to a person convicted of a class A felony as defined in article two hundred twenty of this chapter.

(b) Authorized sentence. The court shall impose a determinate term of imprisonment which shall be imposed by the court in whole or half years and which shall include as a part thereof a period of post-release supervision in accordance with section 70.45 of this article. The terms authorized for such determinate sentences are as follows:

(i) for a class A-I felony, the term shall be at least eight years and shall not exceed twenty years;

(ii) for a class A-II felony, the term shall be at least three years and shall not exceed ten years.

(c) Lifetime probation. Notwithstanding any other provision of law, the court may sentence a defendant convicted of a class A-II felony defined in article two hundred twenty of this chapter to lifetime probation in accordance with the provisions of section 65.00 of this chapter.

3. Sentence of imprisonment for a second felony drug offender.

(a) Applicability. This subdivision shall apply to a second felony drug offender whose prior felony conviction or convictions did not include one or more violent felony offenses.

(b) Authorized sentence. When the court has found pursuant to the provisions of section 400.21 of the criminal procedure law that a defendant is a second felony drug offender who stands convicted of a class A felony as defined in article two hundred twenty or two hundred twenty-one of this chapter, the court shall impose a determinate sentence of imprisonment. Such determinate sentence shall include as a part thereof a period of post-release supervision in accordance with section 70.45 of this article. Such determinate sentence shall be imposed by the court in whole or half years as follows:

(i) for a class A-I felony, the term shall be at least twelve years and shall not exceed twenty-four years;

(ii) for a class A-II felony, the term shall be at least six years and shall not exceed fourteen years.

(c) Lifetime probation. Notwithstanding any other provision of law, the court may sentence a defendant convicted of a class A-II felony defined in article two hundred twenty of this chapter to lifetime probation in accordance with the provisions of section 65.00 of this chapter.

4. Sentence of imprisonment for a second felony drug offender previously convicted of a violent felony offense.

54

(a) Applicability. This subdivision shall apply to a second felony drug offender whose prior felony conviction was a violent felony.

(b) Authorized sentence. When the court has found pursuant to the provisions of section 400.21 of the criminal procedure law that a defendant is a second felony drug offender whose prior felony conviction was a violent felony, who stands convicted of a class A felony as defined in article two hundred twenty or two hundred twenty-one of this chapter, the court shall impose a determinate sentence of imprisonment. Such determinate sentence shall include as a part thereof a period of post-release supervision in accordance with section 70.45 of this article. Such determinate sentence shall be imposed by the court in whole or half years as follows:

(i) for a class A-I felony, the term shall be at least fifteen years and shall not exceed thirty years;

(ii) for a class A-II felony, the term shall be at least eight years and shall not exceed seventeen years.

5. Sentence of imprisonment for operating as a major trafficker.

(a) Applicability. This subdivision shall apply to a person convicted of the class A-I felony of operating as a major trafficker as defined in section 220.77 of this chapter.

(b) Authorized sentence. Except as provided in paragraph (c) of this subdivision, the court shall impose an indeterminate term of imprisonment for an A-I felony, in accordance with the provisions of section 70.00 of this article.

(c) Alternative determinate sentence. If a defendant stands convicted of violating section 220.77 of this chapter, and if the court, having regard to the nature and circumstances of the crime and the history and character of the defendant, is of the opinion that a sentence of imprisonment is necessary but that it would be unduly harsh to impose the indeterminate sentence for a class A-I felony specified under section 70.00 of this article, the court may instead impose the determinate sentence of imprisonment authorized by clause (i) of subparagraph (b) of subdivision two of this section for a class A-I drug felony; in such case, the reasons for the court's opinion shall be set forth on the record.

N.Y. Penal Law § 70.71

Section 70.80 - Sentences of imprisonment for conviction of a felony sex offense

1. Definitions.

(a) For the purposes of this section, a "felony sex offense" means a conviction of any felony defined in article one hundred thirty of this chapter, including a sexually motivated felony, or patronizing a person for prostitution in the first degree as defined in section 230.06 of this chapter, patronizing a person for prostitution in the second degree as defined in section 230.05 of this chapter, aggravated patronizing a minor for prostitution in the third degree as defined in section 230.11 of this chapter, aggravated patronizing a minor for prostitution in the second degree as defined in section 230.12 of this chapter, aggravated patronizing a minor for prostitution in the first degree as defined in section 230.13 of this chapter, incest in the second degree as defined in section 255.26 of this chapter, or incest in the first degree as defined in section 255.27 of this chapter, or a felony attempt or conspiracy to commit any of the above.

(b) A felony sex offense shall be deemed a "violent felony sex offense" if it is for an offense defined as a violent felony offense in section 70.02 of this article, or for a sexually motivated felony as defined in section 130.91 of this chapter where the specified offense is a violent felony offense as defined in section 70.02 of this article.

(c) For the purposes of this section, a "predicate felony sex offender" means a person who stands convicted of any felony sex offense as defined in paragraph (a) of this subdivision, other than a class A-I felony, after having previously been subjected to one or more predicate felony convictions as defined in subdivision one of section 70.06 or subdivision one of section 70.04 of this article.

(d) For purposes of this section, a "violent felony offense" is any felony defined in subdivision one of section 70.02 of this article, and a "non-violent felony offense" is any felony not defined therein.

2. In imposing a sentence within the authorized statutory range for any felony sex offense, the court may consider all relevant factors set forth in section 1.05 of this chapter, and in particular, may consider the defendant's criminal history, if any, including any history of sex offenses; any mental illness or mental abnormality from which the defendant may suffer; the defendant's ability or inability to control his sexual behavior; and, if the defendant has difficulty controlling such behavior, the extent to which that difficulty may pose a threat to society.

3. Except as provided by subdivision four, five, six, seven or eight of this section, or when a defendant is being sentenced for a conviction of the class A-II felonies of predatory sexual assault and predatory sexual assault against a child as defined in sections 130.95 and 130.96 of this chapter, or for any class A-I sexually motivated felony for which a life sentence or a life without parole sentence must be imposed, a sentence imposed upon a defendant convicted of a felony sex offense shall be a determinate sentence. The determinate sentence shall be imposed by the court in whole or half years, and shall include as a part thereof a period of post-release supervision in accordance with subdivision two-a of section 70.45 of this article. Persons eligible for sentencing under section 70.07 of this article governing second child sexual assault felonies shall be sentenced under such section and paragraph (j) of subdivision two-a of section 70.45 of this article.

4.

(a) Sentences of imprisonment for felony sex offenses. Except as provided in subdivision five, six, seven, or eight of this section, the term of the determinate sentence must be fixed by the court as follows:

(i) for a class B felony, the term must be at least five years and must not exceed twenty-five years;

(ii) for a class C felony, the term must be at least three and one-half years and must not exceed fifteen years;

(iii) for a class D felony, the term must be at least two years and must not exceed seven years; and

(iv) for a class E felony, the term must be at least one and one-half years and must not exceed four years.

(b) Probation. The court may sentence a defendant convicted of a class D or class E felony sex offense to probation in accordance with the provisions of section 65.00 of this title.

(c) Alternative definite sentences for class D and class E felony sex offenses. If the court, having regard to the nature and circumstances of the crime and to the history and character of the defendant, is of the opinion that a sentence of imprisonment is necessary but that it would be unduly harsh to impose a determinate sentence upon a person convicted of a class D or class E felony sex offense, the court may impose a definite sentence of imprisonment and fix a term of one year or less.

5. Sentence of imprisonment for a predicate felony sex offender.

(a) Applicability. This subdivision shall apply to a predicate felony sex offender who stands convicted of a non-violent felony sex offense and who was previously convicted of one or more felonies.

(b) Non-violent predicate felony offense. When the court has found, pursuant to the provisions of the criminal procedure law, that a person is a predicate felony sex offender, and the person's predicate conviction was for a non-violent felony offense, the court must impose a determinate sentence of imprisonment, the term of which must be fixed by the court as follows:

(i) for a class B felony, the term must be at least eight years and must not exceed twenty-five years;

(ii) for a class C felony, the term must be at least five years and must not exceed fifteen years;

(iii) for a class D felony, the term must be at least three years and must not exceed seven years; and

(iv) for a class E felony, the term must be at least two years and must not exceed four years.

(c) Violent predicate felony offense. When the court has found, pursuant to the provisions of the criminal procedure law, that a person is a predicate felony sex offender, and the person's predicate conviction was for a violent felony offense, the court must impose a determinate sentence of imprisonment, the term of which must be fixed by the court as follows:

(i) for a class B felony, the term must be at least nine years and must not exceed twenty-five years;

(ii) for a class C felony, the term must be at least six years and must not exceed fifteen years;

(iii) for a class D felony, the term must be at least four years and must not exceed seven years; and

(iv) for a class E felony, the term must be at least two and one-half years and must not exceed four years.

(d) A defendant who stands convicted of a non-violent felony sex offense, other than a class A-I or class A-II felony, who is adjudicated a persistent felony offender under section 70.10 of this article, shall be sentenced pursuant to the provisions of section 70.10 or pursuant to this subdivision.

6. Sentence of imprisonment for a violent felony sex offense. Except as provided in subdivisions seven and eight of this section, a defendant who stands convicted of a violent felony sex offense must be sentenced pursuant to the provisions of section 70.02, section 70.04, subdivision six of section 70.06, section 70.08, or section 70.10 of this article, as applicable.

7. Sentence for a class A felony sex offense. When a person stands convicted of a sexually motivated felony pursuant to section 130.91 of this chapter and the specified offense is a class A felony, the court must sentence the defendant in accordance with the provisions of:

(a) section 60.06 of this chapter and section 70.00 of this article, as applicable, if such offense is a class A-I felony; and

(b) section 70.00, 70.06 or 70.08 of this article, as applicable, if such offense is a class A-II felony.

8. Whenever a juvenile offender stands convicted of a felony sex offense, he or she must be sentenced pursuant to the provisions of sections 60.10 and 70.05 of this chapter.

9. Every determinate sentence for a felony sex offense, as defined in paragraph (a) of subdivision one of this section, imposed pursuant to any section of this article, shall include as a part thereof a period of post-release supervision in accordance with subdivision two-a of section 70.45 of this article.

N.Y. Penal Law § 70.80

Amended by New York Laws 2015, ch. 368,Sec. 4, eff. 1/19/2016.

Section 70.85 - Transitional exception to determinate sentencing laws

This section shall apply only to cases in which a determinate sentence was imposed between September first, nineteen hundred ninety-eight, and the effective date of this section, and was required by law to include a term of post-release supervision, but the court did not explicitly state such a term when pronouncing sentence. When such a case is again before the court pursuant to section six hundred one-d of the correction law or otherwise, for consideration of whether to resentence, the court may, notwithstanding any other provision of law but only on consent of the district attorney, re-impose the originally imposed determinate sentence of imprisonment without any term of post-release supervision, which then shall be deemed a lawful sentence.

N.Y. Penal Law § 70.85

Article 80 - FINES

Section 80.00 - Fine for felony

1. A sentence to pay a fine for a felony shall be a sentence to pay an amount, fixed by the court, not exceeding the higher of

a. five thousand dollars; or

b. double the amount of the defendant's gain from the commission of the crime or, if the defendant is convicted of a crime defined in article four hundred ninety-six of this chapter, any higher amount not exceeding three times the amount of the defendant's gain from the commission of such offense; or

c. if the conviction is for any felony defined in article two hundred twenty or two hundred twenty-one of this chapter, according to the following schedule:

(i) for A-I felonies, one hundred thousand dollars;

(ii) for A-II felonies, fifty thousand dollars;

(iii) for B felonies, thirty thousand dollars;

(iv) for C felonies, fifteen thousand dollars. When imposing a fine pursuant to the provisions of this paragraph, the court shall consider the profit gained by defendant's conduct, whether the amount of the fine is disproportionate to the conduct in which defendant engaged, its impact on any victims, and defendant's economic circumstances, including the defendant's ability to pay, the effect of the fine upon his or her immediate family or any other persons to whom the defendant owes an obligation of support.

2. As used in this section the term "gain" means the amount of money or the value of property derived from the commission of the crime, less the amount of money or the value of property returned to the victim of the crime or seized by or surrendered to lawful authority prior to the time sentence is imposed.

3. When the court imposes a fine for a felony pursuant to paragraph b of subdivision one of this section, the court shall make a finding as to the amount of the defendant's gain from the crime. If the record does not contain sufficient evidence to support such a finding or to permit adequate consideration of the matters specified in paragraph c of subdivision one of this section, the court may conduct a hearing upon such issues.

4. Exception. The provisions of this section shall not apply to a corporation.

5. All moneys in excess of five thousand dollars received or collected in payment of a fine imposed pursuant to paragraph c of subdivision one of this section are the property of the state and the state comptroller shall deposit all such fines to the rehabilitative alcohol and substance treatment fund established pursuant to section ninety-seven-cc of the state finance law.

6. Notwithstanding any inconsistent provision of subdivision one of this section a sentence to pay a fine for a felony set forth in the vehicle and traffic law shall be a sentence to pay an amount fixed by the court in accordance with the provisions of the law that defines the crime.

7. When the court imposes a fine pursuant to section 145.22 or 145.23 of this chapter, the court shall direct that no less than ten percent of such fine be credited to the state cemetery vandalism restoration and administration fund created pursuant to section ninety-seven-r of the state finance law.

N.Y. Penal Law § 80.00

Amended by New York Laws 2014, ch. 55,Sec. H-A-27, eff. 4/30/2014.

Section 80.05 - Fines for misdemeanors and violation

1. Class A misdemeanor. A sentence to pay a fine for a class A misdemeanor shall be a sentence to pay an amount, fixed by the court, not exceeding one thousand dollars, provided, however, that a sentence imposed for a violation of section 215.80 of this chapter may include a fine in an amount equivalent to double the value of the property unlawfully disposed of in the commission of the crime.

2. Class B misdemeanor. A sentence to pay a fine for a class B misdemeanor shall be a sentence to pay an amount, fixed by the court, not exceeding five hundred dollars.

3. Unclassified misdemeanor. A sentence to pay a fine for an unclassified misdemeanor shall be a sentence to pay an amount, fixed by the court, in accordance with the provisions of the law or ordinance that defines the crime.

4. Violation. A sentence to pay a fine for a violation shall be a sentence to pay an amount, fixed by the court, not exceeding two hundred fifty dollars.

In the case of a violation defined outside this chapter, if the amount of the fine is expressly specified in the law or ordinance that defines the offense, the amount of the fine shall be fixed in accordance with that law or ordinance.

5. Alternative sentence. If a person has gained money or property through the commission of any misdemeanor or violation then upon conviction thereof, the court, in lieu of imposing the fine authorized for the offense under one of the above subdivisions, may sentence the defendant to pay an amount, fixed by the court, not exceeding double the amount of the defendant's gain from the commission of the offense; provided, however, that the amount fixed by the court pursuant to this subdivision upon a conviction under section 11-1904 of the environmental conservation law shall not exceed five thousand dollars. In such event the provisions of subdivisions two and three of section 80.00 shall be applicable to the sentence.

6. Exception. The provisions of this section shall not apply to a corporation.

N.Y. Penal Law § 80.05

Section 80.10 - Fines for corporations

1. In general. A sentence to pay a fine, when imposed on a corporation for an offense defined in this chapter or for an offense defined outside this chapter for which no special corporate fine is specified, shall be a sentence to pay an amount, fixed by the court, not exceeding:

(a) Ten thousand dollars, when the conviction is of a felony;

(b) Five thousand dollars, when the conviction is of a class A misdemeanor or of an unclassified misdemeanor for which a term of imprisonment in excess of three months is authorized;

(c) Two thousand dollars, when the conviction is of a class B misdemeanor or of an unclassified misdemeanor for which the authorized term of imprisonment is not in excess of three months;

(d) Five hundred dollars, when the conviction is of a violation;

(e) Any higher amount not exceeding double the amount of the corporation's gain from the commission of the offense or, if the corporation is convicted of a crime defined in article four hundred ninety-six of this chapter, any higher amount not exceeding three times the amount of the corporation's gain from the commission of such offense.

2. Exception. In the case of an offense defined outside this chapter, if a special fine for a corporation is expressly specified in the law or ordinance that defines the offense, the fine fixed by the court shall be as follows:

(a) An amount within the limits specified in the law or ordinance that defines the offense; or

(b) Any higher amount not exceeding double the amount of the corporation's gain from the commission of the offense.

3. Determination of amount or value. When the court imposes the fine authorized by paragraph (e) of subdivision one or paragraph (b) of subdivision two for any offense the provisions of subdivision three of section 80.00 shall be applicable to the sentence.

N.Y. Penal Law § 80.10

Amended by New York Laws 2014, ch. 55,Sec. H-A-28, eff. 4/30/2014.

Section 80.15 - Multiple offenses

Where a person is convicted of two or more offenses committed through a single act or omission, or through an act or omission which in itself constituted one of the offenses and also was a material element of the other, and the court imposes a sentence of imprisonment or a fine or both for one of the offenses, a fine shall not be imposed for the other. The provisions of this section shall not apply to any offense or offenses set forth in the vehicle and traffic law.

N.Y. Penal Law § 80.15

Article 85 - SENTENCE OF INTERMITTENT IMPRISONMENT

Section 85.00 - Sentence of intermittent imprisonment

1. Definition. A sentence of intermittent imprisonment is a revocable sentence of imprisonment to be served on days or during certain periods of days, or both, specified by the court as part of the sentence. A person who receives a sentence of intermittent imprisonment shall be incarcerated in the institution to which he is committed at such times as are specified by the court in the sentence.

2. Authorization for use of sentence. The court may impose a sentence of intermittent imprisonment in any case where:

(a) the court is imposing sentence, upon a person other than a second or persistent felony offender, for a class D or class E felony or for any offense that is not a felony; and

(b) the court is not imposing any other sentence of imprisonment upon the defendant at the same time; and

(c) the defendant is not under any other sentence of imprisonment with a term in excess of fifteen days imposed by any other court; and

3. Duration of sentence. A sentence of intermittent imprisonment may be for any term that could be imposed as a definite sentence of imprisonment for the offense for which such sentence is imposed. The term of the sentence shall commence on the day it is imposed and shall be calculated upon the basis of the duration of its term, rather than upon the basis of the days spent in confinement, so that no person shall be subject to any such sentence for a period that is longer than a period that commences on the date the sentence is imposed and ends on the date the term of the longest definite sentence for the offense would have expired, after deducting the credit that would have been applicable to a definite sentence for jail time but without regard to any credit authorized to be allowed against the term of a definite sentence for good behavior. The provisions of section five hundred-l of the correction law shall not be applicable to a sentence of intermittent imprisonment.

4. Imposition of sentence.

(a) When the court imposes a sentence of intermittent imprisonment the court shall specify in the sentence:

(i) that the court is imposing a sentence of intermittent imprisonment;

(ii) the term of such sentence;

(iii) the days or parts of days on which the sentence is to be served, but except as provided in paragraph (iv) hereof such specification need not include the dates on which such days fall; and

(iv) the first and last dates on which the defendant is to be incarcerated under the sentence.

(b) The court, in its discretion, may specify any day or days or parts thereof on which the defendant shall be confined and may specify a period to commence at the commencement of the sentence and not to exceed fifteen days during which the defendant is to be continuously confined.

N.Y. Penal Law § 85.00

Section 85.05 - Modification and revocation of sentences of intermittent imprisonment

1. Authorization. A sentence of intermittent imprisonment may be modified by the court in its discretion upon application of the defendant; and the court on its own motion may modify or revoke any such sentence if:

(a) the court is satisfied during the term of the sentence that the defendant has committed another offense during such term;

(b) the defendant has failed to report to the institution to which he has been committed, or to the institution designated by the head of the agency to which he has been committed, on a day or dates specified in the commitment and is unable or unwilling to furnish a reasonable and acceptable explanation for such failure; or

(c) the defendant has violated a rule or regulation of the institution or agency to which he has been committed and the head of such institution or agency or someone delegated by him has reported such violation in writing to the court.

2. Interruption of sentence. In any case where the defendant fails to report to the institution or to an institution of the agency to which he has been committed, the term of the sentence shall be interrupted and such interruption shall continue until the defendant either reports to such institution or appears before the court that imposed the sentence, whichever occurs first. If the defendant reports to the institution before he appears before the court, he shall be brought before the court.

3. Action by court. The court shall not modify or revoke a sentence of intermittent imprisonment unless the defendant has been afforded an opportunity to be heard. Any modification of a sentence of intermittent imprisonment:

(a) may provide (i) for different or additional or fewer days or parts of days on which the defendant is to be confined, or (ii) where the defendant has failed to report as specified in the sentence, an extension of the term of the sentence for the period during which it was interrupted, or (iii) for both; and

(b) shall be by written order of the court and shall be delivered and filed in the same manner as the original sentence, as specified in subdivision two of section 85.10 of this article.

4. Jail time. Where a sentence of intermittent imprisonment is revoked and a sentence of imprisonment is imposed in its place for the same offense, time spent in confinement under the sentence of intermittent imprisonment shall be calculated as jail time under subdivision three of section 70.30 of this chapter and shall be added to any jail time accrued against such sentence prior to imposition thereof.

N.Y. Penal Law § 85.05

Section 85.10 - Commitment; notifications; warrants

1. Commitment. Commitment under a sentence of intermittent imprisonment and execution of the judgment shall be in accordance with the procedure applicable to a definite sentence of imprisonment, except that: (a) detention of the defendant under the judgment shall be executed during the times specified in the sentence; and (b) the court may provide that the defendant is to report to a specified institution on a specified date at a specified time to commence service of the sentence and in such case the defendant need not be taken into or retained in custody when sentence is imposed.

2. Notifications. A written copy of the sentence imposed by the court signed by the judge who imposed the sentence shall be delivered to the defendant and shall be annexed to the commitment and to each copy of the commitment required to be delivered or filed. When the defendant is not taken into or retained in custody at the time sentence is imposed, the commitment and copy of the sentence shall forthwith be delivered to the person whose duty it is to execute the judgment. If at any time the defendant fails to report for confinement as provided in the sentence the officer in charge of the institution or department to which such commitment is made or someone designated by such officer shall forthwith notify the court in writing of such failure to report.

3. Warrants. Upon receipt of any such notification the court may issue a warrant to an appropriate police officer or peace officer directing him to take the defendant into custody and bring him before the court. The court may then commit such person to custody or fix bail or release him on his own recognizance for future appearance before the court.

N.Y. Penal Law § 85.10

Section 85.15 - Subsequent sentences

1.[Effective until September 1, 2023] Indeterminate and determinate sentences. The service of an indeterminate or a determinate sentence of imprisonment shall satisfy any sentence of intermittent imprisonment imposed on a person for an offense committed prior to the time the indeterminate or determinate sentence was imposed. A person who is serving a sentence of intermittent imprisonment at the time an indeterminate or a determinate sentence of imprisonment is imposed shall be delivered to the custody of the state department of corrections and community supervision to commence service of the indeterminate or determinate sentence immediately.

1.[Effective September 1, 2023] Indeterminate and reformatory sentences. The service of an indeterminate or a reformatory sentence of imprisonment shall satisfy any sentence of intermittent imprisonment imposed on a person for an offense committed prior to the time the indeterminate or reformatory sentence was imposed. A person who is serving a sentence of intermittent imprisonment at the time an indeterminate or a reformatory sentence of imprisonment is imposed shall be delivered to the custody of the state department of corrections and community supervision to commence service of the indeterminate or reformatory sentence immediately.

2. Definite sentences. If a definite sentence of imprisonment is imposed on a person who is under a previously imposed sentence of intermittent imprisonment, such person shall commence service of the definite sentence immediately. Where such definite sentence is for a term in excess of thirty days, the service of such sentence shall satisfy the sentence of intermittent imprisonment unless the sentence of intermittent imprisonment is revoked, or a warrant is issued pursuant to subdivision three of section 85.10 of this article and prior to satisfaction of, or conditional release under, such definite sentence of imprisonment.

N.Y. Penal Law § 85.15

Amended by New York Laws 2021, ch. 55,Sec. A-19, eff. 4/19/2021.
Amended by New York Laws 2020, ch. 55,Sec. A-19, eff. 4/3/2020.
Amended by New York Laws 2019, ch. 55,Sec. O-19, eff. 4/12/2019.
Amended by New York Laws 2017, ch. 55,Sec. A-19, eff. 4/20/2017.
Amended by New York Laws 2015, ch. 55,Sec. B-19, eff. 4/13/2015.

Part 3 - SPECIFIC OFFENSES

Title G - ANTICIPATORY OFFENSES

Article 100 - CRIMINAL SOLICITATION

Section 100.00 - Criminal solicitation in the fifth degree

A person is guilty of criminal solicitation in the fifth degree when, with intent that another person engage in conduct constituting a crime, he solicits, requests, commands, importunes or otherwise attempts to cause such other person to engage in such conduct.

N.Y. Penal Law § 100.00

Section 100.05 - Criminal solicitation in the fourth degree

A person is guilty of criminal solicitation in the fourth degree when:

1. with intent that another person engage in conduct constituting a felony, he solicits, requests, commands, importunes or otherwise attempts to cause such other person to engage in such conduct; or

2. being over eighteen years of age, with intent that another person under sixteen years of age engage in conduct that would constitute a crime, he solicits, requests, commands, importunes or otherwise attempts to cause such other person to engage in such conduct.

Criminal solicitation in the fourth degree is a class A misdemeanor.

N.Y. Penal Law § 100.05

Section 100.08 - Criminal solicitation in the third degree

A person is guilty of criminal solicitation in the third degree when, being over eighteen years of age, with intent that another person under sixteen years of age engage in conduct that would constitute a felony, he solicits, requests, commands, importunes or otherwise attempts to cause such other person to engage in such conduct.

N.Y. Penal Law § 100.08

Section 100.10 - Criminal solicitation in the second degree

A person is guilty of criminal solicitation in the second degree when, with intent that another person engage in conduct constituting a class A felony, he solicits, requests, commands, importunes or otherwise attempts to cause such other person to engage in such conduct.

N.Y. Penal Law § 100.10

Section 100.13 - Criminal solicitation in the first degree

A person is guilty of criminal solicitation in the first degree when, being over eighteen years of age, with intent that another person under sixteen years of age engage in conduct that would constitute a class A felony, he solicits, requests, commands, importunes or otherwise attempts to cause such other person to engage in such conduct.

N.Y. Penal Law § 100.13

Section 100.15 - Criminal solicitation; no defense

It is no defense to a prosecution for criminal solicitation that the person solicited could not be guilty of the crime solicited owing to criminal irresponsibility or other legal incapacity or exemption, or to unawareness of the criminal nature of the conduct solicited or of the defendant's criminal purpose or to other factors precluding the mental state required for the commission of the crime in question.

N.Y. Penal Law § 100.15

Section 100.20 - Criminal solicitation; exemption

A person is not guilty of criminal solicitation when his solicitation constitutes conduct of a kind that is necessarily incidental to the commission of the crime solicited. When under such circumstances the solicitation constitutes an offense other than criminal solicitation which is related to but separate from the crime solicited, the actor is guilty of such related and separate offense only and not of criminal solicitation.

N.Y. Penal Law § 100.20

Article 105 - CONSPIRACY

Section 105.00 - Conspiracy in the sixth degree

A person is guilty of conspiracy in the sixth degree when, with intent that conduct constituting a crime be performed, he agrees with one or more persons to engage in or cause the performance of such conduct.

N.Y. Penal Law § 105.00

Section 105.05 - Conspiracy in the fifth degree

A person is guilty of conspiracy in the fifth degree when, with intent that conduct constituting:

1. a felony be performed, he agrees with one or more persons to engage in or cause the performance of such conduct; or

2. a crime be performed, he, being over eighteen years of age, agrees with one or more persons under sixteen years of age to engage in or cause the performance of such conduct.

Conspiracy in the fifth degree is a class A misdemeanor.

N.Y. Penal Law § 105.05

Section 105.10 - Conspiracy in the fourth degree

A person is guilty of conspiracy in the fourth degree when, with intent that conduct constituting:

1. a class B or class C felony be performed, he or she agrees with one or more persons to engage in or cause the performance of such conduct; or

2. a felony be performed, he or she, being over eighteen years of age, agrees with one or more persons under sixteen years of age to engage in or cause the performance of such conduct; or

3. the felony of money laundering in the third degree as defined in section 470.10 of this chapter, be performed, he or she agrees with one or more persons to engage in or cause the performance of such conduct.

Conspiracy in the fourth degree is a class E felony.

N.Y. Penal Law § 105.10

Section 105.13 - Conspiracy in the third degree

A person is guilty of conspiracy in the third degree when, with intent that conduct constituting a class B or a class C felony be performed, he, being over eighteen years of age, agrees with one or more persons under sixteen years of age to engage in or cause the performance of such conduct.

N.Y. Penal Law § 105.13

Section 105.15 - Conspiracy in the second degree

A person is guilty of conspiracy in the second degree when, with intent that conduct constituting a class A felony be performed, he agrees with one or more persons to engage in or cause the performance of such conduct.

N.Y. Penal Law § 105.15

Section 105.17 - Conspiracy in the first degree

A person is guilty of conspiracy in the first degree when, with intent that conduct constituting a class A felony be performed, he, being over eighteen years of age, agrees with one or more persons under sixteen years of age to engage in or cause the performance of such conduct.

N.Y. Penal Law § 105.17

Section 105.20 - Conspiracy; pleading and proof; necessity of overt act

A person shall not be convicted of conspiracy unless an overt act is alleged and proved to have been committed by one of the conspirators in furtherance of the conspiracy.

N.Y. Penal Law § 105.20

Section 105.25 - Conspiracy; jurisdiction and venue

1. A person may be prosecuted for conspiracy in the county in which he entered into such conspiracy or in any county in which an overt act in furtherance thereof was committed.

2. An agreement made within this state to engage in or cause the performance of conduct in another jurisdiction is punishable herein as a conspiracy only when such conduct would constitute a crime both under the laws of this state if performed herein and under the laws of the other jurisdiction if performed therein.

3. An agreement made in another jurisdiction to engage in or cause the performance of conduct within this state, which would constitute a crime herein, is punishable herein only when an overt act in furtherance of such conspiracy is committed within this state. Under such circumstances, it is no defense to a prosecution for conspiracy that the conduct which is the objective of the conspiracy would not constitute a crime under the laws of the other jurisdiction if performed therein.

N.Y. Penal Law § 105.25

Section 105.30 - Conspiracy; no defense

It is no defense to a prosecution for conspiracy that, owing to criminal irresponsibility or other legal incapacity or exemption, or to unawareness of the criminal nature of the agreement or the object conduct or of the defendant's criminal purpose or to other factors precluding the mental state required for the commission of conspiracy or the object crime, one or more of the defendant's co-conspirators could not be guilty of conspiracy or the object crime.

N.Y. Penal Law § 105.30

Section 105.35 - Conspiracy; enterprise corruption: applicability

For purposes of this article, conspiracy to commit the crime of enterprise corruption in violation of section 460.20 of this chapter shall not constitute an offense.

N.Y. Penal Law § 105.35

Article 110 - ATTEMPT

Section 110.00 - Attempt to commit a crime

A person is guilty of an attempt to commit a crime when, with intent to commit a crime, he engages in conduct which tends to effect the commission of such crime.

N.Y. Penal Law § 110.00

Section 110.05 - Attempt to commit a crime; punishment

An attempt to commit a crime is a:

1. Class A-I felony when the crime attempted is the A-I felony of murder in the first degree, aggravated murder as defined in subdivision one of section 125.26 of this chapter, criminal possession of a controlled substance in the first degree, criminal sale of a controlled substance in the first degree, criminal possession of a chemical or biological weapon in the first degree or criminal use of a chemical or biological weapon in the first degree;

2. Class A-II felony when the crime attempted is a class A-II felony;

3. Class B felony when the crime attempted is a class A-I felony except as provided in subdivision one hereof;

4. Class C felony when the crime attempted is a class B felony;

5. Class D felony when the crime attempted is a class C felony;

6. Class E felony when the crime attempted is a class D felony;

7. Class A misdemeanor when the crime attempted is a class E felony;

8. Class B misdemeanor when the crime attempted is a misdemeanor;

9. Class D felony when the crime attempted is bribery in the third degree as defined in section 200.00 of this chapter, a class C felony when the crime attempted is bribery in the second degree as defined in section 200.03 of this chapter and a class B felony when the crime attempted is bribery in the first degree as defined in subdivision two of section 200.04 of this chapter.

N.Y. Penal Law § 110.05

Amended by New York Laws 2014, ch. 55,Sec. H-A-8, eff. 4/30/2014.

Section 110.10 - Attempt to commit a crime; no defense

If the conduct in which a person engages otherwise constitutes an attempt to commit a crime pursuant to section 110.00, it is no defense to a prosecution for such attempt that the crime charged to have been attempted was, under the attendant circumstances, factually or legally impossible of commission, if such crime could have been committed had the attendant circumstances been as such person believed them to be.

N.Y. Penal Law § 110.10

Article 115 - CRIMINAL FACILITATION

Section 115.00 - Criminal facilitation in the fourth degree

A person is guilty of criminal facilitation in the fourth degree when, believing it probable that he is rendering aid:
1. to a person who intends to commit a crime, he engages in conduct which provides such person with means or opportunity for the commission thereof and which in fact aids such person to commit a felony; or
2. to a person under sixteen years of age who intends to engage in conduct which would constitute a crime, he, being over eighteen years of age, engages in conduct which provides such person with means or opportunity for the commission thereof and which in fact aids such person to commit a crime.
Criminal facilitation in the fourth degree is a class A misdemeanor.
N.Y. Penal Law § 115.00

Section 115.01 - Criminal facilitation in the third degree

A person guilty of criminal facilitation in the third degree, when believing it probable that he is rendering aid to a person under sixteen years of age who intends to engage in conduct that would constitute a felony, he, being over eighteen years of age, engages in conduct which provides such person with means or opportunity for the commission thereof and which in fact aids such person to commit a felony.
N.Y. Penal Law § 115.01

Section 115.05 - Criminal facilitation in the second degree

A person is guilty of criminal facilitation in the second degree when, believing it probable that he is rendering aid to a person who intends to commit a class A felony, he engages in conduct which provides such person with means or opportunity for the commission thereof and which in fact aids such person to commit such class A felony.
N.Y. Penal Law § 115.05

Section 115.08 - Criminal facilitation in the first degree

A person is guilty of criminal facilitation in the first degree when, believing it probable that he is rendering aid to a person under sixteen years of age who intends to engage in conduct that would constitute a class A felony, he, being over eighteen years of age, engages in conduct which provides such person with means or opportunity for the commission thereof and which in fact aids such person to commit such a class A felony.
N.Y. Penal Law § 115.08

Section 115.10 - Criminal facilitation; no defense

It is no defense to a prosecution for criminal facilitation that:
1. The person facilitated was not guilty of the underlying felony owing to criminal irresponsibility or other legal incapacity or exemption, or to unawareness of the criminal nature of the conduct in question or to other factors precluding the mental state required for the commission of such felony; or
2. The person facilitated has not been prosecuted for or convicted of the underlying felony, or has previously been acquitted thereof; or
3. The defendant himself is not guilty of the felony which he facilitated because he did not act with the intent or other culpable mental state required for the commission thereof.
N.Y. Penal Law § 115.10

Section 115.15 - Criminal facilitation; corroboration

A person shall not be convicted of criminal facilitation upon the testimony of a person who has committed the felony charged to have been facilitated unless such testimony be corroborated by such other evidence as tends to connect the defendant with such facilitation.
N.Y. Penal Law § 115.15

Section 115.20 - Criminal facilitation; definitions and construction

N.Y. Penal Law § 115.20
Added by New York Laws 2013, ch. 1, Sec. 31, eff. 3/16/2013.

Title H - OFFENSES AGAINST THE PERSON INVOLVING PHYSICAL INJURY, SEXUAL CONDUCT, RESTRAINT AND INTIMIDATION

Article 120 - ASSAULT AND RELATED OFFENSES

Section 120.00 - Assault in the third degree

A person is guilty of assault in the third degree when:
1. With intent to cause physical injury to another person, he causes such injury to such person or to a third person; or
2. He recklessly causes physical injury to another person; or
3. With criminal negligence, he causes physical injury to another person by means of a deadly weapon or a dangerous instrument.
Assault in the third degree is a class A misdemeanor.
N.Y. Penal Law § 120.00

Section 120.01 - Reckless assault of a child by a child day care provider

A person is guilty of reckless assault of a child when, being a child day care provider or an employee thereof, he or she recklessly causes serious physical injury to a child under the care of such provider or employee who is less than eleven years of age.
N.Y. Penal Law § 120.01

Section 120.02 - Reckless assault of a child

Reckless assault of a child is a class D felony.

1. A person is guilty of reckless assault of a child when, being eighteen years of age or more, such person recklessly causes serious physical injury to the brain of a child less than five years old by shaking the child, or by slamming or throwing the child so as to impact the child's head on a hard surface or object.

2. For purposes of subdivision one of this section, the following shall constitute "serious physical injury":

a. "serious physical injury" as defined in subdivision ten of section 10.00 of this chapter; or

b.extreme rotational cranial acceleration and deceleration and one or more of the following: (i) subdural hemorrhaging; (ii) intracranial hemorrhaging; or (iii) retinal hemorrhaging.

N.Y. Penal Law § 120.02

Section 120.03 - Vehicular assault in the second degree

A person is guilty of vehicular assault in the second degree when he or she causes serious physical injury to another person, and either:

(1) operates a motor vehicle in violation of subdivision two, three, four or four-a of section eleven hundred ninety-two of the vehicle and traffic law or operates a vessel or public vessel in violation of paragraph (b), (c), (d) or (e) of subdivision two of section forty-nine-a of the navigation law, and as a result of such intoxication or impairment by the use of a drug, or by the combined influence of drugs or of alcohol and any drug or drugs, operates such motor vehicle, vessel or public vessel in a manner that causes such serious physical injury to such other person, or

(2) operates a motor vehicle with a gross vehicle weight rating of more than eighteen thousand pounds which contains flammable gas, radioactive materials or explosives in violation of subdivision one of section eleven hundred ninety-two of the vehicle and traffic law, and such flammable gas, radioactive materials or explosives is the cause of such serious physical injury, and as a result of such impairment by the use of alcohol, operates such motor vehicle in a manner that causes such serious physical injury to such other person, or

(3) operates a snowmobile in violation of paragraph (b), (c) or (d) of subdivision one of section 25.24 of the parks, recreation and historic preservation law or operates an all terrain vehicle as defined in paragraph (a) of subdivision one of section twenty-two hundred eighty-one of the vehicle and traffic law and in violation of subdivision two, three, four, or four-a of section eleven hundred ninety-two of the vehicle and traffic law, and as a result of such intoxication or impairment by the use of a drug, or by the combined influence of drugs or of alcohol and any drug or drugs, operates such snowmobile or all terrain vehicle in a manner that causes such serious physical injury to such other person.

If it is established that the person operating such motor vehicle, vessel, public vessel, snowmobile or all terrain vehicle caused such serious physical injury while unlawfully intoxicated or impaired by the use of alcohol or a drug, then there shall be a rebuttable presumption that, as a result of such intoxication or impairment by the use of alcohol or a drug, or by the combined influence of drugs or of alcohol and any drug or drugs, such person operated the motor vehicle, vessel, public vessel, snowmobile or all terrain vehicle in a manner that caused such serious physical injury, as required by this section. Vehicular assault in the second degree is a class E felony.

N.Y. Penal Law § 120.03

Section 120.04 - Vehicular assault in the first degree

A person is guilty of vehicular assault in the first degree when he or she commits the crime of vehicular assault in the second degree as defined in section 120.03 of this article, and either:

(1) commits such crime while operating a motor vehicle while such person has .18 of one per centum or more by weight of alcohol in such person's blood as shown by chemical analysis of such person's blood, breath, urine or saliva made pursuant to the provisions of section eleven hundred ninety-four of the vehicle and traffic law;

(2) commits such crime while knowing or having reason to know that: (a) his or her license or his or her privilege of operating a motor vehicle in another state or his or her privilege of obtaining a license to operate a motor vehicle in another state is suspended or revoked and such suspension or revocation is based upon a conviction in such other state for an offense which would, if committed in this state, constitute a violation of any of the provisions of section eleven hundred ninety-two of the vehicle and traffic law; or (b) his or her license or his or her privilege of operating a motor vehicle in the state or his or her privilege of obtaining a license issued by the commissioner of motor vehicles is suspended or revoked and such suspension or revocation is based upon either a refusal to submit to a chemical test pursuant to section eleven hundred ninety-four of the vehicle and traffic law or following a conviction for a violation of any of the provisions of section eleven hundred ninety-two of the vehicle and traffic law;

(3) has previously been convicted of violating any of the provisions of section eleven hundred ninety-two of the vehicle and traffic law within the preceding ten years, provided that, for the purposes of this subdivision, a conviction in any other state or jurisdiction for an offense which, if committed in this state, would constitute a violation of section eleven hundred ninety-two of the vehicle and traffic law, shall be treated as a violation of such law;

(4) causes serious physical injury to more than one other person;

(5) has previously been convicted of violating any provision of this article or article one hundred twenty-five of this title involving the operation of a motor vehicle, or was convicted in any other state or jurisdiction of an offense involving the operation of a motor vehicle which, if committed in this state, would constitute a violation of this article or article one hundred twenty-five of this title; or

(6) commits such crime while operating a motor vehicle while a child who is fifteen years of age or less is a passenger in such motor vehicle and causes serious physical injury to such child.

If it is established that the person operating such motor vehicle caused such serious physical injury or injuries while unlawfully intoxicated or impaired by the use of alcohol or a drug, or by the combined influence of drugs or of alcohol and any drug or drugs, then there shall be a rebuttable presumption that, as a result of such intoxication or impairment by the use of alcohol or a drug, or by the combined influence of drugs or of alcohol and any drug or drugs, such person operated the motor vehicle in a manner that caused such serious physical injury or injuries, as required by this section and section 120.03 of this article.

N.Y. Penal Law § 120.04

Section 120.04-A - Aggravated vehicular assault

A person is guilty of aggravated vehicular assault when he or she engages in reckless driving as defined by section twelve hundred twelve of the vehicle and traffic law, and commits the crime of vehicular assault in the second degree as defined in section 120.03 of this article, and either:

(1) commits such crimes while operating a motor vehicle while such person has .18 of one per centum or more by weight of alcohol in such person's blood as shown by chemical analysis of such person's blood, breath, urine or saliva made pursuant to the provisions of section eleven hundred ninety-four of the vehicle and traffic law;

(2) commits such crimes while knowing or having reason to know that: (a) his or her license or his or her privilege of operating a motor vehicle in another state or his or her privilege of obtaining a license to operate a motor vehicle in another state is suspended or revoked and such suspension or revocation is based upon a conviction in such other state for an offense which would, if committed in this state, constitute a violation of any of the provisions of section eleven hundred ninety-two of the vehicle and traffic law; or (b) his or her license or his or her privilege of operating a motor vehicle in this state or his or her privilege of obtaining a license issued by the commissioner of motor vehicles is suspended or revoked and such suspension or revocation is based upon either a refusal to submit to a chemical test pursuant to section eleven hundred ninety-four of the vehicle and traffic law or following a conviction for a violation of any of the provisions of section eleven hundred ninety-two of the vehicle and traffic law;

(3) has previously been convicted of violating any of the provisions of section eleven hundred ninety-two of the vehicle and traffic law within the preceding ten years, provided that, for the purposes of this subdivision, a conviction in any other state or jurisdiction for an offense which, if committed in this state, would constitute a violation of section eleven hundred ninety-two of the vehicle and traffic law, shall be treated as a violation of such law;

(4) causes serious physical injury to more than one other person;

(5) has previously been convicted of violating any provision of this article or article one hundred twenty-five of this title involving the operation of a motor vehicle, or was convicted in any other state or jurisdiction of an offense involving the operation of a motor vehicle which, if committed in this state, would constitute a violation of this article or article one hundred twenty-five of this title; or

(6) commits such crime while operating a motor vehicle while a child who is fifteen years of age or less is a passenger in such motor vehicle and causes serious physical injury to such child.

If it is established that the person operating such motor vehicle caused such serious physical injury or injuries while unlawfully intoxicated or impaired by the use of alcohol or a drug, or by the combined influence of drugs or of alcohol and any drug or drugs, then there shall be a rebuttable presumption that, as a result of such intoxication or impairment by the use of alcohol or a drug, or by the combined influence of drugs or of alcohol and any drug or drugs, such person operated the motor vehicle in a manner that caused such serious physical injury or injuries, as required by this section and section 120.03 of this article.

N.Y. Penal Law § 120.04-A

Section 120.05 - Assault in the second degree

A person is guilty of assault in the second degree when:

1. With intent to cause serious physical injury to another person, he causes such injury to such person or to a third person; or

2. With intent to cause physical injury to another person, he causes such injury to such person or to a third person by means of a deadly weapon or a dangerous instrument; or

3. With intent to prevent a peace officer, a police officer, prosecutor as defined in subdivision thirty-one of section 1.20 of the criminal procedure law, registered nurse, licensed practical nurse, public health sanitarian, New York city public health sanitarian, sanitation enforcement agent, New York city sanitation worker, a firefighter, including a firefighter acting as a paramedic or emergency medical technician administering first aid in the course of performance of duty as such firefighter, an emergency medical service paramedic or emergency medical service technician, or medical or related personnel in a hospital emergency department, a city marshal, a school crossing guard appointed pursuant to section two hundred eight-a of the general municipal law, a traffic enforcement officer , traffic enforcement agent or employee of any entity governed by the public service law in the course of performing an essential service, from performing a lawful duty, by means including releasing or failing to control an animal under circumstances evincing the actor's intent that the animal obstruct the lawful activity of such peace officer, police officer, prosecutor as defined in subdivision thirty-one of section 1.20 of the criminal procedure law, registered nurse, licensed practical nurse, public health sanitarian, New York city public health sanitarian, sanitation enforcement agent, New York city sanitation worker, firefighter, paramedic, technician, city marshal, school crossing guard appointed pursuant to section two hundred eight-a of the general municipal law, traffic enforcement officer , traffic enforcement agent or employee of an entity governed by the public service law, he or she causes physical injury to such peace officer, police officer, prosecutor as defined in subdivision thirty-one of section 1.20 of the criminal procedure law, registered nurse, licensed practical nurse, public health sanitarian, New York city public health sanitarian,

sanitation enforcement agent, New York city sanitation worker, firefighter, paramedic, technician or medical or related personnel in a hospital emergency department, city marshal, school crossing guard, traffic enforcement officer , traffic enforcement agent or employee of an entity governed by the public service law; or

3-a. With intent to prevent an employee of a local social services district directly involved in investigation of or response to alleged abuse or neglect of a child, a vulnerable elderly person or an incompetent or physically disabled person, from performing such investigation or response, the actor, not being such child, vulnerable elderly person or incompetent or physically disabled person, or with intent to prevent an employee of a local social services district directly involved in providing public assistance and care from performing his or her job, causes physical injury to such employee including by means of releasing or failing to control an animal under circumstances evincing the actor's intent that the animal obstruct the lawful activities of such employee; or

3-b. With intent to prevent an employee of the New York city housing authority from performing his or her lawful duties while located on housing project grounds, real property, or a building owned, managed, or operated by such authority he or she causes physical injury to such employee; or

3-c. With intent to prevent an employee providing direct patient care, who is not a nurse pursuant to title eight of the education law, whose principal employment responsibility is to carry out direct patient care for one or more patients in any hospital, nursing home, residential health care facility, general hospital, government agency including any chronic disease hospital, maternity hospital, outpatient department, emergency center or surgical center under article twenty-eight of the public health law, from performing a lawful duty, he or she causes physical injury to such employee providing direct patient care; or

4. He recklessly causes serious physical injury to another person by means of a deadly weapon or a dangerous instrument; or

4-a. He recklessly causes physical injury to another person who is a child under the age of eighteen by intentional discharge of a firearm, rifle or shotgun; or

5. For a purpose other than lawful medical or therapeutic treatment, he intentionally causes stupor, unconsciousness or other physical impairment or injury to another person by administering to him, without his consent, a drug, substance or preparation capable of producing the same; or

6. In the course of and in furtherance of the commission or attempted commission of a felony, other than a felony defined in article one hundred thirty which requires corroboration for conviction, or of immediate flight therefrom, he, or another participant if there be any, causes physical injury to a person other than one of the participants; or

7. Having been charged with or convicted of a crime and while confined in a correctional facility, as defined in subdivision three of section forty of the correction law, pursuant to such charge or conviction, with intent to cause physical injury to another person, he causes such injury to such person or to a third person; or

8. Being eighteen years old or more and with intent to cause physical injury to a person less than eleven years old, the defendant recklessly causes serious physical injury to such person; or

9. Being eighteen years old or more and with intent to cause physical injury to a person less than seven years old, the defendant causes such injury to such person; or

10. Acting at a place the person knows, or reasonably should know, is on school grounds and with intent to cause physical injury, he or she:

(a) causes such injury to an employee of a school or public school district; or

(b) not being a student of such school or public school district, causes physical injury to another, and such other person is a student of such school who is attending or present for educational purposes. For purposes of this subdivision the term "school grounds" shall have the meaning set forth in subdivision fourteen of section 220.00 of this chapter; or

11. With intent to cause physical injury to a train operator, ticket inspector, conductor, signalperson, bus operator , station agent, station cleaner or terminal cleaner employed by any transit agency, authority or company, public or private, whose operation is authorized by New York state or any of its political subdivisions, a city marshal, a school crossing guard appointed pursuant to section two hundred eight-a of the general municipal law, a traffic enforcement officer, traffic enforcement agent, prosecutor as defined in subdivision thirtyone of section 1.20 of the criminal procedure law, sanitation enforcement agent, New York city sanitation worker, registered nurse, licensed practical nurse, emergency medical service paramedic, or emergency medical service technician, he or she causes physical injury to such train operator, ticket inspector, conductor, signalperson, bus operator , station agent, station cleaner or terminal cleaner, city marshal, school crossing guard appointed pursuant to section two hundred eight-a of the general municipal law, traffic enforcement officer, traffic enforcement agent, prosecutor as defined in subdivision thirty-one of section 1.20 of the criminal procedure law, registered nurse, licensed practical nurse, sanitation enforcement agent, New York city sanitation worker, emergency medical service paramedic, or emergency medical service technician, while such employee is performing an assigned duty on, or directly related to, the operation of a train or bus, including the cleaning of a train or bus station or terminal, or such city marshal, school crossing guard, traffic enforcement officer, traffic enforcement agent, prosecutor as defined in subdivision thirty-one of section 1.20 of the criminal procedure law, registered nurse, licensed practical nurse, sanitation enforcement agent, New York city sanitation worker, emergency medical service paramedic, or emergency medical service technician is performing an assigned duty, or

11-a. With intent to cause physical injury to an employee of a local social services district directly involved in investigation of or response to alleged abuse or neglect of a child, vulnerable elderly person or an incompetent or physically disabled person, the actor, not being such child, vulnerable elderly person or incompetent or physically disabled person, or with intent to prevent an employee of a local social services district directly involved in providing public assistance and care from performing his or her job, causes physical injury to such employee; or

11-b. With intent to cause physical injury to an employee of the New York city housing authority performing his or her lawful duties while located on housing project grounds, real property, or a building owned, managed, or operated by such authority he or she causes physical injury to such employee; or

11-c. With intent to cause physical injury to an employee providing direct patient care, who is not a nurse pursuant to title eight of the education law, whose principal employment responsibility is to carry out direct patient care for one or more patients in any hospital, nursing home, residential health care facility, general hospital, government agency including any chronic disease hospital, maternity hospital, outpatient department, emergency center or surgical center under article twenty-eight of the public health law, he or she causes physical injury to such employee providing direct patient care while such employee is performing a lawful duty; or

12. With intent to cause physical injury to a person who is sixty-five years of age or older, he or she causes such injury to such person, and the actor is more than ten years younger than such person; or

13. Being confined to a secure treatment facility, as such term is defined in subdivision (o) of section 10.03 of the mental hygiene law, and with intent to cause physical injury to an employee of such secure treatment facility performing his or her duties, he or she causes such injury to such person; or

14. With intent to prevent or obstruct a process server, as defined in section eighty-nine-t of the general business law, from performing a lawful duty pursuant to article three of the civil practice law and rules, or intentionally, as retaliation against such a process server for the performance of the process server's duties pursuant to such article, including by means of releasing or failing to control an animal evincing the actor's intent that the animal prevent or obstruct the lawful duty of the process server or as retaliation against the process server, he or she causes physical injury to such process server.

N.Y. Penal Law § 120.05

Amended by New York Laws 2016, ch. 281,Sec. 1 and Sec. 2, eff. 11/1/2016.
Amended by New York Laws 2016, ch. 268,Sec. 1, eff. 11/1/2016.
Amended by New York Laws 2016, ch. 267,Sec. 1, eff. 11/1/2016.
Amended by New York Laws 2015, ch. 487,Sec. 1, eff. 2/18/2016.
Amended by New York Laws 2015, ch. 477,Sec. 1, eff. 11/1/2016.
Amended by New York Laws 2015, ch. 472,Sec. 1, eff. 11/1/2016.
Amended by New York Laws 2015, ch. 423,Sec. 1, eff. 11/1/2016.
Amended by New York Laws 2014, ch. 196,Sec. 1, eff. 11/1/2014.
Amended by New York Laws 2013, ch. 1,Sec. 32, eff. 3/16/2013.
See New York Laws 2014, ch. 197, Sec. 2.

Section 120.06 - Gang assault in the second degree
A person is guilty of gang assault in the second degree when, with intent to cause physical injury to another person and when aided by two or more other persons actually present, he causes serious physical injury to such person or to a third person.

N.Y. Penal Law § 120.06

Section 120.07 - Gang assault in the first degree
A person is guilty of gang assault in the first degree when, with intent to cause serious physical injury to another person and when aided by two or more other persons actually present, he causes serious physical injury to such person or to a third person.

N.Y. Penal Law § 120.07

Section 120.08 - Assault on a peace officer, police officer, firefighter or emergency medical services professional
A person is guilty of assault on a peace officer, police officer, firefighter or emergency medical services professional when, with intent to prevent a peace officer, police officer, a firefighter, including a firefighter acting as a paramedic or emergency medical technician administering first aid in the course of performance of duty as such firefighter, or an emergency medical service paramedic or emergency medical service technician, from performing a lawful duty, he or she causes serious physical injury to such peace officer, police officer, firefighter, paramedic or technician.

N.Y. Penal Law § 120.08

Amended by New York Laws 2018, ch. 476,Sec. 240, eff. 12/28/2018.

Section 120.09 - Assault on a judge
A person is guilty of assault on a judge when, with intent to cause serious physical injury and prevent a judge from performing official judicial duties, he or she causes serious physical injury to such judge. For the purposes of this section, the term judge shall mean a judge of a court of record or a justice court.

N.Y. Penal Law § 120.09

Section 120.10 - Assault in the first degree
A person is guilty of assault in the first degree when:

1. With intent to cause serious physical injury to another person, he causes such injury to such person or to a third person by means of a deadly weapon or a dangerous instrument; or

2. With intent to disfigure another person seriously and permanently, or to destroy, amputate or disable permanently a member or organ of his body, he causes such injury to such person or to a third person; or

3. Under circumstances evincing a depraved indifference to human life, he recklessly engages in conduct which creates a grave risk of death to another person, and thereby causes serious physical injury to another person; or

4. In the course of and in furtherance of the commission or attempted commission of a felony or of immediate flight therefrom, he, or another participant if there be any, causes serious physical injury to a person other than one of the participants.

Assault in the first degree is a class B felony.

N.Y. Penal Law § 120.10

Section 120.11 - Aggravated assault upon a police officer or a peace officer

A person is guilty of aggravated assault upon a police officer or a peace officer when, with intent to cause serious physical injury to a person whom he knows or reasonably should know to be a police officer or a peace officer engaged in the course of performing his official duties, he causes such injury by means of a deadly weapon or dangerous instrument.

N.Y. Penal Law § 120.11

Section 120.12 - Aggravated assault upon a person less than eleven years old

A person is guilty of aggravated assault upon a person less than eleven years old when being eighteen years old or more the defendant commits the crime of assault in the third degree as defined in section 120.00 of this article upon a person less than eleven years old and has been previously convicted of such crime upon a person less than eleven years old within the preceding ten years.

N.Y. Penal Law § 120.12

Amended by New York Laws 2013, ch. 172,Sec. 2, eff. 7/29/2013.

Section 120.13 - Menacing in the first degree

A person is guilty of menacing in the first degree when he or she commits the crime of menacing in the second degree and has been previously convicted of the crime of menacing in the second degree or the crime of menacing a police officer or peace officer within the preceding ten years.

N.Y. Penal Law § 120.13

Section 120.14 - Menacing in the second degree

A person is guilty of menacing in the second degree when:

1. He or she intentionally places or attempts to place another person in reasonable fear of physical injury, serious physical injury or death by displaying a deadly weapon, dangerous instrument or what appears to be a pistol, revolver, rifle, shotgun, machine gun or other firearm; or

2. He or she repeatedly follows a person or engages in a course of conduct or repeatedly commits acts over a period of time intentionally placing or attempting to place another person in reasonable fear of physical injury, serious physical injury or death; or

3. He or she commits the crime of menacing in the third degree in violation of that part of a duly served order of protection, or such order which the defendant has actual knowledge of because he or she was present in court when such order was issued, pursuant to article eight of the family court act, section 530.12 of the criminal procedure law, or an order of protection issued by a court of competent jurisdiction in another state, territorial or tribal jurisdiction, which directed the respondent or defendant to stay away from the person or persons on whose behalf the order was issued.

Menacing in the second degree is a class A misdemeanor.

N.Y. Penal Law § 120.14

Section 120.15 - Menacing in the third degree

A person is guilty of menacing in the third degree when, by physical menace, he or she intentionally places or attempts to place another person in fear of death, imminent serious physical injury or physical injury.

N.Y. Penal Law § 120.15

Section 120.16 - Hazing in the first degree

A person is guilty of hazing in the first degree when, in the course of another person's initiation into or affiliation with any organization, he intentionally or recklessly engages in conduct, including, but not limited to, making physical contact with or requiring physical activity of such other person, which creates a substantial risk of physical injury to such other person or a third person and thereby causes such injury.

N.Y. Penal Law § 120.16

Amended by New York Laws 2018, ch. 188,Sec. 1, eff. 8/13/2018.

Section 120.17 - Hazing in the second degree

A person is guilty of hazing in the second degree when, in the course of another person's initiation or affiliation with any organization, he intentionally or recklessly engages in conduct, including, but not limited to, making physical contact with or requiring physical activity of such other person, which creates a substantial risk of physical injury to such other person or a third person.

N.Y. Penal Law § 120.17

Amended by New York Laws 2018, ch. 188,Sec. 2, eff. 8/13/2018.

Section 120.18 - Menacing a police officer or peace officer

A person is guilty of menacing a police officer or peace officer when he or she intentionally places or attempts to place a police officer or peace officer in reasonable fear of physical injury, serious physical injury or death by displaying a deadly weapon, knife, pistol, revolver, rifle, shotgun, machine gun or other firearm, whether operable or not, where such officer was in the course of performing his or her official duties and the defendant knew or reasonably should have known that such victim was a police officer or peace officer.

N.Y. Penal Law § 120.18

Section 120.20 - Reckless endangerment in the second degree

A person is guilty of reckless endangerment in the second degree when he recklessly engages in conduct which creates a substantial risk of serious physical injury to another person.

N.Y. Penal Law § 120.20

Section 120.25 - Reckless endangerment in the first degree

A person is guilty of reckless endangerment in the first degree when, under circumstances evincing a depraved indifference to human life, he recklessly engages in conduct which creates a grave risk of death to another person.

N.Y. Penal Law § 120.25

Section 120.30 - Promoting a suicide attempt

A person is guilty of promoting a suicide attempt when he intentionally causes or aids another person to attempt suicide.

N.Y. Penal Law § 120.30

Section 120.35 - Promoting a suicide attempt; when punishable as attempt to commit murder

A person who engages in conduct constituting both the offense of promoting a suicide attempt and the offense of attempt to commit murder may not be convicted of attempt to commit murder unless he causes or aids the suicide attempt by the use of duress or deception.

N.Y. Penal Law § 120.35

Section 120.40 - Definitions

For purposes of sections 120.45, 120.50, 120.55 and 120.60 of this article:

1. "Kidnapping" shall mean a kidnapping crime defined in article one hundred thirty-five of this chapter.

2. "Unlawful imprisonment" shall mean an unlawful imprisonment felony crime defined in article one hundred thirty-five of this chapter.

3. "Sex offense" shall mean a felony defined in article one hundred thirty of this chapter, sexual misconduct, as defined in section 130.20 of this chapter, sexual abuse in the third degree as defined in section 130.55 of this chapter or sexual abuse in the second degree as defined in section 130.60 of this chapter.

4. "Immediate family" means the spouse, former spouse, parent, child, sibling, or any other person who regularly resides or has regularly resided in the household of a person.

5. "Specified predicate crime" means:

a. a violent felony offense;

b. a crime defined in section 130.20, 130.25, 130.30, 130.40, 130.45, 130.55, 130.60, 130.70, 255.25, 255.26 or 255.27;

c. assault in the third degree, as defined in section 120.00; menacing in the first degree, as defined in section 120.13; menacing in the second degree, as defined in section 120.14; coercion in the first degree, as defined in section 135.65; coercion in the second degree, as defined in section 135.61; coercion in the third degree, as defined in section 135.60; aggravated harassment in the second degree, as defined in section 240.30; harassment in the first degree, as defined in section 240.25; menacing in the third degree, as defined in section 120.15; criminal mischief in the third degree, as defined in section 145.05; criminal mischief in the second degree, as defined in section 145.10, criminal mischief in the first degree, as defined in section 145.12; criminal tampering in the first degree, as defined in section 145.20; arson in the fourth degree, as defined in section 150.05; arson in the third degree, as defined in section 150.10; criminal contempt in the first degree, as defined in section 215.51; endangering the welfare of a child, as defined in section 260.10; or

N.Y. Penal Law § 120.40

Amended by New York Laws 2018, ch. 55,Sec. NN-7, eff. 11/1/2018.

Section 120.45 - Stalking in the fourth degree

A person is guilty of stalking in the fourth degree when he or she intentionally, and for no legitimate purpose, engages in a course of conduct directed at a specific person, and knows or reasonably should know that such conduct:

1. is likely to cause reasonable fear of material harm to the physical health, safety or property of such person, a member of such person's immediate family or a third party with whom such person is acquainted; or

2. causes material harm to the mental or emotional health of such person, where such conduct consists of following, telephoning or initiating communication or contact with such person, a member of such person's immediate family or a third party with whom such person is acquainted, and the actor was previously clearly informed to cease that conduct; or

3. is likely to cause such person to reasonably fear that his or her employment, business or career is threatened, where such conduct consists of appearing, telephoning or initiating communication or contact at such person's place of employment or business, and the actor was previously clearly informed to cease that conduct. For the purposes of subdivision two of this section, "following" shall include the unauthorized tracking of such person's movements or location through the use of a global positioning system or other device. Stalking in the fourth degree is a class B misdemeanor.

N.Y. Penal Law § 120.45

Amended by New York Laws 2014, ch. 184,Sec. 1, eff. 10/21/2014.

Section 120.50 - Stalking in the third degree

A person is guilty of stalking in the third degree when he or she:

1. Commits the crime of stalking in the fourth degree in violation of section 120.45 of this article against three or more persons, in three or more separate transactions, for which the actor has not been previously convicted; or

2. Commits the crime of stalking in the fourth degree in violation of section 120.45 of this article against any person, and has previously been convicted, within the preceding ten years of a specified predicate crime, as defined in subdivision five of section 120.40 of this article, and the victim of such specified predicate crime is the victim, or an immediate family member of the victim, of the present offense; or

3. With intent to harass, annoy or alarm a specific person, intentionally engages in a course of conduct directed at such person which is likely to cause such person to reasonably fear physical injury or serious physical injury, the commission of a sex offense against, or the kidnapping, unlawful imprisonment or death of such person or a member of such person's immediate family; or

4. Commits the crime of stalking in the fourth degree and has previously been convicted within the preceding ten years of stalking in the fourth degree.

Stalking in the third degree is a class A misdemeanor.

N.Y. Penal Law § 120.50

Section 120.55 - Stalking in the second degree

A person is guilty of stalking in the second degree when he or she:

1. Commits the crime of stalking in the third degree as defined in subdivision three of section 120.50 of this article and in the course of and in furtherance of the commission of such offense:

(i) displays, or possesses and threatens the use of, a firearm, pistol, revolver, rifle, shotgun, machine gun, electronic dart gun, electronic stun gun, cane sword, billy, blackjack, bludgeon, plastic knuckles, metal knuckles, chuka stick, sand bag, sandclub, slingshot, slungshot, shirken, "Kung Fu Star", dagger, dangerous knife, dirk, razor, stiletto, imitation pistol, dangerous instrument, deadly instrument or deadly weapon; or (ii) displays what appears to be a pistol, revolver, rifle, shotgun, machine gun or other firearm; or

2. Commits the crime of stalking in the third degree in violation of subdivision three of section 120.50 of this article against any person, and has previously been convicted, within the preceding five years, of a specified predicate crime as defined in subdivision five of section 120.40 of this article, and the victim of such specified predicate crime is the victim, or an immediate family member of the victim, of the present offense; or

3. Commits the crime of stalking in the fourth degree and has previously been convicted of stalking in the third degree as defined in subdivision four of section 120.50 of this article against any person; or

4. Being twenty-one years of age or older, repeatedly follows a person under the age of fourteen or engages in a course of conduct or repeatedly commits acts over a period of time intentionally placing or attempting to place such person who is under the age of fourteen in reasonable fear of physical injury, serious physical injury or death; or

5. Commits the crime of stalking in the third degree, as defined in subdivision three of section 120.50 of this article, against ten or more persons, in ten or more separate transactions, for which the actor has not been previously convicted.

Stalking in the second degree is a class E felony.

N.Y. Penal Law § 120.55

Section 120.60 - Stalking in the first degree

A person is guilty of stalking in the first degree when he or she commits the crime of stalking in the third degree as defined in subdivision three of section 120.50 or stalking in the second degree as defined in section 120.55 of this article and, in the course and furtherance thereof, he or she:

1. intentionally or recklessly causes physical injury to the victim of such crime; or

2. commits a class A misdemeanor defined in article one hundred thirty of this chapter, or a class E felony defined in section 130.25, 130.40 or 130.85 of this chapter, or a class D felony defined in section 130.30 or 130.45 of this chapter.

Stalking in the first degree is a class D felony.

N.Y. Penal Law § 120.60

Section 120.70 - Luring a child

1. A person is guilty of luring a child when he or she lures a child into a motor vehicle, aircraft, watercraft, isolated area, building, or part thereof, for the purpose of committing against such child any of the following offenses: an offense as defined in section 70.02 of this chapter; an offense as defined in section 125.25 or 125.27 of this chapter; a felony offense that is a violation of article one hundred thirty of this chapter; an offense as defined in section 135.25 of this chapter; an offense as defined in sections 230.30, 230.33 , 230.34 or 230.34-a of this chapter; an offense as defined in sections 255.25, 255.26, or 255.27 of this chapter; or an offense as defined in sections 263.05, 263.10, or 263.15 of this chapter. For purposes of this subdivision "child" means a person less than seventeen years of age. Nothing in this section shall be deemed to preclude, if the evidence warrants, a conviction for the commission or attempted commission of any crime, including but not limited to a crime defined in article one hundred thirty-five of this chapter.

2. Luring a child is a class E felony, provided, however, that if the underlying offense the actor intended to commit against such child constituted a class A or a class B felony, then the offense of luring a child in violation of this section shall be deemed respectively, a class C felony or class D felony.

N.Y. Penal Law § 120.70

Amended by New York Laws 2018, ch. 189,Sec. 6, eff. 11/13/2018.

Article 121 - STRANGULATION AND RELATED OFFENSES

Section 121.11 - Criminal obstruction of breathing or blood circulation

A person is guilty of criminal obstruction of breathing or blood circulation when, with intent to impede the normal breathing or circulation of the blood of another person, he or she:

a. applies pressure on the throat or neck of such person; or b. blocks the nose or mouth of such person.

Criminal obstruction of breathing or blood circulation is a class A misdemeanor.

N.Y. Penal Law § 121.11

Section 121.12 - Strangulation in the second degree
A person is guilty of strangulation in the second degree when he or she commits the crime of criminal obstruction of breathing or blood circulation, as defined in section 121.11 of this article, and thereby causes stupor, loss of consciousness for any period of time, or any other physical injury or impairment.
N.Y. Penal Law § 121.12
Section 121.13 - Strangulation in the first degree
A person is guilty of strangulation in the first degree when he or she commits the crime of criminal obstruction of breathing or blood circulation, as defined in section 121.11 of this article, and thereby causes serious physical injury to such other person.
N.Y. Penal Law § 121.13
Section 121.13-A - Aggravated strangulation
Aggravated strangulation. A person is guilty of aggravated strangulation when, being a police officer as defined in subdivision thirty-four of section 1.20 of the criminal procedure law or a peace officer as defined in section 2.10 of the criminal procedure law, he or she commits the crime of criminal obstruction of breathing or blood circulation, as defined in section 121.11 of this article, or uses a chokehold or similar restraint, as described in paragraph b of subdivision one of section eight hundred thirty-seven-t of the executive law, and thereby causes serious physical injury or death to another person. Aggravated strangulation is a class C felony.
N.Y. Penal Law § 121.13-A
Added by New York Laws 2020, ch. 94,Sec. 2, eff. 6/12/2020.
Section 121.14 - Medical or dental purpose
For purposes of section 121.11, 121.12 , 121.13 or 121.13-a of this article, it shall be an affirmative defense that the defendant performed such conduct for a valid medical or dental purpose.
N.Y. Penal Law § 121.14
Amended by New York Laws 2020, ch. 94,Sec. 3, eff. 6/12/2020.

Article 125 - HOMICIDE AND RELATED OFFENSES

Section 125.00 - Homicide defined
Homicide means conduct which causes the death of a person under circumstances constituting murder, manslaughter in the first degree, manslaughter in the second degree, or criminally negligent homicide.
N.Y. Penal Law § 125.00
Amended by New York Laws 2019, ch. 1,Sec. 6, eff. 1/22/2019.
Section 125.05 - Homicide and related offenses; definition
The following definition is applicable to this article:
2. [Repealed]
3. [Repealed]
N.Y. Penal Law § 125.05
Amended by New York Laws 2019, ch. 1,Sec. 7a, eff. 1/22/2019.
Amended by New York Laws 2019, ch. 1,Sec. 7, eff. 1/22/2019.
Section 125.10 - Criminally negligent homicide
A person is guilty of criminally negligent homicide when, with criminal negligence, he causes the death of another person.
N.Y. Penal Law § 125.10
Section 125.11 - Aggravated criminally negligent homicide
A person is guilty of aggravated criminally negligent homicide when, with criminal negligence, he or she causes the death of a police officer or peace officer where such officer was in the course of performing his or her official duties and the defendant knew or reasonably should have known that such victim was a police officer or peace officer.
N.Y. Penal Law § 125.11
Section 125.12 - Vehicular manslaughter in the second degree
A person is guilty of vehicular manslaughter in the second degree when he or she causes the death of another person, and either:
(1) operates a motor vehicle in violation of subdivision two, three, four or four-a of section eleven hundred ninety-two of the vehicle and traffic law or operates a vessel or public vessel in violation of paragraph (b), (c), (d) or (e) of subdivision two of section forty-nine-a of the navigation law, and as a result of such intoxication or impairment by the use of a drug, or by the combined influence of drugs or of alcohol and any drug or drugs, operates such motor vehicle, vessel or public vessel in a manner that causes the death of such other person, or
(2) operates a motor vehicle with a gross vehicle weight rating of more than eighteen thousand pounds which contains flammable gas, radioactive materials or explosives in violation of subdivision one of section eleven hundred ninety-two of the vehicle and traffic law, and such flammable gas, radioactive materials or explosives is the cause of such death, and as a result of such impairment by the use of alcohol, operates such motor vehicle in a manner that causes the death of such other person, or
(3) operates a snowmobile in violation of paragraph (b), (c) or (d) of subdivision one of section 25.24 of the parks, recreation and historic preservation law or operates an all terrain vehicle as defined in paragraph (a) of subdivision one of section twenty-two hundred eighty-one of the vehicle and traffic law in violation of subdivision two, three, four, or four-a of section eleven hundred ninety-two of the vehicle and traffic law, and as a result of such intoxication or impairment by

the use of a drug, or by the combined influence of drugs or of alcohol and any drug or drugs, operates such snowmobile or all terrain vehicle in a manner that causes the death of such other person.

If it is established that the person operating such motor vehicle, vessel, public vessel, snowmobile or all terrain vehicle caused such death while unlawfully intoxicated or impaired by the use of alcohol or a drug, then there shall be a rebuttable presumption that, as a result of such intoxication or impairment by the use of alcohol or a drug, or by the combined influence of drugs or of alcohol and any drug or drugs, such person operated the motor vehicle, vessel, public vessel, snowmobile or all terrain vehicle in a manner that caused such death, as required by this section.

Vehicular manslaughter in the second degree is a class D felony.

N.Y. Penal Law § 125.12

Section 125.13 - Vehicular manslaughter in the first degree

A person is guilty of vehicular manslaughter in the first degree when he or she commits the crime of vehicular manslaughter in the second degree as defined in section 125.12 of this article, and either:

(1) commits such crime while operating a motor vehicle while such person has .18 of one per centum or more by weight of alcohol in such person's blood as shown by chemical analysis of such person's blood, breath, urine or saliva made pursuant to the provisions of section eleven hundred ninety-four of the vehicle and traffic law;

(2) commits such crime while knowing or having reason to know that: (a) his or her license or his or her privilege of operating a motor vehicle in another state or his or her privilege of obtaining a license to operate a motor vehicle in another state is suspended or revoked and such suspension or revocation is based upon a conviction in such other state for an offense which would, if committed in this state, constitute a violation of any of the provisions of section eleven hundred ninety-two of the vehicle and traffic law; or (b) his or her license or his or her privilege of operating a motor vehicle in the state or his or her privilege of obtaining a license issued by the commissioner of motor vehicles is suspended or revoked and such suspension or revocation is based upon either a refusal to submit to a chemical test pursuant to section eleven hundred ninety-four of the vehicle and traffic law or following a conviction for a violation of any of the provisions of section eleven hundred ninety-two of the vehicle and traffic law;

(3) has previously been convicted of violating any of the provisions of section eleven hundred ninety-two of the vehicle and traffic law within the preceding ten years, provided that, for the purposes of this subdivision, a conviction in any other state or jurisdiction for an offense which, if committed in this state, would constitute a violation of section eleven hundred ninety-two of the vehicle and traffic law, shall be treated as a violation of such law;

(4) causes the death of more than one other person;

(5) has previously been convicted of violating any provision of this article or article one hundred twenty of this title involving the operation of a motor vehicle, or was convicted in any other state or jurisdiction of an offense involving the operation of a motor vehicle which, if committed in this state, would constitute a violation of this article or article one hundred twenty of this title; or

(6) commits such crime while operating a motor vehicle while a child who is fifteen years of age or less is a passenger in such motor vehicle and causes the death of such child.

If it is established that the person operating such motor vehicle caused such death or deaths while unlawfully intoxicated or impaired by the use of alcohol or a drug, or by the combined influence of drugs or of alcohol and any drug or drugs, then there shall be a rebuttable presumption that, as a result of such intoxication or impairment by the use of alcohol or a drug, or by the combined influence of drugs or of alcohol and any drug or drugs, such person operated the motor vehicle in a manner that caused such death or deaths, as required by this section and section 125.12 of this article.

N.Y. Penal Law § 125.13

Section 125.14 - Aggravated vehicular homicide

A person is guilty of aggravated vehicular homicide when he or she engages in reckless driving as defined by section twelve hundred twelve of the vehicle and traffic law, and commits the crime of vehicular manslaughter in the second degree as defined in section 125.12 of this article, and either:

(1) commits such crimes while operating a motor vehicle while such person has .18 of one per centum or more by weight of alcohol in such person's blood as shown by chemical analysis of such person's blood, breath, urine or saliva made pursuant to the provisions of section eleven hundred ninety-four of the vehicle and traffic law;

(2) commits such crimes while knowing or having reason to know that: (a) his or her license or his or her privilege of operating a motor vehicle in another state or his or her privilege of obtaining a license to operate a motor vehicle in another state is suspended or revoked and such suspension or revocation is based upon a conviction in such other state for an offense which would, if committed in this state, constitute a violation of any of the provisions of section eleven hundred ninety-two of the vehicle and traffic law; or (b) his or her license or his or her privilege of operating a motor vehicle in this state or his or her privilege of obtaining a license issued by the commissioner of motor vehicles is suspended or revoked and such suspension or revocation is based upon either a refusal to submit to a chemical test pursuant to section eleven hundred ninety-four of the vehicle and traffic law or following a conviction for a violation of any of the provisions of section eleven hundred ninety-two of the vehicle and traffic law;

(3) has previously been convicted of violating any of the provisions of section eleven hundred ninety-two of the vehicle and traffic law within the preceding ten years, provided that, for the purposes of this subdivision, a conviction in any other state or jurisdiction for an offense which, if committed in this state, would constitute a violation of section eleven hundred ninety-two of the vehicle and traffic law, shall be treated as a violation of such law;

(4) causes the death of more than one other person;

(5) causes the death of one person and the serious physical injury of at least one other person;

(6) has previously been convicted of violating any provision of this article or article one hundred twenty of this title involving the operation of a motor vehicle, or was convicted in any other state or jurisdiction of an offense involving the operation of a motor vehicle which, if committed in this state, would constitute a violation of this article or article one hundred twenty of this title; or

(7) commits such crime while operating a motor vehicle while a child who is fifteen years of age or less is a passenger in such motor vehicle and causes the death of such child.

If it is established that the person operating such motor vehicle caused such death or deaths while unlawfully intoxicated or impaired by the use of alcohol or a drug, or by the combined influence of drugs or of alcohol and any drug or drugs, then there shall be a rebuttable presumption that, as a result of such intoxication or impairment by the use of alcohol or a drug, or by the combined influence of drugs or of alcohol and any drug or drugs, such person operated the motor vehicle in a manner that caused such death or deaths, as required by this section and section 125.12 of this article.

Aggravated vehicular homicide is a class B felony.

N.Y. Penal Law § 125.14

Section 125.15 - Manslaughter in the second degree

A person is guilty of manslaughter in the second degree when:

1. He recklessly causes the death of another person; or

2. [Repealed]

3. He intentionally causes or aids another person to commit suicide.

Manslaughter in the second degree is a class C felony.

N.Y. Penal Law § 125.15

Amended by New York Laws 2019, ch. 1,Sec. 8, eff. 1/22/2019.

Section 125.20 - Manslaughter in the first degree

A person is guilty of manslaughter in the first degree when:

1. With intent to cause serious physical injury to another person, he causes the death of such person or of a third person; or

2. With intent to cause the death of another person, he causes the death of such person or of a third person under circumstances which do not constitute murder because he acts under the influence of extreme emotional disturbance, as defined in paragraph (a) of subdivision one of section 125.25. The fact that homicide was committed under the influence of extreme emotional disturbance constitutes a mitigating circumstance reducing murder to manslaughter in the first degree and need not be proved in any prosecution initiated under this subdivision; or

3. [Repealed]

4. Being eighteen years old or more and with intent to cause physical injury to a person less than eleven years old, the defendant recklessly engages in conduct which creates a grave risk of serious physical injury to such person and thereby causes the death of such person.

Manslaughter in the first degree is a class B felony.

N.Y. Penal Law § 125.20

Amended by New York Laws 2019, ch. 1,Sec. 9, eff. 1/22/2019.

Section 125.21 - Aggravated manslaughter in the second degree

A person is guilty of aggravated manslaughter in the second degree when he or she recklessly causes the death of a police officer or peace officer where such officer was in the course of performing his or her official duties and the defendant knew or reasonably should have known that such victim was a police officer or peace officer.

N.Y. Penal Law § 125.21

Section 125.22 - Aggravated manslaughter in the first degree

A person is guilty of aggravated manslaughter in the first degree when:

1. with intent to cause serious physical injury to a police officer or peace officer, where such officer was in the course of performing his or her official duties and the defendant knew or reasonably should have known that such victim was a police officer or a peace officer, he or she causes the death of such officer or another police officer or peace officer; or

2. with intent to cause the death of a police officer or peace officer, where such officer was in the course of performing his or her official duties and the defendant knew or reasonably should have known that such victim was a police officer or peace officer, he or she causes the death of such officer or another police officer or peace officer under circumstances which do not constitute murder because he or she acts under the influence of extreme emotional disturbance, as defined in paragraph (a) of subdivision one of section 125.25. The fact that homicide was committed under the influence of extreme emotional disturbance constitutes a mitigating circumstance reducing murder to aggravated manslaughter in the first degree or manslaughter in the first degree and need not be proved in any prosecution initiated under this subdivision.

Aggravated manslaughter in the first degree is a class B felony.

N.Y. Penal Law § 125.22

Section 125.25 - Murder in the second degree

A person is guilty of murder in the second degree when:

1. With intent to cause the death of another person, he causes the death of such person or of a third person; except that in any prosecution under this subdivision, it is an affirmative defense that:

(a)

(i) The defendant acted under the influence of extreme emotional disturbance for which there was a reasonable explanation or excuse, the reasonableness of which is to be determined from the viewpoint of a person in the defendant's situation

72

under the circumstances as the defendant believed them to be. Nothing contained in this paragraph shall constitute a defense to a prosecution for, or preclude a conviction of, manslaughter in the first degree or any other crime.

(ii) It shall not be a "reasonable explanation or excuse" pursuant to subparagraph (i) of this paragraph when the defendant's conduct resulted from the discovery, knowledge or disclosure of the victim's sexual orientation, sex, gender, gender identity, gender expression or sex assigned at birth; or

(b) The defendant's conduct consisted of causing or aiding, without the use of duress or deception, another person to commit suicide. Nothing contained in this paragraph shall constitute a defense to a prosecution for, or preclude a conviction of, manslaughter in the second degree or any other crime; or

2. Under circumstances evincing a depraved indifference to human life, he recklessly engages in conduct which creates a grave risk of death to another person, and thereby causes the death of another person; or

3. Acting either alone or with one or more other persons, he commits or attempts to commit robbery, burglary, kidnapping, arson, rape in the first degree, criminal sexual act in the first degree, sexual abuse in the first degree, aggravated sexual abuse, escape in the first degree, or escape in the second degree, and, in the course of and in furtherance of such crime or of immediate flight therefrom, he, or another participant, if there be any, causes the death of a person other than one of the participants; except that in any prosecution under this subdivision, in which the defendant was not the only participant in the underlying crime, it is an affirmative defense that the defendant:

(a) Did not commit the homicidal act or in any way solicit, request, command, importune, cause or aid the commission thereof; and

(b) Was not armed with a deadly weapon, or any instrument, article or substance readily capable of causing death or serious physical injury and of a sort not ordinarily carried in public places by law-abiding persons; and

(c) Had no reasonable ground to believe that any other participant was armed with such a weapon, instrument, article or substance; and

(d) Had no reasonable ground to believe that any other participant intended to engage in conduct likely to result in death or serious physical injury; or

4. Under circumstances evincing a depraved indifference to human life, and being eighteen years old or more the defendant recklessly engages in conduct which creates a grave risk of serious physical injury or death to another person less than eleven years old and thereby causes the death of such person; or

5. Being eighteen years old or more, while in the course of committing rape in the first, second or third degree, criminal sexual act in the first, second or third degree, sexual abuse in the first degree, aggravated sexual abuse in the first, second, third or fourth degree, or incest in the first, second or third degree, against a person less than fourteen years old, he or she intentionally causes the death of such person.

Murder in the second degree is a class A-I felony.

N.Y. Penal Law § 125.25

Amended by New York Laws 2019, ch. 45,Sec. 1, eff. 6/30/2019.

Section 125.26 - Aggravated murder

A person is guilty of aggravated murder when:

1. With intent to cause the death of another person, he or she causes the death of such person, or of a third person who was a person described in subparagraph (i), (ii), (ii-a) or (iii) of paragraph (a) of this subdivision engaged at the time of the killing in the course of performing his or her official duties; and

(a) Either:

(i) the intended victim was a police officer as defined in subdivision thirty-four of section 1.20 of the criminal procedure law who was at the time of the killing engaged in the course of performing his or her official duties, and the defendant knew or reasonably should have known that the victim was a police officer; or

(ii) the intended victim was a peace officer as defined in paragraph a of subdivision twenty-one, subdivision twenty-three, twenty-four or sixty-two (employees of the division for youth) of section 2.10 of the criminal procedure law who was at the time of the killing engaged in the course of performing his or her official duties, and the defendant knew or reasonably should have known that the victim was such a uniformed court officer, parole officer, probation officer, or employee of the division for youth; or

(ii-a)the intended victim was a firefighter, emergency medical technician, ambulance driver, paramedic, physician or registered nurse involved in a first response team, or any other individual who, in the course of official duties, performs emergency response activities and was engaged in such activities at the time of killing and the defendant knew or reasonably should have known that the intended victim was such firefighter, emergency medical technician, ambulance driver, paramedic, physician or registered nurse; or

(iii) the intended victim was an employee of a state correctional institution or was an employee of a local correctional facility as defined in subdivision two of section forty of the correction law, who was at the time of the killing engaged in the course of performing his or her official duties, and the defendant knew or reasonably should have known that the victim was an employee of a state correctional institution or a local correctional facility; and

(b) The defendant was more than eighteen years old at the time of the commission of the crime; or

2.

(a) With intent to cause the death of a person less than fourteen years old, he or she causes the death of such person, and the defendant acted in an especially cruel and wanton manner pursuant to a course of conduct intended to inflict and inflicting torture upon the victim prior to the victim's death. As used in this subdivision, "torture" means the intentional and depraved infliction of extreme physical pain that is separate and apart from the pain which otherwise would have been associated with such cause of death; and

(b) The defendant was more than eighteen years old at the time of the commission of the crime.

3. In any prosecution under subdivision one or two of this section, it is an affirmative defense that:

(a)

(i) The defendant acted under the influence of extreme emotional disturbance for which there was a reasonable explanation or excuse, the reasonableness of which is to be determined from the viewpoint of a person in the defendant's situation under the circumstances as the defendant believed them to be. Nothing contained in this paragraph shall constitute a defense to a prosecution for, or preclude a conviction of, aggravated manslaughter in the first degree, manslaughter in the first degree or any other crime except murder in the second degree.

(ii) It shall not be a "reasonable explanation or excuse" pursuant to subparagraph (i) of this paragraph when the defendant's conduct resulted from the discovery, knowledge or disclosure of the victim's sexual orientation, sex, gender, gender identity, gender expression or sex assigned at birth; or

(b) The defendant's conduct consisted of causing or aiding, without the use of duress or deception, another person to commit suicide. Nothing contained in this paragraph shall constitute a defense to a prosecution for, or preclude a conviction of, aggravated manslaughter in the second degree, manslaughter in the second degree or any other crime except murder in the second degree.

Aggravated murder is a class A-I felony.

N.Y. Penal Law § 125.26

Amended by New York Laws 2019, ch. 45,Sec. 2, eff. 6/30/2019.

Amended by New York Laws 2013, ch. 1,Sec. 35, eff. 3/16/2013.

Amended by New York Laws 2013, ch. 1,Sec. 34, eff. 3/16/2013.

See New York Laws 2013, ch. 1, Sec. 33.

Section 125.27 - Murder in the first degree

A person is guilty of murder in the first degree when:

1. With intent to cause the death of another person, he causes the death of such person or of a third person; and

(a) Either:

(i) the intended victim was a police officer as defined in subdivision 34 of section 1.20 of the criminal procedure law who was at the time of the killing engaged in the course of performing his official duties, and the defendant knew or reasonably should have known that the intended victim was a police officer; or

(ii) the intended victim was a peace officer as defined in paragraph a of subdivision twenty-one, subdivision twenty-three, twenty-four or sixty-two (employees of the division for youth) of section 2.10 of the criminal procedure law who was at the time of the killing engaged in the course of performing his official duties, and the defendant knew or reasonably should have known that the intended victim was such a uniformed court officer, parole officer, probation officer, or employee of the division for youth; or

(ii-a)the intended victim was a firefighter, emergency medical technician, ambulance driver, paramedic, physician or registered nurse involved in a first response team, or any other individual who, in the course of official duties, performs emergency response activities and was engaged in such activities at the time of killing and the defendant knew or reasonably should have known that the intended victim was such firefighter, emergency medical technician, ambulance driver, paramedic, physician or registered nurse; or

(iii) the intended victim was an employee of a state correctional institution or was an employee of a local correctional facility as defined in subdivision two of section forty of the correction law, who was at the time of the killing engaged in the course of performing his official duties, and the defendant knew or reasonably should have known that the intended victim was an employee of a state correctional institution or a local correctional facility; or

(iv) at the time of the commission of the killing, the defendant was confined in a state correctional institution or was otherwise in custody upon a sentence for the term of his natural life, or upon a sentence commuted to one of natural life, or upon a sentence for an indeterminate term the minimum of which was at least fifteen years and the maximum of which was natural life, or at the time of the commission of the killing, the defendant had escaped from such confinement or custody while serving such a sentence and had not yet been returned to such confinement or custody; or

(v) the intended victim was a witness to a crime committed on a prior occasion and the death was caused for the purpose of preventing the intended victim's testimony in any criminal action or proceeding whether or not such action or proceeding had been commenced, or the intended victim had previously testified in a criminal action or proceeding and the killing was committed for the purpose of exacting retribution for such prior testimony, or the intended victim was an immediate family member of a witness to a crime committed on a prior occasion and the killing was committed for the purpose of preventing or influencing the testimony of such witness, or the intended victim was an immediate family member of a witness who had previously testified in a criminal action or proceeding and the killing was committed for the purpose of exacting retribution upon such witness for such prior testimony. As used in this subparagraph "immediate family member" means a husband, wife, father, mother, daughter, son, brother, sister, stepparent, grandparent, stepchild or grandchild; or

(vi) the defendant committed the killing or procured commission of the killing pursuant to an agreement with a person other than the intended victim to commit the same for the receipt, or in expectation of the receipt, of anything of pecuniary value from a party to the agreement or from a person other than the intended victim acting at the direction of a party to such agreement; or

(vii) the victim was killed while the defendant was in the course of committing or attempting to commit and in furtherance of robbery, burglary in the first degree or second degree, kidnapping in the first degree, arson in the first degree or second degree, rape in the first degree, criminal sexual act in the first degree, sexual abuse in the first degree, aggravated sexual abuse in the first degree or escape in the first degree, or in the course of and furtherance of immediate flight after committing or attempting to commit any such crime or in the course of and furtherance of immediate flight after attempting to commit the crime of murder in the second degree; provided however, the victim is not a participant in one of the aforementioned crimes and, provided further that, unless the defendant's criminal liability under this subparagraph is based upon the defendant having commanded another person to cause the death of the victim or intended victim pursuant to section 20.00 of this chapter, this subparagraph shall not apply where the defendant's criminal liability is based upon the conduct of another pursuant to section 20.00 of this chapter; or

(viii) as part of the same criminal transaction, the defendant, with intent to cause serious physical injury to or the death of an additional person or persons, causes the death of an additional person or persons; provided, however, the victim is not a participant in the criminal transaction; or

(ix) prior to committing the killing, the defendant had been convicted of murder as defined in this section or section 125.25 of this article, or had been convicted in another jurisdiction of an offense which, if committed in this state, would constitute a violation of either of such sections; or

(x) the defendant acted in an especially cruel and wanton manner pursuant to a course of conduct intended to inflict and inflicting torture upon the victim prior to the victim's death. As used in this subparagraph, "torture" means the intentional and depraved infliction of extreme physical pain; "depraved" means the defendant relished the infliction of extreme physical pain upon the victim evidencing debasement or perversion or that the defendant evidenced a sense of pleasure in the infliction of extreme physical pain; or

(xi) the defendant intentionally caused the death of two or more additional persons within the state in separate criminal transactions within a period of twenty-four months when committed in a similar fashion or pursuant to a common scheme or plan; or

(xii) the intended victim was a judge as defined in subdivision twenty-three of section 1.20 of the criminal procedure law and the defendant killed such victim because such victim was, at the time of the killing, a judge; or

(xiii) the victim was killed in furtherance of an act of terrorism, as defined in paragraph (b) of subdivision one of section 490.05 of this chapter; and

(b) The defendant was more than eighteen years old at the time of the commission of the crime.

2. In any prosecution under subdivision one, it is an affirmative defense that:

(a)

(i) The defendant acted under the influence of extreme emotional disturbance for which there was a reasonable explanation or excuse, the reasonableness of which is to be determined from the viewpoint of a person in the defendant's situation under the circumstances as the defendant believed them to be. Nothing contained in this paragraph shall constitute a defense to a prosecution for, or preclude a conviction of, manslaughter in the first degree or any other crime except murder in the second degree.

(ii) It shall not be a "reasonable explanation or excuse" pursuant to subparagraph (i) of this paragraph when the defendant's conduct resulted from the discovery, knowledge or disclosure of the victim's sexual orientation, sex, gender, gender identity, gender expression or sex assigned at birth; or

(b) The defendant's conduct consisted of causing or aiding, without the use of duress or deception, another person to commit suicide. Nothing contained in this paragraph shall constitute a defense to a prosecution for, or preclude a conviction of, manslaughter in the second degree or any other crime except murder in the second degree.

Murder in the first degree is a class A-I felony.

N.Y. Penal Law § 125.27

Amended by New York Laws 2019, ch. 45,Sec. 3, eff. 6/30/2019.

Amended by New York Laws 2013, ch. 1,Sec. 36, eff. 3/16/2013.

See New York Laws 2013, ch. 1, Sec. 33.

Section 125.40 - [Repealed]

N.Y. Penal Law § 125.40

Repealed by New York Laws 2019, ch. 1,Sec. 5, eff. 1/22/2019.

Section 125.45 - [Repealed]

N.Y. Penal Law § 125.45

Repealed by New York Laws 2019, ch. 1,Sec. 5, eff. 1/22/2019.

Section 125.50 - [Repealed]

N.Y. Penal Law § 125.50

Repealed by New York Laws 2019, ch. 1,Sec. 5, eff. 1/22/2019.

Section 125.55 - [Repealed]

N.Y. Penal Law § 125.55

Repealed by New York Laws 2019, ch. 1,Sec. 5, eff. 1/22/2019.

Section 125.60 - [Repealed]

N.Y. Penal Law § 125.60

Repealed by New York Laws 2019, ch. 1,Sec. 5, eff. 1/22/2019.

Article 130 - SEX OFFENSES

Section 130.00 - Sex offenses; definitions of terms

The following definitions are applicable to this article:

1. "Sexual intercourse" has its ordinary meaning and occurs upon any penetration, however slight.

2.

(a) "Oral sexual conduct" means conduct between persons consisting of contact between the mouth and the penis, the mouth and the anus, or the mouth and the vulva or vagina.

(b) "Anal sexual conduct" means conduct between persons consisting of contact between the penis and anus.

3. "Sexual contact" means any touching of the sexual or other intimate parts of a person for the purpose of gratifying sexual desire of either party. It includes the touching of the actor by the victim, as well as the touching of the victim by the actor, whether directly or through clothing, as well as the emission of ejaculate by the actor upon any part of the victim, clothed or unclothed.

4. For the purposes of this article "married" means the existence of the relationship between the actor and the victim as spouses which is recognized by law at the time the actor commits an offense proscribed by this article against the victim.

5. "Mentally disabled" means that a person suffers from a mental disease or defect which renders him or her incapable of appraising the nature of his or her conduct.

6. "Mentally incapacitated" means that a person is rendered temporarily incapable of appraising or controlling his conduct owing to the influence of a narcotic or intoxicating substance administered to him without his consent, or to any other act committed upon him without his consent.

7. "Physically helpless" means that a person is unconscious or for any other reason is physically unable to communicate unwillingness to an act.

8. "Forcible compulsion" means to compel by either:

a. use of physical force; or

b.a threat, express or implied, which places a person in fear of immediate death or physical injury to himself, herself or another person, or in fear that he, she or another person will immediately be kidnapped.

9. "Foreign object" means any instrument or article which, when inserted in the vagina, urethra, penis, rectum or anus, is capable of causing physical injury.

10. "Sexual conduct" means sexual intercourse, oral sexual conduct, anal sexual conduct, aggravated sexual contact, or sexual contact.

11. "Aggravated sexual contact" means inserting, other than for a valid medical purpose, a foreign object in the vagina, urethra, penis, rectum or anus of a child, thereby causing physical injury to such child.

12. "Health care provider" means any person who is, or is required to be, licensed or registered or holds himself or herself out to be licensed or registered, or provides services as if he or she were licensed or registered in the profession of medicine, chiropractic, dentistry or podiatry under any of the following: article one hundred thirty-one, one hundred thirty-two, one hundred thirty-three, or one hundred forty-one of the education law.

13. "Mental health care provider" shall mean a licensed physician, licensed psychologist, registered professional nurse, licensed clinical social worker or a licensed master social worker under the supervision of a physician, psychologist or licensed clinical social worker.

N.Y. Penal Law § 130.00

Section 130.05 - Sex offenses; lack of consent

1. Whether or not specifically stated, it is an element of every offense defined in this article that the sexual act was committed without consent of the victim.

2. Lack of consent results from:

(a) Forcible compulsion; or

(b) Incapacity to consent; or

(c) Where the offense charged is sexual abuse or forcible touching, any circumstances, in addition to forcible compulsion or incapacity to consent, in which the victim does not expressly or impliedly acquiesce in the actor's conduct; or

(d) Where the offense charged is rape in the third degree as defined in subdivision three of section 130.25, or criminal sexual act in the third degree as defined in subdivision three of section 130.40, in addition to forcible compulsion, circumstances under which, at the time of the act of intercourse, oral sexual conduct or anal sexual conduct, the victim clearly expressed that he or she did not consent to engage in such act, and a reasonable person in the actor's situation would have understood such person's words and acts as an expression of lack of consent to such act under all the circumstances.

3. A person is deemed incapable of consent when he or she is:

(a) less than seventeen years old; or

(b) mentally disabled; or

(c) mentally incapacitated; or

(d) physically helpless; or

(e) committed to the care and custody or supervision of the state department of corrections and community supervision or a hospital, as such term is defined in subdivision two of section four hundred of the correction law, and the actor is an employee who knows or reasonably should know that such person is committed to the care and custody or supervision of such department or hospital. For purposes of this paragraph, "employee" means

(i) an employee of the state department of corrections and community supervision who, as part of his or her employment, performs duties:

(A) in a state correctional facility in which the victim is confined at the time of the offense consisting of providing custody, medical or mental health services, counseling services, educational programs, vocational training, institutional parole services or direct supervision to incarcerated individuals; or

(B) of supervising persons released on community supervision and supervises the victim at the time of the offense or has supervised the victim and the victim is still under community supervision at the time of the offense; or

(ii) an employee of the office of mental health who, as part of his or her employment, performs duties in a state correctional facility or hospital, as such term is defined in subdivision two of section four hundred of the correction law in which the incarcerated individual is confined at the time of the offense, consisting of providing custody, medical or mental health services, or direct supervision to such incarcerated individuals; or

(iii) a person, including a volunteer, providing direct services to incarcerated individuals in a state correctional facility in which the victim is confined at the time of the offense pursuant to a contractual arrangement with the state department of corrections and community supervision or, in the case of a volunteer, a written agreement with such department, provided that the person received written notice concerning the provisions of this paragraph; or

(f) committed to the care and custody of a local correctional facility, as such term is defined in subdivision two of section forty of the correction law, and the actor is an employee, not married to such person, who knows or reasonably should know that such person is committed to the care and custody of such facility. For purposes of this paragraph, "employee" means an employee of the local correctional facility where the person is committed who performs professional duties consisting of providing custody, medical or mental health services, counseling services, educational services, or vocational training for incarcerated individuals. For purposes of this paragraph, "employee" shall also mean a person, including a volunteer or a government employee of the state department of corrections and community supervision or a local health, education or probation agency, providing direct services to incarcerated individuals in the local correctional facility in which the victim is confined at the time of the offense pursuant to a contractual arrangement with the local correctional department or, in the case of such a volunteer or government employee, a written agreement with such department, provided that such person received written notice concerning the provisions of this paragraph; or

(g) committed to or placed with the office of children and family services and in residential care, and the actor is an employee, not married to such person, who knows or reasonably should know that such person is committed to or placed with such office of children and family services and in residential care. For purposes of this paragraph, "employee" means an employee of the office of children and family services or of a residential facility in which such person is committed to or placed at the time of the offense who, as part of his or her employment, performs duties consisting of providing custody, medical or mental health services, counseling services, educational services, vocational training, or direct supervision to persons committed to or placed in a residential facility operated by the office of children and family services; or

(h) a client or patient and the actor is a health care provider or mental health care provider charged with rape in the third degree as defined in section 130.25, criminal sexual act in the third degree as defined in section 130.40, aggravated sexual abuse in the fourth degree as defined in section 130.65-a, or sexual abuse in the third degree as defined in section 130.55, and the act of sexual conduct occurs during a treatment session, consultation, interview, or examination; or

(i) a resident or inpatient of a residential facility operated, licensed or certified by (i) the office of mental health; (ii) the office for people with developmental disabilities; or (iii) the office of alcoholism and substance abuse services, and the actor is an employee of the facility not married to such resident or inpatient. For purposes of this paragraph, "employee" means either: an employee of the agency operating the residential facility, who knows or reasonably should know that such person is a resident or inpatient of such facility and who provides direct care services, case management services, medical or other clinical services, habilitative services or direct supervision of the residents in the facility in which the resident resides; or an officer or other employee, consultant, contractor or volunteer of the residential facility, who knows or reasonably should know that the person is a resident of such facility and who is in direct contact with residents or inpatients; provided, however, that the provisions of this paragraph shall only apply to a consultant, contractor or volunteer providing services pursuant to a contractual arrangement with the agency operating the residential facility or, in the case of a volunteer, a written agreement with such facility, provided that the person received written notice concerning the provisions of this paragraph; provided further, however, "employee" shall not include a person with a developmental disability who is or was receiving services and is also an employee of a service provider and who has sexual contact with another service recipient who is a consenting adult who has consented to such contact; or

(j) detained or otherwise in the custody of a police officer, peace officer, or other law enforcement official and the actor is a police officer, peace officer or other law enforcement official who either:

(i) is detaining or maintaining custody of such person; or

(ii) knows, or reasonably should know, that at the time of the offense, such person was detained or in custody.

N.Y. Penal Law § 130.05

Amended by New York Laws 2021, ch. 322,Sec. 105, eff. 8/2/2021.

Amended by New York Laws 2018, ch. 55,Sec. JJ-1, eff. 5/12/2018.

Amended by New York Laws 2012, ch. 501,Sec. G-2, eff. 1/16/2013.

Section 130.10 - Sex offenses; limitation; defenses

1. In any prosecution under this article in which the victim's lack of consent is based solely upon his or her incapacity to consent because he or she was mentally disabled, mentally incapacitated or physically helpless, it is an affirmative defense that the defendant, at the time he or she engaged in the conduct constituting the offense, did not know of the facts or conditions responsible for such incapacity to consent.

2. Conduct performed for a valid medical or mental health care purpose shall not constitute a violation of any section of this article in which incapacity to consent is based on the circumstances set forth in paragraph (h) of subdivision three of section 130.05 of this article.

3. In any prosecution for the crime of rape in the third degree as defined in section 130.25, criminal sexual act in the third degree as defined in section 130.40, aggravated sexual abuse in the fourth degree as defined in section 130.65-a, or sexual abuse in the third degree as defined in section 130.55 in which incapacity to consent is based on the circumstances set forth in paragraph (h) of subdivision three of section 130.05 of this article it shall be an affirmative defense that the client or patient consented to such conduct charged after having been expressly advised by the health care or mental health care provider that such conduct was not performed for a valid medical purpose.

4. In any prosecution under this article in which the victim's lack of consent is based solely on his or her incapacity to consent because he or she was less than seventeen years old, mentally disabled, a client or patient and the actor is a health care provider, detained or otherwise in custody of law enforcement under the circumstances described in paragraph (j) of subdivision three of section 130.05 of this article, or committed to the care and custody or supervision of the state department of corrections and community supervision or a hospital and the actor is an employee, it shall be a defense that the defendant was married to the victim as defined in subdivision four of section 130.00 of this article.

N.Y. Penal Law § 130.10

Amended by New York Laws 2018, ch. 55,Sec. JJ-2, eff. 5/12/2018.

Section 130.16 - Sex offenses; corroboration

A person shall not be convicted of any offense defined in this article of which lack of consent is an element but results solely from incapacity to consent because of the victim's mental defect, or mental incapacity, or an attempt to commit the same, solely on the testimony of the victim, unsupported by other evidence tending to:

(a) Establish that an attempt was made to engage the victim in sexual intercourse, oral sexual conduct, anal sexual conduct, or sexual contact, as the case may be, at the time of the occurrence; and

(b) Connect the defendant with the commission of the offense or attempted offense.

N.Y. Penal Law § 130.16

Section 130.20 - Sexual misconduct

A person is guilty of sexual misconduct when:

1. He or she engages in sexual intercourse with another person without such person's consent; or

2. He or she engages in oral sexual conduct or anal sexual conduct with another person without such person's consent; or

3. He or she engages in sexual conduct with an animal or a dead human body.

Sexual misconduct is a class A misdemeanor.

N.Y. Penal Law § 130.20

Section 130.25 - Rape in the third degree

A person is guilty of rape in the third degree when:

1. He or she engages in sexual intercourse with another person who is incapable of consent by reason of some factor other than being less than seventeen years old;

2. Being twenty-one years old or more, he or she engages in sexual intercourse with another person less than seventeen years old; or

3. He or she engages in sexual intercourse with another person without such person's consent where such lack of consent is by reason of some factor other than incapacity to consent.

Rape in the third degree is a class E felony.

N.Y. Penal Law § 130.25

Section 130.30 - Rape in the second degree

A person is guilty of rape in the second degree when:

1. being eighteen years old or more, he or she engages in sexual intercourse with another person less than fifteen years old; or

2. he or she engages in sexual intercourse with another person who is incapable of consent by reason of being mentally disabled or mentally incapacitated.

It shall be an affirmative defense to the crime of rape in the second degree as defined in subdivision one of this section that the defendant was less than four years older than the victim at the time of the act.

Rape in the second degree is a class D felony.

N.Y. Penal Law § 130.30

Section 130.35 - Rape in the first degree

A person is guilty of rape in the first degree when he or she engages in sexual intercourse with another person:

1. By forcible compulsion; or

2. Who is incapable of consent by reason of being physically helpless; or

3. Who is less than eleven years old; or

4. Who is less than thirteen years old and the actor is eighteen years old or more.

Rape in the first degree is a class B felony.

N.Y. Penal Law § 130.35

Section 130.40 - Criminal sexual act in the third degree

A person is guilty of criminal sexual act in the third degree when:

1. He or she engages in oral sexual conduct or anal sexual conduct with a person who is incapable of consent by reason of some factor other than being less than seventeen years old;

2. Being twenty-one years old or more, he or she engages in oral sexual conduct or anal sexual conduct with a person less than seventeen years old; or

3. He or she engages in oral sexual conduct or anal sexual conduct with another person without such person's consent where such lack of consent is by reason of some factor other than incapacity to consent.

Criminal sexual act in the third degree is a class E felony.

N.Y. Penal Law § 130.40

Section 130.45 - Criminal sexual act in the second degree

A person is guilty of criminal sexual act in the second degree when:

1. being eighteen years old or more, he or she engages in oral sexual conduct or anal sexual conduct with another person less than fifteen years old; or

2. he or she engages in oral sexual conduct or anal sexual conduct with another person who is incapable of consent by reason of being mentally disabled or mentally incapacitated.

It shall be an affirmative defense to the crime of criminal sexual act in the second degree as defined in subdivision one of this section that the defendant was less than four years older than the victim at the time of the act.

Criminal sexual act in the second degree is a class D felony.

N.Y. Penal Law § 130.45

Section 130.50 - Criminal sexual act in the first degree

A person is guilty of criminal sexual act in the first degree when he or she engages in oral sexual conduct or anal sexual conduct with another person:

1. By forcible compulsion; or

2. Who is incapable of consent by reason of being physically helpless; or

3. Who is less than eleven years old; or

4. Who is less than thirteen years old and the actor is eighteen years old or more.

Criminal sexual act in the first degree is a class B felony.

N.Y. Penal Law § 130.50

Section 130.52 - Forcible touching

A person is guilty of forcible touching when such person intentionally, and for no legitimate purpose:

1. forcibly touches the sexual or other intimate parts of another person for the purpose of degrading or abusing such person, or for the purpose of gratifying the actor's sexual desire; or

2. subjects another person to sexual contact for the purpose of gratifying the actor's sexual desire and with intent to degrade or abuse such other person while such other person is a passenger on a bus, train, or subway car operated by any transit agency, authority or company, public or private, whose operation is authorized by New York state or any of its political subdivisions.

N.Y. Penal Law § 130.52

Amended by New York Laws 2015, ch. 250,Sec. 1, eff. 11/1/2015.

Section 130.53 - Persistent sexual abuse

A person is guilty of persistent sexual abuse when he or she commits the crime of forcible touching, as defined in section 130.52 of this article, sexual abuse in the third degree, as defined in section 130.55 of this article, or sexual abuse in the second degree, as defined in section 130.60 of this article, and, within the previous ten year period, excluding any time during which such person was incarcerated for any reason, has been convicted two or more times, in separate criminal transactions for which sentence was imposed on separate occasions, of forcible touching, as defined in section 130.52 of this article, sexual abuse in the third degree as defined in section 130.55 of this article, sexual abuse in the second degree, as defined in section 130.60 of this article, or any offense defined in this article, of which the commission or attempted commission thereof is a felony.

N.Y. Penal Law § 130.53

Amended by New York Laws 2014, ch. 192,Sec. 1, eff. 11/1/2014.

Section 130.55 - Sexual abuse in the third degree

A person is guilty of sexual abuse in the third degree when he or she subjects another person to sexual contact without the latter's consent; except that in any prosecution under this section, it is an affirmative defense that (a) such other person's lack of consent was due solely to incapacity to consent by reason of being less than seventeen years old, and (b) such other person was more than fourteen years old, and (c) the defendant was less than five years older than such other person.

N.Y. Penal Law § 130.55

Section 130.60 - Sexual abuse in the second degree

A person is guilty of sexual abuse in the second degree when he or she subjects another person to sexual contact and when such other person is:

1. Incapable of consent by reason of some factor other than being less than seventeen years old; or

2. Less than fourteen years old.

Sexual abuse in the second degree is a class A misdemeanor.

N.Y. Penal Law § 130.60

Section 130.65 - Sexual abuse in the first degree

A person is guilty of sexual abuse in the first degree when he or she subjects another person to sexual contact:

1. By forcible compulsion; or

2. When the other person is incapable of consent by reason of being physically helpless; or

3. When the other person is less than eleven years old; or

4. When the other person is less than thirteen years old and the actor is twenty-one years old or older.

Sexual abuse in the first degree is a class D felony.

N.Y. Penal Law § 130.65

Section 130.65-A - Aggravated sexual abuse in the fourth degree

1. A person is guilty of aggravated sexual abuse in the fourth degree when:

(a) He or she inserts a foreign object in the vagina, urethra, penis, rectum or anus of another person and the other person is incapable of consent by reason of some factor other than being less than seventeen years old; or

(b) He or she inserts a finger in the vagina, urethra, penis, rectum or anus of another person causing physical injury to such person and such person is incapable of consent by reason of some factor other than being less than seventeen years old.

2. Conduct performed for a valid medical purpose does not violate the provisions of this section.

Aggravated sexual abuse in the fourth degree is a class E felony.

N.Y. Penal Law § 130.65-A

Section 130.66 - Aggravated sexual abuse in the third degree

1. A person is guilty of aggravated sexual abuse in the third degree when he or she inserts a foreign object in the vagina, urethra, penis, rectum or anus of another person:

(a) By forcible compulsion; or

(b) When the other person is incapable of consent by reason of being physically helpless; or

(c) When the other person is less than eleven years old.

2. A person is guilty of aggravated sexual abuse in the third degree when he or she inserts a foreign object in the vagina, urethra, penis, rectum or anus of another person causing physical injury to such person and such person is incapable of consent by reason of being mentally disabled or mentally incapacitated.

3. Conduct performed for a valid medical purpose does not violate the provisions of this section.

Aggravated sexual abuse in the third degree is a class D felony.

N.Y. Penal Law § 130.66

Section 130.67 - Aggravated sexual abuse in the second degree

1. A person is guilty of aggravated sexual abuse in the second degree when he or she inserts a finger in the vagina, urethra, penis, rectum or anus of another person causing physical injury to such person:

(a) By forcible compulsion; or

(b) When the other person is incapable of consent by reason of being physically helpless; or

(c) When the other person is less than eleven years old.

2. Conduct performed for a valid medical purpose does not violate the provisions of this section.

Aggravated sexual abuse in the second degree is a class C felony.

N.Y. Penal Law § 130.67

Section 130.70 - Aggravated sexual abuse in the first degree

1. A person is guilty of aggravated sexual abuse in the first degree when he or she inserts a foreign object in the vagina, urethra, penis, rectum or anus of another person causing physical injury to such person:

(a) By forcible compulsion; or

(b) When the other person is incapable of consent by reason of being physically helpless; or

(c) When the other person is less than eleven years old.

2. Conduct performed for a valid medical purpose does not violate the provisions of this section.

Aggravated sexual abuse in the first degree is a class B felony.

N.Y. Penal Law § 130.70

Section 130.75 - Course of sexual conduct against a child in the first degree

1. A person is guilty of course of sexual conduct against a child in the first degree when, over a period of time not less than three months in duration:

(a) he or she engages in two or more acts of sexual conduct, which includes at least one act of sexual intercourse, oral sexual conduct, anal sexual conduct or aggravated sexual contact, with a child less than eleven years old; or

(b) he or she, being eighteen years old or more, engages in two or more acts of sexual conduct, which include at least one act of sexual intercourse, oral sexual conduct, anal sexual conduct or aggravated sexual contact, with a child less than thirteen years old.

2. A person may not be subsequently prosecuted for any other sexual offense involving the same victim unless the other charged offense occurred outside the time period charged under this section.

Course of sexual conduct against a child in the first degree is a class B felony.

N.Y. Penal Law § 130.75

Section 130.80 - Course of sexual conduct against a child in the second degree

1. A person is guilty of course of sexual conduct against a child in the second degree when, over a period of time not less than three months in duration:

(a) he or she engages in two or more acts of sexual conduct with a child less than eleven years old; or

(b) he or she, being eighteen years old or more, engages in two or more acts of sexual conduct with a child less than thirteen years old.

2. A person may not be subsequently prosecuted for any other sexual offense involving the same victim unless the other charged offense occurred outside the time period charged under this section.

Course of sexual conduct against a child in the second degree is a class D felony.

N.Y. Penal Law § 130.80

Section 130.85 - Female genital mutilation

1. A person is guilty of female genital mutilation when:

(a) a person knowingly circumcises, excises, or infibulates the whole or any part of the labia majora or labia minora or clitoris of another person who has not reached eighteen years of age; or

(b) being a parent, guardian or other person legally responsible and charged with the care or custody of a child less than eighteen years old, he or she knowingly consents to the circumcision, excision or infibulation of whole or part of such child's labia majora or labia minora or clitoris.

2. Such circumcision, excision, or infibulation is not a violation of this section if such act is:

(a) necessary to the health of the person on whom it is performed, and is performed by a person licensed in the place of its performance as a medical practitioner; or

(b) performed on a person in labor or who has just given birth and is performed for medical purposes connected with that labor or birth by a person licensed in the place it is performed as a medical practitioner, midwife, or person in training to become such a practitioner or midwife.

3. For the purposes of paragraph (a) of subdivision two of this section, no account shall be taken of the effect on the person on whom such procedure is to be performed of any belief on the part of that or any other person that such procedure is required as a matter of custom or ritual.

Female genital mutilation is a class E felony.

N.Y. Penal Law § 130.85

Section 130.90 - Facilitating a sex offense with a controlled substance

A person is guilty of facilitating a sex offense with a controlled substance when he or she:

1. knowingly and unlawfully possesses a controlled substance or any preparation, compound, mixture or substance that requires a prescription to obtain and administers such substance or preparation, compound, mixture or substance that requires a prescription to obtain to another person without such person's consent and with intent to commit against such person conduct constituting a felony defined in this article; and

2. commits or attempts to commit such conduct constituting a felony defined in this article.

Facilitating a sex offense with a controlled substance is a class D felony.

N.Y. Penal Law § 130.90

Section 130.91 - Sexually motivated felony

1. A person commits a sexually motivated felony when he or she commits a specified offense for the purpose, in whole or substantial part, of his or her own direct sexual gratification.

2. A "specified offense" is a felony offense defined by any of the following provisions of this chapter: assault in the second degree as defined in section 120.05, assault in the first degree as defined in section 120.10, gang assault in the second degree as defined in section 120.06, gang assault in the first degree as defined in section 120.07, stalking in the first degree as defined in section 120.60, strangulation in the second degree as defined in section 121.12, strangulation in the first degree as defined in section 121.13, manslaughter in the second degree as defined in subdivision one of section 125.15, manslaughter in the first degree as defined in section 125.20, murder in the second degree as defined in section 125.25, aggravated murder as defined in section 125.26, murder in the first degree as defined in section 125.27, kidnapping in the second degree as defined in section 135.20, kidnapping in the first degree as defined in section 135.25, burglary in the third degree as defined in section 140.20, burglary in the second degree as defined in section 140.25, burglary in the first degree as defined in section 140.30, arson in the second degree as defined in section 150.15, arson in the first degree as defined in section 150.20, robbery in the third degree as defined in section 160.05, robbery in the second degree as defined in section 160.10, robbery in the first degree as defined in section 160.15, promoting prostitution in the second degree as defined in section 230.30, promoting prostitution in the first degree as defined in section 230.32, compelling prostitution as defined in section 230.33, sex trafficking of a child as defined in section 230.34 -a, disseminating indecent material to minors in the first degree as defined in section 235.22, use of a child in a sexual performance as defined in section 263.05, promoting an obscene sexual performance by a child as defined in section 263.10, promoting a sexual performance by a child as defined in section 263.15, or any felony attempt or conspiracy to commit any of the foregoing offenses.

N.Y. Penal Law § 130.91

Amended by New York Laws 2018, ch. 189,Sec. 5, eff. 11/13/2018.

Section 130.92 - Sentencing

1. When a person is convicted of a sexually motivated felony pursuant to this article, and the specified felony is a violent felony offense, as defined in section 70.02 of this chapter, the sexually motivated felony shall be deemed a violent felony offense.

2. When a person is convicted of a sexually motivated felony pursuant to this article, the sexually motivated felony shall be deemed to be the same offense level as the specified offense the defendant committed.

3. Persons convicted of a sexually motivated felony as defined in section 130.91 of this article, must be sentenced in accordance with the provisions of section 70.80 of this chapter.

N.Y. Penal Law § 130.92

Section 130.95 - Predatory sexual assault

A person is guilty of predatory sexual assault when he or she commits the crime of rape in the first degree, criminal sexual act in the first degree, aggravated sexual abuse in the first degree, or course of sexual conduct against a child in the first degree, as defined in this article, and when:

1. In the course of the commission of the crime or the immediate flight therefrom, he or she:

(a) Causes serious physical injury to the victim of such crime; or

(b) Uses or threatens the immediate use of a dangerous instrument; or

2. He or she has engaged in conduct constituting the crime of rape in the first degree, criminal sexual act in the first degree, aggravated sexual abuse in the first degree, or course of sexual conduct against a child in the first degree, as defined in this article, against one or more additional persons; or

3. He or she has previously been subjected to a conviction for a felony defined in this article, incest as defined in section 255.25 of this chapter or use of a child in a sexual performance as defined in section 263.05 of this chapter.

Predatory sexual assault is a class A-II felony.

N.Y. Penal Law § 130.95

Section 130.96 - Predatory sexual assault against a child

A person is guilty of predatory sexual assault against a child when, being eighteen years old or more, he or she commits the crime of rape in the first degree, criminal sexual act in the first degree, aggravated sexual abuse in the first degree, or course of sexual conduct against a child in the first degree, as defined in this article, and the victim is less than thirteen years old.

N.Y. Penal Law § 130.96

Article 135 - KIDNAPPING, COERCION AND RELATED OFFENSES

Section 135.00 - Unlawful imprisonment, kidnapping and custodial interference; definitions of terms

The following definitions are applicable to this article:

1. "Restrain" means to restrict a person's movements intentionally and unlawfully in such manner as to interfere substantially with his liberty by moving him from one place to another, or by confining him either in the place where the restriction commences or in a place to which he has been moved, without consent and with knowledge that the restriction is unlawful. A person is so moved or confined "without consent" when such is accomplished by (a) physical force, intimidation or deception, or (b) any means whatever, including acquiescence of the victim, if he is a child less than sixteen years old or an incompetent person and the parent, guardian or other person or institution having lawful control or custody of him has not acquiesced in the movement or confinement.

2. "Abduct" means to restrain a person with intent to prevent his liberation by either (a) secreting or holding him in a place where he is not likely to be found, or (b) using or threatening to use deadly physical force.

3. "Relative" means a parent, ancestor, brother, sister, uncle or aunt.

N.Y. Penal Law § 135.00

Section 135.05 - Unlawful imprisonment in the second degree

A person is guilty of unlawful imprisonment in the second degree when he restrains another person.

N.Y. Penal Law § 135.05

Section 135.10 - Unlawful imprisonment in the first degree

A person is guilty of unlawful imprisonment in the first degree when he restrains another person under circumstances which expose the latter to a risk of serious physical injury.

N.Y. Penal Law § 135.10

Section 135.15 - Unlawful imprisonment; defense

In any prosecution for unlawful imprisonment, it is an affirmative defense that (a) the person restrained was a child less than sixteen years old, and (b) the defendant was a relative of such child, and (c) his sole purpose was to assume control of such child.

N.Y. Penal Law § 135.15

Section 135.20 - Kidnapping in the second degree

A person is guilty of kidnapping in the second degree when he abducts another person.

N.Y. Penal Law § 135.20

Section 135.25 - Kidnapping in the first degree

A person is guilty of kidnapping in the first degree when he abducts another person and when:

1. His intent is to compel a third person to pay or deliver money or property as ransom, or to engage in other particular conduct, or to refrain from engaging in particular conduct; or

2. He restrains the person abducted for a period of more than twelve hours with intent to:

(a) Inflict physical injury upon him or violate or abuse him sexually; or

(b) Accomplish or advance the commission of a felony; or

(c) Terrorize him or a third person; or

(d) Interfere with the performance of a governmental or political function; or

3. The person abducted dies during the abduction or before he is able to return or to be returned to safety. Such death shall be presumed, in a case where such person was less than sixteen years old or an incompetent person at the time of the abduction, from evidence that his parents, guardians or other lawful custodians did not see or hear from him following the termination of the abduction and prior to trial and received no reliable information during such period persuasively indicating that he was alive. In all other cases, such death shall be presumed from evidence that a person whom the person

abducted would have been extremely likely to visit or communicate with during the specified period were he alive and free to do so did not see or hear from him during such period and received no reliable information during such period persuasively indicating that he was alive.

Kidnapping in the first degree is a class A-I felony.

N.Y. Penal Law § 135.25

Section 135.30 - Kidnapping; defense

In any prosecution for kidnapping, it is an affirmative defense that (a) the defendant was a relative of the person abducted, and (b) his sole purpose was to assume control of such person.

N.Y. Penal Law § 135.30

Section 135.35 - Labor trafficking

A person is guilty of labor trafficking if he or she compels or induces another to engage in labor or recruits, entices, harbors, or transports such other person by means of intentionally:

1. requiring that the labor be performed to retire, repay, or service a real or purported debt that the actor has caused by a systematic ongoing course of conduct with intent to defraud such person;

2. withholding, destroying, or confiscating any actual or purported passport, immigration document, or any other actual or purported government identification document, of another person with intent to impair said person's freedom of movement; provided, however, that this subdivision shall not apply to an attempt to correct a social security administration record or immigration agency record in accordance with any local, state, or federal agency requirement, where such attempt is not made for the purpose of any express or implied threat;

3. using force or engaging in any scheme, plan or pattern to compel or induce such person to engage in or continue to engage in labor activity by means of instilling a fear in such person that, if the demand is not complied with, the actor or another will do one or more of the following:

(a) cause physical injury, serious physical injury, or death to a person; or

(b) cause damage to property, other than the property of the actor; or

(c) engage in other conduct constituting a felony or unlawful imprisonment in the second degree in violation of section 135.05 of this article; or

(d) accuse some person of a crime or cause criminal charges or deportation proceedings to be instituted against such person; provided, however, that it shall be an affirmative defense to this subdivision that the defendant reasonably believed the threatened charge to be true and that his or her sole purpose was to compel or induce the victim to take reasonable action to make good the wrong which was the subject of such threatened charge; or

(e) expose a secret or publicize an asserted fact, whether true or false, tending to subject some person to hatred, contempt or ridicule; or

(f) testify or provide information or withhold testimony or information with respect to another's legal claim or defense; or

(g) use or abuse his or her position as a public servant by performing some act within or related to his or her official duties, or by failing or refusing to perform an official duty, in such manner as to affect some person adversely.

Labor trafficking is a class D felony.

N.Y. Penal Law § 135.35

Amended by New York Laws 2015, ch. 368,Sec. 5, eff. 1/19/2016.

Section 135.36 - Labor trafficking; accomplice

In a prosecution for labor trafficking, a person who has been compelled or induced or recruited, enticed, harbored or transported to engage in labor shall not be deemed to be an accomplice.

N.Y. Penal Law § 135.36

Section 135.37 - Aggravated labor trafficking

A person is guilty of aggravated labor trafficking if he or she compels or induces another to engage in labor or recruits, entices, harbors, or transports such other person to engage in labor by means of intentionally unlawfully providing a controlled substance to such person with intent to impair said person's judgment.

N.Y. Penal Law § 135.37

Added by New York Laws 2015, ch. 368,Sec. 6, eff. 1/19/2016.

Section 135.45 - Custodial interference in the second degree

A person is guilty of custodial interference in the second degree when:

1. Being a relative of a child less than sixteen years old, intending to hold such child permanently or for a protracted period, and knowing that he has no legal right to do so, he takes or entices such child from his lawful custodian; or

2. Knowing that he has no legal right to do so, he takes or entices from lawful custody any incompetent person or other person entrusted by authority of law to the custody of another person or institution.

Custodial interference in the second degree is a class A misdemeanor.

N.Y. Penal Law § 135.45

Section 135.50 - Custodial interference in the first degree

A person is guilty of custodial interference in the first degree when he commits the crime of custodial interference in the second degree:

1. With intent to permanently remove the victim from this state, he removes such person from the state; or

2. Under circumstances which expose the victim to a risk that his safety will be endangered or his health materially impaired.

It shall be an affirmative defense to a prosecution under subdivision one of this section that the victim had been abandoned or that the taking was necessary in an emergency to protect the victim because he has been subjected to or threatened with mistreatment or abuse.

Custodial interference in the first degree is a class E felony.

N.Y. Penal Law § 135.50

Section 135.55 - Substitution of children

A person is guilty of substitution of children when, having been temporarily entrusted with a child less than one year old and intending to deceive a parent, guardian or other lawful custodian of such child, he substitutes, produces or returns to such parent, guardian or custodian a child other than the one entrusted.

N.Y. Penal Law § 135.55

Section 135.60 - Coercion in the third degree

A person is guilty of coercion in the third degree when he or she compels or induces a person to engage in conduct which the latter has a legal right to abstain from engaging in, or to abstain from engaging in conduct in which he or she has a legal right to engage, or compels or induces a person to join a group, organization or criminal enterprise which such latter person has a right to abstain from joining, by means of instilling in him or her a fear that, if the demand is not complied with, the actor or another will:

1. Cause physical injury to a person; or

2. Cause damage to property; or

3. Engage in other conduct constituting a crime; or

4. Accuse some person of a crime or cause criminal charges to be instituted against him or her; or

5. Expose a secret or publicize an asserted fact, whether true or false, tending to subject some person to hatred, contempt or ridicule; or

6. Cause a strike, boycott or other collective labor group action injurious to some person's business; except that such a threat shall not be deemed coercive when the act or omission compelled is for the benefit of the group in whose interest the actor purports to act; or

7. Testify or provide information or withhold testimony or information with respect to another's legal claim or defense; or

8. Use or abuse his or her position as a public servant by performing some act within or related to his or her official duties, or by failing or refusing to perform an official duty, in such manner as to affect some person adversely; or

9. Perform any other act which would not in itself materially benefit the actor but which is calculated to harm another person materially with respect to his or her health, safety, business, calling, career, financial condition, reputation or personal relationships.

Coercion in the third degree is a class A misdemeanor.

N.Y. Penal Law § 135.60

Amended by New York Laws 2018, ch. 55,Sec. NN-1, eff. 11/1/2018.

Section 135.61 - Coercion in the second degree

A person is guilty of coercion in the second degree when he or she commits the crime of coercion in the third degree as defined in section 135.60 of this article and thereby compels or induces a person to engage in sexual intercourse, oral sexual conduct or anal sexual conduct as such terms are defined in section 130 of the penal law.

N.Y. Penal Law § 135.61

Added by New York Laws 2018, ch. 55,Sec. NN-2, eff. 11/1/2018.

Section 135.65 - Coercion in the first degree

A person is guilty of coercion in the first degree when he or she commits the crime of coercion in the third degree, and when:

1. He or she commits such crime by instilling in the victim a fear that he or she will cause physical injury to a person or cause damage to property; or

2. He or she thereby compels or induces the victim to:

(a) Commit or attempt to commit a felony; or

(b) Cause or attempt to cause physical injury to a person; or

(c) Violate his or her duty as a public servant.

Coercion in the first degree is a class D felony.

N.Y. Penal Law § 135.65

Amended by New York Laws 2018, ch. 55,Sec. NN-3, eff. 11/1/2018.

Section 135.70 - Coercion; no defense

The crimes of (a) coercion and attempt to commit coercion, and (b) bribe receiving by a labor official as defined in section 180.20, and bribe receiving as defined in section 200.05, are not mutually exclusive, and it is no defense to a prosecution for coercion or an attempt to commit coercion that, by reason of the same conduct, the defendant also committed one of such specified crimes of bribe receiving.

N.Y. Penal Law § 135.70

Section 135.75 - Coercion; defense

In any prosecution for coercion committed by instilling in the victim a fear that he or another person would be charged with a crime, it is an affirmative defense that the defendant reasonably believed the threatened charge to be true and that his sole purpose was to compel or induce the victim to take reasonable action to make good the wrong which was the subject of such threatened charge.

Title I - OFFENSES INVOLVING DAMAGE TO AND INTRUSION UPON PROPERTY
Article 140 - BURGLARY AND RELATED OFFENSES

Section 140.00 - Criminal trespass and burglary; definitions of terms

The following definitions are applicable to this article:

1. "Premises" includes the term "building," as defined herein, and any real property.

2. "Building," in addition to its ordinary meaning, includes any structure, vehicle or watercraft used for overnight lodging of persons, or used by persons for carrying on business therein, or used as an elementary or secondary school, or an inclosed motor truck, or an inclosed motor truck trailer. Where a building consists of two or more units separately secured or occupied, each unit shall be deemed both a separate building in itself and a part of the main building.

3. "Dwelling" means a building which is usually occupied by a person lodging therein at night.

4. "Night" means the period between thirty minutes after sunset and thirty minutes before sunrise.

5. "Enter or remain unlawfully." A person "enters or remains unlawfully" in or upon premises when he is not licensed or privileged to do so. A person who, regardless of his intent, enters or remains in or upon premises which are at the time open to the public does so with license and privilege unless he defies a lawful order not to enter or remain, personally communicated to him by the owner of such premises or other authorized person. A license or privilege to enter or remain in a building which is only partly open to the public is not a license or privilege to enter or remain in that part of the building which is not open to the public. A person who enters or remains upon unimproved and apparently unused land, which is neither fenced nor otherwise enclosed in a manner designed to exclude intruders, does so with license and privilege unless notice against trespass is personally communicated to him by the owner of such land or other authorized person, or unless such notice is given by posting in a conspicuous manner. A person who enters or remains in or about a school building without written permission from someone authorized to issue such permission or without a legitimate reason which includes a relationship involving custody of or responsibility for a pupil or student enrolled in the school or without legitimate business or a purpose relating to the operation of the school does so without license and privilege.

N.Y. Penal Law § 140.00

Section 140.05 - Trespass

A person is guilty of trespass when he knowingly enters or remains unlawfully in or upon premises.

N.Y. Penal Law § 140.05

Section 140.10 - Criminal trespass in the third degree

A person is guilty of criminal trespass in the third degree when he knowingly enters or remains unlawfully in a building or upon real property

(a) which is fenced or otherwise enclosed in a manner designed to exclude intruders; or

(b) where the building is utilized as an elementary or secondary school or a children's overnight camp as defined in section one thousand three hundred ninety-two of the public health law or a summer day camp as defined in section one thousand three hundred ninety-two of the public health law in violation of conspicuously posted rules or regulations governing entry and use thereof; or

(c) located within a city with a population in excess of one million and where the building or real property is utilized as an elementary or secondary school in violation of a personally communicated request to leave the premises from a principal, custodian or other person in charge thereof; or

(d) located outside of a city with a population in excess of one million and where the building or real property is utilized as an elementary or secondary school in violation of a personally communicated request to leave the premises from a principal, custodian, school board member or trustee, or other person in charge thereof; or

(e) where the building is used as a public housing project in violation of conspicuously posted rules or regulations governing entry and use thereof; or

(f) where a building is used as a public housing project in violation of a personally communicated request to leave the premises from a housing police officer or other person in charge thereof; or

(g) where the property consists of a right-of-way or yard of a railroad or rapid transit railroad which has been designated and conspicuously posted as a no-trespass railroad zone.

Criminal trespass in the third degree is a class B misdemeanor.

N.Y. Penal Law § 140.10

Section 140.15 - Criminal trespass in the second degree

A person is guilty of criminal trespass in the second degree when:

1. he or she knowingly enters or remains unlawfully in a dwelling; or

2. being a person required to maintain registration under article six-C of the correction law and designated a level two or level three offender pursuant to subdivision six of section one hundred sixty-eight-l of the correction law, he or she enters or remains in a public or private elementary, parochial, intermediate, junior high, vocational or high school knowing that the victim of the offense for which such registration is required attends or formerly attended such school. It shall not be an offense subject to prosecution under this subdivision if: the person is a lawfully registered student at such school; the person is a lawful student participant in a school sponsored event; the person is a parent or a legal guardian of a lawfully registered student at such school and enters the school for the purpose of attending their child's or dependent's event or activity; such school is the person's designated polling place and he or she enters such school building for the limited

purpose of voting; or if the person enters such school building for the limited purposes authorized by the superintendent or chief administrator of such school.

Criminal trespass in the second degree is a class A misdemeanor.

N.Y. Penal Law § 140.15

Section 140.17 - Criminal trespass in the first degree

A person is guilty of criminal trespass in the first degree when he knowingly enters or remains unlawfully in a building, and when, in the course of committing such crime, he:

1. Possesses, or knows that another participant in the crime possesses, an explosive or a deadly weapon; or

2. Possesses a firearm, rifle or shotgun, as those terms are defined in section 265.00, and also possesses or has readily accessible a quantity of ammunition which is capable of being discharged from such firearm, rifle or shotgun; or

3. Knows that another participant in the crime possesses a firearm, rifle or shotgun under circumstances described in subdivision two.

Criminal trespass in the first degree is a class D felony.

N.Y. Penal Law § 140.17

Section 140.20 - Burglary in the third degree

A person is guilty of burglary in the third degree when he knowingly enters or remains unlawfully in a building with intent to commit a crime therein.

N.Y. Penal Law § 140.20

Section 140.25 - Burglary in the second degree

A person is guilty of burglary in the second degree when he knowingly enters or remains unlawfully in a building with intent to commit a crime therein, and when:

1. In effecting entry or while in the building or in immediate flight therefrom, he or another participant in the crime:

(a) Is armed with explosives or a deadly weapon; or

(b) Causes physical injury to any person who is not a participant in the crime; or

(c) Uses or threatens the immediate use of a dangerous instrument; or

(d) Displays what appears to be a pistol, revolver, rifle, shotgun, machine gun or other firearm; or

2. The building is a dwelling.

Burglary in the second degree is a class C felony.

N.Y. Penal Law § 140.25

Section 140.30 - Burglary in the first degree

A person is guilty of burglary in the first degree when he knowingly enters or remains unlawfully in a dwelling with intent to commit a crime therein, and when, in effecting entry or while in the dwelling or in immediate flight therefrom, he or another participant in the crime:

1. Is armed with explosives or a deadly weapon; or

2. Causes physical injury to any person who is not a participant in the crime; or

3. Uses or threatens the immediate use of a dangerous instrument; or

4. Displays what appears to be a pistol, revolver, rifle, shotgun, machine gun or other firearm; except that in any prosecution under this subdivision, it is an affirmative defense that such pistol, revolver, rifle, shotgun, machine gun or other firearm was not a loaded weapon from which a shot, readily capable of producing death or other serious physical injury, could be discharged. Nothing contained in this subdivision shall constitute a defense to a prosecution for, or preclude a conviction of, burglary in the second degree, burglary in the third degree or any other crime.

Burglary in the first degree is a class B felony.

N.Y. Penal Law § 140.30

Section 140.35 - Possession of burglar's tools

A person is guilty of possession of burglar's tools when he possesses any tool, instrument or other article adapted, designed or commonly used for committing or facilitating offenses involving forcible entry into premises, or offenses involving larceny by a physical taking, or offenses involving theft of services as defined in subdivisions four, five and six of section 165.15, under circumstances evincing an intent to use or knowledge that some person intends to use the same in the commission of an offense of such character.

N.Y. Penal Law § 140.35

Section 140.40 - Unlawful possession of radio devices

As used in this section, the term "radio device" means any device capable of receiving a wireless voice transmission on any frequency allocated for police use, or any device capable of transmitting and receiving a wireless voice transmission. A person is guilty of unlawful possession of a radio device when he possesses a radio device with the intent to use that device in the commission of robbery, burglary, larceny, gambling or a violation of any provision of article two hundred twenty of the penal law.

N.Y. Penal Law § 140.40

Article 145 - CRIMINAL MISCHIEF AND RELATED OFFENSES

Section 145.00 - Criminal mischief in the fourth degree

A person is guilty of criminal mischief in the fourth degree when, having no right to do so nor any reasonable ground to believe that he or she has such right, he or she:

1. Intentionally damages property of another person; or

2. Intentionally participates in the destruction of an abandoned building as defined in section one thousand nine hundred seventy-one-a of the real property actions and proceedings law; or

3. Recklessly damages property of another person in an amount exceeding two hundred fifty dollars; or

4. With intent to prevent a person from communicating a request for emergency assistance, intentionally disables or removes telephonic, TTY or similar communication sending equipment while that person: (a) is attempting to seek or is engaged in the process of seeking emergency assistance from police, law enforcement, fire or emergency medical services personnel; or (b) is attempting to seek or is engaged in the process of seeking emergency assistance from another person or entity in order to protect himself, herself or a third person from imminent physical injury. The fact that the defendant has an ownership interest in such equipment shall not be a defense to a charge pursuant to this subdivision.

N.Y. Penal Law § 145.00

Section 145.05 - Criminal mischief in the third degree

A person is guilty of criminal mischief in the third degree when, with intent to damage property of another person, and having no right to do so nor any reasonable ground to believe that he or she has such right, he or she:

1. damages the motor vehicle of another person, by breaking into such vehicle when it is locked with the intent of stealing property, and within the previous ten year period, has been convicted three or more times, in separate criminal transactions for which sentence was imposed on separate occasions, of criminal mischief in the fourth degree as defined in section 145.00, criminal mischief in the third degree as defined in this section, criminal mischief in the second degree as defined in section 145.10, or criminal mischief in the first degree as defined in section 145.12 of this article; or

2. damages property of another person in an amount exceeding two hundred fifty dollars.

Criminal mischief in the third degree is a class E felony.

N.Y. Penal Law § 145.05

Section 145.10 - Criminal mischief in the second degree

A person is guilty of criminal mischief in the second degree when with intent to damage property of another person, and having no right to do so nor any reasonable ground to believe that he has such right, he damages property of another person in an amount exceeding one thousand five hundred dollars.

N.Y. Penal Law § 145.10

Section 145.12 - Criminal mischief in the first degree

A person is guilty of criminal mischief in the first degree when with intent to damage property of another person, and having no right to do so nor any reasonable ground to believe that he has such right, he damages property of another person by means of an explosive.

N.Y. Penal Law § 145.12

Section 145.13 - Definitions

For the purposes of sections 145.00, 145.05, 145.10 and 145.12 of this article:

N.Y. Penal Law § 145.13

Section 145.14 - Criminal tampering in the third degree

A person is guilty of criminal tampering in the third degree when, having no right to do so nor any reasonable ground to believe that he has such right, he tampers with property of another person with intent to cause substantial inconvenience to such person or to a third person.

N.Y. Penal Law § 145.14

Section 145.15 - Criminal tampering in the second degree

A person is guilty of criminal tampering in the second degree when, having no right to do so nor any reasonable ground to believe that he has such right, he or she tampers or makes connection with property of a gas, electric, sewer, steam or water-works corporation, telephone or telegraph corporation, common carrier, nuclear powered electric generating facility, or public utility operated by a municipality or district; except that in any prosecution under this section, it is an affirmative defense that the defendant did not engage in such conduct for a larcenous or otherwise unlawful or wrongful purpose.

N.Y. Penal Law § 145.15

Section 145.20 - Criminal tampering in the first degree

A person is guilty of criminal tampering in the first degree when, with intent to cause a substantial interruption or impairment of a service rendered to the public, and having no right to do so nor any reasonable ground to believe that he or she has such right, he or she damages or tampers with property of a gas, electric, sewer, steam or water-works corporation, telephone or telegraph corporation, common carrier, nuclear powered electric generating facility, or public utility operated by a municipality or district, and thereby causes such substantial interruption or impairment of service.

N.Y. Penal Law § 145.20

Section 145.22 - Cemetery desecration in the second degree

A person is guilty of cemetery desecration in the second degree when:

(a) with intent to damage property of another person, and having no right to do so nor any reasonable ground to believe that he has such right, he damages any real or personal property maintained as a cemetery plot, grave, burial place or other place of interment of human remains; or

(b) with intent to steal personal property, he steals personal property which is located at a cemetery plot, grave, burial place or other place of interment of human remains and which property is owned by the person or organization which maintains or owns such place or the estate, next-of-kin or representatives of the deceased person interred there.

Cemetery desecration in the second degree is a class A misdemeanor.

N.Y. Penal Law § 145.22

Section 145.23 - Cemetery desecration in the first degree
A person is guilty of cemetery desecration in the first degree when with intent to damage property of another person, and having no right to do so nor any reasonable ground to believe that he has such right, he:
(a) damages any real or personal property maintained as a cemetery plot, grave, burial place or other place of interment of human remains in an amount exceeding two hundred fifty dollars; or
(b) with intent to steal personal property, he steals personal property, the value of which exceeds two hundred fifty dollars, which is located at a cemetery plot, grave, burial place or other place of interment of human remains and which property is owned by the person or organization which maintains or owns such place or the estate, next-of-kin or representatives of the deceased person interred there; or
(c) commits the crime of cemetery desecration in the second degree as defined in section 145.22 of this article and has been previously convicted of the crime of cemetery desecration in the second degree within the preceding five years.
Cemetery desecration in the first degree is a class E felony.
N.Y. Penal Law § 145.23

Section 145.25 - Reckless endangerment of property
A person is guilty of reckless endangerment of property when he recklessly engages in conduct which creates a substantial risk of damage to the property of another person in an amount exceeding two hundred fifty dollars.
N.Y. Penal Law § 145.25

Section 145.26 - Aggravated cemetery desecration in the second degree
A person is guilty of aggravated cemetery desecration in the second degree when, having no right to do so nor any reasonable ground to believe that he or she has such right, he or she opens a casket, crypt, or similar vessel containing a human body or human remains which has been buried or otherwise interred in a cemetery and unlawfully removes therefrom a body, bodily part, any human remains or any object contained in such casket, crypt or similar vessel for the purpose of obtaining unlawful possession of such body, bodily part, human remains or object for such person or a third person.
N.Y. Penal Law § 145.26

Section 145.27 - Aggravated cemetery desecration in the first degree
A person is guilty of aggravated cemetery desecration in the first degree when such person commits the crime of aggravated cemetery desecration in the second degree and has been previously convicted within the past five years of the crime of cemetery desecration in the second degree as defined in section 145.22 of this article, cemetery desecration in the first degree as defined in section 145.23 of this article or aggravated cemetery desecration in the second degree as defined in section 145.26 of this article.
N.Y. Penal Law § 145.27

Section 145.30 - Unlawfully posting advertisements
1. A person is guilty of unlawfully posting advertisements when, having no right to do so nor any reasonable ground to believe that he has such right, he posts, paints or otherwise affixes to the property of another person any advertisement, poster, notice or other matter designed to benefit a person other than the owner of the property.
2. Where such matter consists of a commercial advertisement, it shall be presumed that the vendor of the specified product, service or entertainment is a person who placed such advertisement or caused it to be placed upon the property.
Unlawfully posting advertisements is a violation.
N.Y. Penal Law § 145.30

Section 145.35 - Tampering with a consumer product; consumer product defined
For the purposes of sections 145.40 and 145.45 of this article, "consumer product" means any drug, food, beverage or thing which is displayed or offered for sale to the public, for administration into or ingestion by a human being or for application to any external surface of a human being.
N.Y. Penal Law § 145.35

Section 145.40 - Tampering with a consumer product in the second degree
A person is guilty of tampering with a consumer product in the second degree when, having no right to do so nor any reasonable ground to believe that he has such right, and with intent to cause physical injury to another or with intent to instill in another a fear that he will cause such physical injury, he alters, adulterates or otherwise contaminates a consumer product.
N.Y. Penal Law § 145.40

Section 145.45 - Tampering with a consumer product in the first degree
A person is guilty of tampering with a consumer product in the first degree when, having no right to do so nor any reasonable ground to believe that he has such right, and with intent to cause physical injury to another or with intent to instill in another a fear that he will cause such physical injury, he alters, adulterates or otherwise contaminates a consumer product and thereby creates a substantial risk of serious physical injury to one or more persons.
N.Y. Penal Law § 145.45

Section 145.50 - Penalties for littering on railroad tracks and rights-of-way
1. No person shall throw, dump, or cause to be thrown, dumped, deposited or placed upon any railroad tracks, or within the limits of the rights-of-way of any railroad, any refuse, trash, garbage, rubbish, litter or any nauseous or offensive matter.
2. Where a highway or road lies in whole or part within a railroad rights-of-way, nothing in this section shall be construed as prohibiting the use in a reasonable manner of ashes, sand, salt or other material for the purpose of reducing the hazard of, or providing traction on snow, ice or sleet situated on such highway or road.

3. A violation of the provisions of subdivision one of this section shall be punishable by a fine not to exceed two hundred fifty dollars and/or a requirement to perform services for a public or not-for-profit corporation, association, institution or agency not to exceed eight hours and for any second or subsequent violation by a fine not to exceed five hundred dollars and/or a requirement to perform services for a public or not-for-profit corporation, association, institution or agency not to exceed eight hours.

4. Nothing in this section shall be deemed to apply to a railroad or its employees when matter deposited by them on the railroad tracks or rights-of-way is done pursuant to railroad rules, regulations or procedures.

N.Y. Penal Law § 145.50

Section 145.60 - Making graffiti

1. For purposes of this section, the term "graffiti" shall mean the etching, painting, covering, drawing upon or otherwise placing of a mark upon public or private property with intent to damage such property.

2. No person shall make graffiti of any type on any building, public or private, or any other property real or personal owned by any person, firm or corporation or any public agency or instrumentality, without the express permission of the owner or operator of said property.

Making graffiti is a class A misdemeanor.

N.Y. Penal Law § 145.60

Section 145.65 - Possession of graffiti instruments

A person is guilty of possession of graffiti instruments when he possesses any tool, instrument, article, substance, solution or other compound designed or commonly used to etch, paint, cover, draw upon or otherwise place a mark upon a piece of property which that person has no permission or authority to etch, paint, cover, draw upon or otherwise mark, under circumstances evincing an intent to use same in order to damage such property.

N.Y. Penal Law § 145.65

Section 145.70 - Criminal possession of a taximeter accelerating device

1. For purposes of this section, a "taximeter" means an instrument or device that automatically calculates and displays the charge to a passenger in a vehicle that is licensed to transport members of the public for hire pursuant to local law.

2. For purposes of this section, a "taximeter accelerating device" means an instrument or device that causes a taximeter to increase the charge displayed by such taximeter to an amount greater than the maximum amount permitted by local law.

3. A person is guilty of criminal possession of a taximeter accelerating device when he knowingly possesses, with intent to use unlawfully, a taximeter accelerating device. If such a device is knowingly possessed there is a rebuttable presumption that it is intended to be used unlawfully.

Criminal possession of a taximeter accelerating device is a class A misdemeanor.

N.Y. Penal Law § 145.70

Article 150 - ARSON

Section 150.00 - Arson; definitions

As used in this article,

1. "Building", in addition to its ordinary meaning, includes any structure, vehicle or watercraft used for overnight lodging of persons, or used by persons for carrying on business therein. Where a building consists of two or more units separately secured or occupied, each unit shall not be deemed a separate building.

2. "Motor vehicle", includes every vehicle operated or driven upon a public highway which is propelled by any power other than muscular power, except (a) electrically-driven invalid chairs being operated or driven by an invalid, (b) vehicles which run only upon rails or tracks, and (c) snowmobiles as defined in article forty-seven of the vehicle and traffic law.

N.Y. Penal Law § 150.00

Section 150.01 - Arson in the fifth degree

A person is guilty of arson in the fifth degree when he or she intentionally damages property of another without consent of the owner by intentionally starting a fire or causing an explosion.

N.Y. Penal Law § 150.01

Section 150.05 - Arson in the fourth degree

1. A person is guilty of arson in the fourth degree when he recklessly damages a building or motor vehicle by intentionally starting a fire or causing an explosion.

2. In any prosecution under this section, it is an affirmative defense that no person other than the defendant had a possessory or proprietary interest in the building or motor vehicle.

Arson in the fourth degree is a class E felony.

N.Y. Penal Law § 150.05

Section 150.10 - Arson in the third degree

1. A person is guilty of arson in the third degree when he intentionally damages a building or motor vehicle by starting a fire or causing an explosion.

2. In any prosecution under this section, it is an affirmative defense that (a) no person other than the defendant had a possessory or proprietary interest in the building or motor vehicle, or if other persons had such interests, all of them consented to the defendant's conduct, and (b) the defendant's sole intent was to destroy or damage the building or motor vehicle for a lawful and proper purpose, and (c) the defendant had no reasonable ground to believe that his conduct might endanger the life or safety of another person or damage another building or motor vehicle.

Arson in the third degree is a class C felony.

N.Y. Penal Law § 150.10

Section 150.15 - Arson in the second degree

A person is guilty of arson in the second degree when he intentionally damages a building or motor vehicle by starting a fire, and when (a) another person who is not a participant in the crime is present in such building or motor vehicle at the time, and (b) the defendant knows that fact or the circumstances are such as to render the presence of such a person therein a reasonable possibility.

N.Y. Penal Law § 150.15

Section 150.20 - Arson in the first degree

1. A person is guilty of arson in the first degree when he intentionally damages a building or motor vehicle by causing an explosion or a fire and when (a) such explosion or fire is caused by an incendiary device propelled, thrown or placed inside or near such building or motor vehicle; or when such explosion or fire is caused by an explosive; or when such explosion or fire either (i) causes serious physical injury to another person other than a participant, or (ii) the explosion or fire was caused with the expectation or receipt of financial advantage or pecuniary profit by the actor; and when (b) another person who is not a participant in the crime is present in such building or motor vehicle at the time; and (c) the defendant knows that fact or the circumstances are such as to render the presence of such person therein a reasonable possibility.

2. As used in this section, "incendiary device" means a breakable container designed to explode or produce uncontained combustion upon impact, containing flammable liquid and having a wick or a similar device capable of being ignited. Arson in the first degree is a class A-I felony.

N.Y. Penal Law § 150.20

Title J - OFFENSES INVOLVING THEFT

Article 155 - LARCENY

Section 155.00 - Larceny; definitions of terms

The following definitions are applicable to this title:

1. "Property" means any money, personal property, real property, computer data, computer program, thing in action, evidence of debt or contract, or any article, substance or thing of value, including any gas, steam, water or electricity, which is provided for a charge or compensation.

2. "Obtain" includes, but is not limited to, the bringing about of a transfer or purported transfer of property or of a legal interest therein, whether to the obtainer or another.

3. "Deprive." To "deprive" another of property means (a) to withhold it or cause it to be withheld from him permanently or for so extended a period or under such circumstances that the major portion of its economic value or benefit is lost to him, or (b) to dispose of the property in such manner or under such circumstances as to render it unlikely that an owner will recover such property.

4. "Appropriate." To "appropriate" property of another to oneself or a third person means (a) to exercise control over it, or to aid a third person to exercise control over it, permanently or for so extended a period or under such circumstances as to acquire the major portion of its economic value or benefit, or (b) to dispose of the property for the benefit of oneself or a third person.

5. "Owner." When property is taken, obtained or withheld by one person from another person, an "owner" thereof means any person who has a right to possession thereof superior to that of the taker, obtainer or withholder.

A person who has obtained possession of property by theft or other illegal means shall be deemed to have a right of possession superior to that of a person who takes, obtains or withholds it from him by larcenous means.

A joint or common owner of property shall not be deemed to have a right of possession thereto superior to that of any other joint or common owner thereof.

In the absence of a specific agreement to the contrary, a person in lawful possession of property shall be deemed to have a right of possession superior to that of a person having only a security interest therein, even if legal title lies with the holder of the security interest pursuant to a conditional sale contract or other security agreement.

6. "Secret scientific material" means a sample, culture, micro-organism, specimen, record, recording, document, drawing or any other article, material, device or substance which constitutes, represents, evidences, reflects, or records a scientific or technical process, invention or formula or any part or phase thereof, and which is not, and is not intended to be, available to anyone other than the person or persons rightfully in possession thereof or selected persons having access thereto with his or their consent, and when it accords or may accord such rightful possessors an advantage over competitors or other persons who do not have knowledge or the benefit thereof.

7. "Credit card" means any instrument or article defined as a credit card in section five hundred eleven of the general business law.

7-a. "Debit card" means any instrument or article defined as a debit card in section five hundred eleven of the general business law.

7-b. "Public benefit card" means any medical assistance card, food stamp assistance card, public assistance card, or any other identification, authorization card or electronic access device issued by the state or a social services district as defined in subdivision seven of section two of the social services law, which entitles a person to obtain public assistance benefits under a local, state or federal program administered by the state, its political subdivisions or social services districts.

7-c. "Access device" means any telephone calling card number, credit card number, account number, mobile identification number, electronic serial number or personal identification number that can be used to obtain telephone service.

8. "Service" includes, but is not limited to, labor, professional service, a computer service, transportation service, the supplying of hotel accommodations, restaurant services, entertainment, the supplying of equipment for use, and the

supplying of commodities of a public utility nature such as gas, electricity, steam and water. A ticket or equivalent instrument which evidences a right to receive a service is not in itself service but constitutes property within the meaning of subdivision one.

9. "Cable television service" means any and all services provided by or through the facilities of any cable television system or closed circuit coaxial cable communications system, or any microwave or similar transmission service used in connection with any cable television system or other similar closed circuit coaxial cable communications system. N.Y. Penal Law § 155.00

Section 155.05 - Larceny; defined

1. A person steals property and commits larceny when, with intent to deprive another of property or to appropriate the same to himself or to a third person, he wrongfully takes, obtains or withholds such property from an owner thereof.

2. Larceny includes a wrongful taking, obtaining or withholding of another's property, with the intent prescribed in subdivision one of this section, committed in any of the following ways:

(a) By conduct heretofore defined or known as common law larceny by trespassory taking, common law larceny by trick, embezzlement, or obtaining property by false pretenses;

(b) By acquiring lost property.

A person acquires lost property when he exercises control over property of another which he knows to have been lost or mislaid, or to have been delivered under a mistake as to the identity of the recipient or the nature or amount of the property, without taking reasonable measures to return such property to the owner;

(c) By committing the crime of issuing a bad check, as defined in section 190.05;

(d) By false promise.

A person obtains property by false promise when, pursuant to a scheme to defraud, he obtains property of another by means of a representation, express or implied, that he or a third person will in the future engage in particular conduct, and when he does not intend to engage in such conduct or, as the case may be, does not believe that the third person intends to engage in such conduct.

In any prosecution for larceny based upon a false promise, the defendant's intention or belief that the promise would not be performed may not be established by or inferred from the fact alone that such promise was not performed. Such a finding may be based only upon evidence establishing that the facts and circumstances of the case are wholly consistent with guilty intent or belief and wholly inconsistent with innocent intent or belief, and excluding to a moral certainty every hypothesis except that of the defendant's intention or belief that the promise would not be performed;

(e) By extortion.

A person obtains property by extortion when he compels or induces another person to deliver such property to himself or to a third person by means of instilling in him a fear that, if the property is not so delivered, the actor or another will:

(i) Cause physical injury to some person in the future; or

(ii) Cause damage to property; or

(iii) Engage in other conduct constituting a crime; or

(iv) Accuse some person of a crime or cause criminal charges to be instituted against him; or

(v) Expose a secret or publicize an asserted fact, whether true or false, tending to subject some person to hatred, contempt or ridicule; or

(vi) Cause a strike, boycott or other collective labor group action injurious to some person's business; except that such a threat shall not be deemed extortion when the property is demanded or received for the benefit of the group in whose interest the actor purports to act; or

(vii) Testify or provide information or withhold testimony or information with respect to another's legal claim or defense; or

(viii) Use or abuse his position as a public servant by performing some act within or related to his official duties, or by failing or refusing to perform an official duty, in such manner as to affect some person adversely; or

(ix) Perform any other act which would not in itself materially benefit the actor but which is calculated to harm another person materially with respect to his health, safety, business, calling, career, financial condition, reputation or personal relationships. N.Y. Penal Law § 155.05

Section 155.10 - Larceny; no defense

The crimes of (a) larceny committed by means of extortion and an attempt to commit the same, and (b) bribe receiving by a labor official as defined in section 180.20, and bribe receiving as defined in section 200.05, are not mutually exclusive, and it is no defense to a prosecution for larceny committed by means of extortion or for an attempt to commit the same that, by reason of the same conduct, the defendant also committed one of such specified crimes of bribe receiving. N.Y. Penal Law § 155.10

Section 155.15 - Larceny; defenses

1. In any prosecution for larceny committed by trespassory taking or embezzlement, it is an affirmative defense that the property was appropriated under a claim of right made in good faith.

2. In any prosecution for larceny by extortion committed by instilling in the victim a fear that he or another person would be charged with a crime, it is an affirmative defense that the defendant reasonably believed the threatened charge to be true and that his sole purpose was to compel or induce the victim to take reasonable action to make good the wrong which was the subject of such threatened charge. N.Y. Penal Law § 155.15

Section 155.20 - Larceny; value of stolen property

For the purposes of this title, the value of property shall be ascertained as follows:

1. Except as otherwise specified in this section, value means the market value of the property at the time and place of the crime, or if such cannot be satisfactorily ascertained, the cost of replacement of the property within a reasonable time after the crime.

2. Whether or not they have been issued or delivered, certain written instruments, not including those having a readily ascertainable market value such as some public and corporate bonds and securities, shall be evaluated as follows:

(a) The value of an instrument constituting an evidence of debt, such as a check, draft or promissory note, shall be deemed the amount due or collectable thereon or thereby, such figure ordinarily being the face amount of the indebtedness less any portion thereof which has been satisfied.

(b) The value of a ticket or equivalent instrument which evidences a right to receive a transportation, entertainment or other service shall be deemed the price stated thereon, if any; and if no price is stated thereon the value shall be deemed the price of such ticket or equivalent instrument which the issuer charges the general public.

(c) The value of any other instrument which creates, releases, discharges or otherwise affects any valuable legal right, privilege or obligation shall be deemed the greatest amount of economic loss which the owner of the instrument might reasonably suffer by virtue of the loss of the instrument.

3. Where the property consists of gas, steam, water or electricity, which is provided for charge or compensation, the value shall be the value of the property stolen in any consecutive twelve-month period.

4. When the value of property cannot be satisfactorily ascertained pursuant to the standards set forth in subdivisions one and two of this section, its value shall be deemed to be an amount less than two hundred fifty dollars.

N.Y. Penal Law § 155.20

Section 155.25 - Petit larceny

A person is guilty of petit larceny when he steals property.

N.Y. Penal Law § 155.25

Section 155.30 - Grand Larceny in the fourth degree

A person is guilty of grand larceny in the fourth degree when he steals property and when:

1. The value of the property exceeds one thousand dollars; or

2. The property consists of a public record, writing or instrument kept, filed or deposited according to law with or in the keeping of any public office or public servant; or

3. The property consists of secret scientific material; or

4. The property consists of a credit card or debit card; or

5. The property, regardless of its nature and value, is taken from the person of another; or

6. The property, regardless of its nature and value, is obtained by extortion; or

7. The property consists of one or more firearms, rifles or shotguns, as such terms are defined in section 265.00 of this chapter; or

8. The value of the property exceeds one hundred dollars and the property consists of a motor vehicle, as defined in section one hundred twenty-five of the vehicle and traffic law, other than a motorcycle, as defined in section one hundred twenty-three of such law; or

9. The property consists of a scroll, religious vestment, a vessel, an item comprising a display of religious symbols which forms a representative expression of faith, or other miscellaneous item of property which:

(a) has a value of at least one hundred dollars; and

(b) is kept for or used in connection with religious worship in any building, structure or upon the curtilage of such building or structure used as a place of religious worship by a religious corporation, as incorporated under the religious corporations law or the education law.

10. The property consists of an access device which the person intends to use unlawfully to obtain telephone service.

11. The property consists of anhydrous ammonia or liquified ammonia gas and the actor intends to use, or knows another person intends to use, such anhydrous ammonia or liquified ammonia gas to manufacture methamphetamine.

Grand larceny in the fourth degree is a class E felony.

N.Y. Penal Law § 155.30

Section 155.35 - Grand larceny in the third degree

A person is guilty of grand larceny in the third degree when he or she steals property and:

1. when the value of the property exceeds three thousand dollars, or

2. the property is an automated teller machine or the contents of an automated teller machine.

Grand larceny in the third degree is a class D felony.

N.Y. Penal Law § 155.35

Section 155.40 - Grand larceny in the second degree

A person is guilty of grand larceny in the second degree when he steals property and when:

1. The value of the property exceeds fifty thousand dollars; or

2. The property, regardless of its nature and value, is obtained by extortion committed by instilling in the victim a fear that the actor or another person will (a) cause physical injury to some person in the future, or (b) cause damage to property, or (c) use or abuse his position as a public servant by engaging in conduct within or related to his official duties, or by failing or refusing to perform an official duty, in such manner as to affect some person adversely.

Grand larceny in the second degree is a class C felony.

N.Y. Penal Law § 155.40

Section 155.42 - Grand larceny in the first degree

A person is guilty of grand larceny in the first degree when he steals property and when the value of the property exceeds one million dollars.

N.Y. Penal Law § 155.42

Section 155.43 - Aggravated grand larceny of an automated teller machine

A person is guilty of aggravated grand larceny of an automated teller machine when he or she commits the crime of grand larceny in the third degree, as defined in subdivision two of section 155.35 of this article and has been previously convicted of grand larceny in the third degree within the previous five years.

N.Y. Penal Law § 155.43

Section 155.45 - Larceny; pleading and proof

1. Where it is an element of the crime charged that property was taken from the person or obtained by extortion, an indictment for larceny must so specify. In all other cases, an indictment, information or complaint for larceny is sufficient if it alleges that the defendant stole property of the nature or value required for the commission of the crime charged without designating the particular way or manner in which such property was stolen or the particular theory of larceny involved.

2. Proof that the defendant engaged in any conduct constituting larceny as defined in section 155.05 is sufficient to support any indictment, information or complaint for larceny other than one charging larceny by extortion. An indictment charging larceny by extortion must be supported by proof establishing larceny by extortion.

N.Y. Penal Law § 155.45

Article 156 - OFFENSES INVOLVING COMPUTERS; DEFINITION OF TERMS

Section 156.00 - Offenses involving computers; definition of terms

The following definitions are applicable to this chapter except where different meanings are expressly specified:

1. "Computer" means a device or group of devices which, by manipulation of electronic, magnetic, optical or electrochemical impulses, pursuant to a computer program, can automatically perform arithmetic, logical, storage or retrieval operations with or on computer data, and includes any connected or directly related device, equipment or facility which enables such computer to store, retrieve or communicate to or from a person, another computer or another device the results of computer operations, computer programs or computer data.

2. "Computer program" is property and means an ordered set of data representing coded instructions or statements that, when executed by computer, cause the computer to process data or direct the computer to perform one or more computer operations or both and may be in any form, including magnetic storage media, punched cards, or stored internally in the memory of the computer.

3. "Computer data" is property and means a representation of information, knowledge, facts, concepts or instructions which are being processed, or have been processed in a computer and may be in any form, including magnetic storage media, punched cards, or stored internally in the memory of the computer.

4. "Computer service" means any and all services provided by or through the facilities of any computer communication system allowing the input, output, examination, or transfer, of computer data or computer programs from one computer to another.

5. "Computer material" is property and means any computer data or computer program which:

(a) contains records of the medical history or medical treatment of an identified or readily identifiable individual or individuals. This term shall not apply to the gaining access to or duplication solely of the medical history or medical treatment records of a person by that person or by another specifically authorized by the person whose records are gained access to or duplicated; or

(b) contains records maintained by the state or any political subdivision thereof or any governmental instrumentality within the state which contains any information concerning a person, as defined in subdivision seven of section 10.00 of this chapter, which because of name, number, symbol, mark or other identifier, can be used to identify the person and which is otherwise prohibited by law from being disclosed. This term shall not apply to the gaining access to or duplication solely of records of a person by that person or by another specifically authorized by the person whose records are gained access to or duplicated; or

(c) is not and is not intended to be available to anyone other than the person or persons rightfully in possession thereof or selected persons having access thereto with his, her or their consent and which accords or may accord such rightful possessors an advantage over competitors or other persons who do not have knowledge or the benefit thereof.

6. "Computer network" means the interconnection of hardwire or wireless communication lines with a computer through remote terminals, or a complex consisting of two or more interconnected computers.

7. "Access" means to instruct, communicate with, store data in, retrieve from, or otherwise make use of any resources of a computer, physically, directly or by electronic means.

8. "Without authorization" means to use or to access a computer, computer service or computer network without the permission of the owner or lessor or someone licensed or privileged by the owner or lessor where such person knew that his or her use or access was without permission or after actual notice to such person that such use or access was without permission. It shall also mean the access of a computer service by a person without permission where such person knew that such access was without permission or after actual notice to such person, that such access was without permission. Proof that such person used or accessed a computer, computer service or computer network through the knowing use of a set of instructions, code or computer program that bypasses, defrauds or otherwise circumvents a security measure installed

or used with the user's authorization on the computer, computer service or computer network shall be presumptive evidence that such person used or accessed such computer, computer service or computer network without authorization.

9. "Felony" as used in this article means any felony defined in the laws of this state or any offense defined in the laws of any other jurisdiction for which a sentence to a term of imprisonment in excess of one year is authorized in this state.

N.Y. Penal Law § 156.00

Section 156.05 - Unauthorized use of a computer

A person is guilty of unauthorized use of a computer when he or she knowingly uses, causes to be used, or accesses a computer, computer service, or computer network without authorization.

N.Y. Penal Law § 156.05

Section 156.10 - Computer trespass

A person is guilty of computer trespass when he or she knowingly uses, causes to be used, or accesses a computer, computer service, or computer network without authorization and:

1. he or she does so with an intent to commit or attempt to commit or further the commission of any felony; or

2. he or she thereby knowingly gains access to computer material.

Computer trespass is a class E felony.

N.Y. Penal Law § 156.10

Section 156.20 - Computer tampering in the fourth degree

A person is guilty of computer tampering in the fourth degree when he or she uses, causes to be used, or accesses a computer, computer service, or computer network without authorization and he or she intentionally alters in any manner or destroys computer data or a computer program of another person.

N.Y. Penal Law § 156.20

Section 156.25 - Computer tampering in the third degree

A person is guilty of computer tampering in the third degree when he commits the crime of computer tampering in the fourth degree and:

1. he does so with an intent to commit or attempt to commit or further the commission of any felony; or

2. he has been previously convicted of any crime under this article or subdivision eleven of section 165.15 of this chapter; or

3. he intentionally alters in any manner or destroys computer material; or

4. he intentionally alters in any manner or destroys computer data or a computer program so as to cause damages in an aggregate amount exceeding one thousand dollars.

Computer tampering in the third degree is a class E felony.

N.Y. Penal Law § 156.25

Section 156.26 - Computer tampering in the second degree

A person is guilty of computer tampering in the second degree when he or she commits the crime of computer tampering in the fourth degree and he or she intentionally alters in any manner or destroys:

1. computer data or a computer program so as to cause damages in an aggregate amount exceeding three thousand dollars; or

2. computer material that contains records of the medical history or medical treatment of an identified or readily identifiable individual or individuals and as a result of such alteration or destruction, such individual or individuals suffer serious physical injury, and he or she is aware of and consciously disregards a substantial and unjustifiable risk that such serious physical injury may occur.

Computer tampering in the second degree is a class D felony.

N.Y. Penal Law § 156.26

Section 156.27 - Computer tampering in the first degree

A person is guilty of computer tampering in the first degree when he commits the crime of computer tampering in the fourth degree and he intentionally alters in any manner or destroys computer data or a computer program so as to cause damages in an aggregate amount exceeding fifty thousand dollars.

N.Y. Penal Law § 156.27

Section 156.29 - Unlawful duplication of computer related material in the second degree

A person is guilty of unlawful duplication of computer related material in the second degree when having no right to do so, he or she copies, reproduces or duplicates in any manner computer material that contains records of the medical history or medical treatment of an identified or readily identifiable individual or individuals with an intent to commit or further the commission of any crime under this chapter.

N.Y. Penal Law § 156.29

Section 156.30 - Unlawful duplication of computer related material in the first degree

A person is guilty of unlawful duplication of computer related in the first degree material when having no right to do so, he or she copies, reproduces or duplicates in any manner:

1. any computer data or computer program and thereby intentionally and wrongfully deprives or appropriates from an owner thereof an economic value or benefit in excess of two thousand five hundred dollars; or

2. any computer data or computer program with an intent to commit or attempt to commit or further the commission of any felony.

Unlawful duplication of computer related material in the first degree is a class E felony.

N.Y. Penal Law § 156.30

Section 156.35 - Criminal possession of computer related material

A person is guilty of criminal possession of computer related material when having no right to do so, he knowingly possesses, in any form, any copy, reproduction or duplicate of any computer data or computer program which was copied, reproduced or duplicated in violation of section 156.30 of this article, with intent to benefit himself or a person other than an owner thereof.

N.Y. Penal Law § 156.35

Section 156.40 - Operating an unlawful electronic sweepstakes

1. As used in this section the following words and terms shall have the following meanings:

(a) "Electronic machine or device" means a mechanically, electrically or electronically operated machine or device that is owned, leased or otherwise possessed by a sweepstakes sponsor or promoter, or any sponsors, promoters, partners, affiliates, subsidiaries or contractors thereof; that is intended to be used by a sweepstakes entrant; that uses energy; and that displays the results of a game entry or game outcome to a participant on a screen or other mechanism at a business location, including a private club; provided, that an electronic machine or device may, without limitation:

(1) be server-based;

(2) use a simulated game terminal as a representation of the prizes associated with the results of the sweepstakes entries;

(3) utilize software such that the simulated game influences or determines the winning or value of the prize;

(4) select prizes from a predetermined finite pool of entries;

(5) utilize a mechanism that reveals the content of a predetermined sweepstakes entry;

(6) predetermine the prize results and stores those results for delivery at the time the sweepstakes entry results are revealed;

(7) utilize software to create a game result;

(8) require deposit of any money, coin or token, or the use of any credit card, debit card, prepaid card or any other method of payment to activate the electronic machine or device;

(9) require direct payment into the electronic machine or device, or remote activation of the electronic machine or device;

(10) require purchase of a related product having legitimate value;

(11) reveal the prize incrementally, even though it may not influence if a prize is awarded or the value of any prize awarded;

(12) determine and associate the prize with an entry or entries at the time the sweepstakes is entered; or

(13) be a slot machine or other form of electrical, mechanical, or computer game.

(b) "Enter" or "entry" means the act or process by which a person becomes eligible to receive any prize offered in a sweepstakes.

(c) "Entertaining display" means any visual information, capable of being seen by a sweepstakes entrant, that takes the form of actual game play or simulated game play.

(d) "Prize" means any gift, award, gratuity, good, service, credit or anything else of value, which may be transferred to a person, whether possession of the prize is actually transferred, or placed on an account or other record as evidence of the intent to transfer the prize.

(e) "Sweepstakes" means any game, advertising scheme or plan, or other promotion, which, with or without payment of any consideration, a person may enter to win or become eligible to receive any prize, the determination of which is based upon chance.

2. A person is guilty of operating an unlawful electronic sweepstakes when he or she knowingly possesses with the intent to operate, or place into operation, an electronic machine or device to:

(a) conduct a sweepstakes through the use of an entertaining display, including the entry process or the reveal of a prize; or

(b) promote a sweepstakes that is conducted through the use of an entertaining display, including the entry process or the reveal of a prize.

3. Nothing in this section shall be construed to make illegal any activity which is lawfully conducted as the New York state lottery for education as authorized by article thirty-four of the tax law; pari-mutuel wagering on horse races as authorized by articles two, three, four, five-A, and ten of the racing, pari-mutuel wagering and breeding law; the game of bingo as authorized pursuant to article fourteen-H of the general municipal law; games of chance as authorized pursuant to article nine-A of the general municipal law; gaming as authorized by article thirteen of the racing, pari-mutuel wagering and breeding law; or pursuant to the federal Indian Gaming Regulatory Act.

Operating an unlawful electronic sweepstakes is a class E felony.

N.Y. Penal Law § 156.40

Added by New York Laws 2013, ch. 174,Sec. 11, eff. 7/30/2013.

Section 156.50 - Offenses involving computers; defenses

In any prosecution:

1. under section 156.05 or 156.10 of this article, it shall be a defense that the defendant had reasonable grounds to believe that he had authorization to use the computer;

2. under section 156.20, 156.25, 156.26 or 156.27 of this article it shall be a defense that the defendant had reasonable grounds to believe that he had the right to alter in any manner or destroy the computer data or the computer program;

3. under section 156.29 or 156.30 of this article it shall be a defense that the defendant had reasonable grounds to believe that he had the right to copy, reproduce or duplicate in any manner the computer data or the computer program.

N.Y. Penal Law § 156.50

Article 158 - WELFARE FRAUD

Section 158.00 - Definitions; presumption; limitation

1. Definitions. The following definitions are applicable to this article:

(a) "Public benefit card" means any medical assistance card, food stamp assistance card, public assistance card, or any other identification, authorization card or electronic access device issued by the state or a social services district, as defined in subdivision seven of section two of the social services law, which entitles a person to obtain public assistance benefits under a local, state, or federal program administered by the state, its political subdivisions, or social services districts.

(b) "Fraudulent welfare act" means knowingly and with intent to defraud, engaging in an act or acts pursuant to which a person:

(1) offers, presents or causes to be presented to the state, any of its political subdivisions or social services districts, or any employee or agent thereof, an oral or written application or request for public assistance benefits or for a public benefit card with knowledge that the application or request contains a false statement or false information, and such statement or information is material, or

(2) holds himself or herself out to be another person, whether real or fictitious, for the purpose of obtaining public assistance benefits, or

(3) makes a false statement or provides false information for the purpose of (i) establishing or maintaining eligibility for public assistance benefits or (ii) increasing or preventing reduction of public assistance benefits, and such statement or information is material.

(c) "Public assistance benefits" means money, property or services provided directly or indirectly through programs of the federal government, the state government or the government of any political subdivision within the state and administered by the department of social services or social services districts.

2. Rebuttable presumption.

(a) A person who possesses five or more public benefit cards in a name or names other than his or her own is presumed to possess the same with intent to defraud, deceive or injure another.

(b) The presumption established by this subdivision shall not apply to:

(1) any employee or agent of the department of social services to the extent that he or she possesses such cards in the course of his or her official duties; or

(2) any person to the extent that he she possesses a public benefit card or cards issued to a member or members of his or her immediate family or household with the consent of the cardholder; or

(3) any person providing home health services or personal care services pursuant to title eleven of article five of the social services law, or any agent or employee of a congregate care or residential treatment facility or foster care provider, to the extent that in the course of his or her duties, he or she possesses public assistance cards issued to persons under his or her care.

(c) The presumption established by this subdivision is rebuttable by evidence tending to show that the defendant did not possess such public benefit card or cards with intent to defraud, deceive or injure another. In any action tried before a jury, the jury shall be so instructed.

(d) The foregoing presumption shall apply to prosecutions for criminal possession of public benefit cards.

3. Limitation. Nothing contained in this article shall be construed to prohibit a recipient of public assistance benefits from pledging his or her public assistance benefits or using his or her public benefit card as collateral for a loan.

N.Y. Penal Law § 158.00

Section 158.05 - Welfare fraud in the fifth degree

A person is guilty of welfare fraud in the fifth degree when he or she commits a fraudulent welfare act and thereby takes or obtains public assistance benefits.

N.Y. Penal Law § 158.05

Section 158.10 - Welfare fraud in the fourth degree

A person is guilty of welfare fraud in the fourth degree when he or she commits a fraudulent welfare act and thereby takes or obtains public assistance benefits, and when the value of the public assistance benefits exceeds one thousand dollars.

N.Y. Penal Law § 158.10

Section 158.15 - Welfare fraud in the third degree

A person is guilty of welfare fraud in the third degree when he or she commits a fraudulent welfare act and thereby takes or obtains public assistance benefits, and when the value of the public assistance benefits exceeds three thousand dollars.

N.Y. Penal Law § 158.15

Section 158.20 - Welfare fraud in the second degree

A person is guilty of welfare fraud in the second degree when he or she commits a fraudulent welfare act and thereby takes or obtains public assistance benefits, and when the value of the public assistance benefits exceeds fifty thousand dollars.

N.Y. Penal Law § 158.20

Section 158.25 - Welfare fraud in the first degree

A person is guilty of welfare fraud in the first degree when he or she commits a fraudulent welfare act and thereby takes or obtains public assistance benefits, and when the value of the public assistance benefits exceeds one million dollars.

N.Y. Penal Law § 158.25

Section 158.30 - Criminal use of a public benefit card in the second degree

A person is guilty of criminal use of a public benefit card in the second degree when he or she knowingly:

1. Loans money or otherwise provides property or services on credit, and accepts a public benefit card as collateral or security for the repayment of such loan or for the provision of such property or services;

2. Obtains a public benefit card in exchange for a benefit; or

3. Transfers or delivers a public benefit card to another (a) in exchange for money or a controlled substance as defined in subdivision five of section 220.00, or (b) for the purpose of committing an unlawful act.

Criminal use of a public benefit card in the second degree is a class A misdemeanor.

N.Y. Penal Law § 158.30

Section 158.35 - Criminal use of a public benefit card in the first degree

A person is guilty of criminal use of a public benefit card in the first degree when he or she, pursuant to an act or a series of acts, knowingly (i) obtains three or more public benefit cards from another or others in exchange for a benefit, or (ii) transfers or delivers three or more public benefit cards to another or others in exchange for money or a controlled substance as defined in subdivision five of section 220.00 of this chapter.

N.Y. Penal Law § 158.35

Section 158.40 - Criminal possession of public benefit cards in the third degree

A person is guilty of criminal possession of public benefit cards in the third degree when he or she with intent to defraud, deceive or injure another, knowingly possesses five or more public benefit cards in a name or names other than the person's own name.

N.Y. Penal Law § 158.40

Section 158.45 - Criminal possession of public benefit cards in the second degree

A person is guilty of criminal possession of public benefit cards in the second degree when he or she with intent to defraud, deceive or injure another, knowingly possesses ten or more public benefit cards in a name or names other than the person's own name.

N.Y. Penal Law § 158.45

Section 158.50 - Criminal possession of public benefit cards in the first degree

A person is guilty of criminal possession of public benefit cards in the first degree when he or she with intent to defraud, deceive or injure another, knowingly possesses twenty-five or more public benefit cards in a name or names other than the person's own name.

N.Y. Penal Law § 158.50

Article 160 - ROBBERY

Section 160.00 - Robbery; defined

Robbery is forcible stealing. A person forcibly steals property and commits robbery when, in the course of committing a larceny, he uses or threatens the immediate use of physical force upon another person for the purpose of:

1. Preventing or overcoming resistance to the taking of the property or to the retention thereof immediately after the taking; or

2. Compelling the owner of such property or another person to deliver up the property or to engage in other conduct which aids in the commission of the larceny.

N.Y. Penal Law § 160.00

Section 160.05 - Robbery in the third degree

A person is guilty of robbery in the third degree when he forcibly steals property.

N.Y. Penal Law § 160.05

Section 160.10 - Robbery in the second degree

A person is guilty of robbery in the second degree when he forcibly steals property and when:

1. He is aided by another person actually present; or

2. In the course of the commission of the crime or of immediate flight therefrom, he or another participant in the crime:

(a) Causes physical injury to any person who is not a participant in the crime; or

(b) Displays what appears to be a pistol, revolver, rifle, shotgun, machine gun or other firearm; or

3. The property consists of a motor vehicle, as defined in section one hundred twenty-five of the vehicle and traffic law.

Robbery in the second degree is a class C felony.

N.Y. Penal Law § 160.10

Section 160.15 - Robbery in the first degree

A person is guilty of robbery in the first degree when he forcibly steals property and when, in the course of the commission of the crime or of immediate flight therefrom, he or another participant in the crime:

1. Causes serious physical injury to any person who is not a participant in the crime; or

2. Is armed with a deadly weapon; or

3. Uses or threatens the immediate use of a dangerous instrument; or

4. Displays what appears to be a pistol, revolver, rifle, shotgun, machine gun or other firearm; except that in any prosecution under this subdivision, it is an affirmative defense that such pistol, revolver, rifle, shotgun, machine gun or other firearm was not a loaded weapon from which a shot, readily capable of producing death or other serious physical injury, could be discharged. Nothing contained in this subdivision shall constitute a defense to a prosecution for, or preclude a conviction of, robbery in the second degree, robbery in the third degree or any other crime.

Robbery in the first degree is a class B felony.

N.Y. Penal Law § 160.15

Article 165 - OTHER OFFENSES RELATING TO THEFT

Section 165.00 - Misapplication of property

1. A person is guilty of misapplication of property when, knowingly possessing personal property of another pursuant to an agreement that the same will be returned to the owner at a future time,

(a) he loans, leases, pledges, pawns or otherwise encumbers such property without the consent of the owner thereof in such manner as to create a risk that the owner will not be able to recover it or will suffer pecuniary loss; or

(b) he intentionally refuses to return personal property valued in excess of one hundred dollars to the owner pursuant to the terms of the rental agreement provided that the owner shall have made a written demand for the return of such personal property in person or by certified mail at an address indicated in the rental agreement and he intentionally refuses to return such personal property for a period of thirty days after such demand has been received or should reasonably have been received by him. Such written demand shall state: (i) the date and time at which the personal property was to have been returned under the rental agreement; (ii) that the owner does not consent to the continued withholding or retaining of such personal property and demands its return; and (iii) that the continued withholding or retaining of the property may constitute a class A misdemeanor punishable by a fine of up to one thousand dollars or by a sentence to a term of imprisonment for a period of up to one year or by both such fine and imprisonment.

(c) as used in paragraph (b) of this subdivision and in subdivision three of this section, the terms owner, personal property, and rental agreement shall be defined as in subdivision one of section three hundred ninety-nine-w of the general business law.

2. In any prosecution under paragraph (a) of subdivision one of this section, it is a defense that, at the time the prosecution was commenced, (a) the defendant had recovered possession of the property, unencumbered as a result of the unlawful disposition, and (b) the owner had suffered no material economic loss as a result of the unlawful disposition.

3. In any prosecution under paragraph (b) of subdivision one of this section, it is a defense that at the time the prosecution was commenced, (a) the owner had recovered possession of the personal property and suffered no material economic loss as a result of the unlawful retention; or (b) the defendant is unable to return such personal property because it has been accidentally destroyed or stolen; or (c) the owner failed to comply with the provisions of section three hundred ninety-nine-w of the general business law.

Misapplication of property is a class A misdemeanor.

N.Y. Penal Law § 165.00

Section 165.05 - Unauthorized use of a vehicle in the third degree

A person is guilty of unauthorized use of a vehicle in the third degree when:

1. Knowing that he does not have the consent of the owner, he takes, operates, exercises control over, rides in or otherwise uses a vehicle. A person who engages in any such conduct without the consent of the owner is presumed to know that he does not have such consent; or

2. Having custody of a vehicle pursuant to an agreement between himself or another and the owner thereof whereby he or another is to perform for compensation a specific service for the owner involving the maintenance, repair or use of such vehicle, he intentionally uses or operates the same, without the consent of the owner, for his own purposes in a manner constituting a gross deviation from the agreed purpose; or

3. Having custody of a vehicle pursuant to an agreement with the owner thereof whereby such vehicle is to be returned to the owner at a specified time, he intentionally retains or withholds possession thereof, without the consent of the owner, for so lengthy a period beyond the specified time as to render such retention or possession a gross deviation from the agreement.

For purposes of this section "a gross deviation from the agreement" shall consist of, but not be limited to, circumstances wherein a person who having had custody of a vehicle for a period of fifteen days or less pursuant to a written agreement retains possession of such vehicle for at least seven days beyond the period specified in the agreement and continues such possession for a period of more than two days after service or refusal of attempted service of a notice in person or by certified mail at an address indicated in the agreement stating (i) the date and time at which the vehicle was to have been returned under the agreement; (ii) that the owner does not consent to the continued withholding or retaining of such vehicle and demands its return; and that continued withholding or retaining of the vehicle may constitute a class A misdemeanor punishable by a fine of up to one thousand dollars or by a sentence to a term of imprisonment for a period of up to one year or by both such fine and imprisonment.

Unauthorized use of a vehicle in the third degree is a class A misdemeanor.

N.Y. Penal Law § 165.05

Section 165.06 - Unauthorized use of a vehicle in the second degree

A person is guilty of unauthorized use of a vehicle in the second degree when:

N.Y. Penal Law § 165.06

Section 165.07 - Unlawful use of secret scientific material

A person is guilty of unlawful use of secret scientific material when, with intent to appropriate to himself or another the use of secret scientific material, and having no right to do so and no reasonable ground to believe that he has such right, he makes a tangible reproduction or representation of such secret scientific material by means of writing, photographing, drawing, mechanically or electronically reproducing or recording such secret scientific material.

N.Y. Penal Law § 165.07

Section 165.08 - Unauthorized use of a vehicle in the first degree

A person is guilty of unauthorized use of a vehicle in the first degree when knowing that he does not have the consent of the owner, he takes, operates, exercises control over, rides in or otherwise uses a vehicle with the intent to use the same in the course of or the commission of a class A, class B, class C or class D felony or in the immediate flight therefrom. A person who engages in any such conduct without the consent of the owner is presumed to know he does not have such consent.

N.Y. Penal Law § 165.08

Section 165.09 - Auto stripping in the third degree

A person is guilty of auto stripping in the third degree when:

1. He or she removes or intentionally destroys or defaces any part of a vehicle, other than an abandoned vehicle, as defined in subdivision one of section one thousand two hundred twenty-four of the vehicle and traffic law, without the permission of the owner; or

2. He or she removes or intentionally destroys or defaces any part of an abandoned vehicle, as defined in subdivision one of section one thousand two hundred twenty-four of the vehicle and traffic law, except that it is a defense to such charge that such person was authorized to do so pursuant to law or by permission of the owner.

Auto stripping in the third degree is a class A misdemeanor.

N.Y. Penal Law § 165.09

Section 165.10 - Auto stripping in the second degree

A person is guilty of auto stripping in the second degree when:

1. He or she commits the offense of auto stripping in the third degree and when he or she has been previously convicted within the last five years of having violated the provisions of section 165.09 or this section; or

2. He or she removes or intentionally destroys, defaces, disguises, or alters any part of two or more vehicles, other than abandoned vehicles, as defined in subdivision one of section one thousand two hundred twenty-four of the vehicle and traffic law, without the permission of the owner, and the value of the parts of vehicles removed, destroyed, defaced, disguised, or altered exceeds an aggregate value of one thousand dollars.

Auto stripping in the second degree is a class E felony.

N.Y. Penal Law § 165.10

Section 165.11 - Auto stripping in the first degree

A person is guilty of auto stripping in the first degree when he or she removes or intentionally destroys, defaces, disguises, or alters any part of three or more vehicles, other than abandoned vehicles, as defined in subdivision one of section one thousand two hundred twenty-four of the vehicle and traffic law, without the permission of the owner, and the value of the parts of vehicles removed, destroyed, defaced, disguised, or altered exceeds an aggregate value of three thousand dollars.

N.Y. Penal Law § 165.11

Section 165.15 - Theft of services

A person is guilty of theft of services when:

1. He obtains or attempts to obtain a service, or induces or attempts to induce the supplier of a rendered service to agree to payment therefor on a credit basis, by the use of a credit card or debit card which he knows to be stolen.

2. With intent to avoid payment for restaurant services rendered, or for services rendered to him as a transient guest at a hotel, motel, inn, tourist cabin, rooming house or comparable establishment, he avoids or attempts to avoid such payment by unjustifiable failure or refusal to pay, by stealth, or by any misrepresentation of fact which he knows to be false. A person who fails or refuses to pay for such services is presumed to have intended to avoid payment therefor; or

3. With intent to obtain railroad, subway, bus, air, taxi or any other public transportation service without payment of the lawful charge therefor, or to avoid payment of the lawful charge for such transportation service which has been rendered to him, he obtains or attempts to obtain such service or avoids or attempts to avoid payment therefor by force, intimidation, stealth, deception or mechanical tampering, or by unjustifiable failure or refusal to pay; or

4. With intent to avoid payment by himself or another person of the lawful charge for any telecommunications service, including, without limitation, cable television service, or any gas, steam, sewer, water, electrical, telegraph or telephone service which is provided for a charge or compensation, he obtains or attempts to obtain such service for himself or another person or avoids or attempts to avoid payment therefor by himself or another person by means of (a) tampering or making connection with the equipment of the supplier, whether by mechanical, electrical, acoustical or other means, or (b) offering for sale or otherwise making available, to anyone other than the provider of a telecommunications service for such service provider's own use in the provision of its service, any telecommunications decoder or descrambler, a principal function of which defeats a mechanism of electronic signal encryption, jamming or individually addressed switching imposed by the provider of any such telecommunications service to restrict the delivery of such service, or (c) any misrepresentation of fact which he knows to be false, or (d) any other artifice, trick, deception, code or device. For the purposes of this subdivision the telecommunications decoder or descrambler described in paragraph (b) above or the device described in paragraph (d) above shall not include any non-decoding and non-descrambling channel frequency converter or any television receiver type-accepted by the federal communications commission. In any prosecution under this subdivision, proof that telecommunications equipment, including, without limitation, any cable television converter, descrambler, or related equipment, has been tampered with or otherwise intentionally prevented from performing its functions of control of service delivery without the consent of the supplier of the service, or that telecommunications equipment, including, without limitation, any cable television converter, descrambler, receiver, or related equipment, has been connected to the equipment of the supplier of the service without the consent of the supplier of the service, shall be presumptive evidence

that the resident to whom the service which is at the time being furnished by or through such equipment has, with intent to avoid payment by himself or another person for a prospective or already rendered service, created or caused to be created with reference to such equipment, the condition so existing. A person who tampers with such a device or equipment without the consent of the supplier of the service is presumed to do so with intent to avoid, or to enable another to avoid, payment for the service involved. In any prosecution under this subdivision, proof that any telecommunications decoder or descrambler, a principal function of which defeats a mechanism of electronic signal encryption, jamming or individually addressed switching imposed by the provider of any such telecommunications service to restrict the delivery of such service, has been offered for sale or otherwise made available by anyone other than the supplier of such service shall be presumptive evidence that the person offering such equipment for sale or otherwise making it available has, with intent to avoid payment by himself or another person of the lawful charge for such service, obtained or attempted to obtain such service for himself or another person or avoided or attempted to avoid payment therefor by himself or another person; or

5. With intent to avoid payment by himself or another person of the lawful charge for any telephone service which is provided for a charge or compensation he (a) sells, offers for sale or otherwise makes available, without consent, an existing, canceled or revoked access device; or (b) uses, without consent, an existing, canceled or revoked access device; or (c) knowingly obtains any telecommunications service with fraudulent intent by use of an unauthorized, false, or fictitious name, identification, telephone number, or access device. For purposes of this subdivision access device means any telephone calling card number, credit card number, account number, mobile identification number, electronic serial number or personal identification number that can be used to obtain telephone service.

6. With intent to avoid payment by himself or another person for a prospective or already rendered service the charge or compensation for which is measured by a meter or other mechanical device, he tampers with such device or with other equipment related thereto, or in any manner attempts to prevent the meter or device from performing its measuring function, without the consent of the supplier of the service. In any prosecution under this subdivision, proof that a meter or related equipment has been tampered with or otherwise intentionally prevented from performing its measuring function without the consent of the supplier of the service shall be presumptive evidence that the person to whom the service which is at the time being furnished by or through such meter or related equipment has, with intent to avoid payment by himself or another person for a prospective or already rendered service, created or caused to be created with reference to such meter or related equipment, the condition so existing. A person who tampers with such a device or equipment without the consent of the supplier of the service is presumed to do so with intent to avoid, or to enable another to avoid, payment for the service involved; or

7. He knowingly accepts or receives the use and benefit of service, including gas, steam or electricity service, which should pass through a meter but has been diverted therefrom, or which has been prevented from being correctly registered by a meter provided therefor, or which has been diverted from the pipes, wires or conductors of the supplier thereof. In any prosecution under this subdivision proof that service has been intentionally diverted from passing through a meter, or has been intentionally prevented from being correctly registered by a meter provided therefor, or has been intentionally diverted from the pipes, wires or conductors of the supplier thereof, shall be presumptive evidence that the person who accepts or receives the use and benefit of such service has done so with knowledge of the condition so existing; or

8. With intent to obtain, without the consent of the supplier thereof, gas, electricity, water, steam or telephone service, he tampers with any equipment designed to supply or to prevent the supply of such service either to the community in general or to particular premises; or

9. With intent to avoid payment of the lawful charge for admission to any theatre or concert hall, or with intent to avoid payment of the lawful charge for admission to or use of a chair lift, gondola, rope-tow or similar mechanical device utilized in assisting skiers in transportation to a point of ski arrival or departure, he obtains or attempts to obtain such admission without payment of the lawful charge therefor.

10. Obtaining or having control over labor in the employ of another person, or of business, commercial or industrial equipment or facilities of another person, knowing that he is not entitled to the use thereof, and with intent to derive a commercial or other substantial benefit for himself or a third person, he uses or diverts to the use of himself or a third person such labor, equipment or facilities.

11. With intent to avoid payment by himself, herself, or another person of the lawful charge for use of any computer, computer service, or computer network which is provided for a charge or compensation he or she uses, causes to be used, accesses, or attempts to use or access a computer, computer service, or computer network and avoids or attempts to avoid payment therefor. In any prosecution under this subdivision proof that a person overcame or attempted to overcome any device or coding system a function of which is to prevent the unauthorized use of said computer or computer service shall be presumptive evidence of an intent to avoid payment for the computer or computer service.

Theft of services is a class A misdemeanor, provided, however, that theft of cable television service as defined by the provisions of paragraphs (a), (c) and (d) of subdivision four of this section, and having a value not in excess of one hundred dollars by a person who has not been previously convicted of theft of services under subdivision four of this section is a violation, that theft of services under subdivision nine of this section by a person who has not been previously convicted of theft of services under subdivision nine of this section is a violation and provided further, however, that theft of services of any telephone service under paragraph (a) or (b) of subdivision five of this section having a value in excess of one thousand dollars or by a person who has been previously convicted within five years of theft of services under paragraph (a) of subdivision five of this section is a class E felony.

12. With intent to avoid payment for services rendered by a barbershop, salon or beauty shop, he or she avoids or attempts to avoid such payment by unjustifiable failure or refusal to pay, by stealth, or by any misrepresentation of fact which he or

she knows to be false. Theft of services is a class A misdemeanor, provided, however, that theft of cable television service as defined by the provisions of paragraphs (a), (c) and (d) of subdivision four of this section, and having a value not in excess of one hundred dollars by a person who has not been previously convicted of theft of services under subdivision four of this section is a violation, that theft of services under subdivision nine of this section by a person who has not been previously convicted of theft of services under subdivision nine of this section is a violation, that theft of services under subdivision twelve of this section by a person who has not previously been convicted of theft of services under subdivision twelve of this section is a violation, and provided further, however, that theft of services of any telephone service under paragraph (a) or (b) of subdivision five of this section having a value in excess of one thousand dollars or by a person who has been previously convicted within five years of theft of services under paragraph (a) of subdivision five of this section is a class E felony.

N.Y. Penal Law § 165.15

Amended by New York Laws 2018, ch. 275,Sec. 1, eff. 12/24/2018.

Section 165.16 - Unauthorized sale of certain transportation services

1. A person is guilty of unauthorized sale of certain transportation services when, with intent to avoid payment by another person to the metropolitan transportation authority, New York city transit authority or a subsidiary or affiliate of either such authority of the lawful charge for transportation services on a railroad, subway, bus or mass transit service operated by either such authority or a subsidiary or affiliate thereof, he or she, in exchange for value, sells access to such transportation services to such person, without authorization, through the use of an unlimited farecard or doctored farecard. This section shall apply only to such sales that occur in a transportation facility, as such term is defined in subdivision two of section 240.00 of this chapter, operated by such metropolitan transportation authority, New York city transit authority or subsidiary or affiliate of such authority, when public notice of the prohibitions of its section and the exemptions thereto appears on the face of the farecard or is conspicuously posted in transportation facilities operated by such metropolitan transportation authority, New York city transit authority or such subsidiary or affiliate of such authority.

2. It shall be a defense to a prosecution under this section that a person, firm, partnership, corporation, or association: (a) selling a farecard containing value, other than a doctored farecard, relinquished all rights and privileges thereto upon consummation of the sale; or (b) sold access to transportation services through the use of a farecard, other than a doctored farecard, when such sale was made at the request of the purchaser as an accommodation to the purchaser at a time when a farecard was not immediately available to the purchaser, provided, however, that the seller lawfully acquired the farecard and did not, by means of an unlawful act, contribute to the circumstances that caused the purchaser to make such request.

3. For purposes of this section:

(a) "farecard" means a value-based, magnetically encoded card containing stored monetary value from which a specified amount of value is deducted as payment of a fare;

(b) "unlimited farecard" means a farecard that is time-based, magnetically encoded and which permits entrance an unlimited number of times into facilities and conveyances for a specified period of time; and

(c) "doctored farecard" means a farecard that has been bent or manipulated or altered so as to facilitate a person's access to transportation services without paying the lawful charge.

Unauthorized sale of transportation service is a class B misdemeanor.

N.Y. Penal Law § 165.16

Section 165.17 - Unlawful use of credit card, debit card or public benefit card

A person is guilty of unlawful use of credit card, debit card or public benefit card when in the course of obtaining or attempting to obtain property or a service, he uses or displays a credit card, debit card or public benefit card which he knows to be revoked or cancelled.

N.Y. Penal Law § 165.17

Section 165.20 - Fraudulently obtaining a signature

A person is guilty of fraudulently obtaining a signature when, with intent to defraud or injure another or to acquire a substantial benefit for himself or a third person, he obtains the signature of a person to a written instrument by means of any misrepresentation of fact which he knows to be false.

N.Y. Penal Law § 165.20

Section 165.25 - Jostling

A person is guilty of jostling when, in a public place, he intentionally and unnecessarily:

1. Places his hand in the proximity of a person's pocket or handbag; or

2. Jostles or crowds another person at a time when a third person's hand is in the proximity of such person's pocket or handbag.

Jostling is a class A misdemeanor.

N.Y. Penal Law § 165.25

Section 165.30 - Fraudulent accosting

1. A person is guilty of fraudulent accosting when he accosts a person in a public place with intent to defraud him of money or other property by means of a trick, swindle or confidence game.

2. A person who, either at the time he accosts another in a public place or at some subsequent time or at some other place, makes statements to him or engages in conduct with respect to him of a kind commonly made or performed in the perpetration of a known type of confidence game, is presumed to intend to defraud such person of money or other property.

Fraudulent accosting is a class A misdemeanor.

N.Y. Penal Law § 165.30

Section 165.35 - Fortune telling

A person is guilty of fortune telling when, for a fee or compensation which he directly or indirectly solicits or receives, he claims or pretends to tell fortunes, or holds himself out as being able, by claimed or pretended use of occult powers, to answer questions or give advice on personal matters or to exorcise, influence or affect evil spirits or curses; except that this section does not apply to a person who engages in the aforedescribed conduct as part of a show or exhibition solely for the purpose of entertainment or amusement.

N.Y. Penal Law § 165.35

Section 165.40 - Criminal possession of stolen property in the fifth degree

A person is guilty of criminal possession of stolen property in the fifth degree when he knowingly possesses stolen property, with intent to benefit himself or a person other than an owner thereof or to impede the recovery by an owner thereof.

N.Y. Penal Law § 165.40

Section 165.45 - Criminal possession of stolen property in the fourth degree

A person is guilty of criminal possession of stolen property in the fourth degree when he knowingly possesses stolen property, with intent to benefit himself or a person other than an owner thereof or to impede the recovery by an owner thereof, and when:

1. The value of the property exceeds one thousand dollars; or

2. The property consists of a credit card, debit card or public benefit card; or

3. He is a collateral loan broker or is in the business of buying, selling or otherwise dealing in property; or

4. The property consists of one or more firearms, rifles and shotguns, as such terms are defined in section 265.00 of this chapter; or

5. The value of the property exceeds one hundred dollars and the property consists of a motor vehicle, as defined in section one hundred twenty-five of the vehicle and traffic law, other than a motorcycle, as defined in section one hundred twenty-three of such law; or

6. The property consists of a scroll, religious vestment, vessel or other item of property having a value of at least one hundred dollars kept for or used in connection with religious worship in any building or structure used as a place of religious worship by a religious corporation, as incorporated under the religious corporations law or the education law.

7. The property consists of anhydrous ammonia or liquified ammonia gas and the actor intends to use, or knows another person intends to use, such anhydrous ammonia or liquified ammonia gas to manufacture methamphetamine.

Criminal possession of stolen property in the fourth degree is a class E felony.

N.Y. Penal Law § 165.45

Section 165.50 - Criminal possession of stolen property in the third degree

A person is guilty of criminal possession of stolen property in the third degree when he knowingly possesses stolen property, with intent to benefit himself or a person other than an owner thereof or to impede the recovery by an owner thereof, and when the value of the property exceeds three thousand dollars.

N.Y. Penal Law § 165.50

Section 165.52 - Criminal possession of stolen property in the second degree

A person is guilty of criminal possession of stolen property in the second degree when he knowingly possesses stolen property, with intent to benefit himself or a person other than an owner thereof or to impede the recovery by an owner thereof, and when the value of the property exceeds fifty thousand dollars.

N.Y. Penal Law § 165.52

Section 165.54 - Criminal possession of stolen property in the first degree

A person is guilty of criminal possession of stolen property in the first degree when he knowingly possesses stolen property, with intent to benefit himself or a person other than an owner thereof or to impede the recovery by an owner, and when the value of the property exceeds one million dollars.

N.Y. Penal Law § 165.54

Section 165.55 - Criminal possession of stolen property; presumptions

1. A person who knowingly possesses stolen property is presumed to possess it with intent to benefit himself or a person other than an owner thereof or to impede the recovery by an owner thereof.

2. A collateral loan broker or a person in the business of buying, selling or otherwise dealing in property who possesses stolen property is presumed to know that such property was stolen if he obtained it without having ascertained by reasonable inquiry that the person from whom he obtained it had a legal right to possess it.

3. A person who possesses two or more stolen credit cards, debit cards or public benefit cards is presumed to know that such credit cards, debit cards or public benefit cards were stolen.

4. A person who possesses three or more tickets or equivalent instrument for air transportation service, which tickets or instruments were stolen by reason of having been obtained from the issuer or agent thereof by the use of one or more stolen or forged credit cards, is presumed to know that such tickets or instruments were stolen.

N.Y. Penal Law § 165.55

Section 165.60 - Criminal possession of stolen property; no defense

In any prosecution for criminal possession of stolen property, it is no defense that:

1. The person who stole the property has not been convicted, apprehended or identified; or

2. The defendant stole or participated in the larceny of the property; or

3. The larceny of the property did not occur in this state.

102

N.Y. Penal Law § 165.60

Section 165.65 - Criminal possession of stolen property; corroboration

1. A person charged with criminal possession of stolen property who participated in the larceny thereof may not be convicted of criminal possession of such stolen property solely upon the testimony of an accomplice in the larceny unsupported by corroborative evidence tending to connect the defendant with such criminal possession.

2. Unless inconsistent with the provisions of subdivision one of this section, a person charged with criminal possession of stolen property may be convicted thereof solely upon the testimony of one from whom he obtained such property or solely upon the testimony of one to whom he disposed of such property.

N.Y. Penal Law § 165.65

Section 165.70 - Definitions

As used in sections 165.71, 165.72, 165.73 and 165.74, the following terms have the following definitions:

1. The term "trademark" means(a) any word, name, symbol, or device, or any combination thereof adopted and used by a person to identify goods made by a person and which distinguish them from those manufactured or sold by others which is in use and which is registered, filed or recorded under the laws of this state or of any other state or is registered in the principal register of the United States patent and trademark office; or (b) the symbol of the International Olympic Committee, consisting of five interlocking rings; the emblem of the United States Olympic Committee, consisting of an escutcheon having a blue chief and vertically extending red and white bars on the base with five interlocking rings displayed on the chief; any trademark, trade name, sign, symbol, or insignia falsely representing association with, or authorization by, the International Olympic Committee or the United States Olympic Committee; or the words "Olympic", "Olympiad", "Citius Altius Fortius", or any combination thereof tending to cause confusion, to cause mistake, to deceive, or to falsely suggest a connection with the United States Olympic Committee or any International Olympic Committee or United States Olympic Committee activity.

2. The term "counterfeit trademark" means a spurious trademark or an imitation of a trademark that is:

(a) used in connection with trafficking in goods; and

(b) used in connection with the sale, offering for sale or distribution of goods that are identical with or substantially indistinguishable from a trademark as defined in subdivision one of this section.

The term "counterfeit trademark" does not include any mark used in connection with goods for which the person using such mark was authorized to use the trademark for the type of goods so manufactured or produced by the holder of the right to use such mark or designation, whether or not such goods were manufactured or produced in the United States or in another country, and does not include imitations of trade dress or packaging such as color, shape and the like unless those features have been registered as trademarks as defined in subdivision one of this section.

3. The term "traffic" means to transport, transfer, or otherwise dispose of, to another, as consideration for anything of value, or to obtain control of with intent to so transport, transfer, or otherwise dispose of.

4. The term "goods" means any products, services, objects, materials, devices or substances which are identified by the use of a trademark.

N.Y. Penal Law § 165.70

Section 165.71 - Trademark counterfeiting in the third degree

A person is guilty of trademark counterfeiting in the third degree when, with the intent to deceive or defraud some other person or with the intent to evade a lawful restriction on the sale, resale, offering for sale, or distribution of goods, he or she manufactures, distributes, sells, or offers for sale goods which bear a counterfeit trademark, or possesses a trademark knowing it to be counterfeit for the purpose of affixing it to any goods.

N.Y. Penal Law § 165.71

Section 165.72 - Trademark counterfeiting in the second degree

A person is guilty of trademark counterfeiting in the second degree when, with the intent to deceive or defraud some other person or with the intent to evade a lawful restriction on the sale, resale, offering for sale, or distribution of goods, he or she manufactures, distributes, sells, or offers for sale goods which bear a counterfeit trademark, or possesses a trademark knowing it to be counterfeit for the purpose of affixing it to any goods, and the retail value of all such goods bearing counterfeit trademarks exceeds one thousand dollars.

N.Y. Penal Law § 165.72

Section 165.73 - Trademark counterfeiting in the first degree

A person is guilty of trademark counterfeiting in the first degree when, with the intent to deceive or defraud some other person, or with the intent to evade a lawful restriction on the sale, resale, offering for sale, or distribution of goods, he or she manufactures, distributes, sells, or offers for sale goods which bear a counterfeit trademark, or possesses a trademark knowing it to be counterfeit for the purpose of affixing it to any goods, and the retail value of all such goods bearing counterfeit trademarks exceeds one hundred thousand dollars.

N.Y. Penal Law § 165.73

Section 165.74 - Seizure and distribution or destruction of goods bearing counterfeit trademarks

Any goods manufactured, sold, offered for sale, distributed or produced in violation of this article may be seized by any police officer. The magistrate must, within forty-eight hours after arraignment of the defendant, determine whether probable cause exists to believe that the goods had been manufactured, sold, offered for sale, distributed or produced in violation of this article, and upon a finding that probable cause exists to believe that the goods had been manufactured, sold, offered for sale, distributed, or produced in violation of this article, the court shall authorize such articles to be retained as evidence pending the trial of the defendant. Upon conviction of the defendant, the articles in respect whereof the defendant stands convicted shall be destroyed or donated. Destruction shall not include auction, sale or distribution of the items in their original form. Donation of the items shall be made at the court's discretion upon the request of any law enforcement agency and pursuant to the restrictions and procedures of section three hundred sixty-m of the general business law, for the benefit of indigent individuals.

N.Y. Penal Law § 165.74

Amended by New York Laws 2014, ch. 507,Sec. 2, eff. 12/17/2014.

Title K - OFFENSES INVOLVING FRAUD

Article 170 - FORGERY AND RELATED OFFENSES

Section 170.00 - Forgery; definitions of terms

1. "Written instrument" means any instrument or article, including computer data or a computer program, containing written or printed matter or the equivalent thereof, used for the purpose of reciting, embodying, conveying or recording information, or constituting a symbol or evidence of value, right, privilege or identification, which is capable of being used to the advantage or disadvantage of some person.

2. "Complete written instrument" means one which purports to be a genuine written instrument fully drawn with respect to every essential feature thereof. An endorsement, attestation, acknowledgment or other similar signature or statement is deemed both a complete written instrument in itself and a part of the main instrument in which it is contained or to which it attaches.

3. "Incomplete written instrument" means one which contains some matter by way of content or authentication but which requires additional matter in order to render it a complete written instrument.

4. "Falsely make." A person "falsely makes" a written instrument when he makes or draws a complete written instrument in its entirety, or an incomplete written instrument, which purports to be an authentic creation of its ostensible maker or drawer, but which is not such either because the ostensible maker or drawer is fictitious or because, if real, he did not authorize the making or drawing thereof.

5. "Falsely complete." A person "falsely completes" a written instrument when, by adding, inserting or changing matter, he transforms an incomplete written instrument into a complete one, without the authority of anyone entitled to grant it, so that such complete instrument appears or purports to be in all respects an authentic creation of or fully authorized by its ostensible maker or drawer.

6. "Falsely alter." A person "falsely alters" a written instrument when, without the authority of anyone entitled to grant it, he changes a written instrument, whether it be in complete or incomplete form, by means of erasure, obliteration, deletion, insertion of new matter, transposition of matter, or in any other manner, so that such instrument in its thus altered form appears or purports to be in all respects an authentic creation of or fully authorized by its ostensible maker or drawer.

7. "Forged instrument" means a written instrument which has been falsely made, completed or altered.

8. "Electronic access device" means a mobile identification number or electronic serial number that can be used to obtain telephone service.

N.Y. Penal Law § 170.00

Section 170.05 - Forgery in the third degree

A person is guilty of forgery in the third degree when, with intent to defraud, deceive or injure another, he falsely makes, completes or alters a written instrument.

N.Y. Penal Law § 170.05

Section 170.10 - Forgery in the second degree

A person is guilty of forgery in the second degree when, with intent to defraud, deceive or injure another, he falsely makes, completes or alters a written instrument which is or purports to be, or which is calculated to become or to represent if completed:

1. A deed, will, codicil, contract, assignment, commercial instrument, credit card, as that term is defined in subdivision seven of section 155.00, or other instrument which does or may evidence, create, transfer, terminate or otherwise affect a legal right, interest, obligation or status; or

2. A public record, or an instrument filed or required or authorized by law to be filed in or with a public office or public servant; or

3. A written instrument officially issued or created by a public office, public servant or governmental instrumentality; or

4. Part of an issue of tokens, public transportation transfers, certificates or other articles manufactured and designed for use as symbols of value usable in place of money for the purchase of property or services; or

5. A prescription of a duly licensed physician or other person authorized to issue the same for any drug or any instrument or device used in the taking or administering of drugs for which a prescription is required by law.

Forgery in the second degree is a class D felony.

N.Y. Penal Law § 170.10

Section 170.15 - Forgery in the first degree

A person is guilty of forgery in the first degree when, with intent to defraud, deceive or injure another, he falsely makes, completes or alters a written instrument which is or purports to be, or which is calculated to become or to represent if completed:

1. Part of an issue of money, stamps, securities or other valuable instruments issued by a government or governmental instrumentality; or

104

2. Part of an issue of stock, bonds or other instruments representing interests in or claims against a corporate or other organization or its property.

Forgery in the first degree is a class C felony.

N.Y. Penal Law § 170.15

Section 170.20 - Criminal possession of a forged instrument in the third degree

A person is guilty of criminal possession of a forged instrument in the third degree when, with knowledge that it is forged and with intent to defraud, deceive or injure another, he utters or possesses a forged instrument.

N.Y. Penal Law § 170.20

Section 170.25 - Criminal possession of a forged instrument in the second degree

A person is guilty of criminal possession of a forged instrument in the second degree when, with knowledge that it is forged and with intent to defraud, deceive or injure another, he utters or possesses any forged instrument of a kind specified in section 170.10.

N.Y. Penal Law § 170.25

Section 170.27 - Criminal possession of a forged instrument in the second degree; presumption

A person who possesses two or more forged instruments, each of which purports to be a credit card or debit card, as those terms are defined in subdivisions seven and seven-a of section 155.00, is presumed to possess the same with knowledge that they are forged and with intent to defraud, deceive or injure another.

N.Y. Penal Law § 170.27

Section 170.30 - Criminal possession of a forged instrument in the first degree

A person is guilty of criminal possession of a forged instrument in the first degree when, with knowledge that it is forged and with intent to defraud, deceive or injure another, he utters or possesses any forged instrument of a kind specified in section 170.15.

N.Y. Penal Law § 170.30

Section 170.35 - Criminal possession of a forged instrument; no defense

In any prosecution for criminal possession of a forged instrument, it is no defense that the defendant forged or participated in the forgery of the instrument in issue; provided that a person may not be convicted of both criminal possession of a forged instrument and forgery with respect to the same instrument.

N.Y. Penal Law § 170.35

Section 170.40 - Criminal possession of forgery devices

A person is guilty of criminal possession of forgery devices when:

1. He makes or possesses with knowledge of its character any plate, die or other device, apparatus, equipment, or article specifically designed for use in counterfeiting or otherwise forging written instruments; or

2. With intent to use, or to aid or permit another to use, the same for purposes of forgery, he makes or possesses any device, apparatus, equipment or article capable of or adaptable to such use.

Criminal possession of forgery devices is a class D felony.

N.Y. Penal Law § 170.40

Section 170.45 - Criminal simulation

A person is guilty of criminal simulation when:

1. With intent to defraud, he makes or alters any object in such manner that it appears to have an antiquity, rarity, source or authorship which it does not in fact possess; or

2. With knowledge of its true character and with intent to defraud, he utters or possesses an object so simulated.

Criminal simulation is a class A misdemeanor.

N.Y. Penal Law § 170.45

Section 170.47 - Criminal possession of an anti-security item

A person is guilty of criminal possession of an anti-security item, when with intent to steal property at a retail mercantile establishment as defined in article twelve-B of the general business law, he knowingly possesses in such an establishment an item designed for the purpose of overcoming detection of security markings or attachments placed on property offered for sale at such an establishment.

N.Y. Penal Law § 170.47

Section 170.50 - Unlawfully using slugs; definitions of terms

The following definitions are applicable to sections 170.55 and 170.60:

1. "Coin machine" means a coin box, turnstile, vending machine or other mechanical or electronic device or receptacle designed (a) to receive a coin or bill or a token made for the purpose, and (b) in return for the insertion or deposit thereof, automatically to offer, to provide, to assist in providing or to permit the acquisition of some property or some service.

2. "Slug" means an object or article which, by virtue of its size, shape or any other quality, is capable of being inserted or deposited in a coin machine as an improper substitute for a genuine coin, bill or token.

3. "Value" of a slug means the value of the coin, bill or token for which it is capable of being substituted.

N.Y. Penal Law § 170.50

Section 170.55 - Unlawfully using slugs in the second degree

A person is guilty of unlawfully using slugs in the second degree when:

1. With intent to defraud the owner of a coin machine, he inserts or deposits a slug in such machine; or

2. He makes, possesses or disposes of a slug with intent to enable a person to insert or deposit it in a coin machine.

Unlawfully using slugs in the second degree is a class B misdemeanor.

N.Y. Penal Law § 170.55

A person is guilty of unlawfully using slugs in the first degree when he makes, possesses or disposes of slugs with intent to enable a person to insert or deposit them in a coin machine, and the value of such slugs exceeds one hundred dollars.

N.Y. Penal Law § 170.60

A person is guilty of forgery of a vehicle identification number when:

(1) He knowingly destroys, covers, defaces, alters or otherwise changes the form or appearance of a vehicle identification number on any vehicle or component part thereof, except tires; or

(2) He removes any such number from a vehicle or component part thereof, except as required by the provisions of the vehicle and traffic law; or

(3) He affixes a vehicle identification number to a vehicle, except in accordance with the provisions of the vehicle and traffic law.

(4) He or she, with intent to defraud, knowingly manufactures, produces or reproduces a vehicle identification number label, sticker or plate which was not manufactured, produced or reproduced in accordance with the rules and regulations promulgated by the United States National Highway Safety Administration and/or in accordance with the provisions of the state vehicle and traffic law.

N.Y. Penal Law § 170.65

Amended by New York Laws 2013, ch. 186,Sec. 1, eff. 11/1/2013.

A person is guilty of illegal possession of a vehicle identification number when:

(1) He knowingly possesses a vehicle identification number label, sticker or plate which has been removed from the vehicle or vehicle part to which such label, sticker or plate was affixed by the manufacturer in accordance with 49 U.S.C. section 32101, et seq. and regulations promulgated thereunder or in accordance with the provisions of the vehicle and traffic law; or

(2) He knowingly possesses a vehicle or vehicle part to which is attached a vehicle identification number label, sticker or plate or on which is stamped or embossed a vehicle identification number which has been destroyed, covered, defaced, altered or otherwise changed, or a vehicle or vehicle part from which a vehicle identification number label, sticker or plate has been removed, which label, sticker or plate was affixed in accordance with 49 U.S.C. section 32101, et seq. or regulations promulgated thereunder, except when he has complied with the provisions of the vehicle and traffic law and regulations promulgated thereunder; or

(3) He knowingly possesses a vehicle, or part of a vehicle to which by law or regulation must be attached a vehicle identification number, either (a) with a vehicle identification number label, sticker, or plate which was not affixed by the manufacturer in accordance with 49 U.S.C. section 32101, et seq. or regulations promulgated thereunder, or in accordance with the provisions of the vehicle and traffic law or regulations promulgated thereunder, or (b) on which is affixed, stamped or embossed a vehicle identification number which was not affixed, stamped or embossed by the manufacturer, or in accordance with 49 U.S.C. section 32101, et seq. or regulations promulgated thereunder or in accordance with the provisions of the vehicle and traffic law or regulations promulgated thereunder.

Illegal possession of a vehicle identification number is a class E felony.

N.Y. Penal Law § 170.70

(1) A person is presumed to knowingly possess a vehicle or vehicle part in violation of subdivision two of section 170.70, when he possesses any combination of five such whole vehicles or individual vehicle parts, none of which are attached to or contained in the same vehicle.

(2) A person is presumed to knowingly possess a vehicle or vehicle part in violation of subdivision three of section 170.70, when he possesses any combination of five such whole vehicles or individual vehicle parts, none of which are attached to or contained in the same vehicle.

N.Y. Penal Law § 170.71

A person is guilty of fraudulent making of an electronic access device in the second degree when, with intent to defraud, deceive or injure another, he falsely makes, completes or alters two or more electronic access devices, as that term is defined in subdivision eight of section 170.00 of this article.

N.Y. Penal Law § 170.75

Article 175 - OFFENSES INVOLVING FALSE WRITTEN STATEMENTS

The following definitions are applicable to this article:

1. "Enterprise" means any entity of one or more persons, corporate or otherwise, public or private, engaged in business, commercial, professional, industrial, eleemosynary, social, political or governmental activity.

2. "Business record" means any writing or article, including computer data or a computer program, kept or maintained by an enterprise for the purpose of evidencing or reflecting its condition or activity.

3. "Written instrument" means any instrument or article, including computer data or a computer program, containing written or printed matter or the equivalent thereof, used for the purpose of reciting, embodying, conveying or recording

information, or constituting a symbol or evidence of value, right, privilege or identification, which is capable of being used to the advantage or disadvantage of some person.

N.Y. Penal Law § 175.00

Section 175.05 - Falsifying business records in the second degree

A person is guilty of falsifying business records in the second degree when, with intent to defraud, he:

1. Makes or causes a false entry in the business records of an enterprise; or

2. Alters, erases, obliterates, deletes, removes or destroys a true entry in the business records of an enterprise; or

3. Omits to make a true entry in the business records of an enterprise in violation of a duty to do so which he knows to be imposed upon him by law or by the nature of his position; or

4. Prevents the making of a true entry or causes the omission thereof in the business records of an enterprise.

Falsifying business records in the second degree is a class A misdemeanor.

N.Y. Penal Law § 175.05

Section 175.10 - Falsifying business records in the first degree

A person is guilty of falsifying business records in the first degree when he commits the crime of falsifying business records in the second degree, and when his intent to defraud includes an intent to commit another crime or to aid or conceal the commission thereof.

N.Y. Penal Law § 175.10

Section 175.15 - Falsifying business records; defense

In any prosecution for falsifying business records, it is an affirmative defense that the defendant was a clerk, bookkeeper or other employee who, without personal benefit, merely executed the orders of his employer or of a superior officer or employee generally authorized to direct his activities.

N.Y. Penal Law § 175.15

Section 175.20 - Tampering with public records in the second degree

A person is guilty of tampering with public records in the second degree when, knowing that he does not have the authority of anyone entitled to grant it, he knowingly removes, mutilates, destroys, conceals, makes a false entry in or falsely alters any record or other written instrument filed with, deposited in, or otherwise constituting a record of a public office or public servant.

N.Y. Penal Law § 175.20

Section 175.25 - Tampering with public records in the first degree

A person is guilty of tampering with public records in the first degree when, knowing that he does not have the authority of anyone entitled to grant it, and with intent to defraud, he knowingly removes, mutilates, destroys, conceals, makes a false entry in or falsely alters any record or other written instrument filed with, deposited in, or otherwise constituting a record of a public office or public servant.

N.Y. Penal Law § 175.25

Section 175.30 - Offering a false instrument for filing in the second degree

A person is guilty of offering a false instrument for filing in the second degree when, knowing that a written instrument contains a false statement or false information, he offers or presents it to a public office or public servant with the knowledge or belief that it will be filed with, registered or recorded in or otherwise become a part of the records of such public office or public servant.

N.Y. Penal Law § 175.30

Section 175.35 - Offering a false instrument for filing in the first degree

A person is guilty of offering a false instrument for filing in the first degree when:

1. knowing that a written instrument contains a false statement or false information, and with intent to defraud the state or any political subdivision, public authority or public benefit corporation of the state, he or she offers or presents it to a public office, public serv ant, public authority or public benefit corporation with the knowledge or belief that it will be filed with, registered or recorded in or otherwise become a part of the records of such public office, public servant, public authority or public benefit corporation; or

2.

(a) he or she commits the crime of offering a false instrument for filing in the second degree; and

(b) such instrument is a financing statement the contents of which are prescribed by section 9--502 of the uniform commercial code, the collat eral asserted to be covered in such statement is the property of a person who is a state or local officer as defined by section two of the public officers law or who otherwise is a judge or justice of the unified court system, such financing statement does not relate to an actual transaction, and he or she filed such financing statement in retaliation for the performance of official duties by such person.

N.Y. Penal Law § 175.35

Amended by New York Laws 2013, ch. 490,Sec. 3, eff. 11/1/2014.

See New York Laws 2013, ch. 490, Sec. 5.

Section 175.40 - Issuing a false certificate

A person is guilty of issuing a false certificate when, being a public servant authorized by law to make or issue official certificates or other official written instruments, and with intent to defraud, deceive or injure another person, he issues such an instrument, or makes the same with intent that it be issued, knowing that it contains a false statement or false information.

N.Y. Penal Law § 175.40

Section 175.45 - Issuing a false financial statement

A person is guilty of issuing a false financial statement when, with intent to defraud:

1. He knowingly makes or utters a written instrument which purports to describe the financial condition or ability to pay of some person and which is inaccurate in some material respect; or

2. He represents in writing that a written instrument purporting to describe a person's financial condition or ability to pay as of a prior date is accurate with respect to such person's current financial condition or ability to pay, whereas he knows it is materially inaccurate in that respect.

Issuing a false financial statement is a class A misdemeanor.

N.Y. Penal Law § 175.45

Article 176 - INSURANCE FRAUD

Section 176.00 - Insurance fraud; definition of terms

The following definitions are applicable to this article:

1. "Insurance policy" has the meaning assigned to insurance contract by subsection (a) of section one thousand one hundred one of the insurance law except it shall include reinsurance contracts, purported insurance policies and purported reinsurance contracts.

2. "Statement" includes, but is not limited to, any notice, proof of loss, bill of lading, invoice, account, estimate of property damages, bill for services, diagnosis, prescription, hospital or doctor records, x-ray, test result, and other evidence of loss, injury or expense.

3. "Person" includes any individual, firm, association or corporation.

4. "Personal insurance" means a policy of insurance insuring a natural person against any of the following contingencies:

(a) loss of or damage to real property used predominantly for residential purposes and which consists of not more than four dwelling units, other than hotels, motels and rooming houses;

(b) loss of or damage to personal property which is not used in the conduct of a business;

(c) losses or liabilities arising out of the ownership, operation, or use of a motor vehicle, predominantly used for non-business purposes;

(d) other liabilities for loss of, damage to, or injury to persons or property, not arising from the conduct of a business;

(e) death, including death by personal injury, or the continuation of life, or personal injury by accident, or sickness, disease or ailment, excluding insurance providing disability benefits pursuant to article nine of the workers' compensation law.

A policy of insurance which insures any of the contingencies listed in paragraphs (a) through (e) of this subdivision as well as other contingencies shall be personal insurance if that portion of the annual premium attributable to the listed contingencies exceeds that portion attributable to other contingencies.

5. "Commercial insurance" means insurance other than personal insurance, and shall also include insurance providing disability benefits pursuant to article nine of the workers' compensation law, insurance providing workers' compensation benefits pursuant to the provisions of the workers' compensation law and any program of self insurance providing similar benefits.

N.Y. Penal Law § 176.00

Section 176.05 - Insurance fraud; defined

A fraudulent insurance act is committed by any person who, knowingly and with intent to defraud presents, causes to be presented, or prepares with knowledge or belief that it will be presented to or by an insurer, self insurer, or purported insurer, or purported self insurer, or any agent thereof:

1. any written statement as part of, or in support of, an application for the issuance of, or the rating of a commercial insurance policy, or certificate or evidence of self insurance for commercial insurance or commercial self insurance, or a claim for payment or other benefit pursuant to an insurance policy or self insurance program for commercial or personal insurance that he or she knows to:

(a) contain materially false information concerning any fact material thereto; or

(b) conceal, for the purpose of misleading, information concerning any fact material thereto; or

2. any written statement or other physical evidence as part of, or in support of, an application for the issuance of a health insurance policy, or a policy or contract or other authorization that provides or allows coverage for, membership or enrollment in, or other services of a public or private health plan, or a claim for payment, services or other benefit pursuant to such policy, contract or plan that he or she knows to:

(a) contain materially false information concerning any material fact thereto; or

(b) conceal, for the purpose of misleading, information concerning any fact material thereto.

Such policy or contract or plan or authorization shall include, but not be limited to, those issued or operating pursuant to any public or governmentally-sponsored or supported plan for health care coverage or services or those otherwise issued or operated by entities authorized pursuant to the public health law. For purposes of this subdivision an "application for the issuance of a health insurance policy" shall not include (i) any application for a health insurance policy or contract approved by the superintendent of financial services pursuant to the provisions of sections three thousand two hundred sixteen, four thousand three hundred four, four thousand three hundred twenty-one or four thousand three hundred twenty-two of the insurance law or any other application for a health insurance policy or contract approved by the superintendent of financial services in the individual or direct payment market; or (ii) any application for a certificate evidencing coverage under a self-insured plan or under a group contract approved by the superintendent of financial services.

N.Y. Penal Law § 176.05

Section 176.10 - Insurance fraud in the fifth degree

A person is guilty of insurance fraud in the fifth degree when he commits a fraudulent insurance act.

N.Y. Penal Law § 176.10

Section 176.15 - Insurance fraud in the fourth degree

A person is guilty of insurance fraud in the fourth degree when he commits a fraudulent insurance act and thereby wrongfully takes, obtains or withholds, or attempts to wrongfully take, obtain or withhold property with a value in excess of one thousand dollars.

N.Y. Penal Law § 176.15

Section 176.20 - Insurance fraud in the third degree

A person is guilty of insurance fraud in the third degree when he commits a fraudulent insurance act and thereby wrongfully takes, obtains or withholds, or attempts to wrongfully take, obtain or withhold property with a value in excess of three thousand dollars.

N.Y. Penal Law § 176.20

Section 176.25 - Insurance fraud in the second degree

A person is guilty of insurance fraud in the second degree when he commits a fraudulent insurance act and thereby wrongfully takes, obtains or withholds, or attempts to wrongfully take, obtain or withhold property with a value in excess of fifty thousand dollars.

N.Y. Penal Law § 176.25

Section 176.30 - Insurance fraud in the first degree

A person is guilty of insurance fraud in the first degree when he commits a fraudulent insurance act and thereby wrongfully takes, obtains or withholds, or attempts to wrongfully take, obtain or withhold property with a value in excess of one million dollars.

N.Y. Penal Law § 176.30

Section 176.35 - Aggravated insurance fraud

A person is guilty of aggravated insurance fraud in the fourth degree when he commits a fraudulent insurance act, and has been previously convicted within the preceding five years of any offense, an essential element of which is the commission of a fraudulent insurance act.

N.Y. Penal Law § 176.35

Section 176.40 - Fraudulent life settlement act; defined

A fraudulent life settlement act is committed by any person who, knowingly and with intent to defraud, presents, causes to be presented, or prepares with knowledge or belief that it will be presented to, or by, a life settlement provider, life settlement broker, life settlement intermediary, or any agent thereof, or to any owner any written statement or other physical evidence as part of, or in support of, an application for a life settlement contract, a claim for payment or other benefit under a life settlement contract, which the person knows to:

(1) contain materially false information concerning any material fact thereto; or

(2) conceal, for the purpose of misleading, information concerning any fact material thereto.

N.Y. Penal Law § 176.40

Section 176.45 - Life settlement fraud in the fifth degree

A person is guilty of life settlement fraud in the fifth degree when he or she commits a fraudulent life settlement act.

N.Y. Penal Law § 176.45

Section 176.50 - Life settlement fraud in the fourth degree

A person is guilty of life settlement fraud in the fourth degree when he or she commits a fraudulent life settlement act and thereby wrongfully takes, obtains or withholds, or attempts to wrongfully take, obtain or withhold property with a value in excess of twenty-five thousand dollars.

N.Y. Penal Law § 176.50

Section 176.55 - Life settlement fraud in the third degree

A person is guilty of life settlement fraud in the third degree when he or she commits a fraudulent life settlement act and thereby wrongfully takes, obtains or withholds, or attempts to wrongfully take, obtain or withhold property with a value in excess of fifty thousand dollars.

N.Y. Penal Law § 176.55

Section 176.60 - Life settlement fraud in the second degree

A person is guilty of life settlement fraud in the second degree when he or she commits a fraudulent life settlement act and thereby wrongfully takes, obtains or withholds, or attempts to wrongfully take, obtain or withhold property with a value in excess of one hundred thousand dollars.

N.Y. Penal Law § 176.60

Section 176.65 - Life settlement fraud in the first degree

A person is guilty of life settlement fraud in the first degree when he or she commits a fraudulent life settlement act and thereby wrongfully takes, obtains or withholds, or attempts to wrongfully take, obtain or withhold property with a value in excess of one million dollars.

N.Y. Penal Law § 176.65

Section 176.70 - Aggravated life settlement fraud

A person is guilty of aggravated life settlement fraud when he or she commits a fraudulent life settlement act, and has been previously convicted within the preceding five years of any offense, an essential element of which is the commission of a fraudulent life settlement act.

N.Y. Penal Law § 176.70

Section 176.75 - Staging a motor vehicle accident in the second degree

A person is guilty of staging a motor vehicle accident in the second degree when, with intent to commit and in furtherance of a fraudulent insurance act, he or she operates a motor vehicle and intentionally causes a collision involving a motor vehicle.

N.Y. Penal Law § 176.75

Added by New York Laws 2019, ch. 151,Sec. 2, eff. 11/1/2019.

Section 176.80 - Staging a motor vehicle accident in the first degree

A person is guilty of staging a motor vehicle accident in the first degree when he or she commits the offense of staging a motor vehicle accident in the second degree and thereby causes serious physical injury or death to another person, other than a participant in such offense.

N.Y. Penal Law § 176.80

Added by New York Laws 2019, ch. 151,Sec. 2, eff. 11/1/2019.

Article 177 - HEALTH CARE FRAUD

Section 177.00 - Definitions

The following definitions are applicable to this article:

1. "Health plan" means any publicly or privately funded health insurance or managed care plan or contract, under which any health care item or service is provided, and through which payment may be made to the person who provided the health care item or service. The state's medical assistance program (Medicaid) shall be considered a single health plan. For purposes of this article, a payment made pursuant to the state's managed care program as defined in paragraph (c) of subdivision one of section three hundred sixty-four-j of the social services law shall be deemed a payment by the state's medical assistance program (Medicaid).

2. "Person" means any individual or entity, other than a recipient of a health care item or service under a health plan unless such recipient acts as an accessory to such an individual or entity.

N.Y. Penal Law § 177.00

Section 177.05 - Health care fraud in the fifth degree

A person is guilty of health care fraud in the fifth degree when, with intent to defraud a health plan, he or she knowingly and willfully provides materially false information or omits material information for the purpose of requesting payment from a health plan for a health care item or service and, as a result of such information or omission, he or she or another person receives payment in an amount that he, she or such other person is not entitled to under the circumstances.

N.Y. Penal Law § 177.05

Section 177.10 - Health care fraud in the fourth degree

A person is guilty of health care fraud in the fourth degree when such person, on one or more occasions, commits the crime of health care fraud in the fifth degree and the payment or portion of the payment wrongfully received, as the case may be, from a single health plan, in a period of not more than one year, exceeds three thousand dollars in the aggregate.

N.Y. Penal Law § 177.10

Section 177.15 - Health care fraud in the third degree

A person is guilty of health care fraud in the third degree when such person, on one or more occasions, commits the crime of health care fraud in the fifth degree and the payment or portion of the payment wrongfully received, as the case may be, from a single health plan, in a period of not more than one year, exceeds ten thousand dollars in the aggregate.

N.Y. Penal Law § 177.15

Section 177.20 - Health care fraud in the second degree

A person is guilty of health care fraud in the second degree when such person, on one or more occasions, commits the crime of health care fraud in the fifth degree and the payment or portion of the payment wrongfully received, as the case may be, from a single health plan, in a period of not more than one year, exceeds fifty thousand dollars in the aggregate.

N.Y. Penal Law § 177.20

Section 177.25 - Health care fraud in the first degree

A person is guilty of health care fraud in the first degree when such person, on one or more occasions, commits the crime of health care fraud in the fifth degree and the payment or portion of the payment wrongfully received, as the case may be, from a single health plan, in a period of not more than one year, exceeds one million dollars in the aggregate.

N.Y. Penal Law § 177.25

Section 177.30 - Health care fraud; affirmative defense

In any prosecution under this article, it shall be an affirmative defense that the defendant was a clerk, bookkeeper or other employee, other than an employee charged with the active management and control, in an executive capacity, of the affairs of the corporation, who, without personal benefit, merely executed the orders of his or her employer or of a superior employee generally authorized to direct his or her activities.

N.Y. Penal Law § 177.30

Article 178 - CRIMINAL DIVERSION OF PRESCRIPTION MEDICATIONS AND PRESCRIPTIONS

Section 178.00 - Criminal diversion of prescription medications and prescriptions; definitions

The following definitions are applicable to this article:

1. "Prescription medication or device" means any article for which a prescription is required in order to be lawfully sold, delivered or distributed by any person authorized by law to engage in the practice of the profession of pharmacy.

2. "Prescription" means a direction or authorization by means of a written prescription form or an oral prescription which permits a person to lawfully obtain a prescription medication or device from any person authorized to dispense such prescription medication or device.

3. "Criminal diversion act" means an act or acts in which a person knowingly:

(a) transfers or delivers, in exchange for anything of pecuniary value, a prescription medication or device with knowledge or reasonable grounds to know that the recipient has no medical need for it; or

(b) receives, in exchange for anything of pecuniary value, a prescription medication or device with knowledge or reasonable grounds to know that the seller or transferor is not authorized by law to sell or transfer such prescription medication or device; or

(c) transfers or delivers a prescription in exchange for anything of pecuniary value; or

(d) receives a prescription in exchange for anything of pecuniary value.

N.Y. Penal Law § 178.00

Section 178.05 - Criminal diversion of prescription medications and prescriptions; limitation

1. The provisions of this article shall not apply to:

(a) a duly licensed physician or other person authorized to issue a prescription acting in good faith in the lawful course of his or her profession; or

(b) a duly licensed pharmacist acting in good faith in the lawful course of the practice of pharmacy; or

(c) a person acting in good faith seeking treatment for a medical condition or assisting another person to obtain treatment for a medical condition.

2. No provision of this article relating to the sale of a prescription medication or device shall be deemed to authorize any act prohibited by article thirty-three of the public health law or article two hundred twenty of this chapter.

N.Y. Penal Law § 178.05

Section 178.10 - Criminal diversion of prescription medications and prescriptions in the fourth degree

A person is guilty of criminal diversion of prescription medications and prescriptions in the fourth degree when he or she commits a criminal diversion act.

N.Y. Penal Law § 178.10

Section 178.15 - Criminal diversion of prescription medications and prescriptions in the third degree

A person is guilty of criminal diversion of prescription medications and prescriptions in the third degree when he or she:

1. commits a criminal diversion act, and the value of the benefit exchanged is in excess of one thousand dollars; or

2. commits the crime of criminal diversion of prescription medications and prescriptions in the fourth degree, and has previously been convicted of the crime of criminal diversion of prescription medications and prescriptions in the fourth degree.

Criminal diversion of prescription medications and prescriptions in the third degree is a class E felony.

N.Y. Penal Law § 178.15

Section 178.20 - Criminal diversion of prescription medications and prescriptions in the second degree

A person is guilty of criminal diversion of prescription medications and prescriptions in the second degree when he or she commits a criminal diversion act, and the value of the benefit exchanged is in excess of three thousand dollars.

N.Y. Penal Law § 178.20

Section 178.25 - Criminal diversion of prescription medications and prescriptions in the first degree

A person is guilty of criminal diversion of prescription medications and prescriptions in the first degree when he or she commits a criminal diversion act, and the value of the benefit exchanged is in excess of fifty thousand dollars.

N.Y. Penal Law § 178.25

Section 178.26 - Fraud and deceit related to controlled substances

1. No person shall willfully:

(a) obtain or attempt to obtain a controlled substance, a prescription for a controlled substance or an official New York state prescription form,

(i) by fraud, deceit, misrepresentation or subterfuge; or

(ii) by the concealment of a material fact; or

(iii) by the use of a false name or the giving of a false address;

(b) make a false statement in any prescription, order, application, report or record required by article thirty-three of the public health law;

(c) falsely assume the title of, or represent himself or herself to be a licensed manufacturer, distributor, pharmacy, pharmacist, practitioner, researcher, approved institutional dispenser, owner or employee of a registered outsourcing facility or other authorized person, for the purpose of obtaining a controlled substance as these terms are defined in article thirty-three of the public health law;

(d) make or utter any false or forged prescription or false or forged written order;

(e) affix any false or forged label to a package or receptacle containing controlled substances; or

(f) imprint on or affix to any controlled substance a false or forged code number or symbol.

2. Possession of a false or forged prescription for a controlled substance by any person other than a pharmacist in the lawful pursuance of his or her profession shall be presumptive evidence of his or her intent to use the same for the purpose of illegally obtaining a controlled substance.

3. Possession of a blank official New York state prescription form by any person to whom it was not lawfully issued shall be presumptive evidence of such person's intent to use same for the purpose of illegally obtaining a controlled substance.

4. Any person who, in the course of treatment, is supplied with a controlled substance or a prescription therefor by one practitioner and who with the intent to deceive, intentionally withholds or intentionally fails to disclose the fact, is supplied during such treatment with a controlled substance or a prescription therefor by another practitioner shall be guilty of a violation of this article.

5. The provisions of subdivision one of section thirty-three hundred ninety-six of the public health law shall apply to this section. Fraud and deceit related to controlled substances is a class A misdemeanor.

N.Y. Penal Law § 178.26

Added by New York Laws 2014, ch. 36,Sec. 1, eff. 6/23/2014.

Article 179 - CRIMINAL DIVERSION OF MEDICAL MARIHUANA

Section 179.00 - [Effective Until 7/5/2028] Criminal diversion of medical cannabis; definitions

The following definitions are applicable to this article:

1. "Medical cannabis" means medical cannabis as defined in section three of the cannabis law.

2. "Certification" means a certification, made under section thirty of the cannabis law.

N.Y. Penal Law § 179.00

Amended by New York Laws 2021, ch. 92,Sec. 47, eff. 3/31/2021.

Amended by New York Laws 2021, ch. 92,Sec. 41, eff. 3/31/2021.

Added by New York Laws 2014, ch. 90,Sec. 9, eff. 7/5/2014.

Section 179.05 - [Effective Until 7/5/2028] Criminal diversion of medical cannabis; limitations

The provisions of this article shall not apply to:

1. a practitioner authorized to issue a certification who acted in good faith in the lawful course of his or her profession; or

2. a registered organization as that term is defined in section thirty-four of the cannabis law who acted in good faith in the lawful course of the practice of pharmacy; or

3. a person who acted in good faith seeking treatment for a medical condition or assisting another person to obtain treatment for a medical condition.

N.Y. Penal Law § 179.05

Amended by New York Laws 2021, ch. 92,Sec. 47, eff. 3/31/2021.

Amended by New York Laws 2021, ch. 92,Sec. 41, eff. 3/31/2021.

Added by New York Laws 2014, ch. 90,Sec. 9, eff. 7/5/2014.

Section 179.10 - [Effective Until 7/5/2028] Criminal diversion of medical cannabis in the first degree

A person is guilty of criminal diversion of medical cannabis in the first degree when he or she is a practitioner, as that term is defined in section three of the cannabis law, who issues a certification with knowledge of reasonable grounds to know that (i) the recipient has no medical need for it, or (ii) it is for a purpose other than to treat a condition as defined in section three of the cannabis law.

N.Y. Penal Law § 179.10

Amended by New York Laws 2021, ch. 92,Sec. 47, eff. 3/31/2021.

Amended by New York Laws 2021, ch. 92,Sec. 41, eff. 3/31/2021.

Added by New York Laws 2014, ch. 90,Sec. 9, eff. 7/5/2014.

Section 179.11 - [Effective Until 7/5/2028] Criminal diversion of medical cannabis in the second degree

A person is guilty of criminal diversion of medical cannabis in the second degree when he or she sells, trades, delivers, or otherwise provides medical cannabis to another with knowledge or reasonable grounds to know that the recipient is not registered under article three of the cannabis law.

N.Y. Penal Law § 179.11

Amended by New York Laws 2021, ch. 92,Sec. 47, eff. 3/31/2021.

Amended by New York Laws 2021, ch. 92,Sec. 41, eff. 3/31/2021.

Added by New York Laws 2014, ch. 90,Sec. 9, eff. 7/5/2014.

Section 179.15 - [Effective Until 7/5/2028]Criminal retention of medical cannabis

A person is guilty of criminal retention of medical cannabis when, being a certified patient or designated caregiver, as those terms are defined in section three of the cannabis law, he or she knowingly obtains, possesses, stores or maintains an amount of cannabis in excess of the amount he or she is authorized to possess under the provisions of article three of the cannabis law.

N.Y. Penal Law § 179.15

Amended by New York Laws 2021, ch. 92,Sec. 47, eff. 3/31/2021.

Amended by New York Laws 2021, ch. 92,Sec. 41, eff. 3/31/2021.

Added by New York Laws 2014, ch. 90,Sec. 9, eff. 7/5/2014.

Article 180 - BRIBERY NOT INVOLVING PUBLIC SERVANTS, AND RELATED OFFENSES

Section 180.00 - Commercial bribing in the second degree

A person is guilty of commercial bribing in the second degree when he confers, or offers or agrees to confer, any benefit upon any employee, agent or fiduciary without the consent of the latter's employer or principal, with intent to influence his conduct in relation to his employer's or principal's affairs.

N.Y. Penal Law § 180.00

Section 180.03 - Commercial bribing in the first degree

A person is guilty of commercial bribing in the first degree when he confers, or offers or agrees to confer, any benefit upon any employee, agent or fiduciary without the consent of the latter's employer or principal, with intent to influence his conduct in relation to his employer's or principal's affairs, and when the value of the benefit conferred or offered or agreed to be conferred exceeds one thousand dollars and causes economic harm to the employer or principal in an amount exceeding two hundred fifty dollars.

N.Y. Penal Law § 180.03

Section 180.05 - Commercial bribe receiving in the second degree

An employee, agent or fiduciary is guilty of commercial bribe receiving in the second degree when, without the consent of his employer or principal, he solicits, accepts or agrees to accept any benefit from another person upon an agreement or understanding that such benefit will influence his conduct in relation to his employer's or principal's affairs.

N.Y. Penal Law § 180.05

Section 180.08 - Commercial bribe receiving in the first degree

An employee, agent or fiduciary is guilty of commercial bribe receiving in the first degree when, without the consent of his employer or principal, he solicits, accepts or agrees to accept any benefit from another person upon an agreement or understanding that such benefit will influence his conduct in relation to his employer's or principal's affairs, and when the value of the benefit solicited, accepted or agreed to be accepted exceeds one thousand dollars and causes economic harm to the employer or principal in an amount exceeding two hundred fifty dollars.

N.Y. Penal Law § 180.08

Section 180.10 - Bribery of labor official; definition of term

As used in this article, "labor official" means any duly appointed representative of a labor organization or any duly appointed trustee or representative of an employee welfare trust fund.

N.Y. Penal Law § 180.10

Section 180.15 - Bribing a labor official

A person is guilty of bribing a labor official when, with intent to influence a labor official in respect to any of his acts, decisions or duties as such labor official, he confers, or offers or agrees to confer, any benefit upon him.

N.Y. Penal Law § 180.15

Section 180.20 - Bribing a labor official; defense

In any prosecution for bribing a labor official, it is a defense that the defendant conferred or agreed to confer the benefit involved upon the labor official as a result of conduct of the latter constituting larceny committed by means of extortion, or an attempt to commit the same, or coercion, or an attempt to commit coercion.

N.Y. Penal Law § 180.20

Section 180.25 - Bribe receiving by a labor official

A labor official is guilty of bribe receiving by a labor official when he solicits, accepts or agrees to accept any benefit from another person upon an agreement or understanding that such benefit will influence him in respect to any of his acts, decisions, or duties as such labor official.

N.Y. Penal Law § 180.25

Section 180.30 - Bribe receiving by a labor official; no defense

The crimes of (a) bribe receiving by a labor official, and (b) larceny committed by means of extortion, attempt to commit the same, coercion or attempt to commit coercion, are not mutually exclusive, and it is no defense to a prosecution for bribe receiving by a labor official that, by reason of the same conduct, the defendant also committed one of such other specified crimes.

N.Y. Penal Law § 180.30

Section 180.35 - Sports bribery and tampering; definitions of terms

As used in this article:

1. "Sports contest" means any professional or amateur sport or athletic game or contest viewed by the public.

2. "Sports participant" means any person who participates or expects to participate in a sports contest as a player, contestant or member of a team, or as a coach, manager, trainer or other person directly associated with a player, contestant or team.

3. "Sports official" means any person who acts or expects to act in a sports contest as an umpire, referee, judge or otherwise to officiate at a sports contest.

4. "Pari-mutuel betting" is such betting as is authorized under the provisions of the pari-mutuel revenue law as set forth in chapter 254 of the laws of 1940 with amendments.

5. "Pari-mutuel horse race" means any horse race upon which betting is conducted under the provisions of the pari-mutuel revenue law as set forth in chapter 254 of the laws of 1940.

N.Y. Penal Law § 180.35

Section 180.40 - Sports bribing

A person is guilty of sports bribing when he:

1. Confers, or offers or agrees to confer, any benefit upon a sports participant with intent to influence him not to give his best efforts in a sports contest; or

2. Confers, or offers or agrees to confer, any benefit upon a sports official with intent to influence him to perform his duties improperly.

Sports bribing is a class D felony.

N.Y. Penal Law § 180.40

Section 180.45 - Sports bribe receiving

A person is guilty of sports bribe receiving when:

1. Being a sports participant, he solicits, accepts or agrees to accept any benefit from another person upon an agreement or understanding that he will thereby be influenced not to give his best efforts in a sports contest; or

2. Being a sports official, he solicits, accepts or agrees to accept any benefit from another person upon an agreement or understanding that he will perform his duties improperly.

Sports bribe receiving is a class E felony.

N.Y. Penal Law § 180.45

Section 180.50 - Tampering with a sports contest in the second degree

A person is guilty of tampering with a sports contest when, with intent to influence the outcome of a sports contest, he tampers with any sports participant, sports official or with any animal or equipment or other thing involved in the conduct or operation of a sports contest in a manner contrary to the rules and usages purporting to govern such a contest.

N.Y. Penal Law § 180.50

Section 180.51 - Tampering with a sports contest in the first degree

A person is guilty of tampering with a sports contest in the first degree when, with intent to influence the outcome of a pari-mutuel horse race:

1. He affects any equine animal involved in the conduct or operation of a pari-mutuel horse race by administering to the animal in any manner whatsoever any controlled substance listed in section thirty-three hundred six of the public health law; or

2. He knowingly enters or furnishes to another person for entry or brings into this state for entry into a pari-mutuel horse race, or rides or drives in any pari-mutuel horse race any running, trotting or pacing horse, mare, gelding, colt or filly under an assumed name, or deceptively out of its proper class, or that has been painted or disguised or represented to be any other or different horse, mare, gelding, colt or filly from that which it actually is; or

3. He knowingly and falsely registers with the jockey club, United States trotting association, American quarter horse association or national steeplechase and hunt association a horse, mare, gelding, colt or filly previously registered under a different name; or

4. He agrees with one or more persons to enter such misrepresented or drugged animal in a pari-mutuel horse race. A person shall not be convicted of a violation of this subdivision unless an overt act is alleged and proved to have been committed by one of said persons in furtherance of said agreement.

Tampering with a sports contest in the first degree is a class E felony.

N.Y. Penal Law § 180.51

Section 180.52 - Impairing the integrity of a pari-mutuel betting system in the second degree

A person is guilty of impairing the integrity of a pari-mutuel betting system in the second degree when, with the intent to obtain either any payment for himself or for a third person or with the intent to defraud any person he:

1. Alters, changes or interferes with any equipment or device used in connection with pari-mutuel betting; or

2. Causes any false, inaccurate, delayed or unauthorized data, impulse or signal to be fed into, or transmitted over, or registered in or displayed upon any equipment or device used in connection with pari-mutuel betting.

Impairing the integrity of a pari-mutuel betting system in the second degree is a class E felony.

N.Y. Penal Law § 180.52

Section 180.53 - Impairing the integrity of a pari-mutuel betting system in the first degree

A person is guilty of impairing the integrity of a pari-mutuel betting system in the first degree when, with the intent to obtain either any payment for himself or for a third person or with the intent to defraud any person, and when the value of the payment exceeds one thousand five hundred dollars he:

1. Alters, changes or interferes with any equipment or device used in connection with pari-mutuel betting; or

2. Causes any false, inaccurate, delayed or unauthorized data, impulse or signal to be fed into, or transmitted over, or registered in or displayed upon any equipment or device used in connection with pari-mutuel betting.

Impairing the integrity of a pari-mutuel betting system in the first degree is a class D felony.

N.Y. Penal Law § 180.53

Section 180.54 - Rent gouging; definition of term

As used in this article, "lawful rental and other lawful charges" means registered, reported or contracted for rent pursuant to chapter four hundred three of the laws of nineteen hundred eighty-three, article two of the private housing finance law or section eight of the federal housing act of nineteen hundred sixty-eight, or, rent contained in a court approved stipulation of settlement, even if such rent or charges are subsequently decreased by order of the department of housing and community renewal or a court of competent jurisdiction.

N.Y. Penal Law § 180.54

Section 180.55 - Rent gouging in the third degree

A person is guilty of rent gouging in the third degree when, in connection with the leasing, rental or use of real property, he solicits, accepts or agrees to accept from a person some consideration of value, less than two hundred fifty dollars, in addition to lawful rental and other lawful charges, upon an agreement or understanding that the furnishing of such consideration will increase the possibility that any person may obtain or renew the lease, rental or use of such property, or that a failure to furnish it will decrease the possibility that any person may obtain or renew the same.

N.Y. Penal Law § 180.55

Section 180.56 - Rent gouging in the second degree

A person is guilty of rent gouging in the second degree when, in connection with the leasing, rental or use of real property, he solicits, accepts or agrees to accept from a person some consideration of value, of two hundred fifty dollars or more, in addition to lawful rental and other lawful charges, upon an agreement or understanding that the furnishing of such consideration will increase the possibility that any person may obtain or renew the lease, rental or use of such property, or that a failure to furnish it will decrease the possibility that any person may obtain or renew the same.

N.Y. Penal Law § 180.56

Section 180.57 - Rent gouging in the first degree

A person is guilty of rent gouging in the first degree when, in the course of a scheme constituting a systematic ongoing course of conduct in connection with the leasing, rental or use of three or more apartment units, the rental price of which is regulated pursuant to the provisions of federal, state or local law, he solicits, accepts or agrees to accept from one or more persons in three separate transactions some consideration of value, knowing that such consideration is in addition to lawful rental and other lawful charges established pursuant to the provisions of such federal, state or local law, and upon an agreement or understanding that the furnishing of such consideration will increase the possibility that any person may obtain or renew the lease, rental or use of such property, or that a failure to furnish it will decrease the possibility that any person may obtain or renew same, and thereby obtains such consideration from one or more persons.

N.Y. Penal Law § 180.57

Article 185 - FRAUDS ON CREDITORS

Section 185.00 - Fraud in insolvency

1. As used in this section, "administrator" means an assignee or trustee for the benefit of creditors, a liquidator, a receiver or any other person entitled to administer property for the benefit of creditors.

2. A person is guilty of fraud in insolvency when, with intent to defraud any creditor and knowing that proceedings have been or are about to be instituted for the appointment of an administrator, or knowing that a composition agreement or other arrangement for the benefit of creditors has been or is about to be made, he

(a) conveys, transfers, removes, conceals, destroys, encumbers or otherwise disposes of any part of or any interest in the debtor's estate; or

(b) obtains any substantial part of or interest in the debtor's estate; or

(c) presents to any creditor or to the administrator any writing or record relating to the debtor's estate knowing the same to contain a false material statement; or

(d) misrepresents or fails or refuses to disclose to the administrator the existence, amount or location of any part of or any interest in the debtor's estate, or any other information which he is legally required to furnish to such administrator.

Fraud in insolvency is a class A misdemeanor.

N.Y. Penal Law § 185.00

Section 185.05 - Fraud involving a security interest

A person is guilty of fraud involving a security interest when, having executed a security agreement creating a security interest in personal property securing a monetary obligation owed to a secured party, and:

1. Having under the security agreement both the right of sale or other disposition of the property and the duty to account to the secured party for the proceeds of disposition, he sells or otherwise disposes of the property and wrongfully fails to account to the secured party for the proceeds of disposition; or

2. Having under the security agreement no right of sale or other disposition of the property, he knowingly secretes, withholds or disposes of such property in violation of the security agreement.

Fraud involving a security interest is a class A misdemeanor.

N.Y. Penal Law § 185.05

Section 185.10 - Fraudulent disposition of mortgaged property

A person is guilty of fraudulent disposition of mortgaged property when, having theretofore executed a mortgage of real or personal property or any instrument intended to operate as such, he sells, assigns, exchanges, secretes, injures, destroys or otherwise disposes of any part of the property, upon which the mortgage or other instrument is at the time a lien, with intent thereby to defraud the mortgagee or a purchaser thereof.

N.Y. Penal Law § 185.10

Section 185.15 - Fraudulent disposition of property subject to a conditional sale contract

A person is guilty of fraudulent disposition of property subject to a conditional sale contract when, prior to the performance of the condition of a conditional sale contract and being the buyer or any legal successor in interest of the buyer, he sells, assigns, mortgages, exchanges, secretes, injures, destroys or otherwise disposes of the goods subject to the conditional sale contract under claim of full ownership, with intent thereby to defraud another.

N.Y. Penal Law § 185.15

Article 187 - RESIDENTIAL MORTGAGE FRAUD

Section 187.00 - Definitions

As used in this article:

1. "Person" means any individual or entity.

2. "Residential mortgage loan" means a loan or agreement to extend credit, including the renewal, refinancing or modification of any such loan, made to a person, which loan is primarily secured by either a mortgage, deed of trust, or other lien upon any interest in residential real property or any certificate of stock or other evidence of ownership in, and a proprietary lease from, a corporation or partnership formed for the purpose of cooperative ownership of residential real property.

3. "Residential real property" means real property improved by a one-to-four family dwelling, or a residential unit in a building including units owned as condominiums or on a cooperative basis, used or occupied, or intended to be used or occupied, wholly or partly, as the home or residence of one or more persons, but shall not refer to unimproved real property upon which such dwellings are to be constructed.

4. "Residential mortgage fraud" is committed by a person who, knowingly and with intent to defraud, presents, causes to be presented, or prepares with knowledge or belief that it will be used in soliciting an applicant for, applying for, underwriting or closing a residential mortgage loan, or filing with a county clerk of any county in the state arising out of and related to the closing of a residential mortgage loan, any written statement which:

(a) contains materially false information concerning any fact material thereto; or

(b) conceals, for the purpose of misleading, information concerning any fact material thereto.

N.Y. Penal Law § 187.00

Section 187.01 - Limitation on prosecution

No individual who applies for a residential mortgage loan and intends to occupy such residential property which such mortgage secures shall be held liable under this article provided, however, any such individual who acts as an accessory to an individual or entity in committing any crime defined in this article may be charged as an accessory to such crime.

N.Y. Penal Law § 187.01

Section 187.05 - Residential mortgage fraud in the fifth degree

A person is guilty of residential mortgage fraud in the fifth degree when he or she commits residential mortgage fraud.

N.Y. Penal Law § 187.05

Section 187.10 - Residential mortgage fraud in the fourth degree

A person is guilty of residential mortgage fraud in the fourth degree when he or she commits residential mortgage fraud and thereby receives proceeds or any other funds in the aggregate in excess of one thousand dollars.

N.Y. Penal Law § 187.10

Section 187.15 - Residential mortgage fraud in the third degree

A person is guilty of residential mortgage fraud in the third degree when he or she commits residential mortgage fraud and thereby receives proceeds or any other funds in the aggregate in excess of three thousand dollars.

N.Y. Penal Law § 187.15

Section 187.20 - Residential mortgage fraud in the second degree

A person is guilty of residential mortgage fraud in the second degree when he or she commits residential mortgage fraud and thereby receives proceeds or any other funds in the aggregate in excess of fifty thousand dollars.

N.Y. Penal Law § 187.20

Section 187.25 - Residential mortgage fraud in the first degree

A person is guilty of residential mortgage fraud in the first degree when he or she commits residential mortgage fraud and thereby receives proceeds or any other funds in the aggregate in excess of one million dollars.

N.Y. Penal Law § 187.25

Article 190 - OTHER FRAUDS

Section 190.00 - Issuing a bad check; definitions of terms

The following definitions are applicable to this article:

1. "Check" means any check, draft or similar sight order for the payment of money which is not post-dated with respect to the time of utterance.

2. "Drawer" of a check means a person whose name appears thereon as the primary obligor, whether the actual signature be that of himself or of a person purportedly authorized to draw the check in his behalf.

3. "Representative drawer" means a person who signs a check as drawer in a representative capacity or as agent of the person whose name appears thereon as the principal drawer or obligor.

4. "Utter." A person "utters" a check when, as a drawer or representative drawer thereof, he delivers it or causes it to be delivered to a person who thereby acquires a right against the drawer with respect to such check. One who draws a check with intent that it be so delivered is deemed to have uttered it if the delivery occurs.

5. "Pass." A person "passes" a check when, being a payee, holder or bearer of a check which previously has been or purports to have been drawn and uttered by another, he delivers it, for a purpose other than collection, to a third person who thereby acquires a right with respect thereto.

6. "Funds" means money or credit.

7. "Insufficient funds." A drawer has "insufficient funds" with a drawee to cover a check when he has no funds or account whatever, or funds in an amount less than that of the check; and a check dishonored for "no account" shall also be deemed to have been dishonored for "insufficient funds."

N.Y. Penal Law § 190.00

Section 190.05 - Issuing a bad check

A person is guilty of issuing a bad check when:

1. (a) As a drawer or representative drawer, he utters a check knowing that he or his principal, as the case may be, does not then have sufficient funds with the drawee to cover it, and (b) he intends or believes at the time of utterance that payment will be refused by the drawee upon presentation, and (c) payment is refused by the drawee upon presentation; or

2. (a) He passes a check knowing that the drawer thereof does not then have sufficient funds with the drawee to cover it, and (b) he intends or believes at the time the check is passed that payment will be refused by the drawee upon presentation, and (c) payment is refused by the drawee upon presentation.

Issuing a bad check is a class B misdemeanor.

N.Y. Penal Law § 190.05

Section 190.10 - Issuing a bad check; presumptions

1. When the drawer of a check has insufficient funds with the drawee to cover it at the time of utterance, the subscribing drawer or representative drawer, as the case may be, is presumed to know of such insufficiency.

2. A subscribing drawer or representative drawer, as the case may be, of an ultimately dishonored check is presumed to have intended or believed that the check would be dishonored upon presentation when:

(a) The drawer had no account with the drawee at the time of utterance; or

(b)

(i) The drawer had insufficient funds with the drawee at the time of utterance, and (ii) the check was presented to the drawee for payment not more than thirty days after the date of utterance, and (iii) the drawer had insufficient funds with the drawee at the time of presentation.

3. Dishonor of a check by the drawee and insufficiency of the drawer's funds at the time of presentation may properly be proved by introduction in evidence of a notice of protest of the check, or of a certificate under oath of an authorized representative of the drawee declaring the dishonor and insufficiency, and such proof shall constitute presumptive evidence of such dishonor and insufficiency.

N.Y. Penal Law § 190.10

Section 190.15 - Issuing a bad check; defenses

In any prosecution for issuing a bad check, it is an affirmative defense that:

1. The defendant or a person acting in his behalf made full satisfaction of the amount of the check within ten days after dishonor by the drawee; or

2. The defendant, in acting as a representative drawer, did so as an employee who, without personal benefit, merely executed the orders of his employer or of a superior officer or employee generally authorized to direct his activities.

N.Y. Penal Law § 190.15

Section 190.20 - False advertising

A person is guilty of false advertising when, with intent to promote the sale or to increase the consumption of property or services, he makes or causes to be made a false or misleading statement in any advertisement or publishes any advertisement in violation of chapter three of the act of congress entitled "Truth in Lending Act" and the regulations thereunder, as such act and regulations may from time to time be amended, addressed to the public or to a substantial number of persons; except that, in any prosecution under this section, it is an affirmative defense that the allegedly false or misleading statement was not knowingly or recklessly made or caused to be made.

N.Y. Penal Law § 190.20

Section 190.23 - False personation

A person is guilty of false personation when after being informed of the consequences of such act, he or she knowingly misrepresents his or her actual name, date of birth or address to a police officer or peace officer with intent to prevent such police officer or peace officer from ascertaining such information.

N.Y. Penal Law § 190.23

Section 190.25 - Criminal impersonation in the second degree

A person is guilty of criminal impersonation in the second degree when he:

1. Impersonates another and does an act in such assumed character with intent to obtain a benefit or to injure or defraud another; or

2. Pretends to be a representative of some person or organization and does an act in such pretended capacity with intent to obtain a benefit or to injure or defraud another; or

3. (a) Pretends to be a public servant, or wears or displays without authority any uniform, badge, insignia or facsimile thereof by which such public servant is lawfully distinguished, or falsely expresses by his words or actions that he is a public servant or is acting with approval or authority of a public agency or department; and (b) so acts with intent to induce another to submit to such pretended official authority, to solicit funds or to otherwise cause another to act in reliance upon that pretense.

4. Impersonates another by communication by internet website or electronic means with intent to obtain a benefit or injure or defraud another, or by such communication pretends to be a public servant in order to induce another to submit to such authority or act in reliance on such pretense.

N.Y. Penal Law § 190.25

Section 190.26 - Criminal impersonation in the first degree

A person is guilty of criminal impersonation in the first degree when he:

1. Pretends to be a police officer or a federal law enforcement officer as enumerated in section 2.15 of the criminal procedure law, or wears or displays without authority, any uniform, badge or other insignia or facsimile thereof, by which such police officer or federal law enforcement officer is lawfully distinguished or expresses by his or her words or actions that he or she is acting with the approval or authority of any police department or acting as a federal law enforcement officer with the approval of any agency that employs federal law enforcement officers as enumerated in section 2.15 of the criminal procedure law; and

2. So acts with intent to induce another to submit to such pretended official authority or otherwise to act in reliance upon said pretense and in the course of such pretense commits or attempts to commit a felony; or

3. Pretending to be a duly licensed physician or other person authorized to issue a prescription for any drug or any instrument or device used in the taking or administering of drugs for which a prescription is required by law, communicates to a pharmacist an oral prescription which is required to be reduced to writing pursuant to section thirty-three hundred thirty-two of the public health law.

Criminal impersonation in the first degree is a class E felony.

N.Y. Penal Law § 190.26

Section 190.27 - Criminal sale of a police uniform

A person is guilty of criminal sale of a police uniform when he or she sells or offers for sale the uniform of any police officer to any person, unless presented with a valid photo identification card showing the purchaser to be a member of the police department which has authorized the requested uniform or an authorization to purchase specified uniforms signed by the police chief or the police commissioner of such police department accompanied by a personal photo identification. For purposes of this section, "police officer" shall include federal law enforcement officers, as defined in section 2.15 of the criminal procedure law; and "uniform" shall include all or any part of the uniform which identifies the wearer as a member of a police department, such as the uniform, shield, badge, numbers or other identifying insignias or emblems.

N.Y. Penal Law § 190.27

Section 190.30 - Unlawfully concealing a will

A person is guilty of unlawfully concealing a will when, with intent to defraud, he conceals, secretes, suppresses, mutilates or destroys a will, codicil or other testamentary instrument.

N.Y. Penal Law § 190.30

Section 190.35 - Misconduct by corporate official

A person is guilty of misconduct by corporate official when:

1. Being a director of a stock corporation, he knowingly concurs in any vote or act of the directors of such corporation, or any of them, by which it is intended:

(a) To make a dividend except in the manner provided by law; or

(b) To divide, withdraw or in any manner pay to any stockholder any part of the capital stock of the corporation except in the manner provided by law; or

(c) To discount or receive any note or other evidence of debt in payment of an installment of capital stock actually called in and required to be paid, or with intent to provide the means of making such payment; or

(d) To receive or discount any note or other evidence of debt with intent to enable any stockholder to withdraw any part of the money paid in by him on his stock; or

(e) To apply any portion of the funds of such corporation, directly or indirectly, to the purchase of shares of its own stock, except in the manner provided by law; or

2. Being a director or officer of a stock corporation:

(a) He issues, participates in issuing, or concurs in a vote to issue any increase of its capital stock beyond the amount of the capital stock thereof, duly authorized by or in pursuance of law; or

(b) He sells, or agrees to sell, or is directly or indirectly interested in the sale of any share of stock of such corporation, or in any agreement to sell the same, unless at the time of such sale or agreement he is an actual owner of such share, provided that the foregoing shall not apply to a sale by or on behalf of an underwriter or dealer in connection with a bona fide public offering of shares of stock of such corporation.

Misconduct by corporate official is a class B misdemeanor.

N.Y. Penal Law § 190.35

Section 190.40 - Criminal usury in the second degree

A person is guilty of criminal usury in the second degree when, not being authorized or permitted by law to do so, he knowingly charges, takes or receives any money or other property as interest on the loan or forbearance of any money or other property, at a rate exceeding twenty-five per centum per annum or the equivalent rate for a longer or shorter period.

N.Y. Penal Law § 190.40

Section 190.42 - Criminal usury in the first degree

A person is guilty of criminal usury in the first degree when, not being authorized or permitted by law to do so, he knowingly charges, takes or receives any money or other property as interest on the loan or forbearance of any money or other property, at a rate exceeding twenty-five per centum per annum or the equivalent rate for a longer or shorter period and either the actor had previously been convicted of the crime of criminal usury or of the attempt to commit such crime, or the actor's conduct was part of a scheme or business of making or collecting usurious loans.

N.Y. Penal Law § 190.42

Section 190.45 - Possession of usurious loan records

A person is guilty of possession of usurious loan records when, with knowledge of the contents thereof, he possesses any writing, paper, instrument or article used to record criminally usurious transactions prohibited by section 190.40.

N.Y. Penal Law § 190.45

Section 190.50 - Unlawful collection practices

A person is guilty of unlawful collection practices when, with intent to enforce a claim or judgment for money or property, he knowingly sends, mails or delivers to another person a notice, document or other instrument which has no judicial or official sanction and which in its format or appearance, simulates a summons, complaint, court order or process, or an insignia, seal or printed form of a federal, state or local government or an instrumentality thereof, or is otherwise calculated to induce a belief that such notice, document or instrument has a judicial or official sanction.

N.Y. Penal Law § 190.50

Section 190.55 - Making a false statement of credit terms

A person is guilty of making a false statement of credit terms when he knowingly and willfully violates the provisions of chapter two of the act of congress entitled "Truth in Lending Act" and the regulations thereunder, as such act and regulations may from time to time be amended, by understating or failing to state the interest rate required to be disclosed, or by failing to make or by making a false or inaccurate or incomplete statement of other credit terms in violation of such act.

N.Y. Penal Law § 190.55

Section 190.60 - Scheme to defraud in the second degree

1. A person is guilty of a scheme to defraud in the second degree when he engages in a scheme constituting a systematic ongoing course of conduct with intent to defraud more than one person or to obtain property from more than one person by false or fraudulent pretenses, representations or promises, and so obtains property from one or more of such persons.

2. In any prosecution under this section, it shall be necessary to prove the identity of at least one person from whom the defendant so obtained property, but it shall not be necessary to prove the identity of any other intended victim.

Scheme to defraud in the second degree is a class A misdemeanor.

N.Y. Penal Law § 190.60

Section 190.65 - Scheme to defraud in the first degree

1. A person is guilty of a scheme to defraud in the first degree when he or she:

(a) engages in a scheme constituting a systematic ongoing course of conduct with intent to defraud ten or more persons or to obtain property from ten or more persons by false or fraudulent pretenses, representations or promises, and so obtains property from one or more of such persons; or

(b) engages in a scheme constituting a systematic ongoing course of conduct with intent to defraud more than one person or to obtain property from more than one person by false or fraudulent pretenses, representations or promises, and so obtains property with a value in excess of one thousand dollars from one or more such persons; or

(c) engages in a scheme constituting a systematic ongoing course of conduct with intent to defraud more than one person, more than one of whom is a vulnerable elderly person as defined in subdivision three of section 260.31 of this chapter or to obtain property from more than one person, more than one of whom is a vulnerable elderly person as defined in subdivision three of section 260.31 of this chapter, by false or fraudulent pretenses, representations or promises, and so obtains property from one or more such persons; or

(d) engages in a systematic ongoing course of conduct, with intent to defraud more than one person by false or fraudulent pretenses, representations or promises, by disposing of solid waste as defined in section 27-0701 of the environmental conservation law on such persons' property, and so damages the property of one or more of such persons in an amount in excess of one thousand dollars.

2. In any prosecution under this section, it shall be necessary to prove the identity of at least one person from whom the defendant so obtained property, but it shall not be necessary to prove the identity of any other intended victim, provided that in any prosecution under paragraph (c) of subdivision one of this section, it shall be necessary to prove the identity of at least one such vulnerable elderly person as defined in subdivision three of section 260.31 of this chapter.

3. In any prosecution under paragraph (d) of subdivision one of this section, it shall be necessary to prove the identity of at least one person on whose property the defendant fraudulently disposed of solid waste pursuant to such paragraph (d), but it shall not be necessary to prove the identity of any other victim or intended victim.

Scheme to defraud in the first degree is a class E felony.

N.Y. Penal Law § 190.65

Amended by New York Laws 2020, ch. 332,Sec. 6, eff. 1/1/2021.

Section 190.70 - Scheme to defraud the state by unlawfully selling prescriptions

A person is guilty of a scheme to defraud the state by unlawfully selling prescriptions when he or she engages, with intent to defraud the state, in a scheme constituting a systematic, ongoing course of conduct to make, sell, deliver for sale or offer for sale one or more prescriptions and so obtains goods or services from the state with a value in excess of one thousand dollars or causes the state to reimburse another in excess of one thousand dollars for the delivery of such goods or services.

N.Y. Penal Law § 190.70

Section 190.72 - Unauthorized radio transmission

A person is guilty of an unauthorized radio transmission when such person knowingly makes or causes to be made a radio transmission in this state, on a radio frequency assigned and licensed by the federal communications commission for use by amplitude modulation (AM) radio stations between the frequencies of five hundred thirty kilohertz (kHz) to seventeen hundred kilohertz (kHz), or frequency modulation (FM) radio stations between the frequencies of eighty-eight megahertz (MHz) to one hundred eight megahertz (MHz), without authorization or having first obtained a license from the federal communications commission or duly authorized federal agency, in violation of federal law.

N.Y. Penal Law § 190.72

Section 190.75 - Criminal use of an access device in the second degree

A person is guilty of criminal use of an access device in the second degree when he knowingly uses an access device without consent of an owner thereof with intent to unlawfully obtain telecommunications services on behalf of himself or a third person. As used in this section, access device shall have the meaning set forth in subdivision seven-c of section 155.00 of this chapter.

N.Y. Penal Law § 190.75

Section 190.76 - Criminal use of an access device in the first degree

A person is guilty of criminal use of an access device in the first degree when he knowingly uses an access device without consent of an owner thereof with intent to unlawfully obtain telecommunications services on behalf of himself or a third person, and so obtains such services with a value in excess of one thousand dollars. As used in this section, access device shall have the meaning set forth in subdivision seven-c of section 155.00 of this chapter.

N.Y. Penal Law § 190.76

Section 190.77 - Offenses involving theft of identity; definitions

1. For the purposes of sections 190.78, 190.79, 190.80 and 190.80-a and 190.85 of this article "personal identifying information" means a person's name, address, telephone number, date of birth, driver's license number, social security number, place of employment, mother's maiden name, financial services account number or code, savings account number or code, checking account number or code, brokerage account number or code, credit card account number or code, debit card number or code, automated teller machine number or code, taxpayer identification number, computer system password, signature or copy of a signature, electronic signature, unique biometric data that is a fingerprint, voice print, retinal image or iris image of another person, telephone calling card number, mobile identification number or code, electronic serial number or personal identification number, or any other name, number, code or information that may be used alone or in conjunction with other such information to assume the identity of another person.

2. For the purposes of sections 190.78, 190.79, 190.80, 190.80-a, 190.81, 190.82 and 190.83 of this article:

a. "electronic signature" shall have the same meaning as defined in subdivision three of section three hundred two of the state technology law.

b. "personal identification number" means any number or code which may be used alone or in conjunction with any other information to assume the identity of another person or access financial resources or credit of another person.

c. "member of the armed forces" shall mean a person in the military service of the United States or the military service of the state, including but not limited to, the armed forces of the United States, the army national guard, the air national guard, the New York naval militia, the New York guard, and such additional forces as may be created by the federal or state government as authorized by law.

N.Y. Penal Law § 190.77

Section 190.78 - Identity theft in the third degree

A person is guilty of identity theft in the third degree when he or she knowingly and with intent to defraud assumes the identity of another person by presenting himself or herself as that other person, or by acting as that other person or by using personal identifying information of that other person, and thereby:

1. obtains goods, money, property or services or uses credit in the name of such other person or causes financial loss to such person or to another person or persons; or

2. commits a class A misdemeanor or higher level crime.

Identity theft in the third degree is a class A misdemeanor.

N.Y. Penal Law § 190.78

Section 190.79 - Identity theft in the second degree

A person is guilty of identify theft in the second degree when he or she knowingly and with intent to defraud assumes the identity of another person by presenting himself or herself as that other person, or by acting as that other person or by using personal identifying information of that other person, and thereby:

1. obtains goods, money, property or services or uses credit in the name of such other person in an aggregate amount that exceeds five hundred dollars; or

2. causes financial loss to such person or to another person or persons in an aggregate amount that exceeds five hundred dollars; or

3. commits or attempts to commit a felony or acts as an accessory to the commission of a felony; or

4. commits the crime of identity theft in the third degree as defined in section 190.78 of this article and has been previously convicted within the last five years of identity theft in the third degree as defined in section 190.78, identity theft in the second degree as defined in this section, identity theft in the first degree as defined in section 190.80, unlawful possession of personal identification information in the third degree as defined in section 190.81, unlawful possession of personal identification information in the second degree as defined in section 190.82, unlawful possession of personal identification information in the first degree as defined in section 190.83, unlawful possession of a skimmer device in the second degree as defined in section 190.85, unlawful possession of a skimmer device in the first degree as defined in section 190.86, grand larceny in the fourth degree as defined in section 155.30, grand larceny in the third degree as defined in section

155.35, grand larceny in the second degree as defined in section 155.40 or grand larceny in the first degree as defined in section 155.42 of this chapter.

Identity theft in the second degree is a class E felony.

N.Y. Penal Law § 190.79

Section 190.80 - Identity theft in the first degree

A person is guilty of identity theft in the first degree when he or she knowingly and with intent to defraud assumes the identity of another person by presenting himself or herself as that other person, or by acting as that other person or by using personal identifying information of that other person, and thereby:

1. obtains goods, money, property or services or uses credit in the name of such other person in an aggregate amount that exceeds two thousand dollars; or

2. causes financial loss to such person or to another person or persons in an aggregate amount that exceeds two thousand dollars; or

3. commits or attempts to commit a class D felony or higher level crime or acts as an accessory in the commission of a class D or higher level felony; or

4. commits the crime of identity theft in the second degree as defined in section 190.79 of this article and has been previously convicted within the last five years of identity theft in the third degree as defined in section 190.78, identity theft in the second degree as defined in section 190.79, identity theft in the first degree as defined in this section, unlawful possession of personal identification information in the third degree as defined in section 190.81, unlawful possession of personal identification information in the second degree as defined in section 190.82, unlawful possession of personal identification information in the first degree as defined in section 190.83, unlawful possession of a skimmer device in the second degree as defined in section 190.85, unlawful possession of a skimmer device in the first degree as defined in section 190.86, grand larceny in the fourth degree as defined in section 155.30, grand larceny in the third degree as defined in section 155.35, grand larceny in the second degree as defined in section 155.40 or grand larceny in the first degree as defined in section 155.42 of this chapter.

Identity theft in the first degree is a class D felony.

N.Y. Penal Law § 190.80

Section 190.80-A - Aggravated identity theft

A person is guilty of aggravated identity theft when he or she knowingly and with intent to defraud assumes the identity of another person by presenting himself or herself as that other person, or by acting as that other person or by using personal identifying information of that other person, and knows that such person is a member of the armed forces, and knows that such member is presently deployed outside of the continental United States and:

1. thereby obtains goods, money, property or services or uses credit in the name of such member of the armed forces in an aggregate amount that exceeds five hundred dollars; or

2. thereby causes financial loss to such member of the armed forces in an aggregate amount that exceeds five hundred dollars.

Aggravated identity theft is a class D felony.

N.Y. Penal Law § 190.80-A

Section 190.81 - Unlawful possession of personal identification information in the third degree

A person is guilty of unlawful possession of personal identification information in the third degree when he or she knowingly possesses a person's financial services account number or code, savings account number or code, checking account number or code, brokerage account number or code, credit card account number or code, debit card number or code, automated teller machine number or code, personal identification number, mother's maiden name, computer system password, electronic signature or unique biometric data that is a fingerprint, voice print, retinal image or iris image of another person knowing such information is intended to be used in furtherance of the commission of a crime defined in this chapter.

N.Y. Penal Law § 190.81

Section 190.82 - Unlawful possession of personal identification information in the second degree

A person is guilty of unlawful possession of personal identification information in the second degree when he or she knowingly possesses two hundred fifty or more items of personal identification information of the following nature: a person's financial services account number or code, savings account number or code, checking account number or code, brokerage account number or code, credit card account number or code, debit card number or code, automated teller machine number or code, personal identification number, mother's maiden name, computer system password, electronic signature or unique biometric data that is a fingerprint, voice print, retinal image or iris image of another person knowing such information is intended to be used in furtherance of the commission of a crime defined in this chapter.

N.Y. Penal Law § 190.82

Section 190.83 - Unlawful possession of personal identification information in the first degree

A person is guilty of unlawful possession of personal identification information in the first degree when he or she commits the crime of unlawful possession of personal identification information in the second degree and:

1. with intent to further the commission of identity theft in the second degree, he or she supervises more than three accomplices; or

2. he or she has been previously convicted within the last five years of identity theft in the third degree as defined in section 190.78, identity theft in the second degree as defined in section 190.79, identity theft in the first degree as defined in section 190.80, unlawful possession of personal identification information in the third degree as defined in section 190.81,

unlawful possession of personal identification information in the second degree as defined in section 190.82, unlawful possession of personal identification information in the first degree as defined in this section, unlawful possession of a skimmer device in the second degree as defined in section 190.85, unlawful possession of a skimmer device in the first degree as defined in section 190.86, grand larceny in the fourth degree as defined in section 155.30, grand larceny in the third degree as defined in section 155.35, grand larceny in the second degree as defined in section 155.40 or grand larceny in the first degree as defined in section 155.42 of this chapter; or

3. with intent to further the commission of identity theft in the second degree:

(a) he or she supervises more than two accomplices, and

(b) he or she knows that the person whose personal identification information that he or she possesses is a member of the armed forces, and

(c) he or she knows that such member of the armed forces is presently deployed outside of the continental United States.

Unlawful possession of personal identification information in the first degree is a class D felony.

N.Y. Penal Law § 190.83

Section 190.84 - Defenses

In any prosecution for identity theft or unlawful possession of personal identification information pursuant to this article, it shall be an affirmative defense that the person charged with the offense:

1. was under twenty-one years of age at the time of committing the offense and the person used or possessed the personal identifying or identification information of another solely for the purpose of purchasing alcohol;

2. was under eighteen years of age at the time of committing the offense and the person used or possessed the personal identifying or identification information of another solely for the purpose of purchasing tobacco products; or

3. used or possessed the personal identifying or identification information of another person solely for the purpose of misrepresenting the person's age to gain access to a place the access to which is restricted based on age.

N.Y. Penal Law § 190.84

Section 190.85 - Unlawful possession of a skimmer device in the second degree

1. A person is guilty of unlawful possession of a skimmer device in the second degree when he or she possesses a skimmer device with the intent that such device be used in furtherance of the commission of the crime of identity theft or unlawful possession of personal identification information as defined in this article.

2. For purposes of this article, "skimmer device" means a device designed or adapted to obtain personal identifying information from a credit card, debit card, public benefit card, access card or device, or other card or device that contains personal identifying information.

Unlawful possession of a skimmer device in the second degree is a class A misdemeanor.

N.Y. Penal Law § 190.85

Section 190.86 - Unlawful possession of a skimmer device in the first degree

A person is guilty of unlawful possession of a skimmer device in the first degree when he or she commits the crime of unlawful possession of a skimmer device in the second degree and he or she has been previously convicted within the last five years of identity theft in the third degree as defined in section 190.78, identity theft in the second degree as defined in section 190.79, identity theft in the first degree as defined in section 190.80, unlawful possession of personal identification information in the third degree as defined in section 190.81, unlawful possession of personal identification information in the second degree as defined in section 190.82, unlawful possession of personal identification information in the first degree as defined in section 190.83, unlawful possession of a skimmer device in the second degree as defined in section 190.85, unlawful possession of a skimmer device in the first degree as defined in this section, grand larceny in the fourth degree as defined in section 155.30, grand larceny in the third degree as defined in section 155.35, grand larceny in the second degree as defined in section 155.40 or grand larceny in the first degree as defined in section 155.42 of this chapter.

N.Y. Penal Law § 190.86

Section 190.87 - Immigrant assistant services fraud in the second degree

A person is guilty of immigrant assistance services fraud in the second degree when, with intent to defraud another person seeking immigrant assistance services, as defined in article twenty-eight-C of the general business law, from such person, he or she violates section four hundred sixty-d of the general business law with intent to obtain property from such other person by false or fraudulent pretenses, representations or promises, and thereby wrongfully obtains such property.

N.Y. Penal Law § 190.87

Added by New York Laws 2014, ch. 206,Sec. 7, eff. 2/2/2015.

Section 190.89 - Immigrant assistance services fraud in the first degree

A person is guilty of immigrant assistance services fraud in the first degree when, with intent to defraud another person seeking immigrant assistance services, as defined in article twenty-eight-C of the general business law, from such person, he or she violates section four hundred sixty-d of the general business law with intent to obtain property from such other person by false or fraudulent pretenses, representations or promises, and thereby wrongfully obtains such property with a value in excess of one thousand dollars.

N.Y. Penal Law § 190.89

Added by New York Laws 2014, ch. 206,Sec. 8, eff. 2/2/2015.

Title L - OFFENSES AGAINST PUBLIC ADMINISTRATION
Article 195 - OFFICIAL MISCONDUCT AND OBSTRUCTION OF PUBLIC SERVANTS GENERALLY

Section 195.00 - Official misconduct

A public servant is guilty of official misconduct when, with intent to obtain a benefit or deprive another person of a benefit:

1. He commits an act relating to his office but constituting an unauthorized exercise of his official functions, knowing that such act is unauthorized; or

2. He knowingly refrains from performing a duty which is imposed upon him by law or is clearly inherent in the nature of his office.

Official misconduct is a class A misdemeanor.

N.Y. Penal Law § 195.00

Section 195.02 - Concealment of a human corpse

A person is guilty of concealment of a human corpse when, having a reasonable expectation that a human corpse or a part thereof will be produced for or used as physical evidence in:

(a) an official proceeding;

(b) an autopsy as part of a criminal investigation; or

(c) an examination by law enforcement personnel as part of a criminal investigation; such person, alone or in concert with another, conceals, alters or destroys such corpse or part thereof with the intent to prevent its production, use or discovery.

Concealment of a human corpse is a class E felony.

N.Y. Penal Law § 195.02

Added by New York Laws 2015, ch. 242, Sec. 2, eff. 11/22/2015.

Section 195.05 - Obstructing governmental administration in the second degree

A person is guilty of obstructing governmental administration when he intentionally obstructs, impairs or perverts the administration of law or other governmental function or prevents or attempts to prevent a public servant from performing an official function, by means of intimidation, physical force or interference, or by means of any independently unlawful act, or by means of interfering, whether or not physical force is involved, with radio, telephone, television or other telecommunications systems owned or operated by the state, or a county, city, town, village, fire district or emergency medical service or by means of releasing a dangerous animal under circumstances evincing the actor's intent that the animal obstruct governmental administration.

N.Y. Penal Law § 195.05

Section 195.06 - Killing or injuring a police animal

A person is guilty of killing or injuring a police animal when such person intentionally kills or injures any animal while such animal is in the performance of its duties and under the supervision of a police or peace officer.

N.Y. Penal Law § 195.06

Section 195.06-A - Killing a police work dog or police work horse

A person is guilty of killing a police work dog or police work horse when such person intentionally kills a police work dog or police work horse while such dog or horse is in the performance of its duties and under the supervision of a police officer. For purposes of this section, "police work dog" or "police work horse," as the case may be, shall mean any dog or horse owned or harbored by any state or municipal police department or any state or federal law enforcement agency, which has been trained to aid law enforcement officers and is actually being used for police work purposes.

N.Y. Penal Law § 195.06-A

Added by New York Laws 2013, ch. 162, Sec. 1, eff. 11/1/2013.

Section 195.07 - Obstructing governmental administration in the first degree

A person is guilty of obstructing governmental administration in the first degree when he commits the crime of obstructing governmental administration in the second degree by means of interfering with a telecommunications system thereby causing serious physical injury to another person.

N.Y. Penal Law § 195.07

Section 195.08 - Obstructing governmental administration by means of a self-defense spray device

A person is guilty of obstructing governmental administration by means of a self-defense spray device when, with the intent to prevent a police officer or peace officer from performing a lawful duty, he causes temporary physical impairment to a police officer or peace officer by intentionally discharging a self-defense spray device, as defined in paragraph fourteen of subdivision a of section 265.20 of this chapter, thereby causing such temporary physical impairment.

N.Y. Penal Law § 195.08

Section 195.10 - Refusing to aid a peace or a police officer

A person is guilty of refusing to aid a peace or a police officer when, upon command by a peace or a police officer identifiable or identified to him as such, he unreasonably fails or refuses to aid such peace or a police officer in effecting an arrest, or in preventing the commission by another person of any offense.

N.Y. Penal Law § 195.10

Section 195.11 - Harming an animal trained to aid a person with a disability in the second degree

A person is guilty of harming an animal trained to aid a person with a disability in the second degree when such person intentionally causes physical injury to such animal while it is in the performance of aiding a person with a disability, and thereby renders such animal incapable of providing such aid to such person, or to another person with a disability.

N.Y. Penal Law § 195.11

Section 195.12 - Harming an animal trained to aid a person with a disability in the first degree

A person is guilty of harming an animal trained to aid a person with a disability in the first degree when such person:

1. intentionally causes physical injury to such animal while it is in the performance of aiding a person with a disability, and thereby renders such animal permanently incapable of providing such aid to such person, or to another person with a disability; or

2. intentionally kills such animal while it is in the performance of aiding a person with a disability.

Harming an animal trained to aid a person with a disability in the first degree is a class A misdemeanor.

N.Y. Penal Law § 195.12

Section 195.15 - Obstructing firefighting operations

A person is guilty of obstructing firefighting operations when he or she intentionally and unreasonably obstructs the efforts of any:

1. firefighter in extinguishing a fire, or prevents or dissuades another from extinguishing or helping to extinguish a fire;

2. firefighter, police officer or peace officer in performing his or her duties in circumstances involving an imminent danger created by an explosion, threat of explosion or the presence of toxic fumes or gases; or

3. firefighter performing emergency medical care on a sick or injured person. Obstructing firefighting operations is a class A misdemeanor.

N.Y. Penal Law § 195.15

Amended by New York Laws 2017, ch. 124,Sec. 1, eff. 11/1/2017.

Section 195.16 - Obstructing emergency medical services

A person is guilty of obstructing emergency medical services when he or she intentionally and unreasonably obstructs the efforts of any service, technician, personnel, system or unit specified in section three thousand one of the public health law in the performance of their duties.

N.Y. Penal Law § 195.16

Section 195.17 - Obstruction of governmental duties by means of a bomb, destructive device, explosive, or hazardous substance

A person is guilty of obstruction of governmental duties by means of a bomb, destructive device, explosive, or hazardous substance when he or she, in furtherance of a felony offense, knowingly and unlawfully installs or causes to be installed a bomb, destructive device, explosive, or hazardous substance, in any object, place, or compartment that is subject to a search so as to obstruct, prevent, hinder or delay the administration of law or performance of a government function.

N.Y. Penal Law § 195.17

Section 195.20 - Defrauding the government

A person is guilty of defrauding the government when, being a public servant or party officer, he or she:

(a) engages in a scheme constituting a systematic ongoing course of conduct with intent to:

(i) defraud the state or a political subdivision of the state or a governmental instrumentality within the state or to obtain property, services or other resources from the state or a political subdivision of the state or a governmental instrumentality within the state by false or fraudulent pretenses, representations or promises; or

(ii) defraud the state or a political subdivision of the state or a governmental instrumentality within the state by making use of property, services or resources of the state, political subdivision of the state or a governmental instrumentality within the state for private business purposes or other compensated non-governmental purposes; and

(b) so obtains property, services or other resources with a value in excess of one thousand dollars from such state, political subdivision or governmental instrumentality.

Defrauding the government is a class E felony.

N.Y. Penal Law § 195.20

Article 200 - BRIBERY INVOLVING PUBLIC SERVANTS AND RELATED OFFENSES

Section 200.00 - Bribery in the third degree

A person is guilty of bribery in the third degree when he confers, or offers or agrees to confer, any benefit upon a public servant upon an agreement or understanding that such public servant's vote, opinion, judgment, action, decision or exercise of discretion as a public servant will thereby be influenced.

N.Y. Penal Law § 200.00

Section 200.03 - Bribery in the second degree

A person is guilty of bribery in the second degree when he confers, or offers or agrees to confer, any benefit valued in excess of five thousand dollars upon a public servant upon an agreement or understanding that such public servant's vote, opinion, judgment, action, decision or exercise of discretion as a public servant will thereby be influenced.

N.Y. Penal Law § 200.03

Amended by New York Laws 2014, ch. 55,Sec. H-A-18, eff. 4/30/2014.

Section 200.04 - Bribery in the first degree

A person is guilty of bribery in the first degree when the person confers, or offers or agrees to confer :

(1) any benefit upon a public servant upon an agreement or understanding that such public servant's vote, opinion, judgment, action, decision or exercise of discretion as a public servant will thereby be influenced in the investigation, arrest, detention, prosecution or incarceration of any person for the commission or alleged commission of a class A felony defined in article two hundred twenty of this part or an attempt to commit any such class A felony; or

(2) any benefit valued in excess of one hundred thousand dollars upon a public servant upon an agreement or understanding that such public servant's vote, opinion, judgment, action, decision or exercise of discretion as a public servant will thereby be influenced.

Bribery in the first degree is a class B felony.

N.Y. Penal Law § 200.04

Amended by New York Laws 2014, ch. 55,Sec. H-A-19, eff. 4/30/2014.

Section 200.05 - Bribery; defense

In any prosecution for bribery, it is a defense that the defendant conferred or agreed to confer the benefit involved upon the public servant involved as a result of conduct of the latter constituting larceny committed by means of extortion, or an attempt to commit the same, or coercion, or an attempt to commit coercion.

N.Y. Penal Law § 200.05

Section 200.10 - Bribe receiving in the third degree

A public servant is guilty of bribe receiving in the third degree when he or she solicits, accepts or agrees to accept any benefit from another person upon an agreement or understanding that his or her vote, opinion, judgment, action, decision or exercise of discretion as a public servant will thereby be influenced.

N.Y. Penal Law § 200.10

Amended by New York Laws 2014, ch. 55,Sec. H-A-21, eff. 4/30/2014.

Section 200.11 - Bribe receiving in the second degree

A public servant is guilty of bribe receiving in the second degree when he or she solicits, accepts or agrees to accept any benefit valued in excess of five thousand dollars from another person upon an agreement or understanding that his or her vote, opinion, judgment, action, decision or exercise of discretion as a public servant will thereby be influenced.

N.Y. Penal Law § 200.11

Amended by New York Laws 2014, ch. 55,Sec. H-A-22, eff. 4/30/2014.

Section 200.12 - Bribe receiving in the first degree

A public servant is guilty of bribe receiving in the first degree when he or she solicits, accepts or agrees to accept:

(a) any benefit from another person upon an agreement or understanding that his or her vote, opinion, judgment, action, decision or exercise of discretion as a public servant will thereby be influenced in the investigation, arrest, detention, prosecution or incarceration of any person for the commission or alleged commission of a class A felony defined in article two hundred twenty of this part or an attempt to commit any such class A felony; or

(b) any benefit valued in excess of one hundred thousand dollars from another person upon an agreement or understanding that such public servant's vote, opinion, judgment, action, decision or exercise of discretion as a public servant will thereby be influenced.

Bribe receiving in the first degree is a class B felony.

N.Y. Penal Law § 200.12

Amended by New York Laws 2014, ch. 55,Sec. H-A-23, eff. 4/30/2014.

Section 200.15 - Bribe receiving; no defense

1. The crimes of (a) bribe receiving, and (b) larceny committed by means of extortion, attempt to commit the same, coercion and attempt to commit coercion, are not mutually exclusive, and it is no defense to a prosecution for bribe receiving that, by reason of the same conduct, the defendant also committed one of such other specified crimes.

2. It is no defense to a prosecution pursuant to the provisions of this article that the public servant did not have power or authority to perform the act or omission for which the alleged bribe, gratuity or reward was given.

N.Y. Penal Law § 200.15

Section 200.20 - Rewarding official misconduct in the second degree

A person is guilty of rewarding official misconduct in the second degree when he knowingly confers, or offers or agrees to confer, any benefit upon a public servant for having violated his duty as a public servant.

N.Y. Penal Law § 200.20

Section 200.22 - Rewarding official misconduct in the first degree

A person is guilty of rewarding official misconduct in the first degree when he knowingly confers, or offers or agrees to confer, any benefit upon a public servant for having violated his duty as a public servant in the investigation, arrest, detention, prosecution, or incarceration of any person for the commission or alleged commission of a class A felony defined in article two hundred twenty of the penal law or the attempt to commit any such class A felony.

N.Y. Penal Law § 200.22

Section 200.25 - Receiving reward for official misconduct in the second degree

A public servant is guilty of receiving reward for official misconduct in the second degree when he solicits, accepts or agrees to accept any benefit from another person for having violated his duty as a public servant.

N.Y. Penal Law § 200.25

Section 200.27 - Receiving reward for official misconduct in the first degree

A public servant is guilty of receiving reward for official misconduct in the first degree when he solicits, accepts or agrees to accept any benefit from another person for having violated his duty as a public servant in the investigation, arrest, detention, prosecution, or incarceration of any person for the commission or alleged commission of a class A felony defined in article two hundred twenty of the penal law or the attempt to commit any such class A felony.

N.Y. Penal Law § 200.27

Section 200.30 - Giving unlawful gratuities

A person is guilty of giving unlawful gratuities when he knowingly confers, or offers or agrees to confer, any benefit upon a public servant for having engaged in official conduct which he was required or authorized to perform, and for which he was not entitled to any special or additional compensation.

N.Y. Penal Law § 200.30

Section 200.35 - Receiving unlawful gratuities

A public servant is guilty of receiving unlawful gratuities when he solicits, accepts or agrees to accept any benefit for having engaged in official conduct which he was required or authorized to perform, and for which he was not entitled to any special or additional compensation.

N.Y. Penal Law § 200.35

Section 200.40 - Bribe giving and bribe receiving for public office; definition of term

As used in sections 200.45 and 200.50, "party officer" means a person who holds any position or office in a political party, whether by election, appointment or otherwise.

N.Y. Penal Law § 200.40

Section 200.45 - Bribe giving for public office

A person is guilty of bribe giving for public office when he confers, or offers or agrees to confer, any money or other property upon a public servant or a party officer upon an agreement or understanding that some person will or may be appointed to a public office or designated or nominated as a candidate for public office.

N.Y. Penal Law § 200.45

Section 200.50 - Bribe receiving for public office

A public servant or a party officer is guilty of bribe receiving for public office when he solicits, accepts or agrees to accept any money or other property from another person upon an agreement or understanding that some person will or may be appointed to a public office or designated or nominated as a candidate for public office.

N.Y. Penal Law § 200.50

Section 200.55 - Impairing the integrity of a government licensing examination

A person is guilty of impairing the integrity of a government licensing examination when, with intent to obtain a benefit for himself or herself, or for another person, he or she:

1. Wrongfully alters or changes an applicant's grade on a government licensing examination; or

2. Causes any false or inaccurate grade to be entered into a government licensing registry; or

3. Provides answers, with an intent to wrongfully benefit another, to current questions on a pending government licensing examination; or

4. Wrongfully provides a copy of a current test used to determine competence in a licensed profession, trade, craft or other vocation.

Impairing the integrity of a government licensing examination is a class D felony.

N.Y. Penal Law § 200.55

Section 200.56 - Corrupt use of position or authority

A person is guilty of corrupt use of position or authority if such person:

1. While holding public office, or being nominated or seeking a nomination therefor, corruptly uses or promises to use, directly, or indirectly, any official authority or influence possessed or anticipated, in the way of conferring upon any person, or in order to secure, or aid any person in securing, any office or public employment, or any nomination, confirmation, promotion or increase of salary, upon consideration that the vote or political influence or action of the person so to be benefited or of any other person, shall be given or used in behalf of any candidate, officer or party or upon any other corrupt condition or consideration; or

2. Being a public officer or employee of the state or a political subdivision having, or claiming to have, any authority or influence affecting the nomination, public employment, confirmation, promotion, removal or increase or decrease of salary of any public officer or employee, corruptly promises or threatens to use any such authority or influence, directly or indirectly to affect the vote or political action of any such public officer or employee, or on account of the vote or political action of such officer or employee; or

3. Corruptly makes, tenders or offers to procure, or cause any nomination or appointment for any public office or place, or accepts or requests any such nomination or appointment, upon the payment or contribution of any valuable consideration, or upon an understanding or promise thereof; or

4. Corruptly makes any gift, promise or contribution to any person, upon the condition or consideration of receiving an appointment or election to a public office or a position of public employment, or for receiving or retaining any such office or position, or promotion, privilege, increase of salary or compensation therein, or exemption from removal or discharge therefrom.

Corrupt use of position or authority is a class E felony.

N.Y. Penal Law § 200.56

Added by New York Laws 2014, ch. 55,Sec. H-A-26, eff. 4/30/2014.

Article 205 - ESCAPE AND OTHER OFFENSES RELATING TO CUSTODY

Section 205.00 - Escape and other offenses relating to custody; definitions of terms

The following definitions are applicable to this article:

1. "Detention Facility" means any place used for the confinement, pursuant to an order of a court, of a person (a) charged with or convicted of an offense, or (b) charged with being or adjudicated a youthful offender, person in need of supervision

or juvenile delinquent, or (c) held for extradition or as a material witness, or (d) otherwise confined pursuant to an order of a court.

2. "Custody" means restraint by a public servant pursuant to an authorized arrest or an order of a court.

3. "Contraband" means any article or thing which a person confined in a detention facility is prohibited from obtaining or possessing by statute, rule, regulation or order.

4. "Dangerous contraband" means contraband which is capable of such use as may endanger the safety or security of a detention facility or any person therein.

N.Y. Penal Law § 205.00

Section 205.05 - Escape in the third degree

A person is guilty of escape in the third degree when he escapes from custody.

N.Y. Penal Law § 205.05

Section 205.10 - Escape in the second degree

A person is guilty of escape in the second degree when:

1. He escapes from a detention facility; or

2. Having been arrested for, charged with or convicted of a class C, class D or class E felony, he escapes from custody; or

3. Having been adjudicated a youthful offender, which finding was substituted for the conviction of a felony, he escapes from custody.

Escape in the second degree is a class E felony.

N.Y. Penal Law § 205.10

Section 205.15 - Escape in the first degree

A person is guilty of escape in the first degree when:

1. Having been charged with or convicted of a felony, he escapes from a detention facility; or

2. Having been arrested for, charged with or convicted of a class A or class B felony, he escapes from custody; or

3. Having been adjudicated a youthful offender, which finding was substituted for the conviction of a felony, he escapes from a detention facility.

Escape in the first degree is a class D felony.

N.Y. Penal Law § 205.15

Section 205.16 - [Expires September 1, 2023] Absconding from temporary release in the second degree

A person is guilty of absconding from temporary release in the second degree when having been released from confinement in a correctional institution or division for youth facility to participate in a program of work release, he intentionally fails to return to the institution or facility of his confinement at or before the time prescribed for his return.

N.Y. Penal Law § 205.16

Section 205.17 - [Expires September 1, 2023] Absconding from temporary release in the first degree

A person is guilty of absconding from temporary release in the first degree when having been released from confinement in a correctional institution under the jurisdiction of the state department of corrections and community supervision or a facility under the jurisdiction of the state office of children and family services to participate in a program of temporary release, he or she intentionally fails to return to the institution or facility of his or her confinement at or before the time prescribed for his or her return.

N.Y. Penal Law § 205.17

Section 205.18 - [Expires Sepember 1, 2023] Absconding from a furlough program

A person is guilty of absconding from a furlough program when, having been released from confinement in an institution under the jurisdiction of the commissioner of correction in a city having a population of one million or more or of a county which elects to have this article apply thereto to participate in a furlough program, he intentionally fails to return to the institution of his confinement at or before the time prescribed for his return.

N.Y. Penal Law § 205.18

Amended by New York Laws 2021, ch. 55,Sec. A-3, eff. 4/19/2021.
Amended by New York Laws 2020, ch. 55,Sec. A-3, eff. 4/3/2020.
Amended by New York Laws 2019, ch. 55,Sec. O-3, eff. 4/12/2019.
Amended by New York Laws 2017, ch. 55,Sec. A-3, eff. 4/20/2017.
Amended by New York Laws 2015, ch. 55,Sec. B-3, eff. 4/13/2015.

Section 205.19 - [Expires September 1, 2023] Absconding from a community treatment facility

A person is guilty of absconding from a community treatment facility when having been released from confinement from a correctional institution under the jurisdiction of the state department of corrections and community supervision by transfer to a community treatment facility, he or she leaves such facility without authorization or he or she intentionally fails to return to the community treatment facility at or before the time prescribed for his or her return.

N.Y. Penal Law § 205.19

Amended by New York Laws 2021, ch. 55,Sec. A-24, eff. 4/19/2021.
Amended by New York Laws 2020, ch. 55,Sec. A-24, eff. 4/3/2020.
Amended by New York Laws 2019, ch. 55,Sec. O-24, eff. 4/12/2019.

Section 205.20 - Promoting prison contraband in the second degree

A person is guilty of promoting prison contraband in the second degree when:

1. He knowingly and unlawfully introduces any contraband into a detention facility; or

2. Being a person confined in a detention facility, he knowingly and unlawfully makes, obtains or possesses any contraband.

Promoting prison contraband in the second degree is a class A misdemeanor.

N.Y. Penal Law § 205.20

Section 205.25 - Promoting prison contraband in the first degree

A person is guilty of promoting prison contraband in the first degree when:

1. He knowingly and unlawfully introduces any dangerous contraband into a detention facility; or

2. Being a person confined in a detention facility, he knowingly and unlawfully makes, obtains or possesses any dangerous contraband.

Promoting prison contraband in the first degree is a class D felony.

N.Y. Penal Law § 205.25

Section 205.30 - Resisting arrest

A person is guilty of resisting arrest when he intentionally prevents or attempts to prevent a police officer or peace officer from effecting an authorized arrest of himself or another person.

N.Y. Penal Law § 205.30

Section 205.50 - Hindering prosecution; definition of term

As used in sections 205.55, 205.60 and 205.65, a person "renders criminal assistance" when, with intent to prevent, hinder or delay the discovery or apprehension of, or the lodging of a criminal charge against, a person who he knows or believes has committed a crime or is being sought by law enforcement officials for the commission of a crime, or with intent to assist a person in profiting or benefiting from the commission of a crime, he:

1. Harbors or conceals such person; or

2. Warns such person of impending discovery or apprehension; or

3. Provides such person with money, transportation, weapon, disguise or other means of avoiding discovery or apprehension; or

4. Prevents or obstructs, by means of force, intimidation or deception, anyone from performing an act which might aid in the discovery or apprehension of such person or in the lodging of a criminal charge against him; or

5. Suppresses, by any act of concealment, alteration or destruction, any physical evidence which might aid in the discovery or apprehension of such person or in the lodging of a criminal charge against him; or

6. Aids such person to protect or expeditiously profit from an advantage derived from such crime.

N.Y. Penal Law § 205.50

Section 205.55 - Hindering prosecution in the third degree

A person is guilty of hindering prosecution in the third degree when he renders criminal assistance to a person who has committed a felony.

N.Y. Penal Law § 205.55

Section 205.60 - Hindering prosecution in the second degree

A person is guilty of hindering prosecution in the second degree when he renders criminal assistance to a person who has committed a class B or class C felony.

N.Y. Penal Law § 205.60

Section 205.65 - Hindering prosecution in the first degree

A person is guilty of hindering prosecution in the first degree when he renders criminal assistance to a person who has committed a class A felony, knowing or believing that such person has engaged in conduct constituting a class A felony.

N.Y. Penal Law § 205.65

Article 210 - PERJURY AND RELATED OFFENSES

Section 210.00 - Perjury and related offenses; definitions of terms

The following definitions are applicable to this article:

1. "Oath" includes an affirmation and every other mode authorized by law of attesting to the truth of that which is stated.

2. "Swear" means to state under oath.

3. "Testimony" means an oral statement made under oath in a proceeding before any court, body, agency, public servant or other person authorized by law to conduct such proceeding and to administer the oath or cause it to be administered.

4. "Oath required by law." An affidavit, deposition or other subscribed written instrument is one for which an "oath is required by law" when, absent an oath or swearing thereto, it does not or would not, according to statute or appropriate regulatory provisions, have legal efficacy in a court of law or before any public or governmental body, agency or public servant to whom it is or might be submitted.

5. "Swear falsely." A person "swears falsely" when he intentionally makes a false statement which he does not believe to be true (a) while giving testimony, or (b) under oath in a subscribed written instrument. A false swearing in a subscribed written instrument shall not be deemed complete until the instrument is delivered by its subscriber, or by someone acting in his behalf, to another person with intent that it be uttered or published as true.

6. "Attesting officer" means any notary public or other person authorized by law to administer oaths in connection with affidavits, depositions and other subscribed written instruments, and to certify that the subscriber of such an instrument has appeared before him and has sworn to the truth of the contents thereof.

7. "Jurat" means a clause wherein an attesting officer certifies, among other matters, that the subscriber has appeared before him and sworn to the truth of the contents thereof.

N.Y. Penal Law § 210.00

Section 210.05 - Perjury in the third degree

A person is guilty of perjury in the third degree when he swears falsely.

N.Y. Penal Law § 210.05

Section 210.10 - Perjury in the second degree

A person is guilty of perjury in the second degree when he swears falsely and when his false statement is (a) made in a subscribed written instrument for which an oath is required by law, and (b) made with intent to mislead a public servant in the performance of his official functions, and (c) material to the action, proceeding or matter involved.

N.Y. Penal Law § 210.10

Section 210.15 - Perjury in the first degree

A person is guilty of perjury in the first degree when he swears falsely and when his false statement (a) consists of testimony, and (b) is material to the action, proceeding or matter in which it is made.

N.Y. Penal Law § 210.15

Section 210.20 - Perjury; pleading and proof where inconsistent statements involved

Where a person has made two statements under oath which are inconsistent to the degree that one of them is necessarily false, where the circumstances are such that each statement, if false, is perjuriously so, and where each statement was made within the jurisdiction of this state and within the period of the statute of limitations for the crime charged, the inability of the people to establish specifically which of the two statements is the false one does not preclude a prosecution for perjury, and such prosecution may be conducted as follows:

1. The indictment or information may set forth the two statements and, without designating either, charge that one of them is false and perjuriously made.

2. The falsity of one or the other of the two statements may be established by proof or a showing of their irreconcilable inconsistency.

3. The highest degree of perjury of which the defendant may be convicted is determined by hypothetically assuming each statement to be false and perjurious. If under such circumstances perjury of the same degree would be established by the making of each statement, the defendant may be convicted of that degree at most. If perjury of different degrees would be established by the making of the two statements, the defendant may be convicted of the lesser degree at most.

N.Y. Penal Law § 210.20

Section 210.25 - Perjury; defense

In any prosecution for perjury, it is an affirmative defense that the defendant retracted his false statement in the course of the proceeding in which it was made before such false statement substantially affected the proceeding and before it became manifest that its falsity was or would be exposed.

N.Y. Penal Law § 210.25

Section 210.30 - Perjury; no defense

It is no defense to a prosecution for perjury that:

1. The defendant was not competent to make the false statement alleged; or

2. The defendant mistakenly believed the false statement to be immaterial; or

3. The oath was administered or taken in an irregular manner or that the authority or jurisdiction of the attesting officer who administered the oath was defective, if such defect was excusable under any statute or rule of law.

N.Y. Penal Law § 210.30

Section 210.35 - Making an apparently sworn false statement in the second degree

A person is guilty of making an apparently sworn false statement in the second degree when (a) he subscribes a written instrument knowing that it contains a statement which is in fact false and which he does not believe to be true, and (b) he intends or believes that such instrument will be uttered or delivered with a jurat affixed thereto, and (c) such instrument is uttered or delivered with a jurat affixed thereto.

N.Y. Penal Law § 210.35

Section 210.40 - Making an apparently sworn false statement in the first degree

A person is guilty of making an apparently sworn false statement in the first degree when he commits the crime of making an apparently sworn false statement in the second degree, and when (a) the written instrument involved is one for which an oath is required by law, and (b) the false statement contained therein is made with intent to mislead a public servant in the performance of his official functions, and (c) such false statement is material to the action, proceeding or matter involved.

N.Y. Penal Law § 210.40

Section 210.45 - Making a punishable false written statement

A person is guilty of making a punishable false written statement when he knowingly makes a false statement, which he does not believe to be true, in a written instrument bearing a legally authorized form notice to the effect that false statements made therein are punishable.

N.Y. Penal Law § 210.45

Section 210.50 - Perjury and related offenses; requirement of corroboration

In any prosecution for perjury, except a prosecution based upon inconsistent statements pursuant to section 210.20, or in any prosecution for making an apparently sworn false statement, or making a punishable false written statement, falsity of a statement may not be established by the uncorroborated testimony of a single witness.

N.Y. Penal Law § 210.50

Article 215 - OTHER OFFENSES RELATING TO JUDICIAL AND OTHER PROCEEDINGS

Section 215.00 - Bribing a witness

A person is guilty of bribing a witness when he confers, or offers or agrees to confer, any benefit upon a witness or a person about to be called as a witness in any action or proceeding upon an agreement or understanding that (a) the testimony of such witness will thereby be influenced, or (b) such witness will absent himself from, or otherwise avoid or seek to avoid appearing or testifying at, such action or proceeding.

N.Y. Penal Law § 215.00

Section 215.05 - Bribe receiving by a witness

A witness or a person about to be called as a witness in any action or proceeding is guilty of bribe receiving by a witness when he solicits, accepts or agrees to accept any benefit from another person upon an agreement or understanding that (a) his testimony will thereby be influenced, or (b) he will absent himself from, or otherwise avoid or seek to avoid appearing or testifying at, such action or proceeding.

N.Y. Penal Law § 215.05

Section 215.10 - Tampering with a witness in the fourth degree

A person is guilty of tampering with a witness when, knowing that a person is or is about to be called as a witness in an action or proceeding,

(a) he wrongfully induces or attempts to induce such person to absent himself from, or otherwise to avoid or seek to avoid appearing or testifying at, such action or proceeding, or (b) he knowingly makes any false statement or practices any fraud or deceit with intent to affect the testimony of such person.

Tampering with a witness in the fourth degree is a class A misdemeanor.

N.Y. Penal Law § 215.10

Section 215.11 - Tampering with a witness in the third degree

A person is guilty of tampering with a witness in the third degree when, knowing that a person is about to be called as a witness in a criminal proceeding:

1. He wrongfully compels or attempts to compel such person to absent himself from, or otherwise to avoid or seek to avoid appearing or testifying at such proceeding by means of instilling in him a fear that the actor will cause physical injury to such person or another person; or

2. He wrongfully compels or attempts to compel such person to swear falsely by means of instilling in him a fear that the actor will cause physical injury to such person or another person.

Tampering with a witness in the third degree is a class E felony.

N.Y. Penal Law § 215.11

Section 215.12 - Tampering with a witness in the second degree

A person is guilty of tampering with a witness in the second degree when he:

1. Intentionally causes physical injury to a person for the purpose of obstructing, delaying, preventing or impeding the giving of testimony in a criminal proceeding by such person or another person or for the purpose of compelling such person or another person to swear falsely; or

2. He intentionally causes physical injury to a person on account of such person or another person having testified in a criminal proceeding.

Tampering with a witness in the second degree is a class D felony.

N.Y. Penal Law § 215.12

Section 215.13 - Tampering with a witness in the first degree

A person is guilty of tampering with a witness in the first degree when:

1. He intentionally causes serious physical injury to a person for the purpose of obstructing, delaying, preventing or impeding the giving of testimony in a criminal proceeding by such person or another person or for the purpose of compelling such person or another person to swear falsely; or

2. He intentionally causes serious physical injury to a person on account of such person or another person having testified in a criminal proceeding.

Tampering with a witness in the first degree is a class B felony.

N.Y. Penal Law § 215.13

Section 215.14 - Employer unlawfully penalizing witness or victim

1. Any person who is the victim of an offense upon which an accusatory instrument is based or, is subpoenaed to attend a criminal proceeding as a witness pursuant to article six hundred ten of the criminal procedure law or who exercises his rights as a victim as provided by section 380.50 or 390.30 of the criminal procedure law or subdivision two of section two hundred fifty-nine-i of the executive law and who notifies his employer or agent of his intent to appear as a witness, to consult with the district attorney, or to exercise his rights as provided in the criminal procedure law, the family court act and the executive law prior to the day of his attendance, shall not on account of his absence from employment by reason of such service be subject to discharge or penalty except as hereinafter provided. Upon request of the employer or agent, the party who sought the attendance or testimony shall provide verification of the employee's service. An employer may, however, withhold wages of any such employee during the period of such attendance. The subjection of an employee to discharge or penalty on account of his absence from employment by reason of his required attendance as a witness at a

criminal proceeding or consultation with the district attorney or exercise of his rights as provided under law shall constitute a class B misdemeanor.

2. For purposes of this section, the term "victim" shall include the aggrieved party or the aggrieved party's next of kin, if the aggrieved party is deceased as a result of the offense, the representative of a victim as defined in subdivision six of section six hundred twenty-one of the executive law, a good samaritan as defined in subdivision seven of section six hundred twenty-one of such law or a person pursuing an application or enforcement of an order of protection under the criminal procedure law or the family court act.

N.Y. Penal Law § 215.14

Section 215.15 - Intimidating a victim or witness in the third degree

A person is guilty of intimidating a victim or witness in the third degree when, knowing that another person possesses information relating to a criminal transaction and other than in the course of that criminal transaction or immediate flight therefrom, he:

1. Wrongfully compels or attempts to compel such other person to refrain from communicating such information to any court, grand jury, prosecutor, police officer or peace officer by means of instilling in him a fear that the actor will cause physical injury to such other person or another person; or

2. Intentionally damages the property of such other person or another person for the purpose of compelling such other person or another person to refrain from communicating, or on account of such other person or another person having communicated, information relating to that criminal transaction to any court, grand jury, prosecutor, police officer or peace officer.

Intimidating a victim or witness in the third degree is a class E felony.

N.Y. Penal Law § 215.15

Section 215.16 - Intimidating a victim or witness in the second degree

A person is guilty of intimidating a victim or witness in the second degree when, other than in the course of that criminal transaction or immediate flight therefrom, he:

1. Intentionally causes physical injury to another person for the purpose of obstructing, delaying, preventing or impeding the communication by such other person or another person of information relating to a criminal transaction to any court, grand jury, prosecutor, police officer or peace officer or for the purpose of compelling such other person or another person to swear falsely; or

2. Intentionally causes physical injury to another person on account of such other person or another person having communicated information relating to a criminal transaction to any court, grand jury, prosecutor, police officer or peace officer; or

3. Recklessly causes physical injury to another person by intentionally damaging the property of such other person or another person, for the purpose of obstructing, delaying, preventing or impeding such other person or another person from communicating, or on account of such other person or another person having communicated, information relating to a criminal transaction to any court, grand jury, prosecutor, police officer or peace officer.

Intimidating a victim or witness in the second degree is a class D felony.

N.Y. Penal Law § 215.16

Section 215.17 - Intimidating a victim or witness in the first degree

A person is guilty of intimidating a victim or witness in the first degree when, other than in the course of that criminal transaction or immediate flight therefrom, he:

1. Intentionally causes serious physical injury to another person for the purpose of obstructing, delaying, preventing or impeding the communication by such other person or another person of information relating to a criminal transaction to any court, grand jury, prosecutor, police officer or peace officer or for the purpose of compelling such other person or another person to swear falsely; or

2. Intentionally causes serious physical injury to another person on account of such other person or another person having communicated information relating to a criminal transaction to any court, grand jury, prosecutor, police officer or peace officer.

Intimidating a victim or witness in the first degree is a class B felony.

N.Y. Penal Law § 215.17

Section 215.19 - Bribing a juror

A person is guilty of bribing a juror when he confers, or offers or agrees to confer, any benefit upon a juror upon an agreement or understanding that such juror's vote, opinion, judgment, decision or other action as a juror will thereby be influenced.

N.Y. Penal Law § 215.19

Section 215.20 - Bribe receiving by a juror

A juror is guilty of bribe receiving by a juror when he solicits, accepts or agrees to accept any benefit from another person upon an agreement or understanding that his vote, opinion, judgment, decision or other action as a juror will thereby be influenced.

N.Y. Penal Law § 215.20

Section 215.22 - Providing a juror with a gratuity

A person is guilty of providing a juror with a gratuity when he or she, having been a party in a concluded civil or criminal action or proceeding or having been a person with regard to whom a grand jury has taken action pursuant to any subdivision of section 190.60 of the criminal procedure law (or acting on behalf of such a party or such a person), directly

131

or indirectly confers, offers to confer or agrees to confer upon a person whom he or she knows has served as a juror in such action or proceeding or on such grand jury any benefit with intent to reward such person for such service.

N.Y. Penal Law § 215.22

Section 215.23 - Tampering with a juror in the second degree

A person is guilty of tampering with a juror in the second degree when, prior to discharge of the jury, he:

1. confers, or offers or agrees to confer, any payment or benefit upon a juror or upon a third person acting on behalf of such juror, in consideration for such juror or third person supplying information in relation to an action or proceeding pending or about to be brought before such juror; or

2. acting on behalf of a juror, accepts or agrees to accept any payment or benefit for himself or for such juror, in consideration for supplying any information in relation to an action or proceeding pending or about to be brought before such juror and prior to his discharge.

Tampering with a juror in the second degree is a class B misdemeanor.

N.Y. Penal Law § 215.23

Section 215.25 - Tampering with a juror in the first degree

A person is guilty of tampering with a juror in the first degree when, with intent to influence the outcome of an action or proceeding, he communicates with a juror in such action or proceeding, except as authorized by law.

N.Y. Penal Law § 215.25

Section 215.28 - Misconduct by a juror in the second degree

A person is guilty of misconduct by a juror in the second degree when, in relation to an action or proceeding pending or about to be brought before him and prior to discharge, he accepts or agrees to accept any payment or benefit for himself or for a third person in consideration for supplying any information concerning such action or proceeding.

N.Y. Penal Law § 215.28

Section 215.30 - Misconduct by a juror in the first degree

A juror is guilty of misconduct by a juror in the first degree when, in relation to an action or proceeding pending or about to be brought before him, he agrees to give a vote, opinion, judgment, decision or report for or against any party to such action or proceeding.

N.Y. Penal Law § 215.30

Section 215.35 - Tampering with physical evidence; definitions of terms

The following definitions are applicable to section 215.40:

1. "Physical evidence" means any article, object, document, record or other thing of physical substance which is or is about to be produced or used as evidence in an official proceeding.

2. "Official proceeding" means any action or proceeding conducted by or before a legally constituted judicial, legislative, administrative or other governmental agency or official, in which evidence may properly be received.

N.Y. Penal Law § 215.35

Section 215.40 - Tampering with physical evidence

A person is guilty of tampering with physical evidence when:

1. With intent that it be used or introduced in an official proceeding or a prospective official proceeding, he (a) knowingly makes, devises or prepares false physical evidence, or (b) produces or offers such evidence at such a proceeding knowing it to be false; or

2. Believing that certain physical evidence is about to be produced or used in an official proceeding or a prospective official proceeding, and intending to prevent such production or use, he suppresses it by any act of concealment, alteration or destruction, or by employing force, intimidation or deception against any person.

Tampering with physical evidence is a class E felony.

N.Y. Penal Law § 215.40

Section 215.45 - Compounding a crime

1. A person is guilty of compounding a crime when:

(a) He solicits, accepts or agrees to accept any benefit upon an agreement or understanding that he will refrain from initiating a prosecution for a crime; or

(b) He confers, or offers or agrees to confer, any benefit upon another person upon an agreement or understanding that such other person will refrain from initiating a prosecution for a crime.

2. In any prosecution under this section, it is an affirmative defense that the benefit did not exceed an amount which the defendant reasonably believed to be due as restitution or indemnification for harm caused by the crime.

Compounding a crime is a class A misdemeanor.

N.Y. Penal Law § 215.45

Section 215.50 - Criminal contempt in the second degree

A person is guilty of criminal contempt in the second degree when he engages in any of the following conduct:

1. Disorderly, contemptuous, or insolent behavior, committed during the sitting of a court, in its immediate view and presence and directly tending to interrupt its proceedings or to impair the respect due to its authority; or

2. Breach of the peace, noise, or other disturbance, directly tending to interrupt a court's proceedings; or

3. Intentional disobedience or resistance to the lawful process or other mandate of a court except in cases involving or growing out of labor disputes as defined by subdivision two of section seven hundred fifty-three-a of the judiciary law; or

4. Contumacious and unlawful refusal to be sworn as a witness in any court proceeding or, after being sworn, to answer any legal and proper interrogatory; or

5. Knowingly publishing a false or grossly inaccurate report of a court's proceedings; or

6. Intentional failure to obey any mandate, process or notice, issued pursuant to articles sixteen, seventeen, eighteen, or eighteen-a of the judiciary law, or to rules adopted pursuant to any such statute or to any special statute establishing commissioners of jurors and prescribing their duties or who refuses to be sworn as provided therein; or

7. On or along a public street or sidewalk within a radius of two hundred feet of any building established as a courthouse, he calls aloud, shouts, holds or displays placards or signs containing written or printed matter, concerning the conduct of a trial being held in such courthouse or the character of the court or jury engaged in such trial or calling for or demanding any specified action or determination by such court or jury in connection with such trial.

Criminal contempt in the second degree is a class A misdemeanor.

N.Y. Penal Law § 215.50

Section 215.51 - Criminal contempt in the first degree

A person is guilty of criminal contempt in the first degree when:

(a) he contumaciously and unlawfully refuses to be sworn as a witness before a grand jury, or, when after having been sworn as a witness before a grand jury, he refuses to answer any legal and proper interrogatory; or

(b) in violation of a duly served order of protection, or such order of which the defendant has actual knowledge because he or she was present in court when such order was issued, or an order of protection issued by a court of competent jurisdiction in this or another state, territorial or tribal jurisdiction, he or she:

(i) intentionally places or attempts to place a person for whose protection such order was issued in reasonable fear of physical injury, serious physical injury or death by displaying a deadly weapon, dangerous instrument or what appears to be a pistol, revolver, rifle, shotgun, machine gun or other firearm or by means of a threat or threats; or

(ii) intentionally places or attempts to place a person for whose protection such order was issued in reasonable fear of physical injury, serious physical injury or death by repeatedly following such person or engaging in a course of conduct or repeatedly committing acts over a period of time; or

(iii) intentionally places or attempts to place a person for whose protection such order was issued in reasonable fear of physical injury, serious physical injury or death when he or she communicates or causes a communication to be initiated with such person by mechanical or electronic means or otherwise, anonymously or otherwise, by telephone, or by telegraph, mail or any other form of written communication; or

(iv) with intent to harass, annoy, threaten or alarm a person for whose protection such order was issued, repeatedly makes telephone calls to such person, whether or not a conversation ensues, with no purpose of legitimate communication; or

(v) with intent to harass, annoy, threaten or alarm a person for whose protection such order was issued, strikes, shoves, kicks or otherwise subjects such other person to physical contact or attempts or threatens to do the same; or

(vi) by physical menace, intentionally places or attempts to place a person for whose protection such order was issued in reasonable fear of death, imminent serious physical injury or physical injury.

(c) he or she commits the crime of criminal contempt in the second degree as defined in subdivision three of section 215.50 of this article by violating that part of a duly served order of protection, or such order of which the defendant has actual knowledge because he or she was present in court when such order was issued, under sections two hundred forty and two hundred fifty-two of the domestic relations law, articles four, five, six and eight of the family court act and section 530.12 of the criminal procedure law, or an order of protection issued by a court of competent jurisdiction in another state, territorial or tribal jurisdiction, which requires the respondent or defendant to stay away from the person or persons on whose behalf the order was issued, and where the defendant has been previously convicted of the crime of aggravated criminal contempt or criminal contempt in the first or second degree for violating an order of protection as described herein within the preceding five years; or

(d) in violation of a duly served order of protection, or such order of which the defendant has actual knowledge because he or she was present in court when such order was issued, or an order issued by a court of competent jurisdiction in this or another state, territorial or tribal jurisdiction, he or she intentionally or recklessly damages the property of a person for whose protection such order was issued in an amount exceeding two hundred fifty dollars.

Criminal contempt in the first degree is a class E felony.

N.Y. Penal Law § 215.51

Section 215.52 - Aggravated criminal contempt

A person is guilty of aggravated criminal contempt when:

1. in violation of a duly served order of protection, or such order of which the defendant has actual knowledge because he or she was present in court when such order was issued, or an order of protection issued by a court of competent jurisdiction in another state, territorial or tribal jurisdiction, he or she intentionally or recklessly causes physical injury or serious physical injury to a person for whose protection such order was issued; or

2. he or she commits the crime of criminal contempt in the first degree as defined in subdivision (b) or (d) of section 215.51 of this article and has been previously convicted of the crime of aggravated criminal contempt; or

3. he or she commits the crime of criminal contempt in the first degree, as defined in paragraph (i), (ii), (iii), (v) or (vi) of subdivision (b) or subdivision (c) of section 215.51 of this article, and has been previously convicted of the crime of criminal contempt in the first degree, as defined in such subdivision (b), (c) or (d) of section 215.51 of this article, within the preceding five years.

Aggravated criminal contempt is a class D felony.

N.Y. Penal Law § 215.52

Section 215.54 - Criminal contempt; prosecution and punishment

Adjudication for criminal contempt under subdivision A of section seven hundred fifty of the judiciary law shall not bar a prosecution for the crime of criminal contempt under section 215.50 based upon the same conduct but, upon conviction thereunder, the court, in sentencing the defendant shall take the previous punishment into consideration.

N.Y. Penal Law § 215.54

Section 215.55 - Bail jumping in the third degree

A person is guilty of bail jumping in the third degree when by court order he has been released from custody or allowed to remain at liberty, either upon bail or upon his own recognizance, upon condition that he will subsequently appear personally in connection with a criminal action or proceeding, and when he does not appear personally on the required date or voluntarily within thirty days thereafter.

N.Y. Penal Law § 215.55

Section 215.56 - Bail jumping in the second degree

A person is guilty of bail jumping in the second degree when by court order he has been released from custody or allowed to remain at liberty, either upon bail or upon his own recognizance, upon condition that he will subsequently appear personally in connection with a charge against him of committing a felony, and when he does not appear personally on the required date or voluntarily within thirty days thereafter.

N.Y. Penal Law § 215.56

Section 215.57 - Bail jumping in the first degree

A person is guilty of bail jumping in the first degree when by court order he has been released from custody or allowed to remain at liberty, either upon bail or upon his own recognizance, upon condition that he will subsequently appear personally in connection with an indictment pending against him which charges him with the commission of a class A or class B felony, and when he does not appear personally on the required date or voluntarily within thirty days thereafter.

N.Y. Penal Law § 215.57

Section 215.58 - Failing to respond to an appearance ticket

1. A person is guilty of failing to respond to an appearance ticket when, having been personally served with an appearance ticket, as defined in subdivision two, based upon his alleged commission of a crime, he does not appear personally in the court in which such appearance ticket is returnable on the return date thereof or voluntarily within thirty days thereafter.

2. As used in this section, an appearance ticket means a written notice, whether referred to as a summons or by any other name, issued by a police officer, peace officer or other non-judicial public servant authorized by law to issue the same, directing a designated person to appear in a designated court at a designated future time in connection with a criminal action to be instituted in such court with respect to his alleged commission of a designated offense.

3. This section does not apply to any case in which an alternative to response to an appearance ticket is authorized by law and the actor complies with such alternative procedure.

Failing to respond to an appearance ticket is a violation.

N.Y. Penal Law § 215.58

Section 215.59 - Bail jumping and failing to respond to an appearance ticket; defense

In any prosecution for bail jumping or failing to respond to an appearance ticket, it is an affirmative defense that:

1. The defendant's failure to appear on the required date or within thirty days thereafter was unavoidable and due to circumstances beyond his control; and

2. During the period extending from the expiration of the thirty day period to the commencement of the action, the defendant either:

(a) appeared voluntarily as soon as he was able to do so, or

(b) although he did not so appear, such failure of appearance was unavoidable and due to circumstances beyond his control.

N.Y. Penal Law § 215.59

Section 215.60 - Criminal contempt of the legislature

A person is guilty of criminal contempt of the legislature when, having been duly subpoenaed to attend as a witness before either house of the legislature or before any committee thereof, he:

1. Fails or refuses to attend without lawful excuse; or

2. Refuses to be sworn; or

3. Refuses to answer any material and proper question; or

4. Refuses, after reasonable notice, to produce books, papers, or documents in his possession or under his control which constitute material and proper evidence.

Criminal contempt of the legislature is a class A misdemeanor.

N.Y. Penal Law § 215.60

Section 215.65 - Criminal contempt of a temporary state commission

A person is guilty of criminal contempt of a temporary state commission when, having been duly subpoenaed to attend as a witness at an investigation or hearing before a temporary state commission, he fails or refuses to attend without lawful excuse.

N.Y. Penal Law § 215.65

Section 215.66 - Criminal contempt of the state commission on judicial conduct

A person is guilty of criminal contempt of the state commission on judicial conduct when, having been duly subpoenaed to attend as a witness at an investigation or hearing before the commission or a referee designated by the commission, he fails or refuses to attend without lawful excuse.

N.Y. Penal Law § 215.66

Section 215.70 - Unlawful grand jury disclosure

A person is guilty of unlawful grand jury disclosure when, being a grand juror, a public prosecutor, a grand jury stenographer, a grand jury interpreter, a police officer or a peace officer guarding a witness in a grand jury proceeding, or a clerk, attendant, warden or other public servant having official duties in or about a grand jury room or proceeding, or a public officer or public employee, he intentionally discloses to another the nature or substance of any grand jury testimony, or any decision, result or other matter attending a grand jury proceeding which is required by law to be kept secret, except in the proper discharge of his official duties or upon written order of the court. Nothing contained herein shall prohibit a witness from disclosing his own testimony.

N.Y. Penal Law § 215.70

Section 215.75 - Unlawful disclosure of an indictment

A public servant is guilty of unlawful disclosure of an indictment when, except in the proper discharge of his official duties, he intentionally discloses the fact that an indictment has been found or filed before the accused person is in custody.

N.Y. Penal Law § 215.75

Section 215.80 - Unlawful disposition of assets subject to forfeiture

Any defendant in a forfeiture action pursuant to article thirteen-A of the civil practice law and rules who knowingly and intentionally conceals, destroys, dissipates, alters, removes from the jurisdiction, or otherwise disposes of, property specified in a provisional remedy ordered by the court or in a judgment of forfeiture in knowing contempt of said order shall be guilty of a class A misdemeanor.

N.Y. Penal Law § 215.80

Title M - OFFENSES AGAINST PUBLIC HEALTH AND MORALS

Article 220 - CONTROLLED SUBSTANCES OFFENSES

Section 220.00 - Controlled substances; definitions

1. "Sell" means to sell, exchange, give or dispose of to another, or to offer or agree to do the same.

2. "Unlawfully" means in violation of article thirty-three of the public health law.

3. "Ounce" means an avoirdupois ounce as applied to solids or semisolids, and a fluid ounce as applied to liquids.

4. "Pound" means an avoirdupois pound.

5. "Controlled substance" means any substance listed in schedule I, II, III, IV or V of section thirty-three hundred six of the public health law .

6. [Repealed]

7. "Narcotic drug" means any controlled substance listed in schedule I(b), I(c), II(b) or II(c) other than methadone.

8. "Narcotic preparation" means any controlled substance listed in schedule II(b-1), III(d) or III(e).

9. "Hallucinogen" means any controlled substance listed in paragraphs (5), (17), (18), (19), (20) and (21) of subdivision (d) of schedule I of section thirty-three hundred six of the public health law.

10. "Hallucinogenic substance" means any controlled substance listed in schedule I(d) other than concentrated cannabis, lysergic acid diethylamide, or an hallucinogen.

11. "Stimulant" means any controlled substance listed in schedule I(f),II(d).

12. "Dangerous depressant" means any controlled substance listed in schedule I(e)(2), (3), II(e), III(c)(3) or IV(c)(2), (31), (32), (40).

13. "Depressant" means any controlled substance listed in schedule IV(c) except (c)(2), (31), (32), (40).

14. "School grounds" means(a) in or on or within any building, structure, athletic playing field, playground or land contained within the real property boundary line of a public or private elementary, parochial, intermediate, junior high, vocational, or high school, or (b) any area accessible to the public located within one thousand feet of the real property boundary line comprising any such school or any parked automobile or other parked vehicle located within one thousand feet of the real property boundary line comprising any such school. For the purposes of this section an "area accessible to the public" shall mean sidewalks, streets, parking lots, parks, playgrounds, stores and restaurants.

15. "Prescription for a controlled substance" means a direction or authorization, by means of an official New York state prescription form, a written prescription form or an oral prescription, which will permit a person to lawfully obtain a controlled substance from any person authorized to dispense controlled substances.

16. For the purposes of sections 220.70, 220.71, 220.72, 220.73, 220.74, 220.75 and 220.76 of this article:

(a) "Precursor" means ephedrine, pseudoephedrine, or any salt, isomer or salt of an isomer of such substances.

(b) "Chemical reagent" means a chemical reagent that can be used in the manufacture, production or preparation of methamphetamine.

(c) "Solvent" means a solvent that can be used in the manufacture, production or preparation of methamphetamine.

(d) "Laboratory equipment" means any items, components or materials that can be used in the manufacture, preparation or production of methamphetamine.

(e) "Hazardous or dangerous material" means any substance, or combination of substances, that results from or is used in the manufacture, preparation or production of methamphetamine which, because of its quantity, concentration, or physical or chemical characteristics, poses a substantial risk to human health or safety, or a substantial danger to the environment.

17. "School bus" means every motor vehicle owned by a public or governmental agency or private school and operated for the transportation of pupils, teachers and other persons acting in a supervisory capacity, to or from school or school

activities or privately owned and operated for compensation for the transportation of pupils, children of pupils, teachers and other persons acting in a supervisory capacity to or from school or school activities.

18. "Controlled substance organization" means four or more persons sharing a common purpose to engage in conduct that constitutes or advances the commission of a felony under this article.

19. "Director" means a person who is the principal administrator, organizer, or leader of a controlled substance organization or one of several principal administrators, organizers, or leaders of a controlled substance organization.

20. "Profiteer" means a person who: (a) is a director of a controlled substance organization; (b) is a member of a controlled substance organization and has managerial responsibility over one or more other members of that organization; or (c) arranges, devises or plans one or more transactions constituting a felony under this article so as to obtain profits or expected profits. A person is not a profiteer if he or she is acting only as an employee; or if he or she is acting as an accommodation to a friend or relative; or if he or she is acting only under the direction and control of others and exercises no substantial, independent role in arranging or directing the transactions in question.

N.Y. Penal Law § 220.00

Amended by New York Laws 2021, ch. 92,Sec. 14, eff. 3/31/2021.

Amended by New York Laws 2021, ch. 92,Sec. 10-a, eff. 3/31/2021.

Amended by New York Laws 2021, ch. 92,Sec. 10, eff. 3/31/2021.

Section 220.03 - Criminal possession of a controlled substance in the seventh degree

A person is guilty of criminal possession of a controlled substance in the seventh degree when he or she knowingly and unlawfully possesses a controlled substance; provided, however, that it shall not be a violation of this section when a person possesses a residual amount of a controlled substance and that residual amount is in or on a hypodermic syringe or hypodermic needle obtained and possessed pursuant to section thirty-three hundred eighty-one of the public health law, which includes the state's syringe exchange and pharmacy and medical provider-based expanded syringe access programs; nor shall it be a violation of this section when a person's unlawful possession of a controlled substance is discovered as a result of seeking immediate health care as defined in paragraph (b) of subdivision three of section 220.78 of the penal law, for either another person or him or herself because such person is experiencing a drug or alcohol overdose or other life threatening medical emergency as defined in paragraph (a) of subdivision three of section 220.78 of the penal law.

N.Y. Penal Law § 220.03

Amended by New York Laws 2015, ch. 57,Sec. I-4, eff. 4/13/2015.

Section 220.06 - Criminal possession of a controlled substance in the fifth degree

A person is guilty of criminal possession of a controlled substance in the fifth degree when he knowingly and unlawfully possesses:

1. a controlled substance with intent to sell it; or

2. one or more preparations, compounds, mixtures or substances containing a narcotic preparation and said preparations, compounds, mixtures or substances are of an aggregate weight of one-half ounce or more; or

3. phencyclidine and said phencyclidine weighs fifty milligrams or more; or

4. [Repealed]

5. cocaine and said cocaine weighs five hundred milligrams or more.

6. ketamine and said ketamine weighs more than one thousand milligrams; or

7. ketamine and has previously been convicted of possession or the attempt to commit possession of ketamine in any amount; or

8. one or more preparations, compounds, mixtures or substances containing gamma hydroxybutyric acid, as defined in paragraph four of subdivision (e) of schedule I of section thirty-three hundred six of the public health law, and said preparations, compounds, mixtures or substances are of an aggregate weight of twenty-eight grams or more.

Criminal possession of a controlled substance in the fifth degree is a class D felony.

N.Y. Penal Law § 220.06

Amended by New York Laws 2021, ch. 92,Sec. 11, eff. 3/31/2021.

Section 220.09 - Criminal possession of a controlled substance in the fourth degree

A person is guilty of criminal possession of a controlled substance in the fourth degree when he knowingly and unlawfully possesses:

1. one or more preparations, compounds, mixtures or substances containing a narcotic drug and said preparations, compounds, mixtures or substances are of an aggregate weight of one-eighth ounce or more; or

2. one or more preparations, compounds, mixtures or substances containing methamphetamine, its salts, isomers or salts of isomers and said preparations, compounds, mixtures or substances are of an aggregate weight of one-half ounce or more; or

3. one or more preparations, compounds, mixtures or substances containing a narcotic preparation and said preparations, compounds, mixtures or substances are of an aggregate weight of two ounces or more; or

4. a stimulant and said stimulant weighs one gram or more; or

5. lysergic acid diethylamide and said lysergic acid diethylamide weighs one milligram or more; or

6. a hallucinogen and said hallucinogen weighs twenty-five milligrams or more; or

7. a hallucinogenic substance and said hallucinogenic substance weighs one gram or more; or

8. a dangerous depressant and such dangerous depressant weighs ten ounces or more; or

9. a depressant and such depressant weighs two pounds or more; or

10. [Repealed]

11. phencyclidine and said phencyclidine weighs two hundred fifty milligrams or more; or

136

12. methadone and said methadone weighs three hundred sixty milligrams or more; or

13. phencyclidine and said phencyclidine weighs fifty milligrams or more with intent to sell it and has previously been convicted of an offense defined in this article or the attempt or conspiracy to commit any such offense; or

14. ketamine and said ketamine weighs four thousand milligrams or more; or

15. one or more preparations, compounds, mixtures or substances containing gamma hydroxybutyric acid, as defined in paragraph four of subdivision (e) of schedule I of section thirty-three hundred six of the public health law, and said preparations, compounds, mixtures or substances are of an aggregate weight of two hundred grams or more.

Criminal possession of a controlled substance in the fourth degree is a class C felony.

N.Y. Penal Law § 220.09

Amended by New York Laws 2021, ch. 92,Sec. 12, eff. 3/31/2021.

Section 220.16 - Criminal possession of a controlled substance in the third degree

A person is guilty of criminal possession of a controlled substance in the third degree when he knowingly and unlawfully possesses:

1. a narcotic drug with intent to sell it; or

2. a stimulant, hallucinogen, hallucinogenic substance, or lysergic acid diethylamide, with intent to sell it and has previously been convicted of an offense defined in article two hundred twenty or the attempt or conspiracy to commit any such offense; or

3. a stimulant with intent to sell it and said stimulant weighs one gram or more; or

4. lysergic acid diethylamide with intent to sell it and said lysergic acid diethylamide weighs one milligram or more; or

5. a hallucinogen with intent to sell it and said hallucinogen weighs twenty-five milligrams or more; or

6. a hallucinogenic substance with intent to sell it and said hallucinogenic substance weighs one gram or more; or

7. one or more preparations, compounds, mixtures or substances containing methamphetamine, its salts, isomers or salts of isomers with intent to sell it and said preparations, compounds, mixtures or substances are of an aggregate weight of one-eighth ounce or more; or

8. a stimulant and said stimulant weighs five grams or more; or

9. lysergic acid diethylamide and said lysergic acid diethylamide weighs five milligrams or more; or

10. a hallucinogen and said hallucinogen weighs one hundred twenty-five milligrams or more; or

11. a hallucinogenic substance and said hallucinogenic substance weighs five grams or more; or

12. one or more preparations, compounds, mixtures or substances containing a narcotic drug and said preparations, compounds, mixtures or substances are of an aggregate weight of one-half ounce or more; or

13. phencyclidine and said phencyclidine weighs one thousand two hundred fifty milligrams or more.

Criminal possession of a controlled substance in the third degree is a class B felony.

N.Y. Penal Law § 220.16

Section 220.18 - Criminal possession of a controlled substance in the second degree

A person is guilty of criminal possession of a controlled substance in the second degree when he or she knowingly and unlawfully possesses:

1. one or more preparations, compounds, mixtures or substances containing a narcotic drug and said preparations, compounds, mixtures or substances are of an aggregate weight of four ounces or more; or

2. one or more preparations, compounds, mixtures or substances containing methamphetamine, its salts, isomers or salts of isomers and said preparations, compounds, mixtures or substances are of an aggregate weight of two ounces or more; or

3. a stimulant and said stimulant weighs ten grams or more; or

4. lysergic acid diethylamide and said lysergic acid diethylamide weighs twenty-five milligrams or more; or

5. a hallucinogen and said hallucinogen weighs six hundred twenty-five milligrams or more; or

6. a hallucinogenic substance and said hallucinogenic substance weighs twenty-five grams or more; or

7. methadone and said methadone weighs two thousand eight hundred eighty milligrams or more.

Criminal possession of a controlled substance in the second degree is a class A-II felony.

N.Y. Penal Law § 220.18

Section 220.21 - Criminal possession of a controlled substance in the first degree

A person is guilty of criminal possession of a controlled substance in the first degree when he or she knowingly and unlawfully possesses:

1. one or more preparations, compounds, mixtures or substances containing a narcotic drug and said preparations, compounds, mixtures or substances are of an aggregate weight of eight ounces or more; or

2. methadone and said methadone weighs five thousand seven hundred sixty milligrams or more.

Criminal possession of a controlled substance in the first degree is a class A-I felony.

N.Y. Penal Law § 220.21

Section 220.25 - Criminal possession of a controlled substance; presumption

1. The presence of a controlled substance in an automobile, other than a public omnibus, is presumptive evidence of knowing possession thereof by each and every person in the automobile at the time such controlled substance was found; except that such presumption does not apply (a) to a duly licensed operator of an automobile who is at the time operating it for hire in the lawful and proper pursuit of his trade, or (b) to any person in the automobile if one of them, having obtained the controlled substance and not being under duress, is authorized to possess it and such controlled substance is in the same container as when he received possession thereof, or (c) when the controlled substance is concealed upon the person of one of the occupants.

2. The presence of a narcotic drug, narcotic preparation, marihuana or phencyclidine in open view in a room, other than a public place, under circumstances evincing an intent to unlawfully mix, compound, package or otherwise prepare for sale such controlled substance is presumptive evidence of knowing possession thereof by each and every person in close proximity to such controlled substance at the time such controlled substance was found; except that such presumption does not apply to any such persons if (a) one of them, having obtained such controlled substance and not being under duress, is authorized to possess it and such controlled substance is in the same container as when he received possession thereof, or (b) one of them has such controlled substance upon his person.

N.Y. Penal Law § 220.25

Section 220.28 - Use of a child to commit a controlled substance offense

For purposes of this section, "child" means a person less than sixteen years of age.

1. A person is guilty of use of a child to commit a controlled substance offense when, being eighteen years old or more, he or she commits a felony sale or felony attempted sale of a controlled substance in violation of this article and, as part of that criminal transaction, knowingly uses a child to effectuate such felony sale or felony attempted sale of such controlled substance.

2. For purposes of this section, "uses a child to effectuate the felony sale or felony attempted sale of such controlled substance" means conduct by which the actor: (a) conceals such controlled substance on or about the body or person of such child for the purpose of effectuating the criminal sale or attempted sale of such controlled substance to a third person; or (b) directs, forces or otherwise requires such child to sell or attempt to sell or offer direct assistance to the defendant in selling or attempting to sell such controlled substance to a third person.

N.Y. Penal Law § 220.28

Section 220.31 - Criminal sale of a controlled substance in the fifth degree

A person is guilty of criminal sale of a controlled substance in the fifth degree when he knowingly and unlawfully sells a controlled substance.

N.Y. Penal Law § 220.31

Section 220.34 - Criminal sale of a controlled substance in the fourth degree

A person is guilty of criminal sale of a controlled substance in the fourth degree when he knowingly and unlawfully sells:

1. a narcotic preparation; or

2. a dangerous depressant or a depressant and the dangerous depressant weighs ten ounces or more, or the depressant weighs two pounds or more; or

3. [Repealed]

4. phencyclidine and the phencyclidine weighs fifty milligrams or more; or

5. methadone; or

6. any amount of phencyclidine and has previously been convicted of an offense defined in this article or the attempt or conspiracy to commit any such offense; or

6-a. ketamine and said ketamine weighs four thousand milligrams or more.

7. a controlled substance in violation of section 220.31 of this article, when such sale takes place upon school grounds or on a school bus; or

8. a controlled substance in violation of section 220.31 of this article, when such sale takes place upon the grounds of a child day care or educational facility under circumstances evincing knowledge by the defendant that such sale is taking place upon such grounds. As used in this subdivision, the phrase "the grounds of a child day care or educational facility" shall have the same meaning as provided for in subdivision five of section 220.44 of this article. For the purposes of this subdivision, a rebuttable presumption shall be established that a person has knowledge that they are within the grounds of a child day care or educational facility when notice is conspicuously posted of the presence or proximity of such facility; or

9. one or more preparations, compounds, mixtures or substances containing gamma hydroxybutyric acid, as defined in paragraph four of subdivision (e) of schedule I of section thirty-three hundred six of the public health law, and said preparations, compounds, mixtures or substances are of an aggregate weight of twenty-eight grams or more.

Criminal sale of a controlled substance in the fourth degree is a class C felony.

N.Y. Penal Law § 220.34

Amended by New York Laws 2021, ch. 92,Sec. 13, eff. 3/31/2021.

Section 220.39 - Criminal sale of a controlled substance in the third degree

A person is guilty of criminal sale of a controlled substance in the third degree when he knowingly and unlawfully sells:

1. a narcotic drug; or

2. a stimulant, hallucinogen, hallucinogenic substance, or lysergic acid diethylamide and has previously been convicted of an offense defined in article two hundred twenty or the attempt or conspiracy to commit any such offense; or

3. a stimulant and the stimulant weighs one gram or more; or

4. lysergic acid diethylamide and the lysergic acid diethylamide weighs one milligram or more; or

5. a hallucinogen and the hallucinogen weighs twenty-five milligrams or more; or

6. a hallucinogenic substance and the hallucinogenic substance weighs one gram or more; or

7. one or more preparations, compounds, mixtures or substances containing methamphetamine, its salts, isomers or salts of isomers and the preparations, compounds, mixtures or substances are of an aggregate weight of one-eighth ounce or more; or

8. phencyclidine and the phencyclidine weighs two hundred fifty milligrams or more; or

9. a narcotic preparation to a person less than twenty-one years old.

Criminal sale of a controlled substance in the third degree is a class B felony.

N.Y. Penal Law § 220.39

Section 220.41 - Criminal sale of a controlled substance in the second degree

A person is guilty of criminal sale of a controlled substance in the second degree when he knowingly and unlawfully sells:

1. one or more preparations, compounds, mixtures or substances containing a narcotic drug and the preparations, compounds, mixtures or substances are of an aggregate weight of one-half ounce or more; or

2. one or more preparations, compounds, mixtures or substances containing methamphetamine, its salts, isomers or salts of isomers and the preparations, compounds, mixtures or substances are of an aggregate weight of one-half ounce or more; or

3. a stimulant and the stimulant weighs five grams or more; or

4. lysergic acid diethylamide and the lysergic acid diethylamide weighs five milligrams or more; or

5. a hallucinogen and the hallucinogen weighs one hundred twenty-five milligrams or more; or

6. a hallucinogenic substance and the hallucinogenic substance weighs five grams or more; or

7. methadone and the methadone weighs three hundred sixty milligrams or more.

Criminal sale of a controlled substance in the second degree is a class A-II felony.

N.Y. Penal Law § 220.41

Section 220.43 - Criminal sale of a controlled substance in the first degree

A person is guilty of criminal sale of a controlled substance in the first degree when he knowingly and unlawfully sells:

1. one or more preparations, compounds, mixtures or substances containing a narcotic drug and the preparations, compounds, mixtures or substances are of an aggregate weight of two ounces or more; or

2. methadone and the methadone weighs two thousand eight hundred eighty milligrams or more.

Criminal sale of a controlled substance in the first degree is a class A-I felony.

N.Y. Penal Law § 220.43

Section 220.44 - Criminal sale of a controlled substance in or near school grounds

A person is guilty of criminal sale of a controlled substance in or near school grounds when he knowingly and unlawfully sells:

1. a controlled substance in violation of any one of subdivisions one through six-a of section 220.34 of this article, when such sale takes place upon school grounds or on a school bus; or

2. a controlled substance in violation of any one of subdivisions one through eight of section 220.39 of this article, when such sale takes place upon school grounds or on a school bus; or

3. a controlled substance in violation of any one of subdivisions one through six of section 220.34 of this article, when such sale takes place upon the grounds of a child day care or educational facility under circumstances evincing knowledge by the defendant that such sale is taking place upon such grounds; or

4. a controlled substance in violation of any one of subdivisions one through eight of section 220.39 of this article, when such sale takes place upon the grounds of a child day care or educational facility under circumstances evincing knowledge by the defendant that such sale is taking place upon such grounds.

5. For purposes of subdivisions three and four of this section, "the grounds of a child day care or educational facility" means(a) in or on or within any building, structure, athletic playing field, a playground or land contained within the real property boundary line of a public or private child day care center as such term is defined in paragraph (c) of subdivision one of section three hundred ninety of the social services law, or nursery, pre-kindergarten or kindergarten, or (b) any area accessible to the public located within one thousand feet of the real property boundary line comprising any such facility or any parked automobile or other parked vehicle located within one thousand feet of the real property boundary line comprising any such facility. For the purposes of this section an "area accessible to the public" shall mean sidewalks, streets, parking lots, parks, playgrounds, stores and restaurants.

6. For the purposes of this section, a rebuttable presumption shall be established that a person has knowledge that they are within the grounds of a child day care or educational facility when notice is conspicuously posted of the presence or proximity of such facility.

Criminal sale of a controlled substance in or near school grounds is a class B felony.

N.Y. Penal Law § 220.44

Section 220.45 - Criminally possessing a hypodermic instrument

A person is guilty of criminally possessing a hypodermic instrument when he or she knowingly and unlawfully possesses or sells a hypodermic syringe or hypodermic needle. It shall not be a violation of this section when a person obtains and possesses a hypodermic syringe or hypodermic needle pursuant to section thirty-three hundred eighty-one of the public health law, which includes the state's syringe exchange and pharmacy and medical provider-based expanded syringe access programs.

N.Y. Penal Law § 220.45

Amended by New York Laws 2015, ch. 57,Sec. I-3, eff. 4/13/2015.

Section 220.46 - Criminal injection of a narcotic drug

A person is guilty of criminal injection of a narcotic drug when he knowingly and unlawfully possesses a narcotic drug and he intentionally injects by means of a hypodermic syringe or hypodermic needle all or any portion of that drug into the body of another person with the latter's consent.

N.Y. Penal Law § 220.46

Section 220.48 - Criminal sale of a controlled substance to a child

A person is guilty of criminal sale of a controlled substance to a child when, being over twenty-one years old, he or she knowingly and unlawfully sells a controlled substance in violation of section 220.34 or 220.39 of this article to a person less than seventeen years old.

N.Y. Penal Law § 220.48

Section 220.50 - Criminally using drug paraphernalia in the second degree

A person is guilty of criminally using drug paraphernalia in the second degree when he knowingly possesses or sells:

1. Diluents, dilutants or adulterants, including but not limited to, any of the following: quinine hydrochloride, mannitol, mannite, lactose or dextrose, adapted for the dilution of narcotic drugs or stimulants under circumstances evincing an intent to use, or under circumstances evincing knowledge that some person intends to use, the same for purposes of unlawfully mixing, compounding, or otherwise preparing any narcotic drug or stimulant; or

2. Gelatine capsules, glassine envelopes, vials, capsules or any other material suitable for the packaging of individual quantities of narcotic drugs or stimulants under circumstances evincing an intent to use, or under circumstances evincing knowledge that some person intends to use, the same for the purpose of unlawfully manufacturing, packaging or dispensing of any narcotic drug or stimulant; or

3. Scales and balances used or designed for the purpose of weighing or measuring controlled substances, under circumstances evincing an intent to use, or under circumstances evincing knowledge that some person intends to use, the same for purpose of unlawfully manufacturing, packaging or dispensing of any narcotic drug or stimulant.

Criminally using drug paraphernalia in the second degree is a class A misdemeanor.

N.Y. Penal Law § 220.50

Section 220.55 - Criminally using drug paraphernalia in the first degree

A person is guilty of criminally using drug paraphernalia in the first degree when he commits the crime of criminally using drug paraphernalia in the second degree and he has previously been convicted of criminally using drug paraphernalia in the second degree.

N.Y. Penal Law § 220.55

Section 220.60 - Criminal possession of precursors of controlled substances

A person is guilty of criminal possession of precursors of controlled substances when, with intent to manufacture a controlled substance unlawfully, he possesses at the same time:

(a) carbamide (urea) and propanedioc and malonic acid or its derivatives; or

(b) ergot or an ergot derivative and diethylamine or dimethylformamide or diethylamide; or

(c) phenylacetone (1-phenyl-2 propanone) and hydroxylamine or ammonia or formamide or benzaldehyde or nitroethane or methylamine.

(d) pentazocine and methyliodide; or

(e) phenylacetonitrile and dichlorodiethyl methylamine or dichlorodiethyl benzylamine; or

(f) diephenylacetonitrile and dimethylaminoisopropyl chloride; or

(g) piperidine and cyclohexanone and bromobenzene and lithium or magnesium; or

(h) 2, 5-dimethoxy benzaldehyde and nitroethane and a reducing agent.

Criminal prossession of precursors of controlled substances is a class E felony.

N.Y. Penal Law § 220.60

Section 220.65 - Criminal sale of a prescription for a controlled substance or of a controlled substance by a practitioner or pharmacist

A person is guilty of criminal sale of a prescription for a controlled substance or of a controlled substance by a practitioner or pharmacist when:

1. being a practitioner, as that term is defined in section thirty-three hundred two of the public health law, he or she knowingly and unlawfully sells a prescription for a controlled substance. For the purposes of this section, a person sells a prescription for a controlled substance unlawfully when he or she does so other than in good faith in the course of his or her professional practice; or

2. being a practitioner or pharmacist, as those terms are defined in section thirty-three hundred two of the public health law, he or she, acting other than in good faith, while purporting to act within the scope of the power, authority and privileges of his or her license, as that term is defined in section thirty-three hundred two of the public health law, knowingly and unlawfully sells a controlled substance.

Criminal sale of a prescription for a controlled substance or of a controlled substance by a practitioner or pharmacist is a class C felony.

N.Y. Penal Law § 220.65

Amended by New York Laws 2014, ch. 31,Sec. 1, eff. 6/23/2014.

Section 220.70 - Criminal possession of methamphetamine manufacturing material in the second degree

A person is guilty of criminal possession of methamphetamine manufacturing material in the second degree when he or she possesses a precursor, a chemical reagent or a solvent with the intent to use or knowing another intends to use such precursor, chemical reagent, or solvent to unlawfully produce, prepare or manufacture methamphetamine.

N.Y. Penal Law § 220.70

Section 220.71 - Criminal possession of methamphetamine manufacturing material in the first degree

A person is guilty of criminal possession of methamphetamine manufacturing material in the first degree when he or she commits the offense of criminal possession of methamphetamine manufacturing material in the second degree, as defined in section 220.70 of this article, and has previously been convicted within the preceding five years of criminal possession of methamphetamine manufacturing material in the second degree, as defined in section 220.70 of this article, or a violation of this section.

N.Y. Penal Law § 220.71

Section 220.72 - Criminal possession of precursors of methamphetamine

A person is guilty of criminal possession of precursors of methamphetamine when he or she possesses at the same time a precursor and a solvent or chemical reagent, with intent to use or knowing that another intends to use each such precursor, solvent or chemical reagent to unlawfully manufacture methamphetamine.

N.Y. Penal Law § 220.72

Section 220.73 - Unlawful manufacture of methamphetamine in the third degree

A person is guilty of unlawful manufacture of methamphetamine in the third degree when he or she possesses at the same time and location, with intent to use, or knowing that another intends to use each such product to unlawfully manufacture, prepare or produce methamphetamine:

1. Two or more items of laboratory equipment and two or more precursors, chemical reagents or solvents in any combination; or

2. One item of laboratory equipment and three or more precursors, chemical reagents or solvents in any combination; or

3. A precursor:

(a) mixed together with a chemical reagent or solvent; or

(b) with two or more chemical reagents and/or solvents mixed together.

Unlawful manufacture of methamphetamine in the third degree is a class D felony.

N.Y. Penal Law § 220.73

Section 220.74 - Unlawful manufacture of methamphetamine in the second degree

A person is guilty of unlawful manufacture of methamphetamine in the second degree when he or she:

1. Commits the offense of unlawful manufacture of methamphetamine in the third degree as defined in section 220.73 of this article in the presence of another person under the age of sixteen, provided, however, that the actor is at least five years older than such other person under the age of sixteen; or

2. Commits the crime of unlawful manufacture of methamphetamine in the third degree as defined in section 220.73 of this article and has previously been convicted within the preceding five years of the offense of criminal possession of precursors of methamphetamine as defined in section 220.72 of this article, criminal possession of methamphetamine manufacturing material in the first degree as defined in section 220.71 of this article, unlawful disposal of methamphetamine laboratory material as defined in section 220.76 of this article, unlawful manufacture of methamphetamine in the third degree as defined in section 220.73 of this article, unlawful manufacture of methamphetamine in the second degree as defined in this section, or unlawful manufacture of methamphetamine in the first degree as defined in section 220.75 of this article.

Unlawful manufacture of methamphetamine in the second degree is a class C felony.

N.Y. Penal Law § 220.74

Section 220.75 - Unlawful manufacture of methamphetamine in the first degree

A person is guilty of unlawful manufacture of methamphetamine in the first degree when such person commits the crime of unlawful manufacture of methamphetamine in the second degree, as defined in subdivision one of section 220.74 of this article, after having previously been convicted within the preceding five years of unlawful manufacture of methamphetamine in the third degree, as defined in section 220.73, unlawful manufacture of methamphetamine in the second degree, as defined in section 220.74 of this article, or unlawful manufacture of methamphetamine in the first degree, as defined in this section.

N.Y. Penal Law § 220.75

Section 220.76 - Unlawful disposal of methamphetamine laboratory material

A person is guilty of unlawful disposal of methamphetamine laboratory material when, knowing that such actions are in furtherance of a methamphetamine operation, he or she knowingly disposes of, or possesses with intent to dispose of, hazardous or dangerous material under circumstances that create a substantial risk to human health or safety or a substantial danger to the environment.

N.Y. Penal Law § 220.76

Section 220.77 - Operating as a major trafficker

A person is guilty of operating as a major trafficker when:

1. Such person acts as a director of a controlled substance organization during any period of twelve months or less, during which period such controlled substance organization sells one or more controlled substances, and the proceeds collected or due from such sale or sales have a total aggregate value of seventy-five thousand dollars or more; or

2. As a profiteer, such person knowingly and unlawfully sells, on one or more occasions within six months or less, a narcotic drug, and the proceeds collected or due from such sale or sales have a total aggregate value of seventy-five thousand dollars or more.

3. As a profiteer, such person knowingly and unlawfully possesses, on one or more occasions within six months or less, a narcotic drug with intent to sell the same, and such narcotic drugs have a total aggregate value of seventy-five thousand dollars or more.

Operating as a major trafficker is a class A-I felony.

N.Y. Penal Law § 220.77

Section 220.78 - Witness or victim of drug or alcohol overdose

1. A person who, in good faith, seeks health care for someone who is experiencing a drug or alcohol overdose or other life threatening medical emergency shall not be charged or prosecuted for a controlled substance offense under this article or a cannabis offense under article two hundred twenty-two of this title, other than an offense involving sale for consideration or other benefit or gain, or charged or prosecuted for possession of alcohol by a person under age twenty-one years under section sixty-five-c of the alcoholic beverage control law, or for possession of drug paraphernalia under article thirty-nine of the general business law, with respect to any controlled substance, cannabis, alcohol or paraphernalia that was obtained as a result of such seeking or receiving of health care.

2. A person who is experiencing a drug or alcohol overdose or other life threatening medical emergency and, in good faith, seeks health care for himself or herself or is the subject of such a good faith request for health care, shall not be charged or prosecuted for a controlled substance offense under this article or a cannabis offense under article two hundred twenty-two of this title, other than an offense involving sale for consideration or other benefit or gain, or charged or prosecuted for possession of alcohol by a person under age twenty-one years under section sixty-five-c of the alcoholic beverage control law, or charged or prosecuted for possession of cannabis or concentrated cannabis by a person under the age of twenty-one under section one hundred thirty-two of the cannabis law, or for possession of drug paraphernalia under article thirty-nine of the general business law, with respect to any substance, cannabis, alcohol or paraphernalia that was obtained as a result of such seeking or receiving of health care.

3. Definitions. As used in this section the following terms shall have the following meanings:

(a) "Drug or alcohol overdose" or "overdose" means an acute condition including, but not limited to, physical illness, coma, mania, hysteria or death, which is the result of consumption or use of a controlled substance or alcohol and relates to an adverse reaction to or the quantity of the controlled substance or alcohol or a substance with which the controlled substance or alcohol was combined; provided that a patient's condition shall be deemed to be a drug or alcohol overdose if a prudent layperson, possessing an average knowledge of medicine and health, could reasonably believe that the condition is in fact a drug or alcohol overdose and (except as to death) requires health care.

(b) "Health care" means the professional services provided to a person experiencing a drug or alcohol overdose by a health care professional licensed, registered or certified under title eight of the education law or article thirty of the public health law who, acting within his or her lawful scope of practice, may provide diagnosis, treatment or emergency services for a person experiencing a drug or alcohol overdose.

4. It shall be an affirmative defense to a criminal sale controlled substance offense under this article or a criminal sale of cannabis offense under article two hundred twenty-two of this title, not covered by subdivision one or two of this section, with respect to any controlled substance or cannabis which was obtained as a result of such seeking or receiving of health care, that:

(a) the defendant, in good faith, seeks health care for someone or for him or herself who is experiencing a drug or alcohol overdose or other life threatening medical emergency; and

(b) the defendant has no prior conviction for the commission or attempted commission of a class A-I, A-II or B felony under this article.

5. Nothing in this section shall be construed to bar the admissibility of any evidence in connection with the investigation and prosecution of a crime with regard to another defendant who does not independently qualify for the bar to prosecution or for the affirmative defense; nor with regard to other crimes committed by a person who otherwise qualifies under this section; nor shall anything in this section be construed to bar any seizure pursuant to law, including but not limited to pursuant to section thirty-three hundred eighty-seven of the public health law.

6. The bar to prosecution described in subdivisions one and two of this section shall not apply to the prosecution of a class A-I felony under this article, and the affirmative defense described in subdivision four of this section shall not apply to the prosecution of a class A-I or A-II felony under this article.

N.Y. Penal Law § 220.78

Amended by New York Laws 2021, ch. 92,Sec. 48, eff. 3/31/2021.

Article 221 - OFFENSES INVOLVING MARIHUANA

Section 221.00 - [Repealed]

N.Y. Penal Law § 221.00

Amended by New York Laws 2021, ch. 92,Sec. 41, eff. 3/31/2021.

Repealed by New York Laws 2021, ch. 92,Sec. 15, eff. 3/31/2021.

Amended by New York Laws 2014, ch. 90,Sec. 8, eff. 7/5/2014.

Section 221.05 - [Repealed]

N.Y. Penal Law § 221.05

Repealed by New York Laws 2021, ch. 92,Sec. 15, eff. 3/31/2021.

Amended by New York Laws 2019, ch. 131,Sec. 1, eff. 8/28/2019.

Section 221.10 - [Repealed]

N.Y. Penal Law § 221.10

Repealed by New York Laws 2021, ch. 92,Sec. 15, eff. 3/31/2021.

Amended by New York Laws 2019, ch. 131,Sec. 2, eff. 8/28/2019.

Section 221.15 - [Repealed]

N.Y. Penal Law § 221.15

Repealed by New York Laws 2021, ch. 92,Sec. 15, eff. 3/31/2021.

Section 221.20 - [Repealed]
N.Y. Penal Law § 221.20
Repealed by New York Laws 2021, ch. 92,Sec. 15, eff. 3/31/2021.
Section 221.25 - [Repealed]
N.Y. Penal Law § 221.25
Repealed by New York Laws 2021, ch. 92,Sec. 15, eff. 3/31/2021.
Section 221.30 - [Repealed]
N.Y. Penal Law § 221.30
Repealed by New York Laws 2021, ch. 92,Sec. 15, eff. 3/31/2021.
Section 221.35 - [Repealed]
N.Y. Penal Law § 221.35
Repealed by New York Laws 2021, ch. 92,Sec. 15, eff. 3/31/2021.
Section 221.40 - [Repealed]
N.Y. Penal Law § 221.40
Repealed by New York Laws 2021, ch. 92,Sec. 15, eff. 3/31/2021.
Section 221.45 - [Repealed]
N.Y. Penal Law § 221.45
Repealed by New York Laws 2021, ch. 92,Sec. 15, eff. 3/31/2021.
Section 221.50 - [Repealed]
N.Y. Penal Law § 221.50
Repealed by New York Laws 2021, ch. 92,Sec. 15, eff. 3/31/2021.
Section 221.55 - [Repealed]
N.Y. Penal Law § 221.55
Repealed by New York Laws 2021, ch. 92,Sec. 15, eff. 3/31/2021.

Article 222 - CANNABIS

Section 222.00 - Cannabis; definitions

1. "Cannabis" means all parts of the plant of the genus Cannabis, whether growing or not; the seeds thereof; the resin extracted from any part of the plant; and every compound, manufacture, salt, derivative, mixture, or preparation of the plant, its seeds or resin. It does not include the mature stalks of the plant, fiber produced from the stalks, oil or cake made from the seeds of the plant, any other compound, manufacture, salt, derivative, mixture, or preparation of the mature stalks (except the resin extracted therefrom), fiber, oil, or cake, or the sterilized seed of the plant which is incapable of germination. It does not include hemp, cannabinoid hemp or hemp extract as defined in section three of the cannabis law or drug products approved by the Federal Food and Drug Administration.
2. "Concentrated cannabis" means:
(a) the separated resin, whether crude or purified, obtained from a plant of the genus Cannabis; or
(b) a material, preparation, mixture, compound or other substance which contains more than three percent by weight of delta-9 tetrahydrocannabinol, or its isomer, delta-8 dibenzopyran numbering system, or delta-1 tetrahydrocannabinol or its isomer, delta 1 (6) monoterpene numbering system.
3. For the purposes of this article, "sell" shall mean to sell, exchange or dispose of for compensation. "Sell" shall not include the transfer of cannabis or concentrated cannabis between persons twenty-one years of age or older without compensation in the quantities authorized in paragraph (b) of subdivision one of section 222.05 of this article.
4. For the purposes of this article, "smoking" shall have the same meaning as that term is defined in section three of the cannabis law.
N.Y. Penal Law § 222.00
Added by New York Laws 2021, ch. 92,Sec. 16, eff. 3/31/2021.

Section 222.05 - Personal use of cannabis

Notwithstanding any other provision of law to the contrary:
1. The following acts are lawful for persons twenty-one years of age or older:
(a) possessing, displaying, purchasing, obtaining, or transporting up to three ounces of cannabis and up to twenty-four grams of concentrated cannabis;
(b) transferring, without compensation, to a person twenty-one years of age or older, up to three ounces of cannabis and up to twenty-four grams of concentrated cannabis;
(c) using, smoking, ingesting, or consuming cannabis or concentrated cannabis unless otherwise prohibited by state law;
(d) possessing, using, displaying, purchasing, obtaining, manufacturing, transporting or giving to any person twenty-one years of age or older cannabis paraphernalia or concentrated cannabis paraphernalia;
(e) planting, cultivating, harvesting, drying, processing or possessing cultivated cannabis in accordance with section 222.15 of this article; and
(f) assisting another person who is twenty-one years of age or older, or allowing property to be used, in any of the acts described in paragraphs (a) through (e) of this subdivision.
2. Cannabis, concentrated cannabis, cannabis paraphernalia or concentrated cannabis paraphernalia involved in any way with conduct deemed lawful by this section are not contraband nor subject to seizure or forfeiture of assets under article four hundred eighty of this chapter, section thirteen hundred eleven of the civil practice law and rules, or other applicable

143

law, and no conduct deemed lawful by this section shall constitute the basis for approach, search, seizure, arrest or detention.

3. Except as provided in subdivision four of this section, in any criminal proceeding including proceedings pursuant to section 710.20 of the criminal procedure law, no finding or determination of reasonable cause to believe a crime has been committed shall be based solely on evidence of the following facts and circumstances, either individually or in combination with each other:

(a) the odor of cannabis;

(b) the odor of burnt cannabis;

(c) the possession of or the suspicion of possession of cannabis or concentrated cannabis in the amounts authorized in this article;

(d) the possession of multiple containers of cannabis without evidence of concentrated cannabis in the amounts authorized in this article;

(e) the presence of cash or currency in proximity to cannabis or concentrated cannabis; or

(f) the planting, cultivating, harvesting, drying, processing or possessing cultivated cannabis in accordance with section 222.15 of this article.

4. Paragraph (b) of subdivision three of this section shall not apply when a law enforcement officer is investigating whether a person is operating a motor vehicle, vessel or snowmobile while impaired by drugs or the combined influence of drugs or of alcohol and any drug or drugs in violation of subdivision four or subdivision four-a of section eleven hundred ninety-two of the vehicle and traffic law, or paragraph (e) of subdivision two of section forty-nine-a of the navigation law, or paragraph (d) of subdivision one of section 25.24 of the parks, recreation and historic preservation law. During such investigations, the odor of burnt cannabis shall not provide probable cause to search any area of a vehicle that is not readily accessible to the driver and reasonably likely to contain evidence relevant to the driver's condition.

N.Y. Penal Law § 222.05

Added by New York Laws 2021, ch. 92, Sec. 16, eff. 3/31/2021.

Section 222.10 - Restrictions on cannabis use

Unless otherwise authorized by law or regulation, no person shall:

1. smoke or vape cannabis in a location where smoking or vaping cannabis is prohibited pursuant to article thirteen-E of the public health law; or

2. smoke, vape or ingest cannabis or concentrated cannabis in or upon the grounds of a school, as defined in subdivision ten of section eleven hundred twenty-five of the education law or in or on a school bus, as defined in section one hundred forty-two of the vehicle and traffic law; provided, however, provisions of this subdivision shall not apply to acts that are in compliance with article three of the cannabis law.

Notwithstanding any other section of law, violations of restrictions on cannabis use are subject to a civil penalty not exceeding twenty-five dollars or an amount of community service not exceeding twenty hours.

N.Y. Penal Law § 222.10

Added by New York Laws 2021, ch. 92, Sec. 16, eff. 3/31/2021.

Section 222.15 - Personal cultivation and home possession of cannabis

1. Except as provided for in section forty-one of the cannabis law, and unless otherwise authorized by law or regulation, no person may:

(a) plant, cultivate, harvest, dry, process or possess more than three mature cannabis plants and three immature cannabis plants at any one time; or

(b) plant, cultivate, harvest, dry, process or possess, within his or her private residence, or on the grounds of his or her private residence, more than three mature cannabis plants and three immature cannabis plants at any one time; or

(c) being under the age of twenty-one, plant, cultivate, harvest, dry, process or possess cannabis plants.

2. No more than six mature and six immature cannabis plants may be cultivated, harvested, dried, or possessed within any private residence, or on the grounds of a person's private residence.

3. The personal cultivation of cannabis shall only be permitted within, or on the grounds of, a person's private residence.

4. Any mature or immature cannabis plant described in paragraph (a) or (b) of subdivision one of this section, and any cannabis produced by any such cannabis plant or plants cultivated, harvested, dried, processed or possessed pursuant to paragraph (a) or (b) of subdivision one of this section shall, unless otherwise authorized by law or regulation, be stored within such person's private residence or on the grounds of such person's private residence. Such person shall take reasonable steps designed to ensure that such cultivated cannabis is in a secured place and not accessible to any person under the age of twenty-one.

5. Notwithstanding any law to the contrary, a person may lawfully possess up to five pounds of cannabis in their private residence or on the grounds of such person's private residence. Such person shall take reasonable steps designed to ensure that such cannabis is in a secured place not accessible to any person under the age of twenty-one.

6. A county, town, city or village may enact and enforce regulations to reasonably regulate the actions and conduct set forth in subdivision one of this section; provided that:

(a) a violation of any such a regulation, as approved by such county, town, city or village enacting the regulation, may constitute no more than an infraction and may be punishable by no more than a discretionary civil penalty of two hundred dollars or less; and

(b) no county, town, city or village may enact or enforce any such regulation or regulations that may completely or essentially prohibit a person from engaging in the action or conduct authorized by subdivision one of this section.

A violation of this section, other than paragraph (a) of subdivision six of this section, may be subject to a civil penalty of up to one hundred twenty-five dollars per violation.

7. The office of cannabis management shall issue regulations for the home cultivation of cannabis. The office of cannabis management shall enact, and may enforce, regulations to regulate the actions and conduct set forth in this section including requirements for, or restrictions and prohibitions on, the use of any compressed flammable gas solvents such as propane, butane, or other hexane gases for cannabis processing; or other forms of home cultivation, manufacturing, or cannabinoid production and processing, which the office determines poses a danger to public safety; and to ensure the home cultivation of cannabis is for personal use by an adult over the age of twenty-one in possession of cannabis plants, and not utilized for unlicensed commercial or illicit activity, provided any regulations issued by the office shall not completely or essentially prohibit a person from engaging in the action or conduct authorized by this section.

8. The office of cannabis management may issue guidance or advisories for the education and promotion of safe practices for activities and conduct authorized in subdivision one of this section.

9. Subdivisions one through five of this section shall not take effect until such a time as the office of cannabis management has issued regulations governing the home cultivation of cannabis. The office shall issue rules and regulations governing the home cultivation of cannabis by certified patients as defined in section three of the cannabis law, no later than six months after the effective date of this article and shall issue rules and regulations governing the home cultivation of cannabis for cannabis consumers as defined by section three of the cannabis law no later than eighteen months following the first authorized retail sale of adult-use cannabis products to a cannabis consumer.

N.Y. Penal Law § 222.15

Added by New York Laws 2021, ch. 92,Sec. 16, eff. 3/31/2021.

Section 222.20 - Licensing of cannabis production and distribution; defense

In any prosecution for an offense involving cannabis under this article or an authorized local law, it is a defense that the defendant was engaged in such activity in compliance with the cannabis law.

N.Y. Penal Law § 222.20

Added by New York Laws 2021, ch. 92,Sec. 16, eff. 3/31/2021.

Section 222.25 - Unlawful possession of cannabis

A person is guilty of unlawful possession of cannabis when he or she knowingly and unlawfully possesses cannabis and such cannabis weighs more than three ounces or concentrated cannabis and such concentrated cannabis weighs more than twenty-four grams.

N.Y. Penal Law § 222.25

Added by New York Laws 2021, ch. 92,Sec. 16, eff. 3/31/2021.

Section 222.30 - Criminal possession of cannabis in the third degree

A person is guilty of criminal possession of cannabis in the third degree when he or she knowingly and unlawfully possesses:

1. cannabis and such cannabis weighs more than sixteen ounces; or

2. concentrated cannabis and such concentrated cannabis weighs more than five ounces.

Criminal possession of cannabis in the third degree is a class A misdemeanor.

N.Y. Penal Law § 222.30

Added by New York Laws 2021, ch. 92,Sec. 16, eff. 3/31/2021.

Section 222.35 - Criminal possession of cannabis in the second degree

A person is guilty of criminal possession of cannabis in the second degree when he or she knowingly and unlawfully possesses:

1. cannabis and such cannabis weighs more than five pounds; or

2. concentrated cannabis and such concentrated cannabis weighs more than two pounds.

Criminal possession of cannabis in the second degree is a class E felony.

N.Y. Penal Law § 222.35

Added by New York Laws 2021, ch. 92,Sec. 16, eff. 3/31/2021.

Section 222.40 - Criminal possession of cannabis in the first degree

A person is guilty of criminal possession of cannabis in the first degree when he or she knowingly and unlawfully possesses:

1. cannabis and such cannabis weighs more than ten pounds; or

2. concentrated cannabis and such concentrated cannabis weighs more than four pounds.

Criminal possession of cannabis in the first degree is a class D felony.

N.Y. Penal Law § 222.40

Added by New York Laws 2021, ch. 92,Sec. 16, eff. 3/31/2021.

Section 222.45 - Unlawful sale of cannabis

A person is guilty of unlawful sale of cannabis when he or she knowingly and unlawfully sells cannabis or concentrated cannabis.

N.Y. Penal Law § 222.45

Added by New York Laws 2021, ch. 92,Sec. 16, eff. 3/31/2021.

Section 222.50 - Criminal sale of cannabis in the third degree

A person is guilty of criminal sale of cannabis in the third degree when:

1. he or she knowingly and unlawfully sells more than three ounces of cannabis or more than twenty-four grams of concentrated cannabis; or

2. being twenty-one years of age or older, he or she knowingly and unlawfully sells or gives, or causes to be given or sold, cannabis or concentrated cannabis to a person less than twenty-one years of age; except that in any prosecution under this subdivision, it is a defense that the defendant was less than three years older than the person under the age of twenty-one at the time of the offense. This subdivision shall not apply to designated caregivers, practitioners, employees of a registered organization or employees of a designated caregiver facility acting in compliance with article three of the cannabis law. Criminal sale of cannabis in the third degree is a class A misdemeanor.

N.Y. Penal Law § 222.50

Added by New York Laws 2021, ch. 92,Sec. 16, eff. 3/31/2021.

Section 222.55 - Criminal sale of cannabis in the second degree

A person is guilty of criminal sale of cannabis in the second degree when:

1. he or she knowingly and unlawfully sells more than sixteen ounces of cannabis or more than five ounces of concentrated cannabis; or

2. being twenty-one years of age or older, he or she knowingly and unlawfully sells or gives, or causes to be given or sold, more than three ounces of cannabis or more than twenty-four grams of concentrated cannabis to a person less than eighteen years of age. This subdivision shall not apply to designated caregivers, practitioners, employees of a registered organization or employees of a designated caregiver facility acting in compliance with article three of the cannabis law. Criminal sale of cannabis in the second degree is a class E felony.

N.Y. Penal Law § 222.55

Added by New York Laws 2021, ch. 92,Sec. 16, eff. 3/31/2021.

Section 222.60 - Criminal sale of cannabis in the first degree

A person is guilty of criminal sale of cannabis in the first degree when he or she knowingly and unlawfully sells more than five pounds of cannabis or more than two pounds of concentrated cannabis.

N.Y. Penal Law § 222.60

Added by New York Laws 2021, ch. 92,Sec. 16, eff. 3/31/2021.

Section 222.65 - Aggravated criminal sale of cannabis

A person is guilty of aggravated criminal sale of cannabis when he or she knowingly and unlawfully sells cannabis or concentrated cannabis weighing one hundred pounds or more.

N.Y. Penal Law § 222.65

Added by New York Laws 2021, ch. 92,Sec. 16, eff. 3/31/2021.

Article 225 - GAMBLING OFFENSES

Section 225.00 - Gambling offenses; definitions of terms

The following definitions are applicable to this article:

1. "Contest of chance" means any contest, game, gaming scheme or gaming device in which the outcome depends in a material degree upon an element of chance, notwithstanding that skill of the contestants may also be a factor therein.

2. "Gambling." A person engages in gambling when he stakes or risks something of value upon the outcome of a contest of chance or a future contingent event not under his control or influence, upon an agreement or understanding that he will receive something of value in the event of a certain outcome.

3. "Player" means a person who engages in any form of gambling solely as a contestant or bettor, without receiving or becoming entitled to receive any profit therefrom other than personal gambling winnings, and without otherwise rendering any material assistance to the establishment, conduct or operation of the particular gambling activity. A person who gambles at a social game of chance on equal terms with the other participants therein does not otherwise render material assistance to the establishment, conduct or operation thereof by performing, without fee or remuneration, acts directed toward the arrangement or facilitation of the game, such as inviting persons to play, permitting the use of premises therefor and supplying cards or other equipment used therein. A person who engages in "bookmaking", as defined in this section is not a "player."

4. "Advance gambling activity." A person "advances gambling activity" when, acting other than as a player, he engages in conduct which materially aids any form of gambling activity. Such conduct includes but is not limited to conduct directed toward the creation or establishment of the particular game, contest, scheme, device or activity involved, toward the acquisition or maintenance of premises, paraphernalia, equipment or apparatus therefor, toward the solicitation or inducement of persons to participate therein, toward the actual conduct of the playing phases thereof, toward the arrangement of any of its financial or recording phases, or toward any other phase of its operation. One advances gambling activity when, having substantial proprietary or other authoritative control over premises being used with his knowledge for purposes of gambling activity, he permits such to occur or continue or makes no effort to prevent its occurrence or continuation.

5. "Profit from gambling activity." A person "profits from gambling activity" when, other than as a player, he accepts or receives money or other property pursuant to an agreement or understanding with any person whereby he participates or is to participate in the proceeds of gambling activity.

6. "Something of value" means any money or property, any token, object or article exchangeable for money or property, or any form of credit or promise directly or indirectly contemplating transfer of money or property or of any interest therein, or involving extension of a service, entertainment or a privilege of playing at a game or scheme without charge.

7. "Gambling device" means any device, machine, paraphernalia or equipment which is used or usable in the playing phases of any gambling activity, whether such activity consists of gambling between persons or gambling by a person involving the playing of a machine. Notwithstanding the foregoing, lottery tickets, policy slips and other items used in the playing phases of lottery and policy schemes are not gambling devices.

7-a. A "coin operated gambling device" means a gambling device which operates as a result of the insertion of something of value. A device designed, constructed or readily adaptable or convertible for such use is a coin operated gambling device notwithstanding the fact that it may require adjustment, manipulation or repair in order to operate as such. A machine which awards free or extended play is not a gambling device merely because such free or extended play may constitute something of value provided that the outcome depends upon the skill of the player and not in a material degree upon an element of chance.

8. "Slot machine" means a gambling device which, as a result of the insertion of a coin or other object, operates, either completely automatically or with the aid of some physical act by the player, in such manner that, depending upon elements of chance, it may eject something of value. A device so constructed, or readily adaptable or convertible to such use, is no less a slot machine because it is not in working order or because some mechanical act of manipulation or repair is required to accomplish its adaptation, conversion or workability. Nor is it any less a slot machine because, apart from its use or adaptability as such, it may also sell or deliver something of value on a basis other than chance. A machine which sells items of merchandise which are of equivalent value, is not a slot machine merely because such items differ from each other in composition, size, shape or color.

9. "Bookmaking" means advancing gambling activity by unlawfully accepting bets from members of the public as a business, rather than in a casual or personal fashion, upon the outcomes of future contingent events.

10. "Lottery" means an unlawful gambling scheme in which (a) the players pay or agree to pay something of value for chances, represented and differentiated by numbers or by combinations of numbers or by some other media, one or more of which chances are to be designated the winning ones; and (b) the winning chances are to be determined by a drawing or by some other method based upon the element of chance; and (c) the holders of the winning chances are to receive something of value provided, however, that in no event shall the provisions of this subdivision be construed to include a raffle as such term is defined in subdivision three-b of section one hundred eighty-six of the general municipal law.

11. "Policy" or "the numbers game" means a form of lottery in which the winning chances or plays are not determined upon the basis of a drawing or other act on the part of persons conducting or connected with the scheme, but upon the basis of the outcome or outcomes of a future contingent event or events otherwise unrelated to the particular scheme.

12. "Unlawful" means not specifically authorized by law.

13. "Authorized gaming establishment" means any structure, structure and adjacent or attached structure, or grounds adjacent to a structure in which casino gaming, conducted pursuant to article thirteen of the racing, pari-mutuel wagering and breeding law, or Class III gaming, as authorized pursuant to a compact reached between the state of New York and a federally recognized Indian nation or tribe under the federal Indian Gaming Regulatory Act of 1988, is conducted and shall include all public and non-public areas of any such building, except for such areas of a building where either Class I or II gaming are conducted or any building or grounds known as a video gaming entertainment facility, including facilities where food and drink are served, as well as those areas not normally open to the public, such as where records related to video lottery gaming operations are kept, except shall not include the racetracks or such areas where such video lottery gaming operations or facilities do not take place or exist, such as racetrack areas or fair grounds which are wholly unrelated to video lottery gaming operations, pursuant to section sixteen hundred seventeen-a and paragraph five of subdivision a of section sixteen hundred twelve of the tax law, as amended and implemented.

14. "Authorized gaming operator" means an enterprise or business entity authorized by state or federal law to operate casino or video lottery gaming.

15. "Casino gaming" means games authorized to be played pursuant to a license granted under article thirteen of the racing, pari-mutuel wagering and breeding law or by federally recognized Indian nations or tribes pursuant to a gaming compact reached in accordance with the federal Indian Gaming Regulatory Act of 1988, Pub. L. 100-497, 102 Stat. 2467, codified at 25 U.S.C. §§ 2701-21 and 18 U.S.C. §§ 1166-68.

16. "Cash equivalent" means a treasury check, a travelers check, wire transfer of funds, transfer check, money order, certified check, cashiers check, payroll check, a check drawn on the account of the authorized gaming operator payable to the patron or to the authorized gaming establishment, a promotional coupon, promotional chip, promotional cheque, promotional token, or a voucher recording cash drawn against a credit card or charge card.

17. "Cheques" or "chips" or "tokens" means nonmetal, metal or partly metal representatives of value, redeemable for cash or cash equivalent, and issued and sold by an authorized casino operator for use at an authorized gaming establishment. The value of such cheques or chips or tokens shall be considered equivalent in value to the cash or cash equivalent exchanged for such cheques or chips or tokens upon purchase or redemption.

18. "Class I gaming" and "Class II gaming" means those forms of gaming that are not Class III gaming, as defined in subsection eight of section four of the federal Indian Gaming Regulatory Act, 25 U.S.C. § 2703.

19. "Class III gaming" means those forms of gaming that are not Class I or Class II gaming, as defined in subsections six and seven of section four of the federal Indian Gaming Regulatory Act, 25 U.S.C. § 2703 and those games enumerated in the Appendix of a gaming compact.

20. "Compact" or "gaming compact" means the agreement between a federally recognized Indian tribe and the state of New York regarding Class III gaming activities entered into pursuant to the federal Indian Gaming Regulatory Act, Pub. L. 100-497, 102 Stat. 2467, codified at 25 U.S.C. §§ 2701-21 and 18 U.S.C. §§ 1166-68 (1988 & Supp. II).

21. "Gaming equipment or device" means any machine or device which is specially designed or manufactured for use in the operation of any Class III or video lottery game.

22. "Gaming regulatory authority" means, with respect to any authorized gaming establishment on Indian lands, territory or reservation, the Indian nation or tribal gaming commission, its authorized officers, agents and representatives acting in their official capacities or such other agency of a nation or tribe as the nation or tribe may designate as the agency responsible for the regulation of Class III gaming, jointly with the state gaming agency, conducted pursuant to a gaming compact between the nation or tribe and the state of New York, or with respect to any casino gaming authorized pursuant to article thirteen of the racing, pari-mutuel wagering and breeding law or video lottery gaming conducted pursuant to section sixteen hundred seventeen-a and paragraph five of subdivision a of section sixteen hundred twelve of the tax law, as amended and implemented.

23. "Premises" includes any structure, parking lot, building, vehicle, watercraft, and any real property.

24. "Sell" means to sell, exchange, give or dispose of to another.

25. "State gaming agency" shall mean the New York state gaming commission, its authorized officials, agents, and representatives acting in their official capacities as the regulatory agency of the state which has responsibility for regulation with respect to video lottery gaming or casino gaming.

26. "Unfair gaming equipment" means loaded dice, marked cards, substituted cards or dice, or fixed roulette wheels or other gaming equipment which has been altered in a way that tends to deceive or tends to alter the elements of chance or normal random selection which determine the result of the game or outcome, or the amount or frequency of the payment in a game.

27. "Unlawful gaming property" means:

(a) any device, not prescribed for use in casinio gaming by its rules, which is capable of assisting a player:

(i) to calculate any probabilities material to the outcome of a contest of chance; or

(ii) to receive or transmit information material to the outcome of a contest of chance; or

(b) any object or article which, by virtue of its size, shape or any other quality, is capable of being used in casino gaming as an improper substitute for a genuine chip, cheque, token, betting coupon, debit instrument, voucher or other instrument or indicia of value; or

(c) any unfair gaming equipment.

28. "Video lottery gaming" has the meaning set forth in subdivision six of section sixteen hundred two of the tax law.

29. "Voucher" means an instrument of value generated by a video lottery terminal representing a monetary amount and/or play value owed to a customer at a specific video lottery terminal based on video lottery gaming winnings and/or amounts not wagered.

N.Y. Penal Law § 225.00

Amended by New York Laws 2015, ch. 59,Sec. OO-2, eff. 5/13/2015.

Amended by New York Laws 2013, ch. 175,Sec. 3, eff. 7/30/2013.

Amended by New York Laws 2013, ch. 174,Sec. 3, eff. 7/30/2013.

Section 225.05 - Promoting gambling in the second degree

A person is guilty of promoting gambling in the second degree when he knowingly advances or profits from unlawful gambling activity.

N.Y. Penal Law § 225.05

Section 225.10 - Promoting gambling in the first degree

A person is guilty of promoting gambling in the first degree when he knowingly advances or profits from unlawful gambling activity by:

1. Engaging in bookmaking to the extent that he receives or accepts in any one day more than five bets totaling more than five thousand dollars; or

2. Receiving, in connection with a lottery or policy scheme or enterprise, (a) money or written records from a person other than a player whose chances or plays are represented by such money or records, or (b) more than five hundred dollars in any one day of money played in such scheme or enterprise.

N.Y. Penal Law § 225.10

Section 225.15 - Possession of gambling records in the second degree

A person is guilty of possession of gambling records in the second degree when, with knowledge of the contents or nature thereof, he possesses any writing, paper, instrument or article:

1. Of a kind commonly used in the operation or promotion of a bookmaking scheme or enterprise; or

2. Of a kind commonly used in the operation, promotion or playing of a lottery or policy scheme or enterprise; except that in any prosecution under this subdivision, it is a defense that the writing, paper, instrument or article possessed by the defendant constituted, reflected or represented plays, bets or chances of the defendant himself in a number not exceeding ten.

3. Of any paper or paper product in sheet form chemically converted to nitrocellulose having explosive characteristics.

4. Of any water soluble paper or paper derivative in sheet form.

Possession of gambling records in the second degree is a class A misdemeanor.

N.Y. Penal Law § 225.15

Section 225.20 - Possession of gambling records in the first degree

A person is guilty of possession of gambling records in the first degree when, with knowledge of the contents thereof, he possesses any writing, paper, instrument or article:

1. Of a kind commonly used in the operation or promotion of a bookmaking scheme or enterprise, and constituting, reflecting or representing more than five bets totaling more than five thousand dollars; or

2. Of a kind commonly used in the operation, promotion or playing of a lottery or policy scheme or enterprise, and constituting, reflecting or representing more than five hundred plays or chances therein.

Possession of gambling records in the first degree is a class E felony.

N.Y. Penal Law § 225.20

Section 225.25 - Possession of gambling records; defense

In any prosecution for possession of gambling records, it is a defense that the writing, paper, instrument or article possessed by the defendant was neither used nor intended to be used in the operation or promotion of a bookmaking scheme or enterprise, or in the operation, promotion or playing of a lottery or policy scheme or enterprise.

N.Y. Penal Law § 225.25

Section 225.30 - Possession of a gambling device

a. A person is guilty of possession of a gambling device when, with knowledge of the character thereof, he or she manufactures, sells, transports, places or possesses, or conducts or negotiates any transaction affecting or designed to affect ownership, custody or use of:

1. A slot machine, unless such possession is permitted pursuant to article nine-A of the general municipal law; or

2. Any other gambling device, believing that the same is to be used in the advancement of unlawful gambling activity; or

3. A coin operated gambling device with intent to use such device in the advancement of unlawful gambling activity.

b. Possession of a slot machine shall not be unlawful where such possession and use is pursuant to a gaming compact, duly executed by the governor and an Indian tribe or Nation, under the Indian Gaming Regulatory Act, as codified at 25 U.S.C. §§§§ 2701-2721 and 18 U.S.C §§§§ 1166-1168, where the use of such slot machine or machines is consistent with such gaming compact and where the state receives a negotiated percentage of the net drop (defined as gross money wagered after payout, but before expenses) from any such slot machine or machines.

c. Transportation and possession of a slot machine shall not be unlawful where such transportation and possession is necessary to facilitate the training of persons in the repair and reconditioning of such machines as are used or are to be used for operations in those casinos authorized pursuant to a tribal-state compact as provided for pursuant to section eleven hundred seventy-two of title fifteen of the United States Code in the state of New York.

d. Transportation and possession of a slot machine shall not be unlawful where such slot machine was transported into this state in a sealed container and possessed for the purpose of product development, research, or additional manufacture or assembly, and such slot machine will be or has been transported in a sealed container to a jurisdiction outside of this state for purposes which are lawful in such outside jurisdiction.

Possession of a gambling device is a class A misdemeanor.

e. Transportation and possession of a gambling device shall not be unlawful where (i) the manufacturer or distributor of the gambling device has filed a statement with the state gaming commission required by subdivision twenty-one of section one hundred four of the racing, pari-mutuel wagering and breeding law, (ii) such gambling device was transported into this state in a sealed container and possessed for the purpose of exhibition or marketing in accordance with such statement, and (iii) such device is thereafter transported in a sealed container to a jurisdiction outside of this state for purposes that are lawful in such outside jurisdiction.

N.Y. Penal Law § 225.30

Amended by New York Laws 2013, ch. 47,Sec. 2, eff. 5/1/2013.

Amended by New York Laws 2013, ch. 46,Sec. 2, eff. 5/1/2013.

Section 225.32 - Possession of a gambling device; defenses

1. In any prosecution for possession of a gambling device specified in subdivision one of section 225.30 of this article, it is an affirmative defense that:

(a) the slot machine possessed by the defendant was neither used nor intended to be used in the operation or promotion of unlawful gambling activity or enterprise and that such slot machine is an antique; for purposes of this section proof that a slot machine was manufactured prior to nineteen hundred forty-one shall be conclusive proof that such a machine is an antique;

(b) the slot machine possessed by the defendant was manufactured or assembled by the defendant for the sole purpose of transporting such slot machine in a sealed container to a jurisdiction outside this state for purposes which are lawful in such outside jurisdiction; or

(c) the slot machine possessed by the defendant was neither used nor intended to be used in the operation or promotion of unlawful gambling activity or enterprise, is more than thirty years old, and such possession takes place in the defendant's home.

2. Where a defendant raises an affirmative defense provided by subdivision one hereof, any slot machine seized from the defendant shall not be destroyed, or otherwise altered until a final court determination is rendered. In a final court determination rendered in favor of said defendant, such slot machine shall be returned, forthwith, to said defendant, notwithstanding any provisions of law to the contrary.

N.Y. Penal Law § 225.32

Section 225.35 - Gambling offenses; presumptions

1. Proof of possession of any gambling device or of any gambling record specified in sections 225.15 and 225.20, is presumptive evidence of possession thereof with knowledge of its character or contents.

2. In any prosecution under this article in which it is necessary to prove the occurrence of a sporting event, a published report of its occurrence in any daily newspaper, magazine or other periodically printed publication of general circulation shall be admissible in evidence and shall constitute presumptive proof of the occurrence of such event.

3. Possession of three or more coin operated gambling devices or possession of a coin operated gambling device in a public place shall be presumptive evidence of intent to use in the advancement of unlawful gambling activity.

N.Y. Penal Law § 225.35

Section 225.40 - Lottery offenses; no defense

Any offense defined in this article which consists of the commission of acts relating to a lottery is no less criminal because the lottery itself is drawn or conducted without the state and is not violative of the laws of the jurisdiction in which it was so drawn or conducted.

N.Y. Penal Law § 225.40

Section 225.55 - Gaming fraud in the second degree

A person is guilty of gaming fraud in the second degree when he or she:

1. with intent to defraud and in violation of the rules of the casino gaming, misrepresents, changes the amount bet or wagered on, or the outcome or possible outcome of the contest or event which is the subject of the bet or wager, or the amount or frequency of payment in the casino gaming; or

2. with intent to defraud, obtains anything of value from casino gaming without having won such amount by a bet or wager contingent thereon.

Gaming fraud in the second degree is a class A misdemeanor.

N.Y. Penal Law § 225.55

Added by New York Laws 2013, ch. 174,Sec. 4, eff. 7/30/2013.

Section 225.60 - Gaming fraud in the first degree

A person is guilty of gaming fraud in the first degree when he or she commits a gaming fraud in the second degree, and:

1. The value of the benefit obtained exceeds one thousand dollars; or

2. He or she has been previously convicted within the preceding five years of any offense of which an essential element is the commission of a gaming fraud.

N.Y. Penal Law § 225.60

Added by New York Laws 2013, ch. 174,Sec. 4, eff. 7/30/2013.

Section 225.65 - Use of counterfeit, unapproved or unlawful wagering instruments

A person is guilty of use of counterfeit, unapproved or unlawful wagering instruments when in playing or using any casino gaming designed to be played with, received or be operated by chips, cheques, tokens, vouchers or other wagering instruments approved by the appropriate gaming regulatory authority, he or she knowingly uses chips, cheques, tokens, vouchers or other wagering instruments other than those approved by the appropriate gaming regulating authority and the state gaming agency or lawful coin or legal tender of the United States of America.

N.Y. Penal Law § 225.65

Added by New York Laws 2013, ch. 174,Sec. 4, eff. 7/30/2013.

Section 225.70 - Possession of unlawful gaming property in the third degree

A person is guilty of possession of unlawful gaming property in the third degree when he or she possesses, with intent to use such property to commit gaming fraud, unlawful gaming property at a premises being used for casino gaming.

N.Y. Penal Law § 225.70

Added by New York Laws 2013, ch. 174,Sec. 4, eff. 7/30/2013.

Section 225.75 - Possession of unlawful gaming property in the second degree

A person is guilty of possession of unlawful gaming property in the second degree when:

1. He or she makes, sells, or possesses with intent to sell, any unlawful gaming property at a casino gaming facility, the value of which exceeds three hundred dollars, with intent that it be made available to a person for unlawful use; or

2. He or she commits possession of unlawful gaming property in the third degree as defined in section 225.70 of this article, and the face value of the improper substitute property exceeds five hundred dollars; or

3. He or she commits the offense of possession of unlawful gaming property in the third degree and has been previously convicted within the preceding five years of any offense of which an essential element is possession of unlawful gaming property.

N.Y. Penal Law § 225.75

Added by New York Laws 2013, ch. 174,Sec. 4, eff. 7/30/2013.

Section 225.80 - Possession of unlawful gaming property in the first degree

A person is guilty of possession of unlawful gaming property in the first degree when:

1. He or she commits the crime of unlawful possession of gaming property in the third degree as defined in section 225.70 of this article and the face value of the improper substitute property exceeds one thousand dollars; or

2. He or she commits the offense of possession of unlawful gaming property in the second degree as defined in subdivision one or two of section 225.75 of this article and has been previously convicted within the preceding five years of any offense of which an essential element is possession of unlawful gaming property.

N.Y. Penal Law § 225.80

Added by New York Laws 2013, ch. 174,Sec. 4, eff. 7/30/2013.

Section 225.85 - Use of unlawful gaming property

A person is guilty of use of unlawful gaming property when he or she knowingly with intent to defraud uses unlawful gaming property at a premises being used for casino gaming.

N.Y. Penal Law § 225.85

Added by New York Laws 2013, ch. 174,Sec. 4, eff. 7/30/2013.

Section 225.90 - Manipulation of gaming outcomes at an authorized gaming establishment

A person is guilty of manipulation of gaming outcomes at an authorized gaming establishment when he or she:

1. Knowingly conducts, operates, deals or otherwise manipulates, or knowingly allows to be conducted, operated, dealt or otherwise manipulated, cards, dice or gaming equipment or device, for themselves or for another, through any trick or sleight of hand performance, with the intent of deceiving or altering the elements of chance or normal random selection which determines the result or outcome of the game, or the amount or frequency of the payment in a game; or

2. Knowingly uses, conducts, operates, deals, or exposes for play, or knowingly allows to be used, conducted, operated, dealt or exposed for play any cards, dice or gaming equipment or device, or any combination of gaming equipment or devices, which have in any manner been altered, marked or tampered with, or placed in a condition, or operated in a manner, the result of which tends to deceive or tends to alter the elements of chance or normal random selection which determine the result of the game or outcome, or the amount or frequency of the payment in a game; or

3. Knowingly uses, or possesses with the intent to use, any cards, dice or other gaming equipment or devices other than that provided by an authorized gaming operator for current use in a permitted gaming activity; or

4. Alters or misrepresents the outcome of a game or other event on which bets or wagers have been made after the outcome is made sure but before it is revealed to players.

Possession of altered, marked or tampered with dice, cards, or gaming equipment or devices at an authorized gambling establishment is presumptive evidence of possession thereof with knowledge of its character or contents and intention to use such altered, marked or tampered with dice, cards, or gaming equipment or devices in violation of this section.

N.Y. Penal Law § 225.90

Added by New York Laws 2013, ch. 174,Sec. 4, eff. 7/30/2013.

Section 225.95 - Unlawful manufacture, sale, distribution, marking, altering or modification of equipment and devices associated with gaming

A person is guilty of unlawful manufacture, sale, distribution, marking, altering or modification of equipment and devices associated with gaming when if he or she:

1. Manufactures, sells or distributes any cards, chips, cheques, tokens, dice, vouchers, game or device and he or she knew or reasonably should have known it was intended to be used to violate any provision of this article; or

2. Marks, alters or otherwise modifies any associated gaming equipment or device in a manner that either affects the result of the wager by determining win or loss or alters the normal criteria of random selection in a manner that affects the operation of a game or determines the outcome of a game, and he or she knew or reasonably should have known that it was intended to be used to violate any provision of this article.

N.Y. Penal Law § 225.95

Added by New York Laws 2013, ch. 174,Sec. 4, eff. 7/30/2013.

Article 230 - PROSTITUTION OFFENSES

Section 230.00 - Prostitution

A person is guilty of prostitution when such person engages or agrees or offers to engage in sexual conduct with another person in return for a fee.

N.Y. Penal Law § 230.00

Section 230.01 - Prostitution; affirmative defense

In any prosecution under section 230.00, section 230.03, section 230.19, section 230.20, subdivision 2 of section 230.25, subdivision 2 of section 230.30 or section 230.34-a of this article, it is an affirmative defense that the defendant's participation in the offense was a result of having been a victim of compelling prostitution under section 230.33 of this article, a victim of sex trafficking under section 230.34 of this article, a victim of sex trafficking of a child under section 230.34 -a of this article or a victim of trafficking in persons under the trafficking victims protection act (United States Code, Title 22, Chapter 78).

N.Y. Penal Law § 230.01

Amended by New York Laws 2021, ch. 23,Sec. 3, eff. 2/2/2021.

Amended by New York Laws 2018, ch. 189,Sec. 2, eff. 11/13/2018.

Added by New York Laws 2015, ch. 368,Sec. 9, eff. 1/19/2016.

Section 230.02 - Patronizing a person for prostitution; definitions

1. A person patronizes a person for prostitution when:

(a) Pursuant to a prior understanding, he or she pays a fee to another person as compensation for such person or a third person having engaged in sexual conduct with him or her; or

(b) He or she pays or agrees to pay a fee to another person pursuant to an understanding that in return therefor such person or a third person will engage in sexual conduct with him or her; or

(c) He or she solicits or requests another person to engage in sexual conduct with him or her in return for a fee.

2. As used in this article, "person who is patronized" means the person with whom the defendant engaged in sexual conduct or was to have engaged in sexual conduct pursuant to the understanding, or the person who was solicited or requested by the defendant to engage in sexual conduct.

N.Y. Penal Law § 230.02

Amended by New York Laws 2015, ch. 368,Sec. 10, eff. 1/19/2016.

Section 230.03 - Prostitution in a school zone

Prostitution in a school zone is a class A misdemeanor.

1. A person is guilty of prostitution in a school zone when, being nineteen years of age or older, and acting during the hours that school is in session, he or she commits the crime of prostitution in violation of section 230.00 of this article at a place that he or she knows, or reasonably should know, is in a school zone, and he or she knows, or reasonably should know, that such act of prostitution is within the direct view of children attending such school.

2. For the purposes of this section, section 230.08 and section 230.19 of this article, "school zone" means (a) in or on or within any building, structure, athletic playing field, playground or land contained within the real property boundary line of a public or private elementary, parochial, intermediate, junior high, vocational, or high school, or (b) any public sidewalk, street, parking lot, park, playground or private land, located immediately adjacent to the boundary line of such school.

N.Y. Penal Law § 230.03

Amended by New York Laws 2015, ch. 368,Sec. 11, eff. 1/19/2016.

Section 230.04 - Patronizing a person for prostitution in the third degree

A person is guilty of patronizing a person for prostitution in the third degree when he or she patronizes a person for prostitution.

N.Y. Penal Law § 230.04

Amended by New York Laws 2015, ch. 368,Sec. 12, eff. 1/19/2016.

Section 230.05 - Patronizing a person for prostitution in the second degree

A person is guilty of patronizing a person for prostitution in the second degree when, being eighteen years old or more, he or she patronizes a person for prostitution and the person patronized is less than fifteen years old.

N.Y. Penal Law § 230.05

Amended by New York Laws 2015, ch. 368,Sec. 13, eff. 1/19/2016.

Section 230.06 - Patronizing a person for prostitution in the first degree

A person is guilty of patronizing a person for prostitution in the first degree when :

1. He or she patronizes a person for prostitution and the person patronized is less than eleven years old; or

2. Being eighteen years old or more, he or she patronizes a person for prostitution and the person patronized is less than thirteen years old.

N.Y. Penal Law § 230.06

Amended by New York Laws 2015, ch. 368,Sec. 14, eff. 1/19/2016.

Section 230.07 - Patronizing a person for prostitution; defense

In any prosecution for patronizing a person for prostitution in the first or second degrees or patronizing a person for prostitution in a school zone, it is a defense that the defendant did not have reasonable grounds to believe that the person was less than the age specified.

N.Y. Penal Law § 230.07

Amended by New York Laws 2015, ch. 368,Sec. 15, eff. 1/19/2016.

Section 230.08 - Patronizing a person for prostitution in a school zone

1. A person is guilty of patronizing a person for prostitution in a school zone when, being twenty-one years old or more, he or she patronizes a person for prostitution and the person patronized is less than eighteen years old at a place that he or she knows, or reasonably should know, is in a school zone.

2. For purposes of this section, "school zone" shall mean "school zone" as defined in subdivision two of section 230.03 of this article. Patronizing a person for prostitution in a school zone is a class E felony.

N.Y. Penal Law § 230.08

Added by New York Laws 2015, ch. 368,Sec. 16, eff. 1/19/2016.

Section 230.10 - Prostitution and patronizing a person for prostitution; no defense

In any prosecution for prostitution or patronizing a person for prostitution, the sex of the two parties or prospective parties to the sexual conduct engaged in, contemplated or solicited is immaterial, and it is no defense that:

1. Such persons were of the same sex; or

2. The person who received, agreed to receive or solicited a fee was a male and the person who paid or agreed or offered to pay such fee was a female.

N.Y. Penal Law § 230.10

Amended by New York Laws 2015, ch. 368,Sec. 17, eff. 1/19/2016.

Section 230.11 - Aggravated patronizing a minor for prostitution in the third degree

A person is guilty of aggravated patronizing a minor for prostitution in the third degree when, being twenty-one years old or more, he or she patronizes a person for prostitution and the person patronized is less than seventeen years old and the person guilty of patronizing engages in sexual intercourse, oral sexual conduct, anal sexual conduct, or aggravated sexual conduct as those terms are defined in section 130.00 of this part, with the person patronized. Aggravated patronizing a minor for prostitution in the third degree is a class E felony.

N.Y. Penal Law § 230.11

Added by New York Laws 2015, ch. 368,Sec. 18, eff. 1/19/2016.

Section 230.12 - Aggravated patronizing a minor for prostitution in the second degree

A person is guilty of aggravated patronizing a minor for prostitution in the second degree when, being eighteen years old or more, he or she patronizes a person for prostitution and the person patronized is less than fifteen years old and the person guilty of patronizing engages in sexual intercourse, oral sexual conduct, anal sexual conduct, or aggravated sexual conduct as those terms are defined in section 130.00 of this part, with the person patronized. Aggravated patronizing a minor for prostitution in the second degree is a class D felony.

N.Y. Penal Law § 230.12

Added by New York Laws 2015, ch. 368,Sec. 18, eff. 1/19/2016.

Section 230.13 - Aggravated patronizing a minor for prostitution in the first degree

A person is guilty of aggravated patronizing a minor for prostitution in the first degree when he or she patronizes a person for prostitution and the person patronized is less than eleven years old, or being eighteen years old or more, he or she patronizes a person for prostitution and the person patronized is less than thirteen years old, and the person guilty of patronizing engages in sexual intercourse, oral sexual conduct, anal sexual conduct, or aggravated sexual conduct as those terms are defined in section 130.00 of this part, with the person patronized. Aggravated patronizing a minor for prostitution in the first degree is a class B felony.

N.Y. Penal Law § 230.13

Added by New York Laws 2015, ch. 368,Sec. 18, eff. 1/19/2016.

Section 230.15 - Promoting prostitution; definitions of terms

The following definitions are applicable to this article:

1. "Advance prostitution." A person "advances prostitution" when, acting other than as a person in prostitution or as a patron thereof, he or she knowingly causes or aids a person to commit or engage in prostitution, procures or solicits patrons for prostitution, provides persons or premises for prostitution purposes, operates or assists in the operation of a house of prostitution or a prostitution enterprise, or engages in any other conduct designed to institute, aid or facilitate an act or enterprise of prostitution.

2. "Profit from prostitution." A person "profits from prostitution" when, acting other than as a person in prostitution receiving compensation for personally rendered prostitution services, he or she accepts or receives money or other property pursuant to an agreement or understanding with any person whereby he or she participates or is to participate in the proceeds of prostitution activity.

N.Y. Penal Law § 230.15

Amended by New York Laws 2015, ch. 368,Sec. 19, eff. 1/19/2016.

Section 230.19 - Promoting prostitution in a school zone

1. A person is guilty of promoting prostitution in a school zone when, being nineteen years old or more, he or she knowingly advances or profits from prostitution that he or she knows or reasonably should know is or will be committed in violation of section 230.03 of this article in a school zone during the hours that school is in session.

2. For purposes of this section, "school zone" shall mean "school zone" as defined in subdivision two of section 230.03 of this article.

Promoting prostitution in a school zone is a class E felony.

N.Y. Penal Law § 230.19

Amended by New York Laws 2015, ch. 368,Sec. 20, eff. 1/19/2016.

Section 230.20 - Promoting prostitution in the fourth degree

A person is guilty of promoting prostitution in the fourth degree when he or she knowingly:

1. Advances or profits from prostitution; or

2. With intent to advance or profit from prostitution, distributes or disseminates to ten or more people in a public place obscene material, as such terms are defined by subdivisions one and two of section 235.00 of this title, or material that depicts nudity, as such term is defined by subdivision one of section 245.10 of this part.

Promoting prostitution in the fourth degree is a class A misdemeanor.

N.Y. Penal Law § 230.20

Section 230.25 - Promoting prostitution in the third degree

A person is guilty of promoting prostitution in the third degree when he or she knowingly:

1. Advances or profits from prostitution by managing, supervising, controlling or owning, either alone or in association with others, a house of prostitution or a prostitution business or enterprise involving prostitution activity by two or more persons in prostitution, or a business that sells travel-related services knowing that such services include or are intended to facilitate travel for the purpose of patronizing a person for prostitution, including to a foreign jurisdiction and regardless of the legality of prostitution in said foreign jurisdiction; or

2. Advances or profits from prostitution of a person less than nineteen years old.

N.Y. Penal Law § 230.25

Amended by New York Laws 2015, ch. 368,Sec. 21, eff. 1/19/2016.

Section 230.30 - Promoting prostitution in the second degree

A person is guilty of promoting prostitution in the second degree when he or she knowingly:

1. Advances prostitution by compelling a person by force or intimidation to engage in prostitution, or profits from such coercive conduct by another; or

2. Advances or profits from prostitution of a person less than eighteen years old.

N.Y. Penal Law § 230.30

Amended by New York Laws 2015, ch. 368,Sec. 22, eff. 1/19/2016.

Section 230.32 - Promoting prostitution in the first degree

A person is guilty of promoting prostitution in the first degree when he or she:

1. knowingly advances or profits from prostitution of a person less than thirteen years old; or

2. being twenty-one years old or more, he or she knowingly advances or profits from prostitution of a person less than fifteen years old.

N.Y. Penal Law § 230.32

Amended by New York Laws 2015, ch. 368,Sec. 23, eff. 1/19/2016.

Section 230.33 - Compelling prostitution

A person is guilty of compelling prostitution when, being eighteen years old or more, he or she knowingly advances prostitution by compelling a person less than eighteen years old, by force or intimidation, to engage in prostitution.

N.Y. Penal Law § 230.33

Amended by New York Laws 2015, ch. 368,Sec. 24, eff. 1/19/2016.

Section 230.34 - Sex trafficking

A person is guilty of sex trafficking if he or she intentionally advances or profits from prostitution by:

1. unlawfully providing to a person who is patronized, with intent to impair said person's judgment: (a) a narcotic drug or a narcotic preparation; (b) concentrated cannabis as defined in paragraph (a) of subdivision four of section thirty-three hundred two of the public health law; (c) methadone; or (d) gamma-hydroxybutyrate (GHB) or flunitrazepan, also known as Rohypnol;

2. making material false statements, misstatements, or omissions to induce or maintain the person being patronized to engage in or continue to engage in prostitution activity;

3. withholding, destroying, or confiscating any actual or purported passport, immigration document, or any other actual or purported government identification document of another person with intent to impair said person's freedom of movement; provided, however, that this subdivision shall not apply to an attempt to correct a social security administration record or immigration agency record in accordance with any local, state, or federal agency requirement, where such attempt is not made for the purpose of any express or implied threat;

4. requiring that prostitution be performed to retire, repay, or service a real or purported debt;

5. using force or engaging in any scheme, plan or pattern to compel or induce the person being patronized to engage in or continue to engage in prostitution activity by means of instilling a fear in the person being patronized that, if the demand is not complied with, the actor or another will do one or more of the following:

(a) cause physical injury, serious physical injury, or death to a person; or

(b) cause damage to property, other than the property of the actor; or

(c) engage in other conduct constituting a felony or unlawful imprisonment in the second degree in violation of section 135.05 of this chapter; or

(d) accuse some person of a crime or cause criminal charges or deportation proceedings to be instituted against some person; provided, however, that it shall be an affirmative defense to this subdivision that the defendant reasonably believed the threatened charge to be true and that his or her sole purpose was to compel or induce the victim to take reasonable action to make good the wrong which was the subject of such threatened charge; or

(e) expose a secret or publicize an asserted fact, whether true or false, tending to subject some person to hatred, contempt or ridicule; or

(f) testify or provide information or withhold testimony or information with respect to another's legal claim or defense; or

(g) use or abuse his or her position as a public servant by performing some act within or related to his or her official duties, or by failing or refusing to perform an official duty, in such manner as to affect some person adversely; or

(h) perform any other act which would not in itself materially benefit the actor but which is calculated to harm the person who is patronized materially with respect to his or her health, safety, or immigration status.

N.Y. Penal Law § 230.34

Section 230.34-a - Sex trafficking of a child

1. A person is guilty of sex trafficking of a child when he or she, being twenty-one years old or more, intentionally advances or profits from prostitution of another person and such person is a child less than eighteen years old. Knowledge by the defendant of the age of such child is not an element of this offense and it is not a defense to a prosecution therefor that the defendant did not know the age of the child or believed such age to be eighteen or over.

2. For purposes of this section:

(a) A person "advances prostitution" when, acting other than as a person in prostitution or as a patron thereof, and with intent to cause prostitution, he or she directly engages in conduct that facilitates an act or enterprise of prostitution.

(b) A person "profits from prostitution" when, acting other than as a person in prostitution receiving compensation for personally rendered prostitution services, and with intent to facilitate prostitution, he or she accepts or receives money or other property pursuant to an agreement or understanding with any person whereby he or she participates in the proceeds of prostitution activity.

Sex trafficking of a child is a class B felony.

N.Y. Penal Law § 230.34-a

Added by New York Laws 2018, ch. 189,Sec. 1, eff. 11/13/2018.

Section 230.35 - Promoting or compelling prostitution; accomplice

In a prosecution for promoting prostitution or compelling prostitution, a person less than eighteen years old from whose prostitution activity another person is alleged to have advanced or attempted to advance or profited or attempted to profit shall not be deemed to be an accomplice.

N.Y. Penal Law § 230.35

Amended by New York Laws 2015, ch. 368,Sec. 25, eff. 1/19/2016.

Section 230.36 - Sex trafficking; accomplice

In a prosecution for sex trafficking, a person from whose prostitution activity another person is alleged to have advanced or attempted to advance or profited or attempted to profit shall not be deemed to be an accomplice.

N.Y. Penal Law § 230.36

Section 230.40 - Permitting prostitution

A person is guilty of permitting prostitution when, having possession or control of premises or vehicle which he or she knows are being used for prostitution purposes or for the purpose of advancing prostitution, he or she fails to make reasonable effort to halt or abate such use.

N.Y. Penal Law § 230.40

Amended by New York Laws 2015, ch. 368,Sec. 26, eff. 1/19/2016.

Article 235 - OBSCENITY AND RELATED OFFENSES

Section 235.00 - Obscenity; definitions of terms

The following definitions are applicable to sections 235.05, 235.10 and 235.15:

1. "Obscene." Any material or performance is "obscene" if (a) the average person, applying contemporary community standards, would find that considered as a whole, its predominant appeal is to the prurient interest in sex, and (b) it depicts or describes in a patently offensive manner, actual or simulated: sexual intercourse, criminal sexual act, sexual bestiality, masturbation, sadism, masochism, excretion or lewd exhibition of the genitals, and (c) considered as a whole, it lacks serious literary, artistic, political, and scientific value. Predominant appeal shall be judged with reference to ordinary adults unless it appears from the character of the material or the circumstances of its dissemination to be designed for children or other specially susceptible audience.

2. "Material" means anything tangible which is capable of being used or adapted to arouse interest, whether through the medium of reading, observation, sound or in any other manner.

3. "Performance" means any play, motion picture, dance or other exhibition performed before an audience.

4. "Promote" means to manufacture, issue, sell, give, provide, lend, mail, deliver, transfer, transmute, publish, distribute, circulate, disseminate, present, exhibit or advertise, or to offer or agree to do the same.

5. "Wholesale promote" means to manufacture, issue, sell, provide, mail, deliver, transfer, transmute, publish, distribute, circulate, disseminate or to offer or agree to do the same for purposes of resale.

6. "Simulated" means the explicit depiction or description of any of the types of conduct set forth in clause (b) of subdivision one of this section, which creates the appearance of such conduct.

7. " Criminal sexual act" means any of the types of sexual conduct defined in subdivision two of section 130.00 provided, however, that in any prosecution under this article the marital status of the persons engaged in such conduct shall be irrelevant and shall not be considered.

N.Y. Penal Law § 235.00

Section 235.05 - Obscenity in the third degree

A person is guilty of obscenity in the third degree when, knowing its content and character, he:

1. Promotes, or possesses with intent to promote, any obscene material; or

2. Produces, presents or directs an obscene performance or participates in a portion thereof which is obscene or which contributes to its obscenity.

Obscenity in the third degree is a class A misdemeanor.

N.Y. Penal Law § 235.05

Section 235.06 - Obscenity in the second degree

A person is guilty of obscenity in the second degree when he commits the crime of obscenity in the third degree as defined in subdivisions one and two of section 235.05 of this chapter and has been previously convicted of obscenity in the third degree.

N.Y. Penal Law § 235.06

Section 235.07 - Obscenity in the first degree

A person is guilty of obscenity in the first degree when, knowing its content and character, he wholesale promotes or possesses with intent to wholesale promote, any obscene material.

N.Y. Penal Law § 235.07

Section 235.10 - Obscenity; presumptions

1. A person who promotes or wholesale promotes obscene material, or possesses the same with intent to promote or wholesale promote it, in the course of his business is presumed to do so with knowledge of its content and character.

2. A person who possesses six or more identical or similar obscene articles is presumed to possess them with intent to promote the same.

The provisions of this section shall not apply to public libraries or association libraries as defined in subdivision two of section two hundred fifty-three of the education law, or trustees or employees of such public libraries or association libraries when acting in the course and scope of their duties or employment.

N.Y. Penal Law § 235.10

Section 235.15 - Obscenity or disseminating indecent material to minors in the second degree; defense

1. In any prosecution for obscenity, or disseminating indecent material to minors in the second degree in violation of subdivision three of section 235.21 of this article, it is an affirmative defense that the persons to whom allegedly obscene or indecent material was disseminated, or the audience to an allegedly obscene performance, consisted of persons or institutions having scientific, educational, governmental or other similar justification for possessing, disseminating or viewing the same.

2. In any prosecution for obscenity, it is an affirmative defense that the person so charged was a motion picture projectionist, stage employee or spotlight operator, cashier, doorman, usher, candy stand attendant, porter or in any other non-managerial or non-supervisory capacity in a motion picture theatre; provided he has no financial interest, other than his employment, which employment does not encompass compensation based upon any proportion of the gross receipts, in the promotion of obscene material for sale, rental or exhibition or in the promotion, presentation or direction of any obscene performance, or is in any way responsible for acquiring obscene material for sale, rental or exhibition.

N.Y. Penal Law § 235.15

Section 235.20 - Disseminating indecent material to minors; definitions of terms

The following definitions are applicable to sections 235.21, 235.22, 235.23 and 235.24 of this article:

1. "Minor" means any person less than seventeen years old.

2. "Nudity" means the showing of the human male or female genitals, pubic area or buttocks with less than a full opaque covering, or the showing of the female breast with less than a fully opaque covering of any portion thereof below the top of the nipple, or the depiction of covered male genitals in a discernably turgid state.

3. "Sexual conduct" means acts of masturbation, homosexuality, sexual intercourse, or physical contact with a person's clothed or unclothed genitals, pubic area, buttocks or, if such person be a female, breast.

4. "Sexual excitement" means the condition of human male or female genitals when in a state of sexual stimulation or arousal.

5. "Sado-masochistic abuse" means flagellation or torture by or upon a person clad in undergarments, a mask or bizarre costume, or the condition of being fettered, bound or otherwise physically restrained on the part of one so clothed.

6. "Harmful to minors" means that quality of any description or representation, in whatever form, of nudity, sexual conduct, sexual excitement, or sado-masochistic abuse, when it:

(a) Considered as a whole, appeals to the prurient interest in sex of minors; and

(b) Is patently offensive to prevailing standards in the adult community as a whole with respect to what is suitable material for minors; and

(c) Considered as a whole, lacks serious literary, artistic, political and scientific value for minors.

7. The term "access software" means software (including client or server software) or enabling tools that do not create or provide the content of the communication but that allow a user to do any one or more of the following:

(a) filter, screen, allow or disallow content;

(b) pick, choose, analyze or digest content; or

(c) transmit, receive, display, forward, cache, search, subset, organize, reorganize or translate content.

N.Y. Penal Law § 235.20

Section 235.21 - Disseminating indecent material to minors in the second degree

A person is guilty of disseminating indecent material to minors in the second degree when:

1. With knowledge of its character and content, he sells or loans to a minor for monetary consideration:

(a) Any picture, photograph, drawing, sculpture, motion picture film, or similar visual representation or image of a person or portion of the human body which depicts nudity, sexual conduct or sado-masochistic abuse and which is harmful to minors; or

(b) Any book, pamphlet, magazine, printed matter however reproduced, or sound recording which contains any matter enumerated in paragraph (a) hereof, or explicit and detailed verbal descriptions or narrative accounts of sexual excitement, sexual conduct or sado-masochistic abuse and which, taken as a whole, is harmful to minors; or

2. Knowing the character and content of a motion picture, show or other presentation which, in whole or in part, depicts nudity, sexual conduct or sado-masochistic abuse, and which is harmful to minors, he:

(a) Exhibits such motion picture, show or other presentation to a minor for a monetary consideration; or

(b) Sells to a minor an admission ticket or pass to premises whereon there is exhibited or to be exhibited such motion picture, show or other presentation; or

(c) Admits a minor for a monetary consideration to premises whereon there is exhibited or to be exhibited such motion picture show or other presentation; or

3. Knowing the character and content of the communication which, in whole or in part, depicts actual or simulated nudity, sexual conduct or sado-masochistic abuse, and which is harmful to minors, he intentionally uses any computer communication system allowing the input, output, examination or transfer, of computer data or computer programs from one computer to another, to initiate or engage in such communication with a person who is a minor.

Disseminating indecent material to minors in the second degree is a class E felony.

N.Y. Penal Law § 235.21

Section 235.22 - Disseminating indecent material to minors in the first degree

A person is guilty of disseminating indecent material to minors in the first degree when:

1. knowing the character and content of the communication which, in whole or in part, depicts or describes, either in words or images actual or simulated nudity, sexual conduct or sado-masochistic abuse, and which is harmful to minors, he intentionally uses any computer communication system allowing the input, output, examination or transfer, of computer data or computer programs from one computer to another, to initiate or engage in such communication with a person who is a minor; and

2. by means of such communication he importunes, invites or induces a minor to engage in sexual intercourse, oral sexual conduct or anal sexual conduct, or sexual contact with him, or to engage in a sexual performance, obscene sexual performance, or sexual conduct for his benefit.

Disseminating indecent material to minors in the first degree is a class D felony.

N.Y. Penal Law § 235.22

Section 235.23 - Disseminating indecent material to minors; presumption and defenses

1. A person who engages in the conduct proscribed by section 235.21 is presumed to do so with knowledge of the character and content of the material sold or loaned, or the motion picture, show or presentation exhibited or to be exhibited.

2. In any prosecution for disseminating indecent material to minors in the second degree pursuant to subdivision one or two of section 235.21 of this article, it is an affirmative defense that:

(a) The defendant had reasonable cause to believe that the minor involved was seventeen years old or more; and

(b) Such minor exhibited to the defendant a draft card, driver's license, birth certificate or other official or apparently official document purporting to establish that such minor was seventeen years old or more.

3. In any prosecution for disseminating indecent material to minors in the second degree pursuant to subdivision three of section 235.21 of this article or disseminating indecent material to minors in the first degree pursuant to section 235.22 of this article, it shall be a defense that:

(a) The defendant made a reasonable effort to ascertain the true age of the minor and was unable to do so as a result of actions taken by the minor; or

(b) The defendant has taken, in good faith, reasonable, effective and appropriate actions under the circumstances to restrict or prevent access by minors to materials specified in such subdivision, which may involve any appropriate measures to restrict minors from access to such communications, including any method which is feasible under available technology; or

(c) The defendant has restricted access to such materials by requiring use of a verified credit card, debit account, adult access code or adult personal identification number; or

(d) The defendant has in good faith established a mechanism such that the labelling, segregation or other mechanism enables such material to be automatically blocked or screened by software or other capabilities reasonably available to responsible adults wishing to effect such blocking or screening and the defendant has not otherwise solicited minors not subject to such screening or blocking capabilities to access that material or to circumvent any such screening or blocking.

N.Y. Penal Law § 235.23

Section 235.24 - Disseminating indecent material to minors; limitations

In any prosecution for disseminating indecent material to minors in the second degree pursuant to subdivision three of section 235.21 of this article or disseminating indecent material to minors in the first degree pursuant to section 235.22 of this article:

1. No person shall be held to have violated such provisions solely for providing access or connection to or from a facility, system, or network not under that person's control, including transmission, downloading, intermediate storage, access software, or other related capabilities that are incidental to providing such access or connection that do not include the creation of the content of the communication.

(a) The limitations provided by this subdivision shall not be applicable to a person who is a conspirator with an entity actively involved in the creation or knowing distribution of communications that violate such provisions, or who knowingly advertises the availability of such communications.

(b) The limitations provided by this subdivision shall not be applicable to a person who provides access or connection to a facility, system, or network engaged in the violation of such provisions that is owned or controlled by such person.

2. No employer shall be held liable under such provisions for the actions of an employee or agent unless the employee's or agent's conduct is within the scope of his employment or agency and the employer having knowledge of such conduct, authorizes or ratifies such conduct, or recklessly disregards such conduct.

N.Y. Penal Law § 235.24

Title N - OFFENSES AGAINST PUBLIC ORDER, PUBLIC SENSIBILITIES AND THE RIGHT TO PRIVACY

Article 240 - OFFENSES AGAINST PUBLIC ORDER

Section 240.00 - Offenses against public order; definitions of terms

The following definitions are applicable to this article:

1. "Public place" means a place to which the public or a substantial group of persons has access, and includes, but is not limited to, highways, transportation facilities, schools, places of amusement, parks, playgrounds, community centers, and hallways, lobbies and other portions of apartment houses and hotels not constituting rooms or apartments designed for actual residence.

2. "Transportation facility" means any conveyance, premises or place used for or in connection with public passenger transportation, whether by air, railroad, motor vehicle or any other method. It includes aircraft, watercraft, railroad cars,

buses, school buses as defined in section one hundred forty-two of the vehicle and traffic law, and air, boat, railroad and bus terminals and stations and all appurtenances thereto.

3. "School grounds" means in or on or within any building, structure, school bus as defined in section one hundred forty-two of the vehicle and traffic law, athletic playing field, playground or land contained within the real property boundary line of a public or private elementary, parochial, intermediate, junior high, vocational or high school.

4. "Hazardous substance" shall mean any physical, chemical, microbiological or radiological substance or matter which, because of its quantity, concentration, or physical, chemical or infectious characteristics, may cause or significantly contribute to an increase in mortality or an increase in serious irreversible or incapacitating reversible illness, or pose a substantial present or potential hazard to human health.

5. "Age" means sixty years old or more.

6. "Disability" means a physical or mental impairment that substantially limits a major life activity.

7. "Gender identity or expression" means a person's actual or perceived gender-related identity, appearance, behavior, expression, or other gender-related characteristic regardless of the sex assigned to that person at birth, including, but not limited to, the status of being transgender.

N.Y. Penal Law § 240.00

Amended by New York Laws 2019, ch. 8,Sec. 23, eff. 11/1/2019.

Amended by New York Laws 2017, ch. 167,Sec. 1, eff. 11/12/2017.

Section 240.05 - Riot in the second degree

A person is guilty of riot in the second degree when, simultaneously with four or more other persons, he engages in tumultuous and violent conduct and thereby intentionally or recklessly causes or creates a grave risk of causing public alarm.

N.Y. Penal Law § 240.05

Section 240.06 - Riot in the first degree

A person is guilty of riot in the first degree when he:

1. Simultaneously with ten or more other persons, engages in tumultuous and violent conduct and thereby intentionally or recklessly causes or creates a grave risk of causing public alarm, and in the course of and as a result of such conduct, a person other than one of the participants suffers physical injury or substantial property damage occurs; or

2. While in a correctional facility or a local correctional facility, as those terms are defined in subdivisions four and sixteen, respectively, of section two of the correction law, simultaneously with ten or more other persons, engages in tumultuous and violent conduct and thereby intentionally or recklessly causes or creates a grave risk of causing alarm within such correctional facility or local correctional facility and in the course of and as a result of such conduct, a person other than one of the participants suffers physical injury or substantial property damage occurs.

Riot in the first degree is a class E felony.

N.Y. Penal Law § 240.06

Section 240.08 - Inciting to riot

A person is guilty of inciting to riot when he urges ten or more persons to engage in tumultuous and violent conduct of a kind likely to create public alarm.

N.Y. Penal Law § 240.08

Section 240.10 - Unlawful assembly

A person is guilty of unlawful assembly when he assembles with four or more other persons for the purpose of engaging or preparing to engage with them in tumultuous and violent conduct likely to cause public alarm, or when, being present at an assembly which either has or develops such purpose, he remains there with intent to advance that purpose.

N.Y. Penal Law § 240.10

Section 240.15 - Criminal anarchy

A person is guilty of criminal anarchy when (a) he advocates the overthrow of the existing form of government of this state by violence, or (b) with knowledge of its contents, he publishes, sells or distributes any document which advocates such violent overthrow, or (c) with knowledge of its purpose, he becomes a member of any organization which advocates such violent overthrow.

N.Y. Penal Law § 240.15

Section 240.20 - Disorderly conduct

A person is guilty of disorderly conduct when, with intent to cause public inconvenience, annoyance or alarm, or recklessly creating a risk thereof:

1. He engages in fighting or in violent, tumultuous or threatening behavior; or

2. He makes unreasonable noise; or

3. In a public place, he uses abusive or obscene language, or makes an obscene gesture; or

4. Without lawful authority, he disturbs any lawful assembly or meeting of persons; or

5. He obstructs vehicular or pedestrian traffic; or

6. He congregates with other persons in a public place and refuses to comply with a lawful order of the police to disperse; or

7. He creates a hazardous or physically offensive condition by any act which serves no legitimate purpose.

Disorderly conduct is a violation.

N.Y. Penal Law § 240.20

Section 240.21 - Disruption or disturbance of a religious service, funeral, burial or memorial service
A person is guilty of disruption or disturbance of a religious service, funeral, burial or memorial service when he or she makes unreasonable noise or disturbance while at a lawfully assembled religious service, funeral, burial or memorial service, or within three hundred feet thereof, with intent to cause annoyance or alarm or recklessly creating a risk thereof.
N.Y. Penal Law § 240.21

Section 240.25 - Harassment in the first degree
A person is guilty of harassment in the first degree when he or she intentionally and repeatedly harasses another person by following such person in or about a public place or places or by engaging in a course of conduct or by repeatedly committing acts which places such person in reasonable fear of physical injury. This section shall not apply to activities regulated by the national labor relations act, as amended, the railway labor act, as amended, or the federal employment labor management act, as amended.
N.Y. Penal Law § 240.25

Section 240.26 - Harassment in the second degree
A person is guilty of harassment in the second degree when, with intent to harass, annoy or alarm another person:
1. He or she strikes, shoves, kicks or otherwise subjects such other person to physical contact, or attempts or threatens to do the same; or
2. He or she follows a person in or about a public place or places; or
3. He or she engages in a course of conduct or repeatedly commits acts which alarm or seriously annoy such other person and which serve no legitimate purpose.
Subdivisions two and three of this section shall not apply to activities regulated by the national labor relations act, as amended, the railway labor act, as amended, or the federal employment labor management act, as amended.
Harassment in the second degree is a violation.
N.Y. Penal Law § 240.26

Section 240.30 - Aggravated harassment in the second degree
A person is guilty of aggravated harassment in the second degree when:
1. With intent to harass another person, the actor either:
(a) communicates , anonymously or otherwise, by telephone, by computer or any other electronic means, or by mail, or by transmitting or delivering any other form of communication, a threat to cause physical harm to, or unlawful harm to the property of, such person, or a member of such person's same family or household as defined in subdivision one of section 530.11 of the criminal procedure law, and the actor knows or reasonably should know that such communication will cause such person to reasonably fear harm to such person's physical safety or property, or to the physical safety or property of a member of such person's same family or household; or
(b) causes a communication to be initiated anonymously or otherwise, by telephone, by computer or any other electronic means, or by mail, or by transmitting or delivering any other form of communication, a threat to cause physical harm to, or unlawful harm to the property of, such person, a member of such person's same family or household as defined in subdivision one of section 530.11 of the criminal procedure law, and the actor knows or reasonably should know that such communication will cause such person to reasonably fear harm to such person's physical safety or property, or to the physical safety or property of a member of such person's same family or household; or
2. With intent to harass or threaten another person, he or she makes a telephone call, whether or not a conversation ensues, with no purpose of legitimate communication; or
3. With the intent to harass, annoy, threaten or alarm another person, he or she strikes, shoves, kicks, or otherwise subjects another person to physical contact, or attempts or threatens to do the same because of a belief or perception regarding such person's race, color, national origin, ancestry, gender, gender identity or expression, religion, religious practice, age, disability or sexual orientation, regardless of whether the belief or perception is correct; or
4. With the intent to harass, annoy, threaten or alarm another person, he or she strikes, shoves, kicks or otherwise subjects another person to physical contact thereby causing physical injury to such person or to a family or household member of such person as defined in section 530.11 of the criminal procedure law; or
5. He or she commits the crime of harassment in the first degree and has previously been convicted of the crime of harassment in the first degree as defined by section 240.25 of this article within the preceding ten years.
Aggravated harassment in the second degree is a class A misdemeanor.
N.Y. Penal Law § 240.30
Amended by New York Laws 2019, ch. 8, Sec. 21, eff. 11/1/2019.
Amended by New York Laws 2014, ch. 188, Sec. 1, eff. 7/23/2014.

Section 240.31 - Aggravated harassment in the first degree
A person is guilty of aggravated harassment in the first degree when with intent to harass, annoy, threaten or alarm another person, because of a belief or perception regarding such person's race, color, national origin, ancestry, gender, gender identity or expression, religion, religious practice, age, disability or sexual orientation, regardless of whether the belief or perception is correct, he or she:
1. Damages premises primarily used for religious purposes, or acquired pursuant to section six of the religious corporation law and maintained for purposes of religious instruction, and the damage to the premises exceeds fifty dollars; or
2. Commits the crime of aggravated harassment in the second degree in the manner proscribed by the provisions of subdivision three of section 240.30 of this article and has been previously convicted of the crime of aggravated harassment in the second degree for the commission of conduct proscribed by the provisions of subdivision three of section 240.30 or

he or she has been previously convicted of the crime of aggravated harassment in the first degree within the preceding ten years; or

3. Etches, paints, draws upon or otherwise places a swastika, commonly exhibited as the emblem of Nazi Germany, on any building or other real property, public or private, owned by any person, firm or corporation or any public agency or instrumentality, without express permission of the owner or operator of such building or real property;

4. Sets on fire a cross in public view; or

5. Etches, paints, draws upon or otherwise places or displays a noose, commonly exhibited as a symbol of racism and intimidation, on any building or other real property, public or private, owned by any person, firm or corporation or any public agency or instrumentality, without express permission of the owner or operator of such building or real property. Aggravated harassment in the first degree is a class E felony.

N.Y. Penal Law § 240.31

Amended by New York Laws 2019, ch. 8,Sec. 22, eff. 11/1/2019.

Section 240.32 - Aggravated harassment of an employee by an incarcerated individual

An incarcerated individual or respondent is guilty of aggravated harassment of an employee by an incarcerated individual when, with intent to harass, annoy, threaten or alarm a person in a facility whom he or she knows or reasonably should know to be an employee of such facility or the board of parole or the office of mental health, or a probation department, bureau or unit or a police officer, he or she causes or attempts to cause such employee to come into contact with blood, seminal fluid, urine, feces, or the contents of a toilet bowl, by throwing, tossing or expelling such fluid or material.

N.Y. Penal Law § 240.32

Amended by New York Laws 2021, ch. 322,Sec. 106, eff. 8/2/2021.

Amended by New York Laws 2013, ch. 180,Sec. 1, eff. 11/1/2013.

Section 240.35 - Loitering

A person is guilty of loitering when he:

2. Loiters or remains in a public place for the purpose of gambling with cards, dice or other gambling paraphernalia; or

4. [Repealed]

5. Loiters or remains in or about school grounds, a college or university building or grounds or a children's overnight camp as defined in section one thousand three hundred ninety-two of the public health law or a summer day camp as defined in section one thousand three hundred ninety-two of the public health law, or loiters, remains in or enters a school bus as defined in section one hundred forty-two of the vehicle and traffic law, not having any reason or relationship involving custody of or responsibility for a pupil or student, or any other specific, legitimate reason for being there, and not having written permission from anyone authorized to grant the same or loiters or remains in or about such children's overnight camp or summer day camp in violation of conspicuously posted rules or regulations governing entry and use thereof; or

6. Loiters or remains in any transportation facility, unless specifically authorized to do so, for the purpose of soliciting or engaging in any business, trade or commercial transactions involving the sale of merchandise or services, or for the purpose of entertaining persons by singing, dancing or playing any musical instrument; or

N.Y. Penal Law § 240.35

Amended by New York Laws 2020, ch. 98,Sec. 1, eff. 6/13/2020.

Section 240.36 - Loitering in the first degree

A person is guilty of loitering in the first degree when he loiters or remains in any place with one or more persons for the purpose of unlawfully using or possessing a controlled substance, as defined in section 220.00 of this chapter.

N.Y. Penal Law § 240.36

Section 240.37 - [Repealed]

N.Y. Penal Law § 240.37

Repealed by New York Laws 2021, ch. 23,Sec. 2, eff. 2/2/2021.

See New York Laws 2021, ch. 23,Sec. 1

Amended by New York Laws 2015, ch. 368,Sec. 27, eff. 1/19/2016.

Section 240.40 - Appearance in public under the influence of narcotics or a drug other than alcohol

A person is guilty of appearance in public under the influence of narcotics or a drug other than alcohol when he appears in a public place under the influence of narcotics or a drug other than alcohol to the degree that he may endanger himself or other persons or property, or annoy persons in his vicinity.

N.Y. Penal Law § 240.40

Section 240.45 - Criminal nuisance in the second degree

A person is guilty of criminal nuisance in the second degree when:

1. By conduct either unlawful in itself or unreasonable under all the circumstances, he knowingly or recklessly creates or maintains a condition which endangers the safety or health of a considerable number of persons; or

2. He knowingly conducts or maintains any premises, place or resort where persons gather for purposes of engaging in unlawful conduct.

Criminal nuisance in the second degree is a class B misdemeanor.

N.Y. Penal Law § 240.45

Section 240.46 - Criminal nuisance in the first degree

A person is guilty of criminal nuisance in the first degree when he knowingly conducts or maintains any premises, place or resort where persons come or gather for purposes of engaging in the unlawful sale of controlled substances in violation of section 220.39, 220.41, or 220.43 of this chapter, and thereby derives the benefit from such unlawful conduct.

N.Y. Penal Law § 240.46

Section 240.48 - Disseminating a false registered sex offender notice

A person is guilty of disseminating a false registered sex offender notice when, knowing the information he or she disseminates or causes to be disseminated to be false or baseless, such person disseminates or causes to be disseminated any notice which purports to be an official notice from a government agency or a law enforcement agency and such notice asserts that an individual is a registered sex offender.

N.Y. Penal Law § 240.48

Section 240.50 - Falsely reporting an incident in the third degree

A person is guilty of falsely reporting an incident in the third degree when, knowing the information reported, conveyed or circulated to be false or baseless, he or she:

1. Initiates or circulates a false report or warning of an alleged occurrence or impending occurrence of a crime, catastrophe or emergency under circumstances in which it is not unlikely that public alarm or inconvenience will result; or

2. Reports, by word or action, to an official or quasi-official agency or organization having the function of dealing with emergencies involving danger to life or property, an alleged occurrence or impending occurrence of a catastrophe or emergency which did not in fact occur or does not in fact exist; or

3. Gratuitously reports to a law enforcement officer or agency (a) the alleged occurrence of an offense or incident which did not in fact occur; or (b) an allegedly impending occurrence of an offense or incident which in fact is not about to occur; or (c) false information relating to an actual offense or incident or to the alleged implication of some person therein; or

4. Reports, by word or action, an alleged occurrence or condition of child abuse or maltreatment or abuse or neglect of a vulnerable person which did not in fact occur or exist to:

(a) the statewide central register of child abuse and maltreatment, as defined in title six of article six of the social services law or the vulnerable persons' central register as defined in article eleven of such law, or

(b) any person required to report cases of suspected child abuse or maltreatment pursuant to subdivision one of section four hundred thirteen of the social services law or to report cases of suspected abuse or neglect of a vulnerable person pursuant to section four hundred ninety-one of such law, knowing that the person is required to report such cases, and with the intent that such an alleged occurrence be reported to the statewide central register or vulnerable persons' central register.

N.Y. Penal Law § 240.50

Amended by New York Laws 2012, ch. 501,Sec. G-1, eff. 1/16/2013.

Section 240.55 - Falsely reporting an incident in the second degree

A person is guilty of falsely reporting an incident in the second degree when, knowing the information reported, conveyed or circulated to be false or baseless, he or she:

1. Initiates or circulates a false report or warning of an alleged occurrence or impending occurrence of a fire, explosion, or the release of a hazardous substance under circumstances in which it is not unlikely that public alarm or inconvenience will result;

2. Reports, by word or action, to any official or quasi-official agency or organization having the function of dealing with emergencies involving danger to life or property, an alleged occurrence or impending occurrence of a fire, explosion, or the release of a hazardous substance which did not in fact occur or does not in fact exist; or

3. Knowing the information reported, conveyed or circulated to be false or baseless and under circumstances in which it is likely public alarm or inconvenience will result, he or she initiates or circulates a report or warning of an alleged occurrence or an impending occurrence of a fire, an explosion, or the release of a hazardous substance upon any private premises.

Falsely reporting an incident in the second degree is a class E felony.

N.Y. Penal Law § 240.55

Section 240.60 - Falsely reporting an incident in the first degree

A person is guilty of falsely reporting an incident in the first degree when he:

1. commits the crime of falsely reporting an incident in the second degree as defined in section 240.55 of this article, and has previously been convicted of that crime; or

2. commits the crime of falsely reporting an incident in the third degree as defined in subdivisions one and two of section 240.50 of this article or falsely reporting an incident in the second degree as defined in subdivisions one and two of section 240.55 of this article and another person who is an employee or member of any official or quasi-official agency having the function of dealing with emergencies involving danger to life or property; or who is a volunteer firefighter with a fire department, fire company, or any unit thereof as defined in the volunteer firefighters' benefit law; or who is a volunteer ambulance worker with a volunteer ambulance corporation or any unit thereof as defined in the volunteer ambulance workers' benefit law suffers serious physical injury or is killed in the performance of his or her official duties in traveling to or working at or returning to a firehouse, police station, quarters or other base facility from the location identified in such report; or

3. commits the crime of falsely reporting an incident in the third degree as defined in subdivisions one and two of section 240.50 of this article or falsely reporting an incident in the second degree as defined in subdivisions one and two of section 240.55 of this article and another person suffers serious physical injury or is killed as a result of any vehicular or other accident involving any emergency vehicle which is responding to, operating at, or returning from the location identified in such report.

4. An emergency vehicle as referred to in subdivision three of this section shall include any vehicle operated by any employee or member of any official or quasi-official agency having the function of dealing with emergencies involving

161

danger to life or property and shall include, but not necessarily be limited to, an emergency vehicle which is operated by a volunteer firefighter with a fire department, fire company, or any unit thereof as defined in the volunteer firefighters' benefit law; or by a volunteer ambulance worker with a volunteer ambulance corporation, or any unit thereof as defined in the volunteer ambulance workers' benefit law.

5. Knowing the information reported, conveyed or circulated to be false or baseless and under circumstances in which it is likely public alarm or inconvenience will result, he or she initiates or circulates a report or warning of an alleged occurrence or an impending occurrence of a fire, an explosion, or the release of a hazardous substance upon school grounds and it is likely that persons are present on said grounds.

6. Knowing the information reported, conveyed or circulated to be false or baseless and under circumstances in which it is likely public alarm or inconvenience will result, he or she initiates or circulates a report or warning of an alleged occurrence or impending occurrence of a fire, explosion or the release of a hazardous substance in or upon a sports stadium or arena, mass transportation facility, enclosed shopping mall, any public building or any public place, and it is likely that persons are present. For purposes of this subdivision, the terms "sports stadium or arena, mass transportation facility or enclosed shopping mall" shall have their natural meaning and the term "public building" shall have the meaning set forth in section four hundred one of the executive law.

Falsely reporting an incident in the first degree is a class D felony.

N.Y. Penal Law § 240.60

Section 240.61 - Placing a false bomb or hazardous substance in the second degree

A person is guilty of placing a false bomb or hazardous substance in the second degree when he or she places, or causes to be placed, any device or object that by its design, construction, content or characteristics appears to be or to contain, a bomb, destructive device, explosive or hazardous substance, but is, in fact, an inoperative facsimile or imitation of such a bomb, destructive device, explosive or hazardous substance and which he or she knows, intends or reasonably believes will appear to be a bomb, destructive device, explosive or hazardous substance under circumstances in which it is likely to cause public alarm or inconvenience.

N.Y. Penal Law § 240.61

Section 240.62 - Placing a false bomb or hazardous substance in the first degree

A person is guilty of placing a false bomb or hazardous substance in the first degree when he or she places, or causes to be placed, in or upon school grounds, a public building, or a public place any device or object that by its design, construction, content or characteristics appears to be or to contain, a bomb, destructive device, explosive or hazardous substance, but is, in fact, an inoperative facsimile or imitation of such a bomb, destructive device, explosive or hazardous substance and which he or she knows, intends or reasonably believes will appear to be a bomb, destructive device, explosive or hazardous substance under circumstances in which it is likely to cause public alarm or inconvenience. For purposes of this section the term "public building" shall have the meaning set forth in section four hundred one of the executive law.

N.Y. Penal Law § 240.62

Section 240.63 - Placing a false bomb or hazardous substance in a sports stadium or arena, mass transportation facility or enclosed shopping mall

A person is guilty of placing a false bomb or hazardous substance in a sports stadium or arena, mass transportation facility or enclosed shopping mall when he or she places, or causes to be placed, in a sports stadium or arena, mass transportation facility or enclosed shopping mall, in which it is likely that persons are present, any device or object that by its design, construction, content or characteristics appears to be or to contain a bomb, destructive device, explosive or hazardous substance, but is, in fact, an inoperative facsimile or imitation of such a bomb, destructive device, explosive or hazardous substance and which he or she knows, intends or reasonably believes will appear to be a bomb, destructive device, explosive or hazardous substance under circumstances in which it is likely to cause public alarm or inconvenience. For purposes of this section, "sports stadium or arena, mass transportation facility or enclosed shopping mall" shall have its natural meaning.

N.Y. Penal Law § 240.63

Section 240.65 - Unlawful prevention of public access to records

A person is guilty of unlawful prevention of public access to records when, with intent to prevent the public inspection of a record pursuant to article six of the public officers law, he willfully conceals or destroys any such record.

N.Y. Penal Law § 240.65

Section 240.70 - Criminal interference with health care services or religious worship in the second degree

1. A person is guilty of criminal interference with health services or religious worship in the second degree when:

(a) by force or threat of force or by physical obstruction, he or she intentionally injures, intimidates or interferes with, or attempts to injure, intimidate or interfere with, another person because such other person was or is obtaining or providing reproductive health services; or

(b) by force or threat of force or by physical obstruction, he or she intentionally injures, intimidates or interferes with, or attempts to injure, intimidate or interfere with, another person in order to discourage such other person or any other person or persons from obtaining or providing reproductive health services; or

(c) by force or threat of force or by physical obstruction, he or she intentionally injures, intimidates or interferes with, or attempts to injure, intimidate or interfere with, another person because such person was or is seeking to exercise the right of religious freedom at a place of religious worship; or

(d) he or she intentionally damages the property of a health care facility, or attempts to do so, because such facility provides reproductive health services, or intentionally damages the property of a place of religious worship.

2. A parent or legal guardian of a minor shall not be subject to prosecution for conduct otherwise prohibited by paragraph (a) or (b) of subdivision one of this section which is directed exclusively at such minor.

3. For purposes of this section:

(a) the term "health care facility" means a hospital, clinic, physician's office or other facility that provides reproductive health services, and includes the building or structure in which the facility is located;

(b) the term "interferes with" means to restrict a person's freedom of movement;

(c) the term "intimidates" means to place a person in reasonable apprehension of physical injury to himself or herself or to another person;

(d) the term "physical obstruction" means rendering impassable ingress to or egress from a facility that provides reproductive health services or to or from a place of religious worship, or rendering passage to or from such a facility or place of religious worship unreasonably difficult or hazardous; and

(e) the term "reproductive health services" means health care services provided in a hospital, clinic, physician's office or other facility and includes medical, surgical, counseling or referral services relating to the human reproductive system, including services relating to pregnancy or the termination of a pregnancy.

Criminal interference with health care services or religious worship in the second degree is a class A misdemeanor.
N.Y. Penal Law § 240.70

Section 240.71 - Criminal interference with health care services or religious worship in the first degree

A person is guilty of criminal interference with health care services or religious worship in the first degree when he or she commits the crime of criminal interference with health care services or religious worship in the second degree and has been previously convicted of the crime of criminal interference with health care services or religious worship in the first or second degree or aggravated interference with health care services in the first or second degree.
N.Y. Penal Law § 240.71

Section 240.72 - Aggravated interference with health care services in the second degree

A person is guilty of the crime of aggravated interference with health care services in the second degree when he or she commits the crime of criminal interference with health care services or religious worship in violation of paragraph (a) of subdivision one of section 240.70 of this article and thereby causes physical injury to such other person who was obtaining or providing, or was assisting another person to obtain or provide reproductive health services.
N.Y. Penal Law § 240.72

Section 240.73 - Aggravated interference with health care services in the first degree

A person is guilty of the crime of aggravated interference with health care services in the first degree when he or she commits the crime of criminal interference with health care services or religious worship in violation of paragraph (a) of subdivision one of section 240.70 of this article and thereby causes serious physical injury to such other person who was obtaining or providing, or who was assisting another person to obtain or provide reproductive health services.
N.Y. Penal Law § 240.73

Section 240.75 - Aggravated family offense

1. A person is guilty of aggravated family offense when he or she commits a misdemeanor defined in subdivision two of this section as a specified offense and he or she has been convicted of one or more specified offenses within the immediately preceding five years. For the purposes of this subdivision, in calculating the five year period, any period of time during which the defendant was incarcerated for any reason between the time of the commission of any of such previous offenses and the time of commission of the present crime shall be excluded and such five year period shall be extended by a period or periods equal to the time served under such incarceration.

2. A "specified offense" is an offense defined in section 120.00 (assault in the third degree); section 120.05 (assault in the second degree); section 120.10 (assault in the first degree); section 120.13 (menacing in the first degree); section 120.14 (menacing in the second degree); section 120.15 (menacing in the third degree); section 120.20 (reckless endangerment in the second degree); section 120.25 (reckless endangerment in the first degree); section 120.45 (stalking in the fourth degree); section 120.50 (stalking in the third degree); section 120.55 (stalking in the second degree); section 120.60 (stalking in the first degree); section 121.11 (criminal obstruction of breathing or blood circulation); section 121.12 (strangulation in the second degree); section 121.13 (strangulation in the first degree); subdivision one of section 125.15 (manslaughter in the second degree); subdivision one, two or four of section 125.20 (manslaughter in the first degree); section 125.25 (murder in the second degree); section 130.20 (sexual misconduct); section 130.30 (rape in the second degree); section 130.35 (rape in the first degree); section 130.40 (criminal sexual act in the third degree); section 130.45 (criminal sexual act in the second degree); section 130.50 (criminal sexual act in the first degree); section 130.52 (forcible touching); section 130.53 (persistent sexual abuse); section 130.55 (sexual abuse in the third degree); section 130.60 (sexual abuse in the second degree); section 130.65 (sexual abuse in the first degree); section 130.66 (aggravated sexual abuse in the third degree); section 130.67 (aggravated sexual abuse in the second degree); section 130.70 (aggravated sexual abuse in the first degree); section 130.91 (sexually motivated felony); section 130.95 (predatory sexual assault); section 130.96 (predatory sexual assault against a child); section 135.05 (unlawful imprisonment in the second degree); section 135.10 (unlawful imprisonment in the first degree); section 135.60 (coercion in the third degree); section 135.61 (coercion in the second degree); section 135.65 (coercion in the first degree); section 140.20 (burglary in the third degree); section 140.25 (burglary in the second degree); section 140.30 (burglary in the first degree); section 145.00 (criminal mischief in the fourth degree); section 145.05 (criminal mischief in the third degree); section 145.10 (criminal mischief in the second degree); section 145.12 (criminal mischief in the first degree); section 145.14 (criminal tampering in the third degree); section 215.50 (criminal contempt in the second degree); section 215.51 (criminal contempt in the first degree);

section 215.52 (aggravated criminal contempt); section 240.25 (harassment in the first degree); subdivision one, two or four of section 240.30 (aggravated harassment in the second degree); aggravated family offense as defined in this section or any attempt or conspiracy to commit any of the foregoing offenses where the defendant and the person against whom the offense was committed were members of the same family or household as defined in subdivision one of section 530.11 of the criminal procedure law.

3. The person against whom the current specified offense is committed may be different from the person against whom the previous specified offense was committed and such persons do not need to be members of the same family or household. Aggravated family offense is a class E felony.

N.Y. Penal Law § 240.75

Amended by New York Laws 2018, ch. 55,Sec. NN-8, eff. 11/1/2018.

Section 240.76 - Directing a laser at an aircraft in the second degree

A person is guilty of directing a laser at an aircraft in the second degree when, with intent to disrupt safe air travel, he or she directs the beam of a laser:

1. onto a specific aircraft intending to thereby disrupt or interfere with such aircraft in the special aircraft jurisdiction of the United States; or

2. in the immediate vicinity of an aircraft in the special aircraft jurisdiction of the United States, and:

(a) the calculated or measured beam irradiance on the aircraft, or in the immediate vicinity of the aircraft, exceeds limits set by the FAA for the FAA-specified laser flight zone (normal, sensitive, critical, or laser-free) where the aircraft was located; and

(b) a pilot in the illuminated aircraft files a laser incident report with the FAA.

3. As used in this section:

(a) the term "laser" shall mean any device designed or used to amplify electromagnetic radiation by stimulated emission that emits a beam; and

(b) the term "FAA" shall mean the Federal Aviation Administration.

4. This section does not prohibit directing a laser beam at an aircraft, or in the immediate vicinity of an aircraft, by:

(a) an authorized individual in the conduct of research and development or flight test operations conducted by an aircraft manufacturer, the FAA, or any other person authorized by the FAA to conduct such research and development or flight test operations; or

(b) members or elements of the United States department of defense or the United States department of homeland security acting in an official capacity for the purpose of research, development, operations, testing or training; or

(c) an individual in an emergency situation using a laser to attract the attention of an aircraft for bona fide rescue purposes; or

(d) an individual whose laser operations have been submitted to and reviewed by the FAA, when:

(i) the FAA has issued a letter not objecting to the laser use; and

(ii) the laser is operated in conformity with the FAA submission. Directing a laser at an aircraft is a class A misdemeanor.

N.Y. Penal Law § 240.76

Added by New York Laws 2014, ch. 98,Sec. 1, eff. 11/1/2014.

Section 240.77 - Directing a laser at an aircraft in the first degree

A person is guilty of directing a laser at an aircraft in the first degree when he or she commits the crime of directing a laser at an aircraft in the second degree in violation of section 240.76 of this article and thereby causes a significant change of course or other serious disruption to the safe travel of an aircraft that threatens the physical safety of the aircraft's passengers or crew. Directing a laser at an aircraft in the first degree is a class E felony.

N.Y. Penal Law § 240.77

Added by New York Laws 2014, ch. 98,Sec. 1, eff. 11/1/2014.

Article 241 - HARASSMENT OF RENT REGULATED TENANTS

Section 241.00 - Harassment of a rent regulated tenant; definition of terms

As used in this article:

1. "Rent regulated tenant" shall mean a person occupying a housing accommodation or any lawful successor to the tenancy which is subject to the regulations and control of residential rents and evictions pursuant to the emergency housing rent control law, the local emergency housing rent control act, the emergency tenant protection act of nineteen seventy-four, the New York city rent and rehabilitation law or the New York city rent stabilization law of nineteen hundred sixty-nine, and such person is either a party to a lease or rental agreement for such housing accommodation, a statutory tenant or a person who lawfully occupies such housing accommodation with such party to a lease or rental agreement or with such statutory tenant. The definition of "rent regulated tenant" as used in this subdivision shall be applicable only to the provisions of this article and shall not be applicable to any other provision of law.

2. "Housing accommodations" shall mean housing accommodations which are subject to the regulations and control of residential rents and evictions pursuant to the emergency housing rent control law, the local emergency housing rent control act, the emergency tenant protection act of nineteen seventy-four, the New York city rent and rehabilitation law or the New York city rent stabilization law of nineteen hundred sixty-nine.

3. "Owner" shall mean an owner, lessor, sublessor, assignee, net lessee, or a proprietary lessee of a housing accommodation in a structure or premises owned by a cooperative corporation or association, or an owner of a condominium unit or the sponsor of such cooperative corporation or association or condominium development, or any

other person or entity receiving or entitled to receive rent for the use or occupation of any housing accommodation, or an agent of or any person acting on behalf of any of the foregoing.

N.Y. Penal Law § 241.00

Amended by New York Laws 2019, ch. 573,Sec. 4, eff. 5/31/2020.

Amended by New York Laws 2019, ch. 36,Sec. A-6, eff. 6/14/2019.

Section 241.02 - Harassment of a rent regulated tenant in the second degree

An owner is guilty of harassment of a rent regulated tenant in the second degree when, with intent to induce a rent regulated tenant to vacate a housing accommodation, such owner intentionally engages in a course of conduct that:

1. impairs the habitability of a housing accommodation; or

2. creates or maintains a condition which endangers the safety or health of the dwelling's tenant; or

3. is reasonably likely to interfere with or disturb, and does interfere with or disturb, the comfort, repose, peace or quiet of such rent regulated tenant in his or her use and occupancy of such housing accommodation including, but not limited to, the interruption or discontinuance of essential services. The good faith commencement and pursuit of a lawful eviction action by an owner against a rent regulated tenant in a court of competent jurisdiction shall not, by itself, constitute a "course of conduct" in violation of this subdivision.

Harassment of a rent regulated tenant in the second degree is a class A misdemeanor.

N.Y. Penal Law § 241.02

Added by New York Laws 2019, ch. 573,Sec. 2, eff. 5/31/2020.

Section 241.05 - Harassment of a rent regulated tenant in the first degree

An owner is guilty of harassment of a rent regulated tenant in the first degree when :

1. With intent to induce a rent regulated tenant to vacate a housing accommodation, such owner:

(a) With intent to cause physical injury to such tenant, causes such injury to such tenant or to a third person; or

(b) Recklessly causes physical injury to such tenant or to a third person; or

2. With intent to induce two or more rent regulated tenants occupying different housing accommodations to vacate such housing accommodations, such owner intentionally engages in a systematic ongoing course of conduct that:

(a) impairs the habitability of such housing accommodations; or

(b) creates or maintains a condition which endangers the safety or health of one or more of the dwellings' rent regulated tenants; or

(c) is reasonably likely to interfere with or disturb, and does interfere with or disturb, the comfort, repose, peace or quiet of one or more of such rent regulated tenants in their use and occupancy of such housing accommodations including, but not limited to, the interruption or discontinuance of essential services; or

3. Such owner commits the crime of harassment of a rent regulated tenant in the second degree as defined in section 241.02 of this article and has previously been convicted within the preceding five years of such crime or the crime of harassment of a rent regulated tenant in the first degree.

The good faith commencement and pursuit of a lawful eviction action by an owner against a rent regulated tenant in a court of competent jurisdiction shall not, by itself, constitute a "systematic ongoing course of conduct" in violation of paragraph (c) of subdivision two of this section.

Harassment of a rent regulated tenant in the first degree is a class E felony.

N.Y. Penal Law § 241.05

Amended by New York Laws 2019, ch. 573,Sec. 3, eff. 5/31/2020.

Amended by New York Laws 2019, ch. 36,Sec. A-6, eff. 6/14/2019.

Article 242 - OFFENSES AGAINST SERVICE ANIMALS AND HANDLERS

Section 242.00 - Definitions

For purposes of this article:

1. "Service animal" shall mean any animal that has been partnered with a person who has a disability and has been trained or is being trained, by a qualified person, to aid or guide a person with a disability.

2. "Disability" shall have the same meaning as provided in section two hundred ninety-two of the executive law.

3. "Handler" shall mean a disabled person using a service animal.

4. "Formal training program" or "certified trainer" shall mean an institution, group or individual who has documentation and community recognition as a provider of service animals.

N.Y. Penal Law § 242.00

Section 242.05 - Interference, harassment or intimidation of a service animal

A person is guilty of interference, harassment or intimidation of a service animal when he or she commits an act with intent to and which does make it impractical, dangerous or impossible for a service animal to perform its assigned responsibilities of assisting a person with a disability.

N.Y. Penal Law § 242.05

Section 242.10 - Harming a service animal in the second degree

A person is guilty of harming a service animal in the second degree when, with the intent to do so, he or she causes physical injury, or causes such injury that results in the death, of a service animal.

N.Y. Penal Law § 242.10

Section 242.15 - Harming a service animal in the first degree

A person is guilty of harming a service animal in the first degree when, he or she commits the crime of harming a service animal in the second degree, and has been convicted of harming a service animal in the first or second degree within the prior five years.

N.Y. Penal Law § 242.15

Article 245 - OFFENSES AGAINST PUBLIC SENSIBILITIES

Section 245.00 - Public lewdness

A person is guilty of public lewdness when he or she intentionally exposes the private or intimate parts of his or her body in a lewd manner or commits any other lewd act:

(a) in a public place, or

(b) (i) in private premises under circumstances in which he or she may readily be observed from either a public place or from other private premises, and with intent that he or she be so observed, or (ii) while trespassing, as defined in section 140.05 of this part, in a dwelling as defined in subdivision three of section 140.00 of this part, under circumstances in which he or she is observed by a lawful occupant.

N.Y. Penal Law § 245.00

Amended by New York Laws 2015, ch. 373,Sec. 1, eff. 11/1/2015.

Section 245.01 - Exposure of a person

A person is guilty of exposure if he appears in a public place in such a manner that the private or intimate parts of his body are unclothed or exposed. For purposes of this section, the private or intimate parts of a female person shall include that portion of the breast which is below the top of the areola. This section shall not apply to the breastfeeding of infants or to any person entertaining or performing in a play, exhibition, show or entertainment.

N.Y. Penal Law § 245.01

Section 245.02 - Promoting the exposure of a person

A person is guilty of promoting the exposure of a person when he knowingly conducts, maintains, owns, manages, operates or furnishes any public premise or place where a person in a public place appears in such a manner that the private or intimate parts of his body are unclothed or exposed. For purposes of this section, the private or intimate parts of a female person shall include that portion of the breast which is below the top of the areola. This section shall not apply to the breastfeeding of infants or to any person entertaining or performing in a play, exhibition, show or entertainment.

N.Y. Penal Law § 245.02

Section 245.03 - Public lewdness in the first degree

A person is guilty of public lewdness in the first degree when:

1. being nineteen years of age or older and intending to be observed by a person less than sixteen years of age in a place described in subdivision (a) or (b) of section 245.00 of this article, he or she intentionally exposes the private or intimate parts of his or her body in a lewd manner for the purpose of alarming or seriously annoying such person, and he or she is thereby observed by such person in such place; or

2. he or she commits the crime of public lewdness, as defined in section 245.00 of this article, and within the preceding year has been convicted of an offense defined in such section 245.00 or this section. Public lewdness in the first degree is a class A misdemeanor.

N.Y. Penal Law § 245.03

Added by New York Laws 2014, ch. 186,Sec. 1, eff. 11/1/2014.

Section 245.05 - Offensive exhibition

A person is guilty of offensive exhibition when he knowingly produces, operates, manages or furnishes premises for, or in any way promotes or participates in, an exhibition in the nature of public entertainment or amusement in which:

1. A person competes continuously without respite for a period of more than eight consecutive hours in a dance contest, bicycle race or other contest involving physical endurance; or

2. A person is held up to ridicule or contempt by voluntarily submitting to indignities such as the throwing of balls or other articles at his head or body; or

3. A firearm is discharged or a knife, arrow or other sharp or dangerous instrument is thrown or propelled at or toward a person.

Offensive exhibition is a violation.

N.Y. Penal Law § 245.05

Section 245.10 - Public display of offensive sexual material; definitions of terms

The following definitions are applicable to section 245.11:

1. "Nudity" means the showing of the human male or female genitals, pubic area or buttocks with less than a full opaque covering, or the showing of the female breast with less than a fully opaque covering of any portion thereof below the top of the nipple, or the depiction of covered male genitals in a discernibly turgid state.

2. "Sexual conduct" means an act of masturbation, homosexuality, sexual intercourse, or physical contact with a person's clothed or unclothed genitals, pubic area, buttocks or, if such person be a female, breast.

3. "Sado-masochistic abuse" means flagellation or torture by or upon a person clad in undergarments, a mask or bizzare costume, or the condition of being fettered, bound or otherwise physically restrained on the part of one so clothed.

4. "Transportation facility" means any conveyance, premises or place used for or in connection with public passenger transportation, whether by air, railroad, motor vehicle or any other method. It includes aircraft, watercraft, railroad cars, buses, and air, boat, railroad and bus terminals and stations and all appurtenances thereto.

166

N.Y. Penal Law § 245.10

Section 245.11 - Public display of offensive sexual material

A person is guilty of public display of offensive sexual material when, with knowledge of its character and content, he displays or permits to be displayed in or on any window, showcase, newsstand, display rack, wall, door, billboard, display board, viewing screen, moving picture screen, marquee or similar place, in such manner that the display is easily visible from or in any: public street, sidewalk or thoroughfare; transportation facility; or any place accessible to members of the public without fee or other limit or condition of admission such as a minimum age requirement and including but not limited to schools, places of amusement, parks and playgrounds but excluding rooms or apartments designed for actual residence; any pictorial, three-dimensional or other visual representation of a person or a portion of the human body that predominantly appeals to prurient interest in sex, and that:

(a) depicts nudity, or actual or simulated sexual conduct or sado-masochistic abuse; or

(b) depicts or appears to depict nudity, or actual or simulated sexual conduct or sado-masochistic abuse, with the area of the male or female subject's unclothed or apparently unclothed genitals, pubic area or buttocks, or of the female subject's unclothed or apparently unclothed breast, obscured by a covering or mark placed or printed on or in front of the material displayed, or obscured or altered in any other manner.

Public display of offensive sexual material is a Class A misdemeanor.

N.Y. Penal Law § 245.11

Section 245.15 - Unlawful dissemination or publication of an intimate image

1. A person is guilty of unlawful dissemination or publication of an intimate image when:

(a) with intent to cause harm to the emotional, financial or physical welfare of another person, he or she intentionally disseminates or publishes a still or video image of such other person, who is identifiable from the still or video image itself or from information displayed in connection with the still or video image, without such other person's consent, which depicts:

(i) an unclothed or exposed intimate part of such other person; or

(ii) such other person engaging in sexual conduct as defined in subdivision ten of section 130.00 of this chapter with another person; and

(b) such still or video image was taken under circumstances when the person depicted had a reasonable expectation that the image would remain private and the actor knew or reasonably should have known the person depicted intended for the still or video image to remain private, regardless of whether the actor was present when the still or video image was taken.

2. For purposes of this section "intimate part" means the naked genitals, pubic area, anus or female nipple of the person.

2-a. For purposes of this section "disseminate" and "publish" shall have the same meaning as defined in section 250.40 of this title.

3. This section shall not apply to the following:

(a) the reporting of unlawful conduct;

(b) dissemination or publication of an intimate image made during lawful and common practices of law enforcement, legal proceedings or medical treatment;

(c) images involving voluntary exposure in a public or commercial setting; or

(d) dissemination or publication of an intimate image made for a legitimate public purpose.

4. Nothing in this section shall be construed to limit, or to enlarge, the protections that 47 U.S.C § 230 confers on an interactive computer service for content provided by another information content provider, as such terms are defined in 47 U.S.C. § 230.

Unlawful dissemination or publication of an intimate image is a class A misdemeanor.

N.Y. Penal Law § 245.15

Added by New York Laws 2019, ch. 109,Sec. 1, eff. 9/21/2019.

Article 250 - OFFENSES AGAINST THE RIGHT TO PRIVACY

Section 250.00 - Eavesdropping; definitions of terms

The following definitions are applicable to this article:

1. "Wiretapping" means the intentional overhearing or recording of a telephonic or telegraphic communication by a person other than a sender or receiver thereof, without the consent of either the sender or receiver, by means of any instrument, device or equipment. The normal operation of a telephone or telegraph corporation and the normal use of the services and facilities furnished by such corporation pursuant to its tariffs or necessary to protect the rights or property of said corporation shall not be deemed "wiretapping."

2. "Mechanical overhearing of a conversation" means the intentional overhearing or recording of a conversation or discussion, without the consent of at least one party thereto, by a person not present thereat, by means of any instrument, device or equipment.

3. "Telephonic communication" means any aural transfer made in whole or in part through the use of facilities for the transmission of communications by the aid of wire, cable or other like connection between the point of origin and the point of reception (including the use of such connection in a switching station) furnished or operated by any person engaged in providing or operating such facilities for the transmission of communications and such term includes any electronic storage of such communications.

4. "Aural transfer" means a transfer containing the human voice at any point between and including the point of origin and the point of reception.

5. "Electronic communication" means any transfer of signs, signals, writing, images, sounds, data, or intelligence of any nature transmitted in whole or in part by a wire, radio, electromagnetic, photoelectronic or photo-optical system, but does not include:

(a) any telephonic or telegraphic communication; or

(b) any communication made through a tone only paging device; or

(c) any communication made through a tracking device consisting of an electronic or mechanical device which permits the tracking of the movement of a person or object; or

(d) any communication that is disseminated by the sender through a method of transmission that is configured so that such communication is readily accessible to the general public.

6. "Intercepting or accessing of an electronic communication" and "intentionally intercepted or accessed" mean the intentional acquiring, receiving, collecting, overhearing, or recording of an electronic communication, without the consent of the sender or intended receiver thereof, by means of any instrument, device or equipment, except when used by a telephone company in the ordinary course of its business or when necessary to protect the rights or property of such company.

7. "Electronic communication service" means any service which provides to users thereof the ability to send or receive wire or electronic communications.

8. "Unlawfully" means not specifically authorized pursuant to article seven hundred or seven hundred five of the criminal procedure law for the purposes of this section and sections 250.05, 250.10, 250.15, 250.20, 250.25, 250.30 and 250.35 of this article.

N.Y. Penal Law § 250.00

Section 250.05 - Eavesdropping

A person is guilty of eavesdropping when he unlawfully engages in wiretapping, mechanical overhearing of a conversation, or intercepting or accessing of an electronic communication.

N.Y. Penal Law § 250.05

Section 250.10 - Possession of eavesdropping devices

A person is guilty of possession of eavesdropping devices when, under circumstances evincing an intent to use or to permit the same to be used in violation of section 250.05, he possesses any instrument, device or equipment designed for, adapted to or commonly used in wiretapping or mechanical overhearing of a conversation.

N.Y. Penal Law § 250.10

Section 250.15 - Failure to report wiretapping

A telephone or telegraph corporation is guilty of failure to report wiretapping when, having knowledge of the occurrence of unlawful wiretapping, it does not report such matter to an appropriate law enforcement officer or agency.

N.Y. Penal Law § 250.15

Section 250.20 - Divulging an eavesdropping warrant

A person is guilty of divulging an eavesdropping warrant when, possessing information concerning the existence or content of an eavesdropping warrant issued pursuant to article seven hundred of the criminal procedure law, or concerning any circumstances attending an application for such a warrant, he discloses such information to another person; except that such disclosure is not criminal or unlawful when permitted by section 700.65 of the criminal procedure law or when made to a state or federal agency specifically authorized by law to receive reports concerning eavesdropping warrants, or when made in a legal proceeding, or to a law enforcement officer or agency connected with the application for such warrant, or to a legislative committee or temporary state commission, or to the telephone or telegraph corporation whose facilities are involved, or to any entity operating an electronic communications service whose facilities are involved.

N.Y. Penal Law § 250.20

Section 250.25 - Tampering with private communications

A person is guilty of tampering with private communications when:

1. Knowing that he does not have the consent of the sender or receiver, he opens or reads a sealed letter or other sealed private communication; or

2. Knowing that a sealed letter or other sealed private communication has been opened or read in violation of subdivision one of this section, he divulges without the consent of the sender or receiver, the contents of such letter or communication, in whole or in part, or a resume of any portion of the contents thereof; or

3. Knowing that he does not have the consent of the sender or receiver, he obtains or attempts to obtain from an employee, officer or representative of a telephone or telegraph corporation, by connivance, deception, intimidation or in any other manner, information with respect to the contents or nature thereof of a telephonic or telegraphic communication; except that the provisions of this subdivision do not apply to a law enforcement officer who obtains information from a telephone or telegraph corporation pursuant to section 250.35; or

4. Knowing that he does not have the consent of the sender or receiver, and being an employee, officer or representative of a telephone or telegraph corporation, he knowingly divulges to another person the contents or nature thereof of a telephonic or telegraphic communication; except that the provisions of this subdivision do not apply to such person when he acts pursuant to section 250.35.

Tampering with private communications is a class B misdemeanor.

N.Y. Penal Law § 250.25

168

Section 250.30 - Unlawfully obtaining communications information

A person is guilty of unlawfully obtaining communications information when, knowing that he does not have the authorization of a telephone or telegraph corporation, he obtains or attempts to obtain, by deception, stealth or in any other manner, from such corporation or from any employee, officer or representative thereof:

1. Information concerning identification or location of any wires, cables, lines, terminals or other apparatus used in furnishing telephone or telegraph service; or

2. Information concerning a record of any communication passing over telephone or telegraph lines of any such corporation.

Unlawfully obtaining communications information is a class B misdemeanor.

N.Y. Penal Law § 250.30

Section 250.35 - Failing to report criminal communications

1. It shall be the duty of a telephone or telegraph corporation, or an entity operating an electronic communications service, and of any employee, officer or representative thereof having knowledge that the facilities of such corporation or entity are being used to conduct any criminal business, traffic or transaction, to furnish or attempt to furnish to an appropriate law enforcement officer or agency all pertinent information within his possession relating to such matter, and to cooperate fully with any law enforcement officer or agency investigating such matter.

2. A person is guilty of failing to report criminal communications when he knowingly violates any duty prescribed in subdivision one of this section.

Failing to report criminal communications is a class B misdemeanor.

N.Y. Penal Law § 250.35

Section 250.40 - Unlawful surveillance; definitions

The following definitions shall apply to sections 250.45, 250.50, 250.55 and 250.60 of this article:

1. "Place and time when a person has a reasonable expectation of privacy" means a place and time when a reasonable person would believe that he or she could fully disrobe in privacy.

2. "Imaging device" means any mechanical, digital or electronic viewing device, camera, cellular phone or any other instrument capable of recording, storing or transmitting visual images that can be utilized to observe a person.

3. "Sexual or other intimate parts" means the human male or female genitals, pubic area or buttocks, or the female breast below the top of the nipple, and shall include such part or parts which are covered only by an undergarment.

4. "Broadcast" means electronically transmitting a visual image with the intent that it be viewed by a person.

5. "Disseminate" means to give, provide, lend, deliver, mail, send, forward, transfer or transmit, electronically or otherwise to another person.

6. "Publish" means to (a) disseminate, as defined in subdivision five of this section, with the intent that such image or images be disseminated to ten or more persons; or (b) disseminate with the intent that such images be sold by another person; or (c) post, present, display, exhibit, circulate, advertise or allows access, electronically or otherwise, so as to make an image or images available to the public; or (d) disseminate with the intent that an image or images be posted, presented, displayed, exhibited, circulated, advertised or made accessible, electronically or otherwise and to make such image or images available to the public.

7. "Sell" means to disseminate to another person, as defined in subdivision five of this section, or to publish, as defined in subdivision six of this section, in exchange for something of value.

N.Y. Penal Law § 250.40

Section 250.45 - Unlawful surveillance in the second degree

A person is guilty of unlawful surveillance in the second degree when:

1. For his or her own, or another person's amusement, entertainment, or profit, or for the purpose of degrading or abusing a person, he or she intentionally uses or installs, or permits the utilization or installation of an imaging device to surreptitiously view, broadcast or record a person dressing or undressing or the sexual or other intimate parts of such person at a place and time when such person has a reasonable expectation of privacy, without such person's knowledge or consent; or

2. For his or her own, or another person's sexual arousal or sexual gratification, he or she intentionally uses or installs, or permits the utilization or installation of an imaging device to surreptitiously view, broadcast or record a person dressing or undressing or the sexual or other intimate parts of such person at a place and time when such person has a reasonable expectation of privacy, without such person's knowledge or consent; or

3.

(a) For no legitimate purpose, he or she intentionally uses or installs, or permits the utilization or installation of an imaging device to surreptitiously view, broadcast or record a person in a bedroom, changing room, fitting room, restroom, toilet, bathroom, washroom, shower or any room assigned to guests or patrons in a motel, hotel or inn, without such person's knowledge or consent.

(b) For the purposes of this subdivision, when a person uses or installs, or permits the utilization or installation of an imaging device in a bedroom, changing room, fitting room, restroom, toilet, bathroom, washroom, shower or any room assigned to guests or patrons in a hotel, motel or inn, there is a rebuttable presumption that such person did so for no legitimate purpose; or

4. Without the knowledge or consent of a person, he or she intentionally uses or installs, or permits the utilization or installation of an imaging device to surreptitiously view, broadcast or record, under the clothing being worn by such person, the sexual or other intimate parts of such person; or

5. For his or her own, or another individual's amusement, entertainment, profit, sexual arousal or gratification, or for the purpose of degrading or abusing a person, the actor intentionally uses or installs or permits the utilization or installation of an imaging device to surreptitiously view, broadcast, or record such person in an identifiable manner:

(a) engaging in sexual conduct, as defined in subdivision ten of section 130.00 of this part;

(b) in the same image with the sexual or intimate part of any other person; and

(c) at a place and time when such person has a reasonable expectation of privacy, without such person's knowledge or consent.

Unlawful surveillance in the second degree is a class E felony.

N.Y. Penal Law § 250.45

Amended by New York Laws 2014, ch. 193,Sec. 1, eff. 11/1/2014.

Section 250.50 - Unlawful surveillance in the first degree

A person is guilty of unlawful surveillance in the first degree when he or she commits the crime of unlawful surveillance in the second degree and has been previously convicted within the past ten years of unlawful surveillance in the first or second degree.

N.Y. Penal Law § 250.50

Section 250.55 - Dissemination of an unlawful surveillance image in the second degree

A person is guilty of dissemination of an unlawful surveillance image in the second degree when he or she, with knowledge of the unlawful conduct by which an image or images of the sexual or other intimate parts of another person or persons were obtained and such unlawful conduct would satisfy the essential elements of the crime of unlawful surveillance in the first or second degree, as defined, respectively, in section 250.50 or 250.45 of this article, intentionally disseminates such image or images.

N.Y. Penal Law § 250.55

Amended by New York Laws 2014, ch. 193,Sec. 2, eff. 11/1/2014.

Section 250.60 - Dissemination of an unlawful surveillance image in the first degree

A person is guilty of dissemination of an unlawful surveillance image in the first degree when:

1. He or she, with knowledge of the unlawful conduct by which an image or images of the sexual or other intimate parts of another person or persons were obtained and such unlawful conduct would satisfy the essential elements of the crime of unlawful surveillance in the first or second degree, 45 of this article, sells or publishes such image or images; or

2. Having created a surveillance image in violation of section 250.45 or 250.50 of this article, or in violation of the law in any other jurisdiction which includes all of the essential elements of either such crime, or having acted as an accomplice to such crime, or acting as an agent to the person who committed such crime, he or she intentionally disseminates such unlawfully created image; or

3. He or she commits the crime of dissemination of an unlawful surveillance image in the second degree and has been previously convicted within the past ten years of dissemination of an unlawful surveillance image in the first or second degree.

N.Y. Penal Law § 250.60

Amended by New York Laws 2014, ch. 193,Sec. 3, eff. 11/1/2014.

Section 250.65 - Additional provisions

1. The provisions of sections 250.45, 250.50, 250.55 and 250.60 of this article do not apply with respect to any: (a) law enforcement personnel engaged in the conduct of their authorized duties; (b) security system wherein a written notice is conspicuously posted on the premises stating that a video surveillance system has been installed for the purpose of security; or (c) video surveillance devices installed in such a manner that their presence is clearly and immediately obvious.

2. With respect to sections 250.55 and 250.60 of this article, the provisions of subdivision two of section 235.15 and subdivisions one and two of section 235.24 of this chapter shall apply.

N.Y. Penal Law § 250.65

Title O - OFFENSES AGAINST MARRIAGE, THE FAMILY, AND THE WELFARE OF CHILDREN AND INCOMPETENTS

Article 255 - OFFENSES AFFECTING THE MARITAL RELATIONSHIP

Section 255.00 - Unlawfully solemnizing a marriage

A person is guilty of unlawfully solemnizing a marriage when:

1. Knowing that he is not authorized by the laws of this state to do so, he performs a marriage ceremony or presumes to solemnize a marriage; or

2. Being authorized by the laws of this state to perform marriage ceremonies and to solemnize marriages, he performs a marriage ceremony or solemnizes a marriage knowing that a legal impediment to such marriage exists.

Unlawfully solemnizing a marriage is a class A misdemeanor.

N.Y. Penal Law § 255.00

Section 255.05 - Unlawfully issuing a dissolution decree

A person is guilty of unlawfully issuing a dissolution decree when, not being a judicial officer authorized to issue decrees of divorce or annulment, he issues a written instrument reciting or certifying that he or some other purportedly but not actually authorized person has issued a valid decree of civil divorce, annulment or other dissolution of a marriage.

N.Y. Penal Law § 255.05

Section 255.10 - Unlawfully procuring a marriage license
A person is guilty of unlawfully procuring a marriage license when he procures a license to marry another person at a time when he has a living spouse, or the other person has a living spouse.
N.Y. Penal Law § 255.10

Section 255.15 - Bigamy
A person is guilty of bigamy when he contracts or purports to contract a marriage with another person at a time when he has a living spouse, or the other person has a living spouse.
N.Y. Penal Law § 255.15

Section 255.17 - Adultery
A person is guilty of adultery when he engages in sexual intercourse with another person at a time when he has a living spouse, or the other person has a living spouse.
N.Y. Penal Law § 255.17

Section 255.20 - Unlawfully procuring a marriage license, bigamy, adultery: defense
In any prosecution for unlawfully procuring a marriage license, bigamy, or adultery, it is an affirmative defense that the defendant acted under a reasonable belief that both he and the other person to the marriage or prospective marriage or to the sexual intercourse, as the case may be, were unmarried.
N.Y. Penal Law § 255.20

Section 255.25 - Incest in the third degree
A person is guilty of incest in the third degree when he or she marries or engages in sexual intercourse, oral sexual conduct or anal sexual conduct with a person whom he or she knows to be related to him or her, whether through marriage or not, as an ancestor, descendant, brother or sister of either the whole or the half blood, uncle, aunt, nephew or niece.
N.Y. Penal Law § 255.25

Section 255.26 - Incest in the second degree
A person is guilty of incest in the second degree when he or she commits the crime of rape in the second degree, as defined in section 130.30 of this part, or criminal sexual act in the second degree, as defined in section 130.45 of this part, against a person whom he or she knows to be related to him or her, whether through marriage or not, as an ancestor, descendant, brother or sister of either the whole or the half blood, uncle, aunt, nephew or niece.
N.Y. Penal Law § 255.26

Section 255.27 - Incest in the first degree
A person is guilty of incest in the first degree when he or she commits the crime of rape in the first degree, as defined in subdivision three or four of section 130.35 of this part, or criminal sexual act in the first degree, as defined in subdivision three or four of section 130.50 of this part, against a person whom he or she knows to be related to him or her, whether through marriage or not, as an ancestor, descendant, brother or sister of either the whole or half blood, uncle, aunt, nephew or niece.
N.Y. Penal Law § 255.27

Section 255.30 - Adultery and incest; corroboration
1. A person shall not be convicted of adultery or of an attempt to commit adultery solely upon the testimony of the other party to the adulterous act or attempted act, unsupported by other evidence tending to establish that the defendant attempted to engage with the other party in sexual intercourse, and that the defendant or the other party had a living spouse at the time of the adulterous act or attempted act.
2. A person shall not be convicted of incest or of an attempt to commit incest solely upon the testimony of the other party unsupported by other evidence tending to establish that the defendant married the other party, or that the defendant was a relative of the other party of a kind specified in section 255.25.
N.Y. Penal Law § 255.30

Article 260 - OFFENSES RELATING TO CHILDREN, DISABLED PERSONS AND VULNERABLE ELDERLY PERSONS

Section 260.00 - Abandonment of a child
Abandonment of a child is a class E felony.
1. A person is guilty of abandonment of a child when, being a parent, guardian or other person legally charged with the care or custody of a child less than fourteen years old, he or she deserts such child in any place with intent to wholly abandon such child.
2. A person is not guilty of the provisions of this section when he or she engages in the conduct described in subdivision one of this section: (a) with the intent that the child be safe from physical injury and cared for in an appropriate manner; (b) the child is left with an appropriate person, or in a suitable location and the person who leaves the child promptly notifies an appropriate person of the child's location; and (c) the child is not more than thirty days old.
N.Y. Penal Law § 260.00

Section 260.05 - Non-support of a child in the second degree
A person is guilty of non-support of a child when:
1. being a parent, guardian or other person legally charged with the care or custody of a child less than sixteen years old, he or she fails or refuses without lawful excuse to provide support for such child when he or she is able to do so, or becomes unable to do so, when, though employable, he or she voluntarily terminates his or her employment, voluntarily reduces his or her earning capacity, or fails to diligently seek employment; or

2. being a parent, guardian or other person obligated to make child support payments by an order of child support entered by a court of competent jurisdiction for a child less than eighteen years old, he or she knowingly fails or refuses without lawful excuse to provide support for such child when he or she is able to do so, or becomes unable to do so, when, though employable, he or she voluntarily terminates his or her employment, voluntarily reduces his or her earning capacity, or fails to diligently seek employment.

Non-support of a child in the second degree is a class A misdemeanor.

N.Y. Penal Law § 260.05

Section 260.06 - Non-support of a child in the first degree

A person is guilty of non-support of a child in the first degree when:

1.

(a) being a parent, guardian or other person legally charged with the care or custody of a child less than sixteen years old, he or she fails or refuses without lawful excuse to provide support for such child when he or she is able to do so; or

(b) being a parent, guardian or other person obligated to make child support payments by an order of child support entered by a court of competent jurisdiction for a child less than eighteen years old, he or she fails or refuses without lawful excuse to provide support for such child when he or she is able to do so; and

2. he or she has previously been convicted in the preceding five years of a crime defined in section 260.05 of this article or a crime defined by the provisions of this section.

Non-support of a child in the first degree is a class E felony.

N.Y. Penal Law § 260.06

Section 260.10 - Endangering the welfare of a child

A person is guilty of endangering the welfare of a child when:

1. He or she knowingly acts in a manner likely to be injurious to the physical, mental or moral welfare of a child less than seventeen years old or directs or authorizes such child to engage in an occupation involving a substantial risk of danger to his or her life or health; or

2. Being a parent, guardian or other person legally charged with the care or custody of a child less than eighteen years old, he or she fails or refuses to exercise reasonable diligence in the control of such child to prevent him or her from becoming an "abused child," a "neglected child," a "juvenile delinquent" or a "person in need of supervision," as those terms are defined in articles ten, three and seven of the family court act.

3. A person is not guilty of the provisions of this section when he or she engages in the conduct described in subdivision one of section 260.00 of this article: (a) with the intent to wholly abandon the child by relinquishing responsibility for and right to the care and custody of such child; (b) with the intent that the child be safe from physical injury and cared for in an appropriate manner; (c) the child is left with an appropriate person, or in a suitable location and the person who leaves the child promptly notifies an appropriate person of the child's location; and (d) the child is not more than thirty days old.

N.Y. Penal Law § 260.10

Section 260.11 - Endangering the welfare of a child; corroboration

A person shall not be convicted of endangering the welfare of a child, or of an attempt to commit the same, upon the testimony of a victim who is incapable of consent because of mental defect or mental incapacity as to conduct that constitutes an offense or an attempt to commit an offense referred to in section 130.16, without additional evidence sufficient pursuant to section 130.16 to sustain a conviction of an offense referred to in section 130.16, or of an attempt to commit the same.

N.Y. Penal Law § 260.11

Section 260.15 - Endangering the welfare of a child; defense

In any prosecution for endangering the welfare of a child, pursuant to section 260.10 of this article, based upon an alleged failure or refusal to provide proper medical care or treatment to an ill child, it is an affirmative defense that the defendant (a) is a parent, guardian or other person legally charged with the care or custody of such child; and (b) is a member or adherent of an organized church or religious group the tenets of which prescribe prayer as the principal treatment for illness; and (c) treated or caused such ill child to be treated in accordance with such tenets.

N.Y. Penal Law § 260.15

Section 260.20 - Unlawfully dealing with a child in the first degree

A person is guilty of unlawfully dealing with a child in the first degree when:

1. He knowingly permits a child less than eighteen years old to enter or remain in or upon a place, premises or establishment where sexual activity as defined by article one hundred thirty, two hundred thirty or two hundred sixty-three of this part or activity involving controlled substances as defined by article two hundred twenty of this part is maintained or conducted, and he knows or has reason to know that such activity is being maintained or conducted; or

2. He gives or sells or causes to be given or sold any alcoholic beverage, as defined by section three of the alcoholic beverage control law, to a person less than twenty-one years old; except that this subdivision does not apply to the parent or guardian of such a person or to a person who gives or causes to be given any such alcoholic beverage to a person under the age of twenty-one years, who is a student in a curriculum licensed or registered by the state education department, where the tasting or imbibing of alcoholic beverages is required in courses that are part of the required curriculum, provided such alcoholic beverages are given only for instructional purposes during classes conducted pursuant to such curriculum.

It is no defense to a prosecution pursuant to subdivision two of this section that the child acted as the agent or representative of another person or that the defendant dealt with the child as such.

It is an affirmative defense to a prosecution pursuant to subdivision two of this section that the defendant who sold, caused to be sold or attempted to sell such alcoholic beverage to a person less than twenty-one years old, had not been, at the time of such sale or attempted sale, convicted of a violation of this section or section 260.21 of this article within the preceding five years, and such defendant, subsequent to the commencement of the present prosecution, has completed an alcohol training awareness program established pursuant to subdivision twelve of section seventeen of the alcoholic beverage control law. A defendant otherwise qualifying pursuant to this paragraph may request and shall be afforded a reasonable adjournment of the proceedings to enable him or her to complete such alcohol training awareness program.

Unlawfully dealing with a child in the first degree is a class A misdemeanor.

N.Y. Penal Law § 260.20

Amended by New York Laws 2021, ch. 92,Sec. 49, eff. 3/31/2021.

Section 260.21 - Unlawfully dealing with a child in the second degree

A person is guilty of unlawfully dealing with a child in the second degree when:

1. Being an owner, lessee, manager or employee of a place where alcoholic beverages are sold or given away, he permits a child less than sixteen years old to enter or remain in such place unless:

(a) The child is accompanied by his parent, guardian or an adult authorized by a parent or guardian; or

(b) The entertainment or activity is being conducted for the benefit or under the auspices of a non-profit school, church or other educational or religious institution; or

(c) Otherwise permitted by law to do so; or

(d) The establishment is closed to the public for a specified period of time to conduct an activity or entertainment, during which the child is in or remains in such establishment, and no alcoholic beverages are sold, served, given away or consumed at such establishment during such period. The state liquor authority shall be notified in writing by the licensee of such establishment, of the intended closing of such establishment, to conduct any such activity or entertainment, not less than ten days prior to any such closing; or

2. He marks the body of a child less than eighteen years old with indelible ink or pigments by means of tattooing; or

3. He or she sells or causes to be sold tobacco in any form to a child less than twenty-one years old.

It is no defense to a prosecution pursuant to subdivision three of this section that the child acted as the agent or representative of another person or that the defendant dealt with the child as such.

Unlawfully dealing with a child in the second degree is a class B misdemeanor.

N.Y. Penal Law § 260.21

Amended by New York Laws 2019, ch. 100,Sec. 9, eff. 11/13/2019.

Section 260.22 - Facilitating female genital mutilation

A person is guilty of facilitating female genital mutilation when, knowing that a person intends to engage in the circumcising, excising or infibulating of the whole or any part of the labia majora or labia minora or clitoris of a person under eighteen years of age, and except as provided in subdivision two of section 130.85 of this chapter, he or she intentionally aids the commission or attempted commission of such conduct.

N.Y. Penal Law § 260.22

Added by New York Laws 2016, ch. 49,Sec. 1, eff. 9/6/2016.

Section 260.24 - Endangering the welfare of an incompetent or physically disabled person in the second degree

A person is guilty of endangering the welfare of an incompetent or physically disabled person in the second degree when he or she reckless ly engages in conduct which is likely to be injurious to the physical, mental or moral welfare of a person who is unable to care for himself or herself because of physical disability, mental disease or defect. Endangering the welfare of an incompetent or physically disabled person in the second degree is a class A misdemeanor.

N.Y. Penal Law § 260.24

Added by New York Laws 2012, ch. 501,Sec. G-3, eff. 1/16/2013.

Section 260.25 - Endangering the welfare of an incompetent or physically disabled person in the first degree

A person is guilty of endangering the welfare of an incompetent or physically disabled person in the first degree when he knowingly acts in a manner likely to be injurious to the physical, mental or moral welfare of a person who is unable to care for himself or herself because of physical disability, mental disease or defect. Endangering the welfare of an incompetent or physically disabled person in the first degree is a class E felony.

N.Y. Penal Law § 260.25

Amended by New York Laws 2012, ch. 501,Sec. G-4, eff. 1/16/2013.

Section 260.31 - [First of two versions]Vulnerable elderly persons; definitions

For the purpose of sections 260.32 and 260.34 of this article, the following definitions shall apply:

1. "Caregiver" means a person who (i) assumes responsibility for the care of a vulnerable elderly person, or an incompetent or physically disabled person pursuant to a court order; or (ii) receives monetary or other valuable consideration for providing care for a vulnerable elderly person, or an incompetent or physically disabled person.

2. "Sexual contact" means any touching of the sexual or other intimate parts of a person for the purpose of gratifying sexual desire of either party. It includes the touching of the actor by the victim, as well as the touching of the victim by the actor, whether directly or through clothing, as well as the emission of ejaculate by the actor upon any part of the victim, clothed or unclothed.

3. "Vulnerable elderly person" means a person sixty years of age or older who is suffering from a disease or infirmity associated with advanced age and manifested by demonstrable physical, mental or emotional dysfunction to the extent that the person is incapable of adequately providing for his or her own health or personal care.

4. "Incompetent or physically disabled person" means an individual who is unable to care for himself or herself because of physical disability, mental disease or defect.

N.Y. Penal Law § 260.31

Section 260.31 - [Second of two versions]Misrepresentation by a child day care provider

A person is guilty of misrepresentation by a child day care provider when, being a child day care provider or holding himself or herself out as such, he or she makes any willful and intentional misrepresentation, by act or omission, to a parent or guardian of a child in the care of such provider (or a child whose prospective placement in such care is being considered by such parent or guardian) to any state or local official having jurisdiction over child day care providers, or to any police officer or peace officer as to the facts pertaining to such child day care provider, including, but not limited to:

(i) the number of children in the facility or home where such number is in violation of the provisions of section three hundred ninety of the social services law, (ii) the area of the facility, home, or center used for child day care, or (iii) the credentials or qualifications of any child day care provider, assistant, employee, or volunteer. A misrepresentation subject to the provisions of this section must substantially place at risk the health or safety of a child in the care of a child day care provider.

Misrepresentation by a child day care provider is a class A misdemeanor.

N.Y. Penal Law § 260.31

Section 260.32 - Endangering the welfare of a vulnerable elderly person, or an incompetent or physically disabled person in the second degree

A person is guilty of endangering the welfare of a vulnerable elderly person, or an incompetent or physically disabled person in the second degree when, being a caregiver for a vulnerable elderly person, or an incompetent or physically disabled person:

1. With intent to cause physical injury to such person, he or she causes such injury to such person; or

2. He or she recklessly causes physical injury to such person; or

3. With criminal negligence, he or she causes physical injury to such person by means of a deadly weapon or a dangerous instrument; or

4. He or she subjects such person to sexual contact without the latter's consent. Lack of consent under this subdivision results from forcible compulsion or incapacity to consent, as those terms are defined in article one hundred thirty of this chapter, or any other circumstances in which the vulnerable elderly person, or an incompetent or physically disabled person does not expressly or impliedly acquiesce in the caregiver's conduct. In any prosecution under this subdivision in which the victim's alleged lack of consent results solely from incapacity to consent because of the victim's mental disability or mental incapacity, the provisions of section 130.16 of this chapter shall apply. In addition, in any prosecution under this subdivision in which the victim's lack of consent is based solely upon his or her incapacity to consent because he or she was mentally disabled, mentally incapacitated or physically helpless, it is an affirmative defense that the defendant, at the time he or she engaged in the conduct constituting the offense, did not know of the facts or conditions responsible for such incapacity to consent.

Endangering the welfare of a vulnerable elderly person, or an incompetent or physically disabled person in the second degree is a class E felony.

N.Y. Penal Law § 260.32

Section 260.34 - Endangering the welfare of a vulnerable elderly person, or an incompetent or physically disabled person in the first degree

A person is guilty of endangering the welfare of a vulnerable elderly person, or an incompetent or physically disabled person in the first degree when, being a caregiver for a vulnerable elderly person, or an incompetent or physically disabled person:

1. With intent to cause physical injury to such person, he or she causes serious physical injury to such person; or

2. He or she recklessly causes serious physical injury to such person.

Endangering the welfare of a vulnerable elderly person, or an incompetent or physically disabled person in the first degree is a class D felony.

N.Y. Penal Law § 260.34

Section 260.35 - Misrepresentation by, or on behalf of, a caregiver for a child or children

1. A person is guilty of misrepresentation by, or on behalf of, a caregiver for a child or children when he or she:

(a) intentionally makes a false written statement about himself, herself, or another person while he or she, or such other person, is being considered for employment, or while under employment as a caregiver to a parent or guardian of a child or children, or the agent of a parent or guardian, and

(b) such statement contains a materially false representation regarding the caregiver's background related to the ability to safely care for a child or children, and

(c) a reasonable person would have relied upon such statement in making an employment decision.

2. For the purposes of this section, "caregiver" shall mean a person employed by or being considered for employment to provide fifteen or more hours of care per week to a child or children in the home of such child or children or in the home of such caregiver, provided that such term shall not apply to a child day care provider required to be licensed pursuant to the social services law.

Misrepresentation by, or on behalf of, a caregiver for a child or children is a class A misdemeanor, provided, however, that if any sentence of imprisonment is imposed for a conviction under this section, term of imprisonment shall not exceed six months.

174

N.Y. Penal Law § 260.35

Added by New York Laws 2018, ch. 195,Sec. 2, eff. 10/15/2018.

Article 263 - SEXUAL PERFORMANCE BY A CHILD

Section 263.00 - Definitions

As used in this article the following definitions shall apply:

1. "Sexual performance" means any performance or part thereof which, for purposes of section 263.16 of this article, includes sexual conduct by a child less than sixteen years of age or, for purposes of section 263.05 or 263.15 of this article, includes sexual conduct by a child less than seventeen years of age.

2. "Obscene sexual performance" means any performance which, for purposes of section 263.11 of this article, includes sexual conduct by a child less than sixteen years of age or, for purposes of section 263.10 of this article, includes sexual conduct by a child less than seventeen years of age, in any material which is obscene, as such term is defined in section 235.00 of this chapter.

3. "Sexual conduct" means actual or simulated sexual intercourse, oral sexual conduct, anal sexual conduct, sexual bestiality, masturbation, sado-masochistic abuse, or lewd exhibition of the genitals.

4. "Performance" means any play, motion picture, photograph or dance. Performance also means any other visual representation exhibited before an audience.

5. "Promote" means to procure, manufacture, issue, sell, give, provide, lend, mail, deliver, transfer, transmute, publish, distribute, circulate, disseminate, present, exhibit or advertise, or to offer or agree to do the same.

6. "Simulated" means the explicit depiction of any of the conduct set forth in subdivision three of this section which creates the appearance of such conduct and which exhibits any uncovered portion of the breasts, genitals or buttocks.

7. "Oral sexual conduct" and "anal sexual conduct" mean the conduct defined by subdivision two of section 130.00 of this chapter.

8. "Sado-masochistic abuse" means the conduct defined in subdivision five of section 235.20 of this chapter.

9. For purposes of sections 263.10, 263.11, 263.15 and 263.16 of this article, the terms "possession," "control" and "promotion" shall not include conduct by an attorney when the performance was provided to such attorney in relation to the representation of a person under investigation or charged under this chapter or as a respondent pursuant to the family court act, and is limited in use for the purpose of representation for the period of such representation.

N.Y. Penal Law § 263.00

Section 263.05 - Use of a child in a sexual performance

A person is guilty of the use of a child in a sexual performance if knowing the character and content thereof he employs, authorizes or induces a child less than seventeen years of age to engage in a sexual performance or being a parent, legal guardian or custodian of such child, he consents to the participation by such child in a sexual performance.

N.Y. Penal Law § 263.05

Section 263.10 - Promoting an obscene sexual performance by a child

A person is guilty of promoting an obscene sexual performance by a child when, knowing the character and content thereof, he produces, directs or promotes any obscene performance which includes sexual conduct by a child less than seventeen years of age.

N.Y. Penal Law § 263.10

Section 263.11 - Possessing an obscene sexual performance by a child

A person is guilty of possessing an obscene sexual performance by a child when, knowing the character and content thereof, he knowingly has in his possession or control, or knowingly accesses with intent to view, any obscene performance which includes sexual conduct by a child less than sixteen years of age.

N.Y. Penal Law § 263.11

Section 263.15 - Promoting a sexual performance by a child

A person is guilty of promoting a sexual performance by a child when, knowing the character and content thereof, he produces, directs or promotes any performance which includes sexual conduct by a child less than seventeen years of age.

N.Y. Penal Law § 263.15

Section 263.16 - Possessing a sexual performance by a child

A person is guilty of possessing a sexual performance by a child when, knowing the character and content thereof, he knowingly has in his possession or control, or knowingly accesses with intent to view, any performance which includes sexual conduct by a child less than sixteen years of age.

N.Y. Penal Law § 263.16

Section 263.20 - Sexual performance by a child; affirmative defenses

1. Under this article, it shall be an affirmative defense that the defendant in good faith reasonably believed the person appearing in the performance was, for purposes of section 263.11 or 263.16 of this article, sixteen years of age or over or, for purposes of section 263.05, 263.10 or 263.15 of this article, seventeen years of age or over.

2. In any prosecution for any offense pursuant to this article, it is an affirmative defense that the person so charged was a librarian engaged in the normal course of his employment, a motion picture projectionist, stage employee or spotlight operator, cashier, doorman, usher, candy stand attendant, porter or in any other non-managerial or non-supervisory capacity in a motion picture theatre; provided he has no financial interest, other than his employment, which employment does not encompass compensation based upon any proportion of the gross receipts, in the promotion of a sexual performance for sale, rental or exhibition or in the promotion, presentation or direction of any sexual performance, or is in any way responsible for acquiring such material for sale, rental or exhibition.

N.Y. Penal Law § 263.20

Section 263.25 - Proof of age of child

Whenever it becomes necessary for the purposes of this article to determine whether a child who participated in a sexual performance was under an age specified in this article, the court or jury may make such determination by any of the following: personal inspection of the child; inspection of a photograph or motion picture which constituted the sexual performance; oral testimony by a witness to the sexual performance as to the age of the child based upon the child's appearance; expert medical testimony based upon the appearance of the child in the sexual performance; and any other method authorized by any applicable provision of law or by the rules of evidence at common law.

N.Y. Penal Law § 263.25

Section 263.30 - Facilitating a sexual performance by a child with a controlled substance or alcohol

1. A person is guilty of facilitating a sexual performance by a child with a controlled substance or alcohol when he or she:

(a)

(i) knowingly and unlawfully possesses a controlled substance as defined in section thirty-three hundred six of the public health law or any controlled substance that requires a prescription to obtain, (ii) administers that substance to a person under the age of seventeen without such person's consent, (iii) intends to commit against such person conduct constituting a felony as defined in section 263.05, 263.10, or 263.15 of this article, and (iv) does so commit or attempt to commit such conduct against such person; or

(b)

(i) administers alcohol to a person under the age of seventeen without such person's consent, (ii) intends to commit against such person conduct constituting a felony defined in section 263.05, 263.10, or 263.15 of this article, and (iii) does so commit or attempt to commit such conduct against such person.

2. For the purposes of this section, "controlled substance" means any substance or preparation, compound, mixture, salt, or isomer of any substance defined in section thirty-three hundred six of the public health law.

Facilitating a sexual performance by a child with a controlled substance or alcohol is a class B felony.

N.Y. Penal Law § 263.30

Title P - OFFENSES AGAINST PUBLIC SAFETY

Article 265 - FIREARMS AND OTHER DANGEROUS WEAPONS

Section 265.00 - Definitions

As used in this article and in article four hundred, the following terms shall mean and include:

1. "Machine-gun" means a weapon of any description, irrespective of size, by whatever name known, loaded or unloaded, from which a number of shots or bullets may be rapidly or automatically discharged from a magazine with one continuous pull of the trigger and includes a sub-machine gun.

2. "Firearm silencer" means any instrument, attachment, weapon or appliance for causing the firing of any gun, revolver, pistol or other firearms to be silent, or intended to lessen or muffle the noise of the firing of any gun, revolver, pistol or other firearms.

3. "Firearm" means (a) any pistol or revolver; or (b) a shotgun having one or more barrels less than eighteen inches in length; or (c) a rifle having one or more barrels less than sixteen inches in length; or (d) any weapon made from a shotgun or rifle whether by alteration, modification, or otherwise if such weapon as altered, modified, or otherwise has an overall length of less than twenty-six inches; or (e) an assault weapon. For the purpose of this subdivision the length of the barrel on a shotgun or rifle shall be determined by measuring the distance between the muzzle and the face of the bolt, breech, or breechlock when closed and when the shotgun or rifle is cocked; the overall length of a weapon made from a shotgun or rifle is the distance between the extreme ends of the weapon measured along a line parallel to the center line of the bore. Firearm does not include an antique firearm.

3-a. "Major component of a firearm, rifle or shotgun" means the barrel, the slide or cylinder, the frame, or receiver of the firearm, rifle, or shotgun.

4. "Switchblade knife" means any knife which has a blade which opens automatically by hand pressure applied to a button, spring or other device in the handle of the knife.

5. "Gravity knife" means any knife which has a blade which is released from the handle or sheath thereof by the force of gravity or the application of centrifugal force which, when released, is locked in place by means of a button, spring, lever or other device.

5-a. "Pilum ballistic knife" means any knife which has a blade which can be projected from the handle by hand pressure applied to a button, lever, spring or other device in the handle of the knife.

5-b. "Metal knuckle knife" means a weapon that, when closed, cannot function as a set of plastic knuckles or metal knuckles, nor as a knife and when open, can function as both a set of plastic knuckles or metal knuckles as well as a knife.

5-c. "Automatic knife" includes a stiletto, a switchblade knife, a cane sword, a pilum ballistic knife, and a metal knuckle knife.

5-d. "Undetectable knife" means any knife or other instrument, which does not utilize materials that are detectable by a metal detector or magnetometer when set at a standard calibration, that is capable of ready use as a stabbing or cutting weapon and was commercially manufactured to be used as a weapon.

6. "Dispose of" means to dispose of, give, give away, lease-loan, keep for sale, offer, offer for sale, sell, transfer and otherwise dispose of.

7. "Deface" means to remove, deface, cover, alter or destroy the manufacturer's serial number or any other distinguishing number or identification mark.

8. "Gunsmith" means any person, firm, partnership, corporation or company who engages in the business of repairing, altering, assembling, manufacturing, cleaning, polishing, engraving or trueing, or who performs any mechanical operation on, any firearm, large capacity ammunition feeding device or machine-gun.

9. "Dealer in firearms" means any person, firm, partnership, corporation or company who engages in the business of purchasing, selling, keeping for sale, loaning, leasing, or in any manner disposing of, any assault weapon, large capacity ammunition feeding device, pistol or revolver.

10. "Licensing officer" means in the city of New York the police commissioner of that city; in the county of Nassau the commissioner of police of that county; in the county of Suffolk the sheriff of that county except in the towns of Babylon, Brookhaven, Huntington, Islip and Smithtown, the commissioner of police of that county; for the purposes of section 400.01 of this chapter the superintendent of state police; and elsewhere in the state a judge or justice of a court of record having his office in the county of issuance.

11. "Rifle" means a weapon designed or redesigned, made or remade, and intended to be fired from the shoulder and designed or redesigned and made or remade to use the energy of the explosive in a fixed metallic cartridge to fire only a single projectile through a rifled bore for each single pull of the trigger.

12. "Shotgun" means a weapon designed or redesigned, made or remade, and intended to be fired from the shoulder and designed or redesigned and made or remade to use the energy of the explosive in a fixed shotgun shell to fire through a smooth bore either a number of ball shot or a single projectile for each single pull of the trigger.

13. "Cane Sword" means a cane or swagger stick having concealed within it a blade that may be used as a sword or stilletto.

14.[First of two versions] "Antique firearm" means:
Any unloaded muzzle loading pistol or revolver with a matchlock, flintlock, percussion cap, or similar type of ignition system, or a pistol or revolver which uses fixed cartridges which are no longer available in the ordinary channels of commercial trade.

14.[Second of two versions] "Chuka stick" means any device designed primarily as a weapon, consisting of two or more lengths of a rigid material joined together by a thong, rope or chain in such a manner as to allow free movement of a portion of the device while held in the hand and capable of being rotated in such a manner as to inflict serious injury upon a person by striking or choking. These devices are also known as nunchakus and centrifugal force sticks.

15. "Loaded firearm" means any firearm loaded with ammunition or any firearm which is possessed by one who, at the same time, possesses a quantity of ammunition which may be used to discharge such firearm.

15-a. "Electronic dart gun" means any device designed primarily as a weapon, the purpose of which is to momentarily stun, knock out or paralyze a person by passing an electrical shock to such person by means of a dart or projectile.

15-b. "Kung Fu star" means a disc-like object with sharpened points on the circumference thereof and is designed for use primarily as a weapon to be thrown.

15-c. "Electronic stun gun" means any device designed primarily as a weapon, the purpose of which is to stun, cause mental disorientation, knock out or paralyze a person by passing a high voltage electrical shock to such person.

16. "Certified not suitable to possess a self-defense spray device, a rifle or shotgun" means that the director or physician in charge of any hospital or institution for mental illness, public or private, has certified to the superintendent of state police or to any organized police department of a county, city, town or village of this state, that a person who has been judicially adjudicated incompetent, or who has been confined to such institution for mental illness pursuant to judicial authority, is not suitable to possess a self-defense spray device, as defined in section 265.20 of this article, or a rifle or shotgun.

17. "Serious offense" means

(a)

any of the following offenses defined in the current penal law and any offense in any jurisdiction or the former penal law that includes all of the essential elements of any of the following offenses: illegally using, carrying or possessing a pistol or other dangerous weapon; possession of burglar's tools; criminal possession of stolen property in the third degree; escape in the third degree; jostling; fraudulent accosting; endangering the welfare of a child; obscenity in the third degree; issuing abortional articles; permitting prostitution; promoting prostitution in the third degree; stalking in the fourth degree; stalking in the third degree; sexual misconduct; forcible touching; sexual abuse in the third degree; sexual abuse in the second degree; criminal possession of a controlled substance in the seventh degree; criminally possessing a hypodermic instrument; criminally using drug paraphernalia in the second degree; criminal possession of methamphetamine manufacturing material in the second degree; and a hate crime defined in article four hundred eighty-five of this chapter.

(b) any of the following offenses defined in the current penal law and any offense in any jurisdiction or in the former penal law that includes all of the essential elements of any of the following offenses, where the defendant and the person against whom the offense was committed were members of the same family or household as defined in subdivision one of section 530.11 of the criminal procedure law and as established pursuant to section 370.15 of the criminal procedure law: assault in the third degree; menacing in the third degree; menacing in the second degree; criminal obstruction of breathing or blood circulation; unlawful imprisonment in the second degree; coercion in the third degree; criminal tampering in the third degree; criminal contempt in the second degree; harassment in the first degree; aggravated harassment in the second degree; criminal trespass in the third degree; criminal trespass in the second degree; arson in the fifth degree; or attempt to commit any of the above-listed offenses.

(c) any misdemeanor offense in any jurisdiction or in the former penal law that includes all of the essential elements of a felony offense as defined in the current penal law.

18. "Armor piercing ammunition" means any ammunition capable of being used in pistols or revolvers containing a projectile or projectile core, or a projectile or projectile core for use in such ammunition, that is constructed entirely (excluding the presence of traces of other substances) from one or a combination of any of the following: tungsten alloys, steel, iron, brass, bronze, beryllium copper, or uranium.

19. "Duly authorized instructor" means (a) a duly commissioned officer of the United States army, navy, marine corps or coast guard, or of the national guard of the state of New York; or (b) a duly qualified adult citizen of the United States who has been granted a certificate as an instructor in small arms practice issued by the United States army, navy or marine corps, or by the adjutant general of this state, or by the national rifle association of America, a not-for-profit corporation duly organized under the laws of this state; (c) by a person duly qualified and designated by the department of environmental conservation under paragraph c of subdivision three of section 11-0713 of the environmental conservation law as its agent in the giving of instruction and the making of certifications of qualification in responsible hunting practices; or (d) a New York state 4-H certified shooting sports instructor.

20. "Disguised gun" means any weapon or device capable of being concealed on the person from which a shot can be discharged through the energy of an explosive and is designed and intended to appear to be something other than a gun.

21. "Semiautomatic" means any repeating rifle, shotgun or pistol, regardless of barrel or overall length, which utilizes a portion of the energy of a firing cartridge or shell to extract the fired cartridge case or spent shell and chamber the next round, and which requires a separate pull of the trigger to fire each cartridge or shell.

22."Assault weapon" means

(a) a semiautomatic rifle that has an ability to accept a detachable magazine and has at least one of the following characteristics:

(i)a folding or telescoping stock;

(ii)a pistol grip that protrudes conspicuously beneath the action of the weapon;

(iii)a thumbhole stock;

(iv)a second handgrip or a protruding grip that can be held by the non-trigger hand;

(v)a bayonet mount;

(vi)a flash suppressor, muzzle break, muzzle compensator, or threaded barrel designed to accommodate a flash suppressor, muzzle break, or muzzle compensator;

(vii)a grenade launcher; or

(b)a semiautomatic shotgun that has at least one of the following characteristics:

(i)a folding or telescoping stock;

(ii)a thumbhole stock;

(iii)a second handgrip or a protruding grip that can be held by the non-trigger hand;

(iv)a fixed magazine capacity in excess of seven rounds;

(v) an ability to accept a detachable magazine; or

(c)a semiautomatic pistol that has an ability to accept a detachable magazine and has at least one of the following characteristics:

(i)a folding or telescoping stock;

(ii)a thumbhole stock;

(iii)a second handgrip or a protruding grip that can be held by the non-trigger hand;

(iv)capacity to accept an ammunition magazine that attaches to the pistol outside of the pistol grip;

(v)a threaded barrel capable of accepting a barrel extender, flash suppressor, forward handgrip, or silencer;

(vi)a shroud that is attached to, or partially or completely encircles, the barrel and that permits the shooter to hold the firearm with the non-trigger hand without being burned;

(vii)a manufactured weight of fifty ounces or more when the pistol is unloaded; or

(viii)a semiautomatic version of an automatic rifle, shotgun or firearm;

(d)a revolving cylinder shotgun;

(e)a semiautomatic rifle, a semiautomatic shotgun or a semiautomatic pistol or weapon defined in subparagraph (v) of paragraph (e) of subdivision twenty-two of section of this chapter as added by chapter one hundred eighty-nine of the laws of two thousand and otherwise lawfully possessed pursuant to such chapter of the laws of two thousand prior to September fourteenth, nineteen hundred ninety-four;

(f)a semiautomatic rifle, a semiautomatic shotgun or a semiautomatic pistol or weapon defined in paragraph (a), (b) or (c) of this subdivision, possessed prior to the date of enactment of the chapter of the laws of two thousand thirteen which added this paragraph;

(g)provided, however, that such term does not include:

(i)any rifle, shotgun or pistol that (A) is manually operated by bolt, pump, lever or slide action; (B) has been rendered permanently inoperable; or (C) is an antique firearm as defined in 18 U.S.C. 921(a)(16);

(ii)a semiautomatic rifle that cannot accept a detachable magazine that holds more than five rounds of ammunition;

(iii)a semiautomatic shotgun that cannot hold more than five rounds of ammunition in a fixed or detachable magazine; or

(iv)a rifle, shotgun or pistol, or a replica or a duplicate thereof, specified in Appendix A to 18 U.S.C. 922 as such weapon was manufactured on October first, nineteen hundred ninety-three. The mere fact that a weapon is not listed in Appendix A shall not be construed to mean that such weapon is an assault weapon;

178

(v)any weapon validly registered pursuant to subdivision sixteen-a of section 400.00 of this chapter. Such weapons shall be subject to the provisions of paragraph (h) of this subdivision;

(vi)any firearm, rifle, or shotgun that was manufactured at least fifty years prior to the current date, but not including replicas thereof that is validly registered pursuant to subdivision sixteen-a of section 400.00 of this chapter;

(h)Any weapon defined in paragraph (e) or (f) of this subdivision and any large capacity ammunition feeding device that was legally possessed by an individual prior to the enactment of the chapter of the laws of two thousand thirteen which added this paragraph, may only be sold to, exchanged with or disposed of to a purchaser authorized to possess such weapons or to an individual or entity outside of the state provided that any such transfer to an individual or entity outside of the state must be reported to the entity wherein the weapon is registered within seventy-two hours of such transfer. An individual who transfers any such weapon or large capacity ammunition device to an individual inside New York state or without complying with the provisions of this paragraph shall be guilty of a class A misdemeanor unless such large capacity ammunition feeding device, the possession of which is made illegal by the chapter of the laws of two thousand thirteen which added this paragraph, is transferred within one year of the effective date of the chapter of the laws of two thousand thirteen which added this paragraph.

23."Large capacity ammunition feeding device" means a magazine, belt, drum, feed strip, or similar device,] that (a) has a capacity of, or that can be readily restored or converted to accept, more than ten rounds of ammunition, or (b) contains more than seven rounds of ammunition, or (c) is obtained after the effective date of the chapter of the laws of two thousand thirteen which amended this subdivision and has a capacity of, or that can be readily restored or converted to accept, more than seven rounds of ammunition; provided, however, that such term does not include an attached tubular device designed to accept, and capable of operating only with, .22 caliber rimfire ammunition or a feeding device that is a curio or relic. A feeding device that is a curio or relic is defined as a device that (i) was manufactured at least fifty years prior to the current date, (ii) is only capable of being used exclusively in a firearm, rifle, or shotgun that was manufactured at least fifty years prior to the current date, but not including replicas thereof, (iii) is possessed by an individual who is not prohibited by state or federal law from possessing a firearm and (iv) is registered with the division of state police pursuant to subdivision sixteen-a of section 400.00 of this chapter, except such feeding devices transferred into the state may be registered at any time, provided they are registered within thirty days of their transfer into the state. Notwithstanding paragraph (h) of subdivision twenty-two of this section, such feeding devices may be transferred provided that such transfer shall be subject to the provisions of section 400.03 of this chapter including the check required to be conducted pursuant to such section

24."Seller of ammunition" means any person, firm, partnership, corporation or company who engages in the business of purchasing, selling or keeping ammunition.

25. "Qualified retired New York or federal law enforcement officer" means an individual who is a retired police officer as police officer is defined in subdivision thirty-four of section 1.20 of the criminal procedure law, a retired peace officer as peace officer is defined in section 2.10 of the criminal procedure law or a retired federal law enforcement officer as federal law enforcement officer is defined in section 2.15 of the criminal procedure law, who:

(a) separated from service in good standing from a public agency located in New York state in which such person served as either a police officer, peace officer or federal law enforcement officer; and

(b) before such separation, was authorized by law to engage in or supervise the prevention, detection, investigation, or prosecution of, or the incarceration of any person for, any violation of law, and had statutory powers of arrest, pursuant to their official duties, under the criminal procedure law; and

(c) (i) before such separation, served as either a police officer, peace officer or federal law enforcement officer for five years or more and at the time of separation, is such an officer; or (ii) separated from service with such agency, after completing any applicable probationary period of such service, due to a service-connected disability, as determined by such agency at or before the time of separation; and

(d) (i) has not been found by a qualified medical professional employed by such agency to be unqualified for reasons relating to mental health; or (ii) has not entered into an agreement with such agency from which the individual is separating from service in which that individual acknowledges he or she is not qualified for reasons relating to mental health; and

(e) is not otherwise prohibited by New York or federal law from possessing any firearm.

26. "Rapid-fire modification device" means any bump stock, trigger crank, binary trigger system, burst trigger system, or any other device that is designed to accelerate the rate of fire of a semi-automatic firearm, rifle or shotgun.

27. "Bump stock" means any device or instrument that increases the rate of fire achievable with a semi-automatic firearm, rifle or shotgun by using energy from the recoil of the weapon to generate a reciprocating action that facilitates repeated activation of the trigger.

28. "Trigger crank" means any device or instrument that repeatedly activates the trigger of a semi-automatic firearm, rifle or shotgun through the use of a lever or other part that is turned in a circular motion and thereby accelerates the rate of fire of such firearm, rifle or shotgun, provided, however, that "trigger crank" shall not include any weapon initially designed and manufactured to fire through the use of a crank or lever.

29. "Binary trigger system" means any device that, when installed in or attached to a semi-automatic firearm rifle, or shotgun causes that weapon to fire once when the trigger is pulled and again when the trigger is released.

30. "Burst trigger system" means any device that, when installed in or attached to a semi-automatic firearm, rifle, or shot gun, allows that weapon to discharge two or more shots with a single pull or the trigger by altering the trigger reset.

31. "New York state 4-H certified shooting instructor" means a certified shooting sports instructor of the National 4-H Shooting Sports, a non-profit organization, engaged in shooting education and youth development programming that is administered by the National Institute of Food and Agriculture of the United States department of agriculture.

179

N.Y. Penal Law § 265.00
Amended by New York Laws 2020, ch. 150,Sec. 3, eff. 8/24/2020.
Amended by New York Laws 2020, ch. 150,Sec. 1, eff. 8/24/2020.
Amended by New York Laws 2020, ch. 55,Sec. N-1, eff. 4/3/2021.
Amended by New York Laws 2019, ch. 146,Sec. 1, eff. 11/1/2019.
Amended by New York Laws 2019, ch. 134,Sec. 1, eff. 1/26/2020.
Amended by New York Laws 2019, ch. 130,Sec. 1, eff. 7/29/2019.
Amended by New York Laws 2019, ch. 34,Sec. 3, eff. 5/30/2019.
Amended by New York Laws 2018, ch. 60,Sec. 1, eff. 6/11/2018.
Amended by New York Laws 2013, ch. 98,Sec. 1, eff. 7/5/2013.
Amended by New York Laws 2013, ch. 1,Sec. 39, eff. 3/16/2013.
Amended by New York Laws 2013, ch. 1,Sec. 38, eff. 4/15/2013.
Amended by New York Laws 2013, ch. 1,Sec. 37, eff. 1/15/2013.
See New York Laws 2020, ch. 55, Sec. N-4.

Section 265.01 - Criminal possession of a weapon in the fourth degree

A person is guilty of criminal possession of a weapon in the fourth degree when:
(1) He or she possesses any firearm, electronic dart gun, electronic stun gun, switchblade knife, pilum ballistic knife, metal knuckle knife, cane sword, billy, blackjack, bludgeon, plastic knuckles, metal knuckles, chuka stick, sand bag, sandclub, wrist-brace type slingshot or slungshot, shirken, or "Kung Fu star";
(2) He or she possesses any dagger, dangerous knife, dirk, machete, razor, stiletto, imitation pistol, undetectable knife or any other dangerous or deadly instrument or weapon with intent to use the same unlawfully against another; or
(3) ; or
(4) He possesses a rifle, shotgun, antique firearm, black powder rifle, black powder shotgun, or any muzzle-loading firearm, and has been convicted of a felony or serious offense; or
(5) He possesses any dangerous or deadly weapon and is not a citizen of the United States; or
(6) He is a person who has been certified not suitable to possess a rifle or shotgun, as defined in subdivision sixteen of section 265.00, and refuses to yield possession of such rifle or shotgun upon the demand of a police officer. Whenever a person is certified not suitable to possess a rifle or shotgun, a member of the police department to which such certification is made, or of the state police, shall forthwith seize any rifle or shotgun possessed by such person. A rifle or shotgun seized as herein provided shall not be destroyed, but shall be delivered to the headquarters of such police department, or state police, and there retained until the aforesaid certificate has been rescinded by the director or physician in charge, or other disposition of such rifle or shotgun has been ordered or authorized by a court of competent jurisdiction.
(7) He knowingly possesses a bullet containing an explosive substance designed to detonate upon impact.
(8) He possesses any armor piercing ammunition with intent to use the same unlawfully against another. Criminal possession of a weapon in the fourth degree is a class A misdemeanor.
N.Y. Penal Law § 265.01
Amended by New York Laws 2019, ch. 146,Sec. 2, eff. 11/1/2019.
Amended by New York Laws 2019, ch. 34,Sec. 1, eff. 5/30/2019.
Amended by New York Laws 2016, ch. 269,Sec. 1, eff. 8/19/2016.
Amended by New York Laws 2013, ch. 1,Sec. 40, eff. 3/16/2013.

Section 265.01-A - Criminal possession of a weapon on school grounds

A person is guilty of criminal possession of a weapon on school grounds when he or she knowingly has in his or her possession a rifle, shotgun, or firearm in or upon a building or grounds, used for educational purposes, of any school, college, or university, except the forestry lands, wherever located, owned , maintained or held in trust for the benefit of the New York State College of Forestry at Syracuse University, now known as the State University of New York college of environmental science and forestry, or upon a school bus as defined in section one hundred forty-two of the vehicle and traffic law, without the written authorization of such educational institution; provided, however no school, as defined in subdivision ten of section eleven hundred twenty-five of the education law, shall issue such written authorization to any teacher, school administrator, or other person employed at the school who is not primarily employed as a school resource officer, police officer, peace officer, or security guard who has been issued a special armed guard registration card as defined in section eighty-nine-f of the general business law, regardless of whether the person is employed directly by such school or by a third party.
N.Y. Penal Law § 265.01-A
Amended by New York Laws 2019, ch. 354,Sec. 1, eff. 11/3/2019.
Amended by New York Laws 2019, ch. 138,Sec. 1, eff. 6/5/2019.
Added by New York Laws 2013, ch. 1,Sec. 41, eff. 3/16/2013.

Section 265.01-B - Criminal possession of a firearm

A person is guilty of criminal possession of a firearm when he or she: (1) possesses any firearm or; (2) lawfully possesses a firearm prior to the effective date of the chapter of the laws of two thousand thirteen which added this section subject to the registration requirements of subdivision sixteen-a of section 400.00 of this chapter and knowingly fails to register such firearm pursuant to such subdivision.
N.Y. Penal Law § 265.01-B
Added by New York Laws 2013, ch. 1,Sec. 41-a, eff. 3/16/2013.

Section 265.01-C - Criminal possession of a rapid-fire modification device

A person is guilty of criminal possession of a rapid-fire modification device when he or she knowingly possesses any rapid-fire modification device.

N.Y. Penal Law § 265.01-C

Added by New York Laws 2019, ch. 130,Sec. 2, eff. 11/26/2019.

Section 265.02 - Criminal possession of a weapon in the third degree

A person is guilty of criminal possession of a weapon in the third degree when:

(1) Such person commits the crime of criminal possession of a weapon in the fourth degree as defined in subdivision one, two, three or five of section 265.01, and has been previously convicted of any crime; or

(2) Such person possesses any explosive or incendiary bomb, bombshell, firearm silencer, machine-gun or any other firearm or weapon simulating a machine-gun and which is adaptable for such use; or

(3) Such person knowingly possesses a machine-gun, firearm, rifle or shotgun which has been defaced for the purpose of concealment or prevention of the detection of a crime or misrepresenting the identity of such machine-gun, firearm, rifle or shotgun; or

(5) (i) Such person possesses three or more firearms; or (ii) such person possesses a firearm and has been previously convicted of a felony or a class A misdemeanor defined in this chapter within the five years immediately preceding the commission of the offense and such possession did not take place in the person's home or place of business; or

(6) Such person knowingly possesses any disguised gun; or

(7) Such person possesses an assault weapon; or

(8) Such person possesses a large capacity ammunition feeding device. For purposes of this subdivision, a large capacity ammunition feeding device shall not include an ammunition feeding device lawfully possessed by such person before the effective date of the chapter of the laws of two thousand thirteen which amended this subdivision, that has a capacity of, or that can be readily restored or converted to accept more than seven but less than eleven rounds of ammunition, or that was manufactured before September thirteenth, nineteen hundred ninety-four, that has a capacity of, or that can be readily restored or converted to accept, more than ten rounds of ammunition; or

(9) Such person possesses an unloaded firearm and also commits a drug trafficking felony as defined in subdivision twenty-one of section 10.00 of this chapter as part of the same criminal transaction; or

(10) Such person possesses an unloaded firearm and also commits any violent felony offense as defined in subdivision one of section 70.02 of this chapter as part of the same criminal transaction.

Criminal possession of a weapon in the third degree is a class D felony.

N.Y. Penal Law § 265.02

Amended by New York Laws 2013, ch. 1,Sec. 41-b, eff. 3/16/2013.

Section 265.03 - Criminal possession of a weapon in the second degree

A person is guilty of criminal possession of a weapon in the second degree when:

(1) with intent to use the same unlawfully against another, such person:

(a) possesses a machine-gun; or

(b) possesses a loaded firearm; or

(c) possesses a disguised gun; or

(2) such person possesses five or more firearms; or

(3) such person possesses any loaded firearm. Such possession shall not, except as provided in subdivision one or seven of section 265.02 of this article, constitute a violation of this subdivision if such possession takes place in such person's home or place of business.

Criminal possession of a weapon in the second degree is a class C felony.

N.Y. Penal Law § 265.03

Section 265.04 - Criminal possession of a weapon in the first degree

A person is guilty of criminal possession of a weapon in the first degree when such person:

(1) possesses any explosive substance with intent to use the same unlawfully against the person or property of another; or

(2) possesses ten or more firearms.

Criminal possession of a weapon in the first degree is a class B felony.

N.Y. Penal Law § 265.04

Section 265.05 - Unlawful possession of weapons by persons under sixteen

It shall be unlawful for any person under the age of sixteen to possess any air-gun, spring-gun or other instrument or weapon in which the propelling force is a spring or air, or any gun or any instrument or weapon in or upon which any loaded or blank cartridges may be used, or any loaded or blank cartridges or ammunition therefor, or any dangerous knife; provided that the possession of rifle or shotgun or ammunition therefor by the holder of a hunting license or permit issued pursuant to article eleven of the environmental conservation law and used in accordance with said law shall not be governed by this section.

N.Y. Penal Law § 265.05

Section 265.06 - Unlawful possession of a weapon upon school grounds

It shall be unlawful for any person age sixteen or older to knowingly possess any air-gun, spring-gun or other instrument or weapon in which the propelling force is a spring, air, piston or CO_2 cartridge in or upon a building or grounds, used for educational purposes, of any school, college or university, without the written authorization of such educational institution.

N.Y. Penal Law § 265.06

Section 265.08 - Criminal use of a firearm in the second degree

A person is guilty of criminal use of a firearm in the second degree when he commits any class C violent felony offense as defined in paragraph (b) of subdivision one of section 70.02 and he either:

(1) possesses a deadly weapon, if the weapon is a loaded weapon from which a shot, readily capable of producing death or other serious injury may be discharged; or

(2) displays what appears to be a pistol, revolver, rifle, shotgun, machine gun or other firearm.

Criminal use of a firearm in the second degree is a class C felony.

N.Y. Penal Law § 265.08

Section 265.09 - Criminal use of a firearm in the first degree

(1) A person is guilty of criminal use of a firearm in the first degree when he commits any class B violent felony offense as defined in paragraph (a) of subdivision one of section 70.02 and he either:

(a) possesses a deadly weapon, if the weapon is a loaded weapon from which a shot, readily capable of producing death or other serious injury may be discharged; or

(b) displays what appears to be a pistol, revolver, rifle, shotgun, machine gun or other firearm.

Criminal use of a firearm in the first degree is a class B felony.

(2)Sentencing. Notwithstanding any other provision of law to the contrary, when a person is convicted of criminal use of a firearm in the first degree as defined in subdivision one of this section, the court shall impose an additional consecutive sentence of five years to the sentence imposed on the underlying class B violent felony offense where the person convicted of such crime displays a loaded weapon from which a shot, readily capable of producing death or other serious injury may be discharged, in furtherance of the commission of such crime, provided, however, that such additional sentence shall not be imposed if the court, having regard to the nature and circumstances of the crime and to the history and character of the defendant, finds on the record that such additional consecutive sentence would be unduly harsh and that not imposing such sentence would be consistent with the public safety and would not deprecate the seriousness of the crime. Notwithstanding any other provision of law to the contrary, the aggregate of the five year consecutive term imposed pursuant to this subdivision and the minimum term of the indeterminate sentence imposed on the underlying class B violent felony shall constitute the new aggregate minimum term of imprisonment, and a person subject to such term shall be required to serve the entire aggregate minimum term and shall not be eligible for release on parole or conditional release during such term. This subdivision shall not apply where the defendant's criminal liability for displaying a loaded weapon from which a shot, readily capable of producing death or other serious injury may be discharged, in furtherance of the commission of crime is based on the conduct of another pursuant to section 20.00 of this chapter.

N.Y. Penal Law § 265.09

Amended by New York Laws 2013, ch. 1,Sec. 42, eff. 3/16/2013.

Section 265.10 - Manufacture, transport, disposition and defacement of weapons and dangerous instruments and appliances

1. Any person who manufactures or causes to be manufactured any machine-gun, assault weapon, large capacity ammunition feeding device or disguised gun is guilty of a class D felony. Any person who manufactures or causes to be manufactured any rapid-fire modification device is guilty of a class E felony.Any person who manufactures or causes to be manufactured any switchblade knife, gravity knife, pilum ballistic knife, metal knuckle knife, undetectable knife, billy, blackjack, bludgeon, plastic knuckles, metal knuckles, Kung Fu star, chuka stick, sandbag, sandclub or slungshot is guilty of a class A misdemeanor.

2. Any person who transports or ships any machine-gun, firearm silencer, assault weapon or large capacity ammunition feeding device or disguised gun, or who transports or ships as merchandise five or more firearms, is guilty of a class D felony. Any person who transports or ships any rapid-fire modification device is guilty of a class E felony.Any person who transports or ships as merchandise any firearm, other than an assault weapon, switchblade knife, gravity knife, pilum ballistic knife, undetectable knife, billy, blackjack, bludgeon, plastic knuckles, metal knuckles, Kung Fu star, chuka stick, sandbag or slungshot is guilty of a class A misdemeanor.

3. Any person who disposes of any machine-gun, assault weapon, large capacity ammunition feeding device or firearm silencer is guilty of a class D felony. Any person who disposes of any rapid-fire modification device is guilty of a class E felony. Any person who knowingly buys, receives, disposes of, or conceals a machine-gun, firearm, large capacity ammunition feeding device, rifle or shotgun which has been defaced for the purpose of concealment or prevention of the detection of a crime or misrepresenting the identity of such machine-gun, firearm, large capacity ammunition feeding device, rifle or shotgun is guilty of a class D felony.

4. Any person who disposes of any of the weapons, instruments or appliances specified in subdivision one of section 265.01, except a firearm, is guilty of a class A misdemeanor, and he is guilty of a class D felony if he has previously been convicted of any crime.

5. Any person who disposes of any of the weapons, instruments, appliances or substances specified in section 265.05 to any other person under the age of sixteen years is guilty of a class A misdemeanor.

6. Any person who wilfully defaces any machine-gun, large capacity ammunition feeding device or firearm is guilty of a class D felony.

7. Any person, other than a wholesale dealer, or gunsmith or dealer in firearms duly licensed pursuant to section 400.00, lawfully in possession of a firearm, who disposes of the same without first notifying in writing the licensing officer in the city of New York and counties of Nassau and Suffolk and elsewhere in the state the executive department, division of state police, Albany, is guilty of a class A misdemeanor.

N.Y. Penal Law § 265.10

Amended by New York Laws 2019, ch. 146,Sec. 3, eff. 11/1/2019.

Amended by New York Laws 2019, ch. 130,Sec. 3, eff. 7/29/2019.

Amended by New York Laws 2019, ch. 34,Sec. 4, eff. 5/30/2019.

Section 265.11 - Criminal sale of a firearm in the third degree

A person is guilty of criminal sale of a firearm in the third degree when such person is not authorized pursuant to law to possess a firearm and such person unlawfully either:

(1) sells, exchanges, gives or disposes of a firearm or large capacity ammunition feeding device to another person; or

(2) possesses a firearm with the intent to sell it.

Criminal sale of a firearm in the third degree is a class D felony.

N.Y. Penal Law § 265.11

Section 265.12 - Criminal sale of a firearm in the second degree

A person is guilty of criminal sale of a firearm in the second degree when such person:

(1) unlawfully sells, exchanges, gives or disposes of to another five or more firearms; or

(2) unlawfully sells, exchanges, gives or disposes of to another person or persons a total of five or more firearms in a period of not more than one year.

Criminal sale of a firearm in the second degree is a class C felony.

N.Y. Penal Law § 265.12

Section 265.13 - Criminal sale of a firearm in the first degree

A person is guilty of criminal sale of a firearm in the first degree when such person:

(1) unlawfully sells, exchanges, gives or disposes of to another ten or more firearms; or

(2) unlawfully sells, exchanges, gives or disposes of to another person or persons a total of ten or more firearms in a period of not more than one year.

Criminal sale of a firearm in the first degree is a class B felony.

N.Y. Penal Law § 265.13

Section 265.14 - Criminal sale of a firearm with the aid of a minor

A person over the age of eighteen years of age is guilty of criminal sale of a weapon with the aid of a minor when a person under sixteen years of age knowingly and unlawfully sells, exchanges, gives or disposes of a firearm in violation of this article, and such person over the age of eighteen years of age, acting with the mental culpability required for the commission thereof, solicits, requests, commands, importunes or intentionally aids such person under sixteen years of age to engage in such conduct.

N.Y. Penal Law § 265.14

Section 265.15 - Presumptions of possession, unlawful intent and defacement

1. The presence in any room, dwelling, structure or vehicle of any machine-gun is presumptive evidence of its unlawful possession by all persons occupying the place where such machine-gun is found.

2. The presence in any stolen vehicle of any weapon, instrument, appliance or substance specified in sections 265.01, 265.02, 265.03, 265.04 and 265.05 is presumptive evidence of its possession by all persons occupying such vehicle at the time such weapon, instrument, appliance or substance is found.

3. The presence in an automobile, other than a stolen one or a public omnibus, of any firearm, large capacity ammunition feeding device, defaced firearm, defaced rifle or shotgun, defaced large capacity ammunition feeding device, firearm silencer, explosive or incendiary bomb, bombshell, switchblade knife, pilum ballistic knife, metal knuckle knife, dagger, dirk, stiletto, billy, blackjack, plastic knuckles, metal knuckles, chuka stick, sandbag, sandclub or slungshot is presumptive evidence of its possession by all persons occupying such automobile at the time such weapon, instrument or appliance is found, except under the following circumstances:

(a) if such weapon, instrument or appliance is found upon the person of one of the occupants therein;

(b) if such weapon, instrument or appliance is found in an automobile which is being operated for hire by a duly licensed driver in the due, lawful and proper pursuit of his or her trade, then such presumption shall not apply to the driver; or

(c) if the weapon so found is a pistol or revolver and one of the occupants, not present under duress, has in his or her possession a valid license to have and carry concealed the same.

4. The possession by any person of the substance as specified in section 265.04 is presumptive evidence of possessing such substance with intent to use the same unlawfully against the person or property of another if such person is not licensed or otherwise authorized to possess such substance. The possession by any person of any dagger, dirk, stiletto, dangerous knife or any other weapon, instrument, appliance or substance designed, made or adapted for use primarily as a weapon, is presumptive evidence of intent to use the same unlawfully against another.

5. The possession by any person of a defaced machine-gun, firearm, rifle or shotgun is presumptive evidence that such person defaced the same.

6. The possession of five or more firearms by any person is presumptive evidence that such person possessed the firearms with the intent to sell same.

N.Y. Penal Law § 265.15

Amended by New York Laws 2019, ch. 34,Sec. 5, eff. 5/30/2019.

Section 265.16 - Criminal sale of a firearm to a minor

A person is guilty of criminal sale of a firearm to a minor when he is not authorized pursuant to law to possess a firearm and he unlawfully sells, exchanges, gives or disposes of a firearm to another person who is or reasonably appears to be less than nineteen years of age who is not licensed pursuant to law to possess a firearm.

N.Y. Penal Law § 265.16

Section 265.17 - Criminal purchase or disposal of a weapon

A person is guilty of criminal purchase or disposal of a weapon when:

1. Knowing that he or she is prohibited by law from possessing a firearm, rifle or shotgun because of a prior conviction or because of some other disability which would render him or her ineligible to lawfully possess a firearm, rifle or shotgun in this state, or knowing that he or she is the subject of an outstanding warrant of arrest issued upon the alleged commission of a felony or serious offense, such person purchases or otherwise acquires a firearm, rifle or shotgun from another person; or

2. Knowing that it would be unlawful for another person to possess a firearm, rifle or shotgun, or knowing that another person is the subject of an outstanding warrant of arrest issued upon the alleged commission of a felony or serious offense, he or she purchases or otherwise acquires a firearm, rifle or shotgun for, on behalf of, or for the use of such other person; or

3. Knowing that another person is prohibited by law from possessing a firearm, rifle or shotgun because of a prior conviction or because of some other disability which would render him or her ineligible to lawfully possess a firearm, rifle or shotgun in this state, or knowing that another person is the subject of an outstanding warrant of arrest issued upon the alleged commission of a felony or serious offense, a person disposes of a firearm, rifle or shotgun to such other person.

Criminal purchase or disposal of a weapon is a class D felony.

N.Y. Penal Law § 265.17

Amended by New York Laws 2021, ch. 236,Sec. 1, eff. 7/1/2021.

Amended by New York Laws 2013, ch. 1,Sec. 43, eff. 3/16/2013.

Section 265.19 - Aggravated criminal possession of a weapon

A person is guilty of aggravated criminal possession of a weapon when he or she commits the crime of criminal possession of a weapon in the second degree as defined in subdivision three of section 03 of this article and also commits any violent felony offense as defined in subdivision one of section 70.02 of this chapter or a drug trafficking felony as defined in subdivision twenty-one of section 10.00 of this chapter arising out of the same criminal transaction Aggravated criminal possession of a weapon is a class C felony

N.Y. Penal Law § 265.19

Added by New York Laws 2013, ch. 1,Sec. 45, eff. 3/16/2013.

Section 265.20 - Exemptions

a.Paragraph (h) of subdivision twenty-two of section 265.00 and sections 265.01, 265.01-a 265.01-b, 265.01-c,265.02, 265.03, 265.04, 265.05, 265.10, 265.11, 265.12, 265.13, 265.15, 265.36, 265.37, 265.50, 265.55 and 270.05 shall not apply to:

1. Possession of any of the weapons, instruments, appliances or substances specified in sections 265.01, 265.01-c,265.02, 265.03, 265.04, 265.05 , 265.50, 265.55 and 270.05 by the following:

(a) Persons in the military service of the state of New York when duly authorized by regulations issued by the adjutant general to possess the same.

(b) Police officers as defined in subdivision thirty-four of section 1.20 of the criminal procedure law.

(c) Peace officers as defined by section 2.10 of the criminal procedure law.

(d) Persons in the military or other service of the United States, in pursuit of official duty or when duly authorized by federal law, regulation or order to possess the same.

(e) Persons employed in fulfilling defense contracts with the government of the United States or agencies thereof when possession of the same is necessary for manufacture, transport, installation and testing under the requirements of such contract.

(f) A person voluntarily surrendering such weapon, instrument, appliance or substance, provided that such surrender shall be made to the superintendent of the division of state police or a member thereof designated by such superintendent, or to the sheriff of the county in which such person resides, or in the county of Nassau or in the towns of Babylon, Brookhaven, Huntington, Islip and Smithtown in the county of Suffolk to the commissioner of police or a member of the police department thereof designated by such commissioner, or if such person resides in a city, town other than one named in this subparagraph, or village to the police commissioner or head of the police force or department thereof or to a member of the force or department designated by such commissioner or head; and provided, further, that the same shall be surrendered by such person in accordance with such terms and conditions as may be established by such superintendent, sheriff, police force or department. Nothing in this paragraph shall be construed as granting immunity from prosecution for any crime or offense except that of unlawful possession of such weapons, instruments, appliances or substances surrendered as herein provided. A person who possesses any such weapon, instrument, appliance or substance as an executor or administrator or any other lawful possessor of such property of a decedent may continue to possess such property for a period not over fifteen days. If such property is not lawfully disposed of within such period the possessor shall deliver it to an appropriate official described in this paragraph or such property may be delivered to the superintendent of state police. Such officer shall hold it and shall thereafter deliver it on the written request of such executor, administrator or other lawful possessor of such property to a named person, provided such named person is licensed to or is otherwise lawfully permitted to possess the same. If no request to deliver the property is received by such official within one year of the delivery of such property, such official shall dispose of it in accordance with the provisions of section 400.05 of this chapter.

2. Possession of a machine-gun, large capacity ammunition feeding device, rapid-fire modification device, firearm, switchblade knife, gravity knife, pilum ballistic knife, billy or blackjack by a warden, superintendent, headkeeper or deputy of a state prison, penitentiary, workhouse, county jail or other institution for the detention of persons convicted or accused of crime or detained as witnesses in criminal cases, in pursuit of official duty or when duly authorized by regulation or order to possess the same.

3.Possession of a pistol or revolver by a person to whom a license therefor has been issued as provided under section 400.00 or 400.01 of this chapter or possession of a weapon as defined in paragraph (e) or (f) of subdivision twenty-two of section 265.00 of this article which is registered pursuant to paragraph (a) of subdivision sixteen-a of section 400.00 of this chapter or is included on an amended license issued pursuant to section 400.00 of this chapter. In the event such license is revoked, other than because such licensee is no longer permitted to possess a firearm, rifle or shotgun under federal or state law, information sufficient to satisfy the requirements of subdivision sixteen-a of section 400.00 of this chapter, shall be transmitted by the licensing officer to the state police, in a form as determined by the superintendent of state police. Such transmission shall constitute a valid registration under such section. Further provided, notwithstanding any other section of this title, a failure to register such weapon by an individual who possesses such weapon before the enactment of the chapter of the laws of two thousand thirteen which amended this paragraph and may so lawfully possess it thereafter upon registration, shall only be subject to punishment pursuant to paragraph (c) of subdivision sixteen-a of section 400.00 of this chapter; provided, that such a license or registration shall not preclude a conviction for the offense defined in subdivision three of section 265.01 of this article or section 265.01-a of this article.

4. Possession of a rifle, shotgun, crossbow or longbow for use while hunting, trapping or fishing, by a person, not a citizen of the United States, carrying a valid license issued pursuant to section 11-0713 of the environmental conservation law.

5. Possession of a rifle or shotgun by a person other than a person who has been convicted of a class A-I felony or a violent felony offense, as defined in subdivision one of section 70.02 of this chapter, who has been convicted as specified in subdivision four of section 265.01 to whom a certificate of good conduct has been issued pursuant to section seven hundred three-b of the correction law.

6. Possession of a switchblade for use while hunting, trapping or fishing by a person carrying a valid license issued to him pursuant to section 11-0713 of the environmental conservation law.

7. Possession, at an indoor or outdoor shooting range for the purpose of loading and firing, of a rifle or shotgun, the propelling force of which is gunpowder by a person under sixteen years of age but not under twelve, under the immediate supervision, guidance and instruction of (a) a duly commissioned officer of the United States army, navy, air force, marine corps or coast guard, or of the national guard of the state of New York; or (b) a duly qualified adult citizen of the United States who has been granted a certificate as an instructor in small arms practice issued by the United States army, navy, air force or marine corps, or by the adjutant general of this state, by the national rifle association of America, a not-for-profit corporation duly organized under the laws of this state, or by a New York state 4-H certified shooting sports instructor; or (c) a parent, guardian, or a person over the age of eighteen designated in writing by such parent or guardian who shall have a certificate of qualification in responsible hunting, including safety, ethics, and landowner relations-hunter relations, issued or honored by the department of environmental conservation; or (d) an agent of the department of environmental conservation appointed to conduct courses in responsible hunting practices pursuant to article eleven of the environmental conservation law.

7-a. Possession and use, at an indoor or outdoor pistol range located in or on premises owned or occupied by a duly incorporated organization organized for conservation purposes or to foster proficiency in small arms or at a target pistol shooting competition under the auspices of or approved by the national rifle association for the purpose of loading and firing the same, by a person duly licensed to possess a pistol or revolver pursuant to section 400.00 or 400.01 of this chapter of a pistol or revolver duly so licensed to another person who is present at the time.

7-b. Possession and use, at an indoor or outdoor pistol range located in or on premises owned or occupied by a duly incorporated organization organized for conservation purposes or to foster proficiency in small arms or at a target pistol shooting competition under the auspices of or approved by the national rifle association for the purpose of loading and firing the same, by a person who has applied for a license to possess a pistol or revolver and pre-license possession of same pursuant to section 400.00 or 400.01 of this chapter, who has not been previously denied a license, been previously convicted of a felony or serious offense, and who does not appear to be, or pose a threat to be, a danger to himself or to others, and who has been approved for possession and use herein in accordance with section 400.00 or 400.01 of this chapter; provided however, that such possession shall be of a pistol or revolver duly licensed to and shall be used under the supervision, guidance and instruction of, a person specified in paragraph seven of this subdivision and provided further that such possession and use be within the jurisdiction of the licensing officer with whom the person has made application therefor or within the jurisdiction of the superintendent of state police in the case of a retired sworn member of the division of state police who has opted to make an application pursuant to section 400.01 of this chapter.

7-c. Possession for the purpose of loading and firing, of a rifle, pistol or shotgun, the propelling force of which may be either air, compressed gas or springs, by a person under sixteen years of age but not under twelve, under the immediate supervision, guidance and instruction of (a) a duly commissioned officer of the United States army, navy, marine corps or coast guard, or of the national guard of the state of New York; or (b) a duly qualified adult citizen of the United States who has been granted a certificate as an instructor in small arms practice issued by the United States army, navy or marine corps, or by the adjutant general of this state, by the national rifle association of America, a not-for-profit corporation duly

185

organized under the laws of this state, or by a New York state 4-H certified shooting sports instructor; or (c) a parent, guardian, or a person over the age of eighteen designated in writing by such parent or guardian who shall have a certificate of qualification in responsible hunting, including safety, ethics, and landowner relations-hunter relations, issued or honored by the department of environmental conservation.

7-d. Possession, at an indoor or outdoor shooting range for the purpose of loading and firing, of a rifle, pistol or shotgun, the propelling force of which may be either air, compressed gas or springs, by a person under twelve years of age, under the immediate supervision, guidance and instruction of (a) a duly commissioned officer of the United States army, navy, marine corps or coast guard, or of the national guard of the state of New York; or (b) a duly qualified adult citizen of the United States who has been granted a certificate as an instructor in small arms practice issued by the United States army, navy or marine corps, or by the adjutant general of this state, by the national rifle association of America, a not-for-profit corporation duly organized under the laws of this state, or by a New York state 4-H certified shooting sports instructor; or (c) a parent, guardian, or a person over the age of eighteen designated in writing by such parent or guardian who shall have a certificate of qualification in responsible hunting, including safety, ethics, and landowner relations-hunter relations, issued or honored by the department of environmental conservation.

7-e. Possession and use of a pistol or revolver, at an indoor or outdoor pistol range located in or on premises owned or occupied by a duly incorporated organization organized for conservation purposes or to foster proficiency in small arms or at a target pistol shooting competition under the auspices of or approved by an association or organization described in paragraph 7-a of this subdivision for the purpose of loading and firing the same by a person at least fourteen years of age but under the age of twenty-one who has not been previously convicted of a felony or serious offense, and who does not appear to be, or pose a threat to be, a danger to himself or to others; provided however, that such possession shall be of a pistol or revolver duly licensed to and shall be used under the immediate supervision, guidance and instruction of, a person specified in paragraph seven of this subdivision.

7-f. Possession and use of a magazine, belt, feed strip or similar device, that contains more than seven rounds of ammunition, but that does not have a capacity of or can readily be restored or converted to accept more than ten rounds of ammunition, at an indoor or outdoor firing range located in or on premises owned or occupied by a duly incorporated organization organized for conservation purposes or to foster proficiency in arms; at an indoor or outdoor firing range for the purpose of firing a rifle or shotgun; at a collegiate, olympic or target shooting competition under the auspices of or approved by the national rifle association; or at an organized match sanctioned by the International Handgun Metallic Silhouette Association.

8. The manufacturer of machine-guns, firearm silencers, assault weapons, large capacity ammunition feeding devices, rapid-fire modification devices, disguised guns, pilum ballistic knives, switchblade or gravity knives, billies or blackjacks as merchandise, or as a transferee recipient of the same for repair, lawful distribution or research and development, and the disposal and shipment thereof direct to a regularly constituted or appointed state or municipal police department, sheriff, police officer or other peace officer, or to a state prison, penitentiary, workhouse, county jail or other institution for the detention of persons convicted or accused of crime or held as witnesses in criminal cases, or to the military service of this state or of the United States; or for the repair and return of the same to the lawful possessor or for research and development.

9. The regular and ordinary transport of firearms as merchandise, provided that the person transporting such firearms, where he knows or has reasonable means of ascertaining what he is transporting, notifies in writing the police commissioner, police chief or other law enforcement officer performing such functions at the place of delivery, of the name and address of the consignee and the place of delivery, and withholds delivery to the consignee for such reasonable period of time designated in writing by such police commissioner, police chief or other law enforcement officer as such official may deem necessary for investigation as to whether the consignee may lawfully receive and possess such firearms.

9-a.

a. Except as provided in subdivision b hereof, the regular and ordinary transport of pistols or revolvers by a manufacturer of firearms to whom a license as a dealer in firearms has been issued pursuant to section 400.00 of this chapter, or by an agent or employee of such manufacturer of firearms who is otherwise duly licensed to carry a pistol or revolver and who is duly authorized in writing by such manufacturer of firearms to transport pistols or revolvers on the date or dates specified, directly between places where the manufacturer of firearms regularly conducts business provided such pistols or revolvers are transported unloaded, in a locked opaque container. For purposes of this subdivision, places where the manufacturer of firearms regularly conducts business includes, but is not limited to places where the manufacturer of firearms regularly or customarily conducts development or design of pistols or revolvers, or regularly or customarily conducts tests on pistols or revolvers, or regularly or customarily participates in the exposition of firearms to the public.

b. The transportation of such pistols or revolvers into, out of or within the city of New York may be done only with the consent of the police commissioner of the city of New York. To obtain such consent, the manufacturer must notify the police commissioner in writing of the name and address of the transporting manufacturer, or agent or employee of the manufacturer who is authorized in writing by such manufacturer to transport pistols or revolvers, the number, make and model number of the firearms to be transported and the place where the manufacturer regularly conducts business within the city of New York and such other information as the commissioner may deem necessary. The manufacturer must not transport such pistols and revolvers between the designated places of business for such reasonable period of time designated in writing by the police commissioner as such official may deem necessary for investigation and to give consent. The police commissioner may not unreasonably withhold his consent.

10. Engaging in the business of gunsmith or dealer in firearms by a person to whom a valid license therefor has been issued pursuant to section 400.00.

11. Possession of a firearm or large capacity ammunition feeding device by a police officer or sworn peace officer of another state while conducting official business within the state of New York.

12. Possession of a pistol or revolver by a person who is a member or coach of an accredited college or university target pistol team while transporting the pistol or revolver into or through New York state to participate in a collegiate, olympic or target pistol shooting competition under the auspices of or approved by the national rifle association, provided such pistol or revolver is unloaded and carried in a locked carrying case and the ammunition therefor is carried in a separate locked container.

12-a. Possession and use of a pistol or revolver, at an indoor or outdoor shooting range, by a registered student of a higher education institution chartered by the state of New York, who is participating in a course in gun safety and proficiency offered by such institution, under the immediate supervision, guidance, and instruction of a person specified in paragraph seven of this subdivision.

13. Possession of pistols and revolvers by a person who is a nonresident of this state while attending or traveling to or from, an organized competitive pistol match or league competition under auspices of, or approved by, the National Rifle Association and in which he is a competitor, within forty-eight hours of such event or by a person who is a non-resident of the state while attending or traveling to or from an organized match sanctioned by the International Handgun Metallic Silhouette Association and in which he is a competitor, within forty-eight hours of such event, provided that he has not been previously convicted of a felony or a crime which, if committed in New York, would constitute a felony, and further provided that the pistols or revolvers are transported unloaded in a locked opaque container together with a copy of the match program, match schedule or match registration card. Such documentation shall constitute prima facie evidence of exemption, providing that such person also has in his possession a pistol license or firearms registration card issued in accordance with the laws of his place of residence. For purposes of this subdivision, a person licensed in a jurisdiction which does not authorize such license by a person who has been previously convicted of a felony shall be presumed to have no prior conviction. The superintendent of state police shall annually review the laws of jurisdictions within the United States and Canada with respect to the applicable requirements for licensing or registration of firearms and shall publish a list of those jurisdictions which prohibit possession of a firearm by a person previously convicted of a felony or crimes which if committed in New York state would constitute a felony.

13-a. Except in cities not wholly contained within a single county of the state, possession of pistols and revolvers by a person who is a nonresident of this state while attending or traveling to or from, an organized convention or exhibition for the display of or education about firearms, which is conducted under auspices of, or approved by, the National Rifle Association and in which he is a registered participant, within forty-eight hours of such event, provided that he has not been previously convicted of a felony or a crime which, if committed in New York, would constitute a felony, and further provided that the pistols or revolvers are transported unloaded in a locked opaque container together with a copy of the convention or exhibition program, convention or exhibition schedule or convention or exhibition registration card. Such documentation shall constitute prima facie evidence of exemption, providing that such person also has in his possession a pistol license or firearms registration card issued in accordance with the laws of his place of residence. For purposes of this paragraph, a person licensed in a jurisdiction which does not authorize such license by a person who has been previously convicted of a felony shall be presumed to have no prior conviction. The superintendent of state police shall annually review the laws of jurisdictions within the United States and Canada with respect to the applicable requirements for licensing or registration of firearms and shall publish a list of those jurisdictions which prohibit possession of a firearm by a person previously convicted of a felony or crimes which if committed in New York state would constitute a felony.

14. Possession in accordance with the provisions of this paragraph of a self-defense spray device as defined herein for the protection of a person or property and use of such self-defense spray device under circumstances which would justify the use of physical force pursuant to article thirty-five of this chapter.

(a) As used in this section "self-defense spray device" shall mean a pocket sized spray device which contains and releases a chemical or organic substance which is intended to produce temporary physical discomfort or disability through being vaporized or otherwise dispensed in the air or any like device containing tear gas, pepper or similar disabling agent.

(b) The exemption under this paragraph shall not apply to a person who:

(i) is less than eighteen years of age; or

(ii) has been previously convicted in this state of a felony or any assault; or

(iii) has been convicted of a crime outside the state of New York which if committed in New York would constitute a felony or any assault crime.

(c) The department of health, with the cooperation of the division of criminal justice services and the superintendent of state police, shall develop standards and promulgate regulations regarding the type of self-defense spray device which may lawfully be purchased, possessed and used pursuant to this paragraph. The regulations shall include a requirement that every self-defense spray device which may be lawfully purchased, possessed or used pursuant to this paragraph have a label which states: "WARNING: The use of this substance or device for any purpose other than self-defense is a criminal offense under the law. The contents are dangerous - use with care. This device shall not be sold by anyone other than a licensed or authorized dealer. Possession of this device by any person under the age of eighteen or by anyone who has been convicted of a felony or assault is illegal. Violators may be prosecuted under the law."

15. Possession and sale of a self-defense spray device as defined in paragraph fourteen of this subdivision by a dealer in firearms licensed pursuant to section 400.00 of this chapter, a pharmacist licensed pursuant to article one hundred thirty-

seven of the education law or by such other vendor as may be authorized and approved by the superintendent of state police.

(a) Every self-defense spray device shall be accompanied by an insert or inserts which include directions for use, first aid information, safety and storage information and which shall also contain a toll free telephone number for the purpose of allowing any purchaser to call and receive additional information regarding the availability of local courses in self-defense training and safety in the use of a self-defense spray device.

(b) Before delivering a self-defense spray device to any person, the licensed or authorized dealer shall require proof of age and a sworn statement on a form approved by the superintendent of state police that such person has not been convicted of a felony or any crime involving an assault. Such forms shall be forwarded to the division of state police at such intervals as directed by the superintendent of state police. Absent any such direction the forms shall be maintained on the premises of the vendor and shall be open at all reasonable hours for inspection by any peace officer or police officer, acting pursuant to his or her special duties. No more than two self-defense spray devices may be sold at any one time to a single purchaser.

16. The terms "rifle," "shotgun," "pistol," "revolver," and "firearm" as used in paragraphs three, four, five, seven, seven-a, seven-b, nine, nine-a, ten, twelve, thirteen and thirteen-a of this subdivision shall not include a disguised gun or an assault weapon.

b. Section 265.01 shall not apply to possession of that type of billy commonly known as a "police baton" which is twenty-four to twenty-six inches in length and no more than one and one-quarter inches in thickness by members of an auxiliary police force of a city with a population in excess of one million persons or the county of Suffolk when duly authorized by regulation or order issued by the police commissioner of such city or such county respectively. Such regulations shall require training in the use of the police baton including but not limited to the defensive use of the baton and instruction in the legal use of deadly physical force pursuant to article thirty-five of this chapter. Notwithstanding the provisions of this section or any other provision of law, possession of such baton shall not be authorized when used intentionally to strike another person except in those situations when the use of deadly physical force is authorized by such article thirty-five.

c. Sections 265.01, 265.10 and 265.15 shall not apply to possession of billies or blackjacks by persons:

1. while employed in fulfilling contracts with New York state, its agencies or political subdivisions for the purchase of billies or blackjacks; or

2. while employed in fulfilling contracts with sister states, their agencies or political subdivisions for the purchase of billies or blackjacks; or

3. while employed in fulfilling contracts with foreign countries, their agencies or political subdivisions for the purchase of billies or blackjacks as permitted under federal law.

d. Subdivision one of section 265.01 and subdivision four of section 265.15 of this article shall not apply to possession or ownership of automatic knives by any cutlery and knife museum established pursuant to section two hundred sixteen-c of the education law or by any director, officer, employee, or agent thereof when he or she is in possession of an automatic knife and acting in furtherance of the business of such museum.

e. Subdivision eight of section 265.02 and sections 265.36 and 265.37 of this chapter shall not apply to a qualified retired New York or federal law enforcement officer as defined in subdivision twenty-five of section 265.00 of this article, with respect to large capacity ammunition feeding devices issued to such officer or purchased by such officer in the course of his or her official duties and owned by such officer at the time of his or her retirement or comparable replacements for such devices, if:

(i) the agency that employed the officer qualified such officer in the use of the weapon which accepts such device in accordance with applicable state or federal standards for active duty law enforcement officers within twelve months prior to his or her retirement; and

(ii) such retired officer meets, at his or her own expense, such applicable standards for such weapon at least once within three years after his or her retirement date and at least once every three years thereafter, provided, however, that any such qualified officer who has been retired for eighteen months or more on the effective date of this subdivision shall have eighteen months from such effective date to qualify in the use of the weapon which accepts such large capacity ammunition feeding device according to the provisions of this subdivision, notwithstanding that such officer did not qualify within three years after his or her retirement date, provided that such officer is otherwise qualified and maintains compliance with the provisions of this subdivision.

N.Y. Penal Law § 265.20

Amended by New York Laws 2020, ch. 150,Sec. 2, eff. 8/24/2020.
Amended by New York Laws 2019, ch. 134,Sec. 3, eff. 1/26/2020.
Amended by New York Laws 2019, ch. 130,Sec. 6, eff. 7/29/2019.
Amended by New York Laws 2019, ch. 130,Sec. 5, eff. 7/29/2019.
Amended by New York Laws 2019, ch. 130,Sec. 4, eff. 7/29/2019.
Amended by New York Laws 2019, ch. 34,Sec. 6, eff. 5/30/2019.
Amended by New York Laws 2018, ch. 476,Sec. 242, eff. 12/28/2018.
Amended by New York Laws 2014, ch. 511,Sec. 1, eff. 12/17/2014.
Amended by New York Laws 2014, ch. 55,Sec. EE-10, eff. 4/1/2014.
Amended by New York Laws 2013, ch. 98,Sec. 2, eff. 7/5/2013.
Amended by New York Laws 2013, ch. 57,Sec. FF-1, eff. 1/15/2013.
Amended by New York Laws 2013, ch. 1,Sec. 46, eff. 3/16/2013.

Section 265.25 - Certain wounds to be reported

Every case of a bullet wound, gunshot wound, powder burn or any other injury arising from or caused by the discharge of a gun or firearm, and every case of a wound which is likely to or may result in death and is actually or apparently inflicted by a knife, icepick or other sharp or pointed instrument, shall be reported at once to the police authorities of the city, town or village where the person reporting is located by:

(a) the physician attending or treating the case; or

(b) the manager, superintendent or other person in charge, whenever such case is treated in a hospital, sanitarium or other institution. Failure to make such report is a class A misdemeanor. This subdivision shall not apply to such wounds, burns or injuries received by a member of the armed forces of the United States or the state of New York while engaged in the actual performance of duty.

N.Y. Penal Law § 265.25

Section 265.26 - Burn injury and wounds to be reported

Every case of a burn injury or wound, where the victim sustained second or third degree burns to five percent or more of the body and/or any burns to the upper respiratory tract or laryngeal edema due to the inhalation of super-heated air, and every case of a burn injury or wound which is likely to or may result in death, shall be reported at once to the office of fire prevention and control. The state fire administrator shall accept the report and notify the proper investigatory agency. A written report shall also be provided to the office of fire prevention and control within seventy-two hours. The report shall be made by (a) the physician attending or treating the case; or (b) the manager, superintendent or other person in charge, whenever such case is treated in a hospital, sanitarium, institution or other medical facility.

N.Y. Penal Law § 265.26

Section 265.30 - Certain convictions to be reported

Every conviction under this article or section 400.00, of a person who is not a citizen of the United States, shall be certified to the proper officer of the United States government by the district attorney of the county in which such conviction was had.

N.Y. Penal Law § 265.30

Section 265.35 - Prohibited use of weapons

1. Any person hunting with a dangerous weapon in any county wholly embraced within the territorial limits of a city is guilty of a class A misdemeanor.

2. Any person who wilfully discharges a loaded firearm or any other gun, the propelling force of which is gunpowder, at an aircraft while such aircraft is in motion in the air or in motion or stationary upon the ground, or at any railway or street railroad train as defined by the public service law, or at a locomotive, car, bus or vehicle standing or moving upon such railway, railroad or public highway, is guilty of a class D felony if thereby the safety of any person is endangered, and in every other case, of a class E felony.

3. Any person who, otherwise than in self defense or in the discharge of official duty, (a) wilfully discharges any species of firearms, air-gun or other weapon, or throws any other deadly missile, either in a public place, or in any place where there is any person to be endangered thereby, or, in Putnam county, within one-quarter mile of any occupied school building other than under supervised instruction by properly authorized instructors although no injury to any person ensues; (b) intentionally, without malice, points or aims any firearm or any other gun, the propelling force of which is gunpowder, at or toward any other person; (c) discharges, without injury to any other person, firearms or any other guns, the propelling force of which is gunpowder, while intentionally without malice, aimed at or toward any person; or (d) maims or injures any other person by the discharge of any firearm or any other gun, the propelling force of which is gunpowder, pointed or aimed intentionally, but without malice, at any such person, is guilty of a class A misdemeanor.

N.Y. Penal Law § 265.35

Section 265.36 - Unlawful possession of a large capacity ammunition feeding device

It shall be unlawful for a person to knowingly possess a large capacity ammunition feeding device manufactured before September thirteenth, nineteen hundred ninety-four, and if such person lawfully possessed such large capacity feeding device before the effective date of the chapter of the laws of two thousand thirteen which added this section, that has a capacity of, or that can be readily restored or converted to accept, more than ten rounds of ammunition.

N.Y. Penal Law § 265.36

Added by New York Laws 2013, ch. 1,Sec. 46-a, eff. 3/16/2013.

Section 265.37 - Unlawful possession of certain ammunition feeding devices

It shall be unlawful for a person to knowingly possess an ammunition feeding device where such device contains more than seven rounds of ammunition.

N.Y. Penal Law § 265.37

Amended by New York Laws 2013, ch. 57,Sec. FF-2, eff. 3/29/2013.

Added by New York Laws 2013, ch. 1,Sec. 46-a, eff. 3/16/2013.

Section 265.40 - Purchase of rifles and/or shotguns in contiguous states

Definitions. As used in this act:

1. "Contiguous state" shall mean any state having any portion of its border in common with a portion of the border of the state of New York;

2. All other terms herein shall be given the meaning prescribed in Public Law 90-618 known as the "Gun Control Act of l968" (18 U.S.C. 921).

It shall be lawful for a person or persons residing in this state, to purchase or otherwise obtain a rifle and/or shotgun in a contiguous state, and to receive or transport such rifle and/or shotgun into this state; provided, however, such person is otherwise eligible to possess a rifle and/or shotgun under the laws of this state.

N.Y. Penal Law § 265.40

Section 265.45 - Failure to safely store rifles, shotguns, and firearms in the first degree

No person who owns or is custodian of a rifle, shotgun or firearm who resides with an individual who:

(i) is under sixteen years of age;

(ii) such person knows or has reason to know is prohibited from possessing a rifle, shotgun or firearm pursuant to a temporary or final extreme risk protection order issued under article sixty-three-A of the civil practice law and rules or 18 U.S.C. § 922(g) (1), (4), (8) or (9); or

(iii) such person knows or has reason to know is prohibited from possessing a rifle, shotgun or firearm based on a conviction for a felony or a serious offense, shall store or otherwise leave such rifle, shotgun or firearm out of his or her immediate possession or control without having first securely locked such rifle, shotgun or firearm in an appropriate safe storage depository or rendered it incapable of being fired by use of a gun locking device appropriate to that weapon. For purposes of this section "safe storage depository" shall mean a safe or other secure container which, when locked, is incapable of being opened without the key, combination or other unlocking mechanism and is capable of preventing an unauthorized person from obtaining access to and possession of the weapon contained therein. Nothing in this section shall be deemed to affect, impair or supersede any special or local act relating to the safe storage of rifles, shotguns or firearms which impose additional requirements on the owner or custodian of such weapons.

(i) a firearm, rifle or shotgun for lawful use as authorized under paragraph seven or seven-e of subdivision a of section 265.20 of this article, or

(ii) a rifle or shotgun for lawful use as authorized by article eleven of the environmental conservation law when such person less than sixteen years of age is the holder of a hunting license or permit and such rifle or shotgun is used in accordance with such law.

Failure to safely store rifles, shotguns, and firearms in the first degree is a class A misdemeanor.

N.Y. Penal Law § 265.45

Amended by New York Laws 2019, ch. 135,Sec. 1-a, eff. 9/28/2019.

Amended by New York Laws 2019, ch. 135,Sec. 1, eff. 9/28/2019.

Amended by New York Laws 2019, ch. 133,Sec. 1, eff. 9/28/2019.

Amended by New York Laws 2019, ch. 19,Sec. 2, eff. 8/24/2019.

Amended by New York Laws 2013, ch. 57,Sec. FF-3, eff. 3/29/2013.

Added by New York Laws 2013, ch. 1,Sec. 47, eff. 3/16/2013.

Section 265.50 - [First of two versions; As added byNew York Laws 2019, ch. 135,Sec. 2] Failure to safely store rifles, shotguns, and firearms in the second degree

No person who owns or is custodian of a rifle, shotgun or firearm and knows, or has reason to know, that a person less than sixteen years of age is likely to gain access to such rifle, shotgun or firearm shall store or otherwise leave such rifle, shotgun or firearm out of his or her immediate possession or control without having first securely locked such rifle, shotgun or firearm in an appropriate safe storage depository or rendered it incapable of being fired by use of a gun locking device appropriate to that weapon. For purposes of this section "safe storage depository" shall have the same meaning as such term is defined in section 265.45 of this article. Nothing in this section shall be deemed to affect, impair or supersede any special or local act relating to the safe storage of rifles, shotguns or firearms which impose additional requirements on the owner or custodian of such weapons.

(i) a firearm, rifle or shotgun for lawful use as authorized under paragraph seven or seven-e of subdivision a of section 265.20 of this article, or

(ii) a rifle or shotgun for lawful use as authorized by article eleven of the environmental conservation law when such person less than sixteen years of age is the holder of a hunting license or permit and such rifle or shotgun is used in accordance with such law.

Failure to safely store rifles, shotguns, and firearms in the second degree is a violation punishable only by a fine of not more than two hundred fifty dollars.

N.Y. Penal Law § 265.50

Amended by New York Laws 2019, ch. 133,Sec. 2, eff. 9/28/2019.

Added by New York Laws 2019, ch. 135,Sec. 2, eff. 9/28/2019.

Section 265.50 - [Second of two versions; As added byNew York Laws 2019, ch. 134,Sec. 2] Criminal manufacture, sale, or transport of an undetectable firearm, rifle or shotgun

A person is guilty of criminal manufacture, sale, or transport of an undetectable firearm, rifle or shotgun when he or she knowingly manufactures, causes to be manufactured, sells, exchanges, gives, disposes of, transports, ships, or possesses with the intent to sell:

1. any firearm, rifle or shotgun that, after the removal of grips, stocks and magazines, is not detectable by a metal detector calibrated to detect the Security Exemplar, as defined pursuant to 18 U.S.C. § 922 (p); or

2. any major component of a firearm, rifle or shotgun that, if subject to the types of detection devices commonly used at airports for security screening, does not generate an image that adequately displays the shape of the component.

Criminal manufacture, sale, or transport of an undetectable firearm, rifle or shotgun is a class D felony.

N.Y. Penal Law § 265.50

Added by New York Laws 2019, ch. 134,Sec. 2, eff. 1/26/2020.

Section 265.55 - Criminal possession of an undetectable firearm, rifle or shotgun

A person is guilty of criminal possession of an undetectable firearm, rifle or shotgun when he or she knowingly possesses:

1. any firearm, rifle or shotgun that, after the removal of grips, stocks and magazines, is not detectable by a metal detector calibrated to detect the Security Exemplar, as defined pursuant to 18 U.S.C. § 922(p); or

2. any major component of a firearm, rifle or shotgun that, if subject to the types of detection devices commonly used at airports for security screening, does not generate an image that adequately displays the shape of the component.

Criminal possession of an undetectable firearm, rifle or shotgun is a class E felony.

N.Y. Penal Law § 265.55

Added by New York Laws 2019, ch. 134,Sec. 2, eff. 1/26/2020.

Article 270 - OTHER OFFENSES RELATING TO PUBLIC SAFETY

Section 270.00 - Unlawfully dealing with fireworks and dangerous fireworks

1. Definition of "fireworks" and "dangerous fireworks".

(a) The term "fireworks," as used in this section, includes:

(i) display fireworks, which means fireworks devices in a finished state, exclusive of mere ornamentation, primarily intended for commercial displays which are designed to produce visible and/or audible effects by combustion, deflagration or detonation, including, but not limited to, salutes containing more than one hundred thirty milligrams (two grains) of explosive composition, aerial shells containing more than forty grams of chemical composition exclusive of lift charge, and other exhibition display items that exceed the limits of consumer fireworks contained in the American Pyrotechnic Association (APA) Standard 87-1, 2001 edition;

(ii) articles pyrotechnic, which means pyrotechnic devices for professional use similar to consumer fireworks in chemical composition and construction but not intended for consumer use and which articles meet the weight limits for consumer fireworks but are not labeled as such and are classified by the United States department of transportation in 49 CFR 172.101 as UN0431;

(iii) special effects, which means any combination of chemical elements or chemical compounds capable of burning independently of the oxygen of the atmosphere, and designed and intended to produce an audible, visual, mechanical, or thermal effect as an integral part of a motion picture, radio, television, theatrical, or opera production, or live entertainment;

(iv) consumer fireworks which are aerial in performance and are commonly referred to as sky rockets, bottle rockets, missile type rockets, helicopters, aerial spinners, roman candles, mines, shell devices, aerial shell kits, reloadables and audible ground devices which are commonly referred to as firecrackers and chasers, as well as metal wire handheld sparklers;

(v) any blank cartridge, blank cartridge pistol, or toy cannon in which explosives are used, firecrackers, or any preparation containing any explosive or inflammable compound or any tablets or other device commonly used and sold as fireworks containing nitrates, chlorates, oxalates, sulphides of lead, barium, antimony, arsenic, mercury, nitroglycerine, phosphorus or any compound containing any of the same or other explosives, or any substance or combination of substances, or article prepared for the purpose of producing a visible or an audible effect by combustion, explosion, deflagration or detonation, or other device containing any explosive substance, other than sparkling devices as defined in subparagraph (vi) of this paragraph; and

(vi) "sparkling devices," as used in this section, includes:

(1) sparkling devices which are ground-based or hand-held devices that produce a shower of white, gold, or colored sparks as their primary pyrotechnic effect. Additional effects may include a colored flame, an audible crackling effect, an audible whistle effect, and smoke. These devices do not rise into the air, do not fire inserts or projectiles into the air, and do not explode or produce a report (an audible crackling-type effect is not considered to be a report). Ground-based or hand-held devices that produce a cloud of smoke as their sole pyrotechnic effect are also included in this category. Types of devices in this category include:

(A) cylindrical fountain: cylindrical tube containing not more than seventy-five grams of pyrotechnic composition that may be contained in a different shaped exterior such as a square, rectangle, cylinder or other shape but the interior tubes are cylindrical in shape. Upon ignition, a shower of colored sparks, and sometimes a whistling effect or smoke, is produced. This device may be provided with a spike for insertion into the ground (spike fountain), a wood or plastic base for placing on the ground (base fountain), or a wood or cardboard handle to be hand held (handle fountain). When more than one tube is mounted on a common base, total pyrotechnic composition may not exceed two hundred grams, and when tubes are securely attached to a base and the tubes are separated from each other on the base by a distance of at least half an inch (12.7 millimeters), a maximum total weight of five hundred grams of pyrotechnic composition shall be allowed.

(B) cone fountain: cardboard or heavy paper cone containing not more than fifty grams of pyrotechnic composition. The effect is the same as that of a cylindrical fountain. When more than one cone is mounted on a common base, total pyrotechnic composition may not exceed two hundred grams, as is outlined in this subparagraph.

(C) wooden sparkler/dipped stick: these devices consist of a wood dowel that has been coated with pyrotechnic composition. Upon ignition of the tip of the device, a shower of sparks is produced. Sparklers may contain up to one hundred grams of pyrotechnic composition per item.

(2) novelties which do not require approval from the United States department of transportation and are not regulated as explosives, provided that they are manufactured and packaged as described below:

(A) party popper: small devices with paper or plastic exteriors that are actuated by means of friction (a string or trigger is typically pulled to actuate the device). They frequently resemble champagne bottles or toy pistols in shape. Upon activation, the device expels flame-resistant paper streamers, confetti, or other novelties and produces a small report. Devices may contain not more than sixteen milligrams (0.25 grains) of explosive composition, which is limited to potassium chlorate and red phosphorus. These devices must be packaged in an inner packaging which contains a maximum of seventy-two devices.

(B) snapper: small, paper-wrapped devices containing not more than one milligram of silver fulminate coated on small bits of sand or gravel. When dropped, the device explodes, producing a small report. Snappers must be in inner packages not to exceed fifty devices each, and the inner packages must contain sawdust or a similar, impact-absorbing material.

(b) The term "dangerous fireworks" means any fireworks capable of causing serious physical injury and which are: firecrackers containing more than fifty milligrams of any explosive substance, torpedoes, skyrockets and rockets including all devices which employ any combustible or explosive substance and which rise in the air during discharge, Roman candles, and bombs, provided, however, that in cities with a population of one million or more, the term "dangerous fireworks" shall also include sparklers more than ten inches in length or one-fourth of one inch in diameter, or chasers including all devices which dart or travel about the surface of the ground during discharge.

(c) "Fireworks" and "dangerous fireworks" shall not be deemed to include the following nor shall the purchase and use of any items listed below be subject to the provisions of section 61 of title 12 of the New York state codes, rules and regulations or section four hundred eighty, four hundred eighty-one, four hundred eighty-two or four hundred eighty-three of the general business law:

(i) flares of the type used by railroads or any warning lights commonly known as red flares, or marine distress signals of a type approved by the United States coast guard, or

(ii) toy pistols, toy canes, toy guns or other devices in which paper caps containing twenty-five hundredths grains or less of explosive compound are used, providing they are so constructed that the hand cannot come in contact with the cap when in place for use, and toy pistol paper caps which contain less than twenty-hundredths grains of explosive mixture, the sale and use of which shall be permitted at all times, or

(iii) bank security devices which contain not more than fifty grams of any compound or substance or any combination thereof, together with an igniter not exceeding 0.2 gram, capable of producing a lachrymating and/or visible or audible effect, where such device is stored or used only by banks, national banking associations, trust companies, savings banks, savings and loan associations, industrial banks, or credit unions, or by any manufacturer, wholesaler, dealer, jobber or common carrier for such devices and where the total storage on any one premises does not exceed one hundred devices, or

(iv) except in cities with a population of one million or more, "fireworks" and "dangerous fireworks" shall not be deemed to include "sparkling devices" as defined in subparagraph (vi) of paragraph (a) of this subdivision. The storage and retail sale of sparkling devices shall be regulated in a manner that is not in conflict with the provisions of NFPA 1124, 2006 edition.

2. Offense.

(a) Except as herein otherwise provided, or except where a permit is obtained pursuant to section 405.00 of this chapter:

(i) any person who shall offer or expose for sale, sell or furnish, any fireworks or dangerous fireworks is guilty of a class B misdemeanor;

(ii) any person who shall offer or expose for sale, sell or furnish any fireworks or dangerous fireworks valued at five hundred dollars or more shall be guilty of a class A misdemeanor;

(iii) any person who shall possess, use, explode or cause to explode any fireworks or dangerous fireworks is guilty of a violation;

(iv) any person who shall offer or expose for sale, sell or furnish, any dangerous fireworks, fireworks or sparkling devices to any person who is under the age of eighteen is guilty of a class A misdemeanor.

(b) A person who has previously been convicted of a violation of subparagraph (iv) of paragraph (a) of this subdivision within the preceding five years and who shall offer or expose for sale, sell or furnish, any dangerous fireworks to any person who is under the age of eighteen, shall be guilty of a class E felony.

(c) Possession of fireworks or dangerous fireworks valued at one hundred fifty dollars or more shall be a presumption that such fireworks were intended to be offered or exposed for sale.

3. Exceptions.

(a) The provisions of this section shall not apply to:

(i) fireworks, dangerous fireworks, and sparkling devices while in possession of railroads, common or contract carriers, retailers, wholesalers, distributors, jobbers and transportation companies or transportation agencies for the purpose of transportation to points without the state, the shipment of which is not prohibited by interstate commerce commission regulations as formulated and published from time to time, unless they be held voluntarily by such railroads, common or contract carriers, retailers, wholesalers, distributors, jobbers and transportation agencies or transporting companies as warehousemen for delivery to points within the state;

(ii) signaling devices used by railroad companies or motor vehicles referred to in subdivision seventeen of section three hundred seventyfive of the vehicle and traffic law;

(iii) high explosives for blasting or similar purposes;

(iv) fireworks, dangerous fireworks and sparkling devices for the use thereof by the United States military, and departments of the state and federal government;

(v) the use, transportation and storage of fireworks, dangerous fireworks and sparkling devices and special effects materials in connection with the production of motion pictures, television programs, commercials, and all entertainment media recorded in any current or to be designed format when such use, transportation and storage has been appropriately permitted by the local governmental subdivision having jurisdiction.

(b) Nothing in this article shall be construed to prohibit:

(i) any manufacturer, wholesaler, retailer, dealer or jobber from manufacturing, possessing or selling at wholesale a sparkling device to municipalities, religious or civic organizations, fair associations, amusement parks, or other organizations authorized by the state to store, transport, possess and use or to individuals to store, transport, possess and use;

(ii) the sale or use of blank cartridges for a motion picture, television program, commercial and all entertainment media, or for signal purposes in athletic sports, or for dog trials or dog training;

(iii) the use, storage, transportation or sale or transfer for use of fireworks and sparkling devices in the preparation for or in connection with motion pictures, television programs, commercials, and all entertainment media recorded in any current or to be designed format when such use, transportation and storage has been appropriately permitted by the local governmental subdivision having jurisdiction;

(iv) the manufacture or sale of sparkling devices provided they are to be shipped directly out of such city and any such items are sold in accordance with the provisions of this article; or

(v) except in cities with a population of one million or more, possession of sparkling devices lawfully obtained in another jurisdiction.

4. Sales of ammunition not prohibited. Nothing contained in this section shall be construed to prevent, or interfere in any way with, the sale of ammunition for revolvers or pistols of any kind, or for rifles, shot guns, or other arms, belonging or which may belong to any persons whether as sporting or hunting weapons or for the purpose of protection to them in their homes, or, as they may go abroad; and manufacturers are authorized to continue to manufacture, and wholesalers and dealers to continue to deal in and freely to sell ammunition to all such persons for such purposes.

5. Notwithstanding the provisions of subdivision four of this section, it shall be unlawful for any dealer in firearms to sell any ammunition designed exclusively for use in a pistol or revolver to any person, not authorized to possess a pistol or revolver. The violation of this section shall constitute a class B misdemeanor.

N.Y. Penal Law § 270.00

Amended by New York Laws 2017, ch. 371,Sec. 1, eff. 1/21/2018.

Amended by New York Laws 2014, ch. 477,Sec. 1, eff. 12/21/2014.

Section 270.05 - Unlawfully possessing or selling noxious material

1. As used in this section, "noxious material" means any container which contains any drug or other substance capable of generating offensive, noxious or suffocating fumes, gases or vapors, or capable of immobilizing a person.

2. A person is guilty of unlawfully possessing noxious material when he possesses such material under circumstances evincing an intent to use it or to cause it to be used to inflict physical injury upon or to cause annoyance to a person, or to damage property of another, or to disturb the public peace.

3. Possession of noxious material is presumptive evidence of intent to use it or cause it to be used in violation of this section.

4. Bank security devices not prohibited. Notwithstanding the provisions of subdivision one of this section, it shall not be unlawful for any bank, national banking association, trust company, savings bank, savings and loan association, industrial bank, or credit union to store, possess, transport, use or cause to discharge any bank security device as described in subdivision one of section 270.00 of this chapter; nor shall it be unlawful for any manufacturer, wholesaler, dealer, jobber or common carrier to manufacture, store, possess, transport, or sell such a device to banks, national banking associations, trust companies, savings banks, savings and loan associations, industrial banks or credit unions.

5. Self-defense spray devices not prohibited. Notwithstanding the provisions of subdivisions two and three of this section, it shall not be unlawful for a person eighteen years of age or older to possess a self-defense spray device as defined in paragraph fourteen of subdivision a of section 265.20 of this chapter in accordance with the provisions set forth therein.

6. A person is guilty of unlawfully selling a noxious material when he or she sells a self-defense spray device as defined in paragraph fourteen of subdivision a of section 265.20 of this chapter and such sale was not authorized in accordance with the provisions of paragraph fifteen of subdivision a of section 265.20 of this chapter.

Unlawfully possessing or selling noxious material is a class B misdemeanor.

N.Y. Penal Law § 270.05

Section 270.10 - Creating a hazard

A person is guilty of creating a hazard when:

1. Having discarded in any place where it might attract children, a container which has a compartment of more than one and one-half cubic feet capacity and a door or lid which locks or fastens automatically when closed and which cannot easily be opened from the inside, he fails to remove the door, lid, locking or fastening device; or

2. Being the owner or otherwise having possession of property upon which an abandoned well or cesspool is located, he fails to cover the same with suitable protective construction.

Creating a hazard is a class B misdemeanor.

N.Y. Penal Law § 270.10

Section 270.15 - Unlawfully refusing to yield a party line

1. As used in this section:

(a) "Party line" means a subscriber's line telephone circuit, consisting of two or more main telephone stations connected therewith, each station with a distinctive ring or telephone number.

(b) "Emergency call" means a telephone call to a police or fire department, or for medical aid or ambulance service, necessitated by a situation in which human life or property is in jeopardy and prompt summoning of aid is essential.

2. A person is guilty of unlawfully refusing to yield a party line when, being informed that a party line is needed for an emergency call, he refuses immediately to relinquish such line.

Unlawfully refusing to yield a party line is a class B misdemeanor.

N.Y. Penal Law § 270.15

Section 270.20 - Unlawful wearing of a body vest

1. A person is guilty of the unlawful wearing of a body vest when acting either alone or with one or more other persons he commits any violent felony offense defined in section 70.02 while possessing a firearm, rifle or shotgun and in the course of and in furtherance of such crime he wears a body vest.

2. For the purposes of this section a "body vest" means a bullet-resistant soft body armor providing, as a minimum standard, the level of protection known as threat level I which shall mean at least seven layers of bullet-resistant material providing protection from three shots of one hundred fifty-eight grain lead ammunition fired from a .38 calibre handgun at a velocity of eight hundred fifty feet per second.

The unlawful wearing of a body vest is a class E felony.

N.Y. Penal Law § 270.20

Section 270.25 - Unlawful fleeing a police officer in a motor vehicle in the third degree

A person is guilty of unlawful fleeing a police officer in a motor vehicle in the third degree when, knowing that he or she has been directed to stop his or her motor vehicle by a uniformed police officer or a marked police vehicle by the activation of either the lights or the lights and siren of such vehicle, he or she thereafter attempts to flee such officer or such vehicle by driving at speeds which equal or exceed twenty-five miles per hour above the speed limit or engaging in reckless driving as defined by section twelve hundred twelve of the vehicle and traffic law.

N.Y. Penal Law § 270.25

Section 270.30 - Unlawful fleeing a police officer in a motor vehicle in the second degree

A person is guilty of unlawful fleeing a police officer in a motor vehicle in the second degree when he or she commits the offense of unlawful fleeing a police officer in a motor vehicle in the third degree, as defined in section 270.25 of this article, and as a result of such conduct a police officer or a third person suffers serious physical injury.

N.Y. Penal Law § 270.30

Section 270.35 - Unlawful fleeing a police officer in a motor vehicle in the first degree

A person is guilty of unlawful fleeing a police officer in a motor vehicle in the first degree when he or she commits the offense of unlawful fleeing a police officer in a motor vehicle in the third degree, as defined in section 270.25 of this article, and as a result of such conduct a police officer or a third person is killed.

N.Y. Penal Law § 270.35

Section 270.40 - Unlawfully installing a gas meter

1. As used in this section "gas meter" means any gas meter that measures usage of any end use customer of gas services.

2. A person is guilty of unlawfully installing a gas meter when he or she installs the gas meter or is the owner of the premises where the meter is unlawfully installed and knows that such gas meter was unlawfully installed. A gas meter is unlawfully installed when it is installed by any person other than a person acting on behalf of a utility corporation subject to the jurisdiction of the public service commission, unless such person has received a permit to install the gas meter from the appropriate permitting authority. Unlawfully installing a gas meter is a class B misdemeanor.

N.Y. Penal Law § 270.40

Added by New York Laws 2021, ch. 274,Sec. 1, eff. 7/16/2021.

Article 275 - OFFENSES RELATING TO UNAUTHORIZED RECORDING

Section 275.00 - Definitions

The following definitions are applicable to this article:

1. "Person" means any individual, firm, partnership, corporation or association.

2. "Owner" means (a) the person who owns, or has the exclusive license in the United States to reproduce or the exclusive license in the United States to distribute to the public copies of the sounds fixed in a master phonograph record, master disc, master tape, master film or any other device used for reproducing sounds on phonograph records, discs, tapes, films, videocassettes, or any other articles upon which sound is recorded, and from which the transferred recorded sounds are directly derived; or (b) the person who owns the rights to record or authorize the recording of a live performance.

3. "Fixed" means embodied in a recording by or under the authority of the author, so that the matter embodied is sufficiently permanent or stable to permit it to be perceived, reproduced, or otherwise communicated for a period of more than transitory duration.

4. "Performer" means the person or persons appearing in a performance.

5. "Performance" means, whether live before an audience or transmitted by wire or through the air by radio or television, a recitation, rendering, or playing of a series of images, musical, spoken, or other sounds, or a combination of images and sounds, in an audible sequence.

6. "Recording" means an original phonograph record, disc, tape, audio or video cassette, wire, film, hard drive, flash drive, memory card or other data storage device or any other medium on which such sounds, images, or both sounds and images are or can be recorded or otherwise stored, or a copy or reproduction that duplicates in whole or in part the original.

N.Y. Penal Law § 275.00

Section 275.05 - Manufacture of unauthorized recordings in the second degree

A person is guilty of the manufacture of unauthorized recordings in the second degree when such person:

1. knowingly, and without the consent of the owner, transfers or causes to be transferred any sound recording, with the intent to rent or sell, or cause to be rented or sold for profit, or used to promote the sale of any product, such article to which such recording was transferred, or

2. transports within this state, for commercial advantage or private financial gain, a recording, knowing that the sounds have been reproduced or transferred without the consent of the owner; provided, however, that this section shall only apply to sound recordings initially fixed prior to February fifteenth, nineteen hundred seventy-two.

Manufacture of unauthorized recordings in the second degree is a class A misdemeanor.

N.Y. Penal Law § 275.05

Section 275.10 - Manufacture of unauthorized recordings in the first degree

A person is guilty of manufacture of unauthorized recordings in the first degree when he commits the crime of manufacture of unauthorized recordings in the second degree as defined in section 275.05 of this article and either:

1. has previously been convicted of that crime within the past five years; or

2. commits that crime by the manufacture of one thousand unauthorized sound recordings; provided, however, that this section shall only apply to sound recordings initially fixed prior to February fifteenth, nineteen hundred seventy-two.

Manufacture of unauthorized recordings in the first degree is a class E felony.

N.Y. Penal Law § 275.10

Section 275.15 - Manufacture or sale of an unauthorized recording of a performance in the second degree

A person commits the crime of manufacture or sale of an unauthorized recording of a performance in the second degree when he knowingly, and without the consent of the performer, records or fixes or causes to be recorded or fixed on a recording a performance, with the intent to sell or rent or cause to be sold or rented such recording, or with the intent to use such recording to promote the sale of any product; or when he knowingly possesses, transports or advertises, for purposes of sale, resale or rental or sells, resells, rents or offers for rental, sale or resale, any recording that the person knows has been produced in violation of this section.

N.Y. Penal Law § 275.15

Section 275.20 - Manufacture or sale of an unauthorized recording of a performance in the first degree

A person commits the crime of unauthorized recording of a performance in the first degree when he commits the crime of manufacture or sale of an unauthorized recording of a performance in the second degree as defined in section 275.15 of this article and either:

1. such person has previously been convicted of that crime within the past five years; or

2. commission of that crime involves at least one thousand unauthorized sound recordings or at least one hundred unauthorized audio-visual recordings.

Manufacture or sale of an unauthorized recording of a performance in the first degree is a class E felony.

N.Y. Penal Law § 275.20

Section 275.25 - Advertisement or sale of unauthorized recordings in the second degree

A person is guilty of the advertisement or sale of unauthorized recordings in the second degree when such person knowingly advertises, offers for sale, resale, or rental, or sells, resells, rents, distributes or possesses for any such purposes, any recording that has been produced or transferred without the consent of the owner; provided, however, that this section shall only apply to sound recordings initially fixed prior to February fifteenth, nineteen hundred seventy-two.

N.Y. Penal Law § 275.25

Section 275.30 - Advertisement or sale of unauthorized recordings in the first degree

A person is guilty of the advertisement or sale of unauthorized recordings in the first degree when such person commits the crime of advertisement or sale of unauthorized recordings in the second degree as defined in section 275.25 of this article and either:

1. such person has previously been convicted of that crime within the past five years; or

2. commission of that crime involves at least one thousand unauthorized sound recordings or at least one hundred unauthorized audiovisual recordings.

Advertisement and sale of unauthorized recordings in the first degree is a class E felony.

N.Y. Penal Law § 275.30

Section 275.32 - Unlawful operation of a recording device in a motion picture or live theater in the third degree

1. A person is guilty of unlawful operation of a recording device in a motion picture or live theater in the third degree when without authority or written permission from the operator of a motion picture theater or live theater, the person operates a recording device in such theater.

2. As used in this section

(a)"recording device" means a photographic or video camera, or any audiovisual recording function of any device used for recording the sound or picture of a motion picture;

(b) "operator" means the owner or lessee of a motion picture theater or live theater or the authorized agent or employee of such owner or lessee;

(c) "motion picture theater" means a theater, screening room, auditorium or other venue that is being utilized primarily for the exhibition of a motion picture at the time of the offense; and

(d) "live theater" means a concert hall, recital hall, theater, or auditorium in which a presentation is rendered, consisting in whole or in part of a musical, dramatic, dance, or other stage rendition by one or more professional performers who appear in person in the immediate presence of their audiences, and admission to which is limited by its operator to persons holding an admission ticket or who have other authority or written permission to enter. Live theater shall not mean or include a musical, dramatic, dance, or other stage rendition that is performed by students enrolled in a school or college or as a part of a children's camp or similar program.

Unlawful operation of a recording device in a motion picture or live theater in the third degree is a violation.

N.Y. Penal Law § 275.32

Section 275.33 - Unlawful operation of a recording device in a motion picture or live theater in the second degree

A person is guilty of unlawful operation of a recording device in a motion picture or live theater in the second degree when he or she violates section 275.32 of this article:

1. for financial profit or commercial purposes; or

2. in circumstances where the material recorded is fifteen or more minutes, or all or a substantial portion, of the motion picture or live theatrical performance; or

3. in circumstances where such person has previously been convicted within the past five years of violating section 275.32 or 275.34 of this article or this section.

Unlawful operation of a recording device in a motion picture or live theater in the second degree is a class A misdemeanor.

N.Y. Penal Law § 275.33

Section 275.34 - Unlawful operation of a recording device in a motion picture or live theater in the first degree

A person is guilty of unlawful operation of a recording device in a motion picture or live theater in the first degree when he or she commits the crime of unlawful operation of a recording device in a motion picture or live theater in the second degree as defined in section 275.33 of this article and has previously been convicted within the past ten years of violating section 275.33 of this article or this section.

N.Y. Penal Law § 275.34

Section 275.35 - Failure to disclose the origin of a recording in the second degree

A person is guilty of failure to disclose the origin of a recording in the second degree when, for commercial advantage or private financial gain, he knowingly advertises or offers for sale, resale, or rental, or sells, resells, or rents, or possesses for such purposes, a recording the cover, box, jacket or label does not clearly and conspicuously disclose the actual name and address of the manufacturer or the name of the performer or principal artist. The omission of the actual name and address of the manufacturer, or the omission of the name of the performer or principal artist, or the omission of both, shall constitute the failure to disclose the origin of a recording.

N.Y. Penal Law § 275.35

Section 275.40 - Failure to disclose the origin of a recording in the first degree

A person is guilty of failure to disclose the origin of a recording in the first degree when such person commits the crime of failure to disclose the origin of a recording in the second degree as defined in section 275.35 of this article and either:

1. such person has been convicted of failure to disclose the origin of a recording in the first or second degree within the past five years; or

2. commission of the crime involves at least one hundred unauthorized sound recordings or at least one hundred unauthorized audiovisual recordings.

Failure to disclose the origin of a recording in the first degree is a class E felony.

N.Y. Penal Law § 275.40

Section 275.45 - Limitations of application

1. This article does not apply to:

(a) any broadcaster who, in connection with or as part of a radio, television, or cable broadcast transmission, or for the purpose of archival preservation, transfers any such recorded sounds or images; or

(b) any person who transfers such sounds or images for personal use, and without profit for such transfer.

2. This article shall neither enlarge nor diminish the rights of parties in civil litigation.

N.Y. Penal Law § 275.45

Part 4 - ADMINISTRATIVE PROVISIONS

Title W - PROVISIONS RELATING TO FIREARMS, FIREWORKS, PORNOGRAPHY EQUIPMENT AND VEHICLES USED IN THE TRANSPORTATION OF GAMBLING RECORDS

Article 400 - LICENSING AND OTHER PROVISIONS RELATING TO FIREARMS

Section 400.00 - Licenses to carry, possess, repair and dispose of firearms

1. Eligibility. No license shall be issued or renewed pursuant to this section except by the licensing officer, and then only after investigation and finding that all statements in a proper application for a license are true. No license shall be issued or renewed except for an applicant (a) twenty-one years of age or older, provided, however, that where such applicant has been honorably discharged from the United States army, navy, marine corps, air force or coast guard, or the national guard of the state of New York, no such age restriction shall apply; (b) of good moral character; (c) who has not been convicted anywhere of a felony or a serious offense or who is not the subject of an outstanding warrant of arrest issued upon the alleged commission of a felony or serious offense; (d) who is not a fugitive from justice; (e) who is not an unlawful user of or addicted to any controlled substance as defined in section 21 U.S.C. 802; (f) who being an alien (i) is not illegally or

unlawfully in the United States or (ii) has not been admitted to the United States under a nonimmigrant visa subject to the exception in 18 U.S.C. 922(y)(2); (g) who has not been discharged from the Armed Forces under dishonorable conditions; (h) who, having been a citizen of the United States, has not renounced his or her citizenship; (i) who has stated whether he or she has ever suffered any mental illness ; (j) who has not been involuntarily committed to a facility under the jurisdiction of an office of the department of mental hygiene pursuant to article nine or fifteen of the mental hygiene law, article seven hundred thirty or section 330.20 of the criminal procedure law, section four hundred two or five hundred eight of the correction law, section 322.2 or 353.4 of the family court act, or has not been civilly confined in a secure treatment facility pursuant to article ten of the mental hygiene law; (k) who has not had a license revoked or who is not under a suspension or ineligibility order issued pursuant to the provisions of section 530.14 of the criminal procedure law or section eight hundred forty-two-a of the family court act; (l) in the county of Westchester, who has successfully completed a firearms safety course and test as evidenced by a certificate of completion issued in his or her name and endorsed and affirmed under the penalties of perjury by a duly authorized instructor, except that: (i) persons who are honorably discharged from the United States army, navy, marine corps or coast guard, or of the national guard of the state of New York, and produce evidence of official qualification in firearms during the term of service are not required to have completed those hours of a firearms safety course pertaining to the safe use, carrying, possession, maintenance and storage of a firearm; and (ii) persons who were licensed to possess a pistol or revolver prior to the effective date of this paragraph are not required to have completed a firearms safety course and test; (m) who has not had a guardian appointed for him or her pursuant to any provision of state law, based on a determination that as a result of marked subnormal intelligence, mental illness, incapacity, condition or disease, he or she lacks the mental capacity to contract or manage his or her own affairs; and (n) concerning whom no good cause exists for the denial of the license. No person shall engage in the business of gunsmith or dealer in firearms unless licensed pursuant to this section. An applicant to engage in such business shall also be a citizen of the United States, more than twenty-one years of age and maintain a place of business in the city or county where the license is issued. For such business, if the applicant is a firm or partnership, each member thereof shall comply with all of the requirements set forth in this subdivision and if the applicant is a corporation, each officer thereof shall so comply. 1-a.[Effective 4/3/2021] For purposes of subdivision one of this section, serious offense shall include an offense in any jurisdiction or the former penal law that includes all of the essential elements of a serious offense as defined by subdivision seventeen of section 265.00 of this chapter. Nothing in this subdivision shall preclude the denial of a license based on the commission of, arrest for or conviction of an offense in any other jurisdiction which does not include all of the essential elements of a serious offense.

2. Types of licenses. A license for gunsmith or dealer in firearms shall be issued to engage in such business. A license for a pistol or revolver, other than an assault weapon or a disguised gun, shall be issued to (a) have and possess in his dwelling by a householder; (b) have and possess in his place of business by a merchant or storekeeper; (c) have and carry concealed while so employed by a messenger employed by a banking institution or express company; (d) have and carry concealed by a justice of the supreme court in the first or second judicial departments, or by a judge of the New York city civil court or the New York city criminal court; (e) have and carry concealed while so employed by a regular employee of an institution of the state, or of any county, city, town or village, under control of a commissioner of correction of the city or any warden, superintendent or head keeper of any state prison, penitentiary, workhouse, county jail or other institution for the detention of persons convicted or accused of crime or held as witnesses in criminal cases, provided that application is made therefor by such commissioner, warden, superintendent or head keeper; (f) have and carry concealed, without regard to employment or place of possession, by any person when proper cause exists for the issuance thereof; and (g) have, possess, collect and carry antique pistols which are defined as follows:

(i) any single shot, muzzle loading pistol with a matchlock, flintlock, percussion cap, or similar type of ignition system manufactured in or before l898, which is not designed for using rimfire or conventional centerfire fixed ammunition; and
(ii) any replica of any pistol described in clause (i) hereof if such replica-
(1) is not designed or redesigned for using rimfire or conventional centerfire fixed ammunition, or
(2) uses rimfire or conventional centerfire fixed ammunition which is no longer manufactured in the United States and which is not readily available in the ordinary channels of commercial trade.

3. Applications.
(a) Applications shall be made and renewed, in the case of a license to carry or possess a pistol or revolver, to the licensing officer in the city or county, as the case may be, where the applicant resides, is principally employed or has his or her principal place of business as merchant or storekeeper; and, in the case of a license as gunsmith or dealer in firearms, to the licensing officer where such place of business is located. Blank applications shall, except in the city of New York, be approved as to form by the superintendent of state police. An application shall state the full name, date of birth, residence, present occupation of each person or individual signing the same, whether or not he or she is a citizen of the United States, whether or not he or she complies with each requirement for eligibility specified in subdivision one of this section and such other facts as may be required to show the good character, competency and integrity of each person or individual signing the application. An application shall be signed and verified by the applicant. Each individual signing an application shall submit one photograph of himself or herself and a duplicate for each required copy of the application. Such photographs shall have been taken within thirty days prior to filing the application. In case of a license as gunsmith or dealer in firearms, the photographs submitted shall be two inches square, and the application shall also state the previous occupation of each individual signing the same and the location of the place of such business, or of the bureau, agency, subagency, office or branch office for which the license is sought, specifying the name of the city, town or village, indicating the street and number and otherwise giving such apt description as to point out reasonably the location thereof. In such case, if the

applicant is a firm, partnership or corporation, its name, date and place of formation, and principal place of business shall be stated. For such firm or partnership, the application shall be signed and verified by each individual composing or intending to compose the same, and for such corporation, by each officer thereof.

(b) Application for an exemption under paragraph seven-b of subdivision a of section 265.20 of this chapter. Each applicant desiring to obtain the exemption set forth in paragraph seven-b of subdivision a of section 265.20 of this chapter shall make such request in writing of the licensing officer with whom his application for a license is filed, at the time of filing such application. Such request shall include a signed and verified statement by the person authorized to instruct and supervise the applicant, that has met with the applicant and that he has determined that, in his judgment, said applicant does not appear to be or poses a threat to be, a danger to himself or to others. He shall include a copy of his certificate as an instructor in small arms, if he is required to be certified, and state his address and telephone number. He shall specify the exact location by name, address and telephone number where such instruction will take place. Such licensing officer shall, no later than ten business days after such filing, request the duly constituted police authorities of the locality where such application is made to investigate and ascertain any previous criminal record of the applicant pursuant to subdivision four of this section. Upon completion of this investigation, the police authority shall report the results to the licensing officer without unnecessary delay. The licensing officer shall no later than ten business days after the receipt of such investigation, determine if the applicant has been previously denied a license, been convicted of a felony, or been convicted of a serious offense, and either approve or disapprove the applicant for exemption purposes based upon such determinations. If the applicant is approved for the exemption, the licensing officer shall notify the appropriate duly constituted police authorities and the applicant. Such exemption shall terminate if the application for the license is denied, or at any earlier time based upon any information obtained by the licensing officer or the appropriate police authorities which would cause the license to be denied. The applicant and appropriate police authorities shall be notified of any such terminations.

4. Investigation. Before a license is issued or renewed, there shall be an investigation of all statements required in the application by the duly constituted police authorities of the locality where such application is made, including but not limited to such records as may be accessible to the division of state police or division of criminal justice services pursuant to section 400.02 of this article. For that purpose, the records of the appropriate office of the department of mental hygiene concerning previous or present mental illness of the applicant shall be available for inspection by the investigating officer of the police authority. Where the applicant is domiciled in a foreign state, the investigation shall include inquiry of the foreign state for records concerning the previous or present mental illness of the applicant, and, to the extent necessary for inspection by the investigating officer, the applicant shall execute a waiver of confidentiality of such record in such form as may be required by the foreign state. In order to ascertain any previous criminal record, the investigating officer shall take the fingerprints and physical descriptive data in quadruplicate of each individual by whom the application is signed and verified. Two copies of such fingerprints shall be taken on standard fingerprint cards eight inches square, and one copy may be taken on a card supplied for that purpose by the federal bureau of investigation; provided, however, that in the case of a corporate applicant that has already been issued a dealer in firearms license and seeks to operate a firearm dealership at a second or subsequent location, the original fingerprints on file may be used to ascertain any criminal record in the second or subsequent application unless any of the corporate officers have changed since the prior application, in which case the new corporate officer shall comply with procedures governing an initial application for such license. When completed, one standard card shall be forwarded to and retained by the division of criminal justice services in the executive department, at Albany. A search of the files of such division and written notification of the results of the search to the licensing officer shall be made without unnecessary delay. Thereafter, such division shall notify the licensing officer and the executive department, division of state police, Albany, of any criminal record of the applicant filed therein subsequent to the search of its files. A second standard card, or the one supplied by the federal bureau of investigation, as the case may be, shall be forwarded to that bureau at Washington with a request that the files of the bureau be searched and notification of the results of the search be made to the investigating police authority. Of the remaining two fingerprint cards, one shall be filed with the executive department, division of state police, Albany, within ten days after issuance of the license, and the other remain on file with the investigating police authority. No such fingerprints may be inspected by any person other than a peace officer, who is acting pursuant to his or her special duties, or a police officer, except on order of a judge or justice of a court of record either upon notice to the licensee or without notice, as the judge or justice may deem appropriate. Upon completion of the investigation, the police authority shall report the results to the licensing officer without unnecessary delay.

4-a. Processing of license applications. Applications for licenses shall be accepted for processing by the licensing officer at the time of presentment. Except upon written notice to the applicant specifically stating the reasons for any delay, in each case the licensing officer shall act upon any application for a license pursuant to this section within six months of the date of presentment of such an application to the appropriate authority. Such delay may only be for good cause and with respect to the applicant. In acting upon an application, the licensing officer shall either deny the application for reasons specifically and concisely stated in writing or grant the application and issue the license applied for.

4-b. Westchester county firearms safety course certificate. In the county of Westchester, at the time of application, the licensing officer to which the license application is made shall provide a copy of the safety course booklet to each license applicant. Before such license is issued, such licensing officer shall require that the applicant submit a certificate of successful completion of a firearms safety course and test issued in his or her name and endorsed and affirmed under the penalties of perjury by a duly authorized instructor.

5. Filing of approved applications.

(a) The application for any license, if granted, shall be filed by the licensing officer with the clerk of the county of issuance, except that in the city of New York and, in the counties of Nassau and Suffolk, the licensing officer shall designate the place of filing in the appropriate division, bureau or unit of the police department thereof, and in the county of Suffolk the county clerk is hereby authorized to transfer all records or applications relating to firearms to the licensing authority of that county. Except as provided in paragraphs (b) through (f) of this subdivision, the name and address of any person to whom an application for any license has been granted shall be a public record. Upon application by a licensee who has changed his place of residence such records or applications shall be transferred to the appropriate officer at the licensee's new place of residence. A duplicate copy of such application shall be filed by the licensing officer in the executive department, division of state police, Albany, within ten days after issuance of the license. The superintendent of state police may designate that such application shall be transmitted to the division of state police electronically. In the event the superintendent of the division of state police determines that it lacks any of the records required to be filed with the division, it may request that such records be provided to it by the appropriate clerk, department or authority and such clerk, department or authority shall provide the division with such records. In the event such clerk, department or authority lacks such records, the division may request the license holder provide information sufficient to constitute such record and such license holder shall provide the division with such information. Such information shall be limited to the license holder's name, date of birth, gender,race, residential address, social security number and firearms possessed by said license holder. Nothing in this subdivision shall be construed to change the expiration date or term of such licenses if otherwise provided for in law. Records assembled or collected for purposes of inclusion in the database established by this section shall be released pursuant to a court order. Records assembled or collected for purposes of inclusion in the database created pursuant to section 400.02 of this chapter shall not be subject to disclosure pursuant to article six of the public officers law.

(b) Each application for a license pursuant to paragraph (a) of this subdivision shall include, on a separate written form prepared by the division of state police within thirty days of the effective date of the chapter of the laws of two thousand thirteen, which amended this section, and provided to the applicant at the same time and in the same manner as the application for a license, an opportunity for the applicant to request an exception from his or her application information becoming public record pursuant to paragraph (a) of this subdivision. Such forms, which shall also be made available to individuals who had applied for or been granted a license prior to the effective date of the chapter of the laws of two thousand thirteen which amended this section, shall notify applicants that, upon discovery that an applicant knowingly provided false information, such applicant may be subject to penalties pursuant to section 175.30 of this chapter, and further, that his or her request for an exception shall be null and void, provided that written notice containing such determination is provided to the applicant. Further, such forms shall provide each applicant an opportunity to specify the grounds on which he or she believes his or her application information should not be publicly disclosed. These grounds, which shall be identified on the application with a box beside each for checking, as applicable, by the applicant, shall be as follows:

(i) the applicant's life or safety may be endangered by disclosure because:

(A) the applicant is an active or retired police officer, peace officer, probation officer, parole officer, or corrections officer;

(B) the applicant is a protected person under a currently valid order of protection;

(C) the applicant is or was a witness in a criminal proceeding involving a criminal charge;

(D) the applicant is participating or previously participated as a juror in a criminal proceeding, or is or was a member of a grand jury; or

(E) the applicant is a spouse, domestic partner or household member of a person identified in this subparagraph or subparagraph (ii) of this paragraph, specifying which subparagraph or subparagraphs and clauses apply.

(ii) the applicant has reason to believe his or her life or safety may be endangered by disclosure due to reasons stated by the applicant.

(iii) the applicant has reason to believe he or she may be subject to unwarranted harassment upon disclosure of such information.

(c) Each form provided for recertification pursuant to paragraph (b) of subdivision ten of this section shall include an opportunity for the applicant to request an exception from the information provided on such form becoming public record pursuant to paragraph (a) of this subdivision. Such forms shall notify applicants that, upon discovery that an applicant knowingly provided false information, such applicant may be subject to penalties pursuant to section 175.30 of this chapter, and further, that his or her request for an exception shall be null and void, provided that written notice containing such determination is provided to the applicant. Further, such forms shall provide each applicant an opportunity to either decline to request the grant or continuation of an exception, or specify the grounds on which he or she believes his or her information should not be publicly disclosed. These grounds, which shall be identified in the application with a box beside each for checking, as applicable, by the applicant, shall be the same as provided in paragraph (b) of this subdivision.

(d) Information submitted on the forms described in paragraph (b) of this subdivision shall be excepted from disclosure and maintained by the entity retaining such information separate and apart from all other records.

(e)

(i) Upon receiving a request for exception from disclosure, the licensing officer shall grant such exception, unless the request is determined to be null and void, pursuant to paragraph (b) or (c) of this subdivision.

(ii) A request for an exception from disclosure may be submitted at any time, including after a license or recertification has been granted.

(iii) If an exception is sought and granted pursuant to paragraph (b) of this subdivision, the application information shall not be public record, unless the request is determined to be null and void. If an exception is sought and granted pursuant to paragraph (c) of this subdivision, the information concerning such recertification application shall not be public record, unless the request is determined to be null and void. Notwithstanding the foregoing provisions of this subparagraph, local and state law enforcement shall, upon request, be granted access to and copies of such application information provided that such information obtained by law enforcement pursuant to this subparagraph shall not be considered a public record of such law enforcement agency.

(f) The information of licensees or applicants for a license shall not be disclosed to the public during the first one hundred twenty days following the effective date of the chapter of the laws of two thousand thirteen, which amended this section. After such period, the information of those who had applied for or been granted a license prior to the preparation of the form for requesting an exception, pursuant to paragraph (b) of this subdivision, may be released only if such individuals did not file a request for such an exception during the first sixty days following such preparation; provided, however, that no information contained in an application for licensure or recertification shall be disclosed by an entity that has not completed processing any such requests received during such sixty days.

(g) If a request for an exception is determined to be null and void pursuant to paragraph (b) or (c) of this subdivision, an applicant may request review of such determination pursuant to article seventy-eight of the civil practice laws and rules. Such proceeding must commence within thirty days after service of the written notice containing the adverse determination. Notice of the right to commence such a petition, and the time period therefor, shall be included in the notice of the determination. Disclosure following such a petition shall not be made prior to the disposition of such review.

6. License: validity. Any license issued pursuant to this section shall be valid notwithstanding the provisions of any local law or ordinance. No license shall be transferable to any other person or premises. A license to carry or possess a pistol or revolver, not otherwise limited as to place or time of possession, shall be effective throughout the state, except that the same shall not be valid within the city of New York unless a special permit granting validity is issued by the police commissioner of that city. Such license to carry or possess shall be valid within the city of New York in the absence of a permit issued by the police commissioner of that city, provided that (a) the firearms covered by such license have been purchased from a licensed dealer within the city of New York and are being transported out of said city forthwith and immediately from said dealer by the licensee in a locked container during a continuous and uninterrupted trip; or provided that (b) the firearms covered by such license are being transported by the licensee in a locked container and the trip through the city of New York is continuous and uninterrupted; or provided that (c) the firearms covered by such license are carried by armored car security guards transporting money or other valuables, in, to, or from motor vehicles commonly known as armored cars, during the course of their employment; or provided that (d) the licensee is a retired police officer as police officer is defined pursuant to subdivision thirty-four of section 1.20 of the criminal procedure law or a retired federal law enforcement officer, as defined in section 2.15 of the criminal procedure law, who has been issued a license by an authorized licensing officer as defined in subdivision ten of section 265.00 of this chapter; provided, further, however, that if such license was not issued in the city of New York it must be marked "Retired Police Officer" or "Retired Federal Law Enforcement Officer", as the case may be, and, in the case of a retired officer the license shall be deemed to permit only police or federal law enforcement regulations weapons; or provided that (e) the licensee is a peace officer described in subdivision four of section 2.10 of the criminal procedure law and the license, if issued by other than the city of New York, is marked "New York State Tax Department Peace Officer" and in such case the exemption shall apply only to the firearm issued to such licensee by the department of taxation and finance. A license as gunsmith or dealer in firearms shall not be valid outside the city or county, as the case may be, where issued. Notwithstanding any inconsistent provision of state or local law or rule or regulation, the premises limitation set forth in any license to have and possess a pistol or revolver in the licensee's dwelling or place of business pursuant to paragraph (a) or (b) of subdivision two of this section shall not prevent the transport of such pistol or revolver directly to or from (i) another dwelling or place of business of the licensee where the licensee is authorized to have and possess such pistol or revolver, (ii) an indoor or outdoor shooting range that is authorized by law to operate as such, (iii) a shooting competition at which the licensee may possess such pistol or revolver consistent with the provisions of subdivision a of section 265.20 of this chapter or consistent with the law applicable at the place of such competition, or (iv) any other location where the licensee is lawfully authorized to have and possess such pistol or revolver; provided however, that during such transport to or from a location specified in clauses (i) through (iv) of this paragraph, the pistol or revolver shall be unloaded and carried in a locked container, and the ammunition therefor shall be carried separately; provided further, however, that a license to have and possess a pistol or revolver in the licensee's dwelling or place of business pursuant to paragraph (a) or (b) of subdivision two of this section that is issued by a licensing officer other than the police commissioner of the city of New York shall not authorize transport of a pistol or revolver into the city of New York in the absence of written authorization to do so by the police commissioner of that city. The term "locked container" shall not include the glove compartment or console of a vehicle.

7. License: form. Any license issued pursuant to this section shall, except in the city of New York, be approved as to form by the superintendent of state police. A license to carry or possess a pistol or revolver shall have attached the licensee's photograph, and a coupon which shall be removed and retained by any person disposing of a firearm to the licensee. Such license shall specify the weapon covered by calibre, make, model, manufacturer's name and serial number, or if none, by any other distinguishing number or identification mark, and shall indicate whether issued to carry on the person or possess on the premises, and if on the premises shall also specify the place where the licensee shall possess the same. If such license is issued to an alien, or to a person not a citizen of and usually a resident in the state, the licensing officer shall state in the license the particular reason for the issuance and the names of the persons certifying to the good character of the applicant. Any license as gunsmith or dealer in firearms shall mention and describe the premises for which it is issued and shall be valid only for such premises.

8. License: exhibition and display. Every licensee while carrying a pistol or revolver shall have on his or her person a license to carry the same. Every person licensed to possess a pistol or revolver on particular premises shall have the license for the same on such premises. Upon demand, the license shall be exhibited for inspection to any peace officer, who is acting pursuant to his or her special duties, or police officer. A license as gunsmith or dealer in firearms shall be prominently displayed on the licensed premises. A gunsmith or dealer of firearms may conduct business temporarily at a location other than the location specified on the license if such temporary location is the location for a gun show or event sponsored by any national, state, or local organization, or any affiliate of any such organization devoted to the collection, competitive use or other sporting use of firearms. Any sale or transfer at a gun show must also comply with the provisions of article thirty-nine-DD of the general business law. Records of receipt and disposition of firearms transactions conducted at such temporary location shall include the location of the sale or other disposition and shall be entered in the permanent records of the gunsmith or dealer of firearms and retained on the location specified on the license. Nothing in this section shall authorize any licensee to conduct business from any motorized or towed vehicle. A separate fee shall not be required of a licensee with respect to business conducted under this subdivision. Any inspection or examination of inventory or records under this section at such temporary location shall be limited to inventory consisting of, or records related to, firearms held or disposed at such temporary locations. Failure of any licensee to so exhibit or display his or her license, as the case may be, shall be presumptive evidence that he or she is not duly licensed.

9. License: amendment. Elsewhere than in the city of New York, a person licensed to carry or possess a pistol or revolver may apply at any time to his or her licensing officer for amendment of his or her license to include one or more such weapons or to cancel weapons held under license. If granted, a record of the amendment describing the weapons involved shall be filed by the licensing officer in the executive department, division of state police, Albany. The superintendent of state police may authorize that such amendment be completed and transmitted to the state police in electronic form. Notification of any change of residence shall be made in writing by any licensee within ten days after such change occurs, and a record of such change shall be inscribed by such licensee on the reverse side of his or her license. Elsewhere than in the city of New York, and in the counties of Nassau and Suffolk, such notification shall be made to the executive department, division of state police, Albany, and in the city of New York to the police commissioner of that city, and in the county of Nassau to the police commissioner of that county, and in the county of Suffolk to the licensing officer of that county, who shall, within ten days after such notification shall be received by him or her, give notice in writing of such change to the executive department, division of state police, at Albany.

10. License: expiration, certification and renewal.

(a) Any license for gunsmith or dealer in firearms and, in the city of New York, any license to carry or possess a pistol or revolver, issued at any time pursuant to this section or prior to the first day of July, nineteen hundred sixty-three and not limited to expire on an earlier date fixed in the license, shall expire not more than three years after the date of issuance. In the counties of Nassau, Suffolk and Westchester, any license to carry or possess a pistol or revolver, issued at any time pursuant to this section or prior to the first day of July, nineteen hundred sixty-three and not limited to expire on an earlier date fixed in the license, shall expire not more than five years after the date of issuance; however, in the county of Westchester, any such license shall be certified prior to the first day of April, two thousand, in accordance with a schedule to be contained in regulations promulgated by the commissioner of the division of criminal justice services, and every such license shall be recertified every five years thereafter. For purposes of this section certification shall mean that the licensee shall provide to the licensing officer the following information only: current name, date of birth, current address, and the make, model, caliber and serial number of all firearms currently possessed. Such certification information shall be filed by the licensing officer in the same manner as an amendment. Elsewhere than in the city of New York and the counties of Nassau, Suffolk and Westchester, any license to carry or possess a pistol or revolver, issued at any time pursuant to this section or prior to the first day of July, nineteen hundred sixty-three and not previously revoked or cancelled, shall be in force and effect until revoked as herein provided. Any license not previously cancelled or revoked shall remain in full force and effect for thirty days beyond the stated expiration date on such license. Any application to renew a license that has not previously expired, been revoked or cancelled shall thereby extend the term of the license until disposition of the application by the licensing officer. In the case of a license for gunsmith or dealer in firearms, in counties having a population of less than two hundred thousand inhabitants, photographs and fingerprints shall be submitted on original applications and upon renewal thereafter only at six year intervals. Upon satisfactory proof that a currently valid original license has been despoiled, lost or otherwise removed from the possession of the licensee and upon application containing an additional photograph of the licensee, the licensing officer shall issue a duplicate license.

(b) All licensees shall be recertified to the division of state police every five years thereafter. Any license issued before the effective date of the chapter of the laws of two thousand thirteen which added this paragraph shall be recertified by the licensee on or before January thirty-first, two thousand eighteen, and not less than one year prior to such date, the state police shall send a notice to all license holders who have not recertified by such time. Such recertification shall be in a form as approved by the superintendent of state police, which shall request the license holder's name, date of birth, gender, race, residential address, social security number, firearms possessed by such license holder, email address at the option of the license holder and an affirmation that such license holder is not prohibited from possessing firearms. The form may be in an electronic form if so designated by the superintendent of state police. Failure to recertify shall act as a revocation of such license. If the New York state police discover as a result of the recertification process that a licensee failed to provide a change of address, the New York state police shall not require the licensing officer to revoke such license.

11. License: revocation and suspension.

(a) The conviction of a licensee anywhere of a felony or serious offense or a licensee at any time becoming ineligible to obtain a license under this section shall operate as a revocation of the license. A license may be revoked or suspended as provided for in section 530.14 of the criminal procedure law or section eight hundred forty-two-a of the family court act. Except for a license issued pursuant to section 400.01 of this article, a license may be revoked and cancelled at any time in the city of New York, and in the counties of Nassau and Suffolk, by the licensing officer, and elsewhere than in the city of New York by any judge or justice of a court of record; a license issued pursuant to section 400.01 of this article may be revoked and cancelled at any time by the licensing officer or any judge or justice of a court of record. The official revoking a license shall give written notice thereof without unnecessary delay to the executive department, division of state police, Albany, and shall also notify immediately the duly constituted police authorities of the locality.

(b) Whenever the director of community services or his or her designee makes a report pursuant to section 9.46 of the mental hygiene law, the division of criminal justice services shall convey such information, whenever it determines that the person named in the report possesses a license issued pursuant to this section, to the appropriate licensing official, who shall issue an order suspending or revoking such license.

(c) In any instance in which a person's license is suspended or revoked under paragraph (a) or (b) of this subdivision, such person shall surrender such license to the appropriate licensing official and any and all firearms, rifles, or shotguns owned or possessed by such person shall be surrendered to an appropriate law enforcement agency as provided in subparagraph (f) of paragraph one of subdivision a of section 265.20 of this chapter. In the event such license, firearm, shotgun, or rifle is not surrendered, such items shall be removed and declared a nuisance and any police officer or peace officer acting pursuant to his or her special duties is authorized to remove any and all such weapons.

12. Records required of gunsmiths and dealers in firearms. Any person licensed as gunsmith or dealer in firearms shall keep a record book approved as to form, except in the city of New York, by the superintendent of state police. In the record book shall be entered at the time of every transaction involving a firearm the date, name, age, occupation and residence of any person from whom a firearm is received or to whom a firearm is delivered, and the calibre, make, model, manufacturer's name and serial number, or if none, any other distinguishing number or identification mark on such firearm. Before delivering a firearm to any person, the licensee shall require him to produce either a license valid under this section to carry or possess the same, or proof of lawful authority as an exempt person pursuant to section 265.20 of this chapter and either (a) the National Instant Criminal Background Check System (NICS) or its successor has issued a "proceed" response to the licensee, or (b) thirty calendar days have elapsed since the date the licensee contacted NICS to initiate a national instant criminal background check and NICS has not notified the licensee that the transfer of the firearm to such person should be denied. In addition, before delivering a firearm to a peace officer, the licensee shall verify that person's status as a peace officer with the division of state police. After completing the foregoing, the licensee shall remove and retain the attached coupon and enter in the record book the date of such license, number, if any, and name of the licensing officer, in the case of the holder of a license to carry or possess, or the shield or other number, if any, assignment and department, unit or agency, in the case of an exempt person. The original transaction report shall be forwarded to the division of state police within ten days of delivering a firearm to any person, and a duplicate copy shall be kept by the licensee. The superintendent of state police may designate that such record shall be completed and transmitted in electronic form. A dealer may be granted a waiver from transmitting such records in electronic form if the superintendent determines that such dealer is incapable of such transmission due to technological limitations that are not reasonably within the control of the dealer, or other exceptional circumstances demonstrated by the dealer, pursuant to a process established in regulation, and at the discretion of the superintendent. Records assembled or collected for purposes of inclusion in the database created pursuant to section 400.02 of this article shall not be subject to disclosure pursuant to article six of the public officers law. The record book shall be maintained on the premises mentioned and described in the license and shall be open at all reasonable hours for inspection by any peace officer, acting pursuant to his special duties, or police officer. In the event of cancellation or revocation of the license for gunsmith or dealer in firearms, or discontinuance of business by a licensee, such record book shall be immediately surrendered to the licensing officer in the city of New York, and in the counties of Nassau and Suffolk, and elsewhere in the state to the executive department, division of state police.

12-a. State police regulations applicable to licensed gunsmiths engaged in the business of assembling or manufacturing firearms. The superintendent of state police is hereby authorized to issue such rules and regulations as he deems reasonably necessary to prevent the manufacture and assembly of unsafe firearms in the state. Such rules and regulations shall establish safety standards in regard to the manufacture and assembly of firearms in the state, including specifications as to materials and parts used, the proper storage and shipment of firearms, and minimum standards of quality control. Regulations issued by the state police pursuant to this subdivision shall apply to any person licensed as a gunsmith under this section engaged in the business of manufacturing or assembling firearms, and any violation thereof shall subject the licensee to revocation of license pursuant to subdivision eleven of this section.

12-c. Firearms records.

(a) Every employee of a state or local agency, unit of local government, state or local commission, or public or private organization who possesses a firearm or machine-gun under an exemption to the licensing requirements under this chapter, shall promptly report in writing to his employer the make, model, calibre and serial number of each such firearm or machine-gun. Thereafter, within ten days of the acquisition or disposition of any such weapon, he shall furnish such information to his employer, including the name and address of the person from whom the weapon was acquired or to whom it was disposed.

(b) Every head of a state or local agency, unit of local government, state or local commission, public authority or public or private organization to whom an employee has submitted a report pursuant to paragraph (a) of this subdivision shall promptly forward such report to the superintendent of state police.

(c) Every head of a state or local agency, unit of local government, state or local commission, public authority, or any other agency, firm or corporation that employs persons who may lawfully possess firearms or machine-guns without the requirement of a license therefor, or that employs persons licensed to possess firearms or machine-guns, shall promptly report to the superintendent of state police, in the manner prescribed by him, the make, model, calibre and serial number of every firearm or machine-gun possessed by it on the effective date of this act for the use of such employees or for any other use. Thereafter, within ten days of the acquisition or disposition of any such weapon, such head shall report such information to the superintendent of the state police, including the name and address of the person from whom the weapon was acquired or to whom it was disposed.

13. Expenses. The expense of providing a licensing officer with blank applications, licenses and record books for carrying out the provisions of this section shall be a charge against the county, and in the city of New York against the city.

14. Fees. In the city of New York and the county of Nassau, the annual license fee shall be twenty-five dollars for gunsmiths and fifty dollars for dealers in firearms. In such city, the city council and in the county of Nassau the Board of Supervisors shall fix the fee to be charged for a license to carry or possess a pistol or revolver and provide for the disposition of such fees. Elsewhere in the state, the licensing officer shall collect and pay into the county treasury the following fees: for each license to carry or possess a pistol or revolver, not less than three dollars nor more than ten dollars as may be determined by the legislative body of the county; for each amendment thereto, three dollars, and five dollars in the county of Suffolk; and for each license issued to a gunsmith or dealer in firearms, ten dollars. The fee for a duplicate license shall be five dollars. The fee for processing a license transfer between counties shall be five dollars. The fee for processing a license or renewal thereof for a qualified retired police officer as defined under subdivision thirty-four of section 1.20 of the criminal procedure law, or a qualified retired sheriff, undersheriff, or deputy sheriff of the city of New York as defined under subdivision two of section 2.10 of the criminal procedure law, or a qualified retired bridge and tunnel officer, sergeant or lieutenant of the triborough bridge and tunnel authority as defined under subdivision twenty of section 2.10 of the criminal procedure law, or a qualified retired uniformed court officer in the unified court system, or a qualified retired court clerk in the unified court system in the first and second judicial departments, as defined in paragraphs a and b of subdivision twenty-one of section 2.10 of the criminal procedure law or a retired correction officer as defined in subdivision twenty-five of section 2.10 of the criminal procedure law shall be waived in all counties throughout the state.

15. Any violation by any person of any provision of this section is a class A misdemeanor.

16-a. Registration.

(a) An owner of a weapon defined in paragraph (e) or (f) of subdivision twenty-two of section 265.00 of this chapter, possessed before the date of the effective date of the chapter of the laws of two thousand thirteen which added this paragraph, must make an application to register such weapon with the superintendent of state police, in the manner provided by the superintendent, or by amending a license issued pursuant to this section within one year of the effective date of this subdivision except any weapon defined under subparagraph (vi) of paragraph (g) of subdivision twenty-two of section 265.00 of this chapter transferred into the state may be registered at any time, provided such weapons are registered within thirty days of their transfer into the state. Registration information shall include the registrant's name, date of birth, gender, race, residential address, social security number and a description of each weapon being registered. A registration of any weapon defined under subparagraph (vi) of paragraph (g) of subdivision twenty-two of section 265.00 or a feeding device as defined under subdivision twenty-three of section 265.00 of this chapter shall be transferable, provided that the seller notifies the state police within seventy-two hours of the transfer and the buyer provides the state police with information sufficient to constitute a registration under this section. Such registration shall not be valid if such registrant is prohibited or becomes prohibited from possessing a firearm pursuant to state or federal law. The superintendent shall determine whether such registrant is prohibited from possessing a firearm under state or federal law. Such check shall be limited to determining whether the factors in 18 USC 922 (g) apply or whether a registrant has been convicted of a serious offense as defined in subdivision sixteen-b of section 265.00 of this chapter, so as to prohibit such registrant from possessing a firearm, and whether a report has been issued pursuant to section 9.46 of the mental hygiene law. All registrants shall recertify to the division of state police every five years thereafter. Failure to recertify shall result in a revocation of such registration.

(a-1) Notwithstanding any inconsistent provisions of paragraph (a) of this subdivision, an owner of an assault weapon as defined in subdivision twenty-two of section 265.00 of this chapter, who is a qualified retired New York or federal law enforcement officer as defined in subdivision twenty-five of section 265.00 of this chapter, where such weapon was issued to or purchased by such officer prior to retirement and in the course of his or her official duties, and for which such officer was qualified by the agency that employed such officer within twelve months prior to his or her retirement, must register such weapon within sixty days of retirement.

(b) The superintendent of state police shall create and maintain an internet website to educate the public as to which semiautomatic rifle, semiautomatic shotgun or semiautomatic pistol or weapon that are illegal as a result of the enactment of the chapter of the laws of two thousand thirteen which added this paragraph, as well as such assault weapons which are illegal pursuant to article two hundred sixty-five of this chapter. Such website shall contain information to assist the public in recognizing the relevant features proscribed by such article two hundred sixty-five, as well as which make and model of weapons that require registration.

(c) A person who knowingly fails to apply to register such weapon, as required by this section, within one year of the effective date of the chapter of the laws of two thousand thirteen which added this paragraph shall be guilty of a class A misdemeanor and such person who unknowingly fails to validly register such weapon within such one year period shall be given a warning by an appropriate law enforcement authority about such failure and given thirty days in which to apply to register such weapon or to surrender it. A failure to apply or surrender such weapon within such thirty-day period shall result in such weapon being removed by an appropriate law enforcement authority and declared a nuisance.

16-b. The cost of the software, programming and interface required to transmit any record that must be electronically transmitted by the dealer or licensing officer to the division of state police pursuant to this chapter shall be borne by the state.

17. Applicability of section. The provisions of article two hundred sixty-five of this chapter relating to illegal possession of a firearm, shall not apply to an offense which also constitutes a violation of this section by a person holding an otherwise valid license under the provisions of this section and such offense shall only be punishable as a class A misdemeanor pursuant to this section. In addition, the provisions of such article two hundred sixty-five of this chapter shall not apply to the possession of a firearm in a place not authorized by law, by a person who holds an otherwise valid license or possession of a firearm by a person within a one year period after the stated expiration date of an otherwise valid license which has not been previously cancelled or revoked shall only be punishable as a class A misdemeanor pursuant to this section.

18. Notice. Upon the issuance of a license, the licensing officer shall issue therewith the following notice in conspicuous and legible twenty-four point type on eight and one-half inches by eleven inches paper stating in bold print the following: WARNING: RESPONSIBLE FIREARM STORAGE IS THE LAW IN NEW YORK STATE. FIREARMS MUST EITHER BE STORED WITH A GUN LOCKING DEVICE OR IN A SAFE STORAGE DEPOSITORY OR NOT BE LEFT OUTSIDE THE IMMEDIATE POSSESSION AND CONTROL OF THE OWNER OR OTHER LAWFUL POSSESSOR IF A CHILD RESIDES IN THE HOME OR IS PRESENT, OR IF THE OWNER OR POSSESSOR RESIDES WITH A PERSON PROHIBITED FROM POSSESSING A FIREARM UNDER STATE OR FEDERAL LAW. FIREARMS SHOULD BE STORED UNLOADED AND LOCKED IN A LOCATION SEPARATE FROM AMMUNITION. LEAVING FIREARMS ACCESSIBLE TO A CHILD OR OTHER PROHIBITED PERSON MAY SUBJECT YOU TO IMPRISONMENT, FINE, OR BOTH.

Nothing in this subdivision shall be deemed to affect, impair or supersede any special or local law relating to providing notice regarding the safe storage of rifles, shotguns or firearms.

N.Y. Penal Law § 400.00

Amended by New York Laws 2020, ch. 55,Sec. N-2, eff. 4/3/2021.
Amended by New York Laws 2019, ch. 244,Sec. 1, eff. 9/3/2019.
Amended by New York Laws 2019, ch. 242,Sec. 1, eff. 11/2/2019.
Amended by New York Laws 2019, ch. 135,Sec. 3, eff. 9/28/2019.
Amended by New York Laws 2019, ch. 129,Sec. 1, eff. 9/12/2019.
Amended by New York Laws 2019, ch. 104,Sec. 1, eff. 7/16/2019.
Amended by New York Laws 2018, ch. 60,Sec. 6, eff. 6/11/2018.
Amended by New York Laws 2013, ch. 98,Sec. 3, eff. 1/15/2014.
Amended by New York Laws 2013, ch. 1,Sec. 48, eff. 1/15/2014.
Amended by New York Laws 2013, ch. 1,Sec. 48, eff. 4/15/2013.
See New York Laws 2020, ch. 55, Sec. N-4.

Section 400.01 - License to carry and possess firearms for retired sworn members of the division of state police

1. A license to carry or possess a firearm for a retired sworn member of the division of state police shall be granted in the same manner and upon the same terms and conditions as licenses issued under section 400.00 of this article provided, however, that applications for such license may be made to, and the licensing officer may be, the superintendent of state police.

2. For purposes of this section, a "retired sworn member of the division of state police" shall mean a former sworn member of the division of state police, who upon separation from the division of state police was immediately entitled to receive retirement benefits under the provisions of the retirement and social security law.

3. The provisions of this section shall only apply to license applications made or renewals which must be made on or after the effective date of this section. A license to carry or possess a pistol or revolver issued pursuant to the provisions of section 400.00 of this article to a person covered by the provisions of this section shall be valid until such license would have expired pursuant to the provisions of section 400.00 of this article; provided that, on or after the effective date of this section, an application or renewal of such license shall be made pursuant to the provisions of this section.

4. Except for the designation of the superintendent of state police as the licensing officer for retired sworn members of the division of state police who have opted to obtain such license under this section, all of the provisions and requirements of section 400.00 of this article and any other provision of law shall be applicable to individuals licensed pursuant to this section. In addition all provisions of section 400.00 of this article, except for the designation of the superintendent of state police as licensing officer are hereby deemed applicable to individuals licensed pursuant to this section.

N.Y. Penal Law § 400.01

Amended by New York Laws 2014, ch. 511,Sec. 2, eff. 12/17/2014.

Section 400.02 - Statewide license and record database

There shall be a statewide license and record database which shall be created and maintained by the division of state police the cost of which shall not be borne by any municipality. Records assembled or collected for purposes of inclusion in such database shall not be subject to disclosure pursuant to article six of the public officers law. Records containing granted license applications shall be periodically checked by the division of criminal justice services against criminal conviction, mental health, and all other records as are necessary to determine their continued accuracy as well as whether an individual is no longer a valid license holder. The division of criminal justice services shall also check pending applications made pursuant to this article against such records to determine whether a license may be granted. All state agencies shall cooperate with the division of criminal justice services, as otherwise authorized by law, in making their records available for such checks. The division of criminal justice services, upon determining that an individual is ineligible to possess a license, or is no longer a valid license holder, shall notify the applicable licensing official of such determination and such licensing official shall not issue a license or revoke such license and any weapons owned or possessed by such individual shall be removed consistent with the provisions of subdivision eleven of section 400.00 of this article. Local and state law enforcement shall have access to such database in the performance of their duties. Records assembled or collected for purposes of inclusion in the database established by this section shall be released pursuant to a court order.

N.Y. Penal Law § 400.02

Amended by New York Laws 2019, ch. 244,Sec. 2, eff. 9/3/2019.

Added by New York Laws 2013, ch. 1,Sec. 49, eff. 1/15/2014.

Section 400.03 - Sellers of ammunition

A seller of ammunition that fails to keep any record required pursuant to this section, for a first offense shall be guilty of a violation and subject to a fine of five hundred dollars, and for a second offense shall be guilty of a class B misdemeanor, and the registration of such seller shall be revoked

1. A seller of ammunition as defined in subdivision twenty-four of section 265.00 of this chapter shall register with the superintendent of state police in a manner provided by the superintendent Any dealer in firearms that is validly licensed pursuant to section 400.00 of this article shall not be required to complete such registration.

2. Any seller of ammunition or dealer in firearms shall keep a record book approved as to form by the superintendent of state police In the record book shall be entered at the time of every transaction involving ammunition the date, name, age, occupation and residence of any person from whom ammunition is received or to whom ammunition is delivered, and the amount, calibre, manufacturer's name and serial number, or if none, any other distinguishing number or identification mark on such ammunition The record book shall be maintained on the premises mentioned and described in the license and shall be open at all reasonable hours for inspection by any peace officer, acting pursuant to his or her special duties, or police officer Any record produced pursuant to this section and any transmission thereof to any government agency shall not be considered a public record for purposes of article six of the public officers law.

3.No later than thirty days after the superintendent of the state police certifies that the statewide license and record database established pursuant to section 400.02 of this article is operational for the purposes of this section, a dealer in firearms licensed pursuant to section 400.00 of this article, a seller of ammunition as defined in subdivision twenty-four of section 265.00 of this chapter shall not transfer any ammunition to any other person who is not a dealer in firearms as defined in subdivision nine of such section 265.00or a seller of ammunition as defined in subdivision twenty-four of section 265.00 of this chapter, unless:

(a) before the completion of the transfer, the licensee or seller contacts the statewide license and record database and provides the database with information sufficient to identify such dealer or seller, transferee based on information on the transferee's identification document as defined in paragraph (c) of this subdivision, as well as the amount, calibre, manufacturer's name and serial number, if any, of such ammunition;

(b) the system provides the licensee or seller with a unique identification number; and

(c) the transferor has verified the identity of the transferee by examining a valid state identification document of the transferee issued by the department of motor vehicles or if the transferee is not a resident of the state of New York, a valid identification document issued by the transferee's state or country of residence containing a photograph of the transferee.

4. If the database determines that the purchaser of ammunition is eligible to possess ammunition pursuant to state and federal laws, the system shall:

(a) assign a unique identification number to the transfer; and

(b) provide the licensee or seller with the number.

5. If the statewide license and record database notifies the licensee or seller that the information available to the database does not demonstrate that the receipt of ammunition by such other person would violate 18 U.S.C. 922(g) or state law, and the licensee transfers ammunition to such other person, the licensee shall indicate to the database that such transaction has been completed at which point a record of such transaction shall be created which shall be accessible by the division of state police and maintained for no longer than one year from point of purchase, which shall not be incorporated into the database established pursuant to section 400.02 of this article or the registry established pursuant to subdivision sixteen-a of section 400.00 of this article The division of state police may share such information with a local law enforcement agency Evidence of the purchase of ammunition is not sufficient to establish probable cause to believe that the purchaser has committed a crime absent other information tending to prove the commission of a crime Records assembled or accessed pursuant to this section shall not be subject to disclosure pursuant to article six of the public officers law This requirement of this section shall not apply (i) if a background check cannot be completed because the system is not operational as determined by the superintendent of state police, or where it cannot be accessed by the practitioner due to a

temporary technological or electrical failure, as set forth in regulation, or (ii) a dealer or seller has been granted a waiver from conducting such background check if the superintendent of state police determines that such dealer is incapable of such check due to technological limitations that are not reasonably within the control of the dealer, or other exceptional circumstances demonstrated by the dealer, pursuant to a process established in regulation, and at the discretion of such superintendent.

6. If the superintendent of state police certifies that background checks of ammunition purchasers may be conducted through the national instant criminal background check system, use of that system by a dealer or seller shall be sufficient to satisfy subdivisions four and five of this section and such checks shall be conducted through such system, provided that a record of such transaction shall be forwarded to the state police in a form determined by the superintendent.

7. No commercial transfer of ammunition shall take place unless a licensed dealer in firearms or registered seller of ammunition acts as an intermediary between the transferor and the ultimate transferee of the ammunition for the purposes of contacting the statewide license and record database pursuant to this section Such transfer between the dealer or seller, and transferee must occur in person.

8. A seller of ammunition who fails to register pursuant to this section and sells ammunition, for a first offense, shall be guilty of a violation and subject to the fine of one thousand dollars and for a second offense, shall be guilty of a class A misdemeanor.

N.Y. Penal Law § 400.03

Added by New York Laws 2013, ch. 1,Sec. 50, eff. 1/15/2014.

Section 400.05 - Disposition of weapons and dangerous instruments, appliances and substances

1. Any weapon, instrument, appliance or substance specified in article two hundred sixty-five, when unlawfully possessed, manufactured, transported or disposed of, or when utilized in the commission of an offense, is hereby declared a nuisance. When the same shall come into the possession of any police officer or peace officer, it shall be surrendered immediately to the official mentioned in paragraph (f) of subdivision one of section 265.20, except that such weapon, instrument, appliance or substance coming into the possession of the state police shall be surrendered to the superintendent of state police.

2. The official to whom the weapon, instrument, appliance or substance which has subsequently been declared a nuisance pursuant to subdivision one of this section is so surrendered shall, at any time but at least once each year, destroy the same or cause it to be destroyed, or render the same or cause it to be rendered ineffective and useless for its intended purpose and harmless to human life.

3. Notwithstanding subdivision two of this section, the official to whom the weapon, instrument, appliance or substance is so surrendered shall not destroy the same if (a) a judge or justice of a court of record, or a district attorney, shall file with the official a certificate that the non-destruction thereof is necessary or proper to serve the ends of justice; or (b) the official directs that the same be retained in any laboratory conducted by any police or sheriff's department for the purpose of research, comparison, identification or other endeavor toward the prevention and detection of crime.

4. In the case of any machine-gun or firearm taken from the possession of any person, the official to whom such weapon is surrendered pursuant to subdivision one of this section shall immediately notify the executive department, division of state police, Albany, giving the calibre, make, model, manufacturer's name and serial number, or if none, any other distinguishing number or identification mark. A search of the files of such division and notification of the results of the search to such official shall immediately be made.

5. Before any machine-gun or firearm is destroyed pursuant to subdivision two of this section, (a) the official to whom the same has been surrendered shall forward to the executive department, division of state police, Albany, a notice of intent to destroy and the calibre, make, model, manufacturer's name and serial number, or if none, any other distinguishing number or identification mark of the machine-gun or firearm; (b) such division shall make and keep a record of such description together with the name and address of the official reporting the same and the date such notice was received; and (c) a search of the files of such division and notification of the results of the search to such official shall be made without unnecessary delay.

6. A firearm or other weapon which is surrendered, or is otherwise voluntarily delivered pursuant to section 265.20 of this chapter and which has not been declared a nuisance pursuant to subdivision one of this section, shall be retained by the official to whom it was delivered for a period not to exceed one year. Prior to the expiration of such time period, a person who surrenders a firearm shall have the right to arrange for the sale, or transfer, of such firearm to a dealer in firearms licensed in accordance with this chapter or for the transfer of such firearm to himself or herself provided that a license therefor has been issued in accordance with this chapter. If no lawful disposition of the firearm or other weapon is made within the time provided, the firearm or weapon concerned shall be declared a nuisance and shall be disposed of in accordance with the provisions of this section.

N.Y. Penal Law § 400.05

Section 400.10 - Report of theft or loss of a firearm,

1.

(a) Any owner or other person lawfully in possession of: (i) a firearm, rifle or, shotgun who suffers the loss or theft of said weapon; (ii) ammunition as well as a firearm, rifle or shotgun who suffers the loss or theft of such ammunition as well as a firearm, rifle or shotgun; or (iii) ammunition and is a dealer in firearms or seller of ammunition who suffers the loss or theft of such ammunition shall within twenty-four hours of the discovery of the loss or theft report the facts and circumstances of the loss or theft to a police department or sheriff's office.

(b) Whenever a person reports the theft or loss of a firearm, rifle , shotgun or ammunition to any police department or sheriff's office, the officer or department receiving such report shall forward notice of such theft or loss to the division of state police via the New York Statewide Police Information Network. The notice shall contain information in compliance with the New York Statewide Police Information Network Operating Manual, including the caliber, make, model, manufacturer's name and serial number, if any, and any other distinguishing number or identification mark on the weapon.

2. The division of state police shall receive, collect and file the information referred to in subdivision one of this section. The division shall cooperate, and undertake to furnish or make available to law enforcement agencies this information, for the purpose of coordinating law enforcement efforts to locate such weapons.

3. Notwithstanding any other provision of law, a violation of paragraph (a) of subdivision one of this section shall be a class A misdemeanor.

N.Y. Penal Law § 400.10

Amended by New York Laws 2013, ch. 1,Sec. 51, eff. 3/16/2013.

Section 400.20 - Waiting period in connection with the sale or transfer of a rifle or shotgun

When a national instant criminal background check is required pursuant to state or federal law to be conducted through the National Instant Criminal Background Check System (NICS) or its successor in connection with the sale or transfer of a rifle or shotgun to any person, before delivering a rifle or shotgun to such person, either (a) NICS has issued a "proceed" response to the seller or transferor, or (b) thirty calendar days shall have elapsed since the date the seller or transferor contacted NICS to initiate a national instant criminal background check and NICS has not notified the seller or transferor that the transfer of the rifle or shotgun to such person should be denied.

N.Y. Penal Law § 400.20

Added by New York Laws 2019, ch. 129,Sec. 2, eff. 9/12/2019.

Article 405 - LICENSING AND OTHER PROVISIONS RELATING TO FIREWORKS

Section 405.00 - Permits for public displays of fireworks

1. Definition of "permit authority." The term "permit authority," as used in this section, means and includes the agency authorized to grant and issue the permits provided in this section. The permit authority on or within state property shall be the office of fire prevention and control. The permit authority for territory within a county park shall be the county park commission, or such other agency having jurisdiction, control and/or operation of the parks or parkways within which any fireworks are to be displayed. The permit authority in a city shall be the duly constituted licensing agency thereof and, in the absence of such agency, shall be an officer designated for the purpose by the legislative body thereof. The permit authority in a village shall be an officer designated for the purpose by the board of trustees thereof and the permit authority in the territory of a town outside of villages shall be an officer designated for the purpose by the town board thereof.

2. Permits for fireworks displays. Notwithstanding the provisions of section 270.00 of this chapter, the permit authority for state property, county parks, cities, villages, or towns may grant a permit for the display of fireworks to municipalities, fair associations, amusement parks, persons, or organizations of individuals that submit an application in writing. The application for such permit shall set forth:

(a) The name of the body sponsoring the display and the names of the persons actually to be in charge of the firing of the display who shall possess a valid certificate of competence as a pyrotechnician as required under the general business law and article sixteen of the labor law. The permit application shall further contain a verified statement from the applicant identifying the individuals who are authorized to fire the display including their certificate numbers, and that such individuals possess a valid certificate of competence as a pyrotechnician.

(b) The date and time of day at which the display is to be held.

(c) The exact location planned for the display.

(d) The number and kind of fireworks to be discharged.

(e) The manner and place of storage of such fireworks prior to the display.

(f) A diagram of the grounds on which the display is to be held showing the point at which the fireworks are to be discharged, the location of all buildings, highways and other lines of communication, the lines behind which the audience will be restrained and the location of all nearby trees, telegraph or telephone lines or other overhead obstructions.

(g) Such other information as the permit authority may deem necessary to protect persons or property.

3. Applications for permits. All applications for permits for the display of fireworks shall be made at least five days in advance of the date of the display and the permit shall contain provisions that the actual point at which the fireworks are to be fired be in accordance with the rules promulgated by the commissioner of labor pursuant to section four hundred sixty-two of the labor law and that all the persons in actual charge of firing the fireworks shall be over the age of eighteen years, competent and physically fit for the task, that there shall be at least two such operators constantly on duty during the discharge and that at least two approved type fire extinguishers shall be kept at as widely separated points as possible within the actual area of the display. For any applications made for the display of fireworks on state property, the state fire administrator shall coordinate the issuance of such permits with the head of the police or fire department or both, where there are such departments. The legislative body of a county park, city, village or town may provide for approval of such permit by the head of the police or fire department or both where there are such departments. No permit granted and issued hereunder shall be transferable. After such permit shall have been granted, sales, possession, use and distribution of fireworks for such display shall be lawful solely therefor.

3-a. Notwithstanding the provisions of subdivision three of this section, no permit may be issued to conduct a display of fireworks upon any property where the boundary line of such property is less than five hundred yards from the boundary line of any property which is owned, leased or operated by any breeder as defined in subdivision four of section two hundred fifty-one of the racing, pari-mutuel wagering and breeding law.

4. Bonds. Before granting and issuing a permit for a display of fireworks as herein provided, the permit authority shall require an adequate bond from the applicant therefor, unless it is a state entity, county park, city, village or town, in a sum to be fixed by the permit authority, which, however, shall not be less than one million dollars, conditioned for the payment of all damages, which may be caused to a person or persons or to property, by reason of the display so permitted and arising from any acts of the permittee, his or her agents, employees, contractors or subcontractors. Such bond shall run to the state if the permit is granted for a display on state property, or to the county park, city, village or town in which the permit is granted and issued and shall be for the use and benefit of any person or persons or any owner or owners of any property so injured or damaged, and such person or persons or such owner or owners are hereby authorized to maintain an action thereon, which right of action also shall accrue to the heirs, executors, administrators, successors or assigns of such person or persons or such owner or owners. The permit authority may accept, in lieu of such bond, an indemnity insurance policy with liability coverage and indemnity protection equivalent to the terms and conditions upon which such bond is predicated and for the purposes provided in this section.

5. Local ordinances superseded.

(a) All local ordinances regulating or prohibiting the display of fireworks are hereby superseded by the provisions of this section. Every city, town or village shall have the power to enact ordinances or local laws regulating or prohibiting the use, or the storage, transportation or sale for use of fireworks in the preparation for or in connection with television broadcasts.

(b) Notwithstanding any inconsistent provision of law, a county may enact a local law to prohibit the sale and use of "sparkling devices", as such term is defined in section 270.00 of this chapter, provided, however, any such local law shall not establish:

(i) an offense greater than a violation for a person who shall use, explode or cause to be exploded a sparkling device; or

(ii) an offense greater than a class B misdemeanor for a person who shall offer or expose for sale, sell or furnish a sparkling device valued at less than five hundred dollars unless such offer, sale or furnishing is to a person less than eighteen years of age.

(c) Notwithstanding paragraph (b) of this subdivision, any city wholly contained within the county of Orange may enact a local law to prohibit the sale and use of "sparkling devices" as defined in section 270.00 of this chapter, in accordance with subparagraphs (i) and (ii) of paragraph (b) of this subdivision, notwithstanding that such county has not enacted a local law to prohibit the sale and use of such sparkling devices.

N.Y. Penal Law § 405.00

Amended by New York Laws 2017, ch. 371,Sec. 2, eff. 1/21/2018.
Amended by New York Laws 2016, ch. 458,Sec. 1, eff. 11/28/2016.
Amended by New York Laws 2014, ch. 477,Sec. 2, eff. 12/21/2014.
Amended by New York Laws 2013, ch. 127,Sec. 2, eff. 7/12/2013.

Section 405.05 - Seizure and destruction of fireworks

Fireworks possessed unlawfully may be seized by any peace officer, acting pursuant to his special duties, or police officer, who must deliver the same to the magistrate before whom the person arrested is required to be taken. The magistrate must, upon the examination of the defendant, or if such examination is delayed or prevented, without awaiting such examination, determine whether the fireworks had been possessed by the defendant in violation of the provisions of section 270.00; and if he finds that the fireworks had been so possessed by the defendant, he must cause such fireworks to be destroyed, in a way safe for the particular type of such fireworks, or to be delivered to the district attorney of the county in which the defendant is liable to indictment or trial, as the interests of justice and public safety may, in his opinion, require. Upon the conviction of the defendant, the district attorney must cause to be destroyed, in a way safe for the particular type of such fireworks, the fireworks in respect whereof the defendant stands convicted, and which remain in the possession or under the control of the district attorney.

N.Y. Penal Law § 405.05

Section 405.10 - Permits for indoor pyrotechnics

1. Definitions. For the purposes of this section, the following terms have the following meanings:

a. Airburst. A pyrotechnic device that is suspended in the air to simulate outdoor aerial fireworks shells without producing hazardous debris.

b. Areas of public assembly. All buildings or portions of buildings used for gathering together fifty or more persons for amusement, athletic, civic, dining, educational, entertainment, patriotic, political, recreational, religious, social, or similar purposes, the entire fire area of which they are a part, and the means of egress therefrom.

c. Assistant. A person who works under the supervision of the pyrotechnic operator.

d. Audience. Spectators whose primary purpose is to view a performance.

e. Building. A combination of any materials, whether portable or fixed, having a roof, to form a structure affording shelter for persons, animals, or property. The word "building" shall be construed for the purposes of this section as though followed by the words "or part or parts thereof", unless the context clearly requires a different meaning.

f. Concussion mortar. A device specifically designed and constructed to produce a loud noise and a violent jarring shock for dramatic effect without producing any damage.

g. Fallout area. The area in which any hazardous debris falls after a pyrotechnic device is fired. The fallout area is defined as a circle that, in turn, is defined by the fallout radius.

h. Fallout radius. A line that defines the fallout area of a pyrotechnic device. The line is defined by two points. The first point is at the center of a pyrotechnic device. The second point is the point most distant from the center of the pyrotechnic device at which any hazardous debris from the device can fall.

i. Fire area. The floor area of a story of a building within exterior walls, party walls, fire walls, or any combination thereof.

j. Hazardous debris. Any debris, produced or expelled by the functioning of a pyrotechnic device, that is capable of causing personal injury or unpredicted property damage. This includes, but is not limited to, hot sparks, heavy casing fragments, and unignited components. Materials such as confetti, lightweight foam pieces, feathers, or novelties are not to be construed as hazardous debris.

k. Owner. Any person, agent, firm, association, limited liability company, partnership, or corporation having a legal or equitable interest in the property.

l. Performance. The enactment of a musical, dramatic, operatic, or other entertainment production. The enactment may begin and progress to its end according to a script, plan, or other preconceived list of events, or deviate therefrom. A performance includes any encores.

m. Performer. Any person active in a performance during which pyrotechnics are used and who is not part of the audience or support personnel. Among others, performers include, but are not limited to, actors, singers, musicians, and acrobats.

n. Permit authority. The agency authorized to grant and issue the permits provided for in this section on or within state property shall be the office of fire prevention and control, in the territory within a county park shall be the county park commission, or such other agency having jurisdiction, control, and/or operation of the parks or parkways within which any pyrotechnics are to be used, in a city shall be the duly constituted licensing agency thereof and, in the absence of such agency, shall be an officer designated for the purpose by the legislative body thereof, in a village shall be an officer designated for the purpose by the board of trustees thereof, and, in the territory of a town outside of villages, shall be an officer designated for the purpose by the town board thereof.

o. Permittee.

(1) The person or persons who are responsible, as provided in subparagraph two of this paragraph, for obtaining the necessary permit or permits for the use of indoor pyrotechnics in areas of public assembly or for a production, or who are responsible for obtaining such permit or permits under an applicable local law or ordinance authorized pursuant to subdivision five of this section.

(2) The owner of a place of public assembly or building in which pyrotechnics are to be used shall be responsible for obtaining such permit or permits; provided, however, that such owner, in writing, by agreement or lease, may require or otherwise authorize a lessee, licensee, pyrotechnic operator, or other party to be responsible for obtaining such permit or permits, in which case such other party or parties shall be deemed responsible for obtaining such permit or permits and shall be the permittee for purposes of this article; provided further that the structure is otherwise appropriate for such use under the New York state fire prevention and building code or other such applicable code.

p. Producer. An individual who has overall responsibility for the operation and management of the performance where the pyrotechnics are to be used. Generally, the producer is an employee of the promotion company, entertainment company, festival, theme park, or other entertainment group.

q. Production. All the performances of a musical, dramatic, operatic, or other show or series of shows.

r. Pyrotechnic device. Any device containing pyrotechnic materials and capable of producing a special effect as defined in this subdivision.

s. Pyrotechnic material (Pyrotechnic special effects material). A chemical mixture used in the entertainment industry to produce visible or audible effects by combustion, deflagration, or detonation. Such a chemical mixture consists predominantly of solids capable of producing a controlled, self-sustaining, and self-contained exothermic chemical reaction that results in heat, gas, sound, light, or a combination of these effects. The chemical reaction functions without external oxygen.

t. Pyrotechnic operator (Special effects operator). An individual who has responsibility for pyrotechnic safety and who controls, initiates, or otherwise creates special effects.

u. Pyrotechnic special effect. A special effect created through the use of pyrotechnic materials and devices.

v. Pyrotechnics. Controlled exothermic chemical reactions that are timed to create the effects of heat, gas, sound, dispersion of aerosols, emission of visible electromagnetic radiation, or a combination of these effects to provide the maximum effect from the least volume.

w. Rocket. A pyrotechnic device that moves by the ejection of matter produced by the internal combustion of propellants.

x. Special effect. A visual or audible effect used for entertainment purposes, often produced to create an illusion. For example, smoke might be produced to create the impression of fog being present, or a puff of smoke, a flash of light, and a loud sound might be produced to create the impression that a cannon has been fired.

y. Support personnel. Any individual who is not a performer or member of the audience. Among others, support personnel include the road crew of any production, stage hands, property masters, security guards, fire watch officers, janitors, or any other employee.

z. Venue manager. An individual who has overall responsibility for the operation and management of the facility where pyrotechnics are to be used in a performance.

2. Permit requirements.

a. All uses of all pyrotechnics in areas of public assembly shall be approved by the permit authority. The permit authority shall determine that appropriate measures are established to provided acceptable crowd management, security, fire protection, (including sprinklers), and other emergency services. All planning and use of pyrotechnics shall be coordinated with the venue manager and producer.

b. Before the performance of any production, the permittee shall submit a plan for the use of pyrotechnics to the permit authority. After a permit has been granted, the permittee shall keep the plan available at the site for safety inspectors or other designated agents of the permit authority. Any addition of pyrotechnics to a performance or any significant change in the presentation of pyrotechnics shall require approval by the permit authority, except that reducing the number or size of pyrotechnics to be used in a performance shall not be considered to be a significant change in the presentation.

c.

(1) The plan for the use of pyrotechnics shall be made in writing or such other form as is required or approved by the permit authority.

(2) The plan shall provide the following:

(a) Name of the person, group, organization, or other entity sponsoring the production.

(b) Date and time of day of the production.

(c) Exact location of the production.

(d) Name of the person actually in charge of firing the pyrotechnics (i.e., the pyrotechnic operator).

(e) Number, names, and ages of all assistants who are to be present.

(f) Qualifications of the pyrotechnic operator.

(g) Pyrotechnic experience of the operator.

(h) Confirmation of any applicable local, state, and federal licenses held by the operator or assistant.

(i) Evidence of the permittee's insurance carrier or financial responsibility.

(j) Number and types of pyrotechnic devices and materials to be used, the operator's experience with those devices and effects, and a definition of the general responsibilities of assistants.

(k) Diagram of the grounds or facilities where the production is to be held. This diagram shall show the point at which the pyrotechnic devices are to be fired, the fallout radius for each pyrotechnic device used in the performance, the lines behind which the audience shall be restrained, and the placement of sprinkler systems.

(l) Point of on-site assembly of pyrotechnic devices.

(m) Manner and place of storage of the pyrotechnic materials and devices.

(n) Material safety data sheet (MSDS) for the pyrotechnic materials to be used.

(o) Certification that the set, scenery, and rigging materials are inherently flame-retardant or have been treated to achieve flame retardancy.

(p) Certification that all materials worn by performers in the fallout area during use of pyrotechnic effects shall be inherently flame-retardant or have been treated to achieve flame retardancy.

(3) All plans shall be submitted as soon as is possible so that the permit authority has time to be present and to notify other interested parties. In no event shall such advance notice be less than five business days.

d. A walk-through and a representative demonstration of the pyrotechnics shall be approved by the permit authority before a permit is approved. The permit authority may waive this requirement based on past history, prior knowledge, and other factors; provided that the authority is confident that the discharge of pyrotechnics can be conducted safely. The demonstration shall be scheduled with sufficient time allowed to reset/reload the pyrotechnics before the arrival of the audience.

e. All pyrotechnic operators shall be at least twenty-one years old and licensed or approved by the permit authority in accordance with all applicable laws, if any. All assistants shall be at least eighteen years old.

3. Conduct of pyrotechnic performances.

a. Two or more fire extinguishers of the proper classification and size as approved by the permit authority shall be readily accessible while the pyrotechnics are being loaded, prepared for firing, or fired. In all cases, at least two pressurized water or pump extinguishers shall be available. Additional fire extinguishing equipment shall be provided as required by the permit authority. Personnel who have a working knowledge of the use of the applicable fire extinguishers shall be present while the pyrotechnics are being handled, used, or removed. No personnel shall use or handle pyrotechnic materials or devices while under the influence of intoxicating beverages, narcotics, controlled substances, and prescription or nonprescription drugs that can impair judgment. Fire detection and life safety systems shall not be interrupted during the operation of pyrotechnic effects.

b.

(1) All pyrotechnic devices shall be mounted in a secure manner to maintain their proper positions and orientations so that, when they are fired, the pyrotechnic effects described in the plan submitted by the permittee are produced. Pyrotechnic devices shall be mounted so that no fallout from the device endangers human lives, results in personal injury, or damages property. Pyrotechnic materials shall be fired only from equipment specifically constructed for the purpose of firing pyrotechnic materials. The pyrotechnic operator shall be responsible for selecting equipment and materials that are compatible.

(2) Where rockets are launched before an audience, performers, or support personnel, the rockets shall be attached securely to a guide wire or cable with both ends securely attached and placed on an impact-resistant surface located at the terminal end of the guide. This guide wire or cable shall be of sufficient strength and flame resistance to withstand the exhaust from the rocket. An effective arrangement to stop the rocket shall be provided.

(3) Pyrotechnics shall be: (a) placed so that any hazardous debris falls into a safe, flame-resistant area; (b) fired so that the trajectory of their pyrotechnic material is not carried over the audience; and (c) placed for firing so that no flammable materials are within their fallout area.

(4) Pyrotechnic devices and materials used indoors shall be specifically manufactured and marked for indoor use by the manufacturer.

(5) Airbursts shall be permitted to be fired above the assembled audience, subject to the following conditions:

(a) The airburst shall be suspended by a minimum 30-gauge metal wire that is attached securely to a secure support acceptable to the authority having jurisdiction.

(b) The airburst shall occur at a minimum height of three times the diameter of the effect.

(c) Where the effect is demonstrated, there shall be no burning or glowing particles below the fifteen-foot level above the floor.

c. Each pyrotechnic device fired during a performance shall be separated from the audience by at least fifteen feet but not by less than twice the fallout radius of the device. Concussion mortars shall be separated from the audience by a minimum of twenty-five feet. There shall be no glowing or flaming particles within ten feet of the audience.

d.

(1) The facility where pyrotechnic materials and devices are handled and used shall be maintained in a neat and orderly condition and shall be kept free of any conditions that can create a fire hazard.

(2) Smoking shall not be permitted within twenty-five feet of the area where pyrotechnics are being handled or fired; provided that smoking by performers as part of the performance shall be permitted as blocked in rehearsals and if expressly approved by the pyrotechnic operator and the permit authority.

e.

(1) The pyrotechnic effect operator shall advise all performers and support personnel that they are exposed to a potentially hazardous situation when performing or otherwise carrying out their responsibilities in the vicinity of a pyrotechnic effect. Performers and support personnel familiar and experienced with the pyrotechnic effects being used shall be permitted to be in the area of a pyrotechnic effect, but only voluntarily and in the performance of their duties.

(2) No part, projectile, or debris from the pyrotechnic material or device shall be propelled so that it damages overhead properties, overhead equipment, or the ceiling and walls of the facility.

(3) Immediately before any performance, the pyrotechnic operator shall make a final check of wiring, positions, hook-ups, and pyrotechnic devices to ensure that they are in proper working order. The pyrotechnic operator also shall verify safety distances.

(4) The placement and wiring of all pyrotechnic devices shall be designed to minimize the possibility of performers and support personnel disturbing the devices during a performance.

(5) The pyrotechnic operator shall exercise extreme care throughout the performance to ensure that the pyrotechnic devices function correctly and that the performers, support personnel, and audience are clear of the devices.

(6) When pyrotechnics are fired, the quantity of smoke developed shall be controlled so as not to obscure the visibility of exit signs or paths of egress.

4. Bonds. Before granting and issuing a permit for a use of pyrotechnics as provided in this section, the permit authority shall require an adequate bond from the applicant therefor, unless such applicant is a state entity, county park, city, village, or town, or from the person to whom a contract for such use shall be awarded, in a sum to be fixed by the permit authority, which, however, shall not be less than five hundred thousand dollars, conditioned for the payment of all damages which may be caused to a person or persons or to property by reason of the use so permitted and arising from any acts of the permittee, his or her agents, employees, contractors, or subcontractors. Such bond shall run to the owner of the facility for which the permit is granted and issued and shall be for the use and benefit of any person or persons or any owner or owners of any property so injured or damaged, and such person or persons or such owner or owners are hereby authorized to maintain an action thereon, which right of action also shall accrue to the heirs, executors, administrators, successors, or assigns of such person or persons or such owner or owners. The permit authority may accept, in lieu of such bond, an indemnity insurance policy with liability coverage and indemnity protection equivalent to the terms and conditions upon which such bond is predicated and for the purposes herein provided.

5. Local laws or ordinances superseded. All local laws or ordinances regulating the use of pyrotechnics within the contemplation of this section are hereby superseded by the provisions of this section, with the exception of:

a. all laws or ordinances enacted by a city of one million or more; and

b.other local laws or ordinances that prohibit the use of indoor pyrotechnics.

N.Y. Penal Law § 405.10

Amended by New York Laws 2013, ch. 127,Sec. 3, eff. 7/12/2013.

Section 405.12 - Unpermitted use of indoor pyrotechnics in the second degree

A person is guilty of unpermitted use of indoor pyrotechnics in the second degree when he or she is responsible for obtaining a necessary permit to use indoor pyrotechnics, as required by paragraph o of subdivision one of section 405.10 of this article, and, without obtaining such permit or knowing that he or she is not in compliance with the terms of a permit, he or she intentionally ignites or detonates pyrotechnics for which such permit is required, or knowingly permits another to ignite or detonate such pyrotechnics, in a building, as defined in paragraph e of subdivision one of section 405.10 of this article.

N.Y. Penal Law § 405.12

Section 405.14 - Unpermitted use of indoor pyrotechnics in the first degree

A person is guilty of unpermitted use of indoor pyrotechnics in the first degree when he or she commits the crime of unpermitted use of indoor pyrotechnics in the second degree, as defined in section 405.12 of this article, and, within the previous five year period, he or she has been convicted one or more times of the crime of unpermitted use of indoor pyrotechnics in the second degree, as defined in section 405.12 of this article, or unpermitted use of indoor pyrotechnics in the first degree, as defined in this section.

N.Y. Penal Law § 405.14

Section 405.16 - Aggravated unpermitted use of indoor pyrotechnics in the second degree

A person is guilty of aggravated unpermitted use of indoor pyrotechnics in the second degree when he or she commits the crime of unpermitted use of indoor pyrotechnics in the second degree, as defined in section 405.12 of this article, and, by means of igniting or detonating such indoor pyrotechnics, he or she recklessly:

(1) causes physical injury to another person; or (2) damages the property of another person in an amount that exceeds two hundred fifty dollars.

Aggravated unpermitted use of indoor pyrotechnics in the second degree is a class E felony.

N.Y. Penal Law § 405.16

Section 405.18 - Aggravated unpermitted use of indoor pyrotechnics in the first degree

A person is guilty of aggravated unpermitted use of indoor pyrotechnics in the first degree when he or she commits the crime of unpermitted use of indoor pyrotechnics in the second degree, as defined in section 405.12 of this article, and, by means of igniting or detonating such indoor pyrotechnics, he or she recklessly causes serious physical injury or death to another person.

N.Y. Penal Law § 405.18

Article 410 - SEIZURE AND FORFEITURE OF EQUIPMENT USED IN PROMOTING PORNOGRAPHY

Section 410.00 - Seizure and forfeiture of equipment used in photographing, filming, producing, manufacturing, projecting or distributing pornographic still or motion

§ 410.00 Seizure and forfeiture of equipment used in photographing, filming, producing, manufacturing, projecting or distributing pornographic still or motion pictures.

1. Any peace officer, acting pursuant to his special duties, or police officer of this state may seize any equipment used in the photographing, filming, printing, producing, manufacturing or projecting of pornographic still or motion pictures and may seize any vehicle or other means of transportation, other than a vehicle or other means of transportation used by any person as a common carrier in the transaction of business as such common carrier, used in the distribution of such obscene prints and articles and such equipment or vehicle or other means of transportation shall be subject to forfeiture as hereinafter in this section provided.

2. The seized property shall be delivered by the police officer or peace officer having made the seizure to the custody of the district attorney of the county wherein the seizure was made, except that in the cities of New York, Yonkers and Buffalo, the seized property shall be delivered to the custody of the police department of such cities, together with a report of all the facts and circumstances of the seizure.

3. It shall be the duty of the district attorney of the county wherein the seizure was made, if elsewhere than in the cities of New York or Buffalo, and where the seizure is made in either such city it shall be the duty of the corporation counsel of the city, to inquire into the facts of the seizure so reported to him and if it appears probable that a forfeiture has been incurred, for the determination of which the institution of proceedings in the supreme court is necessary, to cause the proper proceedings to be commenced and prosecuted, at any time after thirty days from the date of seizure, to declare such forfeiture, unless, upon inquiry and examination such district attorney or corporation counsel decides that such proceedings can not probably be sustained or that the ends of public justice do not require that they should be instituted or prosecuted, in which case, the district attorney or corporation counsel shall cause such seized property to be returned to the owner thereof.

4. Notice of the institution of the forfeiture proceeding shall be served either (a) personally on the owners of the seized property or (b) by registered mail to the owners' last known address and by publication of the notice once a week for two successive weeks in a newspaper published or circulated in the county wherein the seizure was made.

5. Forfeiture shall not be adjudged where the owners established by preponderance of the evidence that (a) the use of such seized property was not intentional on the part of any owner, or (b) said seized property was used by any person other than an owner thereof, while such seized property was unlawfully in the possession of a person who acquired possession thereof in violation of the criminal laws of the United States, or of any state.

6. The district attorney or the police department having custody of the seized property, after such judicial determination of forfeiture, shall, by a public notice of at least five days, sell such forfeited property at public sale. The net proceeds of any such sale, after deduction of the lawful expenses incurred, shall be paid into the general fund of the county wherein the seizure was made except that the net proceeds of the sale of property seized in the cities of New York and Buffalo shall be paid into the respective general funds of such cities.

7. Whenever any person interested in any property which is seized and declared forfeited under the provisions of this section files with a justice of the supreme court a petition for the recovery of such forfeited property, the justice of the supreme court may restore said forfeited property upon such terms and conditions as he deems reasonable and just, if the petitioner establishes either of the affirmative defenses set forth in subdivision five of this section and that the petitioner

was without personal or actual knowledge of the forfeiture proceeding. If the petition be filed after the sale of the forfeited property, any judgment in favor of the petitioner shall be limited to the net proceeds of such sale, after deduction of the lawful expenses and costs incurred by the district attorney, police department or corporation counsel.

8. No suit or action under this section for wrongful seizure shall be instituted unless such suit or action is commenced within two years after the time when the property was seized.

9. For the purposes of this section only, a pornographic still or motion picture, is defined as a still or motion picture showing acts of sexual intercourse or acts of sexual perversion. This section shall not be construed as applying to bona fide medical photographs or films.

N.Y. Penal Law § 410.00

Article 415 - SEIZURE AND FORFEITURE OF VEHICLES, VESSELS AND AIRCRAFT USED TO TRANSPORT OR CONCEAL GAMBLING RECORDS

Section 415.00 - Seizure and forfeiture of vehicles, vessels and aircraft used to transport or conceal gambling records

1. It shall be unlawful to transport, carry, convey or conceal in, upon or by means of any vehicle, vessel or aircraft, with knowledge of the contents thereof, any writing, paper, instrument or article:

(a) Of a kind commonly used in the operation or promotion of a bookmaking scheme or enterprise, and constituting, reflecting or representing more than five bets totaling more than five thousand dollars; or

(b) Of a kind commonly used in the operation, promotion or playing of a lottery or policy scheme or enterprise, and constituting, reflecting or representing more than five hundred plays or chances therein.

2. Any vehicle, vessel or aircraft which has been or is being used in violation of subdivision one by a person other than a bettor, player or shareholder whose bets, plays or shares are represented by all such writings, papers, instruments or articles, shall be seized by any peace officer, who is acting pursuant to his special duties, or police officer, and forfeited as provided in this section. However, such forfeiture and seizure provisions shall not apply to any vehicle, vessel or aircraft used by any person as a common carrier in the transaction of business as such common carrier.

3. The seized property shall be delivered by the police officer or peace officer having made the seizure to the custody of the district attorney of the county wherein the seizure was made, except that in the cities of New York, Yonkers and Buffalo, the seized property shall be delivered to the custody of the police department of such cities, together with a report of all the facts and circumstances of the seizure.

4. It shall be the duty of the district attorney of the county wherein the seizure is made, if elsewhere than in the cities of New York, Yonkers or Buffalo, and where the seizure is made in either such city it shall be the duty of the corporation counsel of the city, to inquire into the facts of the seizure so reported to him and if it appears probable that a forfeiture has been incurred by reason of a violation of this section, for the determination of which the institution of proceedings in the supreme court is necessary, to cause the proper proceedings to be commenced and prosecuted, at any time after thirty days from the date of seizure, to declare such forfeiture, unless, upon inquiry and examination, such district attorney or corporation counsel decides that such proceedings can not probably be sustained or that the ends of public justice do not require that they should be instituted or prosecuted, in which case, the district attorney or corporation counsel shall cause such seized property to be returned to the owner thereof.

5. Notice of the institution of the forfeiture proceeding shall be served either (a) personally on the owners of the seized property, or (b) by registered mail to the owners' last known address and by publication of the notice once a week for two successive weeks in a newspaper published or circulated in the county wherein the seizure was made.

6. Forfeiture shall not be adjudged where the owners establish by preponderance of the evidence that (a) the use of such seized property, in violation of subdivision one of this section, was not intentional on the part of any owner, or (b) said seized property was used in violation of subdivision one of this section by any person other than an owner thereof, while such seized property was unlawfully in the possession of a person who acquired possession thereof in violation of the criminal laws of the United States, or of any state.

7. The district attorney or the police department having custody of the seized property, after such judicial determination of forfeiture, shall, at their discretion, either retain such seized property for the official use of their office or department, or, by a public notice of at least five days, sell such forfeited property at public sale. The net proceeds of any such sale, after deduction of the lawful expenses incurred, shall be paid into the general fund of the county wherein the seizure was made except that the net proceeds of the sale of property seized in the cities of New York, Yonkers and Buffalo shall be paid into the respective general funds of such cities.

8. Whenever any person interested in any property which is seized and declared forfeited under the provisions of this section files with a justice of the supreme court a petition for the recovery of such forfeited property, the justice of the supreme court may restore said forfeited property upon such terms and conditions as he deems reasonable and just, if the petitioner establishes either of the affirmative defenses set forth in subdivision six of this section and that the petitioner was without personal or actual knowledge of the forfeiture proceeding. If the petition be filed after the sale of the forfeited property, any judgment in favor of the petitioner shall be limited to the net proceeds of such sale after deduction of the lawful expenses and costs incurred by the district attorney, police department or corporation counsel.

9. No suit or action under this section for wrongful seizure shall be instituted unless such suit or action is commenced within two years after the time when the property was seized.

N.Y. Penal Law § 415.00

Article 420 - SEIZURE AND DESTRUCTION OF UNAUTHORIZED RECORDINGS OF SOUND AND FORFEITURE OF EQUIPMENT USED IN THE PRODUCTION THEREOF

Section 420.00 - Seizure and destruction of unauthorized recordings

Any article produced in violation of article two hundred seventy-five of this chapter may be seized by any police officer upon the arrest of any individual in possession of same. Upon final determination of the charges, the court shall, upon proper notice by the district attorney or representative of the crime victim or victims, after prior notice to the district attorney and custodian of the seized property, enter an order preserving any goods manufactured, sold, offered for sale, distributed or produced in violation of this article, as evidence for use in other cases, including a civil action. This notice must be received within thirty days of final determination of the charges. The cost of storage, security, and destruction of goods so ordered for preservation and use as evidence in a civil action, other than a civil action under article thirteen-A of the civil practice law and rules initiated by the district attorney, shall be paid by the party seeking preservation of the evidence for a civil action. If no such order is entered within the thirty day period, the district attorney or custodian of the seized property must cause such articles to be destroyed. Destruction shall not include auction, sale, or distribution of the items in their original form.

N.Y. Penal Law § 420.00

Section 420.05 - Seizure and forfeiture of equipment used in the production of unauthorized recordings

1. Any police officer of this state may seize any equipment, or components, used in the manufacture or production of unauthorized recordings and may seize any vehicle or other means of transportation, other than a vehicle or means of transportation used by any person as a common carrier in the transaction of business as such common carrier, used in the distribution of such unauthorized recordings and such equipment or vehicle or other means of transportation shall be subject to forfeiture as provided in this section.

2. The seized property shall be delivered by the police officer having made the seizure to the custody of the district attorney of the county wherein the seizure was made, except that in the cities of New York, Yonkers and Buffalo, the seized property shall be delivered to the custody of the police department of such cities, together with a report of all the facts and circumstances of the seizure.

3. It shall be the duty of the district attorney of the county wherein the seizure was made, if elsewhere than in the city of New York, Yonkers or Buffalo, and where the seizure is made in either such city, it shall be the duty of the corporation counsel of the city, to inquire into the facts of the seizure so reported to him and if it appears probable that a forfeiture has been incurred for the determination of which the institution of proceedings in the supreme court is necessary, to cause the proper proceedings to be commenced and prosecuted, at any time after thirty days from the date of seizure, to declare such forfeiture, unless, upon inquiry and examination such district attorney or corporation counsel decides that such proceedings cannot probably be sustained or that the ends of public justice do not require that they should be instituted or prosecuted, in which case, the district attorney or corporation counsel shall cause such seized property to be returned to the owner thereof.

4. Notice of the institution of the forfeiture proceeding shall be served either:

(a) personally on the owners of the seized property; or

(b) by registered mail to the owners' last known address and by publication of the notice once a week for two successive weeks in a newspaper published or circulated in the county wherein the seizure was made.

5. Forfeiture shall not be adjudged where the owners established by preponderance of the evidence that:

(a) the use of such seized property was not intentional on the part of any owner; or

(b) said seized property was used by any person other than an owner thereof, while such seized property was unlawfully in the possession of a person who acquired possession thereof in violation of the criminal laws of the United States, or of any state.

6. The district attorney or the police department having custody of the seized property, after such judicial determination of forfeiture, shall, by a public notice of at least five days, sell such forfeited property at public sale. The net proceeds of any such sale, after deduction of the lawful expenses incurred, shall be paid into the general fund of the county wherein the seizure was made except that the net proceeds of the sale of property seized in the cities of New York, Yonkers and Buffalo shall be paid into the respective general funds of such cities.

7. Whenever any person interested in any property which is seized and declared forfeited under the provisions of this section files with a justice of the supreme court a petition for the recovery of such forfeited property, the justice of the supreme court may restore said forfeited property upon such terms and conditions as he deems reasonable and just, if the petitioner establishes either of the affirmative defenses set forth in subdivision five of this section and that the petitioner was without personal or actual knowledge of the forfeiture proceeding. If the petition be filed after the sale of the forfeited property, any judgment in favor of the petitioner shall be limited to the net proceeds of such sale, after deduction of the lawful expenses and costs incurred by the district attorney, police department or corporation counsel.

8. No suit or action under this section for wrongful seizure shall be instituted unless such suit or action is commenced within two years after the time when the property was seized.

N.Y. Penal Law § 420.05

Article 450 - DISPOSAL OF STOLEN PROPERTY

Section 450.10 - Disposal of stolen property

1. When property, other than contraband including but not limited to those items subject to the provisions of sections 410.00, 415.00, 420.00 and 420.05 of this chapter, alleged to have been stolen is in the custody of a police officer, a peace

officer or a district attorney and a request for its release is made prior to or during the criminal proceeding, it may not be released except as provided in subdivisions two, three and four of this section. When a request is made for the return of stolen property under this section, the police officer, peace officer or district attorney in possession of such property must provide written notice to the defendant or his counsel of such request as soon as practicable. Such notice shall advise the defendant or his counsel of the date on which the property will be released and the name and address of a person with whom arrangements can be made for the examination, testing, photographing, photocopying or other reproduction of said property.

2. Both the defendant's counsel and the prosecutor thereafter shall make a diligent effort to examine, test and photograph, photocopy or otherwise reproduce the property. Either party may apply to the court for an extension of any period allowed for examination, testing, photographing, photocopying or otherwise reproducing the property. For good cause shown the court may order retention of the property for use as evidence by either party. Unless extended by a court order sought by either party on notice to the other, the property shall be released no later than the time periods for retention set forth in subdivisions three and four of this section to the person making such request after satisfactory proof of such person's entitlement to the possession thereof. Unless a court, upon applicaton of either party with notice to the other, orders otherwise, the release of property in accordance with the provisions of this section shall be unconditional.

3. Except as provided in subdivision four of this section, when a request is made for the release of property described in subdivision one of this section, the property shall be retained until either the expiration of a fifteen day period from receipt by the defendant or his counsel of the notice of the request, or the examination testing and photographing, photocopying or other reproduction of such property, by the parties, whichever event occurs first. The fifteen day period may be extended by up to five additional days by agreement between the parties.

4.

(a) Except as provided in paragraphs (b) and (c) of this subdivision and in subdivision eleven of this section, when a request is made for the release of property described in subdivision one of this section, and the property shall consist of perishables, fungible retail items, motor vehicles or any other property release of which is necessary for either the operation of a business or the health or welfare of any person, the property shall be retained until either the expiration of a forty-eight hour period from the receipt by the defendant's counsel of the notice of the request, or the examination, testing and photocopying, photographing or other reproduction of such property, by the parties whichever event occurs first. The forty-eight hour period may be extended by up to twenty-four additional hours by agreement between the parties. For the purposes of this section, perishables shall mean any property likely to spoil or decay or diminish significantly in value within twenty days of the initial retention of the property.

(b) If, upon oral or written application by the district attorney with notice to the defendant or his counsel, a court determines that immediate release of property described in paragraph (a) of this subdivision is required under the attendant circumstances, the court shall issue an order releasing the property and, if requested by either party, setting, as a part of such order, any condition appropriate in the furtherance of justice.

(c) A motor vehicle alleged to have been stolen but not alleged to have been used in connection with any crime or criminal transaction other than the theft or unlawful use of said motor vehicle, which is in the custody of a police officer, a peace officer or a district attorney, may be released expeditiously to its registered owner or the owner's representative without prior notice to the defendant. Before such release, evidentiary photographs shall be taken of such motor vehicle. Such photographs shall include the vehicle identification number, registration on windshield, license plates, each side of the vehicle, including vent windows, door locks and handles, the front and back of the vehicle, the interior of the vehicle, including ignition lock, seat to floor clearance, center console, radio receptacle and dashboard area, the motor, and any other interior or exterior surfaces showing any and all damage to the vehicle. Notice of such release, and the photographs taken of said vehicle, shall be furnished to the defendant within fifteen days after arraignment or after counsel initially appears on behalf of the defendant or respondent, whichever occurs later.

5. If stolen property comes into the custody of a court, it must, unless temporary retention be deemed necessary in furtherance of justice, be delivered to the owner, on satisfactory proof of his title, and on his paying the necessary expenses incurred in its preservation, to be certified by the court.

6. If stolen property has not been delivered to the owner, the court before which a trial is had for stealing it, may, on proof of his title, order it to be restored to the owner.

7. If stolen property is not claimed by the owner, before the expiration of six months from the conviction of a person for stealing it, the court or other officer having it in custody must, on payment of the necessary expenses incurred in its preservation, deliver it to the county commissioner of social services, or in the city of New York, to the commissioner of social services, to be applied for the benefit of the poor of the county or city, as the case may be.

8. Except in the city of New York, when money or other property is taken from a defendant, arrested upon a charge of an offense, the officer taking it must, at the time, give duplicate receipts therefor, specifying particularly the amount of property taken, one of which receipts he must deliver to the defendant, and the other of which he must forthwith file with the court in which the criminal action is pending.

9. The commissioners of police of the city of New York may designate some person to take charge of all property alleged to be stolen, and which may be brought into the police office, and all property taken from the person of a prisoner, and may prescribe regulations in regard to the duties of the clerk or clerks so designated, and to require and take security for the faithful performance of the duties imposed by this subdivision, and it shall be the duty of every officer into whose possession such property may come, to deliver the same forthwith to the person so designated.

10. Where there has been a failure to comply with the provisions of this section, and where the district attorney does not demonstrate to the satisfaction of the court that such failure has not caused the defendant prejudice, the court shall instruct the jury that it may consider such failure in determining the weight to be given such evidence and may also impose any other sanction set forth in subdivision one of section 245.80 of the criminal procedure law; provided, however, that unless the defendant has convinced the court that such failure has caused him undue prejudice, the court shall not preclude the district attorney from introducing into evidence the property, photographs, photocopies, or other reproductions of the property or, where appropriate, testimony concerning its value and condition, where such evidence is otherwise properly authenticated and admissible under the rules of evidence. Failure to comply with any one or more of the provisions of this section shall not for that reason alone be grounds for dismissal of the accusatory instrument.

11. When a request for the release of stolen property is made pursuant to paragraph (a) of subdivision four of this section and the defendant is not represented by counsel the notice required pursuant to subdivision one of this section shall be personally delivered to the defendant and release of said property shall not occur for a period less than five days: from (a) the delivery of such notice; or (b) in the case of delivery to such person in custody, from the first appearance before the court, whichever is later.

N.Y. Penal Law § 450.10

Amended by New York Laws 2019, ch. 59,Sec. LLL-11, eff. 1/1/2020.

Title X - ORGANIZED CRIME CONTROL ACT

Article 460 - ENTERPRISE CORRUPTION

Section 460.00 - Legislative findings

The legislature finds and determines as follows:

N.Y. Penal Law § 460.00

Section 460.10 - Definitions

The following definitions are applicable to this article.

1. "Criminal act" means conduct constituting any of the following crimes, or conspiracy or attempt to commit any of the following felonies:

(a) Any of the felonies set forth in this chapter: sections 120.05, 120.10 and 120.11 relating to assault; sections 121.12 and 121.13 relating to strangulation; sections 125.10 to 125.27 relating to homicide; sections 130.25, 130.30 and 130.35 relating to rape; sections 135.20 and 135.25 relating to kidnapping; sections 135.35 and 135.37 relating to labor trafficking; section 135.65 relating to coercion; sections 140.20, 140.25 and 140.30 relating to burglary; sections 145.05, 145.10 and 145.12 relating to criminal mischief; article one hundred fifty relating to arson; sections 155.30, 155.35, 155.40 and 155.42 relating to grand larceny; sections 177.10, 177.15, 177.20 and 177.25 relating to health care fraud; article one hundred sixty relating to robbery; sections 165.45, 165.50, 165.52 and 165.54 relating to criminal possession of stolen property; sections 165.72 and 165.73 relating to trademark counterfeiting; sections 170.10, 170.15, 170.25, 170.30, 170.40, 170.65 and 170.70 relating to forgery; sections 175.10, 175.25, 175.35, 175.40 and 210.40 relating to false statements; sections 176.15, 176.20, 176.25 and 176.30 relating to insurance fraud; sections 178.20 and 178.25 relating to criminal diversion of prescription medications and prescriptions; sections 180.03, 180.08, 180.15, 180.25, 180.40, 180.45, 200.00, 200.03, 200.04, 200.10, 200.11, 200.12, 200.20, 200.22, 200.25, 200.27, 200.56, 215.00, 215.05 and 215.19 relating to bribery; sections 187.10, 187.15, 187.20 and 187.25 relating to residential mortgage fraud, sections 190.40 and 190.42 relating to criminal usury; section 190.65 relating to schemes to defraud; any felony defined in article four hundred ninety-six; sections 205.60 and 205.65 relating to hindering prosecution; sections 210.10, 210.15, and 215.51 relating to perjury and contempt; section 215.40 relating to tampering with physical evidence; sections 220.06, 220.09, 220.16, 220.18, 220.21, 220.31, 220.34, 220.39, 220.41, 220.43, 220.46, 220.55, 220.60, 220.65 and 220.77 relating to controlled substances; sections 225.10 and 225.20 relating to gambling; sections 230.25, 230.30, and 230.32 relating to promoting prostitution; section 230.34 relating to sex trafficking; section 230.34 -a relating to sex trafficking of a child; sections 235.06, 235.07, 235.21 and 235.22 relating to obscenity; sections 263.10 and 263.15 relating to promoting a sexual performance by a child; sections 265.02, 265.03, 265.04, 265.11, 265.12, 265.13 and the provisions of section 265.10 which constitute a felony relating to firearms and other dangerous weapons; sections 265.14 and 265.16 relating to criminal sale of a firearm; section 265.50 relating to the criminal manufacture, sale or transport of an undetectable firearm, rifle or shotgun; section 275.10, 275.20, 275.30, or 275.40 relating to unauthorized recordings; and sections 470.05, 470.10, 470.15 and 470.20 relating to money laundering; or

(b) Any felony set forth elsewhere in the laws of this state and defined by the tax law relating to alcoholic beverage, cigarette, gasoline and similar motor fuel taxes; article seventy-one of the environmental conservation law relating to water pollution, hazardous waste or substances hazardous or acutely hazardous to public health or safety of the environment; article twenty-three-A of the general business law relating to prohibited acts concerning stocks, bonds and other securities, article twenty-two of the general business law concerning monopolies.

2. "Enterprise" means either an enterprise as defined in subdivision one of section 175.00 of this chapter or criminal enterprise as defined in subdivision three of this section.

3. "Criminal enterprise" means a group of persons sharing a common purpose of engaging in criminal conduct, associated in an ascertainable structure distinct from a pattern of criminal activity, and with a continuity of existence, structure and criminal purpose beyond the scope of individual criminal incidents.

4. "Pattern of criminal activity" means conduct engaged in by persons charged in an enterprise corruption count constituting three or more criminal acts that:

(a) were committed within ten years of the commencement of the criminal action;

(b) are neither isolated incidents, nor so closely related and connected in point of time or circumstance of commission as to constitute a criminal offense or criminal transaction, as those terms are defined in section 40.10 of the criminal procedure law; and

(c) are either:

(i) related to one another through a common scheme or plan or

(ii) were committed, solicited, requested, importuned or intentionally aided by persons acting with the mental culpability required for the commission thereof and associated with or in the criminal enterprise.

N.Y. Penal Law § 460.10

Amended by New York Laws 2019, ch. 134,Sec. 6, eff. 1/26/2020.

Amended by New York Laws 2018, ch. 189,Sec. 4, eff. 11/13/2018.

Amended by New York Laws 2015, ch. 368,Sec. 7, eff. 1/19/2016.

Amended by New York Laws 2014, ch. 37,Sec. 2, eff. 6/23/2014.

Amended by New York Laws 2014, ch. 55,Sec. H-A-16, eff. 4/30/2014.

Section 460.20 - Enterprise corruption

1. A person is guilty of enterprise corruption when, having knowledge of the existence of a criminal enterprise and the nature of its activities, and being employed by or associated with such enterprise, he:

(a) intentionally conducts or participates in the affairs of an enterprise by participating in a pattern of criminal activity; or

(b) intentionally acquires or maintains any interest in or control of an enterprise by participating in a pattern of criminal activity; or

(c) participates in a pattern of criminal activity and knowingly invests any proceeds derived from that conduct, or any proceeds derived from the investment or use of those proceeds, in an enterprise.

2. For purposes of this section, a person participates in a pattern of criminal activity when, with intent to participate in or advance the affairs of the criminal enterprise, he engages in conduct constituting, or, is criminally liable for pursuant to section 20.00 of this chapter, at least three of the criminal acts included in the pattern, provided that:

(a) Two of his acts are felonies other than conspiracy;

(b) Two of his acts, one of which is a felony, occurred within five years of the commencement of the criminal action; and

(c) Each of his acts occurred within three years of a prior act.

3. For purposes of this section, the enterprise corrupted in violation of subdivision one of this section need not be the criminal enterprise by which the person is employed or with which he is associated, and may be a legitimate enterprise. Enterprise corruption is a class B felony.

N.Y. Penal Law § 460.20

Section 460.22 - Aggravated enterprise corruption

A person is guilty of aggravated enterprise corruption when he or she commits the crime of enterprise corruption and two or more of the acts that constitute his or her pattern of criminal activity are class B felonies or higher, and at least two acts are armed felonies as defined in paragraph (a) of subdivision forty-one of section 1.20 of the criminal procedure law or one act is such an armed felony and one act is a violation of subdivision two of section 265.17 of this chapter or one act is a class B violent felony and two are violations of subdivision two of section 265.17 of this chapter.

N.Y. Penal Law § 460.22

Added by New York Laws 2013, ch. 1,Sec. 52, eff. 3/16/2013.

Section 460.25 - Enterprise corruption; limitations

1. For purposes of subdivision one of section 460.20 of this article, a person does not acquire or maintain an interest in an enterprise by participating in a pattern of criminal activity when he invests proceeds derived from a pattern of criminal activity in such enterprise.

2. For purposes of subdivision one of section 460.20 of this article, it shall not be unlawful to:

(a) purchase securities on the open market with intent to make an investment, and without the intent of controlling or participating in the control of the issuer, or of assisting another to do so, if the securities of the issuer held by the purchaser, the members of his immediate family, and his or their accomplices in any pattern of criminal activity do not amount in the aggregate to five percent of the outstanding securities of any one class and do not confer, either in the law or in fact, the power to elect one or more directors of the issuer;

(b) make a deposit in an account maintained in a savings and loan association, or a deposit in any other such financial institution, that creates an ownership interest in that association or institution;

(c) purchase shares in co-operatively owned residential or commercial property;

(d) purchase non-voting shares in a limited partnership, with intent to make an investment, and without the intent of controlling or participating in the control of the partnership.

N.Y. Penal Law § 460.25

Section 460.30 - Enterprise corruption; forfeiture

1. Any person convicted of enterprise corruption may be required pursuant to this section to criminally forfeit to the state:

(a) any interest in, security of, claim against or property or contractual right of any kind affording a source of influence over any enterprise whose affairs he has controlled or in which he has participated in violation of subdivision one of section 460.20 of this article and for which he was convicted and the use of which interest, security, claim or right by him contributed directly and materially to the crime for which he was convicted unless such forfeiture is disproportionate to the defendant's gain from his association or employment with the enterprise, in which event the jury may recommend forfeiture of a portion thereof;

(b) any interest, including proceeds, he has acquired or maintained in an enterprise in violation of subdivision one of section 460.20 of this article and for which he was convicted unless such forfeiture is disproportionate to the conduct he engaged in and on which the forfeiture is based, in which event the jury may recommend forfeiture of a portion thereof; or

(c) any interest, including proceeds he has derived from an investment of proceeds in an enterprise in violation of subdivision one of section 460.20 of this article and for which he was convicted unless such forfeiture is disproportionate to the conduct he engaged in and on which the forfeiture is based, in which event the jury may recommend forfeiture of a portion thereof.

2.

(a) Forfeiture may be ordered when the grand jury returning an indictment charging a person with enterprise corruption has received evidence legally sufficient to establish, and providing reasonable cause to believe, that the property or other interest is subject to forfeiture under this section. In that event, the grand jury shall file a special information, not to be disclosed to the jury in the criminal action prior to verdict on the criminal charges, specifying the property or other interest for which forfeiture is sought and containing a plain and concise factual statement which sets forth the basis for the forfeiture. Alternatively, where the defendant has waived indictment and consented to be prosecuted by superior court information pursuant to article one hundred ninety-five of the criminal procedure law, the prosecutor may file, in addition to the superior court information charging enterprise corruption, a special information specifying the property or other interest for which forfeiture is sought and containing a plain and concise factual statement which sets forth the basis for the forfeiture.

(b) After returning a verdict of guilty on an enterprise corruption count or counts, the jury shall be given the special information and hear any additional evidence which is relevant and legally admissible upon the forfeiture count or counts of the special information. After hearing such evidence, the jury shall then deliberate upon the forfeiture count or counts and, based upon all the evidence received in connection with the indictment or superior court information and the special information, may, if satisfied by proof beyond a reasonable doubt that the property or other interest, or a portion thereof, is subject to forfeiture under this section return a verdict determining such property or other interest, or portion thereof, is subject to forfeiture, provided, however, where a defendant has waived a jury trial pursuant to article three hundred twenty of the criminal procedure law, the court may hear and receive all of the evidence upon the indictment or superior court information and the special information and render a verdict upon the enterprise corruption count or counts and the forfeiture count or counts.

(c) After the verdict of forfeiture, the court shall hear arguments and may receive additional evidence upon a motion of the defendant that the verdict of forfeiture (i) is against the weight of the evidence, or (ii) is, with respect to a forfeiture pursuant to paragraph (a) of subdivision one of this section, disproportionate to the defendant's gain from his association or employment with the enterprise, or, with respect to a forfeiture pursuant to paragraph (b) or (c) of subdivision one of this section, disproportionate to the conduct he engaged in on which the forfeiture is based. Upon such a finding the court may in the interests of justice set aside, modify, limit or otherwise condition an order of forfeiture.

3.

(a) An order of criminal forfeiture shall authorize the prosecutor to seize all property or other interest declared forfeited under this section upon such terms and conditions as the court shall deem proper. If a property right or other interest is not exercisable or transferable for value by the prosecutor, it shall expire and shall not revert to the convicted person. The court ordering any forfeiture may remit such forfeiture or any portion thereof.

(b) No person shall forfeit any right, title or interest in any property or enterprise under this article who has not been convicted of a violation of section 460.20 of this article. Any person other than the convicted person claiming an interest in forfeited property or other interest may bring a special proceeding to determine that claim, before or after trial, pursuant to section thirteen hundred twenty-seven of the civil practice law and rules, provided, however, that if such an action is brought before trial, it may, upon motion of the prosecutor, and in the court's discretion, be postponed by the court until completion of the trial. In addition, any person claiming an interest in property subject to forfeiture may petition for remission as provided in subdivision seven of section thirteen hundred eleven of such law and rules.

4. All property and other interests which are criminally forfeited following the commencement of an action under this article, whether by plea, verdict or other agreement, shall be disposed of in accordance with the provisions of section thirteen hundred forty-nine of the civil practice law and rules. In any case where one or more of the counts upon which a person is convicted specifically includes as a criminal act a violation of any offense defined in article two hundred twenty of this chapter, the court shall determine what portion of that property or interest derives from or relates to such criminal act, and direct that distribution of that portion be conducted in the manner prescribed for actions grounded upon offenses in violation of article two hundred twenty.

5. Any person convicted of a violation of section 460.20 of this article through which he derived pecuniary value, or by which he caused personal injury or property damage or other loss, may be sentenced to pay a fine not in excess of three times the gross value he gained or three times the gross loss he caused, whichever is greater. Moneys so collected shall be paid as restitution to victims of the crime for medical expenses actually incurred, loss of earnings or property loss or damage caused thereby. Any excess after restitution shall be paid to the state treasury. In any case where one or more of the counts upon which a person is convicted specifically includes as a criminal act a violation of any offense defined in article two hundred twenty of this chapter, the court shall determine what proportion of the entire pattern such criminal acts constitute and distribute such portion in the manner prescribed by section three hundred forty-nine of the civil practice law

and rules for forfeiture actions grounded upon offenses in violation of article two hundred twenty. When the court imposes a fine pursuant to this subdivision, the court shall make a finding as to the amount of the gross value gained or the gross loss caused. If the record does not contain sufficient evidence to support such a finding the court may conduct a hearing upon the issue. In imposing a fine, the court shall consider the seriousness of the conduct, whether the amount of the fine is disproportionate to the conduct in which he engaged, its impact on victims and the enterprise corrupted by that conduct, as well as the economic circumstances of the convicted person, including the effect of the imposition of such a fine upon his immediate family.

6. The imposition of an order of criminal forfeiture pursuant to subdivision one of this section, a judgment of civil forfeiture pursuant to article thirteen-A of the civil practice law and rules, or a fine pursuant to subdivision five of this section or paragraph (b) of subdivision one of section 80.00 of this chapter, shall preclude the imposition of any other such order or judgment of forfeiture or fine based upon the same criminal conduct, provided however that where an order of criminal forfeiture is imposed pursuant to subdivision one of this section, an action pursuant to article thirteen-A of the civil practice law and rules may nonetheless be brought, and an order imposed in that action, for forfeiture of the proceeds of a crime or the substituted proceeds of a crime where such proceeds are not subject to criminal forfeiture pursuant to subdivision one of this section. The imposition of a fine pursuant to subdivision five of this section or paragraph (b) of subdivision one of section 80.00 of this chapter, shall preclude the imposition of any other fine pursuant to any other provision of this chapter.

7. Other than as provided in subdivision six, the imposition of a criminal penalty, forfeiture or fine under this section shall not preclude the application of any other criminal penalty or civil remedy under this article or under any other provision of law.

8. Any payment made as restitution to victims pursuant to this section shall not limit, preclude or impair any liability for damages in any civil action or proceeding for an amount in excess of such payment.

N.Y. Penal Law § 460.30

Section 460.40 - Enterprise corruption; jurisdiction

A person may be prosecuted for enterprise corruption:

1. in any county in which the principal place of business, if any, of the enterprise was located at the time of the offense, and, if the enterprise had a principal place or business located in more than one county, then in any such county in which any conduct occurred constituting or requisite to the completion of the offense of enterprise corruption; or

2. in any county in which any act included in the pattern of criminal activity could have been prosecuted pursuant to article twenty of the criminal procedure law; provided, however, that such person may not be prosecuted for enterprise corruption in such county based on this subdivision if the jurisdiction of such county is based solely on section 20.60 of the criminal procedure law; or

3. in any county in which he:

(a) conducts or participates in the affairs of the enterprise in violation of subdivision one of section 460.20 of this article,

(b) acquires or maintains an interest in or control of the enterprise in violation of subdivision one of section 460.20 of this article,

(c) invests proceeds in an enterprise in violation of subdivision one of section 460.20 of this article; or

4. in any county in which the conduct of the actor had or was likely to have a particular effect upon such county or a political subdivision or part thereof, and was performed with intent that it would, or with knowledge that it was likely to, have such particular effect therein.

N.Y. Penal Law § 460.40

Section 460.50 - Enterprise corruption; prosecution

1. Subject to the provisions of section 460.60 of this article, a charge of enterprise corruption may be prosecuted by: (a) the district attorney of any county with jurisdiction over the offense pursuant to section 460.40 of this article; (b) the deputy attorney general in charge of the statewide organized crime task force when authorized by subdivision seven of section seventy-a of the executive law; or (c) the attorney general when he is otherwise authorized by law to prosecute each of the criminal acts specifically included in the pattern of criminal activity alleged in the enterprise corruption charge.

2. For purposes of paragraph (c) of subdivision one of this section, a criminal act or an offense is specifically included in a pattern of criminal activity when the count of the accusatory instrument charging a person with enterprise corruption alleges a pattern of criminal activity and the act is alleged to be a criminal act within the pattern of criminal activity.

N.Y. Penal Law § 460.50

Section 460.60 - Enterprise corruption; consent to prosecute

1. For purposes of this section, when a grand jury proceeding concerns a possible charge of enterprise corruption, or when an accusatory instrument includes a count charging a person with enterprise corruption, the affected district attorneys are the district attorneys otherwise empowered to prosecute any of the underlying acts of criminal activity in a county with jurisdiction over the offense of enterprise corruption pursuant to section 460.40 of this article, in which:

(a) there has been substantial and significant activity by the particular enterprise; or

(b) conduct occurred constituting a criminal act specifically included in the pattern of criminal activity charged in the accusatory instrument and not previously prosecuted; or

(c) the particular enterprise has its principal place of business.

2. A grand jury proceeding concerning a possible charge of enterprise corruption may be instituted only with the consent of the affected district attorneys. Should the possibility of such a charge develop after a grand jury proceeding has been

instituted, the consent of the affected district attorneys shall be sought as soon as is practical, and an indictment charging a person with enterprise corruption may not be voted upon by the grand jury without such consent.

3. A person may be charged in an accusatory instrument with enterprise corruption only with the consent of the affected district attorneys. When it is impractical to obtain the consent specified in subdivision two of this section prior to the filing of the accusatory instrument, then that consent must be secured within twenty days thereafter.

4. When the prosecutor is the deputy attorney general in charge of the statewide organized crime task force, the consent required by subdivisions two and three of this section shall be in addition to that required by subdivision seven of section seventy-a of the executive law.

5. Within fifteen days after the arraignment of any person on an indictment charging a person with the crime of enterprise corruption the prosecutor shall provide a copy of the indictment to those district attorneys whose consent was required pursuant to subdivision three of this section, and shall notify the court and defendant of those district attorneys whose consent the prosecutor has secured. The court shall then review the indictment and the grand jury minutes, notify any district attorney whose consent under subdivision one of this section should have been but was not obtained, direct that the prosecutor provide that district attorney with the portion of the indictment and grand jury minutes that are relevant to a determination whether that district attorney is an "affected district attorney" within the meaning of subdivision one of this section.

6. The failure to obtain from any district attorney the consent required by subdivision two or three of this section shall not be grounds for dismissal of the accusatory instrument or for any other relief upon motion of a defendant in the criminal action.

Upon motion of a district attorney whose consent, pursuant to subdivision three of this section, the court determines was required but not obtained, the court may not dismiss the accusatory instrument or any count thereof but may grant any appropriate relief. Such relief may include, but is not limited to:

(a) ordering that any money forfeited by a defendant in the criminal action, or the proceeds from the sale of any other property forfeited in the criminal action by a defendant, which would have been paid to the county of that district attorney pursuant to section thirteen hundred forty-nine of the civil practice law and rules had the forfeiture action been prosecuted in the county of that district attorney, be paid in whole or in part to the county of that district attorney; or

(b) upon consent of the defendant, ordering the transfer of the prosecution, or any part thereof, to that district attorney or to any other prosecutor with jurisdiction over the prosecution, of the part thereof to be transferred. However, prior to ordering any transfer of the prosecution, the court shall provide to those district attorneys who have previously consented to the prosecution an opportunity to intervene and be heard concerning such transfer.

7. A district attorney whose consent, pursuant to subdivision three of this section, the court determines was required but not obtained may seek the relief described in subdivision six of this section exclusively by a pre-trial motion in the criminal action based on the indictment charging the crime of enterprise corruption. Such relief must be sought within forty-five days of the receipt of notice from the court pursuant to subdivision five of this section.

N.Y. Penal Law § 460.60

Section 460.70 - Provisional remedies

1. The provisional remedies authorized by article thirteen-A of the civil practice law and rules shall be available in all criminal actions in which criminal forfeiture or a fine pursuant to section 460.60 is sought to the extent and under the same terms and conditions as provided in article thirteen-A of such law and rules.

2. Upon the filing of an indictment and special information seeking criminal forfeiture under this article all further proceedings with respect to provisional remedies shall be heard by the judge or justice in the criminal part to which the indictment and special information are assigned.

3. For purposes of this section, the indictment and special information seeking criminal forfeiture shall constitute the summons and complaint referred to in article thirteen-A of the civil practice law and rules.

N.Y. Penal Law § 460.70

Section 460.80 - Court ordered disclosure

Notwithstanding the provisions of article two hundred forty-five of the criminal procedure law, when forfeiture is sought pursuant to section 460.30 of this article, the court may order discovery of any property not otherwise disclosed which is material and reasonably necessary for preparation by the defendant with respect to the forfeiture proceeding pursuant to such section. The court may issue a protective order denying, limiting, conditioning, delaying or regulating such discovery where a danger to the integrity of physical evidence or a substantial risk of physical harm, intimidation, economic reprisal, bribery or unjustified annoyance or embarrassment to any person or an adverse effect upon the legitimate needs of law enforcement, including the protection of the confidentiality of informants, or any other factor or set of factors outweighs the usefulness of the discovery.

N.Y. Penal Law § 460.80

Amended by New York Laws 2019, ch. 59,Sec. LLL-12, eff. 1/1/2020.

Article 470 - MONEY LAUNDERING

Section 470.00 - Definitions

The following definitions are applicable to this article.

1. "Monetary instrument" means coin and currency of the United States or of any other country; personal checks; bank checks; traveler's checks; money orders; and investment securities and negotiable instruments, in bearer form or otherwise, in such form that title thereto passes on delivery, except that "monetary instrument" shall not include payments to attorneys for legal services.

2. "Conducts" includes initiating, concluding or participating in initiating or concluding a transaction.

3. "Transaction" includes a payment, purchase, sale, loan, pledge, gift, transfer, or delivery, and with respect to a financial institution includes a deposit, withdrawal, transfer between accounts, exchange of currency, loan, extension of credit, purchase or sale of any stock, bond, certificate of deposit, or other monetary instrument, use of a safe deposit box, or any other payment, transfer, or delivery by, through, or to a financial institution, by whatever means effected, except that "transaction" shall not include payments to attorneys for legal services.

4. "Criminal conduct" means conduct which is a crime under the laws of this state or conduct committed in any other jurisdiction which is or would be a crime under the laws of this state.

5. "Specified criminal conduct" means criminal conduct committed in this state constituting a criminal act, as the term criminal act is defined in section 460.10 of this chapter, or constituting the crime of enterprise corruption, as defined in section 460.20 of this chapter, or conduct committed in any other jurisdiction which is or would be specified criminal conduct if committed in this state.

6. "Financial institution" means :

(a) an insured bank, as defined in section 3(b) of the Federal Deposit Insurance Act, 12 U.S.C. 1813(h);

(b) a commercial bank or trust company;

(c) a private banker;

(d) an agency or branch of a foreign bank in the United States;

(e) a credit union;

(f) a thrift institution;

(g) a broker or dealer registered with the Securities and Exchange Commission under the Securities and Exchange Act of 1934, U.S.C. 78a et seq.;

(h) a broker or dealer in securities or commodities;

(i) an investment banker or investment company;

(j) a currency exchange;

(k) an issuer, redeemer, or cashier of travelers' checks, checks, money orders, or similar instruments;

(l) an operator of a credit card system;

(m) an insurance company;

(n) a dealer in precious metals, stones, or jewels;

(o) a pawnbroker;

(p) a loan or finance company;

(q) a travel agency;

(r) a person licensed to engage in the business of receiving money for transmission or transmitting the same by whatever means, or any other person engaged in such business as an agent of a licensee or engaged in such business without a license;

(s) a telegraph company;

(t) a business engaged in vehicle sales, including automobile, airplane and boat sales;

(u) persons involved in real estate closings and settlements;

(v) the United States Postal Service;

(w) an agency of the United States government or of a state or local government carrying out a duty or power of a business described in this subdivision;

(x) a casino, gambling casino, or gaming establishment with an annual gaming revenue of more than a million dollars which:

(i) is licensed as a casino, gambling casino or gaming establishment under the laws of any state or any political subdivision of any state; or

(ii) is an Indian gaming operation conducted under or pursuant to the Indian Gaming Regulatory Act other than an operation which is limited to class 1 gaming as defined in subdivision six of section four of such act; or

(y) any business or agency engaged in any activity which the superintendent of financial services or the United States Secretary of the Treasury determines, by regulation, to be an activity which is similar to, related to, or a substitute for activity which any business as described in this subdivision is authorized to engage.

7. "Financial transaction" means a transaction involving:

(a) the movement of funds by wire or other means; or

(b) one or more monetary instruments; or

(c) the transfer of title to any real property, vehicle, vessel or aircraft; or

(d) the use of a financial institution.

8. "Represented" means any representation made by a law enforcement officer, or by another person at the direction of, or with the approval of, such law enforcement officer.

9. "Law enforcement officer" means any public servant, federal or state, who is authorized to conduct an investigation, prosecute or make an arrest for a criminal offense.

10. For the purpose of this article, each of the five counties in the city of New York shall be considered as a separate county.

N.Y. Penal Law § 470.00

Section 470.03 - Money laundering: aggregation of value; other matters

1. For purposes of subdivisions one and three of sections 470.05, 470.10, 470.15, 470.21, 470.22 and 470.23, and for purposes of subdivisions one and two of sections 470.20 and 470.24 of this article, financial transactions may be considered together and the value of the property involved may be aggregated, provided that the transactions are all part of a single "criminal transaction" as defined in subdivision two of section 40.10 of the criminal procedure law.

2. For purposes of subdivision two of sections 470.05, 470.10, 470.15, 470.21, 470.22 and 470.23 of this article, separate occasions involving the transport, transmittal or transfer of monetary instruments may be considered together and the value of the monetary instruments involved may be aggregated, provided that the occasions are all part of a single "criminal transaction" as defined in subdivision two of section 40.10 of the criminal procedure law.

3. Nothing in sections 470.05, 470.21, 470.22, 470.23 and 470.24; paragraph (b) of subdivision one, paragraph (b) of subdivision two and paragraph (b) of subdivision three of section 470.10; paragraph (b) of subdivision one, paragraph (b) of subdivision two and paragraph (b) of subdivision three of section 470.15; or paragraph (b) of subdivision one and paragraph (b) of subdivision two of section 470.20 of this article shall make it unlawful to return funds held in escrow:
(a) as a portion of a purchase price for real property pursuant to a contract of sale; or
(b) to satisfy the tax or other lawful obligations arising out of an administrative or judicial proceeding concerning the person who provided the escrow funds.
N.Y. Penal Law § 470.03

Section 470.05 - Money laundering in the fourth degree

A person is guilty of money laundering in the fourth degree when:
1. Knowing that the property involved in one or more financial transactions represents the proceeds of criminal conduct:
(a) he or she conducts one or more such financial transactions which in fact involve the proceeds of specified criminal conduct:
(i) With intent to:
(A) promote the carrying on of criminal conduct; or
(B) engage in conduct constituting a felony as set forth in section eighteen hundred three, eighteen hundred four, eighteen hundred five, or eighteen hundred six of the tax law; or
(ii) Knowing that the transaction or transactions in whole or in part are designed to:
(A) conceal or disguise the nature, the location, the source, the ownership or the control of the proceeds of criminal conduct; or
(B) avoid any transaction reporting requirement imposed by law; and
(b) The total value of the property involved in such financial transaction or transactions exceeds five thousand dollars; or
2. Knowing that one or more monetary instruments represents the proceeds of criminal conduct:
(a) he or she transports, transmits, or transfers on one or more occasions, monetary instruments which in fact represent the proceeds of specified criminal conduct:
(i) With intent to promote the carrying on of criminal conduct; or
(ii) Knowing that such transportation, transmittal, or transfer is designed in whole or in part to:
(A) conceal or disguise the nature, the location, the source, the ownership, or the control of the proceeds of criminal conduct; or
(B) avoid any transaction reporting requirement imposed by law; and
(b) The total value of such monetary instrument or instruments exceeds ten thousand dollars; or
3. He or she conducts one or more financial transactions:
(a) involving property represented to be the proceeds of specified criminal conduct, or represented to be property used to conduct or facilitate specified criminal conduct, with intent to:
(i) promote the carrying on of specified criminal conduct; or
(ii) conceal or disguise the nature, the location, the source, the ownership or the control of property believed to be the proceeds of specified criminal conduct; or
(iii) avoid any transaction reporting requirement imposed by law; and
(b) the total value of the property involved in such financial transaction or transactions exceeds ten thousand dollars.
Money laundering in the fourth degree is a class E felony.
N.Y. Penal Law § 470.05

Section 470.10 - Money laundering in the third degree

A person is guilty of money laundering in the third degree when:
1. Knowing that the property involved in one or more financial transactions represents:
(a) the proceeds of the criminal sale of a controlled substance, he or she conducts one or more such financial transactions which in fact involve the proceeds of the criminal sale of a controlled substance:
(i) With intent to:
(A) promote the carrying on of specified criminal conduct; or
(B) engage in conduct constituting a felony as set forth in section eighteen hundred three, eighteen hundred four, eighteen hundred five, or eighteen hundred six of the tax law; or
(ii) Knowing that the transaction or transactions in whole or in part are designed to:
(A) conceal or disguise the nature, the location, the source, the ownership or the control of the proceeds of specified criminal conduct; or
(B) avoid any transaction reporting requirement imposed by law; and

(iii) The total value of the property involved in such financial transaction or transactions exceeds ten thousand dollars; or

(b) the proceeds of criminal conduct, he or she conducts one or more such financial transactions which in fact involve the proceeds of specified criminal conduct:

(i) With intent to:

(A) promote the carrying on of criminal conduct; or

(B) engage in conduct constituting a felony as set forth in section eighteen hundred three, eighteen hundred four, eighteen hundred five, or eighteen hundred six of the tax law; or

(ii) knowing that the transaction or transactions in whole or in part are designed to:

(A) conceal or disguise the nature, the location, the source, the ownership or the control of the proceeds of criminal conduct; or

(B) avoid any transaction reporting requirement imposed by law; and

(iii) The total value of the property involved in such financial transaction or transactions exceeds fifty thousand dollars; or

2. Knowing that one or more monetary instruments represent:

(a) the proceeds of the criminal sale of a controlled substance, he or she transports, transmits, or transfers or attempts to transport, transmit or transfer, on one or more occasions, monetary instruments which in fact represent the proceeds of the criminal sale of a controlled substance from a place in any county in this state to or through a place outside that county or to a place in any county in this state from or through a place outside that county:

(i) With intent to promote the carrying on of specified criminal conduct; or

(ii) Knowing that such transportation, transmittal or transfer is designed in whole or in part to:

(A) conceal or disguise the nature, the location, the source, the ownership or the control of the proceeds of specified criminal conduct; or

(B) avoid any transaction reporting requirement imposed by law; and

(iii) The total value of such monetary instrument or instruments exceeds ten thousand dollars; or

(b) the proceeds of criminal conduct, he or she transports, transmits, or transfers or attempts to transport, transmit or transfer, on one or more occasions monetary instruments which in fact represent the proceeds of specified criminal conduct from a place in any county in this state to or through a place outside that county or to a place in any county in this state from or through a place outside that county:

(i) With intent to promote the carrying on of criminal conduct; or

(ii) Knowing that such transportation, transmittal or transfer is designed in whole or in part to:

(A) conceal or disguise the nature, the location, the source, the ownership, or the control of the proceeds of criminal conduct; or

(B) avoid any transaction reporting requirement imposed by law; and

(iii) The total value of such monetary instrument or instruments exceeds fifty thousand dollars; or

3. He or she conducts one or more financial transactions involving property represented to be:

(a) the proceeds of the criminal sale of a controlled substance, or represented to be property used to conduct or facilitate the criminal sale of a controlled substance:

(i) With intent to:

(A) promote the carrying on of specified criminal conduct; or

(B) conceal or disguise the nature, the location, the source, the ownership or the control of property believed to be the proceeds of specified criminal conduct; or

(C) avoid any transaction reporting requirement imposed by law; and

(ii) The total value of the property involved in such financial transaction or transactions exceeds ten thousand dollars; or

(b) the proceeds of specified criminal conduct, or represented to be property used to conduct or facilitate specified criminal conduct:

(i) With intent to:

(A) promote the carrying on of specified criminal conduct; or

(B) conceal or disguise the nature, the location, the source, the ownership or the control of property believed to be the proceeds of specified criminal conduct; or

(C) avoid any transaction reporting requirement imposed by law; and

(ii) The total value of the property involved in such financial transaction or transactions exceeds fifty thousand dollars.

Money laundering in the third degree is a class D felony.

N.Y. Penal Law § 470.10

Section 470.15 - Money laundering in the second degree

A person is guilty of money laundering in the second degree when:

1. Knowing that the property involved in one or more financial transactions represents:

(a) the proceeds of the criminal sale of a controlled substance, he or she conducts one or more such financial transactions which in fact involve the proceeds of the criminal sale of a controlled substance:

(i) With intent to:

(A) promote the carrying on of specified criminal conduct; or

(B) engage in conduct constituting a felony as set forth in section eighteen hundred three, eighteen hundred four, eighteen hundred five, or eighteen hundred six of the tax law; or

(ii) Knowing that the transaction or transactions in whole or in part are designed to:

(A) conceal or disguise the nature, the location, the source, the ownership or the control of the proceeds of specified criminal conduct; or

(B) avoid any transaction reporting requirement imposed by law; and

(iii) The total value of the property involved in such financial transaction or transactions exceeds fifty thousand dollars; or

(b) the proceeds of specified criminal conduct, he or she conducts one or more such financial transactions which in fact involve the proceeds of specified criminal conduct:

(i) With intent to:

(A) promote the carrying on of specified criminal conduct; or

(B) engage in conduct constituting a felony as set forth in section eighteen hundred three, eighteen hundred four, eighteen hundred five, or eighteen hundred six of the tax law; or

(ii) Knowing that the transaction or transactions in whole or in part are designed to:

(A) conceal or disguise the nature, the location, the source, the ownership or the control of the proceeds of specified criminal conduct; or

(B) avoid any transaction reporting requirement imposed by law; and

(iii) The total value of the property involved in such financial transaction or transactions exceeds one hundred thousand dollars; or

2. Knowing that one or more monetary instruments represent:

(a) the proceeds of the criminal sale of a controlled substance, he or she transports, transmits, or transfers or attempts to transport, transmit or transfer, on one or more occasions, monetary instruments which in fact represent the proceeds of the criminal sale of a controlled substance from a place in any county in this state to or through a place outside that county or to a place in any county in this state from or through a place outside that county:

(i) With intent to promote the carrying on of specified criminal conduct; or

(ii) Knowing that such transportation, transmittal or transfer is designed in whole or in part to:

(A) conceal or disguise the nature, the location, the source, the ownership or the control of the proceeds of specified criminal conduct; or

(B) avoid any transaction reporting requirement imposed by law; and

(iii) The total value of such monetary instrument or instruments exceeds fifty thousand dollars; or

(b) the proceeds of specified criminal conduct, he or she transports, transmits, or transfers or attempts to transport, transmit or transfer, on one or more occasions, monetary instruments which in fact represent the proceeds of specified criminal conduct from a place in any county in this state to or through a place outside that county or to a place in any county in this state from or through a place outside that county:

(i) With intent to promote the carrying on of specified criminal conduct; or

(ii) Knowing that such transportation, transmittal or transfer is designed in whole or in part to:

(A) conceal or disguise the nature, the location, the source, the ownership or the control of the proceeds of specified criminal conduct; or

(B) avoid any transaction reporting requirement imposed by law; and

(iii) The total value of such monetary instrument or instruments exceeds one hundred thousand dollars; or

3. He or she conducts one or more financial transactions involving property represented to be:

(a) the proceeds of the criminal sale of a controlled substance, or represented to be property used to conduct or facilitate the criminal sale of a controlled substance:

(i) With intent to:

(A) promote the carrying on of specified criminal conduct; or

(B) conceal or disguise the nature, the location, the source, the ownership or the control of property believed to be the proceeds of specified criminal conduct; or

(C) avoid any transaction reporting requirement imposed by law; and

(ii) The total represented value of the property involved in such financial transaction or transactions exceeds fifty thousand dollars; or

(b) the proceeds of specified criminal conduct, or represented to be property used to conduct or facilitate specified criminal conduct:

(i) With intent to:

(A) promote the carrying on of specified criminal conduct;

(B) conceal or disguise the nature, the location, the source, the ownership or the control of property believed to be the proceeds of specified criminal conduct; or

(C) avoid any transaction reporting requirement imposed by law; and

(ii) The total represented value of the property involved in such financial transaction or transactions exceeds one hundred thousand dollars.

Money laundering in the second degree is a class C felony.

N.Y. Penal Law § 470.15

Section 470.20 - Money laundering in the first degree

A person is guilty of money laundering in the first degree when:

1. Knowing that the property involved in one or more financial transactions represents:

(a) the proceeds of the criminal sale of a controlled substance, he or she conducts one or more such financial transactions which in fact involve the proceeds of the criminal sale of a controlled substance:

(i) With intent to:

(A) promote the carrying on of specified criminal conduct; or

(B) engage in conduct constituting a felony as set forth in section eighteen hundred three, eighteen hundred four, eighteen hundred five, or eighteen hundred six of the tax law; or

(ii) Knowing that the transaction or transactions in whole or in part are designed to:

(A) conceal or disguise the nature, the location, the source, the ownership or the control of the proceeds of specified criminal conduct; or

(B) avoid any transaction reporting requirement imposed by law; and

(iii) The total value of the property involved in such financial transaction or transactions exceeds five hundred thousand dollars; or

(b) the proceeds of a class A, B or C felony, or of a crime in any other jurisdiction that is or would be a class A, B or C felony under the laws of this state, he or she conducts one or more such financial transactions which in fact involve the proceeds of any such felony:

(i) With intent to:

(A) promote the carrying on of specified criminal conduct; or

(B) engage in conduct constituting a felony as set forth in section eighteen hundred three, eighteen hundred four, eighteen hundred five, eighteen hundred six of the tax law; or

(ii) Knowing that the transaction or transactions in whole or in part are designed to:

(A) conceal or disguise the nature, the location, the source, the ownership or the control of the proceeds of specified criminal conduct; or

(B) avoid any transaction reporting requirement imposed by law; and

(iii) The total value of the property involved in such financial transaction or transactions exceeds one million dollars.

2. He or she conducts one or more financial transactions involving property represented to be:

(a) the proceeds of the criminal sale of a controlled substance, or represented to be property used to conduct or facilitate the criminal sale of a controlled substance:

(i) With intent to:

(A) promote the carrying on of specified criminal conduct; or

(B) conceal or disguise the nature, the location, the source, the ownership or the control of property believed to be the proceeds of specified criminal conduct; or

(C) avoid any transaction reporting requirement imposed by law; and

(ii) The total represented value of the property involved in such financial transaction or transactions exceeds five hundred thousand dollars; or

(b) the proceeds of a class A, B or C felony or of a crime in any other jurisdiction that is or would be a class A, B or C felony under the laws of this state, or represented to be property used to conduct or facilitate such crimes:

(i) With intent to:

(A) promote the carrying on of specified criminal conduct; or

(B) conceal or disguise the nature, the location, the source, the ownership or the control of property believed to be the proceeds of specified criminal conduct; or

(C) avoid any transaction reporting requirement imposed by law; and

(ii) The total represented value of the property involved in such financial transaction or transactions exceeds one million dollars.

Money laundering in the first degree is a class B felony.

N.Y. Penal Law § 470.20

Section 470.21 - Money laundering in support of terrorism in the fourth degree

A person is guilty of money laundering in support of terrorism in the fourth degree when:

1. Knowing that the property involved in one or more financial transactions represents either the proceeds of an act of terrorism as defined in subdivision one of section 490.05 of this part, or a monetary instrument given, received or intended to be used to support a violation of article four hundred ninety of this part:

(a) he or she conducts one or more such financial transactions which in fact involve either the proceeds of an act of terrorism as defined in subdivision one of section 490.05 of this part, or a monetary instrument given, received or intended to be used to support a violation of article four hundred ninety of this part:

(i) With intent to:

(A) promote the carrying on of criminal conduct; or

(B) engage in conduct constituting a felony as set forth in section eighteen hundred three, eighteen hundred four, eighteen hundred five, or eighteen hundred six of the tax law; or

(ii) Knowing that the transaction or transactions in whole or in part are designed to:

(A) conceal or disguise the nature, the location, the source, the ownership or the control of either the proceeds of an act of terrorism as defined in subdivision one of section 490.05 of this part, or a monetary instrument given, received or intended to be used to support a violation of article four hundred ninety of this part; or

(B) avoid any transaction reporting requirement imposed by law; and

(b) the total value of the property involved in such financial transaction or transactions exceeds one thousand dollars; or

2. Knowing that one or more monetary instruments represents either the proceeds of an act of terrorism as defined in subdivision one of section 490.05 of this part, or a monetary instrument given, received or intended to be used to support a violation of article four hundred ninety of this part:

(a) he or she transports, transmits, or transfers on one or more occasions, monetary instruments which in fact represent either the proceeds of an act of terrorism as defined in subdivision one of section 490.05 of this part, or a monetary instrument given, received or intended to be used to support a violation of article four hundred ninety of this part:

(i) With intent to promote the carrying on of criminal conduct; or

(ii) Knowing that such transportation, transmittal, or transfer is designed in whole or in part to:

(A) conceal or disguise the nature, the location, the source, the ownership, or the control of either the proceeds of an act of terrorism as defined in subdivision one of section 490.05 of this part, or a monetary instrument given, received or intended to be used to support a violation of article four hundred ninety of this part; or

(B) avoid any transaction reporting requirement imposed by law; and

(b) the total value of such monetary instrument or instruments exceeds two thousand dollars; or

3. He or she conducts one or more financial transactions:

(a) involving property represented to be either the proceeds of an act of terrorism as defined in subdivision one of section 490.05 of this part, or a monetary instrument given, received or intended to be used to support a violation of article four hundred ninety of this part, with intent to:

(i) promote the carrying on of specified criminal conduct; or

(ii) conceal or disguise the nature, the location, the source, the ownership or the control of property believed to be either the proceeds of an act of terrorism as defined in subdivision one of section 490.05 of this part, or a monetary instrument given, received or intended to be used to support a violation of article four hundred ninety of this part; or

(iii) avoid any transaction reporting requirement imposed by law; and

(b) the total value of the property involved in such financial transaction or transactions exceeds two thousand dollars.

Money laundering in support of terrorism in the fourth degree is a class E felony.

N.Y. Penal Law § 470.21

Section 470.22 - Money laundering in support of terrorism in the third degree

A person is guilty of money laundering in support of terrorism in the third degree when:

1. Knowing that the property involved in one or more financial transactions represents either the proceeds of an act of terrorism as defined in subdivision one of section 490.05 of this part, or a monetary instrument given, received or intended to be used to support a violation of article four hundred ninety of this part:

(a) he or she conducts one or more such financial transactions which in fact involve either the proceeds of an act of terrorism as defined in subdivision one of section 490.05 of this part, or a monetary instrument given, received or intended to be used to support a violation of article four hundred ninety of this part:

(i) With intent to:

(A) promote the carrying on of specified criminal conduct; or

(B) engage in conduct constituting a felony as set forth in section eighteen hundred three, eighteen hundred four, eighteen hundred five, or eighteen hundred six of the tax law; or

(ii) Knowing that the transaction or transactions in whole or in part are designed to:

(A) conceal or disguise the nature, the location, the source, the ownership or the control of either the proceeds of an act of terrorism as defined in subdivision one of section 490.05 of this part, or a monetary instrument given, received or intended to be used to support a violation of article four hundred ninety of this part; or

(B) avoid any transaction reporting requirement imposed by law; and

(b) the total value of the property involved in such financial transaction or transactions exceeds five thousand dollars; or

2. Knowing that one or more monetary instruments represent either the proceeds of an act of terrorism as defined in subdivision one of section 490.05 of this part, or a monetary instrument given, received or intended to be used to support a violation of article four hundred ninety of this part:

(a) he or she transports, transmits, or transfers or attempts to transport, transmit or transfer, on one or more occasions, monetary instruments which in fact represent either the proceeds of an act of terrorism as defined in subdivision one of section 490.05 of this part, or a monetary instrument given, received or intended to be used to support a violation of article four hundred ninety of this part from a place in any county in this state to or through a place outside that county or to a place in any county in this state from or through a place outside that county:

(i) With intent to promote the carrying on of specified criminal conduct; or

(ii) Knowing that such transportation, transmittal or transfer is designed in whole or in part to:

(A) conceal or disguise the nature, the location, the source, the ownership or the control of either the proceeds of an act of terrorism as defined in subdivision one of section 490.05 of this part, or a monetary instrument given, received or intended to be used to support a violation of article four hundred ninety of this part; or

(B) avoid any transaction reporting requirement imposed by law; and

(b) The total value of such monetary instrument or instruments exceeds five thousand dollars; or

3. He or she conducts one or more financial transactions involving property represented to be either the proceeds of an act of terrorism as defined in subdivision one of section 490.05 of this part, or a monetary instrument given, received or intended to be used to support a violation of article four hundred ninety of this part:

(a) With intent to:

(i) promote the carrying on of specified criminal conduct; or

(ii) conceal or disguise the nature, the location, the source, the ownership or the control of property believed to be either the proceeds of an act of terrorism as defined in subdivision one of section 490.05 of this part, or a monetary instrument given, received or intended to be used to support a violation of article four hundred ninety of this part; or

(iii) avoid any transaction reporting requirement imposed by law; and

(b) The total value of the property involved in such financial transaction or transactions exceeds five thousand dollars.

Money laundering in support of terrorism in the third degree is a class D felony.

N.Y. Penal Law § 470.22

Section 470.23 - Money laundering in support of terrorism in the second degree

A person is guilty of money laundering in support of terrorism in the second degree when:

1. Knowing that the property involved in one or more financial transactions represents either the proceeds of an act of terrorism as defined in subdivision one of section 490.05 of this part, or a monetary instrument given, received or intended to be used to support a violation of article four hundred ninety of this part:

(a) he or she conducts one or more such financial transactions which in fact involve either the proceeds of an act of terrorism as defined in subdivision one of section 490.05 of this part, or a monetary instrument given, received or intended to be used to support a violation of article four hundred ninety of this part:

(i) With intent to:

(A) promote the carrying on of specified criminal conduct; or

(B) engage in conduct constituting a felony as set forth in section eighteen hundred three, eighteen hundred four, eighteen hundred five, or eighteen hundred six of the tax law; or

(ii) Knowing that the transaction or transactions in whole or in part are designed to:

(A) conceal or disguise the nature, the location, the source, the ownership or the control of either the proceeds of an act of terrorism as defined in subdivision one of section 490.05 of this part, or a monetary instrument given, received or intended to be used to support a violation of article four hundred ninety of this part; or

(B) avoid any transaction reporting requirement imposed by law; and

(b) the total value of the property involved in such financial transaction or transactions exceeds twenty-five thousand dollars; or

2. Knowing that one or more monetary instruments represent either the proceeds of an act of terrorism as defined in subdivision one of section 490.05 of this part, or a monetary instrument given, received or intended to be used to support a violation of article four hundred ninety of this part:

(a) he or she transports, transmits, or transfers or attempts to transport, transmit or transfer, on one or more occasions, monetary instruments which in fact represent either the proceeds of an act of terrorism as defined in subdivision one of section 490.05 of this part, or a monetary instrument given, received or intended to be used to support a violation of article four hundred ninety of this part from a place in any county in this state to or through a place outside that county or to a place in any county in this state from or through a place outside that county:

(i) With intent to promote the carrying on of specified criminal conduct; or

(ii) Knowing that such transportation, transmittal or transfer is designed in whole or in part to:

(A) conceal or disguise the nature, the location, the source, the ownership or the control of either the proceeds of an act of terrorism as defined in subdivision one of section 490.05 of this part, or a monetary instrument given, received or intended to be used to support a violation of article four hundred ninety of this part; or

(B) avoid any transaction reporting requirement imposed by law; and

(b) the total value of such monetary instrument or instruments exceeds twenty-five thousand dollars; or

3. He or she conducts one or more financial transactions involving property represented to be either the proceeds of an act of terrorism as defined in subdivision one of section 490.05 of this part, or a monetary instrument given, received or intended to be used to support a violation of article four hundred ninety of this part:

(a) With intent to:

(i) promote the carrying on of specified criminal conduct; or

(ii) conceal or disguise the nature, the location, the source, the ownership or the control of property believed to be either the proceeds of an act of terrorism as defined in subdivision one of section 490.05 of this part, or a monetary instrument given, received or intended to be used to support a violation of article four hundred ninety of this part; or

(iii) avoid any transaction reporting requirement imposed by law; and

(b) The total value of the property involved in such financial transaction or transactions exceeds twenty-five thousand dollars.

Money laundering in support of terrorism in the second degree is a class C felony.

N.Y. Penal Law § 470.23

Section 470.24 - Money laundering in support of terrorism in the first degree

A person is guilty of money laundering in support of terrorism in the first degree when:

1. Knowing that the property involved in one or more financial transactions represents either the proceeds of an act of terrorism as defined in subdivision one of section 490.05 of this part, or a monetary instrument given, received or intended to be used to support a violation of article four hundred ninety of this part:

(a) he or she conducts one or more financial transactions which in fact involve either the proceeds of an act of terrorism as defined in subdivision one of section 490.05 of this part, or a monetary instrument given, received or intended to be used to support a violation of article four hundred ninety of this part:

(i) With intent to:

(A) promote the carrying on of specified criminal conduct; or

(B) engage in conduct constituting a felony as set forth in section eighteen hundred three, eighteen hundred four, eighteen hundred five, or eighteen hundred six of the tax law; or

(ii) Knowing that the transaction or transactions in whole or in part are designed to:

(A) conceal or disguise the nature, the location, the source, the ownership or the control of the proceeds of either the proceeds of an act of terrorism as defined in subdivision one of section 490.05 of this part, or a monetary instrument given, received or intended to be used to support a violation of article four hundred ninety of this part; or

(B) avoid any transaction reporting requirement imposed by law; and

(iii) The total value of the property involved in such financial transaction or transactions exceeds seventy-five thousand dollars.

2. He or she conducts one or more financial transactions involving property represented to be either the proceeds of an act of terrorism as defined in subdivision one of section 490.05 of this part, or a monetary instrument given, received or intended to be used to support a violation of article four hundred ninety of this part:

(a) With intent to:

(i) promote the carrying on of specified criminal conduct; or

(ii) conceal or disguise the nature, the location, the source, the ownership or the control of property believed to be either the proceeds of an act of terrorism as defined in subdivision one of section 490.05 of this part, or a monetary instrument given, received or intended to be used to support a violation of article four hundred ninety of this part; or

(iii) avoid any transaction reporting requirement imposed by law; and

(b) The total represented value of the property involved in such financial transaction or transactions exceeds one hundred twenty-five thousand dollars.

N.Y. Penal Law § 470.24

Section 470.25 - Money laundering; fines

1. Any person convicted of a violation of section 470.05, 470.10, 470.15, or 470.20 of this article may be sentenced to pay a fine not in excess of two times the value of the monetary instruments which are the proceeds of specified criminal activity. When a fine is imposed pursuant to this subdivision, the court shall make a finding as to the value of such monetary instrument or instruments. If the record does not contain sufficient evidence to support such a finding the court may conduct a hearing upon the issue. In imposing a fine, the court shall consider the seriousness of the conduct, whether the amount of the fine is disproportionate to the conduct in which he engaged, its impact on victims, as well as the economic circumstances of the convicted person, including the effect of the imposition of such a fine upon his immediate family.

2. The imposition of a fine pursuant to subdivision one of this section or paragraph b of subdivision one of section 80.00 of this chapter, shall preclude the imposition of any other order or judgment of forfeiture or fine based upon the same criminal conduct.

N.Y. Penal Law § 470.25

Article 480 - CRIMINAL FORFEITURE - FELONY CONTROLLED SUBSTANCE OFFENSES

Section 480.00 - Definitions

The following definitions are applicable to this article.

1. "Felony offense" means only a felony defined in article two hundred twenty of this chapter, or an attempt or conspiracy to commit any such felony, provided such attempt or conspiracy is punishable as a felony, or solicitation of any such felony provided such solicitation is punishable as a felony.

2. "Property" means real property, personal property, money, negotiable instruments, securities, or anything of value or an interest in a thing of value.

3. "Proceeds" means any property obtained by a defendant through the commission of a felony controlled substance offense, and includes any appreciation in value of such property.

4. "Substituted proceeds" means any property obtained by a defendant by the sale or exchange of proceeds of a felony controlled substance offense, and any gain realized by such sale or exchange.

5. "Instrumentality of a felony controlled substance offense" means any property, other than real property and any buildings, fixtures, appurtenances, and improvements thereon, whose use contributes directly and materially to the commission of a felony controlled substance offense.

6. "Real property instrumentality of a crime" means an interest in real property the use of which contributes directly and materially to the commission of a specified felony offense.

7. "Specified felony offense" means:

(a) a conviction of a person for a violation of section 220.18, 220.21, 220.41, 220.43, or 220.77 of this chapter, or where the accusatory instrument charges one or more of such offenses, conviction upon a plea of guilty to any of the felonies for which such plea is otherwise authorized by law or a conviction of a person for conspiracy to commit a violation of section 220.18, 220.21, 220.41, 220.43, or 220.77 of this chapter, where the controlled substances which are the object of the conspiracy are located in the real property which is the subject of the forfeiture action; or

(b) three or more violations of any of the felonies defined in section 220.09, 220.16, 220.18, 220.21, 220.31, 220.34, 220.39, 220.41, 220.43 or 220.77 of this chapter, which violations do not constitute a single criminal offense as defined in subdivision one of section 40.10 of the criminal procedure law, or a single criminal transaction, as defined in paragraph (a) of subdivision two of section 40.10 of the criminal procedure law, and at least one of which resulted in a conviction of such offense, or where the accusatory instrument charges one or more of such felonies, conviction upon a plea of guilty to a felony for which such plea is otherwise authorized by law; or

(c) a conviction of a person for a violation of section 220.09, 220.16, 220.34 or 220.39 of this chapter, or where the accusatory instrument charges any such felony, conviction upon a plea of guilty to a felony for which the plea is otherwise authorized by law, together with evidence which:

(i) provides substantial indicia that the defendant used the real property to engage in a continual, ongoing course of conduct involving the unlawful mixing, compounding, manufacturing, warehousing, or packaging of controlled substances as part of an illegal trade or business for gain; and

(ii) establishes, where the conviction is for possession of a controlled substance , that such possession was with the intent to sell it.

N.Y. Penal Law § 480.00

Amended by New York Laws 2021, ch. 92,Sec. 31, eff. 3/31/2021.

Section 480.05 - Felony controlled substance offenses; forfeiture

1. When any person is convicted of a felony offense, the following property is subject to forfeiture pursuant to this article:

(a) any property constituting the proceeds or substituted proceeds of such offense, unless the forfeiture is disproportionate to the defendant's gain from or participation in the offense, in which event the trier of fact may direct forfeiture of a portion thereof; and

(b) any property constituting an instrumentality of such offense, other than a real property instrumentality of a crime, unless such forfeiture is disproportionate to the defendant's gain from or participation in the offense, in which event the trier of fact may direct forfeiture of a portion thereof.

2. When any person is convicted of a specified offense, the real property instrumentality of such specified offense is subject to forfeiture pursuant to this article, unless such forfeiture is disproportionate to the defendant's gain from or participation in the offense, in which event the trier of fact may direct forfeiture of a portion thereof.

3. Property acquired in good faith by an attorney as payment for the reasonable and bona fide fees of legal services or reimbursement of reasonable and bona fide expenses related to the representation of a defendant in connection with a civil or criminal forfeiture proceeding or a related criminal matter, shall be exempt from a judgment of forfeiture. For purposes of this subdivision, "bona fide" means that the attorney who acquired such property had no reasonable basis to believe that the fee transaction was a fraudulent or sham transaction designed to shield property from forfeiture, hide its existence from governmental investigative agencies, or was conducted for any purpose other than legitimate.

N.Y. Penal Law § 480.05

Section 480.10 - Procedure

1. After the grand jury votes to file an indictment charging a person with a felony offense as that term is defined in section 480.00 of this article, it may subsequently receive evidence that property is subject to forfeiture under this article. If such evidence is legally sufficient and provides reasonable cause to believe that such property is subject to forfeiture under this article, the grand jury shall file together with the indictment a special forfeiture information specifying the property for which forfeiture is sought and containing a plain and concise factual statement which sets forth the basis for the forfeiture. Alternatively, where the defendant has waived indictment and has consented to be prosecuted for a felony offense by superior court information pursuant to article one hundred ninety-five of the criminal procedure law, the prosecutor may, in addition to the superior court information, file a special forfeiture information specifying the property for which the forfeiture is sought and containing a plain and concise factual statement which sets forth the basis for the forfeiture.

2. At any time before entry of a plea of guilty to an indictment or commencement of a trial thereof, the prosecutor may file a superseding special forfeiture information in the same court in accordance with the provisions of subdivision one of this section. Upon the filing of such a superseding forfeiture information the court must, upon application of the defendant, order any adjournment of the proceedings which may, by reason of such superseding special forfeiture information, be necessary to accord the defendant adequate opportunity to prepare his defense of the forfeiture action.

3. A motion to inspect and reduce made pursuant to section 210.20 of the criminal procedure law may seek modification of a special forfeiture information dismissing a claim with respect to any property interest therein where the court finds the evidence before the grand jury was legally insufficient to support a claim against such interest.

4. The prosecutor shall promptly file a copy of the special forfeiture information, including the terms thereof, with the state division of criminal justice services and with the local agency responsible for criminal justice planning. Failure to file such information shall not be grounds for any relief under this chapter. The prosecutor shall also report such demographic data as required by the state division of criminal justice services when filing a copy of the special forfeiture information with the state division of criminal justice services.

5. In addition to information required to be disclosed pursuant to article two hundred forty-five of the criminal procedure law, when forfeiture is sought pursuant to this article, and following the defendant's arraignment on the special forfeiture information, the court shall order discovery of any information not otherwise disclosed which is material and reasonably necessary for preparation by the defendant with respect to a forfeiture proceeding brought pursuant to this article. Such material shall include those portions of the grand jury minutes and such other information which pertain solely to the special forfeiture information and shall not include information which pertains to the criminal charges. Upon application of the prosecutor, the court may issue a protective order pursuant to section 245.70 of the criminal procedure law with respect to any information required to be disclosed pursuant to this subdivision.

6.

(a) Trial of forfeiture counts by jury or by the court. Evidence which relates solely to the issue of forfeiture shall not be presented during the trial on the underlying felony offense or specified felony offense, and the defendant shall not be required to present such evidence prior to the verdict on such offense. A defendant who does not present evidence in his defense with respect to the trial of the underlying offense is not precluded on account thereof from presenting evidence during the trial of the forfeiture count or counts.

(b) Trial of forfeiture counts by the jury. After returning a verdict of guilty of a felony offense or specified felony offense, or where the defendant has pled guilty to a felony offense or a specified felony offense and has not waived a jury trial of the forfeiture count or counts pursuant to article three hundred twenty of the criminal procedure law, the jury shall be given the forfeiture information and shall hear any additional evidence which is relevant and legally admissible upon the forfeiture count or counts. After hearing such evidence, the jury shall then deliberate upon the forfeiture count or counts, and based upon all the evidence admitted in connection with the indictment or superior court information and the forfeiture information, may, if satisfied by proof beyond a reasonable doubt that the property, or a portion thereof, is subject to forfeiture pursuant to this article, return a verdict directing that such property, or portion thereof, is subject to forfeiture.

(c) Trial of forfeiture counts by the court. Where a defendant has waived a jury trial of the forfeiture count or counts pursuant to article three hundred twenty of the criminal procedure law, the court shall hear all evidence upon the forfeiture information and may, if satisfied by proof beyond a reasonable doubt that the property, or a portion thereof, is subject to forfeiture under this article, render a verdict determining that such property, or a portion thereof, is subject to forfeiture under this article.

(d) After the verdict of forfeiture, the court shall hear arguments and may receive additional evidence upon a motion of the defendant that the verdict of forfeiture (i) is against the weight of the evidence, or (ii) is, with respect to a forfeiture pursuant to this article, disproportionate to the defendant's gain from the offense, or the defendant's interest in the property, or the defendant's participation in the conduct upon which the forfeiture is based. Upon such a finding, the court may in the interest of justice set aside, modify, limit or otherwise condition the verdict of forfeiture.

7. A final judgment or order of forfeiture issued pursuant to this article shall authorize the prosecutor to seize all property directed to be forfeited under this article upon such terms and conditions as the court deems proper. If a property right is not exercisable or transferable for value by the prosecutor, it shall expire and shall not revert to the convicted person.

8. Where the forfeited property consists of real property, the court may at any time prior to a verdict of forfeiture, enter an order pursuant to subdivision four-a of section thirteen hundred eleven of the civil practice law and rules.

9. No person shall forfeit any right, title, or interest in any property under this article who has not been convicted of a felony offense or specified felony offense, as the case may be. Any person claiming an interest in property subject to forfeiture may institute a special proceeding to determine that claim, before or after the trial, pursuant to section thirteen hundred twenty-seven of the civil practice law and rules; provided, however, that if such special proceeding is initiated before trial on the forfeiture count or counts, it may, upon written motion of the prosecutor, and in the court's discretion, be postponed by the court until completion of the trial. In addition, any person claiming an interest in property subject to forfeiture may petition for remission as provided for in subdivision seven of section thirteen hundred eleven of the civil practice law and rules.

10. Testimony of the defendant or evidence derived therefrom introduced in the trial of the forfeiture count may not be used by the prosecution in any post-trial motion proceedings, appeals, or retrials relating to the defendant's criminal liability for the underlying criminal offense unless the defendant has previously referred to such evidence in such post-trial proceeding, appeal, or retrial relating to the underlying offense and the evidence is presented by the prosecutor in response thereto. Upon vacatur or reversal on appeal of a judgment of conviction upon which a verdict of forfeiture is based, any verdict of forfeiture which is based upon such conviction shall also be vacated or reversed.

N.Y. Penal Law § 480.10

Amended by New York Laws 2019, ch. 59,Sec. LLL-13, eff. 1/1/2020.

Amended by New York Laws 2019, ch. 55,Sec. PP-11, eff. 10/9/2019.

Section 480.20 - Disposal of property

All property which is forfeited pursuant to this article shall be disposed of in accordance with the provisions of section thirteen hundred forty-nine of the civil practice law and rules. All reports required to be filed pursuant to article thirteen-A of such law and rules by a claiming authority shall be filed by the prosecutor in a forfeiture action brought pursuant to this article.

N.Y. Penal Law § 480.20

Section 480.25 - Election of remedies

The imposition of a judgment or order of forfeiture pursuant to this article with respect to a defendant's interest in property shall preclude the imposition of a judgment or order of forfeiture with respect to such interest in property pursuant to the provisions of any other state or local law based upon the same criminal conduct.

N.Y. Penal Law § 480.25

Section 480.30 - Provisional remedies

1. The provisional remedies authorized by article thirteen-A of the civil practice law and rules shall be available in an action for criminal forfeiture pursuant to this article to the extent and under the same terms, conditions and limitations as provided in article thirteen-A of such law and rules, except as specifically provided herein.

2. Upon the filing of an indictment and special forfeiture information, or a superior court information and special forfeiture information, seeking forfeiture pursuant to this article, all further proceedings with respect to provisional remedies shall be heard by the judge or justice in the criminal part to which the criminal action is assigned.

3. For purposes of this section, the indictment and special forfeiture information or superior court information and special forfeiture information seeking criminal forfeiture shall constitute the summons with notice or summons and verified complaint referred to in article thirteen-A of the civil practice law and rules.

N.Y. Penal Law § 480.30

Section 480.35 - Rebuttable presumption

1. In a criminal forfeiture proceeding commenced pursuant to this article, the following rebuttable presumption shall apply: all currency or negotiable instruments payable to the bearer shall be presumed to be the proceeds of a felony offense when such currency or negotiable instruments are (i) found in close proximity to a controlled substance unlawfully possessed by the defendant in an amount sufficient to constitute a violation of section 220.18 or 220.21 of the penal law, or (ii) found in close proximity to any quantity of a controlled substance or marihuana unlawfully possessed by such defendant in a room, other than a public place, under circumstances evincing an intent to unlawfully mix, compound, package, distribute or otherwise prepare for sale such controlled substance or marihuana.

2. The presumption established by this section shall be rebutted by credible and reliable evidence which tends to show that such currency or negotiable instruments payable to the bearer is not the proceeds of a felony offense. In an action tried before a jury, the jury shall be so instructed. Any sworn testimony of a defendant offered to rebut the presumption and any other evidence which is obtained as a result of such testimony, shall be inadmissible in any subsequent proceeding relating to the forfeiture action, or in any other civil or criminal action, except in a prosecution for a violation of article two hundred ten of this chapter. In an action tried before a jury, at the commencement of the trial, or at such other time as the court reasonably directs, the prosecutor shall provide notice to the court and to the defendant of its intent to request that the court charge such presumption.

N.Y. Penal Law § 480.35

Title Y - HATE CRIMES ACT OF 2000

Article 485 - HATE CRIMES

Section 485.00 - Legislative findings

The legislature finds and determines as follows: criminal acts involving violence, intimidation and destruction of property based upon bias and prejudice have become more prevalent in New York state in recent years. The intolerable truth is that in these crimes, commonly and justly referred to as "hate crimes", victims are intentionally selected, in whole or in part, because of their race, color, national origin, ancestry, gender, gender identity or expression, religion, religious practice, age, disability or sexual orientation. Hate crimes do more than threaten the safety and welfare of all citizens. They inflict on victims incalculable physical and emotional damage and tear at the very fabric of free society. Crimes motivated by invidious hatred toward particular groups not only harm individual victims but send a powerful message of intolerance and discrimination to all members of the group to which the victim belongs. Hate crimes can and do intimidate and disrupt entire communities and vitiate the civility that is essential to healthy democratic processes. In a democratic society, citizens cannot be required to approve of the beliefs and practices of others, but must never commit criminal acts on account of them. However, these criminal acts do occur and are occurring more and more frequently. Quite often, these crimes of hate are also acts of terror. The recent attacks in Monsey, New York as well as the shootings in El Paso, Texas; Pittsburgh, Pennsylvania; Sutherland Springs, Texas; Orlando, Florida; and Charleston, South Carolina illustrate that mass killings are often apolitical, motivated by the hatred of a specific group coupled with a desire to inflict mass casualties. The current law emphasizes the political motivation of an act over its catastrophic effect and does not adequately recognize the harm to public order and individual safety that hate crimes cause. Therefore, our laws must be strengthened to provide clear recognition of the gravity of hate crimes and the compelling importance of preventing their recurrence.

N.Y. Penal Law § 485.00

Amended by New York Laws 2020, ch. 55,Sec. R-2, eff. 11/1/2020.
Amended by New York Laws 2019, ch. 8,Sec. 19, eff. 11/1/2019.

Section 485.05 - Hate crimes

1. A person commits a hate crime when he or she commits a specified offense and either:

(a) intentionally selects the person against whom the offense is committed or intended to be committed in whole or in substantial part because of a belief or perception regarding the race, color, national origin, ancestry, gender, gender identity or expression, religion, religious practice, age, disability or sexual orientation of a person, regardless of whether the belief or perception is correct, or

(b) intentionally commits the act or acts constituting the offense in whole or in substantial part because of a belief or perception regarding the race, color, national origin, ancestry, gender, gender identity or expression, religion, religious practice, age, disability or sexual orientation of a person, regardless of whether the belief or perception is correct.

2. Proof of race, color, national origin, ancestry, gender, gender identity or expression, religion, religious practice, age, disability or sexual orientation of the defendant, the victim or of both the defendant and the victim does not, by itself, constitute legally sufficient evidence satisfying the people's burden under paragraph (a) or (b) of subdivision one of this section.

3. A "specified offense" is an offense defined by any of the following provisions of this chapter: section 120.00 (assault in the third degree); section 120.05 (assault in the second degree); section 120.10 (assault in the first degree); section 120.12 (aggravated assault upon a person less than eleven years old); section 120.13 (menacing in the first degree); section 120.14 (menacing in the second degree); section 120.15 (menacing in the third degree); section 120.20 (reckless endangerment in the second degree); section 120.25 (reckless endangerment in the first degree); section 121.12 (strangulation in the second

degree); section 121.13 (strangulation in the first degree); subdivision one of section 125.15 (manslaughter in the second degree); subdivision one, two or four of section 125.20 (manslaughter in the first degree); section 125.25 (murder in the second degree); section 120.45 (stalking in the fourth degree); section 120.50 (stalking in the third degree); section 120.55 (stalking in the second degree); section 120.60 (stalking in the first degree); subdivision one of section 130.35 (rape in the first degree); subdivision one of section 130.50 (criminal sexual act in the first degree); subdivision one of section 130.65 (sexual abuse in the first degree); paragraph (a) of subdivision one of section 130.67 (aggravated sexual abuse in the second degree); paragraph (a) of subdivision one of section 130.70 (aggravated sexual abuse in the first degree); section 135.05 (unlawful imprisonment in the second degree); section 135.10 (unlawful imprisonment in the first degree); section 135.20 (kidnapping in the second degree); section 135.25 (kidnapping in the first degree); section 135.60 (coercion in the third degree); section 135.61 (coercion in the second degree); section 135.65 (coercion in the first degree); section 140.10 (criminal trespass in the third degree); section 140.15 (criminal trespass in the second degree); section 140.17 (criminal trespass in the first degree); section 140.20 (burglary in the third degree); section 140.25 (burglary in the second degree); section 140.30 (burglary in the first degree); section 145.00 (criminal mischief in the fourth degree); section 145.05 (criminal mischief in the third degree); section 145.10 (criminal mischief in the second degree); section 145.12 (criminal mischief in the first degree); section 150.05 (arson in the fourth degree); section 150.10 (arson in the third degree); section 150.15 (arson in the second degree); section 150.20 (arson in the first degree); section 155.25 (petit larceny); section 155.30 (grand larceny in the fourth degree); section 155.35 (grand larceny in the third degree); section 155.40 (grand larceny in the second degree); section 155.42 (grand larceny in the first degree); section 160.05 (robbery in the third degree); section 160.10 (robbery in the second degree); section 160.15 (robbery in the first degree); section 240.25 (harassment in the first degree); subdivision one, two or four of section 240.30 (aggravated harassment in the second degree); section 490.10 (soliciting or providing support for an act of terrorism in the second degree); section 490.15 (soliciting or providing support for an act of terrorism in the first degree); section 490.20 (making a terroristic threat); section 490.25 (crime of terrorism); section 490.30 (hindering prosecution of terrorism in the second degree); section 490.35 (hindering prosecution of terrorism in the first degree); section 490.37 (criminal possession of a chemical weapon or biological weapon in the third degree); section 490.40 (criminal possession of a chemical weapon or biological weapon in the second degree); section 490.45 (criminal possession of a chemical weapon or biological weapon in the first degree); section 490.47 (criminal use of a chemical weapon or biological weapon in the third degree); section 490.50 (criminal use of a chemical weapon or biological weapon in the second degree); section 490.55 (criminal use of a chemical weapon or biological weapon in the first degree); or any attempt or conspiracy to commit any of the foregoing offenses.

4. For purposes of this section:

(a) the term "age" means sixty years old or more;

(b) the term "disability" means a physical or mental impairment that substantially limits a major life activity;

(c) the term "gender identity or expression" means a person's actual or perceived gender-related identity, appearance, behavior, expression, or other gender-related characteristic regardless of the sex assigned to that person at birth, including, but not limited to, the status of being transgender.

N.Y. Penal Law § 485.05

Amended by New York Laws 2020, ch. 55, Sec. R-3, eff. 11/1/2020.

Amended by New York Laws 2019, ch. 8, Sec. 20, eff. 11/1/2019.

Amended by New York Laws 2018, ch. 55, Sec. NN-9, eff. 11/1/2018.

Section 485.10 - Sentencing

1. When a person is convicted of a hate crime pursuant to this article, and the specified offense is a violent felony offense, as defined in section 70.02 of this chapter, the hate crime shall be deemed a violent felony offense.

2. When a person is convicted of a hate crime pursuant to this article and the specified offense is a misdemeanor or a class C, D or E felony, the hate crime shall be deemed to be one category higher than the specified offense the defendant committed, or one category higher than the offense level applicable to the defendant's conviction for an attempt or conspiracy to commit a specified offense, whichever is applicable.

3. Notwithstanding any other provision of law, when a person is convicted of a hate crime pursuant to this article and the specified offense is a class B felony:

(a) the maximum term of the indeterminate sentence must be at least six years if the defendant is sentenced pursuant to section 70.00 of this chapter;

(b) the term of the determinate sentence must be at least eight years if the defendant is sentenced pursuant to section 70.02 of this chapter;

(c) the term of the determinate sentence must be at least twelve years if the defendant is sentenced pursuant to section 70.04 of this chapter;

(d) the maximum term of the indeterminate sentence must be at least four years if the defendant is sentenced pursuant to section 70.05 of this chapter; and

(e) the maximum term of the indeterminate sentence or the term of the determinate sentence must be at least ten years if the defendant is sentenced pursuant to section 70.06 of this chapter.

4. Notwithstanding any other provision of law, when a person is convicted of a hate crime pursuant to this article and the specified offense is a class A-1 felony, the minimum period of the indeterminate sentence shall be not less than twenty years.

5. In addition to any of the dispositions authorized by this chapter, the court may require as part of the sentence imposed upon a person convicted of a hate crime pursuant to this article, that the defendant complete a program, training session or

counseling session directed at hate crime prevention and education, where the court determines such program, training session or counseling session is appropriate, available and was developed or authorized by the court or local agencies in cooperation with organizations serving the affected community.

N.Y. Penal Law § 485.10

Title Y-1 - Enacted without title heading

Article 490 - TERRORISM

Section 490.00 - Legislative findings

The devastating consequences of the recent barbaric attack on the World Trade Center and the Pentagon underscore the compelling need for legislation that is specifically designed to combat the evils of terrorism. Indeed, the bombings of American embassies in Kenya and Tanzania in 1998, the federal building in Oklahoma City in 1995, Pan Am Flight number 103 in Lockerbie in 1988, the 1997 shooting atop the Empire State Building, the 1994 murder of Ari Halberstam on the Brooklyn Bridge and the 1993 bombing of the World Trade Center, will forever serve to remind us that terrorism is a serious and deadly problem that disrupts public order and threatens individual safety both at home and around the world. Terrorism is inconsistent with civilized society and cannot be tolerated.

N.Y. Penal Law § 490.00

Section 490.01 - Liability protection

1. Any person who makes a qualified disclosure of suspicious behavior shall be immune from civil and criminal liability for reporting such behavior.

2. For purposes of this article, "qualified disclosure of suspicious behavior" means any disclosure of allegedly suspicious behavior of another individual or individuals to any person that is made in good faith and with the reasonable belief that such suspicious behavior constitutes, is indicative of, or is in furtherance of a crime or an act of terrorism.

3. An action alleging that a statement or disclosure by a person of any suspicious transaction, activity or occurrence indicating that an individual may be engaging in or preparing to engage in suspicious behavior which constitutes, is indicative of, or is in furtherance of, a crime or an act of terrorism was not made in good faith and with the reasonable belief that such suspicious behavior constitutes, is indicative of, or is in furtherance of, a crime or an act of terrorism must be pled with particularity pursuant to subdivision (b) of rule three thousand sixteen of the civil practice law and rules.

N.Y. Penal Law § 490.01

Section 490.05 - Definitions

As used in this article, the following terms shall mean and include:

1. "Act of terrorism":

(a) for purposes of this article means an act or acts constituting a specified offense as defined in subdivision three of this section for which a person may be convicted in the criminal courts of this state pursuant to article twenty of the criminal procedure law, or an act or acts constituting an offense in any other jurisdiction within or outside the territorial boundaries of the United States which contains all of the essential elements of a specified offense, that is intended to:

(i) intimidate or coerce a civilian population;

(ii) influence the policy of a unit of government by intimidation or coercion; or

(iii) affect the conduct of a unit of government by murder, assassination or kidnapping; or

(b) for purposes of subparagraph (xiii) of paragraph (a) of subdivision one of section 125.27 of this chapter means activities that involve a violent act or acts dangerous to human life that are in violation of the criminal laws of this state and are intended to:

(i) intimidate or coerce a civilian population;

(ii) influence the policy of a unit of government by intimidation or coercion; or

(iii) affect the conduct of a unit of government by murder, assassination or kidnapping.

2. "Material support or resources" means currency or other financial securities, financial services, lodging, training, safehouses, false documentation or identification, communications equipment, facilities, weapons, lethal substances, explosives, personnel, transportation, and other physical assets, except medicine or religious materials.

3.

(a) "Specified offense" for purposes of this article means a class A felony offense other than an offense as defined in article two hundred twenty, a violent felony offense as defined in section 70.02, manslaughter in the second degree as defined in section 125.15, criminal tampering in the first degree as defined in section 145.20, identity theft in the second degree as defined in section 190.79, identity theft in the first degree as defined in section 190.80, unlawful possession of personal identification information in the second degree as defined in section 190.82, unlawful possession of personal identification information in the first degree as defined in section 190.83, money laundering in support of terrorism in the fourth degree as defined in section 470.21, money laundering in support of terrorism in the third degree as defined in section 470.22, money laundering in support of terrorism in the second degree as defined in section 470.23, money laundering in support of terrorism in the first degree as defined in section 470.24 of this chapter, and includes an attempt or conspiracy to commit any such offense.

(b) Notwithstanding the provisions of paragraph (a) of this subdivision, a specified offense shall not mean an offense defined in sections 490.37, 490.40, 490.45, 490.47, 490.50, and 490.55 of this article, nor shall a specified offense mean an attempt to commit any such offense.

4. "Renders criminal assistance" for purposes of sections 490.30 and 490.35 of this article shall have the same meaning as in section 205.50 of this chapter.

5. "Biological agent" means any micro-organism, virus, infectious substance, or biological product that may be engineered as a result of biotechnology, or any naturally occurring or bioengineered component of any such micro-organism, virus, infectious substance, or biological product, capable of causing:

(a) death, disease, or other biological malfunction in a human, an animal, a plant, or another living organism;

(b) deterioration of food, water, equipment, supplies, or material of any kind; or

(c) deleterious alteration of the environment.

6. "Toxin" means the toxic material of plants, animals, micro-organisms, viruses, fungi, or infectious substances, or a recombinant molecule, whatever its origin or method of production, including:

(a) any poisonous substance or biological product that may be engineered as a result of biotechnology produced by a living organism; or

(b) any poisonous isomer or biological product, homolog, or derivative of such a substance.

7. "Delivery system" means:

(a) any apparatus, equipment, device, or means of delivery specifically designed to deliver or disseminate a biological agent, toxin, or vector; or

(b) any vector.

8. "Vector" means a living organism, or molecule, including a recombinant molecule, or biological product that may be engineered as a result of biotechnology, capable of carrying a biological agent or toxin to a host.

9. "Biological weapon" means any biological agent, toxin, vector, or delivery system or combination thereof.

10. "Chemical weapon" means the following, together or separately:

(a) a toxic chemical or its precursors;

(b) a munition or device specifically designed to cause death or other harm through the toxic properties of a toxic chemical or its precursors, which would be released as a result of the employment of such munition or device;

(c) any equipment specifically designed for use directly in connection with the employment of munitions or devices; or

(d) any device that is designed to release radiation or radioactivity at a level dangerous to human life.

11. "Precursor" means any chemical reactant that takes part at any stage in the production by whatever method of a toxic chemical, including any key component of a binary or multicomponent chemical system, and includes precursors which have been identified for application of verification measures under article VI of the convention in schedules contained in the annex on chemicals of the chemical weapons convention.

12. "Key component of a binary or multicomponent chemical system" means the precursor which plays the most important role in determining the toxic properties of the final product and reacts rapidly with other chemicals in the binary or multicomponent system.

13. "Toxic chemical" means any chemical which through its chemical action on life processes can cause death, serious physical injury or permanent harm to humans or animals, including all such chemicals, regardless of their origin or of their method of production, and regardless of whether they are produced in facilities, in munitions or elsewhere, and includes toxic chemicals which have been identified by the commissioner of health and included on the list of toxic chemicals pursuant to subdivision twenty of section two hundred six of the public health law.

14. The terms "biological agent", "toxin", and "toxic chemical" do not include any biological agent, toxin or toxic chemical that is in its naturally occurring environment, if the biological agent, toxin or toxic chemical has not been cultivated, collected, or otherwise extracted from its natural source.

15. "Select chemical agent" shall mean a chemical weapon which has been identified in regulations promulgated pursuant to subdivision twenty of section two hundred six of the public health law.

16. "Select biological agent" shall mean a biological weapon which has been identified in regulations promulgated pursuant to subdivision twenty-one of section two hundred six of the public health law.

17. "Chemical weapons convention" and "convention" mean the convention on the prohibition of the development, production, stockpiling and use of chemical weapons and on their destruction, opened for signature on January thirteenth, nineteen hundred ninety-three.

N.Y. Penal Law § 490.05

Section 490.10 - Soliciting or providing support for an act of terrorism in the second degree

A person commits soliciting or providing support for an act of terrorism in the second degree when, with intent that material support or resources will be used, in whole or in part, to plan, prepare, carry out or aid in either an act of terrorism or the concealment of, or an escape from, an act of terrorism, he or she raises, solicits, collects or provides material support or resources.

N.Y. Penal Law § 490.10

Section 490.15 - Soliciting or providing support for an act of terrorism in the first degree

A person commits soliciting or providing support for an act of terrorism in the first degree when he or she commits the crime of soliciting or providing support for an act of terrorism in the second degree and the total value of material support or resources exceeds one thousand dollars.

N.Y. Penal Law § 490.15

Section 490.20 - Making a terroristic threat

1. A person is guilty of making a terroristic threat when with intent to intimidate or coerce a civilian population, influence the policy of a unit of government by intimidation or coercion, or affect the conduct of a unit of government by murder, assassination or kidnapping, he or she threatens to commit or cause to be committed a specified offense and thereby causes a reasonable expectation or fear of the imminent commission of such offense.

234

2. It shall be no defense to a prosecution pursuant to this section that the defendant did not have the intent or capability of committing the specified offense or that the threat was not made to a person who was a subject thereof.

Making a terroristic threat is a class D felony.

N.Y. Penal Law § 490.20

Section 490.25 - Crime of terrorism

1. A person is guilty of a crime of terrorism when, with intent to intimidate or coerce a civilian population, influence the policy of a unit of government by intimidation or coercion, or affect the conduct of a unit of government by murder, assassination or kidnapping, he or she commits a specified offense.

2. Sentencing.

(a) When a person is convicted of a crime of terrorism pursuant to this section, and the specified offense is a class B, C, D or E felony offense, the crime of terrorism shall be deemed a violent felony offense.

(b) When a person is convicted of a crime of terrorism pursuant to this section, and the specified offense is a class C, D or E felony offense, the crime of terrorism shall be deemed to be one category higher than the specified offense the defendant committed, or one category higher than the offense level applicable to the defendant's conviction for an attempt or conspiracy to commit the offense, whichever is applicable.

(c) When a person is convicted of a crime of terrorism pursuant to this section, and the specified offense is a class B felony offense, the crime of terrorism shall be deemed a class A-I felony offense and the sentence imposed upon conviction of such offense shall be in accordance with section 70.00 of this chapter.

(d) Notwithstanding any other provision of law, when a person is convicted of a crime of terrorism pursuant to this section, and the specified offense is a class A-I felony offense, the sentence upon conviction of such offense shall be life imprisonment without parole; provided, however, that nothing herein shall preclude or prevent a sentence of death when the specified offense is murder in the first degree as defined in section 125.27 of this chapter.

N.Y. Penal Law § 490.25

Section 490.27 - Domestic act of terrorism motivated by hate in the second degree

A person is guilty of the crime of domestic act of terrorism motivated by hate in the second degree when, acting with the intent to cause the death of, or serious physical injury to, five or more other persons, in whole or in substantial part because of the perceived race, color, national origin, ancestry, gender, gender identity or expression, religion, religious practice, age, disability, or sexual orientation of such other persons, regardless of whether that belief or perception is correct, he or she, as part of the same criminal transaction, attempts to cause the death of, or serious physical injury to, such five or more persons, provided that the victims are not participants in the criminal transaction.

N.Y. Penal Law § 490.27

Added by New York Laws 2020, ch. 55,Sec. R-4, eff. 11/1/2020.

Section 490.28 - Domestic act of terrorism motivated by hate in the first degree

A person is guilty of the crime of domestic act of terrorism motivated by hate in the first degree when, acting with the intent to cause the death of, or serious physical injury to, five or more other persons, in whole or in substantial part because of the perceived race, color, national origin, ancestry, gender, gender identity or expression, religion, religious practice, age, disability, or sexual orientation of such other person or persons, regardless of whether that belief or perception is correct, he or she, as part of the same criminal transaction:

1. causes the death of at least one other person, provided that the victim or victims are not a participant in the criminal transaction; and

2. causes or attempts to cause the death of four or more additional other persons, provided that the victims are not a participant in the criminal transaction; and

3. the defendant was more than eighteen years old at the time of the commission of the crime.

N.Y. Penal Law § 490.28

Added by New York Laws 2020, ch. 55,Sec. R-4, eff. 11/1/2020.

Section 490.30 - Hindering prosecution of terrorism in the second degree

A person is guilty of hindering prosecution of terrorism in the second degree when he or she renders criminal assistance to a person who has committed an act of terrorism, knowing or believing that such person engaged in conduct constituting an act of terrorism.

N.Y. Penal Law § 490.30

Section 490.35 - Hindering prosecution of terrorism in the first degree

A person is guilty of hindering prosecution of terrorism in the first degree when he or she renders criminal assistance to a person who has committed an act of terrorism that resulted in the death of a person other than one of the participants, knowing or believing that such person engaged in conduct constituting an act of terrorism.

N.Y. Penal Law § 490.35

Section 490.37 - Criminal possession of a chemical weapon or biological weapon in the third degree

A person is guilty of criminal possession of a chemical weapon or biological weapon in the third degree when he or she possesses any select chemical agent or select biological agent under circumstances evincing an intent by the defendant to use such weapon to cause serious physical injury or death to another person.

N.Y. Penal Law § 490.37

Section 490.40 - Criminal possession of a chemical weapon or biological weapon in the second degree

A person is guilty of criminal possession of a chemical weapon or biological weapon in the second degree when he or she possesses any chemical weapon or biological weapon with intent to use such weapon to:

1.

(a) cause serious physical injury to, or the death of, another person; and

(b)

(i) intimidate or coerce a civilian population;

(ii) influence the policy of a unit of government by intimidation or coercion; or

(iii) affect the conduct of a unit of government by murder, assassination, or kidnapping.

2. cause serious physical injury to, or the death of, more than two persons.

Criminal possession of a chemical weapon or biological weapon in the second degree is a class B felony.

N.Y. Penal Law § 490.40

Section 490.45 - Criminal possession of a chemical weapon or biological weapon in the first degree

A person is guilty of criminal possession of a chemical weapon or biological weapon in the first degree when he or she possesses:

1. any select chemical agent, with intent to use such agent to:

(a) cause serious physical injury to, or the death of, another person; and

(b)

(i) intimidate or coerce a civilian population;

(ii) influence the policy of a unit of government by intimidation or coercion; or

(iii) affect the conduct of a unit of government by murder, assassination, or kidnapping.

2. any select chemical agent, with intent to use such agent to cause serious physical injury to, or the death of, more than two other persons; or

3. any select biological agent, with intent to use such agent to cause serious physical injury to, or the death of, another person.

Criminal possession of a chemical weapon or biological weapon in the first degree is a class A-I felony.

N.Y. Penal Law § 490.45

Section 490.47 - Criminal use of a chemical weapon or biological weapon in third degree

§ 490.47 Criminal use of a chemical weapon or biological weapon in the third degree.

N.Y. Penal Law § 490.47

Section 490.50 - Criminal use of a chemical weapon or biological weapon in second degree

§ 490.50 Criminal use of a chemical weapon or biological weapon in the second degree.

1. cause serious physical injury to, or the death of, another person; and

2.

(a) intimidate or coerce a civilian population;

(b) influence the policy of a unit of government by intimidation or coercion; or

(c) to affect the conduct of a unit of government by murder, assassination, or kidnapping.

Criminal use of a chemical weapon or biological weapon in the second degree is a class A-II felony.

N.Y. Penal Law § 490.50

Section 490.55 - Criminal use of a chemical weapon or biological weapon in first degree

§ 490.55 Criminal use of a chemical weapon or biological weapon in the first degree.

1. with intent to:

(a) cause serious physical injury to, or the death of, another person; and

(b)

(i) intimidate or coerce a civilian population;

(ii) influence the policy of a unit of government by intimidation or coercion; or

(iii) affect the conduct of a unit of government by murder, assassination, or kidnapping; he or she uses, deploys, releases, or causes to be used, deployed, or released any select chemical agent and thereby causes serious physical injury to, or the death of, another person who is not a participant in the crime.

2. with intent to cause serious physical injury to, or the death of, more than two persons, he or she uses, deploys, releases, or causes to be used, deployed, or released any select chemical agent and thereby causes serious physical injury to, or the death of, more than two persons who are not participants in the crime; or

3. with intent to cause serious physical injury to, or the death of, another person, he or she uses, deploys, releases, or causes to be used, deployed, or released any select biological agent and thereby causes serious physical injury to, or the death of, another person who is not a participant in the crime.

Criminal use of a chemical weapon or biological weapon in the first degree is a class A-I felony.

N.Y. Penal Law § 490.55

Section 490.70 - Limitations

1. The provisions of sections 490.37, 490.40, 490.45, 490.47, 490.50, and 490.55 of this article shall not apply where the defendant possessed or used:

(a) any household product generally available for sale to consumers in this state in the quantity and concentration available for such sale;

(b) a self-defense spray device in accordance with the provisions of paragraph fourteen of subdivision a of section 265.20 of this chapter;

(c) a chemical weapon solely for a purpose not prohibited under this chapter, as long as the type and quantity is consistent with such a purpose; or

(d) a biological agent, toxin, or delivery system solely for prophylactic, protective, bona fide research, or other peaceful purposes.

2. For the purposes of this section, the phrase "purposes not prohibited by this chapter" means the following:

(a) any peaceful purpose related to an industrial, agricultural, research, medical, or pharmaceutical activity or other peaceful activity;

(b) any purpose directly related to protection against toxic chemicals and to protection against chemical weapons;

(c) any military purpose of the United States that is not connected with the use of a chemical weapon or that is not dependent on the use of the toxic or poisonous properties of the chemical weapon to cause death or other harm; and

(d) any law enforcement purpose, including any domestic riot control purpose and including imposition of capital punishment.

N.Y. Penal Law § 490.70

Title Y-2 - CORRUPTING THE GOVERNMENT

Article 496 - CORRUPTING THE GOVERNMENT

Section 496.01 - Definitions

For the purposes of this article, "scheme" means any plan, pattern, device, contrivance, or course of action.

N.Y. Penal Law § 496.01

Added by New York Laws 2014, ch. 55, Sec. H-A-14, eff. 4/30/2014.

Section 496.02 - Corrupting the government in the fourth degree

A person is guilty of corrupting the government in the fourth degree when, being a public servant, or acting in concert with a public servant, he or she engages in a scheme constituting a systematic ongoing course of conduct with intent to defraud the state or one or more political subdivisions of the state or one or more governmental instrumentalities within the state to obtain property, actual services or other resources, or obtain property, actual services or other resources from the state, or any political subdivision or governmental instrumentality of the state by false or fraudulent pretenses, representations or promises, and thereby wrongfully obtains such property, actual services or other resources.

N.Y. Penal Law § 496.02

Added by New York Laws 2014, ch. 55, Sec. H-A-14, eff. 4/30/2014.

Section 496.03 - Corrupting the government in the third degree

A person is guilty of corrupting the government in the third degree when, being a public servant, or acting in concert with a public servant, he or she engages in a scheme constituting a systematic ongoing course of conduct with intent to defraud the state or one or more political subdivisions of the state or one or more governmental instrumentalities within the state to obtain property, actual services or other resources, or obtain property, actual services or other resources from the state, or any political subdivision or governmental instrumentality of the state by false or fraudulent pretenses, representations or promises, and thereby wrongfully obtains such property, actual services or other resources with a value in excess of one thousand dollars.

N.Y. Penal Law § 496.03

Added by New York Laws 2014, ch. 55, Sec. H-A-14, eff. 4/30/2014.

Section 496.04 - Corrupting the government in the second degree

A person is guilty of corrupting the government in the second degree when, being a public servant, or acting in concert with a public servant, he or she engages in a scheme constituting a systematic ongoing course of conduct with intent to defraud the state or one or more political subdivisions of the state or one or more governmental instrumentalities within the state to obtain property, actual services or other resources, or obtain property, actual services or other resources from the state, or any political subdivision or governmental instrumentality of the state by false or fraudulent pretenses, representations or promises, and thereby wrongfully obtains such property, actual services or other resources with a value in excess of twenty thousand dollars.

N.Y. Penal Law § 496.04

Added by New York Laws 2014, ch. 55, Sec. H-A-14, eff. 4/30/2014.

Section 496.05 - Corrupting the government in the first degree

A person is guilty of corrupting the government in the first degree when, being a public servant, or acting in concert with a public servant, he or she engages in a scheme constituting a systematic ongoing course of conduct with intent to defraud the state or one or more political subdivisions of the state or one or more governmental instrumentalities within the state to obtain property, actual services or other resources, or to obtain property, actual services or other resources from the state, or any political subdivision or governmental instrumentality of the state by false or fraudulent pretenses, representations or promises, and thereby wrongfully obtains such property, actual services or other resources with a value in excess of one hundred thousand dollars.

N.Y. Penal Law § 496.05

Added by New York Laws 2014, ch. 55, Sec. H-A-14, eff. 4/30/2014.

Section 496.06 - Public corruption

1. A person commits the crime of public corruption when:

(a)

(i) being a public servant he or she commits a specified offense through the use of his or her public office, or

(ii) being a person acting in concert with such public servant he or she commits a specified offense, and

237

(b) the state or any political subdivision thereof or any governmental instrumentality within the state is the owner of the property.

2. A "specified offense" is an offense defined by any of the following provisions of this chapter: section 155.25 (petit larceny); section 155.30 (grand larceny in the fourth degree); section 155.35 (grand larceny in the third degree); section 155.40 (grand larceny in the second degree); section 155.42 (grand larceny in the first degree); section 190.60 (scheme to defraud in the second degree); or section 190.65 (scheme to defraud in the first degree).

N.Y. Penal Law § 496.06

Added by New York Laws 2014, ch. 55,Sec. H-A-14, eff. 4/30/2014.

Section 496.07 - Sentencing

When a person is convicted of the crime of public corruption pursuant to section 496.06 of this article and the specified offense is a class C, D or E felony, the crime shall be deemed to be one category higher than the specified offense the defendant committed, or one category higher than the offense level applicable to the defendant's conviction for an attempt or conspiracy to commit a specified offense, whichever is applicable.

N.Y. Penal Law § 496.07

Added by New York Laws 2014, ch. 55,Sec. H-A-14, eff. 4/30/2014.

Title Z - LAWS REPEALED; TIME OF TAKING EFFECT

Article 500 - LAWS REPEALED; TIME OF TAKING EFFECT

Section 500.05 - Laws repealed

Chapter eighty-eight of the laws of nineteen hundred nine, entitled "An act providing for the punishment of crime, constituting chapter forty of the consolidated laws," and all acts amendatory thereof and supplemental thereto, constituting the penal law as heretofore in force, are hereby repealed.

N.Y. Penal Law § 500.05

Section 500.10 - Time of taking effect

This act shall take effect September first, nineteen hundred sixty-seven.

N.Y. Penal Law § 500.10

Made in United States
Orlando, FL
22 August 2022

21380375R00133